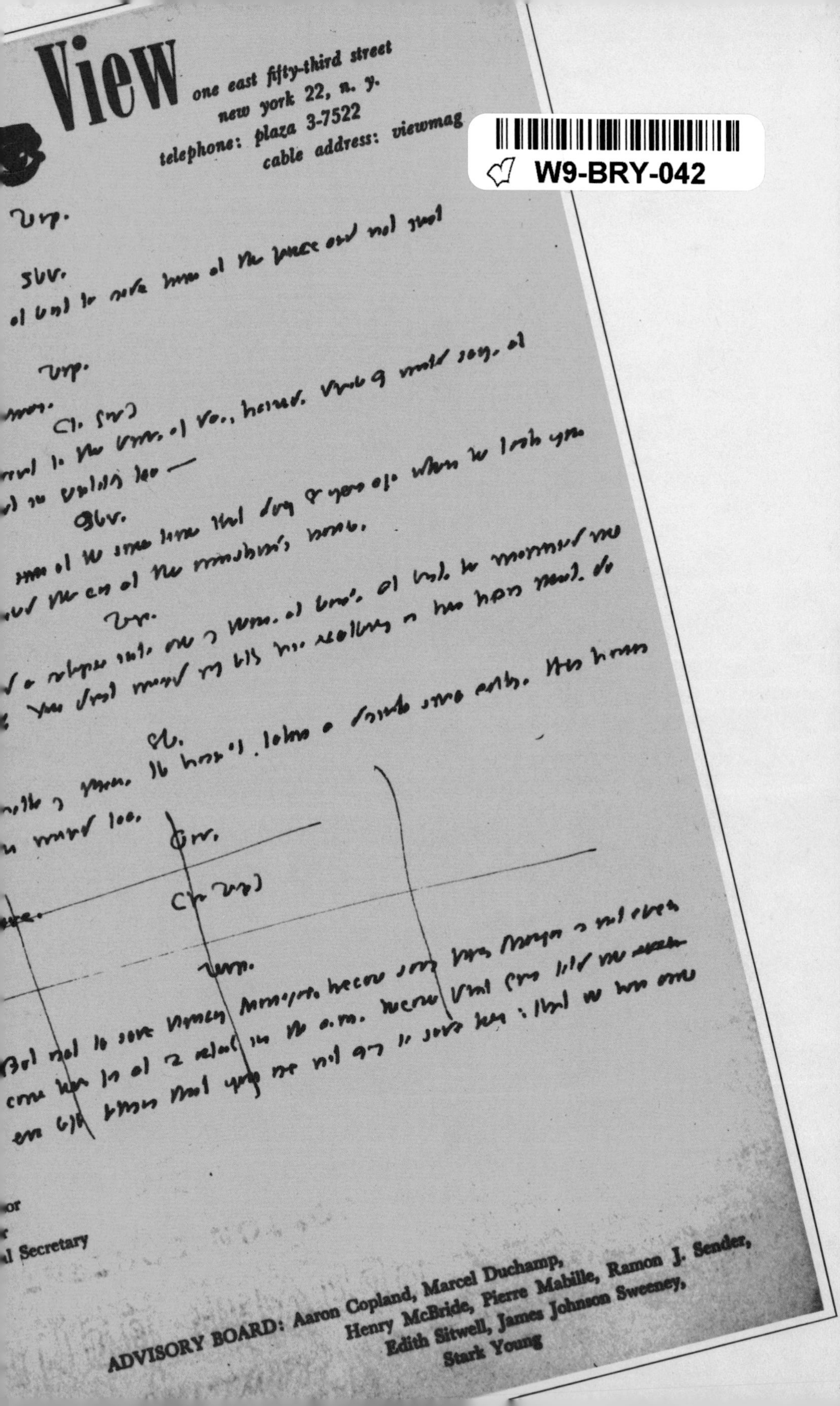
View
one east fifty-third street
new york 22, n. y.
telephone: plaza 3-7522
cable address: viewmag

...or
...r
...l Secretary

ADVISORY BOARD: Aaron Copland, Marcel Duchamp,
Henry McBride, Pierre Mabille, Ramon J. Sender,
Edith Sitwell, James Johnson Sweeney,
Stark Young

Faulkner

A Comprehensive Guide to the Brodsky Collection

Volume V: Manuscripts and Documents

Faulkner

A Comprehensive Guide to the Brodsky Collection

Volume V: Manuscripts and Documents

Edited by
Louis Daniel Brodsky
and
Robert W. Hamblin

UNIVERSITY PRESS OF MISSISSIPPI
JACKSON AND LONDON

Center for the Study of Southern Culture Series

Manufactured in the United States of America
93 92 91 90 89 5 4 3 2 1

The paper in this book meets the guidelines for permanence and durability of the Committee on Production Guidelines for Book Longevity on the Council of Library Resources.

Library of Congress Cataloging-in-Publication Data
(Revised for vol. 5)

Faulkner, a comprehensive guide to the Brodsky Collection.

(Center for the Study of Southern Culture series)
Includes bibliographical references and index.
Contents: v. 1. The biobibliography—v. 2. The letters—[etc.]—v. 5. Manuscripts and documents.
1. Faulkner, William, 1897–1962—Bibliography—Catalogs. 2. Faulkner, William, 1897–1962—Manuscripts—Catalogs. 3. Faulkner, William, 1897–1962—Miscellanea—Catalogs. 4. Faulkner, William 1897–1962—Correspondence. 5. Novelists, American—20th century—Correspondence. 6. Brodsky, Louis Daniel—Library—Catalogs. I. Brodsky, Louis Daniel. II. Hamblin, Robert W. III. Series.
Z8288.F38 1982 016.813′52 82-6966
[PS3511.A86]
ISBN 0-87805-320-4
ISBN 0-87805-240-2 (set)

British Cataloguing in Publication data available

CONTENTS

List of Illustrations vii

Preface ix

Editorial Notes xiii

I Drawings 3

II Poetry 25

III Fiction 91

IV Non-Fiction 201

V Plays 257

VI Biographical Documents 315

VII Last Wills and Testaments 359

Index 383

LIST OF ILLUSTRATIONS

1 Faulkner, 1914 2
2 Cartoon: Speeding Auto, 1913 5
3 Cartoon: "De Faculty," 1913 6
4 Cartoon: "We Have Put Away Childish Things," 1913 7
5 Cartoon: "Basket Ball Champions of C.M.A.A.," 1913 8
6 Cartoon: "Eleventh Grade Special," 1913 9
7 Cartoon: "Burning the Midnight Oil," 1913 10
8 Cartoon: Hogshead of "Knowledge," 1913 11
9 Cartoon: "This Is How He Looks to Us," 1913 12
10 Cartoon: "Taking His Medicine," 1913 13
11 Cartoon: "Them's My Sentiments," 1913 14
12 Man and woman dancing, c. 1916 15
13 Faun and nymph, c. 1918 16
14 Airplanes, c. 1918 17
15 Nude figure, 1920 18
16 Santa Monica residence, 1936 19
17 Map of Yoknapatawpha County, 1945 20
18 Princeton map, 1952 21
19 London map, 1952 22
20 Drawing of pipe, 1953 22
21 Balch Hangar-Flying Squadron insignia, 1958 23
22 Balch "Pipe of American Literature," 1958 23
23 "The black bird swung in the white rose tree," c. 1916–1921 31
24 "L'Apres-Midi d'un Faune," c. 1918 34
25 "The Lilacs," c. 1918 36
26 "A Dead Dancer," c. 1918 40
27 Fragment of *The Lilacs,* 1920 44
28 Fragment of *The Lilacs,* 1920 45
29 Poem fragment, c. 1920 61
30 Poem fragment, c. 1920 62
31 Poem fragment, c. 1920 64
32 Poem fragment, c. 1920 66
33 Poem fragment, c. 1920 67

34 "Mississippi Hills: My Epitaph," 1924 81
35 "November 11th," 1924 83
36 "Ode to the Louver," 1925 86
37 "Ode to the Louver," 1925 87
38 Faulkner in Paris, 1925 88
39 "The Wishing-Tree," 1948 93
40 "Wash," c. 1933 116
41 "Wash," c. 1933 127
42 *Requiem for a Nun,* c. 1950 150
43 *Requiem for a Nun,* c. 1950 160
44 "Weekend Revisited" ("Mr. Acarius"), c. 1953 164
45 *A Fable,* c. 1952 180
46 Pine Manor commencement address, 1953 211
47 "Foreword" to *The Faulkner Reader,* 1953 213
48 "Mississippi," 1954 215
49 "Sepulchure South," 1954 220
50 "Sepulchure South," 1954 223
51 "Freedom: American Style," 1955 230
52 Gold Medal for Fiction presentation address, 1957 250
53 Andrés Bello Award acceptance speech, 1961 252
54 Impressions of Danzas Venezuela, 1961 254
55 Faulkner's Warner Bros. Starting Record, 1942 316
56 Faulkner's recipe for curing pork, 1942 319
57 Warner Bros. Off Payroll Notice, 1945 321
58 Jill Faulkner's report card, 1945–1946 322
59 Ministers' anti-beer broadside, 1950 323
60 Faulkner's "Beer Broadside," 1950 324
61 "Tuesday" outline *(A Fable),* c. 1952 329
62 "First Experimental Balch Hangar-Flying Squadron" citation, 1958 356
63 Faulkner's Hotel Algonquin registration folio, 1958–1962 357
64 Faulkner's Hotel Algonquin registration folio, 1958–1962 357
65 Last Will and Testament, 1940 364
66 Faulkner, 1949 367
67 Last Will and Testament, 1951 368
68 Last Will and Testament, 1951 369

PREFACE

THIS VOLUME CONTINUES the developing series that is making available to literary scholars and the general public the William Faulkner materials housed in the private collection of Louis Daniel Brodsky. Previous volumes have, respectively, catalogued more than 3,000 items belonging to the collection; published some five hundred letters by, to, or about Faulkner; and printed two unproduced screenplays (*The De Gaulle Story* and *Battle Cry*) and three story treatments ("Country Lawyer," "The Life and Death of a Bomber," and "The Damned Don't Cry") that Faulkner wrote for Warner Bros. Pictures in the early 1940s. This present book reproduces an extensive gathering of original manuscripts, as well as legal and biographical documents, that are among the most significant materials in the Brodsky Collection.

The contents of this volume have been selected from a much larger body of manuscripts and documents acquired by Brodsky over the past thirty years. A considerable number of the items have not been previously published. Materials in this category include the succession of last wills and testaments executed by Faulkner over three decades; *The Lilacs,* the handmade booklet of poems that Faulkner presented to Phil Stone in 1920; working draft segments of *Requiem for a Nun* and *A Fable*; "Requiem," Faulkner's own stage adaptation of *Requiem for a Nun;* and "Innocent's Return," a telescript that Faulkner authored, possibly in collaboration with Joan Williams. Other works printed herein, like certain of the early poems, the progressive versions of "Wash," the Margaret Brown copy of "The Wishing-Tree," and "By the People," have previously appeared but only in books or periodicals that are not readily available to the reading public. Still other works, such as "Sepulchure South," the "Foreword" to *The Faulkner Reader,* "Freedom: American Style," and "On Fear: Deep South in Labor," have formerly been given wide circulation, but in versions considerably different from the copies in the Brodsky Collection. This book, therefore, not only expands the existing Faulkner bibliography but also, in key instances, offers privileged views into Faulkner's compositional process.

This volume is divided into seven sections, the first five of which present materials representing different phases of Faulkner's artistic and literary career: drawings, poetry, fiction, non-fiction, and plays. The last two sections contain selected biographical documents and four variants of Faulkner's Last Will and Testament. Within each section the organization is chronological, and both a general introduction and individual headnotes have been provided to identify and date the respective documents and to place them within the overall context of Faulkner's life and career. Where applicable, identifying numbers have been assigned to the entries as a convenient cross-reference to Volume I of the Brodsky series, *The Biobibliography*. (Items lacking numbers have been added to the collection since the compilation of Volume I; these are indicated by a wedge preceeding the entry.)

Because this volume, like its predecessors, is based on the holdings of an individual collector, no attempt has been made to offer a comprehensive record of Faulkner's literary achievements. Neither have we sought, except in a few necessary instances, to collate the Brodsky texts with manuscripts in other Faulkner repositories, such as the Universities of Virginia, Texas, and Mississippi. The sole purpose of this book is to present a thorough and accurate transcription of the principal manuscripts and documents in the Brodsky Collection.

Many of the selections in this volume owe their presence here to an extraordinary provenance: they were acquired from persons who at one time held Faulkner's trust and respect and who (or whose heirs), in turn, have respected the Brodsky Collection enough to entrust their holdings to it. Phil Stone, Faulkner's mentor, friend, and personal lawyer, prepared the legal documents transcribed herein; they came to Brodsky through the cooperation of Stone's widow, Emily Whitehurst Stone. So, too, did the seventeen burned fragments of poems that became part of *The Marble Faun* and *Vision in Spring,* as well as the copy of "The Wishing-Tree" which Faulkner personally typed, bound, and inscribed for his godson, Phil and Emily's son Philip, as a Christmas gift in 1948.

Several of the prose selections, both fiction and non-fiction, were preserved by Faulkner's long-time Random House editor and confidant, Saxe Commins. These materials, deposited in the Brodsky Collection by Commins's widow Dorothy, include the manuscripts and typescripts of *Requiem for a Nun, A Fable,* "By the People," "On Fear," "Sepulchure South," "A Guest's Impression of New England," the *Faulkner Reader* "Foreword," "Freedom: American Style," and the transcribed notes of the People-to-People committee meeting. Myrtle Ramey (Demarest), a grade school friend of Faulkner, kept for almost fifty years the presentation typescript of *Mississippi Poems,* along with the set of ten pen-and-ink cartoons that Faulkner drew for the aborted 1913 Oxford Graded School yearbook. Additional poems came to the collection through Faulkner's great-aunt, 'Bama McLean, who at her death bequeathed her Faulkner memorabilia to her nephew, Vance Carter Broach.

The manuscript drafts of "Wash" were given by Estelle Faulkner, following her husband's death, to her son Malcolm Franklin, who in turn gave them to his good friend, Professor James Silver, at that time head of the history department at Ole Miss. From Silver also came Faulkner's 1945 hand-drawn map of Yoknapatawpha County. Ruth Ford made available her files relating to the stage production of *Requiem for a Nun;* among these materials was a mimeographed copy of "Requiem," Faulkner's adaptation of his 1951 novel.

Victoria Fielden Johnson, Faulkner's step-granddaughter, supplied Faulkner's address upon receiving the Andrés Bello award, the impressions of Danzas Venezuela, and Faulkner's personal recipe for curing pork. Phil Mullen, former editor of the *Oxford Eagle,* provided the typescript of the commencement address that Faulkner delivered at Oxford High School in 1951. Joan Williams, a young writer whom Faulkner befriended, contributed two manuscript pages that Faulkner had drafted for her as exercises in narration. Joseph Blotner, Faulkner's biographer, supplied the copies of the Pine Manor and Gold Medal speeches, the Balch Hangar citation and insignia, and other miscellaneous biographical items.

In addition to these persons who have so graciously deposited materials in the Brodsky Collection, we wish to thank several other individuals who have assisted in the making of this book. We are particularly indebted to Jill Faulkner Summers, Faulkner's daughter, for her kind cooperation and support. We are also deeply appreciative to Donald Lamm and Renee Schwartz, president and legal counsel respectively of W. W. Norton and Company, for permission to publish the Faulkner texts.

Like the series of which it is a part, this book is the result of the friendly cooperation of the University Press of Mississippi, the University of Mississippi's Center for the Study of Southern Culture, and Southeast Missouri State University. We wish especially to acknowledge the contributions of Barney McKee, Richard Abel, JoAnne Prichard, Hunter Cole, Seetha Srinivasan, and John Langston of the Press; William Ferris and Ann J. Abadie of the Center; and Bill W. Stacy, Leslie H. Cochran, Fred B. Goodwin, Sheila Caskey, Henry Sessoms, and James K. Zink of Southeast Missouri.

We are also extremely grateful for the financial support and personal encouragement provided by Saul and Charlotte Brodsky, Biltwell Company, and the Grants and Research Funding Committee of Southeast Missouri State University.

We want to thank photographer Paul Lueders for his painstaking efforts in producing the quality illustrations for this volume.

Our greatest debt is to our families—Jan, Trilogy, and Troika Brodsky and Kaye, Laurie, and Stephen Hamblin—for their love, patience, and understanding.

Louis Daniel Brodsky
Robert W. Hamblin

EDITORIAL NOTES

In preparing the contents of this volume for publication, the editors have employed two different methods of transcription. In the cases of manuscripts handwritten or typed by Faulkner we have recorded the texts as faithfully and meticulously as possible, even to the point of retaining Faulkner's inconsistencies and idiosyncracies of spelling, punctuation, and capitalization. Except for silently correcting obvious typographical errors (*e.g.*, accidental transposition of letters and strikeovers) and for slightly altering the play formats (for *Requiem for a Nun* and "Innocent's Return") in order to conserve space, we have sought to present these materials precisely as Faulkner left them. His deletions *(del.)* and illegible words and phrases *(illeg.)* have been noted in square brackets, while interlinear and marginal *(marg.)* insertions have been recorded in angle brackets. Bracketed numbers within the texts indicate page breaks in the manuscripts. The abbreviation *n.n.* is used to identify unnumbered pages.

We have been less reluctant to make emendations in those documents not written or typed for Faulkner: for example, the last wills and testaments, the *Omnibus* telescript, and the Random House press release. Here, in the interest of clarity and consistency, we have occasionally altered spellings and regularized punctuation and capitalization.

Faulkner

A Comprehensive Guide
to the Brodsky Collection

Volume V: Manuscripts and Documents

1. Faulkner, 1914

I

Drawings

POSSIBLY WILLIAM FAULKNER'S earliest artistic tendency was that of drawing, sketching, painting. During his formative years, his mother, Maud Falkner, not only filled countless sketchbooks herself but encouraged her oldest son to express himself visually. Throughout grade school Faulkner was continually producing sketches of locomotives, cowboys and broncos, guns and airships. In his early manhood he developed an impressive mastery of pen and ink and water color. But by April 1925, as he revealed in an autobiographical prose "sketch" entitled "Out of Nazareth," which appeared in the New Orleans *Times-Picayune,* Faulkner had come to recognize that art was neither his forte nor destiny: "I remarked to Spratling how no one since Cezanne had really dipped his brush in light. Spratling, whose hand has been shaped to a brush as mine has (alas!) not, here became discursive on the subject of transferring light to canvas." In a patently autobiographical novel which Faulkner began slightly later that same year during a walking tour of Europe with his artist-friend from New Orleans, William Spratling, and which at one turn he titled *Elmer,* he explored the fate of a failed artist named Elmer Hodge. That Faulkner was unable to conclude this novel is as inferentially revealing as any singular fact documenting his ultimate abandonment of painting and making illustrations as a way of life.

The Brodsky Collection contains several examples of the various kinds of "art" that Faulkner produced during the years prior to his transformation into a writer—forms which he would pursue amateurishly for the rest of his lifetime. Among these is a group of ten cartoon drawings he executed in pen and ink for a proposed Oxford High School yearbook in 1913. The Collection also contains Faulkner's sketches and drawings evoking his experiences in the RAF as a pilot training cadet in Toronto, Canada; these are similar to other art works from this same period now in the Faulkner Collections at the University of Virginia's Alderman Library.

By 1916, when Faulkner produced the first of several drawings to appear in a series of the University of Mississippi's *Ole Miss* yearbooks during the late teens and early twenties, he had evidenced considerable skill with pen and ink rendering. Typical of his talent and of his potential as an illustrator in the manner of John Held, Jr., is the pen and ink sketch of a young man and woman dancing. Equally impressive is his line drawing of a Pan and nymph which evokes and parallels images he was then exploring in the poems that would culminate in his first book, *The Marble Faun.*

From 1920 through mid-decade, Faulkner painted striking, brightly hued, mystical water colors, some of which adorned the covers and leaves of booklets *(Helen: A Courtship, Mayday, The Wishing-Tree)* he meticulously made by hand for certain friends and lady-loves. The single water color which introduces the poems comprising *The Lilacs,* a booklet Faulkner presented to Phil Stone in January 1920, is badly damaged; but the pen and ink endpiece of a naked female remains intact, revealing the artist's sensitivity to the possibilities of silhouette.

Although early in his professional career as a writer Faulkner relinquished whatever ambitions he might have had of developing into a painter or illustrator, sketches which he made from the thirties until his death in 1962—of houses, self-portraits, cartoons, pipes, insignia, maps drawn for the practical purpose of assisting with directions, and as an enhancement to a compilation of his fiction (*The Portable Faulkner* [1946])—indicate that he never completely abandoned his impulse to express himself graphically.

14 Eleventh grade yearbook drawings, 1913

While a student at Oxford High School, Faulkner completed ten cartoons with pen and ink to be used as illustrations for a proposed class yearbook. The drawings were produced on four 8-by-5 inch sheets of plain white paper, with one leaf containing sketches on both recto and verso. Plans for the yearbook were eventually abandoned, and Faulkner subsequently gave the sketches to his friend and classmate, Myrtle Ramey.

The drawings are arranged on the four sheets as follows:
1 leaf (recto: sketches **a** and **b;** verso: sketches **c, d,** and **e**)
1 leaf (recto: sketches **f** and **g;** verso: blank)
1 leaf (recto: sketches **h** and **i;** verso: blank)
1 leaf (recto: sketch **j;** verso: blank)

a. Drawing, 2 by 5 inches. Speeding auto, with "11 GRADE" written on the side, headed toward an arched gate labeled (in reversed letters) "SUCCESS." Dust cloud in rear forms "FAIL[URE]" in block letters. No caption. Signed "F." Upper right corner is torn away.

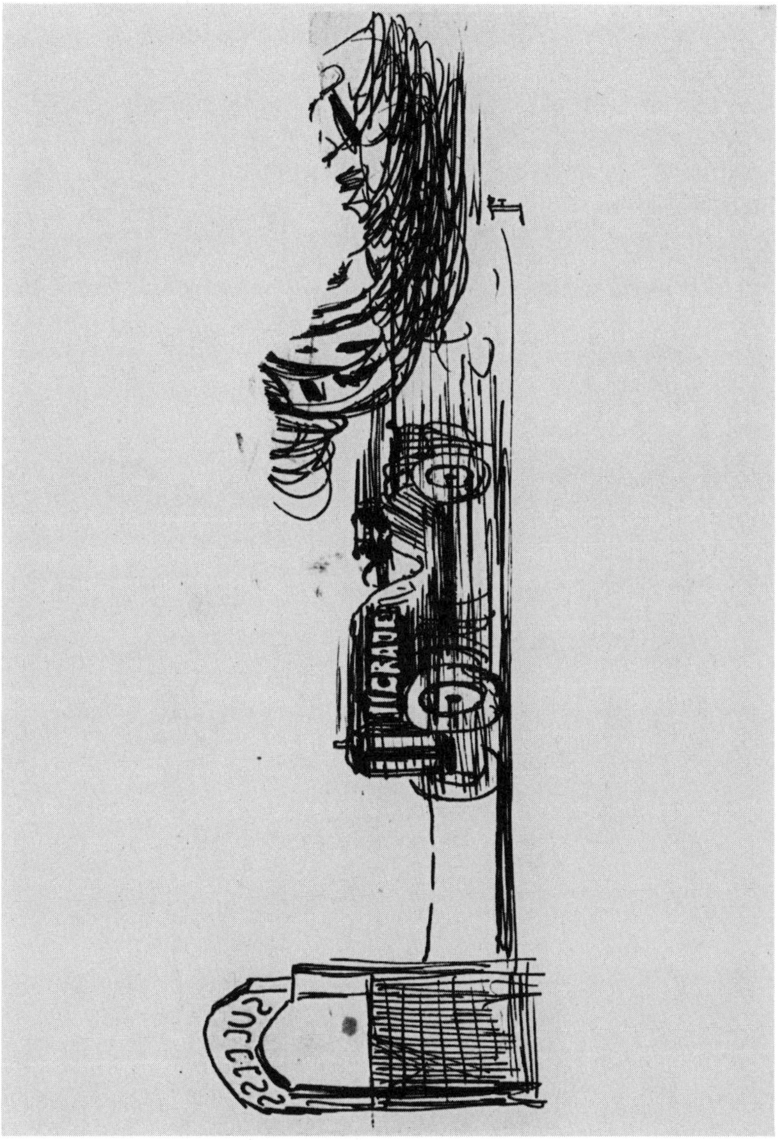

2. Cartoon for proposed high school yearbook, 1913

b. Drawing, 5 by 6 inches. Lineup of five teachers, four holding signs designating their subject areas as "AGRICULTURE," "ENGLISH," "MATH," and "LATIN." The other figure, apparently the principal [G.G. Hurst], is labeled "THE WHOLE SHOW." Caption, printed in Faulkner's hand: "DE FACULTY." Unsigned.

3. Cartoon for proposed high school yearbook, 1913

c. Drawing, 3½ by 5 inches. Figure in cap and gown pushing to the rear four childhood toys—a small horse on wheels, a ball, a soldier, and a top—and facing toward some books. Caption, printed in Faulkner's hand: "WE HAVE PUT AWAY CHILDISH / THINGS." Signed "F." Upper left corner is torn away.

4. Cartoon for proposed high school yearbook, 1913

d. Drawing, 4½ by 2 inches. Seated figure, smiling and winking, wearing a top hat and a basketball uniform with "O H S" [Oxford High School] across front of jersey. Caption, printed in Faulkner's hand: "BASKET BALL / CHAMPIONS OF / C.M.A.A. / [rule] / 1913." Signed "F."

5. Cartoon for proposed high school yearbook, 1913

e. Drawing, 2½ by 4 inches. Bus loaded with students and driven by a teacher [G. G. Hurst] wearing goggles. On side of bus is written: "ELEVENTH GRADE / SPECIAL. / CONDUC[TOR], G. G. HURST / CLAS[S] OF '13." Road sign in foreground points to "KNOWLEDGE" and "SUCCESS." One figure is shown diving from the bus and another is clinging to the back of the vehicle by his fingertips. No caption. Unsigned.

6. Cartoon for proposed high school yearbook, 1913

f. Drawing, 3½ by 5 inches. Figure asleep in armchair with lamp and books on table beside him. Caption, printed in Faulkner's hand: "BURNING THE MIDNIGHT OIL———" Signed "F."

7. Cartoon for proposed high school yearbook, 1913

g. Drawing, 4½ by 5 inches. Bearded figure with mug in left hand removing the top from a hogshead labeled "KNOWLEDGE." Caption, printed in Faulkner's hand: "BY GUM, THAT 'AR 'LEVENTH GRADE NEVER / LEFT NARY DRAP IN TH' KAIG!" Signed "F."

8. Cartoon for proposed high school yearbook, 1913

h. Drawing, 5 by 3½ inches. Stern-looking teacher [G. G. Hurst] sitting at desk on raised platform, aiming a cannon at quaking student seated below. Teacher holds bunch of switches in right hand. Knife, tomahawk, and pistol hang from ceiling. Skull and crossbones in lower right corner. Caption, printed in Faulkner's hand: "THIS IS HOW HE LOOKS TO US." Unsigned.

9. Cartoon for proposed high school yearbook, 1913

i. Drawing, 5 by 4½ inches. Teacher pouring liquid from a large container labeled "KNOWLEDGE" into a funnel placed on top of a student's head. On shelf in background are mortar and pestle and stoppered bottles of "LATIN" and "MATH." Caption, printed in Faulkner's hand: "TAKING HIS MEDIC[I]NE." Signed, in artistic script, "WFalkner."

10. Cartoon for proposed high school yearbook, 1913

j. Drawing, 5 by 8 inches. Female teacher [Ella Wright] preparing to grind out punishment from "DEMERIT MILL" for fierce, bearded figure standing beside her. Culprit has "A. LINCOLN" printed across his chest. At Lincoln's feet, in miniature, a bully holding aloft a Union flag and brandishing a knife is attacking a much smaller figure holding a Confederate flag. Caption, printed in Faulkner's hand: "THEM'S MY SENTIMENTS." Signed, in artistic script, "WFalkner."

11. Cartoon for proposed high school yearbook, 1913

17 Drawing of man and woman dancing. On leaf 14 by 8½ inches, unwatermarked. Executed in black and white with pen and ink. Signed, in artistic script, "William Faulkner."

This drawing, given by Faulkner to Myrtle Ramey, is similar in style to some of those Faulkner produced for the *Ole Miss;* but Ben Wasson, a close associate of Faulkner at the University of Mississippi, has dated this sketch c. 1916, earlier than any of those appearing in the yearbooks.

12. Pen and ink drawing by Faulkner, c. 1916

21 Line drawings by Faulkner, c. 1918, 1 page, 14 by 8½ inches, Hammermill Bond. On verso of early draft of opening of "The Lilacs (see page 35).

These drawings may have been produced during the period (July 10 to December 5, 1918) when Faulkner was a pilot cadet with the Canadian Royal Air Force Squadron stationed in Toronto. The manuscript was for a long time in the possession of Faulkner's mother, Mrs. Maud Falkner, and was stored with a group of materials that included Faulkner's RAF uniform and the trunk he used during his tenure of service.

a. Drawing, 3½ by 2½ inches, in black ink. Faun and nymph.

13. Faun and nymph by Faulkner, c. 1918

b. Drawing, 2 by 5 inches, in pencil. World War I biplane (side view). The tail of this aircraft slightly overlaps the sketch of the faun and nymph.

c. Drawing, 2¾ by 7¼ inches, in pencil. World War I biplane (front view).

d. Drawing, 2¼ by 6¾ inches, in pencil. World War I triplane (rear side view).

14. Sketches by Faulkner, c. 1918

26 Drawing of nude female figure on black escutcheon, 7/8 by 3/8 inches, in black ink. On page [35] of *The Lilacs,* the handmade book of poems Faulkner presented to Phil Stone on January 1, 1920 (see page 43).

15. Nude figure from *The Lilacs,* 1920

409 Line drawing of house at 620 El Cerco Drive, Santa Monica, California, 1936, 8½ by 11 inches, in pencil.

The Faulkners lived in this house during one of their tenures in California. The drawing by Faulkner, with penciled note at bottom by Mrs. Faulkner, was enclosed with a letter Mrs. Faulkner wrote to her son, Malcolm Franklin, on July 27, 1936. A detailed description of this house and its setting appears in Meta Carpenter Wilde and Orin Borsten, *A Loving Gentleman*, pp. 166–175.

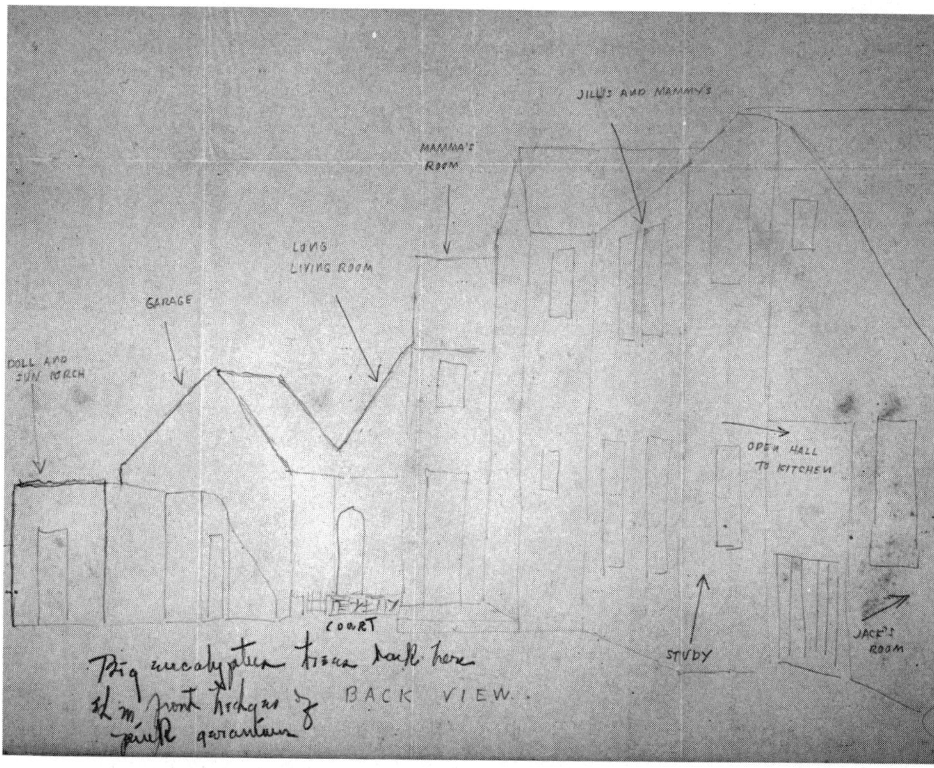

16. Faulkner's drawing of his Santa Monica residence, 1936

606 "Jefferson & Yoknapatawpha Co. Mississippi 1945." Handlettered map by Faulkner in red and black ink, 1 page, 11 by 8½ inches, Millers Falls Onion Skin.

A slightly revised version of this map appears as the endpapers of *The Portable Faulkner.*

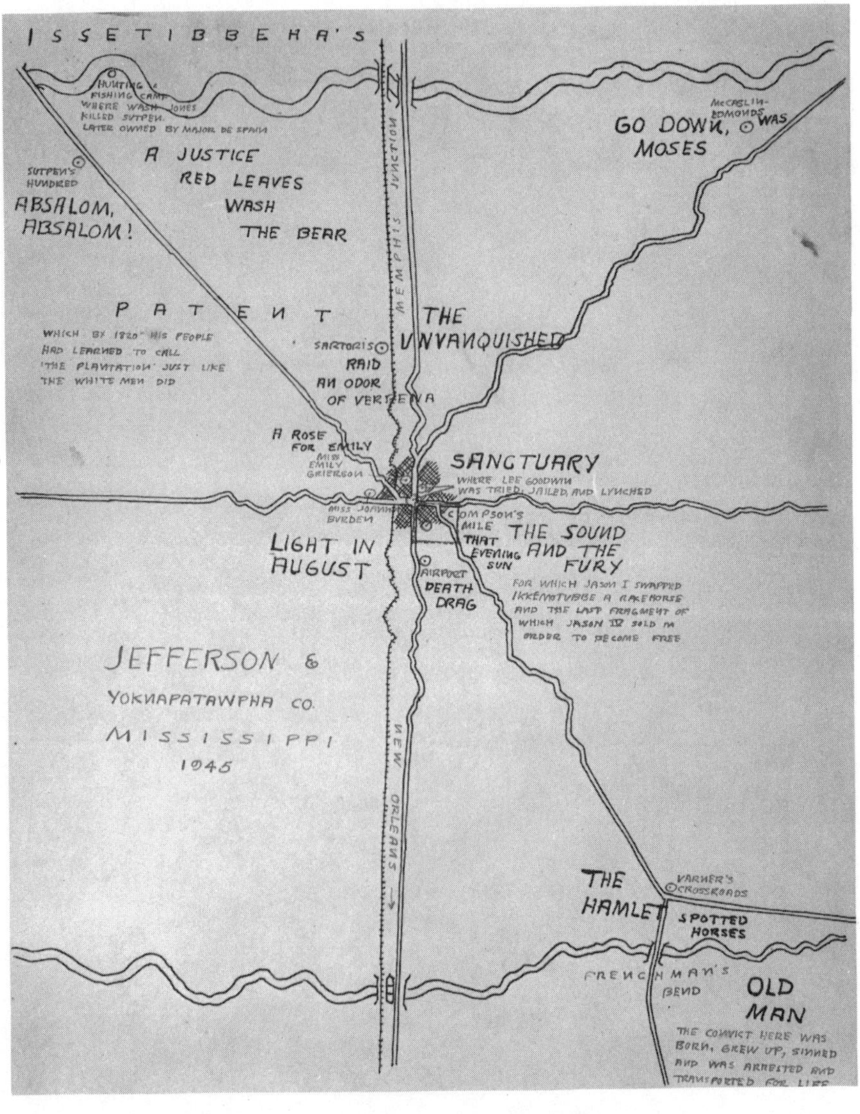

17. Faulkner's 1945 map of Yoknapatawpha County

▶ Map of section of Princeton, New Jersey, sketched by Faulkner, c. November 1952, in black ink, 1 page, 9½ by 6 inches.

Prepared for Joan Williams, this map shows directions from the Princeton railroad station to Saxe Commins's residence at 85 Elm Road. The drawing appears on a leaf of stationery with letterhead of The Princeton Inn.

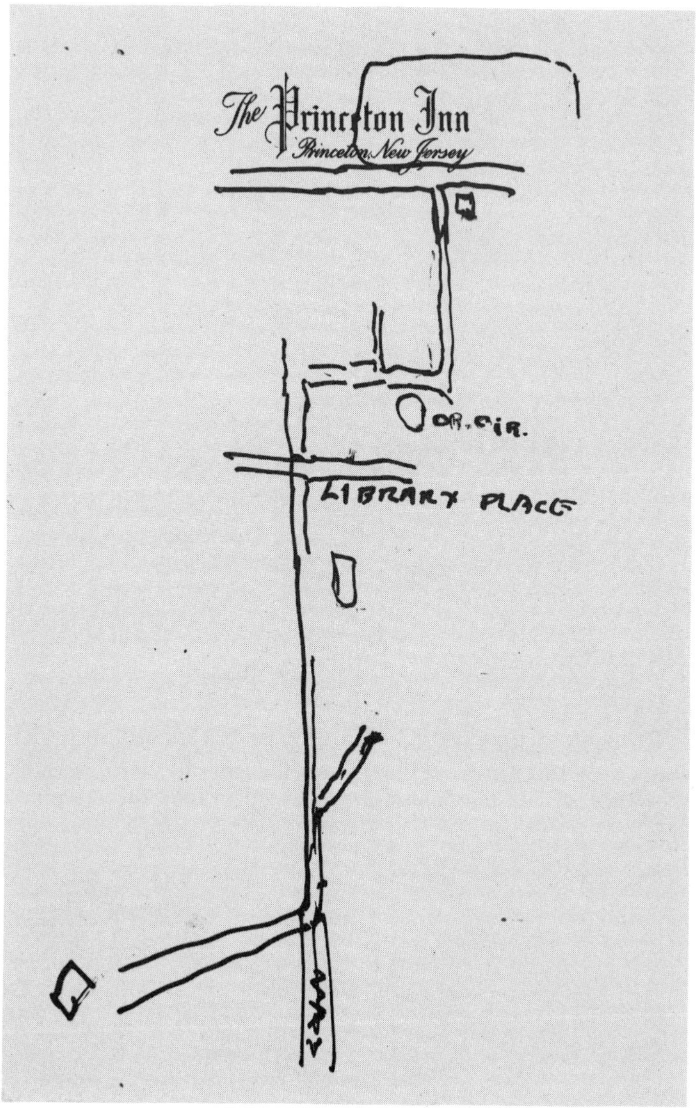

18. Faulkner's map of a section of Princeton, 1952

▶ Map of Brown's Hotel area of London, sketched by Faulkner, c. May 1952, in pencil, 1 page, 11 by 8½ inches, Hammermill Bond.

Upper left corner lists, in Faulkner's hand, in pencil, English currency equivalents. On verso is "Tuesday" outline of *A Fable* (see page 328).

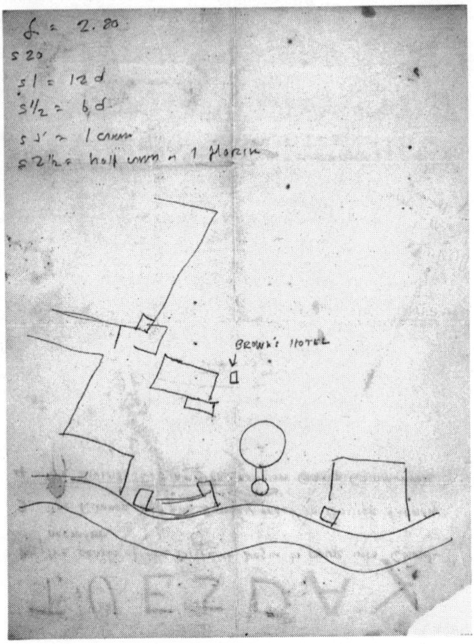

19. Faulkner's map of a section of London, 1952

941 Drawing of pipe, April 1953, 1½ by 6¾ inches, in pencil.

Faulkner drew this picture at the bottom of a letter to Saxe Commins, dated "Friday" [April 24, 1953]. Commins was asked to look for the pipe, which Faulkner had mislaid.

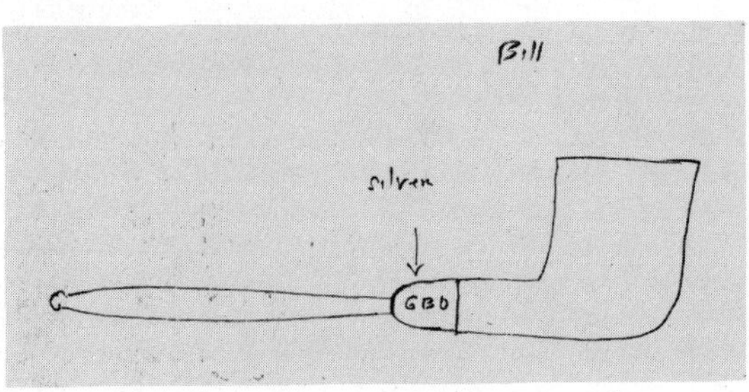

20. Faulkner's sketch of a lost pipe, 1953

▶ Drawing of insignia for "First Experimental Balch Hangar-Flying Squadron," February 5, 1958, 1¹¹⁄₁₆ by 3⅛ inches, in pencil.

Faulkner sketched this humorous imitation of the winged insignia of the Royal Air Force on Joseph Blotner's transcription of the text for a drinking club citation composed by Faulkner, Blotner, and Frederick Gwynn (see page 355).

21. Blotner and Faulkner's notes for Balch Hangar-Flying Squadron citation, 1958

▶ Drawing of pipe, c. May 1958, ½ inch by 1½ inches, in pencil.

Faulkner drew this pipe, at the request of Joseph Blotner, to guide the English Department in its purchase of a gift for Faulkner upon the occasion of his retirement as writer-in-residence at the University of Virginia. The drawing appears on one of two pages of handwritten notes by Blotner pertaining to the gift. "The Emily Clark Balch Pipe of American Literature" was presented to Faulkner on May 26, 1958.

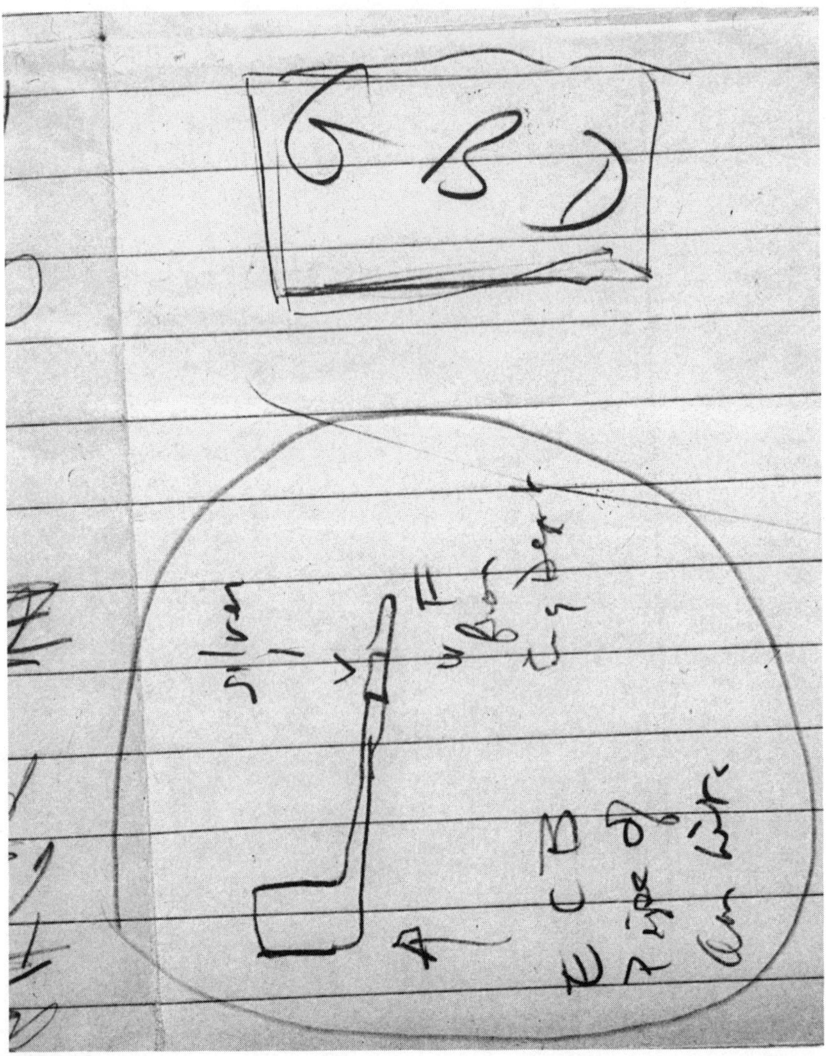

22. Faulkner's drawing of "The Emily Clark Balch Pipe of American Literature," 1958

II

Poetry

ALMOST CERTAINLY, Billy Falkner's interests in reading poetry and in writing verse were more than dilatory or improvisational fancies by 1914 when at the age of seventeen he met Phil Stone. Indeed, it was at Maud Falkner's instigation that introductions were initiated; she wanted her son to have the benefit of the Ole Miss- and Yale-educated Stone boy's erudition. In the ensuing years, Faulkner derived from Stone's direction a vast exposure to avant garde trends in art, psychology, philosophy, and, most singularly important to Faulkner, poetry. Not only did Stone attempt to purchase many of the little magazines and obscure volumes of "modern" poetry that were appearing in the teens and early twenties, but he also was able to make readily available to Faulkner the resources of the Stone family library. Stone's encouragement even extended to providing the money the Four Seas Company required to print Faulkner's first book of poems, *The Marble Faun,* for which Stone also contributed the Prologue. After publication, Stone spent laborious energies promoting and hawking "his" writer's book. For his part, Faulkner would repay his indebtedness and reaffirm his loyalty to his early friend and literary mentor all his life; one manifestation would take the form of dedications: first, to the 1920 handmade booklet, *The Lilacs,* and decades later, to three successive volumes comprising the Snopes trilogy (*The Hamlet* [1940], *The Town* [1957], and *The Mansion* [1959]), components of which he and Stone had shared in concocting during the early twenties.

Although Faulkner's compulsion to compose poetry and arrange various poems into sequences, cycles, or entire books would diminish by the mid-twenties, his admiration for the distilled essences of poetry never did fade. In fact, the prose style which he developed during the years of his greatest achievement is characterized by a lyricism of intense poetic beauty. That in later years Faulkner would occasionally refer to himself as a "failed poet" was no mere understated facetiousness or modest posturing.

The forty-one poems that are included in the Brodsky Collection represent a broad spectrum of the kinds and quality of verse Faulkner produced between 1916 and 1925. In their aggregate, they constitute the complete or partial texts of no less than seven volumes of poems Faulkner either intended for publication or limited distribution as handmade gift volumes. If the ten "'Bama Poems" appear to be juvenalia, they nevertheless contain examples which Faulkner would select to appear in his 1933 poetry volume, *A Green Bough.* And among the earliest surviving holograph drafts of any Faulkner poems are those which formed "A Dead Dancer," "The Lilacs," and "L'Apres-Midi d'un Faune," three poems which appeared in the single edition booklet Faulkner made in 1920.

Also included in the Collection is another "book" of verse which Faulkner gave a grade school girlfriend, Myrtle Ramey, and which existed in a single typescript edition of one copy titled *Mississippi Poems* (1924). Another book from this period was entitled *Vision in Spring* (1921): Faulkner made this one in a "single impression" edition and gave it to Estelle Oldham Franklin, his recently married sweetheart. Certain stanzas, lines, and image clusters from the "Stone fragments" can be identified as belonging to three poems from that volume: "The Dancer," "A Symphony," and "After the Concert." Like *The Lilacs,* these fragments were salvaged from a calamitous 1942 fire that ravaged the Stone house in Oxford where so much of Faulkner's earliest work, primarily poetry, had been stored. Three other fragments from this group of seventeen pieces appear to be from an earlier, shorter version of *The Marble Faun,* written between 1919 and 1920.

In 1926, Faulkner assembled a special group of poems he intended to give to Helen Baird; some of these were written in New Orleans prior to his European walking tour, others during the trip. He called this single impression book which he meticulously copied out in characteristically minute penmanship and bound by hand, *Helen: A Courtship.* The Brodsky Collection contains one poem from this book; titled "Leaving Her," this manuscript is possibly the first holograph draft of what became Sonnet XIII in the book. With one or two exceptions after this date, these poems marked the end of one era in Faulkner's writing career and set the stage for another, that splendid period between 1929 and 1942 when he would publish his most masterful, indeed poetic, fiction. Yet, as attested by the seven-line fragment ("As when from dark the vernal equinox") discovered among materials Saxe Commins kept from his close association with Faulkner during the 1950s, verse for Faulkner was always somewhere close by, waiting to be given voice, once again take flight, sing even in old age of youth's longings.

18 The 'Bama poems

Sometime early in his career, probably on different occasions between 1916 and 1921, Faulkner presented to his beloved great-aunt, Alabama Falkner McLean ("Aunt 'Bama"), of Memphis, Tennessee, thirteen poems in ribbon typescript. Only five of the poems were given titles, but seven others were arranged in sequence and assigned Roman numerals "I." through "VII." Most of these poems quite clearly belong to Faulkner's early phase, when Swinburne and Housman were principal influences.

Three poems from the 'Bama group—"Aubade," "Hymn," and "Pastoral"—were acquired by the University of Virginia and are part of the William Faulkner Collections at that institution. The remaining ten poems, now in the Brodsky Collection, were typed with a purple ribbon on eight sheets of plain white paper, 14 by 8½ inches, and one sheet of plain white paper, 10 by 7¾ inches. The eight legal-size leaves display a watermark depicting a replica of the Great Seal of the United States of America, while the smaller leaf is unwatermarked.

The numbered sequence of seven poems occupies four leaves (recto only), 14 by 8½ inches, and is arranged as follows:

[1] Poems "I." and "II."
[2] Poem "III." and first two stanzas of "IV."
[3] Remainder of poem "IV.," and "V."
[4] Poems "VI." and "VII."

a. "I." First line, "The sun lay long upon the hills." Revised and published as IX, *A Green Bough.*

b. "II." First line, "When I rose up with morning."

c. "III." First line, "Turn again, Dick Whittington."

d. "IV." First line, "When evening shadows grew around." Published as XI, *A Green Bough,* with the omission of stanza two.

e. "V." First line, "I give the world to love you."

f. "VI." First line, "When I was young and proud and gay." Slightly revised when published as XIII, *A Green Bough.*

g. "VII." First line, "Green grow the rushes O."

The other three poems in the 'Bama group are the following:

h. First line, "The black bird swung in the white rose tree." 1 page. Beneath last line of this poem Faulkner has written in black ink: "Mrs. Oldham, of Oxford, who has musical talent, is composing music / for this one."

i. "AN OLD MAN SAYS:" 1 page, 10 by 7¾ inches. Slightly altered version, entitled "I Will Not Weep for Youth," first published in *Contempo,* 1 (February 1, 1932), 1, and reprinted in *An Anthology of the Younger Poets* (1932).

j. "Eunice." 3 pages. First published in *Mississippi Quarterly,* 31 (Summer 1978), 449–452.

I

The sun lay long upon the hills,
The plowman slowly homeward wends;
Cattle low, uneased of milk,
The lush grass to their passing bends.

Mockingbirds in the ancient oak
In golden madness swing and shake;
Sheep, like surf against the cliff
Of quiet green hills, flow and break.

The sun sank down, and with him went
A pageantry whose swords are sheathed
At last, as warriors long ago
Laid their armor by and breathed

This air and found this peace as he
Who, across this sunset moves to rest,
Finds but simple scents and sounds
And this is all—but this is best.

II

When I rose up with morning
I was as brave a lad
As ever broke a furrow
In sunlight garment-clad.

I knew that death came after
But he was far away,
And naught save he could hurt me
While I was strong and gay.

But now my furrow's ended
And, ah, I know, I know
That naught save breaking furrow
Could e'er half hurt me so.

III

Turn again, Dick Whittington,
Sang voices in a wood;—
We'll not wait to call you thrice
So take your tide at flood.

But it was ever the way of youth
To think that Time will wait,
That he may choose his day to climb
The long blue stairs of fate.

"When I'm Lord Mayor of London town
—As tomorrow I shall be—
You'll have a golden canopied throne
And a young page at your knee.

But that is that, and it will keep:
Tonight let's think of naught.
The world is soft and sweet as sleep,
As though for us 'twas wrought."

Turn back, turn back, Dick Whittington!
For we'll not call again.

But young Dick with a maid was lost
Within a twilit lane.

IV

When evening shadows grew around
And the young moon filled the lane,
Their slowing feet made scarce a sound
As Richard strolled with Jane.

They clung and kissed in the leafy shade
And life was fine and clear;
A prince and princess, boy and maid—
Let's stop a little here.

The world was empty of all save they
And spring itself was snared.
Ah, poor's the fare of any day
When none has lesser fared.

Young breasts hollowed out with fire,
A singing fire that spun
The gusty tree of his desire
Till tree and gale were one;

And a small white belly yielded up
That they might try to make
Of youth and dark and spring a cup
That cannot fail nor slake.

V

I give the world to love you:
Now, cross your heart and say—
By moon and stars above,
You'll be true for aye.

So her sweet fire had filled them
With song of youth to youth
And the solemn moment stilled them
Inarticulate with truth.

But again, when skies were lighted,
'Twas easier to say:
She another Harry plighted
And he another May.

VI

When I was young and proud and gay
And flowers in fields were thicking,

There was Tad and Ralph and Ray
All waiting for my picking.

And who, with such a page to spell
And the hand of spring to spread it,
Could like the tale told just as well
By another who had read it?

Ah, not I! and if I had
—When I was young and pretty—
Learned to spell not, there was Tad
And Ralph and Ray to pity.

There was Tad and Ray and Ralph
And field and lane were sunny;
And, oh, I spelled my page myself
Long ere I married Johnny.

VII

Green grow the rushes O
And merry blows the mead;
Now youth his golden penny O
The spending he'll not heed.

Brown turn the rushes O
And flowers blow and die;
And never so gay the spending O
He'll cry it by and by.

[untitled]

The black bird swung in the white rose tree:
Heigh ho, lads; its [*sic*] going to rain!
Though they tell you 'ware of a maid's soft eye
Lest the heart within you break and die;
But when you're old, ah, then you'll sigh
For sweet is the fruit that's once passed by!
Heigh ho, lads; for its going to rain.

The black bird swung in the white rose tree:
Heigh ho, lassies; its going to rain!
And the maiden's sad whose breast must yearn
Over last year's roses in this year's urn
For the rose that's withered will not return.
An[d] the bridge be aflame? ah, let it burn!
Heigh ho, lassies; for its going to rain.

The black bird swung in the white rose tree:
Heigh ho, youth; its going to rain!

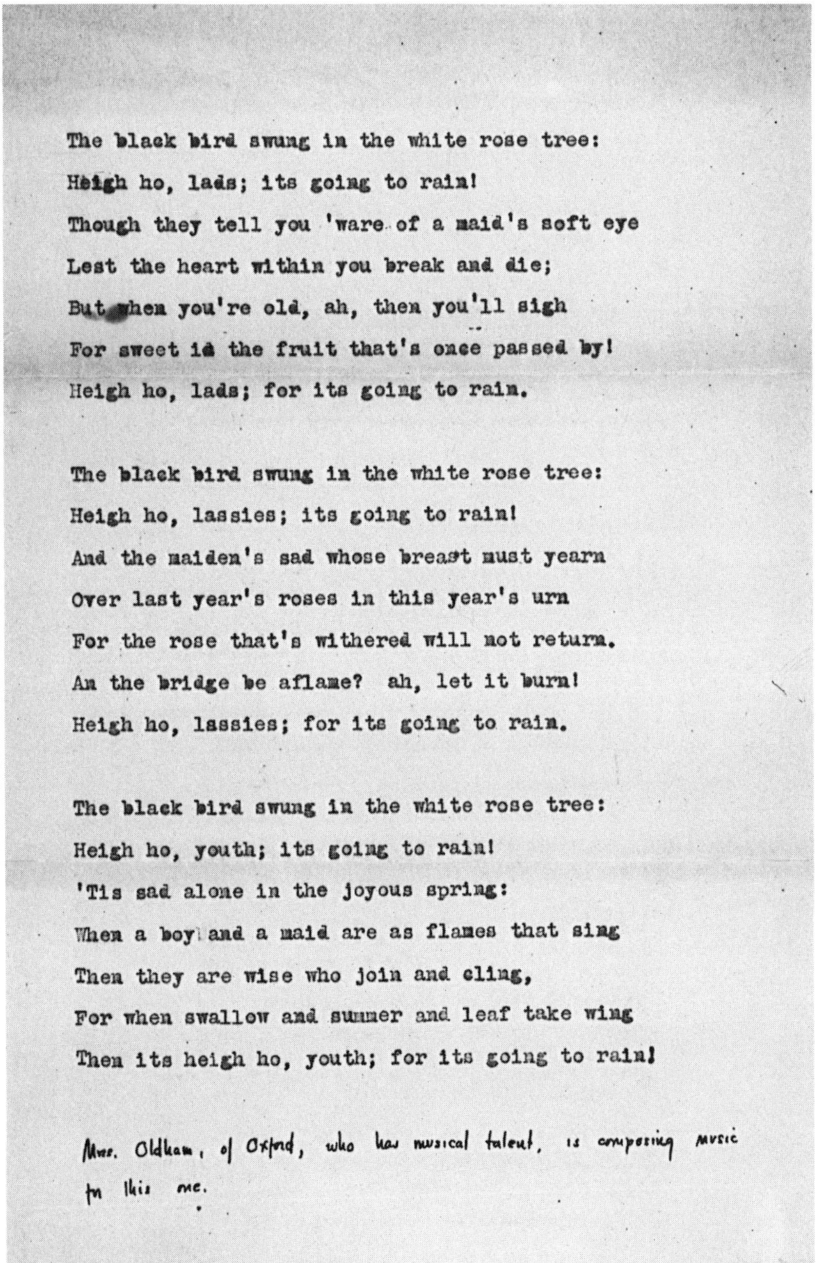

The black bird swung in the white rose tree:
Heigh ho, lads; its going to rain!
Though they tell you 'ware of a maid's soft eye
Lest the heart within you break and die;
But when you're old, ah, then you'll sigh
For sweet is the fruit that's once passed by!
Heigh ho, lads; for its going to rain.

The black bird swung in the white rose tree:
Heigh ho, lassies; its going to rain!
And the maiden's sad whose breast must yearn
Over last year's roses in this year's urn
For the rose that's withered will not return.
An the bridge be aflame? ah, let it burn!
Heigh ho, lassies; for its going to rain.

The black bird swung in the white rose tree:
Heigh ho, youth; its going to rain!
'Tis sad alone in the joyous spring:
When a boy and a maid are as flames that sing
Then they are wise who join and cling,
For when swallow and summer and leaf take wing
Then its heigh ho, youth; for its going to rain!

Mrs. Oldham, of Oxford, who has musical talent, is composing music for this one.

23. "The black bird swung in the white rose tree," c. 1916–1921

'Tis sad alone in the joyous spring:
When a boy and a maid are as flames that sing
Then they are wise who join and cling,
For when swallow and summer and leaf take wing
Then its heigh ho, youth; for its going to rain!

AN OLD MAN SAYS:

I do not weep for youth, in after years
Nor does there haunt me, when I am old,
The world's face in its springtime, blurred with tears
That healed to dust harsh pageantries of gold.

Nor can dulled brain, or ears at a sound scarce heard
Trouble old bones asleep from a sun to a sun
With a dream forgot, a scent or a senseless bird,
That now with earth and silence are brethren: one.

The poplar leaves swirl sunward, bright with rime
To a stately minuet of wind and wheat;
But spring is blown on ruins of old time,
Cruel, incurious, superbly sweet;

And swallows that arch and tighten across the heart
Can strike no hidden chord, when it is mute:
A caught breath, flash of limbs in the myrtles apart—
Dancing girls to a shrilling of lyre and lute.

Death and I amicably wrangle, face to face,
Mouthing dried crumbs of pains and ecstasies;
And regard without alarm cold seas of space—
Eternity is simple where sunlight is.

EUNICE

Is this the house where Eunice lived,
So blank of door, shutter-eyed;
Whose gable streams with star-bright hair?
Is this the house where Eunice died?

Yes, this is the house, that's now so still.
But, ah, when Eunice was a girl
It was bright with happy din
Till every leaf would laugh and whirl

As Eunice danced along the paths
To stroke the flowers with her hands,
And then her tinselled hollyhocks
Bowed in fragile sarabands.

Here is still the sunny nook
Where a boy once climbed the wall,
And together they were crowned
By the cherry's snowy fall.

And this, too, is just such a night
With spring in oak and spring in beech,
When Eunice' lips at last were locked
And words were naught and lost was speech.

Beneath this oak would Eunice sit
To plan and play with lace and thread;
This tree that saw her rosy dream,
This tree that saw her lover dead;

That saw poor Eunice, brave and gay,
And passionate with youth and grief
And wept for her: it knew how sharp
In love, that cannot last, how brief!

But Eunice now, though years have passed,
Is passionate still for spring and youth
When in the April world the rain
Sings as does a singing mouth

And scraps of sky are lost in pools
Blown like silk along the ground;
And above the terrace, through the trees,
The wind goes with a silken sound.

Ah, Eunice; would you seek
Fauns and nymphs in formal ways;
Narcissus, to the garden pool,
Chained by his reflected gaze?

But who can know what Eunice sought
Who was so gently touched by time,
To whom both lad and lass must go
When youth like bells in tune would chime?

In the long and level afternoon
Of summer Eunice always sat
To the gracious rite of tea.
Upon the emerald grass her hat

Bravely flowered, change disdained
Of style and shape and seemed, like her,
More gracious for the grace and strength
That would withdraw, but not defer.

Or in her twilit music room:
Wistaria in inverted flame

Lapping the window, who can know
What thoughts to hurt, what longings came

Moth-like to the candles' gold
Mimic sea upon the ceiling,
While songs of Eunice' yesterday
Set its soundless tide to wheeling?

And, ah, her sorry recompense:
Though youth is lost, her dream is gain—
Who eats his fruit alone can know
That bitter's the husk which must remain.

Is this old garden, choked with weeds,
The sward where she walked to and fro?
Is this the house where Eunice died?
Yes, long ago; ah, long ago.

24 ["L'Apres-Midi d'un Faune"], c. 1918. Autograph manuscript, in pencil, on torn fragment (7 by 11 inches) of front cover of *Saturday Evening Post,* August 31, 1918.

This is quite possibly the first draft of the opening stanza of this poem. The text is markedly different from other known versions. For a detailed discussion of the relationship of this draft to other versions of the poem, see Robert W. Hamblin and Louis Daniel Brodsky, "Faulkner's 'L'Apres-Midi d'un Faune': The Evolution of a Poem," *Studies in Bibliography,* 33 (1980), 254–263.

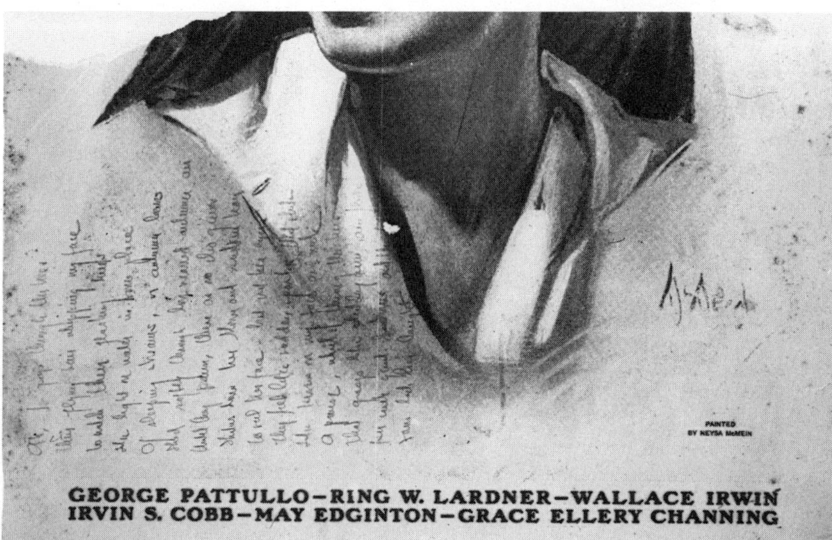

24. Early draft of "L'Apres-Midi d'un Faune," c. 1918

Ah, I peep through the trees
Their flying hair whipping my face
To watch their flashing knees
Like light on water in some place
Of sleeping streams, or autumn leaves
Shed softly through long wearied autumn air
Until they pause, then as one who grieves
Shakes down her blown and sudden hair
To veil her face—but not her eyes.
They feel like sudden sparks that strike
Like kisses on my face and neck.
A pause, whirls through the trees
That grasp like glidding [*sic*] arms, and fleck
Her with quick shadows and the breeze
Fans back her laughter.

22 ["The Lilacs"], c. 1918, autograph manuscript in pencil, 5 pages (3 leaves).

These pages contain early drafts, with deletions and revisions, of material which eventually became lines 1–25, 67–78, and 88–98 of poem published as "The Lilacs." Like other materials in the Brodsky Collection from this period, such as "L'Apres-Midi d'un Faune," "A Dead Dancer," and World War I airplane drawings, these manuscripts were for more than a half century stored in Mrs. Maud Falkner's house among memorabilia from Faulkner's service days as a cadet in the RAF training camp at Long Branch, Toronto, Ontario, Canada. For a full discussion of these pages in relation to other relevant manuscripts, see Louis Daniel Brodsky, "The Autograph Manuscripts of Faulkner's 'The Lilacs'," *Studies in Bibliography,* 36 (1983), 240–252.

a. Recto: first line, "We sit, drinking tea." 1 page, 14 by 8½ inches, Hammermill Bond. On verso: pencil drawings of three World War I airplanes and ink drawing of faun and nymph (see page 16).

We sit, drinking tea
Beneath the lilacs of a summer afternoon
Comfortably, at our ease
[We are in Blighty *del.*]
With real, fresh linen napkins on our knees
We are in Blighty
And we sit, we three
In diffident contentedness
Lest we let each other guess
How pleased we are
Together watching the young moon
Lying [on her ba *del.*] shyly on her back, and the first star

There are women here
Smooth shouldered creatures in sheer scarves, that pass

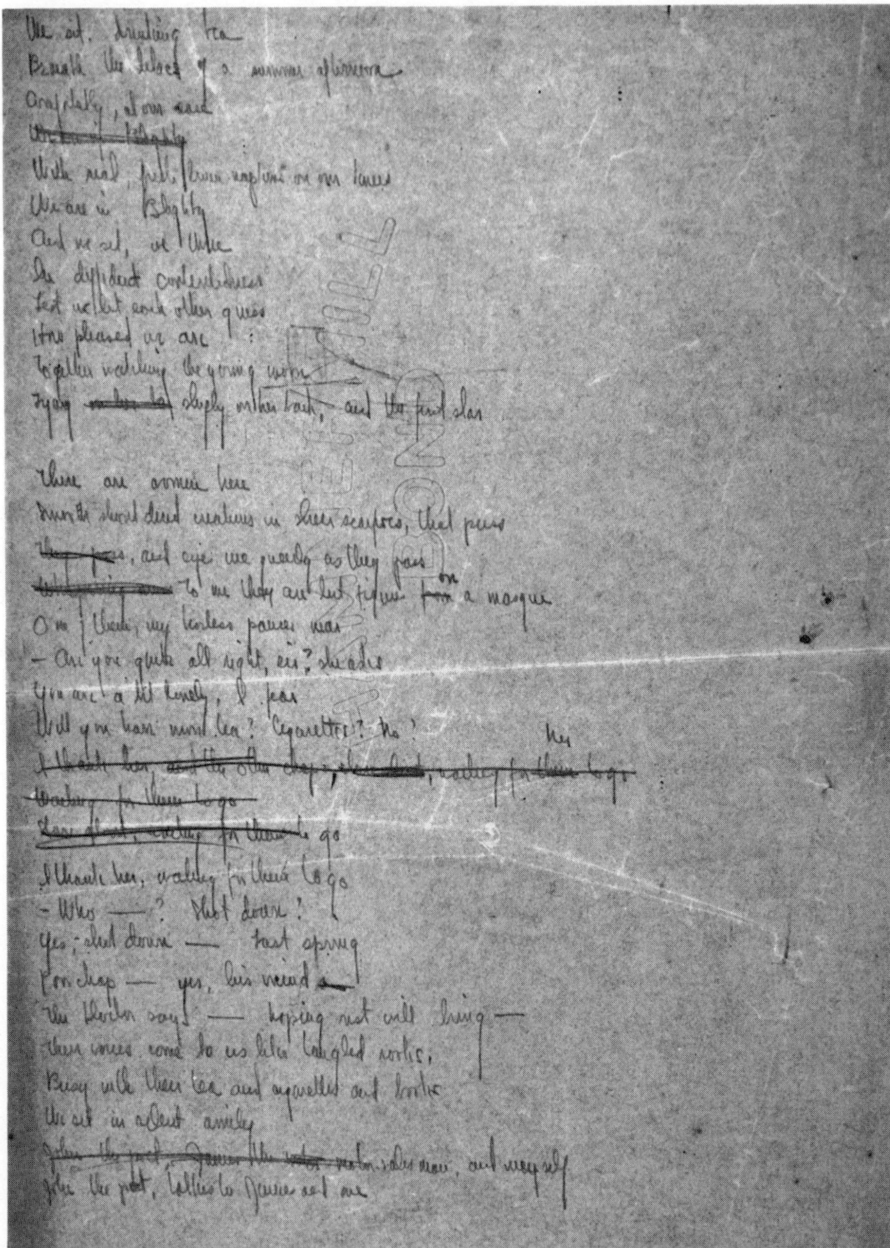

25. Manuscript page of "The Lilacs," c. 1918

[They pass, *del.*] and eye me queerly as they pass
[Whispering across *del.*] To me they are but figures [from *del.*] <on> a
masque
One of them, my hostess pauses near
—Are you quite all right, sir? she asks
You are a bit lonely, I fear
Will you have more tea? Cigarettes? No?
[I thank her, and the other chaps, [stare about, *del.*] waiting for [them *del.*]
<her> to go *del.*]
[Waiting for them to go *del.*]
[Stare about, waiting for them to go *del.*]
I thank her, waiting for them to go
—Who—? Shot down?
Yes, shot down—Last spring
Poor chap—yes, his mind—
The Doctor says—hoping rest will bring—
Their voices come to us like tangled rooks,
Busy with their tea and cigarettes and books
We sit in silent amity
[John the poet, James the [motor *del.*] motor *del.*] salesman, and myself
John the poet, talks to James and me

c. Verso: first line, "We had been." 1 page, 11 by 8½ inches, Hammermill Bond.

We had been
Raiding over Mannheim. Youve seen
The place? Then you know
How one hangs just beneath the stars, and seems
To see the incandescent entrails of the Hun,
And you doubtless know
Those strong sharp searchlight gleams
That cross and recross like sounds
[And [*illeg.*] *del.*]
[To the chap who is impaled on two of them *del.*]
[For the bloody Hun, when all is said and done *del.*]
And the racket of engines and the slow
Coughing unfolding of Archie shell.
Well
[They boxed us in the whirl *del.*]
We had released our bombs and started home
There were Huns everywhere by now
Like wasps around a bat
[Crosses, crosses, crosses *del.*]
[Then the first tracers *del.*]
And tracer bullets like fireflies in dew laden thickets

They boxed us in the whirl
And did us in

b. Verso: first line, “We had been [raiding over M *del.*],” 1 page, 11 by 8½ inches, Hammermill Bond.

We had been [raiding over M *del.*]
Raiding over Mannheim. Youve seen
The place? Then you know
How one hangs just beneath the stars, and seems
To see the incandescent entrails of the Hun
And you doubtless know
[The searchlight gleams *del.*]
[Like wheeling sounds that search for sky for us *del.*]
[And the racket of engines and the slow *del.*]
[Unfolding of the shells *del.*]
[We had released our bombs and started *del.*]
The Huns lurking in the high air
To drop on us [[*illeg.*] the spewing of machine guns *del.*] <with a spewing of guns> and a dance
Of tracers like fireflies in a dew laden thicket
And the great black earth reaching up hungry hands for us
I wonder that any [of the fel *del.*] people even got back alive
Well
The boxed

To drop on us like wasps around a bat

b. Recto: first line, “And the air was alive with Huns.” 1 page, 11 by 8½ inches, Hammermill Bond, letterhead: “M. C. Falkner / Hardware / Oxford, Miss.”

And the air was alive with Huns
And the great black earth reaching [after us *del.*] up for us
<*marg.* A spewing of guns>
And a dance
Of tracers like fireflies over a deep meadow
They boxed us and did us in
Three Huns followed [us, *del.*] after us
Until the machine began to break
And scream from the speed of falling
And I threw away my goggles

There is an end to this somewhere

I

The black earth pulled us down, that night
Out of the bullet tortured air

That was like [an enorm *del.*] a great bowl full of fireflies
There is an end to this somewhere
[We are too young to die *del.*]
One should not die like this

c. Recto: first line, "We sit in silent thoughtfulness." 1 page, 11 by 8½ inches, Hammermill Bond.

We sit in silent thoughtfulness
I shiver suddenly, the sun has gone
And the air is cooler where we three
Sit I can scarcely see
[Them *del.*] And the after glow of the west has followed the sun
The light has gone from the worlds rim
And the pale lilacs stir against a lilac pale sky
The poet bends his head

We sit in silent amity
I shiver suddenly, the sun has gone
And the air is cooler where we three
Are sitting. The light has gone from the worlds rim
Following the sun
And I can scarcely see
The stirring of the pale lilacs against the lilac pale sky
They bend their heads toward me as one head
—Old man—they say—when did you die?
I—I am not dead
[They eye each other as people who have committed a gaucherie *del.*]
[In consternation tinged with pity *del.*]
I hear their whisper as from a great distance—Not dead
Not dead—Poor chap, he isnt dead.
We sit, drinking tea

23 ["A Dead Dancer"], c. 1918, autograph manuscript in pencil and ink, 4 pages (4 leaves).

These are early drafts, including rewrites, of portions of poem which became "A Dead Dancer." For a further discussion of these materials, see Louis Daniel Brodsky, "Additional Manuscripts of Faulkner's 'A Dead Dancer'," *Studies in Bibliography,* 34 (1981), 267–270.

a. First line, "The hurdy-gurdy in the street below." 1 page, 14 by 8½ inches, Hammermill Bond, in brown ink with revisions in pencil.

The hurdy-gurdy in the street below
Still weaves the song across the silent street
Like gold threads in an ancient tapestry

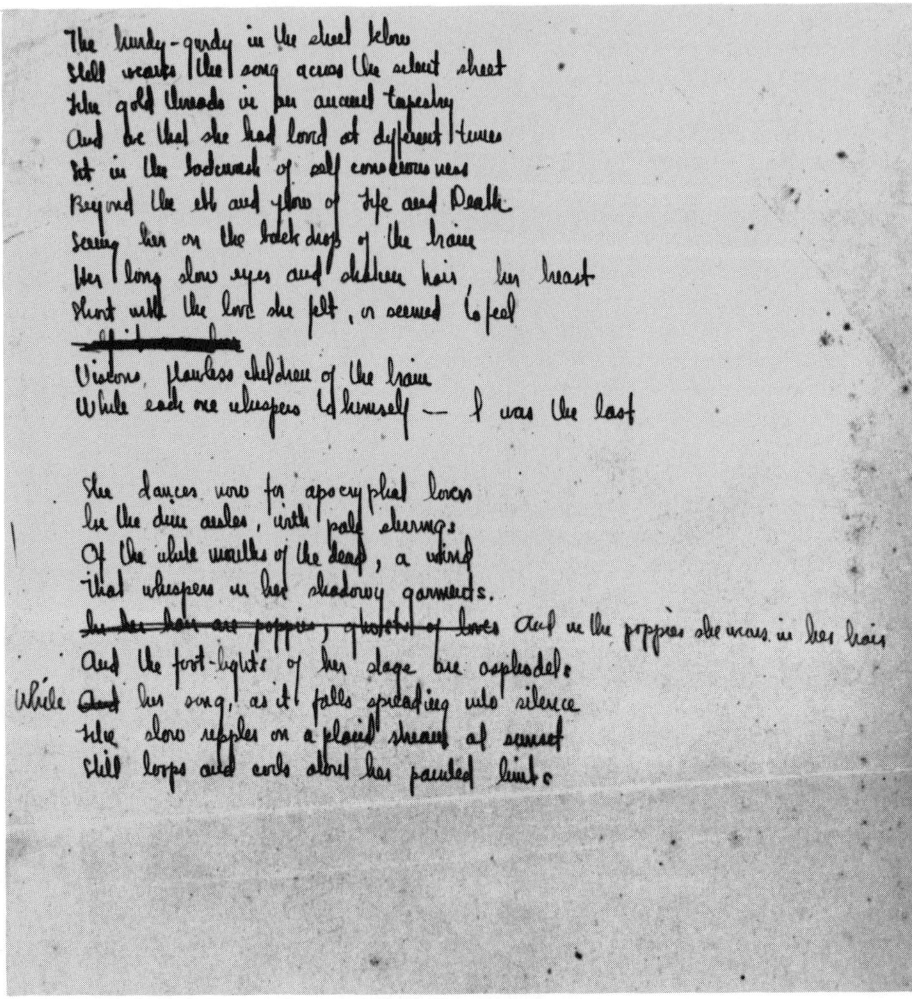

The hurdy-gurdy in the street below
Still weaves the song across the silent street
Like gold threads in an ancient tapestry
And she that she had loved at different times
Set in the backwash of self consciousness
Beyond the ebb and flow of Life and Death
Seeing her on the black drop of the brain
Her long slow eyes and shaken hair, her breast
Burnt with the love she felt, or seemed to feel
~~[illegible]~~
Visions, flawless children of the brain
While each one whispers to himself — I was the last

She dances now for apocryphal lovers
In the dim aisles, with pale stirrings
Of the white wraiths of the dead, a wind
That whispers in her shadowy garments.
~~In her hair are poppies, ghostetal of loves~~ And in the poppies she wears in her hair
And the foot-lights of her stage are asphodel.
While ~~And~~ her song, as it falls spreading into silence
Like slow ripples on a placid stream at sunset
Still loops and curls about her painted limbs.

26. Early draft of "A Dead Dancer," c. 1918

And we that she had loved at different times
Sit in the backwash of self consciousness
Beyond the ebb and flow of Life and Death
Seeing her on the backdrop of the brain
Her long slow eyes and shaken hair, her breast
Short with the love she felt, or seemed to feel
[—If it was love *del.*]
Visions, flawless children of the brain
While each one whispers to himself—I was the last.

She dances now for apocryphal lovers
In the dim aisles, with pale stirrings
Of the white mouths of the dead, a wind
That whispers in her shadowy garments.
[In her hair are poppies, ghosts of loves *del.*]
<*marg.* And in the poppies she wears in her hair>
And the foot-lights of her stage are asphodels
[And *del.*] <*marg.* While> her song, as it falls spreading into silence
Like slow ripples on a placid stream at sunset
Still loops and coils about her painted limbs

d. Verso: first line, "She goes through calm vistas of the shadows." 1 page, 11 by 8½ inches, Hammermill Bond, in pencil. Also on this page are portions of a draft of "The Lilacs" (see page 37). Recto: additional experimental lines from "The Lilacs" (see page 39).

She goes through calm vistas of the shadows
Pale with stirrings of the white mouths of the dead

About her are the white mouths of the dead
Their voices, like a wind that whispers in her garments
And in the poppies wreathed about her head
While the foot lights of her stage are asphodels
And her song, as it falls spreading into silence
Still loops and coils about her painted legs

About her now the white mouths of the dead
Stir like a wind that whispers in her garments
And in the poppies wreathed about her head
While the foot lights of her stage are asphodels
And her song, as it falls spreading into silence
Still loops and coils about her painted legs

b. First line, "The long rain wheels across the sad slow sky." 1 page, 14 by 8½ inches, Hammermill Bond, in pencil. Experimental lines containing images and phrases incorporated into the finished poem.

The long rain wheels across the sad slow sky
Shaking its brooding hair, stiffened formless gleams
Like dreams to haunt our dreams
While summer dies from trees into grey air
Stiff with rain; the long rain shakes its hair

And we sit dreaming dreams beyond the ebb and flow
Of days, blown bits of dirty paper
Stiff with rain; the long rain shakes its hair

And we sit dreaming dreams beyond the ebb and flow
Of insistent shadows, a threading of violins
Horns draw sensuously in darkness
Stiff with rain; the long rain shakes its hair

The long rain wheels across the sad slow sky
Shaking its brooding hair, stiffened formless gleams
Like dreams to haunt our dreams
While summer dies in trees into grey air
And we sit dreaming dreams beyond the ebb and flow
Of dripping shadows, a threading of violins
Horns draw sensuously in darkness
Stiff with rain; the long rain shakes its hair

c. Verso: first line, "The long rain wheels across the sky." 1 page, 11 by 8½ inches, Hammermill Bond, in pencil. Additional experimental lines, very few of which found their way into the poem. Recto: letterhead: "M. C. Falkner / Hardware / Oxford, Miss."

The long rain wheels across the sky
Shaking its brooding hair in formless gleams—
S[low *ov.* ad] dreams to haunt our dreams, a threading of violins
And Horns draw sensuously in darkness
And crowding shadows liquid in the darkness
[And the *ov.* Stiff with] rain; the long rain shakes its hair
Stiff with the backwash

While summer dies in trees into grey air
And we sit dreaming dreams beyond the ebb and flow
Of dying years

The long rain wheels across the stiff sad sky
Shaking its brooding hair in formless gleams
Slow dreams to haunt our dreams [with *ov.* of] with crowding shadows
Stiffened in the rain; the long rain shakes its hair
While summer dies in trees into grey air
Liquid

26 *The Lilacs,* 1920

On January 1, 1920, Faulkner presented to his lawyer friend and literary mentor, Phil Stone, a 36-page booklet of poems, handlettered in India ink, illustrated with ink and water color drawings, and handbound in a red velvet cover. Printed in Faulkner's hand on both the cover and the title page is "THE LILACS / W. FAULKNER."

The verso of the title page carries a dedication to Stone, including a quotation in French, "[. . .] *luit quand il fait Sombre,*" as well as the place and the date, "[. . .]ON* JAN 1 1920." The text contains Faulkner's characteristic reversed s's, like those appearing in the *Ole Miss* poems and cartoons, *Marionettes,* and other contemporaneous works.

Although this gift booklet has been severely damaged, with roughly the outside half of each page having been burned away by the fire that destroyed Stone's home in 1942, enough of the contents remain to allow a collation of most of the poems with other extant copies and thus an approximate restoration of the original texts. The sources relied upon for the restoration that appears on the following pages are identified in parentheses in the outline of the contents of the book.

The material in the booklet, now disassembled in order to protect the fragile leaves, was originally ordered by Faulkner as follows:

[1] Title page

[2] Dedication page

[3] Blank page

[4] Water color of female figure

[5–14] "The Lilacs." Subsequently published in *Double Dealer,* 7 (June 1925), 185–187; *A Green Bough* (I); *Anthology of Magazine Verse for 1925; Salmagundi* (1932); and *Anthology of Poems from the Seventeen Previously Published Braithwaite Anthologies* (1958). (Fair ink copy, University of Virginia; *Double Dealer,* June 1925).

[15–16] "Cathay." Previously published in *The Mississippian,* November 12, 1919, p. 8. *(Early Prose and Poetry)*

[17] "To a Co-ed." Subsequently published in *Ole Miss,* 1919–1920. *(Early Prose and Poetry)*

[18] Unidentified poem.

[19] "O Atthis" (first line). Content and form altered significantly when published as XVII, *A Green Bough.*

[20] "[ ]t Living." Unidentified poem.

[21–23] "L'Apres-Midi d'un Faune." Slightly different from the versions published in the *New Republic,* 20 (August 6, 1919), 24, and *The Mississippian,* October 29, 1919, p. 4. *(Early Prose and Poetry)*

[24–25] "Une Ballade des Femmes Perdues." Published shortly after its appearance here (with slight changes in punctuation) in *The Mississippian,* January 28, 1920, p. 3. *(Early Prose and Poetry)*

[26] "[ ] Bathing." Unidentified poem.

*These letters, barely visible in the charred edge of the page, almost certainly are the remains of the word "Charleston." Stone lived in Charleston, Mississippi, from 1918 into the early '20s, where, with his brother Jack, he managed a branch of the family law firm. Faulkner was a frequent visitor to Charleston during this period and may very well have compiled this booklet of poems during one of these visits.

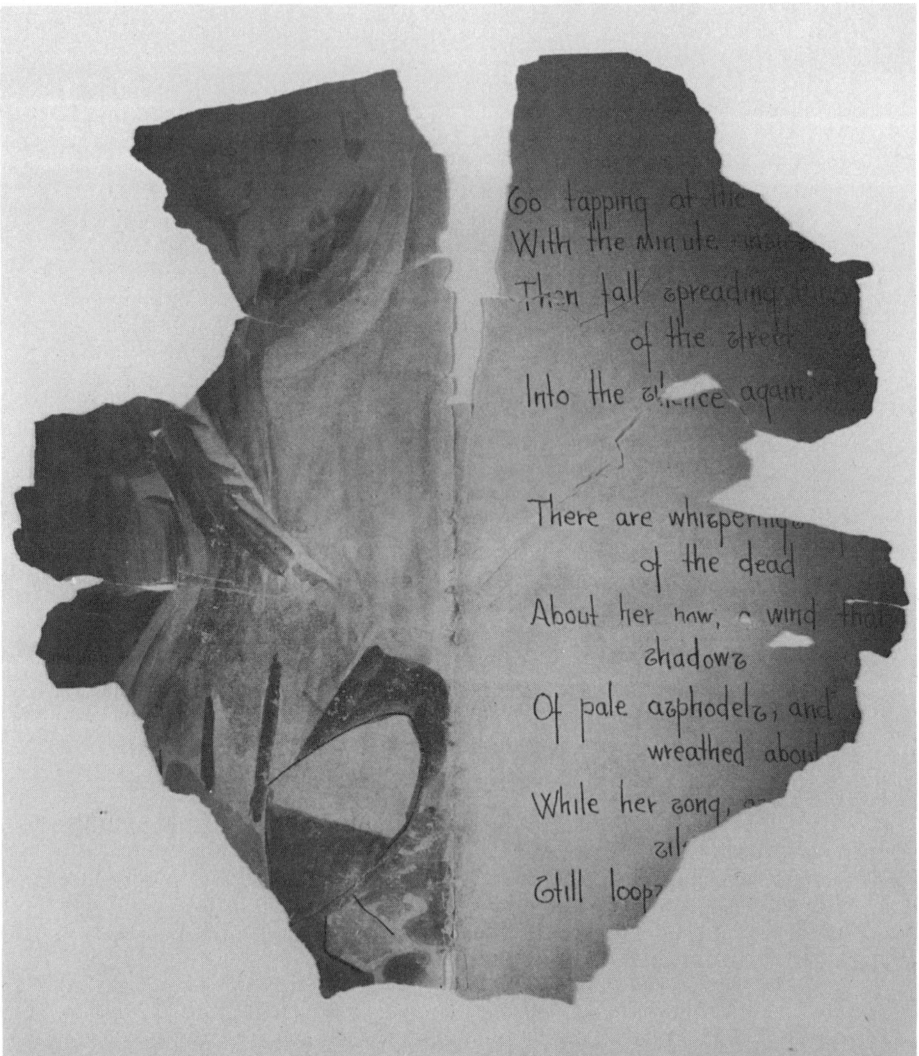

27. Pages 4 (water color) and 33 ("A Dead Dancer") of *The Lilacs*

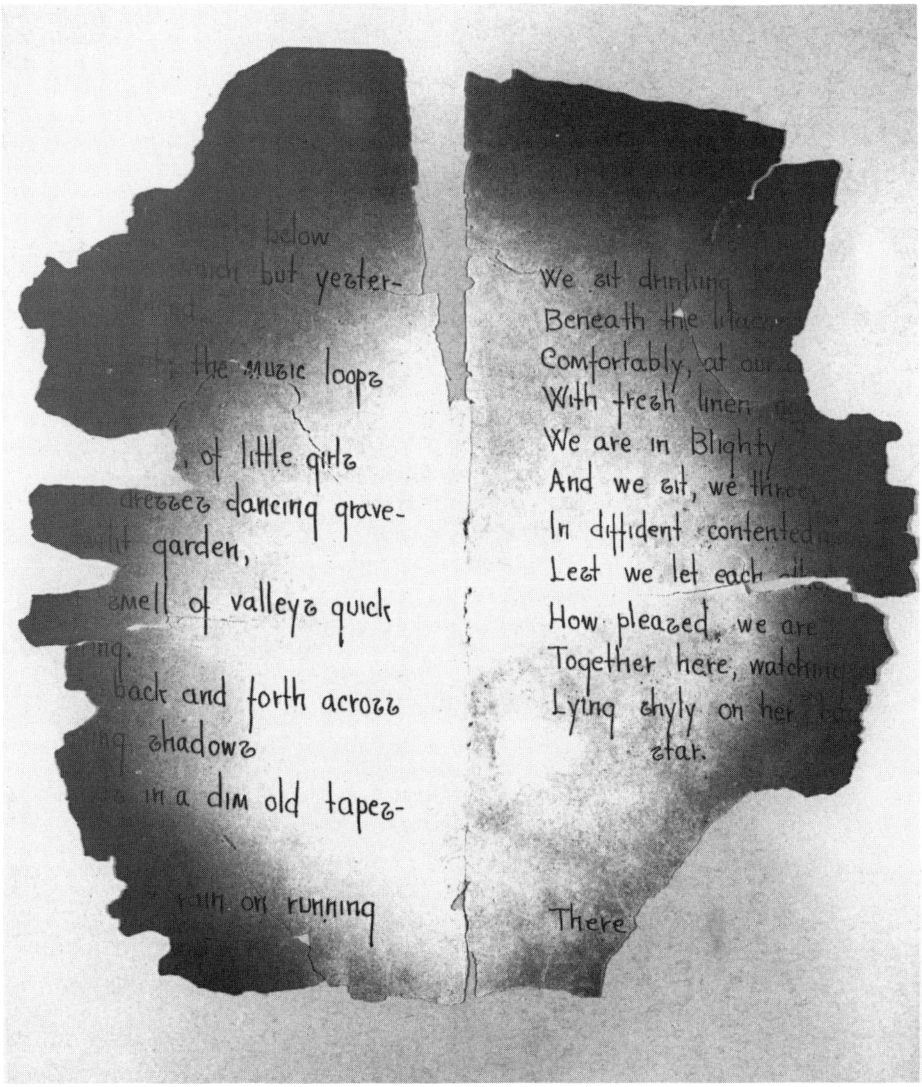

28. Pages 32 ("A Dead Dancer") and 5 ("The Lilacs") of *The Lilacs*

[27] "After Fifty Years." Previously published in *The Mississippian,* December 10, 1919, p. 4. *(Early Prose and Poetry)*

[28–30] "Sapphics." Previously published in *The Mississippian,* November 26, 1919, p. 3. *(Early Prose and Poetry)*

[31–33] "A Dead Dancer." (Manuscripts in Brodsky and University of Virginia Collections)

[34] "[ ] Storm." Unidentified poem.

[35] Black and white, pen and ink drawing of nude female

[36] Apparently a blank endpaper

THE LILACS

W. FAULKNER

[1]

[ ] AVERNOG, PHIL STONE
THIS BOOK IS
[ ]CTIONATELY DEDICATED:
[ ] luit quand il fait Sombre.'
[ ]ON JAN 1 1920

[2]

[Blank Page]

[3]

[Water Color Drawing]

[4]

THE LI[L]ACS

We sit drinking tea
Beneath the lilacs on a su[mmer afternoon]
Comfortably, at our ease
With fresh linen napkins [on our knees]
We are in Blighty
And we sit, we three,
In diffident contentedness
Lest we let each other guess
How pleased we are

Together here, watching th[e young moon]
Lying shyly on her bac[k, and the first]
star.

There [are women here,]

[5]

[Smooth shouldered] creatures in sheer
[Scarves, that] pass
[And eye me s]trangely as they pass.
[One of them,] my hostess, pauses near.
[—Are you quite] all right, sir?—she stops
[to ask.]
[Will you] have more tea? Cigarettes?
[No?—]
[I thank her], waiting for them to go,
[To me they] are as figures on a masque.
[—Who?— Sh]ot down—
[Yes, shot down—Las]t spring—
[Poor chap—Yes,] his mind—
[Hoping rest will bring]—
[Their voices come to me like] tangled
[rooks]

[6]

Busy with their tea a[nd cigarettes]
and books.
We sit in silent am[ity]

—It was a morning in la[te May]
A white woman,
A white wanton at the edg[e of a brake]
A rising whiteness mirrore[d in a lake]
And I, old chap, was o[ut before the]
day
Stalking her through t[he shimmering]
reaches [of the sky]
In my lit[tle pointed-eared machine.]
I kne[w that we could catch her]
[when we liked]

[7]

[For no nymphs] ran as swiftly as
[they c]ould.

[We mounted up an]d up,
[And found her at] the border of a wood
[A cloud forest],
[And pausing] at its brink
[We felt her] arms and her cool breath
[A red rose] on white snows, the kiss
[of] Death.

[The bullet] struck me here, I think,
[In my left] breast
[And killed my] little pointed-eared
[machine.] I watched it fall
[The last wine in a cu]p. . . .
[I thought that we could find] her when
[we liked]

[8]

But now I wonder if I [found her, after]
all.

One should not die [like this]
On such a day
From hot angry bullets, o[r other mod-]
ern way. From angry bullets
One should fall I think [to some]
Etruscan dart
On such a day as this
And become a tall wr[eathed column;]
I should like t[o be]
An ilex tre[e on some white lifting]
isl[e.]
Instead[, I had a bullet through my heart—]

[9]

[—Yes, you are] right
[One should] not die like this,
[And for no c]ause nor reason in the
[world.]
[Tis right enough] for one like you to
[talk]
[Of going into] the far thin sky to stalk
[The mouth] of Death, you did not
[know the] bliss
[Of home a]nd children and the se-
[rene]

[Of living, and] of work and joy that
    [was our] heritage,
[And best of all, of age.]
[We were too young.]

[10]

Still—he draws his [hand across]
    his eyes
—Still, it could not be [otherwise.]

We had been
Raiding over Man[nheim. You've seen]
The place? Then [you know]
How one hangs jus[t beneath the stars]
    and seems to se[e]
The incandescent entr[ails of the Hun.]
The great earth drew [us down, that]
    night. [The black earth drew us]
Out of the bullet [tortured air]
A black bowl of [fireflies. . .]

[11]

[There is an en]d to this, somewhere;
[One should n]ot die like this—

[One should] not [die li]ke this—
[His voice has dropp]ed and the wind
    [is mouthing h]is words
[While the lilacs n]od their heads on
    [slender stal]ks,
[Agreeing while] he talks
[And care] not if he is heard, or is
    [not hear]d.
[One should not die] like this—
[Half audible, half] silent words
[That hover like] grey birds
[About our heads]

[12]

We sit in silent amity
I shiver, for the sun is [gone]
And the air is cooler wh[ere we three]
Are sitting. The light h[as followed]
    the sun,

And I no longer see
The pale lilacs stirri[ng against the]
lilac-pale [sky.]

They bend their h[eads toward me]
as one head
—Old man—the[y say—]
When d[id you die? . . .]

[13]

[I—I am not] dead.

[I hear their] voices as from a great
[distance]—Not dead

[He's not dea]d, [poor] chap; he didn't
[die]—
[We sit, drinki]ng tea.

[14]

CATHA[Y]

Sharp sands, those blind de[sert horsemen, sweep]
Where yesterday tall shining [caravels]
Swam in thy golden past. [What Fate foretells]
That now the winds go light[ly, lest thy sleep]
Be broken. Whe[re] once th[y splendors rose,]
And cast their banners bri[ght against the]
sky,
Now go the empty years [infinitely]
Rich with thy ghos[ts. So is it: who sows]
The seed of Fame mak[es the grain for Death]
to reap.

Wanderers, with faces [sharp as spears,]
And flocks and her[ds on aimless muffled]
feet

[15]

[Drift where glittering] kings went through
[each] street
[Of thy white va]nished cities; and the years
[Have closed lik]e walls behind them. Still
[Through the sp]awn of [le]sser destinies

[We stare, whe]re once thy star burned, lest
[like t]hese
[We lose faith. They know thee not, nor
[will]
[To see thy mag]ic empire when the hand
[Thrusts back t]he curtain of the shifting
(sand,]
[On singing stars] and lifting golden hill.

[16]

[TO A CO-ED]

The dawn herself could no[t more beauty wear]
Than you, mid other women [crowned in grace,]
Nor have the sages known [a fairer face]
Than yours, gold shadowed [by your bright]
sweet hair.
Than you does Venus seem l[ess heavenly fair;]
The twilit hidden stillness of [your eyes,]
And throat, a singing bri[dge of still replies,]
A slender bridg[e], [yet all dreams hover there.]

I could have turned unm[oved from Helen's brow,]
Who found no beauty in the[ir Beatrice;]
Their Thäis seemed les[s lovely than as now,]
Though some had barte[red Athens for her kiss.]
For down Time's arras f[aint and fair and far,]
Your face still beckon[s like a lonely star.]

[17]

[ ]

[ ] the dusk
[ ] garden
[ ]
[ ] dies in grey
[ ]
[ ]spering candles.

[18]

[ ]

O Atthis

For a moment, an eon
I pause, blind

Drawn down
Consumed
In the blaze of the sap[ ]
That burns on thy [ ]

O Atthis

[19]

[ ]T LIVING

[ ] are scattered through the
[ ]
[ ] young beseeching hands. Her hair
[ ]d with them, and the
[ ]
[ ] of her breasts, as young and
[ ]
[ ] now bear kisses for the
[ ]
[ ] dead; nor sighs nor any tears
[ ]er: she only hears the slight
[ ]ing down the years
[ ]ken birds in evening

[20]

L'APRES-MIDI D'UN [FAUNE]

I follow through the [singing trees]
Her streaming clouded h[air and face]
And lascivious dreaming k[nees]
Like gleaming water from [some place]
Of sleeping streams, or a[utumn leaves]
Slow shed through still lo[ve-wearied air.]
She pauses, and as one [who grieves]
Shakes down her blown [and vagrant hair]
To veil her face, but [not her eyes—]
A hot quick spark, each [sudden glance,]
Or as the wild brown b[ee that flies]
Sweet winged, a sharp [extravagance]
Of kisses on my limbs [and neck.]
She whirls, and dan[ces through the trees]
That lift and sway [like arms and fleck]
Her with quick sh[adows, and the breeze]

[21]

[Lies on her short] and circled breast.
[Now hand in ha]nd with her I go,

[The green nig]ht in the silver West,
[Of virgin st]ars, pale row on row
[Like ghostly] hands, and ere she sleep
[The dusk will] take her by some stream
[In silent mea]dows, dim and deep—
[In dreams of] stars and dreaming dream.

[I have a nam]eless wish to go
[To some far s]ilent midnight noon
[Where lonely] streams whisper and flow
[And sigh on san]ds blanched by the moon.
[And blond limbe]d dancers whirling past,
[The senile worn moo]n staring through

[22]

The sighing trees, unt[il at last,]
Their hair is powdered [bright with dew.]
And their sad slow limbs [and brows]
Are petals drifting with t[he breeze]
Shed from the fingers [of the boughs;]
Then suddenly, on all of [these,]
A sound, like some great [deep bell stroke]
Falls, and they dance, uncla[d and cold—]
It was the earth's [great heart that broke]
For springs before the [world grew old.]

[23]

[UNE BALLADE DES FEMMES PE]RDUES

[I sing in the green] dusk
[Fatuously]
[Of ladies that] I have loved
[—Ca ne fait] rein! Helas, vraiment, vraiment

[Gay little gh]osts of love[s] in silver sandals
[They dance] with quick feet on my lute-
    [strin]gs
[With the ab]andon of boarding-school virgins
[While unbidden mot]hs
[Amorous of my] white seraglio
[Call them with] soundless love-songs
[A sort of eth]ereal seduction

[They hear, alas]
[My women]
[And brush my lips with] little ghostly kisses

[24]

Stealing away
Singly
Their tiny ardent faces
Like windflowers from some [blown garden of]
dreams
To their love-nights am[ong the roses]

I am old, and alone
And the star-dust from thei[r] wings
Has dimmed my eyes
I sing in the soft dus[k]
Of lost ladies—Si vrai[ment charmant,]
charmant

[25]

[ ] BATHING

[ ]th sprite
[ ] of white
[ ]
[ ]
[ ]
[ ]
[ ]gainst the moon,
[ ]s o'June
[ ] her knees
[ ]
[ ]iteness in gleams
[ ] sing birds in dreams
[ ] still is
[ ]
[ ]a'en my eyes
[ ]nder thighs
[ ]s

[26]

AFTER FIF[TY YEARS]

Her house is empty and [her heart is old,]
And filled with shades and [echoes that deceive]
No one save her, for still [she tries to weave]
With blind bent fingers, nets [that cannot hold.]
Once all men's arms rose [up to her, 'tis told,]
And hovered like white bird[s for her caress:]
A crown she could have had [to bind each tress]
Of hair, and her sweet arms the [Witches' Gold.]

Her mirrors know her whiteness, [for there]
She rose in dreams from ot[her dreams that lent]
Her softness as she stood, c[rowned with soft hair.]
And with his straight heart [and his young eyes]
    bent
And blind, he feels her pres[ence like shed scent,]
Holding him body and li[fe within its snare.]

[27]

[SAPPHICS]

[So it is: sleep] comes not on my eyelids
[Nor in my eyes], with shaken hair and
    [white]
[Aloof pale hand]s, and lips and breasts
    [of iron,]
    [So] she beholds me,

[And yet th]ough sleep comes not to
    [me t]here comes
[A vision fro]m the full smooth brow of
    [sleep,]
[The white Ap]hrodite moving unbounded
    [By her] own hair

[28]

In the purple beaks [of the doves]
    that draw her,
Beaks straight without [desire, necks]
    bent backward
Toward Lesbos and the [flying feet]
    of Loves
    Weeping behind he[r.]

She looks not back, [she looks not]
    back to where
The nine crowned mu[ses about]
    Apollo
Stand like nine Corinth[ian columns]
    singing
    in clear eve[ning.]

[29]

[She sees not the] Lesbians kissing
    [mouth]

[To mouth acr]oss lute strings, drunken
[with] singing.
[Nor the white] feet of the Oceanides
[Shini]ng and unsandalled;

[Before her go cr]yings and lamentations
[Of barren wo]men, a thunder of wings,
[While outcast] Lethan women, lamen-
[ting,]
[Stiffen] the twilight.

[30]

A DEA[D DANCER]

We, that she had [loved at different]
times
Sit at dusk in diffident gutt[ering silence,]
a ring
Of ill-trimmed lamps, for [we dare not meet]
Each other naked in the dark
—Is it relief we feel? As [yet one can-]
not say,
We are so many trees that [knew the]
spring.
So we sit here in the [backwash of self]
consciousness,
Dreaming dreams beyon[d the ebb and flow]
Of Life and Death, w[hile each one whis-]
pers to himself [—I was the last.]

[31]

[A hurdy gurdy in t]he street below
[Reiterates a so]ng to which but yester-
[day] she danced
[On slender] gilded feet; the music loops
[and] coils
[ ]xically sad, of little girls
[ ] white dresses dancing grave-
[ly in] a twilit garden,
[The faint s]weet smell of valleys quick
[with] spring.
[The notes wea]ve back and forth across
[the gr]owing shadows
[Like gold thr]eads in a dim old tapes-
[try,]
[And delicate as] the rain on running
[feet]

[32]

Go tapping at the [consciousness]
With the minute insist[ence of the rain,]
Then fall spreading throu[gh the stillness]
of the street
Into the silence again.

There are whisperings [of the white mouths]
of the dead
About her now, a wind that [stirs the]
shadows
Of pale asphodels, and [in the poppies]
wreathed about [her head,]
While her song, a[s it falls spreading into]
sil[ence,]
Still loops [and coils about her painted legs.]

[33]

[ ] STORM

[ ]s
[ ] dripping hair
[ ] thin garments to the sun
[ ]ar
[ ] in Chicago

[34]

[Pen and Ink Escutcheon]

[35]

[Blank Endpaper]

[36]

27 The Stone fragments, c. 1920

The Brodsky Collection includes ten partially burned leaves containing autograph and typescript fragments of early Faulkner poems. These fragments, like the damaged "Lilacs" booklet described on pages 43–57, were salvaged by Carvel Collins and Emily Stone from the ruins of Phil Stone's house a decade after its destruction by fire in 1942.

Three leaves, one of which is dated "April, 1920," apparently come from an early typescript version of *The Marble Faun.* The other seven leaves contain autograph (recto) and typescript (verso) lines from various poems. In three instances the text of the holograph fragment corresponds with that of a typescript fragment on a different leaf. No watermark is visible on any of the ten sheets.

Some eighty pieces of related materials were acquired from Stone by the University of Texas at Austin in 1959. The Texas and Brodsky fragments, taken as an aggregate, appear to comprise drafts of three distinguishable books of poems: *Vision in Spring; Orpheus, and Other Poems;* and *The Marble Faun.* The first of these Faulkner presented in a single impression copy, typed and handbound, to Estelle Franklin in 1921. (Judith L. Sensibar's edition of this text was published by the University of Texas Press in 1984.) *Orpheus* was never published, though some of its passages were subsequently incorporated into the version of *The Marble Faun* that was published in 1924.

a. Burned fragment, ribbon typescript (black ink), 1 page. Subject matter and wording suggest *The Marble Faun,* although this passage does not appear in published version. Contains two emendations in Faulkner's hand.

[ ] spills
[ ]g toothed hills
[ ]ke water down the sides
[ ]e va[ ]e; a deep stream glides
[ ]de me here, murmuring cool
[ ] the Naids [*sic*] in their pool.
Below the misted rainbow falls
Circled by its dim blue walls
The Naiads dwell in cool retreat.
The waters sing about their feet
Where all day sunlight sleeps in it,
And the slender moon weeps in it,
While sunsets burn between the two,
And rose-grey daws [*sic*] petalled with dew.
Flowers blow on either hand
Where wide-eyed narcissi stand
And [low *del.*] <bow> in unison beneath,
Where scarce-moving winds breathe,
<*marg.* Where the moving winds scarce brea>
Day on day they dream and sigh
Until the night comes brooding by.
Then they look up through their pool
To watch the sunset flame and cool;
And stars like sparks blow in the sky
As hills in slumber turn and sigh,
Then Naiads spread soft mouths in song
Of the days quiet and long,
Of the forward-turning year.
Winter they can never fear,

b. Burned fragment, ribbon typescript (black ink), 1 page. Fourteen-line section beginning "The stream flows calmly without so[und]" and ending "Throbs her sorrow out to them" appears, in slightly altered form, in *The Marble Faun* (pp. 31–32).

[ ] wing [ ]ded stream,
[ ]ughing and weeping in their [ ]

The stream flows calmly without so[ ]
[ ] the darkness gathered round;
[ ]mbling to the wandering breeze,
Above me stand the inky trees
Peopled by some bird's loud cries
Until it seems as though the skies
Had shaken down their blossomed stars
To seek through the trees' dim bars,
Crying aloud each for his mate
About the old earth, insensate
Seemingly to their white woe;
But their sorrow does she know
And her breast, unkempt and dim,
Throbs her sorrow out to them.
The loud bird's oft-repeated cries
Fill the night with peering eyes
From every dimly-crouching brake,
Also without sound or shake.
The wind so softly shivers by
That all the trees unstirringly
——That arm in arm about me stand——
Part it like water on each hand.

c. Burned fragment, ribbon typescript (black ink), 1 page. Apparently the last page of the typescript; typed below last line: "WILLIAM FAULKNER. / April, 1920." Includes "[. . .]th things that I would know / [. . .]wixt sky above and earth below" (cf. *The Marble Faun,* pp. 12, 49).

[ ]; and my own
[ ]th things that I would know
[ ]wixt sky above and earth below,
[ ]d the earth is blinded too:
Her tears are what men call dew,
Trembling on the hedges, where
They shine like fireflies prisoned there.

d. Burned fragment, recto: autograph manuscript in pencil, 1 page. Similar phrasing and imagery (for example, "surf," "hissing brain," and "spark") appear in lines 85–86 of "The Dancer," in *Vision in Spring*. Cf. also II, *A Green Bough.*

[ ] watched great
[ ] of rain upon
[ ] saw great solemn
[ ] the silence like pale monstrous flowers.

[ ], the specter at my side
[ ] me, and fawned and clung and cried.
It was you who, in a certain dark,
Beneath a surf of blind desire in which you strayed
In a wind that fanned your brain a hissing spark,
You slew me, and my slender body laid
On crusted salty stones roughened with cold.
You laid my body and brought my soul
And in this floorless grass you stole
To hide us both from mortal sight,
For here, perhaps, you thought: I'll die
And wake to walk in clam eternal night
But while you will choir the sky
What of me? whom you have slain?

j. Burned fragment, verso: ribbon typescript (purple ink), 1 page. Second and third stanzas bear strong affinity with lines 72–74, 79–80, in "The Dancer," in *Vision in Spring.*

[ ]er the same, always the same.
[ ] you, for a strange far music sang
[ ] me, a music that I must have heard
[ ]en forgot, for it was strange,
[ ] not strange at all. And when I heard
[ ] I always knew that you were near,
[ ] until I called you to appear.

[ ]alk, then, of a thousand things—
[ ] we have heard, that we have played,
[ ]ave formed of silence when our hands
[ ]nd clung and strayed.

[ ]ppiness, of life,
[ ]arkness cool as rain,
[ ] stars in slim processionals
[ ]ce from the skies again.

XXVII

f. Burned fragment, recto: autograph manuscript in pencil, 1 page. Lines 9–15 are virtually identical to lines 35–39 and 26–27 of "After the Concert," in *Vision in Spring.*

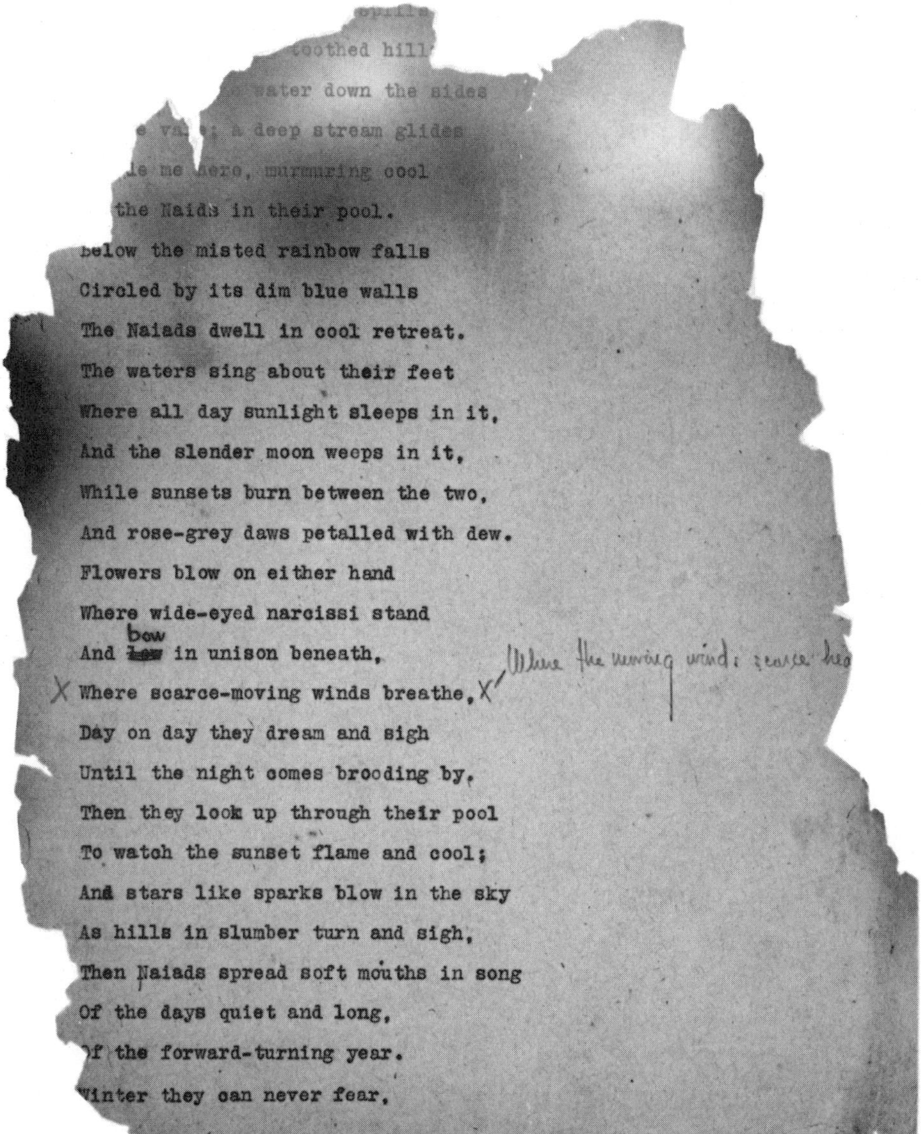

spills
toothed hill
water down the sides
e vale; a deep stream glides
de me here, murmuring cool
the Naids in their pool.
Below the misted rainbow falls
Circled by its dim blue walls
The Naiads dwell in cool retreat.
The waters sing about their feet
Where all day sunlight sleeps in it,
And the slender moon weeps in it,
While sunsets burn between the two,
And rose-grey daws petalled with dew.
Flowers blow on either hand
Where wide-eyed narcissi stand
And ~~low~~ bow in unison beneath,
X Where scarce-moving winds breathe, X' Where the moving winds scarce bre
Day on day they dream and sigh
Until the night comes brooding by,
Then they look up through their pool
To watch the sunset flame and cool;
And stars like sparks blow in the sky
As hills in slumber turn and sigh,
Then Naiads spread soft mouths in song
Of the days quiet and long,
Of the forward-turning year.
Winter they can never fear,

29. Burned fragment of poem, c. 1920

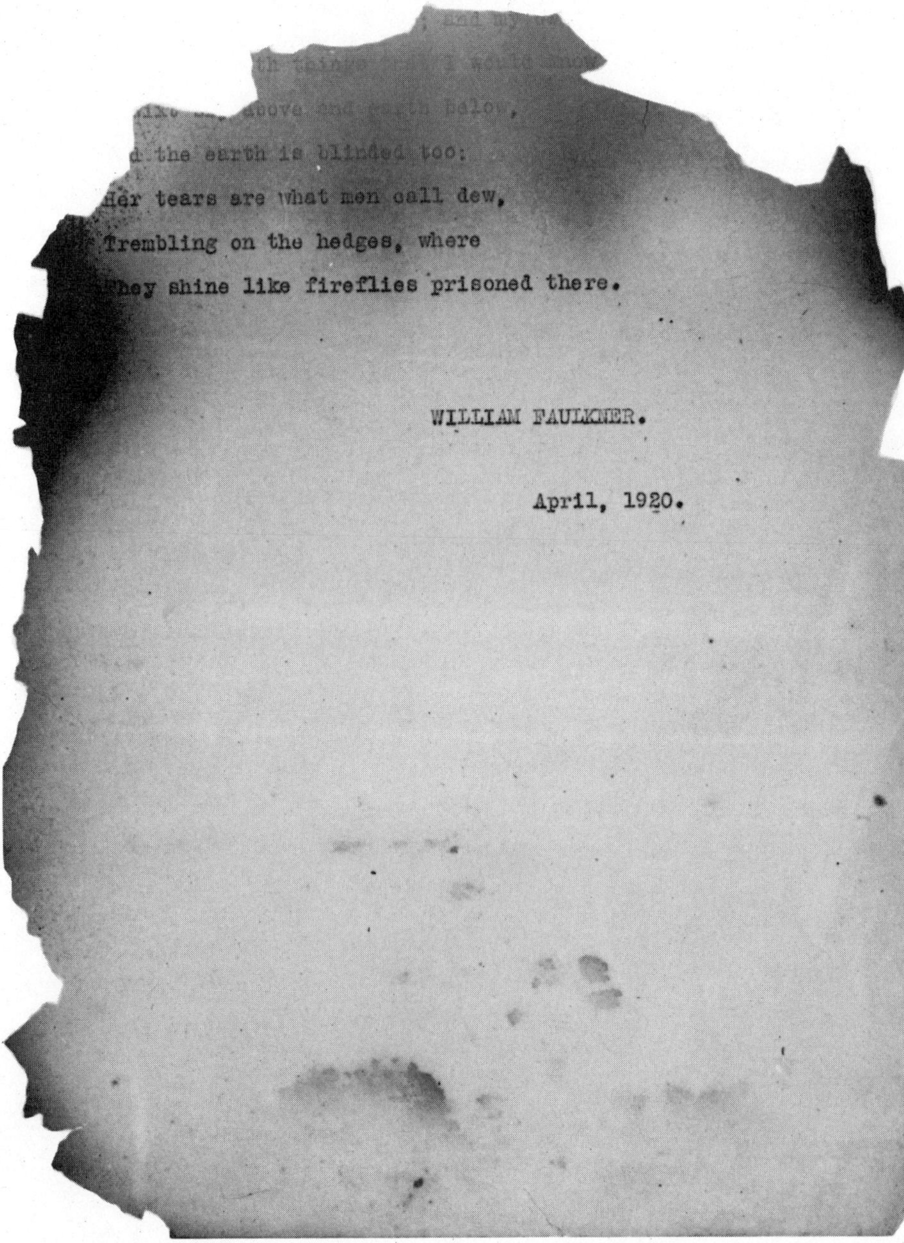

d the earth is blinded too:
Her tears are what men call dew,
Trembling on the hedges, where
They shine like fireflies prisoned there.

WILLIAM FAULKNER.

April, 1920.

30. Burned fragment of early typescript of *The Marble Faun*

[ ] in armor, greave by greave
[ ]nd lances are hurled and fall again.
[ ]ere is something yet, still unattained,
A fuller word than flesh, a stranger thing.
We hear an untouched music pause and sing:—
More than flesh, and more than brain,
More than joy or peace or pain,
More than life and death, this thing—
When it is gained, then all is gained.

Weave, you luminous flowers, weave
A gold device upon dark's lowered shield.
We rise, to a hidden music, out of night,
We laugh and weep, and then to night we yie[ ]

We cry, and raise our joined hands to the far
Still eternal gesture of a star.

e. Burned fragment, recto: autograph manuscript in pencil, 1 page. Virtually identical to lines 14–27 52–65, of poem VII ("A Symphony") in *Vision in Spring*

[ ] and knock
[ ] in flock on flock
[ ]the world
[ ] and whirl
[ ] hands linked in dance
[ ] called life, extravagance.
[ ] drum, and mutter horn
[ ] the dark whence all are born,
[ ] the dark whence all return,
[ ] that freeze, clays that burn!
[ ]ise from dust and walk to dust,
[ ]eauty cries, and falls in lust.
[ ] wild, you far winds, hurl,
[ ] this dead dust from the world.

j. Burned fragment, recto: autograph manuscript in pencil, 1 page. Unidentified poem. This page of holograph roughly corresponds to the typescript appearing on **i** verso.

[ ]d say—This smile I never knew?

No, dont let's talk of partings, forgetting.
Let us accept life as it is, of this
Bright immortal beauty we have found.
Let us forget the mouth, but keep the kiss.
Do you remember that [strange *del.*] first strange passionate spring

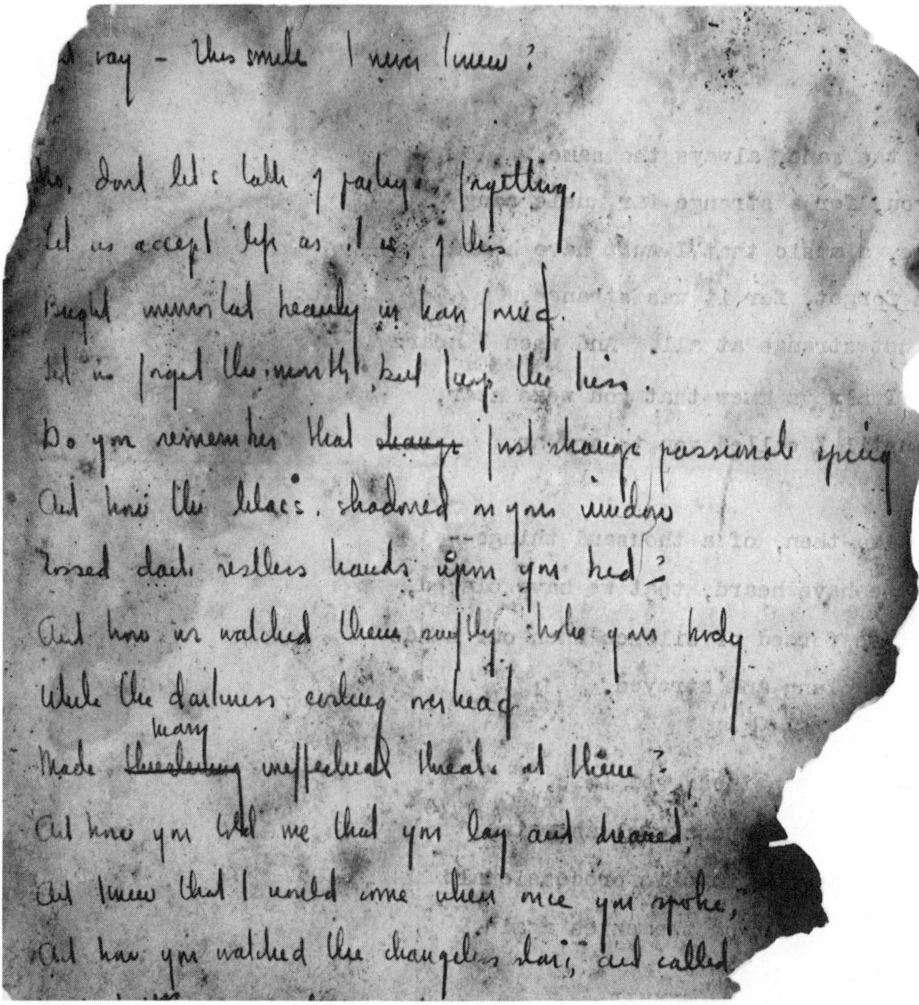

...say — this smile I never knew?

No, don't let's talk of parting, forgetting,
Let us accept life as it is, of this
Bright [illegible] beauty in keen grief.
Let us forget the mouth, but keep the kiss.
Do you remember that ~~strange~~ first strange passionate spring
And how the lilacs, shadowed on your window
Tossed dark restless hands upon your bed?
And how we watched them swiftly stroke your body
While the darkness circling overhead
Made ~~threatening~~ many ineffectual threats at them?
And how you told me that you lay and dreamed,
And knew that I would come when once you spoke,
And how you watched the changeless stars, and called

31. Burned fragment of unidentified poem, c. 1920

And how the lilacs, shadowed on your window
Tossed dark restless hands upon your bed?
And how we watched them swiftly stroke your body
While the darkness coiling overhead
Made [threatening *del.*] <heavy> ineffectual threats at them?
And how you told me that you lay and dreamed,
And knew that I would come when once you spoke?
And how you watched the changeless stars, and called

i. Burned fragment, verso: ribbon typescript (purple ink), 1 page. Unidentified poem. This page of typescript roughly corresponds to the autograph manuscript on **j** recto.

[Let us accept life as] it is, take this
[Bright immortal beauty] we have found.
[Let us forget the mou]th, but keep the kiss.

[Do you remem]ber that first strange passionate spring,
[And how the] lilacs, shadowed on your window
[Tossed da]rk restless hands upon your bed?
[And how] we watched them swiftly stroke your body,
[While th]e darkness coiling overhead
[Made h]eavy ineffectual threats at them?
[And ho]w you told me that you lay and dreamed
[And kn]ew that I would come when once you spoke?
[And how y]ou watched the changeless stars and called my name
[ ]ss in your garden, and I came?

[ ] you call whole springs and springs away. . . .
[ ]irst I thought a spirit spoke
[ ] in beauty was your voice, like wings;
[ ] lay sleepless in your bed
[ ] spring walk in your garden ways.

[ ] saw your face
[ ] when I closed my eyes,
[ ] and different ways

i. Burned fragment, recto: autograph manuscript in pencil, 1 page. Unidentified poem. This page of holograph roughly corresponds to the typescript on **h** verso.

[ ] of pai[n]

[ ] slender magic, called my soul
[ ]ealed by yours, restored it me again.

[Y]es, let us talk of those dark silent days
Yet beautiful to me, also, for I knew

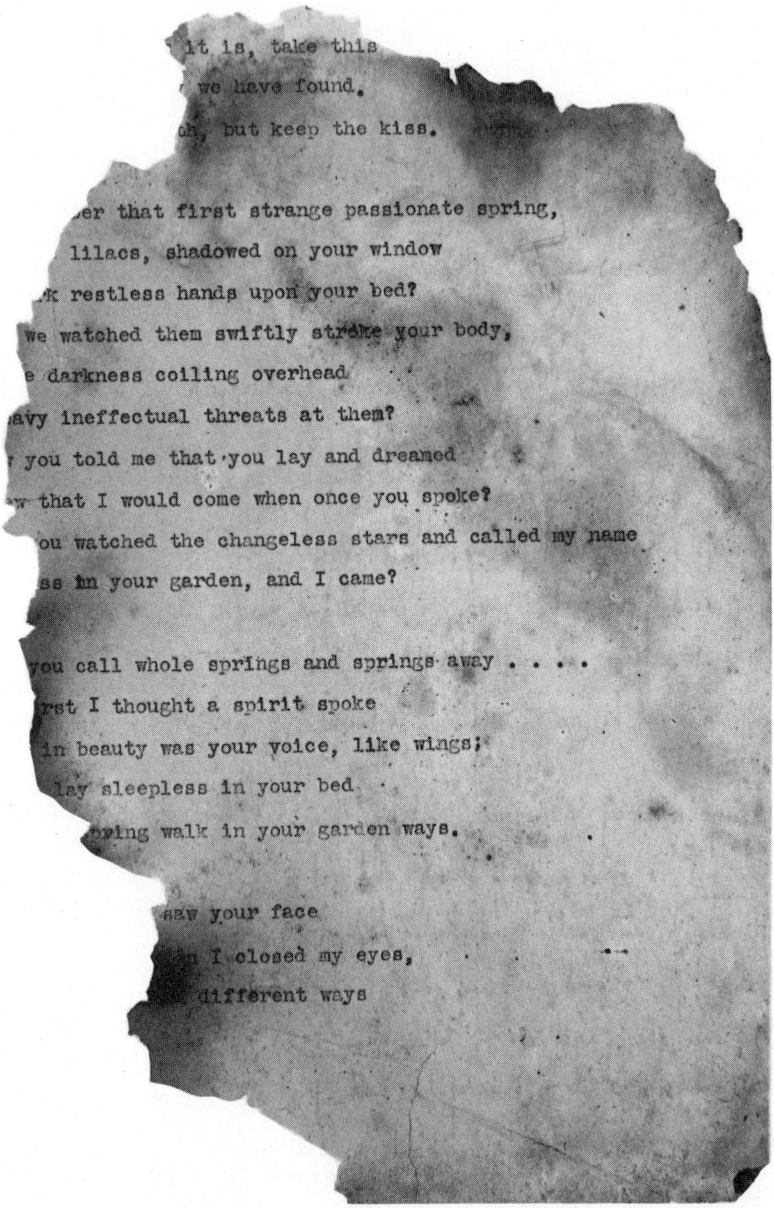

it is, take this
we have found.
th, but keep the kiss.

er that first strange passionate spring,
lilacs, shadowed on your window
k restless hands upon your bed?
we watched them swiftly stroke your body,
e darkness coiling overhead
avy ineffectual threats at them?
you told me that you lay and dreamed
w that I would come when once you spoke?
ou watched the changeless stars and called my name
ss in your garden, and I came?

you call whole springs and springs away . . . .
rst I thought a spirit spoke
in beauty was your voice, like wings;
lay sleepless in your bed
pring walk in your garden ways.

saw your face
I closed my eyes,
different ways

32. Burned fragment of unidentified poem, c. 1920

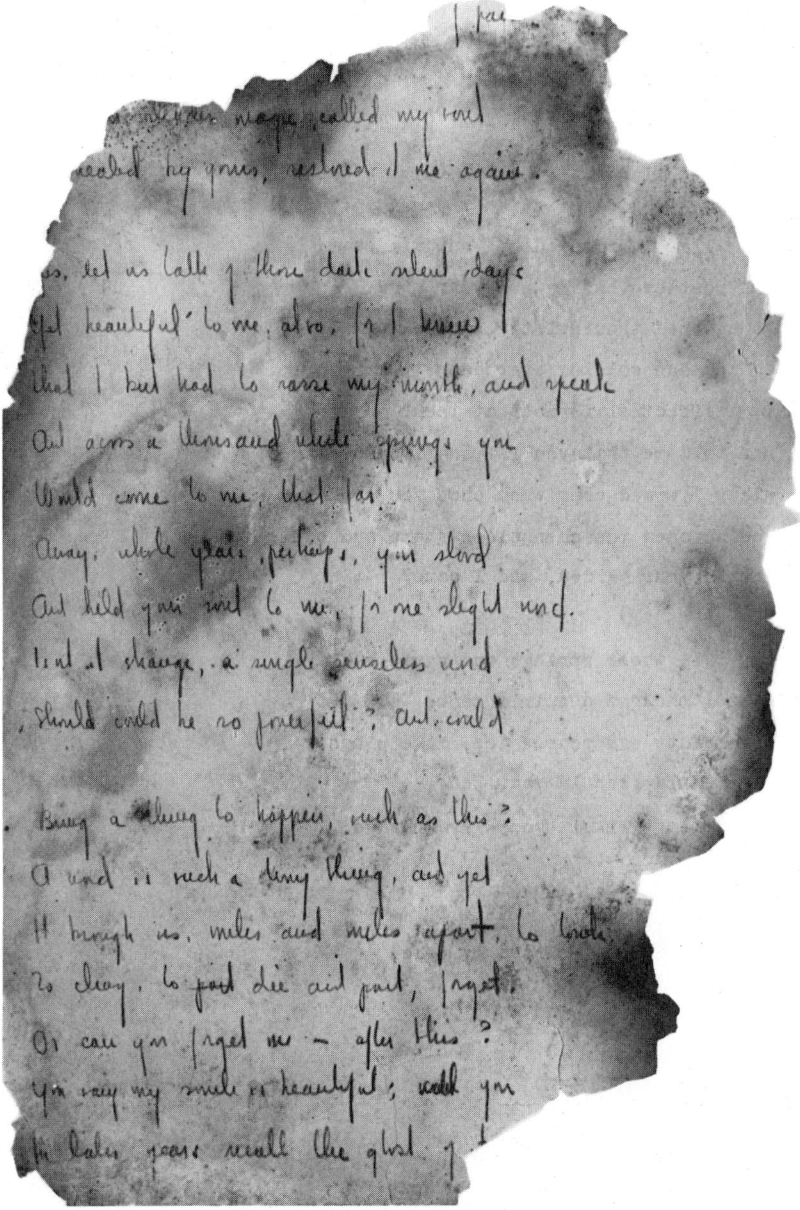
magic, called my soul
by yours, restored it me again.

let us talk of those dark silent days
Yet beautiful to me, also, for I knew
That I but had to raise my mouth, and speak
And across a thousand white springs you
Would come to me, that far
Away, whole years, perhaps, you stood
And held your soul to me, for one slight word.
That it should, a single senseless word
Should could be so powerful? And could

Bring a thing to happen, such as this?
A word is such a tiny thing, and yet
It brought us, miles and miles apart, to look
To stay, to past die and part, forget.
Or can you forget me — after this?
You say my smile is beautiful; would you
In later years recall the ghost of

33. Burned fragment of unidentified poem, c. 1920

That I but had to raise my mouth, and speak
And across a thousand white springs you
Would come to me, that far
Away, whole years, perhaps, you stood
And held your soul to me, for one slight word.
Isnt it strange, a single senseless word
Should could be so powerful? And could

Bring a thing to happen, such as this?
A word is such a tiny thing, and yet
It brough[t] us, miles and miles apart, to touch,
To cling, to [part *del.*] die and part, forget.
Or can you forget me—after this?
You say my smile is beautiful; will you
In later years recall the ghost of [it]

h. Burned fragment, verso: ribbon typescript (purple ink), 1 page. Unidentified poem. This page of typescript roughly corresponds to the autograph manuscript on **i** recto.

[ ]ars,
[ ] in your slim hands,
[ ]ng of your smile
[ ] youth and made it whole,
[ ]ight stiffened vales of pain
[ ] slender magic, called my soul
[ ] it with yours, restored it me again.

[Yes, l]et us talk of those dark silent days
[Yet b]eautiful, to me, also; for I knew
[That I] but had to raise my mouth and speak,
[And] across a thousand white springs you
[Would] come to me; that far
[Away,] whole years away, perhaps, you stood
[And hel]d your soul to me for one slight word.
[Isnt i]t strange, a single senseless word
[ ] be so powerful? And could

[Bring] a thing to happen, such as this?
[A word is] such a tiny thing, and yet
[It brought u]s, miles and miles apart, to touch,
[To cling, to p]art and die, forget. . . .
[Or can you] forget me—after this?
[You say m]y smile is beautiful; will you
[In later y]ears recall the ghost of it
[ ] This smile I never knew?

h. Burned fragment, recto: autograph manuscript in pencil, 1 page. Unidentified poem. This page of holograph roughly corresponds to the typescript on **g** verso.

[ ]s last beauty
[ ] Lamia which all men
[ ]d stormed the door that dark her beauty
This witch woman, who [beside her *del.*] upon her tower
Silent, subtly smiling stood,
[And laid her glances *del.*]
And, lowered eyed, her glances lightly laid
Like flowers from a [pale quick *del.*] narrow fugitive hand

And at my cry the enigmatic door
Swung backward, and the monster, bare of claw,
Stood erect, but at her scarce formed word
Sank back and disappeared, and I saw
My carnate dream wait, slender like a flower
In a casket of dark scented wood
[From this *del.*] Whence in strange white silence she had strayed
And straying yet, she slowly raised her hand.

And all my life flowed back into my eyes,
And my mouth grew thin and sharp with fire,
While she lightly swayed
[ ] her own soft gleamed hair, and all desire,

g. Burned fragment, verso: ribbon typescript (purple ink), 1 page. Unidentified poem. This typescript roughly corresponds to the autograph manuscript on **h** recto.

[ ]ads
[ ] ant space into a violin
[ ] silence runs at will,
[ ]arkness and alone
[ ]oor where this last beauty sleeps,
[ ]ented pale Lamia which all men
[ ] , and stormed the tower where her beauty keeps;
[This wi]tch woman who, upon her tower,
[Silent,] subtly smiling stood
[And, l]owered eyed, her glances lightly laid
[Like flow]ers from a narrow fugitive hand.

[And at my] cry the enigmatic door
[Swung bac]kward, and the monster, bare of claw,
[Stood er]ect, but at her scarce formed word
[Sank back] and disappeared, and I saw
[My carnat]e dream wait, slender like a flower,

[In a cas]ket of dark scented wood
[Whence in] strange white silence she had strayed
[And stray]ing yet, she slowly raised her hand.

[And all my life f]lowed back into my eyes,
[And my mouth grew] thin and sharp with fire
[While she light]ly swayed
[ ] [her own soft] gleamed hair, and all desire,

f. Burned fragment, verso: ribbon typescript (purple ink), 1 page. Unidentified poem with echoes from Eliot's "Preludes" and "The Love Song of J. Alfred Prufrock."

[ ]ly

[ ] window, senselessly staring down,
[ ]rey light pause above the town
[ ]ly fall, and swing between the houses,
[ ]y like a water soaked curtain, blown
[ ]eaking wind from limbs of trees
[ ] the gutters in silent streets of stone.

[ ]treets rattle countless loosened wheels.
[ ]oof beats measure silent streets, and now
[ ]st lone trolley thrusts the silence from a street
[ ]ging heaves above the windy roofs.

[ ] life or death to which one wakes, like this?
[ ] in unison from a thousand beds,
[ ] our shades and face a thousand petty mornings
[ ]ing mirrors to a weak pale flare of gas;
[ ]s of livid hopes and stale regrets
[ ]nd coffee spoons.
[ ] dance, we weep to the same refrain,
[ ] weary ways to dark, then draw our shades again.

XX

d. Burned fragment, verso: ribbon typescript (purple ink), 1 page. Unidentified poem.

[ ] rose and leaned its breast upon the horizon
[ ] breast on sharpened roofs of houses,
[ ]bled on the rigid boughs of trees
[ ]old stone window ledge he stood
[ ]ross the vague and formless city
[ ] the east bared black and ragged teeth.

[ ] thought, is life cruelly asleep below me

[ ] dim oblivion for the sign
[ ]ain, take up its chant of pain,
[ ]ths and deaths, then at red roots of pain
[ ]arkness falls, in oblivion sink again.
[ ]e thought, is the sleeper []ho, in sleep
[ ] secret thoughts and hopes, desires,
[ ] span of consciousness so closely guards
[ ] his breast.

[ ]r who, in slumber bares
[ ]s to which he strives, aspires;
[ ] from fear of ridicule,

e. Burned fragment, verso: ribbon typescript (purple ink), 1 page. Unidentified poem.

[ ]n grown up to the sky.
[ ] in a caverned brain.
[ ] and sleepily opens an eye
[ ]eavy dark like lead upon his eyelids,
[ ] knees lying at length upon him
[ ] heavy mouthed, taking his trembling flesh.

[ ]ike this, I waked between two walls
[ ]tretched my two hands darkly forth to touch them.
[ ]ld not see the sky across them laid,
[ ] see the walls again, I was afraid,
[ ]und that in a floorless passage leading nowhere
[ ]ing whence I knew not, I reclined.

[ ]t my hands, and felt them break
[ ]eard my fingers rattle on sharp stones,
[ ] raised my wrists and beat the wall
[ ]ard a sudden body beside me fall,
[ ] This was my youth that I had slain.

[ ]pectral youth that rose and walked again
[ ] with voice and restless hands,
[ ]t the skyless wall
[ ] like smoke above it, or to fall

g. Burned fragment, recto: autograph manuscript in pencil, 1 page. Unidentified poem.

[ ]es like faces blown
[ ] [go *del.*] slowly go
[ ] may lie
[ ] bark

[ ] along the sky
[ ] down past the somber hills,
[ ]er bells that [lie *del.*] <hang> so still
[ ]der throats with silent dark

[ ]ady flame,
[ ] climbed the dim walled sea
[ ] silence, shod with dew
[ ]flower bells,
[ ] dark with sweet slow [slants *del.*] slants of sound.

[ ] silver flowers dimly ringing
[ ]ing, singing

18 "Pierrot, Sitting Beside The Body of Colombine, suddenly Sees Himself in a Mirror," 3 pages, 14 by 8½ inches, unwatermarked. Signed in typescript at foot of poem, "William Faulkner, / Oxford, Miss."

Faulkner presented this copy of the poem to Mrs. Ben Wasson, Sr. A penciled note at the bottom of the last page, presumably in Mrs. Wasson's hand, states: "Written while visiting in the house / of Mr & Mrs Ben F. Wasson / in 1921." In 1942 Robert W. Daniel acquired the typescript from Mrs. Wasson for display in a Faulkner exhibit at Yale University. The poem was first published in *Mississippi Quarterly,* 35 (Summer 1982), 306–308.

PIERROT, SITTING BESIDE THE BODY OF COLOMBINE, SUDDENLY SEES HIMSELF IN A MIRROR

Pierrot, cramped from sitting so long, felt darkness
Coldly descending like water upon him, and saw his hands
Dissolve from his knees and the crumpled wrists of his jacket:
Pierrot saw his face in the mirror before him
Slowly extinguished like a match, then washed into darkness
By a wind which stirred the curtains there at the window,
Leaving the mirror empty, inscrutable, smooth.

And he dropped his eyes to the couch between him and the mirror
Like two worn pennies, and his memory dived behind them
Like a lithe boy, down through a long blue wave of darkness
To grope in the opaque lambent silence, to waver and pause
Where Colombine lay, so young, and dead and timeless
Between her thin arms, straight in the dusk, and lustrous
And poignantly quiet beside her, beneath her hair.

He turned his head to stare between the restless curtains
Above his garden of roses, across a silence
Murmurous with the slumber of a fountain, above a darkness
Laced with exhalations of dreams woven in slumber.

Below him were houses, and hills beyond: a bland wall somber in starlight,
Beyond the hills, cities: a cumulous flickering of fireflies;
Then once more a room and a window, and aimless curtains
And a face like an extinguished flame staring between them at nothing,
At cumulate cities and hills, and stars and the long grey sound of rain.
Steadily gazing across the dark, he raised his hand
And lightly touched her hair, faintly expecting
To find that it had no substance, was but a shadow
Shaken across her small breasts, tightly confined, that under
His fingers had trembled like captured birds, and that now
Were curiously relaxed and fallen. Yet surely it could not be a shadow
Which had once been so shrill with motion, that once had snared him
And intricately bound his heart with threads of fire.

Quietly he withdrew his hand, while silence
Flowed into the room on the wind, to a stirring of curtains,
While the scent of flowers came up on the wind
And blossomed about him in impalpable haunting fragrance;
Quietly he sat, cramped with long sitting, and saw
A slender bough reach down and pluck the moon
Out of the east, and roundly hold it up to him.

And he thought how all his life, his youth so bright and beautiful,
That had mazed him, had raised him beyond his world of hills and cities
And dust, and the remote long sound of rain, in a net of blue and silver,
Had parted beneath him. Timidly he touched her hair again
And thought that he, in his turn, lay finally quiet, and lifeless
Among the shattered petals of his youth, that another
Lightly touched a hand to his hair, staring beyond him
At a world of hills and cities and rain and dust
In a motionless silence and the immaculate chiming of stars.

. . . .He stirred, expecting to see—What had he thought to see there?
Had he thought, perhaps, to feel the life that was in him
Swirl once more to the heart breaking swirl of her skirts
That once had seemed to enclose them, to knit
The strings of his heart and her heart together?
But there was no movement to tighten his heart in the darkness,
No sharp slender turn of a palm, nor flick of a skirt
About her childish legs which had mazed his life with their swiftness,
And which now were quiet at last, eternal, more childish than ever.

Pierrot, grown cramped from sitting so long, stirred at last
And, turning to the mirror, saw, in its mutable shadow,
His face like a dead match held there before him
Beyond the body of Colombine, so young, and dead and timeless
Whose skirts, which had drawn them and whirled them together
Until they were wearied of a motion sustained and swift and meaningless,

Now lying crushed and lifeless and infinitely pitiful, seemed to him
The symbol of his own life: a broken gesture in tinsel.

18 "Elder Watson in Heaven," 2 pages, 14 by 8½ inches, unwatermarked. Signed in typescript at foot of poem, "William Faulkner, / Oxford, Miss."

Faulkner presented this copy of the poem to Mrs. Ben Wasson, Sr., in 1921. For a detailed discussion of the poem see Louis Daniel Brodsky, "'Elder Watson in Heaven': Poet Faulkner as Satirist," *Faulkner Journal,* 1 (Fall 1985), 2–7.

ELDER WATSON IN HEAVEN

Elder Watson, lying still,
Protrudes a red haired meagre shank;
Treasure above has he, as well
Ten thousand dollars in the bank.

Elder Watson, when erect
And circumscribed with moral good,
Presents the world an iron curve
Of dogma and of platitude

In which his soul, that sober flame,
And presbyterian, and dight
With subtleties equivocal,
Need fear no sudden change of light

When through the shining gates he moves
While music mounts the golden air;
And his reward, as promised him,
Is spread before him everywhere.

Here there is no five percent.
Nor driven bargains, we are told;
Nor bankers' checques: this is a life
Insurance premium, paid in gold.

This, too, will be a recompense
For that ten thousand left behind;
And, feeling Fate's incurious hand,
He drew the shroud across his mind

And to his waiting children, said:
"Walk upright in the sight of God"
Nor did he look back on his clay
As through the opening gates he trod

With confidence, and gravely smiled,
Pausing on the shining stairs

As passionately to him rose
The hurried mourning of his heirs.

Perhaps he smiled, and then, like God,
Saw Elder Watson in the wrack
Of worn theology, sleeping there
Profound, defenseless, on his back.

38 "Pregnacy" [*sic*], autograph manuscript in brown ink and pencil, 1 page, 8½ by 5½ inches, Requisition Bond, signed in pencil, "William Faulkner." On verso of letterhead stationery of "Dr. Willis C. Campbell / Clinic / 869 Madison Ave. / Memphis, Tenn."

This manuscript is a presentation copy which Faulkner recalled from memory and wrote out for Mrs. Homer K. Jones while visiting her Memphis home during the week of November 23, 1924. Faulkner subsequently included the poem in *Mississippi Poems.* See Louis Daniel Brodsky, "William Faulkner: Poet at Large," *Southern Review,* 18 (Fall 1982), 767–775.

PREGNACY

As to an ancient music's hidden fall
Her seed in the huddled dark was warm and wet,
And three cold stars were riven in the wall:
Rain and dark and death above her door were set.

Her hands moaned on her breast in blind
  and supple fire,
Made light within her cave: she saw her harried
Body wrung to a strange and tortured lyre,
Whose music [was once *del.*]<once was>pure
  strings simply married

One to another in simple diffidence
Her strange and happy sorrows once were wed:
But what tomorrow's [song *del.*]
  chords be recompense,
For yesterday's simple song unravishèd?

Three stars in her heart, when she awakes
As winter's [sleep *del.*] sleep [*illeg. del.*]
  breaks greening in the rain,
And in the caverned [earth *del.*]
  earth spring's rumor shakes,
As in her loins, the tilled and quickened grain

45 *Mississippi Poems,* 1924

On December 30, 1924, in Phil Stone's law office, Faulkner presented to his friend and former schoolmate, Myrtle Ramey, a group of twelve poems in carbon typescript. The typed cover sheet listed the title of the collection as

"Mississippi Poems" and showed the place and time of composition or compilation as "Oxford, Mississippi, / October, 1924." In holograph Faulkner added to this title page: "Autographed for Myrtle Ramey / 30 day of December, 1924 / William Faulkner." This date of inscription, together with the fact that four of the typescripts in the group (**i–l** below) bear November or December dates, would suggest that Faulkner had expanded the scope of his manuscript beyond his original intention and now saw the work as a completed entity.

Further evidence of the unity of the twelve poems is that across the top of each page of typescript, including the title page, Stone has written: "Publication rights reserved. Not to be published without the written consent of the author or that of Phil Stone."

The first seven poems in the Ramey group have been assigned Roman numerals, whereas the last five are unnumbered. Nine of the twelve poems have titles. Each poem carries Faulkner's signature in both typescript and holograph. Eleven of the poems occupy one page each; "He furrows the brown earth" is two pages in length. All thirteen pages of text, as well as the title page, are on unwatermarked onionskin, 11 by 8½ inches.

Nine of the poems presented to Miss Ramey were subsequently published by Faulkner, though in considerably altered versions. In 1979 Yoknapatawpha Press issued a limited facsimile edition of *Mississippi Poems* from the Brodsky typescripts. In 1981 a joint trade edition of *Mississippi Poems* and *Helen: A Courtship* was published by Tulane University and Yoknapatawpha Press.

a. "I." First line, "Shall I recall this tree, when I am old." First published in slightly different version in Linton R. Massey, comp., *"Man Working," 1919–1962, William Faulkner,* p. 77.

b. "II." First line, "Moon of death, moon of bright despair." First published in *Mississippi Poems,* p. 15.

c. "III. / INDIAN SUMMER." Published in altered form as XXXV, *A Green Bough.*

d. "IV. / WILD GEESE." Published with alterations as "Over the World's Rim," *New Republic,* 74 (April 12, 1933), 253, and as XXVIII, *A Green Bough.*

e. "V." First line, "He furrows the brown earth, doubly sweet." Revised and published as VIII, *A Green Bough.*

f. "VI. / THE POET GOES BLIND." First published in *Mississippi Poems,* p. 25.

g. "VII. / Mississippi Hills: "MY EPITAPH." Typescript title is "MY EPITAPH"; added, possibly in Faulkner's hand, "Mississippi Hills." Published as "My Epitaph" in *Contempo,* 1 (February 1, 1932), 2, and in *An Anthology of the Younger Poets* (1932); considerably revised versions appear as *This Earth* (1932), as XLIV in *A Green Bough,* and as "If There Be Grief" in *Mississippi Verse* (1934).

h. "THE GALLOWS." Published, with the addition of three final quatrains not included in this typescript, as XIV, *A Green Bough.*

i. "PREGNACY." Revised slightly for publication as XXIX, *A Green Bough.*

j. "NOVEMBER 11TH." Published, with only slight changes in punctuation and capitalization, as "Gray the Day," *New Republic,* 74 (April 12, 1933), 253, and as XXX, *A Green Bough.* Last stanza appears as epigraph for *Soldiers' Pay.*

k. "DECEMBER / TO ELISE." First published in *Mississippi Poems,* p. 37.

l. "MARCH." Revised and published as XLII, *A Green Bough.* Also appears in *Helen: A Courtship,* p. 113.

MISSISSIPPI POEMS

I

Shall I recall this tree, when I am old,
This hill, or how this valley fills with sun
And green afternoon is bought for morning's gold
And sold again for sleep when day is done?

As well to ask the wine to say what grapes
Distilled their purple suns when full and hot,
Or me what body hands' remembering shapes
To trouble heart when mind has long forgot.

The hushèd wings of wind are feathered high
And shape the tree-tops, vaguely fugitive,
To shake my heart with hill and vale for aye
When vale and hill itself no longer live.

But let me take this silver-minted moon
And bridle me the wind centaurs that whirled
Out of Hellas, grained at beauty's noon,
And ride the cold old sorrow of the world.

II

Moon of death, moon of bright despair:
Deep in a silver sea the earth is drowned
And the trees her dead and restless hair
Seeking the surface like a troubled sound.

How oft to this despair must I awake
To feel a bleeding wound within my side
As though with Time I had exchanged, to take
His own cold place where He is crucified.

Shall Time lie here, where I was young and lay
This body by for bright heart's ravishment,
Graved in these thighs where I sought death for aye?
Shall Time such dry the mouth where mine was blent?

Time, the heir to all, might leave me this
Since the heart-break is so soon forgot:
O mother earth, be kind: who gave us bliss
Can give a night where moon and bird are not.

III
INDIAN SUMMER

The courtesan is dead, for all her subtle ways,
Her bonds are loosed in brittle and bitter leaves,

Her last long backward look's to see who grieves
The imminent night toward her reverted gaze.

Another will reign supreme, now she is dead
And winter's lean clean rain sweeps out her room,
For man's delight and anguish: with old new bloom
Crowning his desire, garlanding his head.

So, too, the world, turning to cold and dead
When swallows empty the blue and drowsy days
And clean rain scatters the ghost of Summer's breath—
The courtesan that's dead, for all her subtle ways—

Spring will come! Rejoice! But still is there
An old sorrow sharp as wood-smoke on the air.

IV

WILD GEESE

Over the world's rim, drawing bland November
Reluctant behind them, drawing the moons of cold;
What their lonely voices stir to remember
This dust ere it was flesh? what restless old

Dream a thousand years was safely sleeping,
Wakes my blood to sharp unease? what horn
Rings out to them? Was I free once, sweeping
Their wild and lonely skies ere I was born?

This hand that shaped my body, that gave me vision,
Made me a slave to clay for a fee of breath.
Sweep on, O wild and lonely! Mine the derision,
Thine the splendor and speed, the cleanness, of death.

Over the world's rim, out of some splendid noon,
Seeking some high desire, and not in vain!
They fill and empty the red and dying moon
And crying, cross the rim of the world again.

V

He furrows the brown earth, doubly sweet
To a hushed great passage of wind
Dragging its shadow. Beneath his feet
The furrow breaks, and at its end

He turns. With peace about his head
Traverses he again the earth: his own,
Still with enormous promises of bread
And clean its odorous strength about him blown.

From the shimmering azure of the wood
A blackbird whistles, cool and mellow;
And here, where for a space he stood
To fill his lungs, a spurting yellow

Rabbit bursts, its hurtling gold
Muscled to erratic lines
Of fluid fear across the mold.
He shouts. The darkly liquid pines

Mirror his falling voice as leaf
Raises clear cool depths to meet its falling self;
And then again the blackbird, thief
Of silence in a glossy pelf,

Inscribes the answer to its life
Upon the white page of the sky:
The furious emptiness of strife
For him to read who passes by.

He moves again, to bells of sheep
Slow as clouds on hills of green;
Somewhere rumorous waters sleep
Beyond a faint-leaved willow screen.

Wind and sun and sleep: he can
Furrow the brown earth, doubly sweet
To a simple heart, for here a man
Might bread him with his hands and feet.

VI
THE POET GOES BLIND

You, who so soon with night would break
My day in half, before it reached its noon:
What sport is this—the sleeper to awake
Into a day he sought not, then to take
His waking span and rieve its sun and moon?

Three score and ten were short enough for learning—
Before the dark descends for aye on me—
These streams and hills, so give me time for burning
Upon my heart their eve- and dawnward-turning
Past all forgetting, if I must not see.

The wind blows from the world, upon my cheek,
Molding unseen hills, and I despair.
You are strong: there's hate and fear to wreak
Your might upon! O leave me eyes to seek,
To wing my heart through golden-chambered air.

You, who to leaf and bud and tree,
Raised me from dust and crimson roots of pain,
Take not mine eyes! take limbs; let me be
Tongueless, dead to sound: take breath from me
Or give me back my golden world again.

VII
MISSISSIPPI HILLS: MY EPITAPH

Far blue hills, where I have pleasured me,
Where on silver feet in dogwood cover
Spring follows, singing close the bluebird's "Lover!"
When to the road I trod an end I see,

Let this soft mouth, shapèd to the rain,
Be but golden grief for grieving's sake,
And these green woods be dreaming here to wake
Within my heart when I return again.

Return I will! Where is there the death
While in these blue hills slumbrous overhead
I'm rooted like a tree? Though I be dead,
This soil that holds me fast will find me breath.

The stricken tree has no young green to weep
The golden years we spend to buy regret.
So let this be my doom, if I forget
That there's still spring to shake and break my sleep.

THE GALLOWS

His mother said: I'll make him
A lad as ne'er has been
(And racked him closely, stroking
His soft hair's golden sheen)
His bright youth will be metal
No alchemist has seen.

His mother said: I'll give him
A bright and high desire
'Till all the dross of living
Burns clean within his fire.
He'll be strong and merry
And he'll be clean and brave,
And all the world will rue it
When he is dark in grave.

But dark will treat him kinder
Than man would anywhere

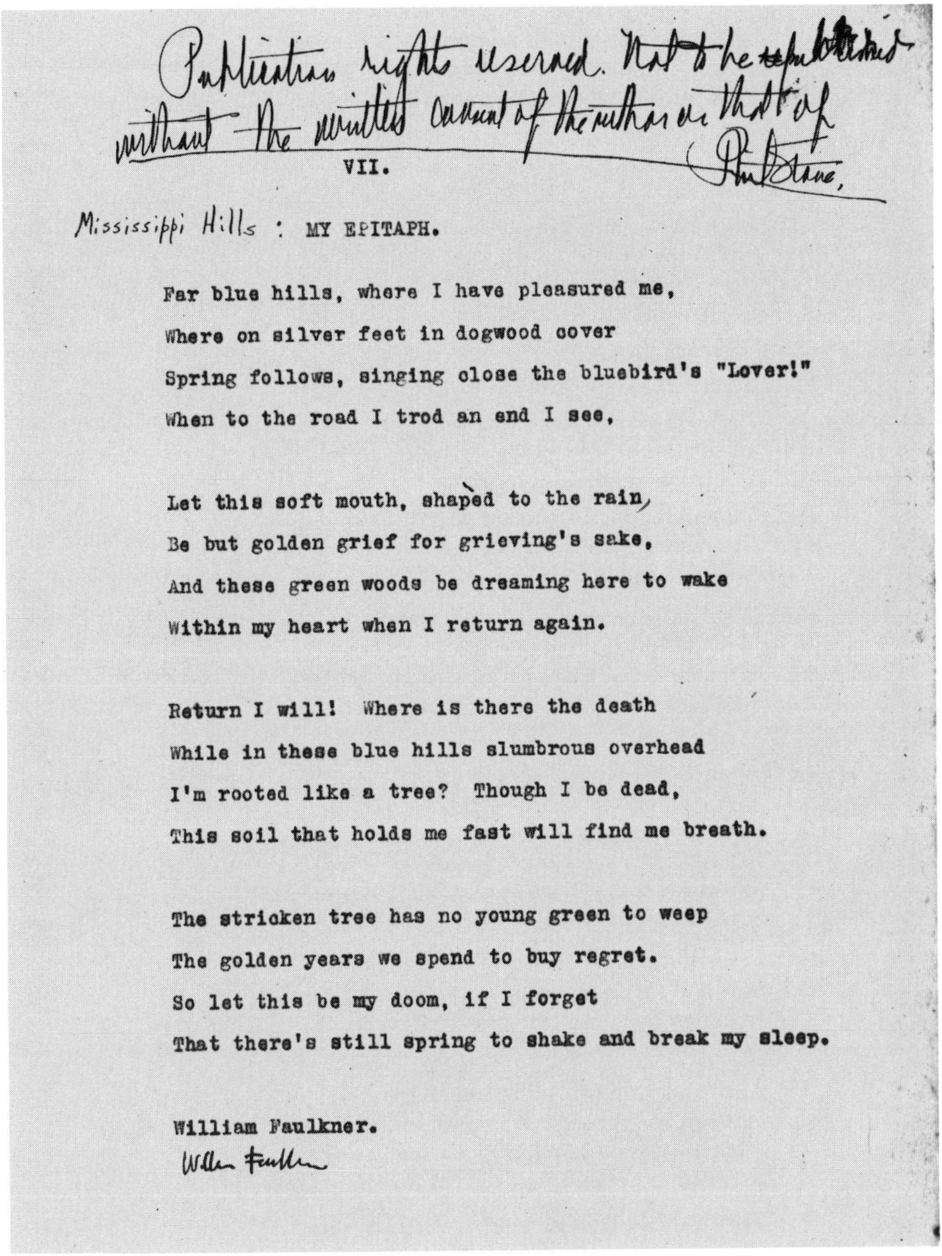

Publication rights reserved. Not to be reproduced without the written consent of the author or that of Phil Stone,

VII.

Mississippi Hills : MY EPITAPH.

Far blue hills, where I have pleasured me,
Where on silver feet in dogwood cover
Spring follows, singing close the bluebird's "Lover!"
When to the road I trod an end I see,

Let this soft mouth, shaped to the rain,
Be but golden grief for grieving's sake,
And these green woods be dreaming here to wake
Within my heart when I return again.

Return I will! Where is there the death
While in these blue hills slumbrous overhead
I'm rooted like a tree? Though I be dead,
This soil that holds me fast will find me breath.

The stricken tree has no young green to weep
The golden years we spend to buy regret.
So let this be my doom, if I forget
That there's still spring to shake and break my sleep.

William Faulkner.
William Faulkner

34. "Mississippi Hills: My Epitaph," 1924

(With barren winds to rock him
—Though now he doesn't care—
And hushed and haughty starlight
To stroke his golden hair)

PREGNACY

As to an ancient music's hidden fall
Her seed in the huddled dark was warm and wet,
And three cold stars were riven in the wall:
Rain and fire and death above her door were set.

Her hands moaned on her breast in blind and supple fire,
Made light within her cave: she saw her harried
Body wrung to a strange and bitter lyre,
Whose music once was pure strings simply married.

One to another in sleepy diffidence
Her thin and happy sorrows once were wed,
And what tomorrow's chords be recompense
For yesterday's single song unravishèd?

Three stars in her heart when she awakes
As winter's sleep breaks greening in the rain,
And in the caverned earth spring's rumor shakes,
As in her loins, the tilled and quickened grain.

NOVEMBER 11TH

Gray the day, and all the year is cold,
Across the empty land the swallows' cry
Marks the south-flown spring: naught is bowled
Save winter, in the sky.

O sorry earth, when this bleak bitter sleep
Stirs and turns, and time once more is green,
In empty path and lane grass will creep,
With none to tread it clean.

April and May and June, and all the dearth
Of heart to green it for, to hurt and wake;
What good is budding, gray November earth,
No need to break your sleep for greening's sake.

The hushèd plaint of wind in stricken trees
Shivers the grass in path and lane
And Grief and Time are tideless golden seas—
Hush, hush! he's home again.

Publication rights reserved. Not to be published without the written consent of the author or that of Phil Stone

NOVEMBER 11TH.

Gray the day, and all the year is cold,
Across the empty land the swallows' cry
Marks the south-flown spring; naught is bowled
Save winter, in the sky.

O sorry earth, when this bleak bitter sleep
Stirs and turns, and time once more is green,
In empty path and lane grass will creep,
With none to tread it clean.

April and May and June, and all the dearth
Of heart to green it for, to hurt and wake;
What good is budding, gray November earth,
No need to break your sleep for greening's sake.

The hushed plaint of wind in stricken trees
Shivers the grass in path and lane
And Grief and Time are tideless golden seas----
Hush, hush! he's home again.

William Faulkner.

Oxford, Mississippi.
November 11, 1924.

William Faulkner

35. "November 11th," 1924

DECEMBER

TO ELISE

Where has flown the spring we knew together?
Barren are the boughs of yesteryear;
But I have seen your hands take wintry weather
And smoothe the rain from it, and leave it fair.

If from sleep's tree these brown and sorry leaves,
If but regret could drown when springs depart,
No more would be each day that drips and grieves
A bare and bitter year within my heart.

In my heart's winter you were budding tree,
And spring seemed all the sweeter, being late;
You the wind that brought the spring to be
Within a garden that was desolate.

You were all the spring, and May and June
Greened brighter in your flesh, but now is dull
The year with rain, and dead the sun and moon,
And all the world is dark, O beautiful.

MARCH

Beneath the apple tree Eve's tortured shape
Glittered in the snake's, her riven breast
Sloped his coils and took the sun's escape
To augur black her sin from east to west.

Through winter's night man can take for warm
Forgiveness of old sins he did commit,
With fetiches the whip of blood to charm,
Forgetting that, with birth, he's heir to it.

But old gods fall away—the ancient Snake
Is throned and crowned instead, who has for minion
That golden apple which will never slake
But feeds and fans man's crumb of fire—when plover
And eagle and shrill northing brids whip over
Nazarine and Roman and Virginian.

▶ "Leaving her," autograph manuscript in brown ink, 1 page, 12¾ by 8⁷⁄₁₆ inches, Hammermill Bond.

This manuscript appears to be the first draft of the poem that became sonnet XIII in *Helen: A Courtship.* (Cf. also lines 13–16, XXV, *A Green Bough.)* The manuscript was originally a part of a large group of papers that Faulkner left with his roommate in New Orleans upon departing for a walking tour of

Europe in July 1925. These materials surfaced in the early 1970s, through the efforts of bookdealer Robert A. Wilson, who channeled all of the manuscripts except this one poem into the Berg Collection of the New York Public Library. See Robert A. Wilson, *Faulkner on Fire Island* (New York, 1979).

[ABSENCE *del.*] LEAVING HER

O I have heard the evening [hushed and *del.*] trumpeted
Beneath swept [harried *del.*] <evening> skies where [geese *del.*] <hawks> have flown
In loneliness of pride where each his own
Marries the hushèd silence whence has fled
His loneliness with him. [And soon has bled *del.*] <O I have seen>

The bitter hawk of loneliness and pride
[Upon the evening swoon his singleness
[Across *del.*] <That on> the evening swooned and curved and died *del.*]
That was my heart, <that> swooning curved and died,
Immaculating skies where he has been.

Here he had hung [to see *del.*] <and [saw *del.*]> <seen> [the *del.*] <her> sweet young flight,
[Marking *del.*] <Tracing *del.*> <Followed> [the *del.*] her cool and passionate loneliness, <singleness,>
Taking for mate his bitter clean distress,
Locked beak to beak in bitter ecstasy

Then beak to beak in bitter ecstasy
Locked with the shadow of his own distress

[*open space*]

Falling dead yet sullen <troubled> down the night

[*space*]

Here he had hung, had seen her sweet young flight,
[Had followed *del.*]
In rain pursued her passionate singleness,
Then beak to beak in bitter ecstasy
Locks with the shadow of his own distress

When she the evening swift with sweet young flight,
The void sky of her passionate singleness <*marg.* Oh I have seen when she with>
Then [beak *del.*] <mouth> to [beak *del.*] <mouth> in bitter ecstasy
[Locked beak to beak her with his curved distress *del.*]

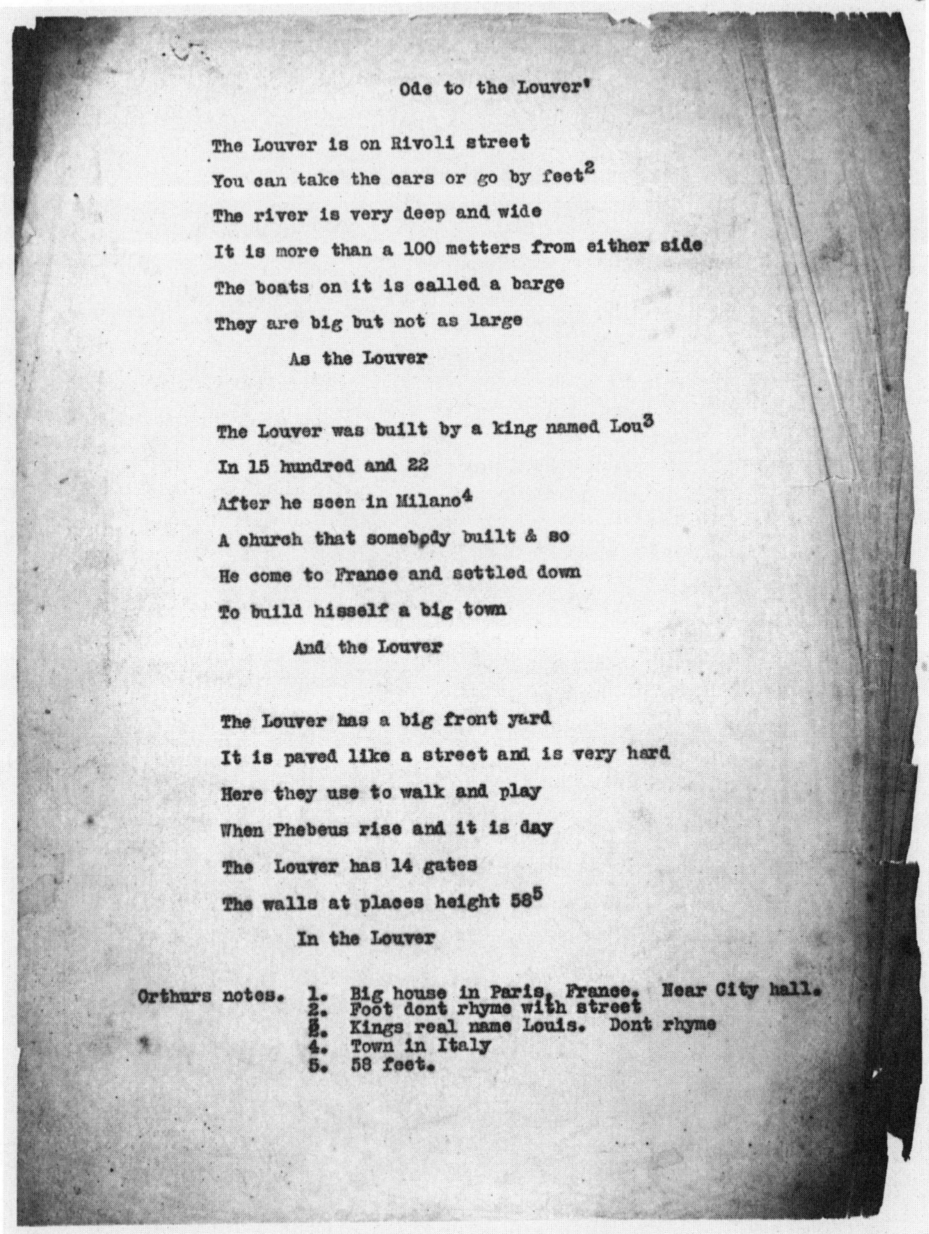

Ode to the Louver[1]

The Louver is on Rivoli street
You can take the cars or go by feet[2]
The river is very deep and wide
It is more than a 100 metters from either side
The boats on it is called a barge
They are big but not as large
As the Louver

The Louver was built by a king named Lou[3]
In 15 hundred and 22
After he seen in Milano[4]
A church that somebpdy built & so
He come to France and settled down
To build hisself a big town
And the Louver

The Louver has a big front yard
It is paved like a street and is very hard
Here they use to walk and play
When Phebeus rise and it is day
The Louver has 14 gates
The walls at places height 58[5]
In the Louver

Orthurs notes.
1. Big house in Paris, France. Near City hall.
2. Foot dont rhyme with street
3. Kings real name Louis. Dont rhyme
4. Town in Italy
5. 58 feet.

36. Page 1 of "Ode to the Louver"

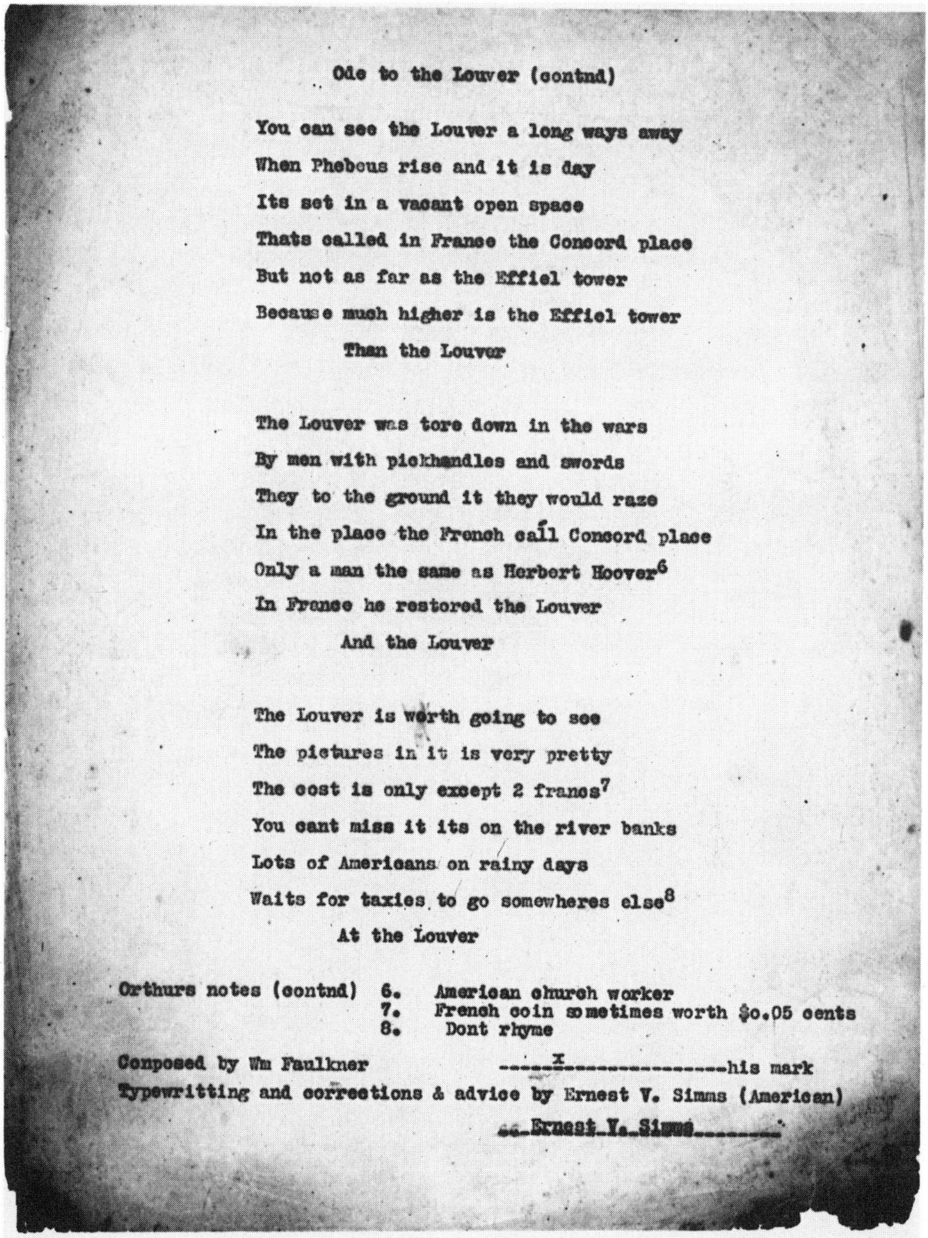

Ode to the Louver (contnd)

You can see the Louver a long ways away
When Phebous rise and it is day
Its set in a vacant open space
Thats called in France the Concord place
But not as far as the Effiel tower
Because much higher is the Effiel tower
Than the Louver

The Louver was tore down in the wars
By men with pickhandles and swords
They to the ground it they would raze
In the place the French call Concord place
Only a man the same as Herbert Hoover[6]
In France he restored the Louver
And the Louver

The Louver is worth going to see
The pictures in it is very pretty
The cost is only except 2 francs[7]
You cant miss it its on the river banks
Lots of Americans on rainy days
Waits for taxies to go somewheres else[8]
At the Louver

Orthurs notes (contnd) 6. American church worker
7. French coin sometimes worth $0.05 cents
8. Dont rhyme

Composed by Wm Faulkner ----x---------------his mark
Typewritting and corrections & advice by Ernest V. Simms (American)
--Ernest V. Simms-------

37. Page 2 of "Ode to the Louver"

38. Faulkner in Paris, 1925

Locks with the shadow of his curved distress
[A hawk *del.*] <In> wild and cooling [notes *del.*] <plunge> he

O I have seen when she with sweet young flight
The void sky [with her *del.*] <rieves with> passionate
singleness,
Beak to beak in bitter ecstasy
[With her own sha *del.*]
Locks with the shadow of his curved distress
In wild and cooling plunge
In wild and cooling arc of death and he
Falling dies still troubled down the night

54 "Ode to the Louver," ribbon typescript, 2 pages, 11 by 8½ inches, unwatermarked.

Faulkner mailed this humorous poem, along with a satirical letter by "Ernest V. Simms," to Phil Stone from Paris in November 1925. The copy of the poem and letter in the Brodsky Collection varies slightly from the one at the University of Texas, Austin, which was published in *Mississippi Quarterly,* 27 (Summer 1974), 333–335.

976 "As when from dark the vernal equinox," c. 1953, autograph manuscript in pencil, 1 page, 11 by 8½ inches, unwatermarked. Fragment of an unidentified poem.

As when from [winter *del.*] dark the <vernal> equinox
Marks [cold away *del.*] <winter's end>, and all the year is May,
So [did *del.*] that simple schoolboy's act unlocks
From barren time a birth: new ecstasy:
[A better man, since he must *del.*] For him who must deserve
<to keep> for aye
[In that soft magic, <where he> finds eternity. *del.*]
That soft magic's immortality

III

Fiction

THE SELECTIONS in this section have been drawn from a much larger group of fiction manuscripts and typescripts in the Brodsky Collection. These have been chosen because, as early or intermediate drafts, they are uniquely distinct from the final, published versions of the works.

The holograph and typescript pages from *Requiem for a Nun* and *A Fable,* as well as the typescript of "By the People" and the brief fragments from *Big Woods* and "Weekend Revisited," were originally left by Faulkner in the keeping of his trusted editor and personal confidant, Saxe Commins. The revisionary drafts of portions of the two novels are particularly significant, since they supplement the manuscript holdings relating to these works at the University of Virginia.

The text of *The Wishing-Tree* printed here has been transcribed from the copy Faulkner gave Phil Stone's son, Philip, as a Christmas gift in 1948. Comparison of this version with that issued by Random House in 1967 reveals vast distinctions in style, particularly in Faulkner's handling of the Negro dialect.

The "Wash" manuscripts in the Brodsky Collection were formerly in the possession of James W. Silver, a history professor at the University of Mississippi and a close friend who shared with Faulkner many conversations focusing on race relations and Southern politics during the 1940s and '50s. The inclusion of the Revised Holograph Draft, together with its experimental drafts, allows the careful, curious reader to follow the evolutionary composition of what is not only one of Faulkner's most impressive short stories but also a crucial segment of *Absalom, Absalom!*.

Like the other manuscripts reproduced in this volume, these pages of fiction show Faulkner to be a consummate craftsman, meticulously revising and rearranging his material to capture the intended style and effect. To trace Faulkner's method of composition is to appreciate not only his innate creative genius but also his painstaking efforts to control and direct that genius toward the formation of an orderly, artistic design.

663 *The Wishing-Tree,* 1927, 1948, ribbon typescript, 44 pages, 10⅝ by 8$\frac{5}{16}$ inches, Hammermill Bond, stapled and bound in manila wrappers with brown tape on spine. Typed on cover: "THE WISHING-TREE / BY / WILLIAM FAULKNER."

This is a presentation copy typed by Faulkner and inscribed on page 1 in blue ink: "For Philip Stone II, / from his god-father. / William Faulkner / Oxford. / Xmas 1948." This text, which differs significantly from the published version (Random House, 1967), is one of two (the other, the carbon of this typescript, was given to Ruth Ford's daughter) that Faulkner copied in 1948 from the version of the story he had presented to Dr. and Mrs. Calvin Brown's daughter in 1927. For a treatment of the complex history of this story, as well as a line-by-line collation of the original typescripts, see Louis Daniel Brodsky, "A Textual History of William Faulkner's *The Wishing-Tree* and *The Wishing Tree,*" *Studies in Bibliography,* 38 (1985), 330–374.

THE WISHING-TREE

She was still asleep, but she could feel herself rising up out of sleep just like a balloon: it was like she was a goldfish in a round bowl of sleep, rising and rising through the warm waters of sleep, to the top. And then she would be awake.

And so she was awake, but she didn't open her eyes at once. Instead, she lay quite still and warm in her bed, and it was like there was another little balloon inside her, getting bigger and bigger and rising and rising. Soon it would be at her mouth, then it would pop out and jump up against the ceiling as though it were laughing at her. The little balloon inside her got bigger and bigger, making all her body and her arms and legs tingle, as if she had just eaten peppermint. What can it be? she wondered, keeping her eyes shut tight, trying to remember from yesterday. What can it be?

"It's your birthday," a voice said near her, and her eyes flew open. There, standing beside the bed, was a strange boy with a thin ugly face and hair so red that it made a glow in the room. He wore a black velvet suit with red stockings and [1] shoes, and from his shoulder hung a huge empty book-satchel.

"Who are you?" she asked, looking at the redheaded boy in astonishment.

"Name's Maurice," the redheaded boy answered. His eyes had queer golden flecks in them, like sparks. "Get up."

She lay still again and looked about the room. The funniest thing was, there was nobody in the room except the redheaded boy and herself. Every morning when she waked, her mother and Dicky would be in the room, and soon afterward Alice would come in to help her dress and get ready for school. But today there was nobody in the room except the strange redheaded boy standing beside her bed and looking at her with his queer yellowflecked eyes.

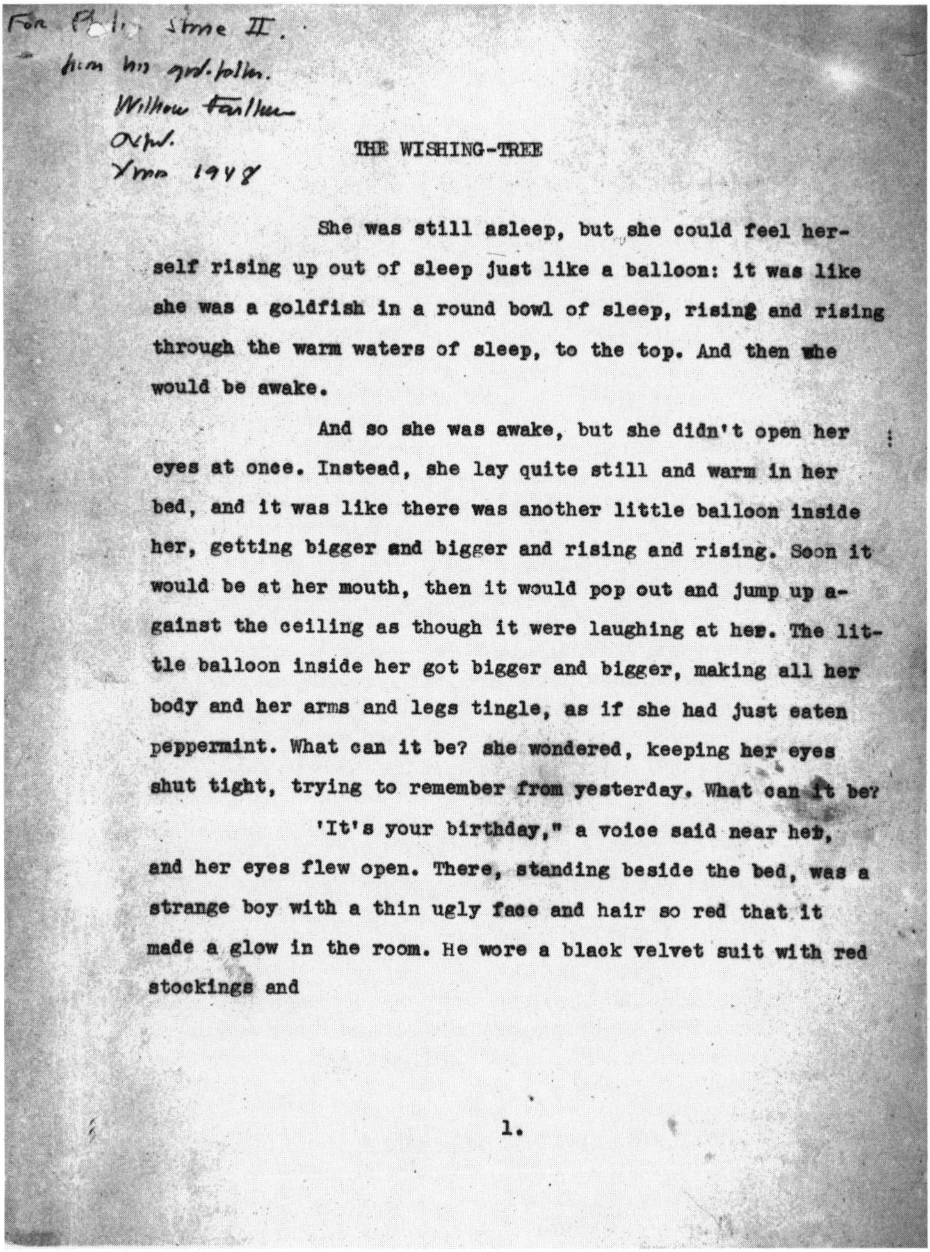

For Philip Stone II.
from his god-father.
William Faulkner
Oxford
Xmas 1948

THE WISHING-TREE

She was still asleep, but she could feel herself rising up out of sleep just like a balloon: it was like she was a goldfish in a round bowl of sleep, rising and rising through the warm waters of sleep, to the top. And then she would be awake.

And so she was awake, but she didn't open her eyes at once. Instead, she lay quite still and warm in her bed, and it was like there was another little balloon inside her, getting bigger and bigger and rising and rising. Soon it would be at her mouth, then it would pop out and jump up against the ceiling as though it were laughing at her. The little balloon inside her got bigger and bigger, making all her body and her arms and legs tingle, as if she had just eaten peppermint. What can it be? she wondered, keeping her eyes shut tight, trying to remember from yesterday. What can it be?

'It's your birthday," a voice said near her, and her eyes flew open. There, standing beside the bed, was a strange boy with a thin ugly face and hair so red that it made a glow in the room. He wore a black velvet suit with red stockings and

1.

39. Dedication page of "The Wishing-Tree," 1948

"Get up," the redheaded boy repeated.

"I'm not dressed," she said.

"Yes, you are," the redheaded boy answered. "Get up."

So she threw the covers back and got out of bed, and sure enough, she was fully dressed—shoes and stockings, and her new lilac dress with the ribbon that matched her eyes. It was the funniest thing! The redheaded boy had gone over to the window and he stood with his face pressed to the windowpane.

"Is it still raining?" she asked. "It was raining last night."

"Come and see," the redheaded boy replied, and she came over beside him and saw through the window the black trees with their bare dripping branches in the rain. "They're sorrying [2] themselves," the redheaded boy murmured.

"I wish it wouldn't rain on my birthday," she said with disappointment. "I think it might stop raining today, don't you?" The redheaded boy glanced at her and then away, then he raised the windowsash. "Oh, don't do that!" she exclaimed, then she stopped in surprise, for as soon as the sash rose, instead of rain and black winter trees, she saw a soft gray mist that smelled of wisteria, and far down in it she heard little far voices calling, "Come down, Daphne." When she looked through the upper sash, there was the rain falling against the glass in crawling streaks, and the black sad trees; but beyond the open sash that soft wisteria scented mist and the little voices saying, "Come down, Daphne; Come down, Daphne."

"Well, this is the funniest thing!" she exclaimed, looking at the redheaded boy, who was digging busily in his huge satchel.

"It's because it's your birthday," the redheaded boy explained.

"But nothing like this ever happened before on my birthday."

"But it might have," the redheaded boy pointed out, taking something out of the satchel. "That's why birthdays are. And, on the night before your birthday—" he glanced at her with his queer goldflecked eyes "—if you get into bed left foot first and turn the pillow over before you got [*i.e.* go] to sleep, anything might happen," he added wisely.

"That's exactly what I did last night!" she said. "But who is that calling me?" [3]

"Why not look down and see?" the redheaded boy suggested. So she leaned out the window into the warm, scented mist, and there, looking up at her from the ground, were Alice and Dicky, and George, a fat boy who lived across the street.

"Come down, Daphne!"

"Wait for me!" she cried down to them, and the redheaded boy was again beside her. In his hand was a toy ladder about six inches long, and he raised the ladder and put one end of it to his mouth and blew through it, and at once the ladder began to grow. The redheaded boy puffed and blew, and the ladder got longer and longer until at last the end of it touched the ground, and Alice caught it and held it steady while she climbed down to them.

"Got up at last, did you, Sleepyhead?" George asked, and Dicky chanted "Sleepyhead, Sleepyhead!" He was a little boy, and he always said whatever the others did.

The redheaded boy climbed down the ladder, and he bent over and pressed his finger on a little shiny button on the ladder, and the air went Whsssssshhhhhhhhhhhh out to [*i.e.* of] the ladder and it was once more a toy ladder about six inches long. The redheaded boy put it back in his satchel. "Name's Maurice," he said shortly, looking from Alice to Dicky and then to George with his queer yellowflecked eyes. "Come on."

The mist was like a big gray tent above them and around them, and a warm little breeze blew through it, smelling of wisteria. They went across the lawn to the street, and the redheaded boy stopped again. [4]

"Well," he said, "how shall we go? walk, or in a car, or on ponies?"

"Ponies! Ponies!" Daphne and George shouted, and Dicky chanted. "Wide a pony! Wide a pony!"

But Alice didn't want to.

"Naw, suh," Alice said, "Me and Dicky ain't goin' to ride on no hawss; and Daphne you ain't got no business with no hawss, neither."

"Oh, Alice!"

"Naw, suh," Alice repeated. "You knows yo' mommer don't allow you to ride no hawss."

"How do you know?" Daphne said, "she didn't say I couldn't."

"How could she, when she don't know you's goin' to? I reckon we kin git wherever we's goin' just like we is."

"Oh, Alice!" Daphne said, and Dicky chanted, "Wide a pony, wide a pony!"

"Alice and Dicky can ride in the ponycart," the redheaded boy suggested. "You aren't scared of a ponycart, are you?"

"I guess I ain't," Alice answered doubtfully. "Daphne better ride in the cart, too."

"No," said Daphne, "I want to ride a pony. Please, Alice."

"They're gentle ponies," the redheaded boy said. "See?" He reached into his satchel and brought out a Shetland pony no larger than a mouse, with a little red bridle with silver, tiny bells, and a red saddle on it. Daphne squealed with delight, and Dicky tried to climb right up the redheaded boy's leg. [5]

"Mine! Mine!" Dicky shouted. "My first choss pony!"

"My pony! My pony!" Dicky [*i.e.* George] shouted. "First choice: I claim first choice!"

"Here, you all wait," the redheaded boy said, holding the pony above his head while its little hooves pawed and scrambled in his hand, "Stand back, now."

So they stood back and the redheaded boy knelt and set the pony on the ground, and he put his mouth to the pommel of the saddle and began to blow. And as he blew the pony began to grow larger. It got bigger and bigger, stamping its feet and shaking its bridle until the bells jingled and tinkled; and the redheaded boy rose to his knees and still puffed and blew, and the pony was as large as a dog now; and the redheaded boy blew and puffed, and he got to his feet and the pony was as large as a calf and still it got bigger and bigger. At last the redheaded boy raised his head.

"There," he said. "Is that big enough?"

"Who's dat 'un for?" Alice asked quickly.

"Mine! Mine!" shouted George and Dicky together.

"No, this one is Daphne's," the redheaded boy said.

"Den you let some of dat air right back out," Alice said promptly. "Dat's too big for Daphne."

"No, no!" Daphne protested. "Look, Alice! See how gentle he is!" She pulled up a handful of grass, and the pony nibbled it and shook his head until the silver bells on the bridle jingled like mad. Then Daphne held the reins and the redheaded boy took two more [6] ponies from his satchel, and Dicky chanted, "First choss pony! First choss pony!"

"How can your satchel hold so much, and yet look like it's empty?" Daphne asked.

"Because I'm Maurice," the redheaded boy answered. "Besides, anything is likely to happen on birthdays," he added gravely.

"Oh," said Daphne.

Then the redheaded boy blew these two ponies up and gave the reins to George to hold, and he took from his satchel a fourth pony hitched to a little wicker cart with bells all over it, and Dicky was just wild. The redheaded boy blew this one up too. Alice watched him nervously.

"Don't blow him up too big now, for me and Dicky," Alice said.

The redheaded boy puffed and blew.

"Ain't dat plenty big enough?" suggested Alice uneasily.

"Alice don't want him any bigger than a rabbit," George said. "He can't pull the cart if he's not any bigger than that, Alice."

The redheaded boy puffed and blew, and soon the pony and cart were the right size. "You'll need a whip," he said, and he reached again into his satchel and got out a red whip.

"Naw, suh," Alice said quickly, "we don't need no whip. You kin put dat right back."

But Dicky had already seen the whip, and when the redheaded boy put the whip back in his satchel, Dicky yelled. So the redheaded boy gave Dicky the whip, and Dicky and Alice got in the cart and [7] Dicky held the end of the reins in one hand and the whip in the other.

"You mustn't hit de hawss wid yo' whup, honey," Alice said. "You'll make him run away."

"Drive first choss pony," Dicky said.

"Shetland pony, darling," Daphne corrected, "Not first choice pony."

"Drive Shetlun pony," Dicky said. Then Daphne and George and the redheaded boy got on their ponies and they rode down the street.

They reached the end of the street and passed the last house, and then all of a sudden they rode out of the mist and into the sunshine. Behind them they could see the mist like a huge gray tent, but everywhere else the sun shone and the trees were green as summer, and the grass was green and little blue and yellow flowers were everywhere in the grass. Birds were singing in the trees, and flying from one tree to another; and the three ponies flew along the road, faster and faster, until Alice and Dicky in the cart were left far behind. They came to the edge of a forest, and they stopped here to wait for the cart.

The cart came trotting up, and Alice was holding her hat one, [*i.e.* on,] and she looked a little alarmed. So they promised not to go fast any more, and they rode of [*i.e.* on] into the forest and after a while they came to a small gray cottage beside the road. The cottage had roses growing up over the door, and sitting in the door was a little old man wi[th] [8] a long gray beard, whittling on a piece of wood.

"Good morning," the redheaded boy said politely.

"Good morning," the little old man replied politely.

"We're looking for the Wishing-Tree," the redheaded boy said.

"You are?" the little old man said. He wagged his head gravely. "It's a far ways," he said. "I don't hardly believe you could find it."

"We are going to ask along the road," the redheaded boy explained.

"There ain't anybody in these parts that ever seen it," the little old man said.

"How do you know it's so far, then?" the redheaded boy asked.

"Oh, I been to it lots of times," the little old man answered. "I used to go to it every day, almost, when I was your age. But I aint been to it now in several years."

"Why not come with us and show us the way?" the redheaded boy suggested. "You can ride in the cart with Alice and Dicky." Alice was mumbling to herself, and Daphne asked,

"What did you say, Alice?"

"I says, we dont want no old trash like him with us. I bet he's a tramp. I bet yo' mommer wouldn't like it if she knowed."

"Could I ride in your ponycart?" the little old man asked.

"Yes," the redheaded boy answered. "If you'll come and show us the way to the Wishing-Tree." [9]

The little old man looked cautiously over his shoulder into the house.

"I believe I will," he said. He shut his knife and he put it and the thing he was carving into his pocket. He rose, and peered again around the edge of the door into the house. "I guess I better go and show you the way, because——"

Then the little old man's wife came to the door and threw a rolling pin at the little old man, and a flatiron.

"You lazy old scoundrel!" the little old man's wife shouted at him, "Sitting out here all day long, gassing with strangers, and not a stick of wood in the house to cook dinner with."

"Mattie——" the little old man said. His wife reached her hand back into the house and she threw an alarm clock at the little old man, and so he ran around the corner of the house. The little old man's wife stood in the door and glared at them.

"And you all with nothing better to do than keep folks from their honest work!" she said. She glared at them again, and slammed the door.

"There now, what I tell you?" Alice said. "White trash!"

"Well, I guess we'll have to ask somebody else where the Wishing-Tree is," the redheaded boy said. "Come on."

They rode on past the house and along the garden fence. At the corner of the garden fence someone called cautiously to them as they passed, and they saw the little old man peering out from behind a row of tomato plants.

"Is she gone?" the little old man hissed. [10]

"Yes," the redheaded boy answered. The little old man came out and climbed the garden fence.

"Wait a minute for me," he said, "and I'll go with you." So they waited for him, and the little old man sneaked along the fence to the house, and grabbed up the alarm clock and the flatiron and the rollingpin and ran back down the road and climbed the garden fence again and hid the alarm clock and the rollingpin and the flatiron in the fence corner. "So she cant throw them at me when we come back," he explained cunningly. "Where can I ride?"

"You can ride in the cart with Alice and Dicky," the readheaded boy told him. Alice mumbled again, and Daphne asked.

"What did you say, Alice?"

"I says, me and Dicky dont want that old trash in the cart with us. Yo' mommer wont like it."

"Why, cant I ride, too?" the little old man said in a hurt tone. "I wouldn't aim to hurt."

"Let him ride in the cart, Alice," the redheaded boy said. "He wont bother you and Dicky."

"Of course I wont, ma'am," the little old man said quickly, "I wouldn't think of it."

"Let him ride in the cart, Alice," they all said.

"Well, git in, then," Alice said ungraciously. "But yo' mommer wont like it."

The little old man hopped nimbly into the cart, and they rode on. Alice turned her back on him. The ponies trotted on along the road. [11]

After a while the little old man said: "I can whittle things with a knife."

Alice sniffed.

"I can whittle most anything I ever seen," the little old man said.

Alice sniffed. The ponies trotted on beneath the trees. There were a lot of butterflies flying around, and squirrels and rabbits and birds.

"This is a nice pony and cart you have," the little old man said.

"First choss pony," Dicky said.

"Shetland pony, darling," Daphne corrected. "Not first choice pony."

"Shetlun pony," Dicky said.

"I used to have a lot of ponies," the little old man said. "But we got shed of them. They et too much."

Alice sniffed again. "Bet you never had nothing in your life except flati'ons throwed at you."

They came to a fork in the road and [the] redheaded boy stopped. "Which way?" he asked.

"That way," the little old man answered immediately, pointing. They rode on that way.

"What were you carving when we came up?" Daphne asked. The little old man reached in his pocket and took the piece of wood out, and they all crowded about the cart to see it.

"Little puppy," Dicky said. [12]

"It's a lizard," George said.

"No, it's a dragon," said Daphne. "Isn't it?"

"It aint nothing," Alice said. "He nor nobody else never saw nothing like that thing."

"What is it?" Daphne asked.

"I dont know," the little old man answered. "I dont know what it is, but I think it's a gillypus."

"What's a gillypus?" asked George.

"I dont know. But I bet it looks something like this."

"Why do you call it a gillypus, then, if you dont know what a gillypus looks like?" George asked.

"Well," the little old man answered, "it looks more like a gillypus than anything I ever seen."

"It dont look like nothing, to me," Alice said. "Not like nothing I ever saw, even in a circus."

"Did you ever go to a circus?" Daphne asked the little old man. "Alice has been."

"I dont know," the little old man answered. "It used to be like I could kind of remember going to one, but that was a long time ago, and now I dont know if I remember or not."

"It's in a big tent," George said. "A tent big enough to hold our house. I wish I had a circus tent."

"It has flags on it," Daphne added, "colored flags flying on top of it."

"I wants to go to a circus," Dicky said. [13]

"We are going to the next one," Daphne said. "Mother has already said we could. Alice is going to take us, aren't you, Alice?"

"And a band," Alice added, "and a elefump bigger'n all dese ponies rolled into one, and all of us on top of 'em. That elefump was the biggest thing I ever seen in my bawn days. Lawd, Lawd."

"I wants to go to a circus, Alice," Dicky said.

"So does I, honey. Spotted hawses, and folks spanglin' through de air . . . . . . Listen: dont I hear a band now?"

It was a horn they heard, and they trotted on through the forest and came in sight of a huge gray castle, with a flag on top of it. A soldier stood on the wall of the castle, blowing the horn. ["]Once Alice's husband was a corporal in the army. I mean, a husband that Alice used to have was a soldier, too.["]

"I wouldn't give nothing for a whole war full of soldiers," Alice said. "Not nothing."

The redheaded boy stopped again. "Which way?" he asked.

"That way," the little old man answered, pointing. They rode on that way, and soon they couldn't hear the horn any more, and still further on they found a curious tree beside the road. It was a white tree, and at first they thought it was a dogwood tree in bloom, but when they came up to it, they saw that the leaves on it were perfectly white.

"What a funny tree," Daphne said. "What kind of a tree is it?"

"It's a—a—it's a mellomax tree," the little old man said. "There's a lot of them in this forest."

"I never saw a tree with white leaves before," Daphne said, [14] and she pulled one of the leaves off. And as soon as she touched it, the leaf turned to a lovely blue color. "If that isn't the funniest thing!" Daphne exclaimed. "Look!"

Then they each pulled a leaf from the tree. George's leaf turned purple, and the redheaded boy's was gold; and Alice took one and hers became a bright red, and she held Dicky up so he could pull one, and his was not any color especially: a kind of faint blending of all colors, with a blue the same shade as Daphne's, but paler, for the dominant note.

"What color is yours?" Daphne asked of the little old man, who showed them his leaf, but his hadn't changed at all.

"That's the color of everybody's wishes," the redheaded boy explained. "Daphne's are blue wishes, and Dicky's are a little of everything and not much of anything yet, because he's little, but when he's bigger they'll be blue like Daphne's because he's Daphne's brother; and Alice's are red wishes, and George's are purple ones; and yours—" he turned to the little old man "—yours are not anything, because you are satisfied with things as they are."

"Why, this must be the Wishing-Tree," Daphne said.

"No, no," the little old man answered, "This is not the Wishing-Tree: I've been to the Wishing-Tree too many times not to know it. This is just a mellomax tree."

"Well, which way is the Wishing-Tree, then?" the redheaded boy asked.

"That way," the little old man answered promptly. And so [15] they went on that way.

"It's an awful long way," George said, "and I'm hungry. I wish I had a sandwich."

And then George nearly fell off his pony in surprise, because there in his hand was a sandwich. George stared at the sandwich, then he smelled it, then he bit it, and whooped for joy.

"Look what George has got," everybody cried, and Dicky said:

"I want something to eat, too." And as soon as he said it, there was something in his hand.

"What you got in your hand, honey?" Alice asked. The others crowded about the cart to see too.

"What in the world is it?" Daphne asked. The redheaded boy pinched a bit of it off and put it in his mouth.

"What does it taste like?" asked George.

"It doesn't taste like anything," the redheaded boy answered, "because it isn't anything. It's just something. That was what Dicky wished for, you see: he didn't say bread or candy, he just said he wanted something."

"I wants candy," Dicky said, and immediately it was a cake of chocolate which he had in his hand.

"Alice, you know he cant have candy," Daphne said.

"Wants candy," Dicky insisted.

"You have something else, honey. Here, gimme yo' candy." You dont want no old candy, does you?" Alice took the candy out of Dicky's hand, but as soon as she did so, the candy disappeared.

Alice sat for a moment in astonishment. Then she whirled upon the little old man. [16]

"You old man," Alice said. "You gimme back that candy, you hear? Taking his candy right out a baby's hand, like that! You gimme that candy, you hear?"

"Why," the little old man said with surprise, "I didn't take it. You taken it yourself."

"Dont you try to prank wid us!" Alice exclaimed. "Didn't somebody took it right outen my hand?"

"Why, Alice!" said Daphne, "He didn't take it!"

"Somebody did, then. And he is the closest!" Alice glared at the little old man.

"I never taken it," the little old man repeated.

"It just went," the redheaded boy explained. "Dicky was the one who wished it, and when Alice took it, it just went, because Alice hadn't wished for any candy."

"Well, I dont like no such goingson around me," Alice said. "I think we better turn around a [*i.e.* and] go home."

"I'm hungry," Dicky said. "I wants——"

"Don't you want some bread and butter and sugar?" Daphne asked quickly. "Or cookies?"

"Wants cookies," Dicky said, and as soon as he said it, he had a cookie in each hand.

"Well, if that isn't the funniest thing!" Daphne exclaimed. "That must have been the Wishing-Tree back there."

"No, no," the little old man said, "I know the Wishing-Tree too well. That was just a mellomax tree."

"Well," the redheaded boy said, "Whatever it was, I'm hungry too. Suppose we stop and all wish ourselves something to eat," [17] he suggested. So they stopped and got down and hitched the ponies, and they sat in a circle beneath a tree.

"Now, Daphne," the redheaded boy said, "You wish first."

"I want——I want——Let me think what I want. Oh, yes: I want some green peas and lady-fingers and an alligator pear and a chocolate malted milk." And as soon as she said it, there they were on the grass in front of her.

"Now, Dicky," said the redheaded boy.

"Alice will have to wish for him," Daphne said. "What do you want, darling?"

"You wants some rice and gravy, dont you, honey?" asked Alice.

"Wants wice and gwavy," said Dicky, and there it was in front of him.

"Now, George," said the redheaded boy.

"I want so much strawberries and chocolate cake that I'll be sick for a week." And immediately there was a huge bowl of strawberries and a fresh chocolate cake in front of him.

"Now, Alice," said the redheaded boy.

"I wants some ham and gravy and a piece of cornbread and a cup of coffee," Alice said, and there it was in front of her.

Now, you choose," the redheaded boy said to the little old man.

"I'll take apple pie and icecream," the little old man said. "We dont have icecream very much at home," he explained.

"Now, it's my turn," the redheaded boy said. "I want [18] some hot gingerbread and an apple."

They sat on the grass and ate, and Alice helped Dicky because he was little.

"George," Daphne said, "You're going to be terribly sick if you eat all those strawberries and that cake by yourself."

"Dont care," mumbled George. "That's what I want."

When they had all finished, they got on the ponies again. The redheaded boy turned to the little old man. "Which way now?" he asked.

"That way," the little old man answered, and they went on that way through the forest.

"I ate too much," George said. "I wish now I hadn't."

"I wish we'd find the Wishing-Tree pretty soon. That's what I wish," Daphne said. A little further on the road forked again.

"That way," the little old man said, and they went on that way.

"I dont feel good," George said.

"Why, there's that white tree again," Daphne said in surprise, "We've come back to it."

"No, no," the little old man said quickly. "That's not the same tree. That's just another mellomax tree. There's a lot of them in this forest."

"I believe it's the same tree, myself," the redheaded boy said.

"So does I," Alice agreed. "I don't think he knows where that Wishing-Tree is not [*i.e.* no] more than I does. Did you ever see the Wishing-Tree?" [19]

"I've been to it more than a million times," the little old man answered hotly. "I know exactly where it is."

"Have you been to it, really?" Daphne asked.

"I cross my heart, I have," the little old man said. "I used to go to it every day when I was a young man. Cross my throat and hope to die."

"Well, this certainly looks like the same tree to me," the redheaded boy repeated. "Which way, then?"

"Dont you all pay no more mind to him," Alice said, "He dont no more know where that tree is than I does," Alice's voice mumbled on, and Daphne asked,

"What did you say, Alice?"

"I says, he aint no better than a ole tramp, that's what I says." She turned and glared at the little old man, who cringed back into the corner of the cart and began to talk to Dicky.

"If we just had a gun," the little old man said, "we could shoot some of these squirrels and rabbits and birds, couldn't we, now? There's a sight of game in this forest."

"I wants a gun," said Dicky, and Alice flung up her hands and shrieked, for there was the gun in Dicky's hands, a gun so big that Dicky couldn't hold it, and it dropped on the little old man's foo[t.]

"You—" said Alice, and she shrieked again. "You, young redheaded man, you take us right back home this minute, 'fo' dis ole fool kills us all dead. You come here and get dis here gun away from him. Look at him, pullin' a gun on me and dis baby!" [20]

"Why, Alice!" exclaimed Daphne, "he didn't do it! It was Dicky himself that wished the gun!"

"I dont care who done it," Alice replied. "Just look at him yonder, grinnin' at us like a 'possum, waitin' a chance to rob and kill us all." She glared at the little old man.

"Honest, ma'am," the little old man said, bewildered, "I never done it. I wouldn't even think——"

"Hush yo' mouf and get dat gun outen dis cart."

The little old man stooped and put his hand on the gun, but as soon as he touched it, it disappeared, because he hadn't wished the gun.

"Well," said Alice, watching him, "where is it? What you done with it? Take it right out from under yo' coat, 'fo' I calls a policeman."

"Alice!" Daphne exclaimed. "Don't you see it's gone? It's gone, Alice! He didn't wish for the gun: It was Dicky who wished for a gun."

Alice flopped around on the seat. "We's goin' right straight home: you tell that redhead boy to pick out the first road he kin find. I'se had about all this goingson I kin stand." Alice fell to mumbling again, and they rode on, and after a while they came again to the gray castle. There were some soldiers marching through the gate of the castle, with a flag at the head of the company.

"Look at the soldiers," Daphne said.

"I dont feel very good," George said. [21]

"Soldiers is de most triflin' folks in de Lord's creatium," Alice said. "Eatin' all day and on de prowl half de night. Thank de Lawd de army dont depend on me be [*i.e.* to] boa'd um."

"I want a soldier," Dicky said.

"You black nigger," Alice exclaimed, "Where you been?"

"The soldier that Dicky had wished for touched his soldier hat. "Why, if it aint Alice," he said.

"And I'll Alice you!" Alice shouted at him. "If I jes' had a stick of stovewood in my hand—" Alice blinked her eyes at the stick of wood, then she threw it at the soldier, but as soon as it touched him, it disappeared. "Jes' gimme one mo' stick," Alice said, and there was another stick in her hand and she threw it and it disappeared also. The soldier jumped behind a tree.

"Lawd a mussy, woman," the soldier said, "what is you chunkin' me wid? Hants?"

"You triflin' villyun," said Alice, and she started to climb out of the cart.

"Alice!" exclaimed Daphne, "What in the world!"

"It's dat husband I used to have. The one dat run off on me and lef' me wid a month house rent and not even a hunk of sidemeat in de house, and me payin' a lawyer to fin' out what de gov'ment done wid him. Him and his army! I'll war him, I will: he aint never seen no war like what I kin aggravoke. You come out from behine that tree, nigger man."

"Don't you hurt my soldier!" Dicky shouted. [22]

"She aint got a flatiron nor a rollinpin neither," the little old man called to the soldier.

"And I dont need none," Alice said. "I don't need—"

"Hol' up," the soldier said, "I kin explain how come I never come back."

"I bet you kin," Alice retorted. "You come right up here and git in this buggy and save yo' explainin' twell we gits home."

The soldier came and got in the cart.

"Don't you hurt my soldier," Dicky repeated.

"He's Alice's soldier, darling," Daphne said. "Is that the soldier you lost in the war, Alice?"

"He's de one," Alice answered. "And a good losin', too. Look at 'im! Even de war dont want him!"

They rode on. The soldier and the little old man sat side by side in the back of the cart.

"What's your husband's name, Alice?" asked Daphne.

"Name Exodus," Alice answered. "De one before him was name Genesis. I never did know what become of him. But you kin bet yo' money dat if meanness aint kilt him, de law's got 'im somewhere."

"I was in a war once," the little old man said to Alice's husband.

"Which one?" Alice's husband asked.

"I never did know," the little old man answered. "There was a lot of folks in it, I remember."

"Sounds like de one I wuz at," Alice's husband said. [23]

"They're all about alike, I reckon," the little old man said.

"I 'speck you's right," Alice's husband agreed. "Wuz it across de water?"

"Across the water?" the little old man repeated.

"Across de big up and down water," Alice's husband explained. "Man, man, dat wuz a war. A hundred days, and jes' water, up and down and up and down, and when ever you looked out de window, all you seen wuz dat restless water. Not even no sagegrass to look at and tell how far you come. I heard day killed folks in dat war, but it seemed like day after day I jes' couldn't die. I dont know how in de worl' folks ever dammed up a pond dat big, nor what dey can do wid it. Dat water 'ud hole all de inscursion boats in de rentire world."

"No, this wasn't that war," the little old man said. "They come right down in my pappy's pasture and fit the war I used to go to."

"Well, now," said Alice's husband, "If dat aint makin' war conveniump!"

"And there was another war I went to," the little old man added, "It was the Seven Pines war."

"Were you behind one of the trees?" asked Daphne.

"No, ma'am," the little old man answered. "There were a lot of generals at that war."

"Well, now," said Alice's husband again. "Wars dont change much, does dey?"

"I don't feel good," George said. "I think . . . . . ." George's eyes had a far away look in them. "I think I'm going to be sick," [24] George said.

"Who won the war you went to?" Daphne asked the little old man.

"I dont know, ma'am," the little old man answered. "I didn't".

"Dat's right, too", Alice's husband agreed. "I never seed a soldier yet dat ever won anything in a war except trouble gittin' in and mo' trouble gittin' loose. But den, white folks' wars is always run funny. Next time de white folks has a war, I think I aint goin'. I think I'll jes' stay in de army instead."

"I reckon that's better," the little old man agreed.

"I think," said George, "that I'm going to be sick." And George sat right on his pony and became dreadfully ill.

"He sho' did," Alice's husband said, "He couldn't be got no sicker goin' to the far offest war in de whole world."

They all stopped, and pretty soon George stopped being ill, and they helped him into the cart.

"Can I ride on this pony, mister?" the little old man asked the redheaded boy, and the redheaded boy said he could, and the little old man hopped out of the cart and mounted the pony.

"Why didn't you wish for a pony before, if you wanted to ride on one?" Daphne asked the little old man. "You haven't wished for anything except apple pie and icecream. Cant you think of anything you'd like to wish for?"

"I don't know," the little old man said. "I hadn't thought about it. But I will think of something to wish for. Let's see . . . I wish we all had a bag of pink and white candy." And as soon as he said it, everyone had a sack of candy in his hand. [25]

"Dicky cant have candy, Alice," Daphne said "You know we have to promise not to let anybody give him candy when we're walking."

So Alice took Dicky's sack, and they all thought up something for Dicky, and the little old man wished Dicky some more cookies. The little old man opened his sack.

"Mine are soft ones," the little old man said. "I'm glad of that. I used to like the hard ones best, but now I have to eat soft ones, because my teeth aint what they used to be when I was a young man."

"Let me see your teeth," Daphne said, and the little old man opened his mouth. He had no teeth at all.

"Why dont you wish for some false teeth?" Daphne asked.

"What are false teeth?" the little old man asked.

"Wish for some, and see," Daphne suggested.

"All right," the little old man agreed. "I wish I had some false teeth", he said, and he clapped his hand to his mouth and looked at Daphne in astonishment.

"Dont you like them?" Daphne asked.

"I dont really believe I do," the little old man answered. "I've kind of got used to not having any, you see." He took the false teeth out and looked at them. "They're right pretty, now, aint they? They'd look right nice on the mantleshelf, wouldn't they? I think I'll just keep them for that."

They rode on through the forest, under the huge oak trees, eating their candy. Except George. George didn't want any candy right now, and he put his sack in his pocket to take home with [26] him. There were a lot of birds in the trees chirping to one another, and squirrels scudded across the grass from one tree to another, and there were flowers of all kinds and colors in the grass.

The little old man kicked his pony with his heels until he lept and pranced and the little silver bells on the bridle jingled madly, "We rode horses in that war I used to go to," the little old man said. "This is the way I used to do." And he made the pony dash down the road until the little old man's beard streamed out behind him in the wind, then he made the pony whirl around and come dashing back.

"I bet you never went to no war in your life," Alice said.

"I bet so too," George said. George was feeling better now. "I bet if you ever saw a enemy, you'd run."

"I bet I wouldn't", the little old man replied quickly. "I bet I'd cut a enemy right in two with my sword. If I just had a sword in my hand———" And there was the sword in his hand—a new shiny one, with a gold handle, and the little old man looked at the sword, and then he rubbed it on his coat until it shone like a mirror, and he showed his sword to Alice's husband. Alice's husband said it was a fine sword, but he said it was a little too long to suit him, because he liked a knife you could hang on a string down your back, inside your shirt.

"This is the way I used to do at a war," the little old man said. "Look at me." And he waved his sword and made the pony dash down the road again and then come flying back.

"I bet you'd be scared as scared," George said. [27]

"I bet I wouldn't be scared of a hundred enemies," the little old man said, "with a fine sword like this. I bet I'd just ride right into 'em and slice 'em right in two."

"I bet you couldn't slice a—a—rabbit in two," George said. "I bet you'd be scared."

"I bet you'd be scared of a tiger or a lion," George said.

"I bet I've killed a hundred tigers and lions in this very forest," the little old man said, "with a sword just like this. . . . No, I used the sword at them wars. I dont remember what I killed the tigers and lions with. It was something else."

"I guess you kilt 'um dodgin' rollin' pins and flati'ons," Alice said.

"If I wuz runnin' a war," Alice's husband said, "I'd get me a bunch of married women and I'd blindfold 'em and I'd p'int 'um and I'd say, 'Go right straight like you's headed and when you hits somethin', it's yo' husband'. That's de way I'd conduck a war."

"It would save a lot of money, wouldn't it?" the little old man agreed, "because they could pick up the rollingpins and flatirons and use them again, couldn't they?"

"I've knowed 'um dat dont need no flati'ons and rollin'pins," Alice's husband said. "Wait twell you's been married as fr[e]quent as I is." [28]

"I don't believe I'll marry any more," the little old man said. "Even if I could, I mean."

"All husbands thinks dat," Alice's husband said. "De trouble is, convincin' de womenfolks. De man what's got any business sayin' he dont think he'll marry no mo' is dead."

"Yaah," said George. "I bet if a lion jumped out from behind that tree, you'd fall dead."

"I bet I wouldn't," the little old man answered, waving his sword again, "I bet I'd just——"

"I wish a lion would ju——"

Daphne screamed, and George didn't even complete his wish, and Alice's husband bellowed like a foghorn and climbed a tree. But Alice's voice drowned them all, and she caught Dicky up in one arm and dragged Daphne by the other and flew down the road. Behind them came George howling at the top of his voice, but the little old man, still carrying his sword, distanced them all.

"Stop! Stop!" the redheaded boy shouted, and Alice stopped and leaned against a tree, painting for breath. There, in the middle of the road, was the lion, and beside it the redheaded boy on his snorting pony. "Come back," the redheaded boy called to them, "He wont hurt you."

"Not twell you gits dat thing outen here!" Alice said. "You Daphne! Dont you go back up there."

"All you have to do," the redheaded boy said, "Is for the one who wished the lion, to unwish him. Who was it that wished him? It was George, wasn't it?" [29]

"I guess so," answered George, who was hiding behind Alice.

"Well, do you want him any longer?" the redheaded boy asked.

"Not me," George replied. "I hope I never see another lion as long as I live." And as soon as George said this, the lion was gone.

"Now we can go back," Daphne said.

"You, Daphne!" Alice exclaimed. "Dont you go up there! Dat thing jes' jumped back behind that tree: I seen him!"

"No, no," the redheaded boy said, "He's gone. Come on back."

They went back, and the little old man who had run still further down the road, came back too, with his sword; and Alice's husband climbed down from the tree and came back also. The lion was gone, but Alice wasn't satisfied until she had looked behind all the trees. But the lion was really gone.

"Why didn't he run after us?" Daphne asked.

"Because none of you wished he would," the redheaded boy explained. "You certainly didn't look like you were wishing he'd run after you. And now the ponies are gone, too. You all wished them away when you saw the lion.

Everybody wished they could run, you know, and you cant run when you're sitting on a pony or in a cart."

They looked at one another in astonishment.

"Will we have to walk?" Daphne asked.

"Well, I haven't any more ponies in my satchel," the redheaded boy replied. [30]

"I 'speck us better walk," Alice said. "De mo' us rides, de further us gits from home. Dey's somethin' mighty curious about this," Alice added and she glared at the little old man, who now wore his sword thrust through his left gallus. "And you kin jes' do somethin' wid dat knife, too," Alice said.

"I aint going to hurt no one with it," the little old man [said]. "Besides, I've lost my gillypus. It fell out of my pocket and now I cant find it."

"That's too bad," Daphne said. "It was a nice gillypus. Don't you wish it could walk and talk, and then you could find it."

"I sure do," the little old man said. "It was the best gillypus I ever seen." And then they heard a rustling in the grass, and a little thin voice crying:

"Here I come, Egbert; here I come."

"That's my name," the little old man said, stooping down to see where the gillypus was. The rustling came nearer, and soon they saw the gillypus running through the grass.

"Little puppy," said Dicky, and he caught up a stick from the ground and hit the gillypus, and the gillypus got larger, and Dicky hit it again, and the gillypus got larger still.

"Darling!" Daphne exclaimed. The gillypus was as big as a rabbit now, and Dicky hit it again.

"Dont hit Mr. Egbert's gillypus!" Daphne cried. The gillypus was as big as a dog now, and Dicky hit it again.

"Alice! Alice!" Daphne exclaimed, trying to catch the stick Dicky was hitting the gillypus with. [31]

"Kill little puppy," Dicky said, and the gillypus fell dead. "Cut little puppy in two," Dicky said, and the gillypus flew in two pieces.

"Look what you done!" the little old man said, and he hid his face in the bend of his arm, and wept.

"I'm awful sorry," said Daphne. "Dicky's a bad boy to kill your gillypus."

Then another little voice wailed up from the grass at their feet, and they looked down and there was Dicky, no bigger than a lead soldier in a clump of grass.

"That's because he made a bad wish," the redheaded boy explained. "A wish that hurt something."

"Dont step on him!" Daphne shrieked, and almost at the same moment Daphne and Alice were little like Dicky, and Alice picked Dicky up and drew Daphne to her with the other arm.

"You ole fool," Alice shouted up to the little old man in her thin tiny voice, "Look what you done! Dont you step on us!"

"I dont know what to do, now," the redheaded boy said. "Dicky'll have to stay little until he does a good deed for somebody; and Daphne and Alice wont wish themselves big again as long as Dicky must stay little."

"I think we all better get little, too," the little old man said, "so we can stay together."

"I guess that's the best idea," the redheaded boy agreed. "But before we do, let's be sure we still have our colored leaves, so we can get big again." [32]

"Not me," said George quickly. " I dont want to be that little. I wish I was home." And George just disappeared.

"I'm sorry he's gone," the little old man said. "I could have killed that lion, if I hadn't been so surprised."

The redheaded boy and the little old man had their leaves in their pockets, but Alice's husband didn't have a leaf, so they had to wish for him; and they did, and then they were all little like Alice and Daphne and Dicky.

"Golly," said the little old man. They were in a huge forest of the funniest trees. The trees were green all over, and they were flat, like huge sword blades stuck into the ground, and there were no branches and leaves on them at all.

"That's grass," the redheaded boy explained. "We better go this way."

They went on among the funny flat trees, and soon they came to a yellow mountain.

"This is a funny mountain," the little old man said. "It's made out of wood, like somebody whittled it with a big knife."

They went on along the foot of the mountain, looking for a road that went over it or around it. But there didn't seem to be any way that they could get around it.

"I know what it is," the redheaded boy said, "It's Mr. Egbert's gillypus."

"I wish I had my gillypus, the little old man said, and they stopped in astonishment, because the mountain disappeared, and then the little old man clapped his hand to his pocket and said, "Some-[33]thing jumped into my pocket." And he put his hand in his pocket and took out his gillypus. "Well," the little old man said, "I'm certainly glad to get this gillypus back again. It's the best gillypus I ever made."

So they went one, [*i.e.* on,] and they came out of the flat forest into a great wide desert, and standing in the middle of the desert was the biggest beast Alice had ever seen, or Alice's husband either.

"It's bigger'n dat elefump," Alice said.

"It's just my pony," the redheaded boy explained. "But he'll come on home by himself: he always does that."

They went on across the desert, and all of a sudden something whooshed through the air and a jaybird as big as two eagles flew down at them. Alice caught Dicky up and caught Daphne to her, and the jaybird whirled about them, trying to peck Dicky up with his beak. Alice's husband aimed his soldier gun and shot at the jaybird, but the jaybird kept on whirling around them trying to eat Dicky up. The jaybird thought Dicky was a bug, because Dicky was so little.

"Put your hat on the ground!" the redheaded boy shouted to the little old man, while Alice's husband was fighting with the jaybird, and the little old man put his hat on the ground and the redheaded boy wished it was as big as a soup plate, and it was, and they all got under it. They could hear the jaybird pecking at the hat, but he couldn't get in.

After a while they couldn't hear the jaybird any more, and Alice's husband raised the hat and looked out. [34]

"He's gone," Alice's husband said. Then he dropped the hat and jumped back inside. "Lawd save us," he shouted. "Here comes a earthquake!"

And before he finished saying it, the ground rose up under them and they tumbled over one another and rolled down a hill, and the hat rolled off of them and they could see the earthquake going on past them. They could see the ground hunching up like there was something burrowing along under it.

"It's a mole," the redheaded boy said. "That's what it was. Come on, we better get back into the forest and think what to do."

They ran back among the flat funny trees again, and Alice sat down against one of the trees to get her breath.

"I think," the redheaded boy said, "that we'd better wish Alice's husband big again, and we'll all get in his hat and he can carry us."

So they wished Alice's husband big again, and he put his hat on the ground and picked them up carefully and put them in the hat.

"You big fool," Alice shouted at him in her tiny thin voice, "you pick me and dis baby up careful, or I'll tear yo' head off and unravel yo' backbone clean down to yo' belt."

So Alice's huband put them in carefully, and he picked up his hat and went on. Daphne and Dicky and Alice and the redheaded boy and the little old man sat in the hat. They couldn't see anything except Alice's husband's head, and the sky and the tree-[35]tops, and the hat had a kind of swinging motion like a hammock when Alice's husband walked; and after a while Dicky went to sleep, and Daphne began to get drowsy, too. But she couldn't get comfortable, because there wasn't [*i.e.* weren't] any pillows in Alice's husband's hat.

I wish I was in my nice soft bed, Daphne said to herself. "No, I don't! I dont!" she screamed, but it was too late, for she was once more at home in her bed, in her room by herself. "I don't want to be here!" Daphne wailed. "I want to find Mr. Egbert so he can tell me where they went to!"

And once more she stood in the road before a small gray cottage with roses growing over the door. "This is not where I left them!" Daphne said. "I want to be where Alice and Dicky and Maurice and Mr. Egbert and Alice's husband are." But nothing happened. Daphne waited a moment, then she wished again. But still nothing happened, and then she remembered her blue leaf and put her hand in the pocket of her dress. The leaf was gone.

Daphne didn't know what to do, but she expected she was going to cry. She stood in the road in front of the house, and then she heard somebody chopping wood behind the house, and she opened the gate and entered the yard. The door of the house was shut, and on the ground near the stoop were some slivers of wood where someone had been whittling, and scattered about the yard were a flatiron and a rollingpin and an alarm clock. The axe was still chopping behind the house, and Daphne went on around the corner toward the sound, and there at the woodpile a little old man with a long white beard worked [36] busily. Daphne flew across the yard to him.

"Where are the others, Mr. Egbert?" Daphne asked.

The little old man stopped in the middle of a stroke and turned with the axe held about his head. Then he lowered the axe.

"Ma'am?" the little old man said.

"I've lost them," Daphne explained.

"We were all together there, and I got lost, and now I dont know where they are," she wailed.

The little old man dropped the axe, "Was it a picnic?" he asked with interest. "I used to go to a lot of picnics, in my time."

"Why, you were with us," said Daphne in surprise. "Did you get lost, too?"

The little old man had the kindest blue eyes, bright and innocent and kind. "I used to go to a lot of picnics," the little old man said. "But I aint been to one now in a long while."

"Why, you were with us this morning!" Daphne exclaimed. "Dont you remember? You had apple pie and icecream!"

"Did I, now?" the little old man said with pleasure. Then he wagged his long white beard. "I used to be a great hand for icecream, in my day. But we dont have icecream very often now, icecream and apple pie. Well, sir." He pushed the wood he had been chopping aside. "Wont you have a seat on this log?" he said politely.

Daphne sat down sadly. "Then you dont know where they are?" she asked.

The little old man sat down also. "Lordy, Lordy," he said, and he wagged his beard again, "It's been a power of years since I went to a picnic. But then, I aint as spry as I once was, and I've [37] kind of got lazy. That's the reason I chop wood, you see. We got a nigger to do it, but I like to chop occasionally for a little exercise."

"How old are you?" Daphne asked.

"Well," the little old man answered, "one April I turned ninety two, but that's been . . . . . . let's see. . . . Well, I dont think it's been so long ago, and so I expect I'm still about ninety two."

"And so you dont know where they are," Daphne said. "I was with them, and then I got l-lost, and now I c-cant f-find them, and I'm sc-cared," Daphne wept.

The little old man jumped up nervously, and he made a clucking sound with his tongue. Suddenly he reached into his pocket. "Look what I got," he said.

Daphne dried her eyes and looked. "Why, it's the gillypus!" she exclaimed.

"Is that what it is?" the little old man said, pleased. "I made it myself, but I didn't know what it was. You can have it, if you want," he added.

"I want Alice and Dicky," Daphne wa[i]led, and she wept again.

The little old man clicked his tongue again and put his hands back into his pockets. "Look", he said, "Look here what I found in the road this morning. I thought at first it was a leaf, but now I believe it's a dragon's scale or a roc's feather."

Daphne looked at the leaf, and clapped her hands. In the old man's hand the leaf was white, but as soon as Daphne touched it, it began to turn blue. "You can have it, if you want," the little old man said. [38]

"Oh, thank you, thank you!" Daphne exclaimed, clutching the leaf tight in her palm. "And when we go on another picnic, we'll come for you," Daphne promised the little old man. "Thank you, thank you!"

"I used to go to a sight of picnics," the little old man said, and the little old man's wife opened the kitchen door and glared at the little old man.

"You, Egbert!" the little old man's wife shouted, and she glared at him again and slammed the door. The little old man caught up the axe again and began chopping wood furiously.

"Now," said Daphne, clasping her blue leaf tightly and shutting her eyes, "I want to be where Dicky and Alice and Maurice and Alice's husband———"

"Hello, Daphne, hello, Daphne!" they all shouted, and Daphne hugged Dicky and Alice, and Alice and Dicky hugged Daphne, and Alice's husband gashed his mouth from ear to ear until all his teeth shown, and the redheaded boy watched them with his queer yellowflecked eyes.

"How did Dicky get big again?" Daphne asked.

"Dat ole tramp los' his gillymus in one of de wrinkles in Exodus' hat, and Dicky foun' it for him," Alice explained, and Daphne hugged Alice and Dicky again, and Dicky and Alice hugged Daphne again.

"Come on," the redheaded boy said. And they went on and passed from out the forest, into a valley. This was the valley through which, in the old days, young Sir Galwyn of Arthgyyl, with the green [39] design called Hunger at his right hand and the red design called Pain at his left hand, had ridden. It was full of sweet odors, and gray, and presently they would reach a river; and they went on and in a while they saw a tree covered with leaves of a thousand different colors.

"It's the Wishing-Tree!" Daphne exclaimed.

"I guess that's what it is," the redheaded boy agreed, but when they drew near the tree the leaves whirled up into the air and spun about it, and they saw that the tree was a tall old man with a long shining beard like silver, and that the leaves were birds of all kinds and colors.

"Good morning, Father Francis," the redheaded boy said.

"Good morning, Maurice," the good Saint Francis replied, and the colored birds spun and whirled and sang about his head.

"This is Daphne, and Dicky, and Alice, and Alice's husband," the redheaded boy said.

"We are looking for the Wishing-Tree," Daphne explained.

The good Saint Francis looked at them, and his eyes twinkled. "And did you find it?"

"We dont know," Daphne replied. "We thought perhaps this was it."

The good Saint Francis thought a while, and the birds settled again about him like a colored cloud. Then he spoke, and once more the birds whirled up into the air and spun and sang around his head.

"Didn't each of you pull a leaf from [a] white tree back yonder in the forests?" the good Saint Francis asked.

"Yes, Father Francis." [40]

"Well, that was the Wishing-Tree. But suppose there are a thousand leaves on that tree, and a thousand boys and girls come along and pull a leaf off; when the next boy or girl comes to it, there wont be any leaves for them, will there?"

"No, Father Francis."

"So a wish you make this way, is a selfish wish, isn't it?"

"Yes, Father Francis."

"Then," the good Saint Francis said, "Let each of you give me the leaf you pulled from the Wishing-Tree so I can put them back, and instead I'll give each of you a bird. And a bird is better than a leaf, because if you'll feed it and care for it, you'll never make a selfish wish, because people who care for and protect helpless things cannot have selfish wishes. Will you do this?"

"Yes, Father Francis," they all answered. So they gave their leaves to the good Saint Francis, and the good Saint Francis took from beneath his gown four wicker cages, and he put a bluebird in a cage for Daphne, and an oriole in a cage for the redheaded boy, and he gave Alice a redbird, and to Dicky a little white bird with pale blue feathertips, because Dicky was little and because he was Daphne's brother.

"What about Alice's husband?" Daphne asked.

"He will help Alice take care of her redbird," the good Saint Francis replied, "Because if he leaves her again, he will be a selfish wisher and he wont deserve a bird."

"And George?" Daphne asked. [41]

"Wishing is not good for George," the good Saint Francis replied. "The first wish George made, he made himself sick and was punished for it; the second wish he made, he frightened you all and himself too for no reason whatever; and the third wish he made, he deserted you when you were in trouble."

"But Mr. Egbert," Daphne said. "He deserves one, doesn't he?"

"Ah," answered the good Saint Francis, "he already has more than I can give him: he is old, and so he no longer has any wishes at all. What became of him, by the way?"

"His wife came and got him," Alice answered.

"Then," the good Saint Francis said, "he doesn't even need anything else."

He ceased speaking, and birds settled down again about his head and shoulders.

"Goodbye, Father Francis," the [*i.e.* they] said. "And thank you." But the good Saint Francis only smiled at them from amid his birds, and they went on.

They came to the bank of the river. But the funniest thing was, it wasn't a flat river, but it stood up on its edge, like a gray wall.

"If that isn't the funniest thing!" Daphne said, because the river was like a mist, it was like the mist this morning had been, and in it she could see a dim thing like a street in a fog stretching on between rows of houses, and the mist smelled of wisteria.

"We'll have to go through it," the redheaded boy said.

"Oh, but I'm afraid to," Daphne said, "Wait." But the redheaded boy had already stepped into it, and Alice and Dicky and [42] Alice's husband followed him. "Wait!" called Daphne again, but they had passed into the mist and were only dim shapes fading on into the mist, and the redheaded boy turned his thin ugly face and his queer yellowflecked eyes, and his hair made a faint glow about them, and beckoned to her. "Wait," called Daphne a third time, and she too passed into the mist, carrying her bluebird in one hand and stretching the other before her, feeling her way. But the others had gone on and disappeared, and the glow of the redheaded boy's hair was gone too; and it was like she was in a round bowl, rising and rising through warm water like sleep, to the top. And then she would be awake.

And she was awake, but she didn't open her eyes at once, and she lay there and her body and arms and legs tingled as though she had just eaten peppermint. What is it? she thought. What can it be?

"Birthday! Birthday!" cried a voice, and her eyes flew open, and there was Dicky jumping up and down on her bed, and leaning over her, her mother. Daphne's mother was awfully beautiful, so slim and tall, with her grave unhappy eyes changeable as seawater, and her slender hands that came so softly about you when you are [*i.e.* were) sick.

"Look," her mother said, and she held out a wicker cage with a bluebird in it, and Daphne squealed with delight.

"I wants a bird, mamma," Dicky chanted," I wants a bird, mamma."

"You can have half of mine, darling," Daphne said, and she let Dicky hold the cage and she closed her eyes again and her mother's [43] hand came onto her face and smoothed the hair back from her brow, and she remembered the good Saint Francis, and Maurice with his queer eyes and his flaming hair, and Mr. Egbert and his gillypus; and dreams and birthdays seemed beautiful and sad to her, but being Daphne was beautifullest and saddest of all.

Well, she still had her bluebird, even if it had been all a dream; and the good Saint Francis had said that if you are kind to helpless creatures, you dont need a Wishing-Tree to make things come true. And next year she would have another birthday, and if she just remembered to get into bed left foot first and to turn the pillow over before she went to sleep, who knows what might happen? [n.n.]

▶"Wash," c. 1933

The Brodsky Collection includes three distinct groups of "Wash" manuscripts arranged in the apparent sequences Faulkner gave them at the time of composition. Each of the groups is secured by and separated from each other with contemporary squarish paper clips and enclosed in an accordian-like, terra-cotta-hued pocket folder with flap and cloth ties. One set of gatherings (called below, "revised complete holograph"), carrying the twice-lined-through title "Wash," consists of eight numbered holograph pages, 10 15/16 by 8 1/2 inches, in Faulkner's fastidious blue-ink scrawl; all eight sheets are characterized by black horizontal and vertical margin rules and no watermarks. A second set of holograph leaves (referred to as "holograph working draft"), also entitled "Wash," comprises twelve pages of similarly margined and unwatermarked 10 15/16-by-8 1/2-inch paper. A third sheaf consists of twenty-two numbered pages of ribbon typescript on Howard Bond paper, 10 7/8 by 8 3/8 inches, the first page of which bears the title "Wash" and the typed superscription in the upper left margin: "William Faulkner / Oxford, Mississippi."

Close inspection supports the assumption that these materials have survived just as Faulkner must have arranged them before clipping and inserting them into the folder. Most obviously, all pages of the typescript, numbered 1–22 at the bottom of each page, are in proper order. Similarly, all eight pages of the revised complete holograph run in perfect sequence, numbered 2 (superimposed over the numeral 1) through 9. Finally, the remaining twelve pages from the holograph working draft also appear to be in sequential order, despite the fact that there are several identically-paginated leaves. Also, it is visually evident that these pages comprise Faulkner's early drafts which, supplanted by revised copies, were set aside. Predictably, in contrast to the revised complete holograph, these pages of the holograph working draft are characterized by numerous interlineations, transpositions of sentences and even entire paragraphs, deletions, marginal insertions, and partial pages representing false starts.

Printed below are the holograph working draft and the revised complete holograph. The typescript copy has been omitted, since it is not substantially different from the version of the story first published in the February 1934 issue of *Harper's Magazine.* For a detailed collation of these various texts, see Louis Daniel Brodsky, "The Textual Development of William Faulkner's "Wash": An Examination of Manuscripts in the Brodsky Collection," *Studies in Bibliography,* 37 (1984), 248–281.

———"Wash," holograph working draft in blue ink, 1 page, numbered "1." Cf. p. "2[*ov. 1*]" of revised complete holograph.

WASH

[He was probably watching, hidden, when Sutpen walked out of the house that a.m. He may have been in the scuppernong arbor, where he and Sutpen often sat with a pail of spring water and a demijohn between them. Thru the long, empty, barren, bitter afternoons of the 4 summers since 1865; until at last [he would practically carry Sutpen into the house and *del.*] Sutpen would reach that state of impotent undefeat [where, swaying, plunging, he would *del.*] when he would rise, swaying and plunging,—an old man, 58 in years but 10 years older thru [*illeg.*] marching on his violent dream—and declare again that he would take his pistol and horse and ride single-handed into Washington and kill Lincoln, already dead, and Sherman, now a private citizen with a monument in New York city. "Kill them!" he would shout. "Shoot them down like dogs, the——" *del.*]

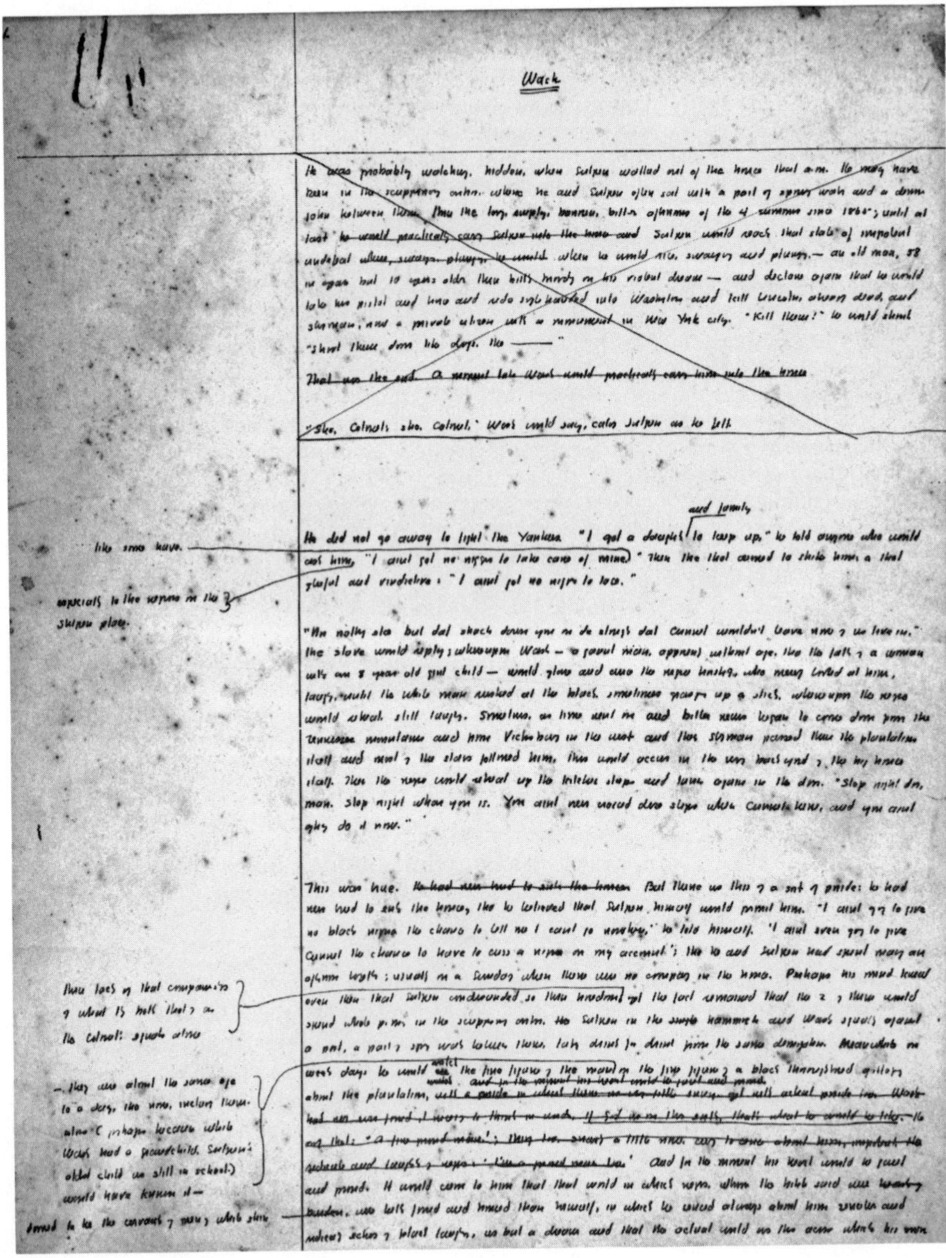
Wash

40. Title page of working draft of "Wash," c. 1933

[That was the end. A moment later Wash would practically carry him into the house *del.*]

["Sho, Colonel; sho, Colonel," Wash would say, catching Sutpen as he fell. *del.*]

He did not go away to fight the Yankees. "I got a daughter <and family> to keep up," he told anyone who would ask him, <*marg.* especially to the negroes on the Sutpen place.> "I aint got no niggers to take care of mine. <*marg.* like some have.>" Then the thot seemed to strike him: a thot gleeful and vindictive: "I aint got no niggers to lose."

"Nor nothing else but dat shack down yon in de slough dat Cunnel wouldn't leave none of us live in," the slave would reply; whereupon Wash—a gaunt man, appearing without age, tho the father of a woman with an 8 year old girl child—would glare and curse the negro house servant, who never looked at him, laughing, until the white man rushed at the black, sometimes grasping up a stick, whereupon the negro would retreat, still laughing. Sometimes, as time went on and bitter news began to come down from the Tennessee mountains and from Vicksburg in the west and then Sherman passed thru the plantation itself and most of the slaves followed him, this would occur in the very back yard of the big house itself. There the negro would retreat up the kitchen steps and turn again in the door. "Stop right dar, man. Stop right whar you is. You aint never crossed dese steps when Cunnel here, and you aint ghy do it now."

This was true. [He had never tried to enter the house. *del.*] But there was this of a sort of pride: he had never tried to enter the house, tho he believed that Sutpen himself would permit him. "I aint going to give no black nigger the chance to tell me I cant go nowhere,' he told himself. 'I aint even going to give Cunnel the chance to have to cuss a nigger on my account'; tho he and Sutpen had spent many an afternoon together; usually on a Sunday when there were no company in the house. Perhaps his mind knew even then that Sutpen condescended so thru boredom. <*marg.* thru lack of that companionship of what [*illeg.*] half thot of as the Colonel: squatting alone> Yet the fact remained that the 2 of them would spend whole p.m.s. in the scuppernong arbor. [He *del.*] Sutpen in the [single *del.*] hammock and Wash squatting against a post, a pail of spring water between them, taking a drink for drink from the same demijohn. Meanwhile on week days, he would [see *del.*] <watch *del.*> <watch> the fine figure of the man <*marg.*—they were almost the same age to a day, tho none, including themselves (perhaps because while Wash had a grandchild, Sutpen's oldest child was still in school.) would have known it—> on the fine figure of a black thoroughbred galloping about the plantation, [with a pride in which there was very little envy. Yet with actual pride for Wash had never ever found it necessary to think in words, *If God was on this earth, that's what he would be like.* He once thot: 'A fine proud man.'; thinking too, [*illeg.*] a little now, seeming to come about him, impotent, the ridicule and laughter of negros: 'I'm a proud man too.' *del.*] And for the moment his heart would be quiet and proud. It would seem to him that that world in which negroes, whom the bible said were [beasts of burden *del.*] <*marg.* doomed to be the servants of men of white skin>, were better found and housed than himself, in which he sensed always about him [*illeg.*] and ridiculing echoes of black laughter, was but a dream and that the actual world was this across which his own

———"Wash," holograph working draft in blue ink, 1 page, numbered "2." Cf. last paragraph of p. "2[*ov. 1*]" of revised complete holograph.

lonely apotheosis seemed to gallop free upon the black horse, thinking how the bible said too that man was made in the image of God, and hence all men were in the same image, [thinking *del.*] thus quieting his heart so that he could say as tho speaking of himself: 'A fine proud man. If God [rode the natural earth, that is what He would want to look like.' *del.*] himself <was to> come down to ride the natural earth, that's what He would aim to look like.'

———"Wash," holograph working draft in blue ink, 1 page, numbered "[2 *del.*] 3." Cf. p. "3" of revised complete holograph.

a man whose own company bored him. Yet the fact remained that the 2 of them would spend whole p.ms [together *del.*] in the scuppernong arbor, Sutpen in the hammock and Wash squatting against a post, a pail of spring water between them, taking drink for drink from the same demijohn. Meanwhile on week days he would watch the fine figure of the man—they were the same age almost to a day, tho neither of them (perhaps because Wash had a grandchild while [his *del.*] Sutpen's oldest child was still in school) [I knew it *del.*] thot it—on the fine figure of a black thoroughbred galloping about the plantation. [And *del.*] <Then *del.*> For that moment his heart would be quiet and proud. It would seem to him that that world in which negroes, whom the Bible told him were cursed <*marg.* and created] by God to be the inferior of all men of white skin, were better found and housed than he and his blood—that world in which he sensed always about him [ec *del.*] mocking echoes of black laughter—was but a dream and an illusion, and that the actual world was this across which his own lonely apotheosis seemed to gallop on the black horse, thinking how the Book [said *del.*] also said how man was made in God's own image and hence all men had the same image in the eyes of God at least, so that he could say, as tho speaking of himself: "A fine proud man. If God Himself was to come down and ride the natural earth, that's what He would aim to look like."

[When in 1865 Sutpen came home, looking like he had aged 10 years, wifeless and sonless (the son had been killed in action) <*marg.* [and *del.*] <then> his wife had died of a combination of pneumonia and grief in the same year *del.*> bringing with him nothing but his saber and the black horse and finding a ruined plantation and a daughter who had been living [by the bounty of a few negroes. *del.*] <*marg.* [to an extent *del.*] <partly> on the meagre bounty of the man to whom he once gave permission to dwell in a tumbledown fish camp of whose very existence he had forgotten about. *del.*> Wash was there to meet him. "Well, Kernel," he said, "they kilt us but they aint whupped us yit, air they?" *del.*]

When in 1865 Sutpen returned home, looking 10 years older, [wifeless *del.*] a widower [and sonle *del.*] (his wife had died of pneumonia the same winter in which his son was killed in action) bringing with him nothing but his [saber *del.*] <*marg.* citation for gallantry signed by General Lee> and the black thoroughbred, finding a ruined plantation and a daughter who had been subsisting partially on the meagre bounty of the man to whom 15 years ago he had granted the use of a tumbledown fishcamp whose very existence he had at the time forgotten, Wash was there to meet him.

"Well, Kernel," Wash said, "they kilt us but they aint whupped us yit, air they?"

[And even 5 years later, when on the graying dawn he looked down at the quilt pallet on which his granddaughter lay with a newborn child, his heart was still quiet. An old negro woman had tended the girl (she was just 17) [and the negress, [now sq *del.*] her duty done, now squatted above the rusted slip scraps which served them for warmth, putting a coal into her pipe *del.*] tho for the time he had forgot her presence as he looked down at the wan, spent face of his granddaughter and the *del.*]

———"Wash," holograph working draft in blue ink, 1 page, numbered "3." Cf. last two paragraphs of p. "3" of revised complete holograph.

5 years later, <when> in a gray dawn he looked down at the quilt pallet on which his granddaughter, now 17, lay with a newborn child, his heart was still quiet. An old negro woman had officiated; she now stopped above the rusted slip scraps which served them for warmth, [and cast *del.*] lifting a coal into her pipe. He watched her as she [began to *del.*] puffed the pipe into life.

"Well?" he said. He spoke harsher than he intended, because he would have to ask her, a negro, to wait for her money. "Will she—hit—Will they be all right now?"

"Dat's for [Him *del.*] Lord to say," the negress answered. "I done all I kin."

———"Wash," holograph working draft in blue ink, 1 page, numbered "4." Cf. p. "4" of revised complete holograph.

Sutpen home. He entered the house now. He had been doing so for some years, taking Sutpen home thus, actually carrying him, talking him into locomotion with cajoling murmurs as tho he almost were a horse, a stallion himself, being met by Sutpen's daughter who without a word would hold open the door for them to enter. He would carry his [half wit *del.*] burden through a once white [doorw *del.*] entrance [surrounded by a fanlight *del.*] surmounted by a fanlight imported piece by piece from France and with a board now nailed over a missing pane, across a velvet carpet from which all knap was now gone, and up a stairway where carpet, runner, was now but a fading ghost of bare board between 2 strips of fading paint, and into a bedroom. It was usually dusk by now and he would help his burden to sprawl onto the bed and straighten its legs and then he would sit quietly in a chair beside it. After a time the daughter would come to the door. "Nome," Wash would tell her. "We're all right. Dont you worry none."

Then it would be dark and after a while he would lie on the floor beside the bed, tho not to sleep, because after a time—maybe before midnight—the man in the bed would stir. "Wash?" Sutpen would say.

"Hyer I am, Kernel. You go back to sleep. We aint whupped yit. Me and you kin do hit."

That is what he thot when he saw the first ribbon of his granddaughter. She was now a girl of 15, already mature, after the way of her kind. He knew where the ribbon came from, even if the girl had lied about where she got it, which she did not. Yet his heart did not surge then with triumph or pride, nor yet with fear. [He was merely quite grave when he approached Sutpen when the store was closed that p.m. *del.*] He just waited. [until he saw the *del.*] He didn't try to spy on the girl or Sutpen, not even when after 3 or 4 ["Get the jug, Wash," Sutpen directed. *del.*] pms, when Sutpen quitted the store in midafternoon, directing him to lock up at sundown. He waited until he saw the new dress, [until she just showed it to him *del.*]

["Wait," Wash said. "Not yit for a minute. *del.*]

"Miss Judith help me to make hit," she said, almost too quietly.

"Sho, now," Wash said. "Hit's right pretty."

Then he approached Sutpen, waiting until he had closed the store for the day: "Get the jug," Sutpen directed.

"Wait," Wash said. "Not for a minute yit." Neither did Sutpen deny the dress; perhaps he realised it would be fruitless.

"What about it?" he said. "I'm 5 [0[*ov.* 8] *del.*] <50> years old, Wash. You and me are old men. Too old to [*illeg.*] any [*illeg.*], even if I wanted to."

"That's hit. Any other man your age would be old. But you air different from other men."

"How different?"

———"Wash," holograph working draft in blue ink, 1 page, numbered "5."

Now it was Sutpen who looked away, turning suddenly, almost brusquely. "Get the jug," he said, sharply.

"Sho, Kernel," Wash said.

There were some, negroes, others poor whites like himself, who believed that Wash was watching his granddaughter's presently changing shape with triumph and even glee. "Wash Jones has fixed old Sutpen at last," they said. "Hit taken him 20 years, but he has done hit at last."

———"Wash," holograph working draft in blue ink, 1 page, numbered "5." Cf. p. "5" of the revised complete holograph.

[Now it was Sutpen who looked away, turning suddenly, brusquely. "Get the jug," he said, sharply. *del.*]

["Sho, Kernel," Wash said. *del.*]

[There were some, negroes, other poor whites, who believed that Wash was watching his granddaughter's presently changing shape with triumph and even glee. They said, "Wash Jones has fixed old Sutpen at last. It taken him 20 years to do hit, but he has done hit at last." *del.*]

Now Wash's gaze no longer questioned. It was tranquil, serene. "I aint afraid. Because you air brave. It aint that you were a brave man and got a paper to show hit from General Lee. But you air brave. That's where hit's different. Hit dont need no ticket from nobody to know that. And I know that whatever you handle or tech, whether hit's a regiment or a ignorant gal or a hound dog, you will make hit right."

Now it was Sutpen who looked away, turning suddenly, brusquely. "Get the jug," he said sharply.

"Sho, Kernel," Wash said. [It was 2 years before the girl's shape began to change and become obvious. *del.*]

[Two years later <when the girl's shape began to change an *del.*> there were some, negroes or poor whites like himself, who believed that he was watching *del.*] [Two years later, when the girl's shape began to change and become [apparent *del.*] obvious, there were some, negroes or poor whites like himself, who believed that Wash was *del.*] It was 2 years before the girl's shape began to change and become obvious. Then the occasional negro <*marg.* who passed> and the half drunk poor whites of Wash's kind who loafed all day before the store, [to watch the 3 of them *del.*] [began to watch the 3 of them like [figures *del.*] actors that came and went upon a stage: the grandfather, the old [*illeg.*], the girl with her air half brazen and half shrinking *del.*] believed that Wash contemplated his granddaughter with triumph and glee. They said: "Wash Jones has fixed old Sutpen at last. Hit taken him 20 years, but he has done hit at last."

———"Wash," holograph working draft in blue ink, 1 page, numbered "6." Cf. p. "6" of revised complete holograph.

"A girl," he repeated. "A girl," in astonishment, hearing the galloping hooves, [thinking *del.*] <seeing> for an astonished moment [of *del.*] the proud galloping figure beneath a brandished saber and a shot torn rushing flag; thinking of the other for the first time as being perhaps an old man like himself, after all. <*marg.* 'Yes, sir,' he thot in a kind of infantile astonishment: 'be dawg if I aint a great grandpaw now for sho.'> He entered the house. He moved clumsily, as tho he no longer lived there, as tho the infant which had just [cried *del.*] drawn breath and cried had dispossessed him, be it his own blood too tho it might. But even above the pallet he could see little save the blur of his granddaughter's exhausted face in a frame of hair, yet even then it took the negress' voice to warn him.

"You better gawn tell him efn you going to." "Hit's daylight already."

["I reckon I had," he said *del.*]. <"I reckon I had," he said.> It was daylight; light had come while he stood above the pallet; soon the swift sun of Miss. latitudes. It seemed to lie just beyond the swamp across the slough like the yolk of an egg about to break and spurt where he descended [the crazy steps *del.*] <into the weeds> and passed the end of the porch where the scythe still leaned which he had borrowed 3 months ago to cut them away. 'You might say that he was represented in a way, anyhow,' he thot, going on. Almost at once he heard the horse. He stepped out of the path to let the old stallion pass, his face lifted, [bright, weary, *del.*]

[Hi *del.*] "Hit's a gal, Kernel," he shouted. But Sutpen only lifted his whip hand and went on. He looked as tho he too had not slept much.

So Wash followed. He could not keep up with the horse and he passed it already tethered to the end of the porch, [and he reached the door just in time to hear Sutpen say, "Too bad you're not a *del.*] But he reached the door in time to hear Sutpen's voice as he straddled his legs above the pallet.

He was standing in the path when Sutpen emerged, tho they were not 5 feet apart when Sutpen seemed to notice him. "Well?" Sutpen said.

"You called [my grand *del.*] her a mare. You said if she was a mare, you would give her a stall in the stable."

"Well?" Wash advanced toward him. "Stand back. Dont touch me, Wash."

"I'm going to tech you, Kernel," [*illeg. del.*] Wash said.

Sutpen struck him across the face with the whip. Wash fell back. When he advanced this time, he held the scythe in his hands. "I'm going to tech you, Kernel," he said.

———"Wash," holograph working draft in blue ink, 1 page, numbered "7."

door with the black gargoyle face of a worn gnome. He raised the hand which held the riding whip. "Stand back, Wash," he said. Then he struck. The old negress sprang down into the weeds as nimble as a goat, and fled. Neither of them saw her. Sutpen slashed Wash again across the face, the force of the blow knocking Wash to his knees. But he rose again, turning toward the porch beside him. When he turned back he held in his hands the scythe which he had borrowed from Sutpen 3 months ago and which Sutpen would never need again.

He hid the scythe carefully before he departed, as tho he intended to need it again, as tho the act iself symbolised the fact that he was not fleeing [he thot without self pity, 'I aint got nowhere to run to. [Besides, I *del.*] No matter how far I was to run, hit would be this same land and these same people. That aint worth running from. Hyer hit is 5 years and I am just seeing [what hit *del.*] how hit was the Yankees whupped us, since ef his kind was the best we had to fight, then who am I and my kind? *del.*] It seemed to him that he had nowhere to run to, even if he would. He could see himself an old man, too old to flee very far, to flee beyond the boundaries of this same land in which [these *del.*] this same kind of man lived, set the order and rule of living. He seemed to see for the first time now, after 5 years, how it was that the Yankees had whupped them: the gallant, the proud, the brave: the thot struck him with a kind of despair: *Maybe if I'd a went to hit, I'd a learned sooner.* and then thinking: *But what would I have done with my life since; how could I a borne to remember what my life had been before?*

He was lying hidden now, thru a long bright sunny day, not so far but he could see, feel them galloping with their horses and guns and dogs, to pursue him and hunt him down. He even knew what they were saying: *Old Wash Jones he come a craping at last. He thot he had Sutpen but Sutpen fooled him. He thot he had Kernel where he would have to marry the gal or pay up and Kernel refused.* "But I never expected that, Kernel," he said, cried, aloud (he was safe enough there, back in the swamp then at the site of an abandoned sawmill, squatting among sawdust piles, a mute and rusty stiff shaft with a rusty wheel half buried in the [*illeg.*] undergrowth.) "You know that. You know that I aint never expected nothing from no man in my life, least of all from you. That I aint never asked you for nothing. For me to do for you was enough, was all I wanted. You knew that."

———"Wash," holograph working draft in blue ink, 1 page, numbered "[8 *del.*] 7."

door with the black gargoyle face of a worn gnome. He raised the hand which held the riding whip. "Stand back, Wash," he said. Then he struck. The old negress leaped down into the weeds with the agility of a goat, and fled. [Neither of them even saw her. *del.*] Sutpen slashed Wash again across the face, striking him to his knees. When he rose and advanced once more he held in his hands the scythe which he had borrowed from Sutpen 3 months ago and which Sutpen would never need again. Before he departed he hid it carefully beneath the porch, as tho he knew even then that he would require it once more. It was as tho the very act itself symbolised or stipulated the fact that he was not fleeing.

During all that long, bright sunny day he was never so far away but he could see, sense, feel, the men gathering with horses and guns and dogs to hunt him down—men mostly of Sutpen's own kind, who had made the company about his table in the time when Wash had yet to approach nearer to the house than the scuppernong arbor—men who had also led soldiers in battles, who maybe also had signed papers from the generals like as not to say that they were among the best of the brave; who had also galloped in the old days arrogant and proud on the fine horses over the fine plantations—symbols of admiration and desire, instruments of despair and grief.

That was who they thot that he would run from. It seemed to him that he had no more to run from than he had to run to. He saw now that he must flee (if he were to flee) bragging and evil shadows, into and across other bragging and evil shadows just like them, since they were all of a kind and he was old, too old to flee far, even if he were to flee. He could never escape them, no matter how much or how far he ran: a man going on 60 could not run that far. Not far enough to escape beyond the boundaries of earth where such men lived, set the order and the rule for living. He [believed that *del.*] saw now for the first time, after 5 years, how it was that Yankees or any other living men had managed to whip them: the gallant, the proud, the brave; the acknowledged and chosen best among them all to carry courage and honor and pride. Maybe if he had gone to the war with them he would have discovered them without having to see all that he had believed in stripped from him like shucks from an ear of corn. But if he had discovered them sooner, what would he have done with his life since? how could he have born for 5 years to remember what his life had been before?

At first he had been worried about his granddaughter.

——— "Wash," holograph working draft in blue ink, 1 page, numbered "7." Cf. p. "7" of revised complete holograph.

door with the black gargoyle face of a worn gnome. He raised the hand which held the riding whip. "Stand back, Wash," he said. Then he struck. The old negress leaped down into the weeds with the agility of a goat and fled. Neither of them saw her. Sutpen slashed Wash again across the face, [the *del.*] striking him to his knees. When he rose and advanced again he held in his hands the scythe which he had borrowed from Sutpen 3 months ago and which Sutpen would never need again, and which Wash hid carefully before he departed, as tho he knew even then that he would require it once more, it was as tho the very act itself symbolised or stipulated the fact that he was not fleeing.

All during the long, bright, sunny day he was never so far away but he could see, sense, feel the men gathering with horses and guns and dogs to hunt him down—men mostly of Sutpen's own kind, who had made the company about his table in the time when Wash had not yet approached nearer to the house than the scuppernong arbor—men who had led soldiers in the war alive, who maybe also had signed papers from the generals like as not, who had also galloped in the old days arrogant and proud on the fine horses across the fine plantations.

That was who they thot he would run from. It seemed to him that he had no more to run from than to run to. He could not escape them, no matter how much or how far he ran: a man going on to 60 [h *del.*] could not run that far. Not far enough to escape beyond the boundaries of [the land w *del.*] earth where such men lived, set the order and the rule of living. He seemed to see for the first time now, after 5 years, how it was that Yankees or any other men had managed to whip them: the gallant, the proud, the brave, [Maybe if he had gone to the war with them he would have discovered them sooner. But if he had discovered sooner, what would he have done with since if they were the self acknowledged best, and he and his kind were less, apparently designated so by God Himself to be. *del.*] the acknowledged and the chosen best to carry courage and honor and pride. Maybe if he had gone to the war with them he would have discovered them sooner. But if he had discovered them sooner, what would he have done with his life since; how could he have born for 5 years to remember what his life had been before?

He had sat thru most of the long p.m. not a half mile from [his home *del.*] what for 20 years he had called home, squatting on his heels after the timeless fashion of his kind among the sawdust piles of an abandoned sawmill in the swamp—a pale gray bowl of sandlike substance as tho he might be on the edge of the sea; squatting so he heard them ride past along the very logging road itself not 50 yards away. He did not attempt to better his positon, tho men came to look into the bowl. They rode on, talking quiet: he could almost hear what they were saying because he already knew what it was, what they had been saying and thinking ever since the old negress reached the first [cabin: *del.*] house: *Old Wash Jones he come a tumble at last. He thot he had Sutpen but Sutpen fooled him. He thot he had Kernel where he would have to marry old Wash's gal or pay up. And Kernel refused.* "But I never expected that, Kernel!" he cried, aloud suddenly, his voice so sudden and so loud in the bright silence as to cause him to start, to leave him a little aghast at his own voice, tho still without alarm yet or fear. Nevertheless some old instinct of hiding and flight held him [*illeg.*], looking this way and that while thinking went smoothly on: 'You know I never. You know how I aint never expected [ara thing from ara man in my life but you. That what I expected from you wasn't nothing that could be teched or helt in the hand *del.*] or asked ara thing from ara living man but what

——— "Wash," holograph working draft in blue ink, 1 page, numbered "8." Cf. p. "8" of revised complete holograph.

I expected from you. And I didn't ask that. I didn't think hit would need. I says to myself, *I dont need to. What need has a fellow like Wash Jones to question* <*marg.* or doubt> *the man that General Lee himself says in a handwrote ticket that he was brave?*

Now it was almost sunset. It would be dark [before he *del.*] by the time he reached home, and he was stiffening, his old man's joints stiff from long squatting. [Yes, home. The closest word to it for a mistake that had lasted 20 years. *del.*] Home. The closest word to it for a mistake that had lasted 20 years. 'His kind looked on my kind as less than niggers,' he thot, walking. ['But hit waited for him to look on me and mine, ay hisn too, as less than mares in a stall *del.*] 'All right. He was born so. Hit's times watching him when I thot maybe he was right. But hit waited for him to look on me and mine—ay, hisn too—as less than mares in a stall. Better if his kind and mine too had never drawn breath on this earth. Better if nara a one of them had ever rid home in '65: Better if all of us that's left was blasted from the face of the earth than that another Wash Jones should see his whole life enter him and [throwed *del.*] [*illeg.*] away like a shuck throwed into the john.'

It was dark when he neared home, because he moved cautious, listening as he moved. He believed that there would be some of them concealed about the house; he was a little surprised when he reached it and heard his granddaughter whimpering and moaning in the darkness. He had forgotten about her. 'I reckon she's been here alone all day,' he thot. 'Hit's plenty of them can spend the day on the chance of getting a shot at me, but nara a one of them had time to see that she had a sup of water even.'

He entered the house. Now that he had penetrated where the line of pistols would be, he ceased trying for stealth, tho moving quietly. His granddaughter [heard him and spoke in the pale darkness, her *del.*] continued to whimper and moan. "Milly," he said quietly, "Milly." She continued to whimper and moan. He moved carefully and found the pallet and knelt beside it, and fumbled and found her face. It was hot and dry.

——— "Wash," revised complete holograph, autograph manuscript in blue ink, 8 pages, 10$^{15}/_{16}$ by 8½ inches, unwatermarked.

[WASH *del.*]

[He did not go away to fight the Yankees. "I'm looking after Colonel Sutpen's place and niggers," he would tell those who asked—a gaunt, malariaridden

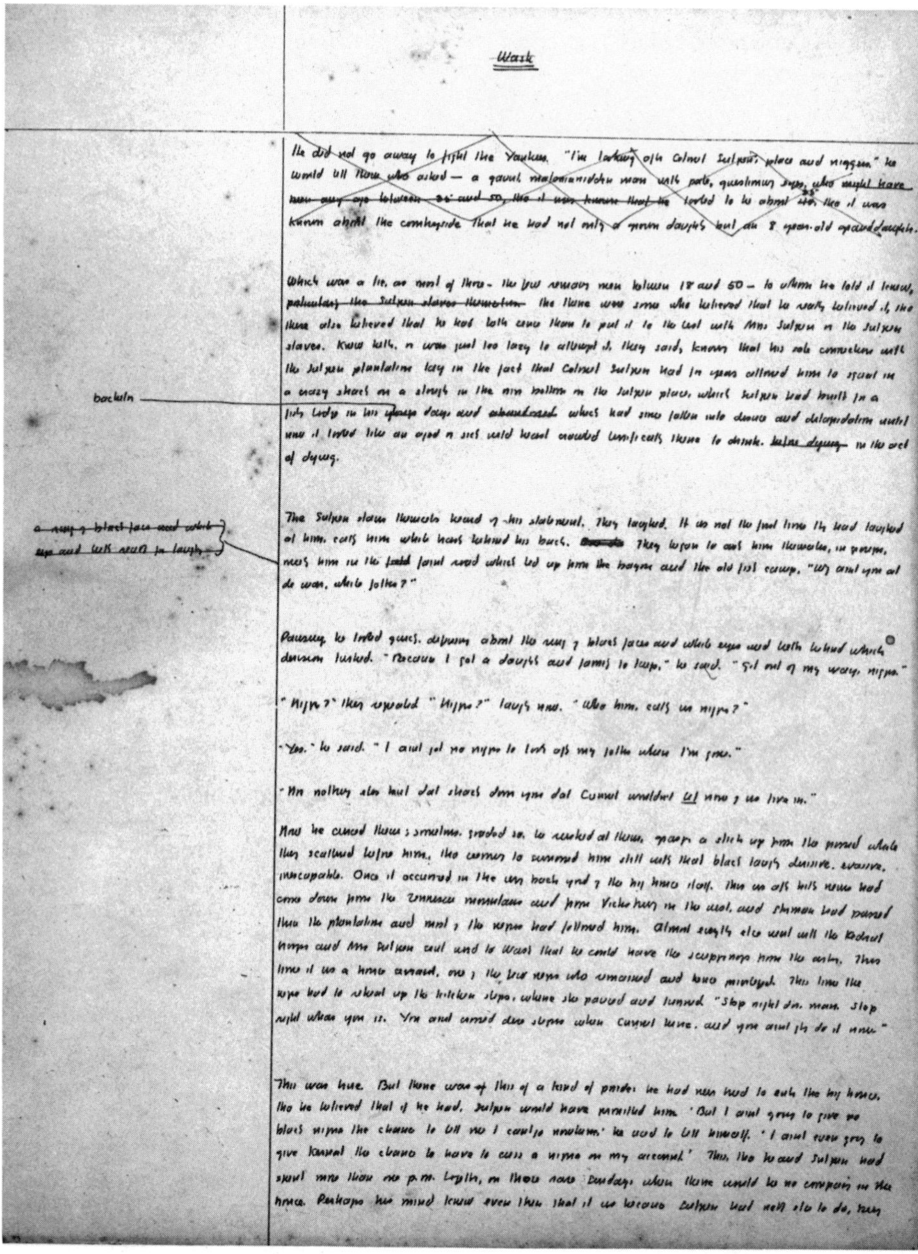

Wash

41. Title page of intermediate version of "Wash," c. 1933

man with pale, questioning eyes, who [might have been any age between 35 and 50, tho it was known that he *del.*] looked to be about [40 *del.*] <35>, tho it was known about the countryside that he had not only a grown daughter but an 8 year-old granddaughter. *del.*]

Which was a lie, as most of those—the few remaining men between 18 and 50—to whom he told it knew, [particularly the Sutpen slaves themselves *del.*] tho there were some who believed that he really believed it, tho these also believed that he had better sense than to put it to the test with Mrs Supen or the Sutpen slaves. Knew better, or was just too lazy to attempt it, they said, knowing that his sole connection with the Sutpen plantation lay in the fact that Colonel Sutpen had for years allowed him to squat in a crazy shack on a slough in the river bottom on the Sutpen place, which Sutpen had built for a fishing lodge in his [younger *del.*] <*marg.* bachelor> days and [abandoned *del.*] which had since fallen into disuse and dilapidation until now it looked like an aged or sick wild beast crawled terrifically there to drink. [before dying *del.*] in the act of dying.

The Sutpen slaves themselves heard of his statement. They laughed. It was not the first time they had laughed at him, calling him white trash behind his back. [One da *del.*] They began to ask him themselves, in groups, <*marg.* a ring of black faces and white eyes and teeth [*illeg.*] for laughing *del.*> meeting him in the [field *del.*] faint road which led up from the bayou and the old fish camp. "Why aint you at de war, white folks?"

Pausing, he looked quick, defensive about the ring of black faces and white eyes and teeth behind which derision lurked. "Because I got a daughter and family to keep," he said. "Git out of my way, niggers."

"Niggers?" they repeated. "Niggers?" laughing now. "Who him, calling us niggers?"

"Yes," he said, "I aint got no niggers to look after my folks when I'm gone."

"Nor nothing else but dat shack down yon dat Cunnel wouldn't *let* none of us live in."

Now he cursed them; sometimes, goaded so, he rushed at them, grasping a stick up from the ground while they scattered before him, tho seeming to surround him still with that black laughing derisive, evasive, inescapable. Once it occurred in the very back yard of the big house itself. This was after bitter news had come down from the Tennessee mountains and from Vicksburg in the west, and Sherman had passed thru the plantation and most of the negros had followed him. Almost everything else went with the Federal troops and Mrs Sutpen sent word to Wash that he could have the scuppernongs from the arbor. This time it was a house servant, one of the few negros who remained and hence privileged. This time the negro had to retreat up the kitchen steps, where she paused and turned. "Stop right dar, man. Stop right whar you is. You aint crossed dese steps when Cunnel here, and you aint ghy do it now."

This was true. But there was [of *del.*] this of a kind of pride: he had never tried to enter the big house, tho he believed that if he had, Sutpen would have permitted him. 'But I aint going to give no black nigger the chance to tell me I cant go nowhere,' he used to tell himself. 'I aint ever going to give Kernal the chance to have to cuss a nigger on my account.' This, tho he and Sutpen had spent more than one p.m. together, on those rare Sundays when there would be no company in the house. Perhaps his mind knew even then that it was because Sutpen had nothing else to do, being [2(*ov.* 1)] a man whose own company bored him. Yet the fact remained that the 2 of them would spend whole p.ms. in the scuppernong arbor, Sutpen in the hammock and Wash squatting against a post, a pail of [spring *del.*] [well water between *del.*] cistern water between them, taking drink for drink from the same demijohn. Meanwhile on week days he would watch the fine figure of the man—they were the same age almost to a day, tho neither of them (perhaps because Wash had a grandchild while Sutpen's oldest child was a youth in school) thot [it *del.*] of themselves as being so—on the fine figure of a black [thoroughbred *del.*] <stallion> galloping about the plantation. For that moment his heart would be quiet and proud. It would seem to him that that world in which negroes, whom the Bible told him had been created and cursed by God to be brute and vassal to all men of white skin, were better found and housed and even clothed than him and his—that world in which he sensed always about him mocking echoes of black laughing—was but a dream and an illusion, and that the actual world was this one across which his own lonely apotheosis seemed to gallop on the black thoroughbred, thinking how the Book said also that all men were created in the image of God and hence all men made the same image in God's eyes at least; so that he could say, as tho speaking of himself: "A fine proud man. If God Himself was to come down and ride the natural earth, that's what He would aim to look like."

Sutpen returned in 1865, [bringing with him *del.*] on the black [thoroughbred *del.*] <stallion>, the 2 of them looking 10 years older. His son had been killed in action in the same winter in which his wife had died; he returned [to a *del.*] with his citation for gallantry at the hand of General Lee to a ruined plantation, where for a year now his daughter had subsisted partially on the [bounty *del.*] meagre bounty of the man to whom 15 years ago he had granted permission to squat in a tumbledown fish camp whose very existence he had at the time forgotten. Wash was there to meet him. "Well, Kernel," Wash said, "they kilt us but they aint whupped us yit, air they?"

That was the tenor of their talk for the next 5 years. It was inferior whiskey which they drank together now, and it was not in the scuppernong arbor [: *del.*]. It was in the rear of the tiny store which Sutpen had contrived to set up on the highroad: a frame [room *del.*] shelved room where, with Wash for clerk, he dispensed meagrely kerosene and staple food and stale gaudy [candy *del.*] [a *del.*] sweets and cheap beads and ribbons to negroes [and *del.*] <or> poor whites [stock *del.*] of Wash's [kind *del.*] own kind, who came afoot to haggle tediously [with them *del.*] for dimes and quarters with the man who at one time could gallop (Sutpen still had the black stallion; the stable in which the stallion's [get [*illeg.*] *del.*] jealous get lived was in better repair than the house where the owner lived) for 10 miles on his own fertile land who had led troops gallantly in battle, until Sutpen in fury would empty the store, close and lock the doors from the inside. Then he and Wash would repair to the rear and the jug. But the talk would not be quiet now, as when Sutpen lay in the hammock [talking *del.*] delivering [a monologue *del.*] an arrogant monologue while Wash squatted guffawing against his post. They both sat now, tho Sutpen had the single chair while Wash used wahtever box or keg was handy, and this for just a little while because soon Sutpen would reach that stage of impotent undefeat [and [*illeg.*] *del.*] when he would rise, swaying and plunging, and declare again that he would take his pistol and the black stallion [(now a year dead) *del.*] and ride singlehanded into Washington and kill Lincoln, [also *del.*] dead now, and Sherman, now a private citizen. "Kill them!" he would shout. "Shoot them down like dogs——"

"Sho, Kernel; sho, Kernel," Wash would say, catching Sutpen as he fell. Then he would commandeer the first passing wagon, or lacking that, he would walk a mile down the road and borrow one and take [3] Sutpen home. He entered the house now. He had been doing so for some years, taking Stupen home in whatever borrowed wagon, talking him into locomotion with cajoling murmurs as tho he were a horse, a stallion himself. The daughter would meet them and hold <open> the paintless door without a word. He would carry his burden thru the once white formal entrance surmounted by a fanlight [brot *del.*] imported piece by piece from Europe and with a board now nailed over a missing pane, across a velvet carpet from which all nap was gone, and up a formal stair where carpet, runner, was now but a fading ghost of bare boards between 2 strips of fading paint, and into the bedroom. It would be dusk by now and he would help his burden to sprawl onto the bed and undress it and then he would sit quietly in a chair beside. After a time the daughter would enter. "We're all right now," Wash would say. "Dont you worry none, Miss Judith."

Then it would be dark and after a while he would lie on the floor beside the bed, tho not to sleep, because after a time—[per *del.*] sometimes before midnight—the man on the bed would stir: "Wash?"

"Hyer I am, Kernel. You go back to sleep. We aint whupped yit, air we. Me and you kin do hit."

Even then, he had already seen the ribbon about his daughter's waist. She was now 15, already mature, after the way of her kind. He knew where the ribbon came from; he had been seeing it and its kind daily for 3 [*ov.*4] years, [He knew now *del.*] even if she had lied about where she got it, which she did not, with a kind of defiant watchfulness. "Sho now," he said. "Efn Kernel wants to give hit to you, I hope you thanked him."

His heart did not surge with triumph or pride, nor yet with fear; not even when he saw the dress, saw her secret, defensive, almost frightened face when she told him that Miss Judith, the daughter, had helped her to make it. He was merely quite grave when he approached Sutpen when he closed the store that p.m. "Get the jug," Sutpen [said *del.*] directed.

"Wait," Wash said. "Not right yit, for a minute."

Neither did Sutpen deny the dress. "What about it?" he said.

But Wash met his arrogant stare. "I've knowed you going on 20 years. I aint never [yet failed *del.*] yit denied to do what you told me to. And I'm a man. And she aint nothing but a 15 year old gal."

"Meaning that I'd harm a girl? [Me, I'm 50 years old. *del.*] I, a man more than 50 years old, as old as you are?"

"If you was any other, I would say you was as old as me. And old or no old, I wouldn't let her keep that dress or nothing else that came from you. But you are different."

"How different?" But the other never looked at him with his pale, questioning, [*illeg. del.*] sober eyes. ["Then, if I am different, what are you afraid of *del.*] "So that's why you are afraid of me?"

[Now Wash's gaze no longer questioned. It was tranquil, serene. "I aint afraid. Because you air brave. Hit dont need no ticket from General Lee for me to know that. And I know that whatever you handle or tech, if hit's a regiment or a gal or even a dog, you will make hit right." *del.*] [4]

Now Wash's gaze no longer questioned. It was tranquil, serene. "I aint afraid. Because you air brave. It aint that you were a brave man once and got a paper to show hit from General Lee. But you air brave, the same like you air breathing. That's where hit's different. Hit dont need no ticket from nobody to know that. And I know that whatever you handle and tech, whether hit's a regiment of men or a ignorant gal or just a hound dog, you will make hit right."

Now it was Sutpen who looked away, turning suddenly, brusquely. "Get the jug," he said sharply.

"Sho, Kernel," Wash said.

So [when *del.*] on that <Sunday> dawn 2 years later, watching the negro midwife which he had walked 3 miles to fetch enter the crazy [house *del.*] door beyond which he could hear his granddaughter's wailing, his heart was concerned tho still not troubled. He knew what they had been saying—the occasional negro who passed, the poor whites of his own kind who loafed all day long about the store, watching quietly the 3 of them—Sutpen, himself, his granddaughter with her air of brazen and shrinking defiance as her condition daily became more and more obvious—like 3 actors that came and went upon a stage. 'I know what they say to one another,' he thot. 'I can almost hyer them: *Wash Jones has fixed old Sutpen at last. Hit taken him 20 years, but he has done hit at last.* [Durn yapping dogs that dont know. That dont know. . . . . .

del.] 'Durn yapping dogs.' It would be dawn after a while, tho not yet. From the house, where the lamp shined [bey *del.*] dim beyond the warped door frame, his granddaughter's voice came steadily as tho run by a clock, while thinking went slowly and terrifically, fumbling, involved somehow with a sound of galloping hooves until there broke suddenly free in gallops the fine proud figure of the man on the fine proud stallion, galloping; and then that at which thinking fumbled broke free too and quite clear, not in justification nor even in explanation, but as the apotheosis, lonely, explicable, beyond all fouling by human touch: 'He is bigger than all them Yankees that kilt his son and his wife and [ruined his pla *del.*] taken his niggers and ruined his land, bigger than this hyer durn country that he fit for and that denied him, bigger than the denial hit helt to his lips like the cup the Book tells about. And how could I have lived this nigh to him for 20 years without being teched [by *del.*] and changed by him? I aint as big as him. But I done been drug along. 'Hit's like I telt him and telt Miss Judith: We aint whupped yet. Me and him kin do hit.'

[So when it was dawn (he realised it by the fact that he could now see the house itself and the old negress standing in the door) and [she *del.*] his granddaughter's voice had ceased *del.*]

He realised it was dawn suddenly, by the fact that he could now see the house and the old negress in the door looking at him. Then he realised that his granddaughter's voice had ceased. "It's a girl," the negress said. "You can [tell him *del.*] go tell him if you wants to." She reentered the house.

["A girl," he repeated. "A girl. Sho, now." It was getting light fast; soon the sun of Miss. latitudes. He turned and looked toward the east. "Hit'll ketch me before I git thar,' he thot, moving on, passing the corner of the porch where the scythe leaned which he had borrowed 3 months ago to cut away the weeds which choked the steps. He looked at it, passing. 'In a way, you might say that he was represented, anyhow.' Then he paused; his pale eyes filled with a sort of pleased and infantile astonishment; he said aloud: "Be dawg if I aint a great-grandpaw now. I just thot of that." *del.*] [5]

"A girl," he repeated; "a girl"; in astonishment, hearing the galloping hooves, [seeing for an instant the proud galloping *del.*] seeing the proud galloping figure emerge again and seem to pass before his eyes thru avatars culminating in [that *del.*] one where it galloped beneath a brandished saber and a shot torn flag rushing down a sky in color like sulphur, thinking for the first time in his life that perhaps Sutpen was an old man like himself, after all. 'Gittin a gal,' he thot in that astonishment; then he thot [in *del.*] with the pleased surprise of a child: 'Yes, sir. Be dawg if I aint lived to be a great grandpaw, after all.'

He entered the house. He moved clumsily, on tiptoe, as tho he no longer lived there, as tho the infant which had just drawn breath and cried had dispossessed him, be it his own blood too tho it might. But even above the pallet he could see little save the blur of his granddaughter's exhausted face in a frame of hair. Then the negress squatting on the [*illeg.*] fire spoke. "You better gawn tell him ef you going to. Hit' [it *del.*]s daylight now."

But this was not necessary. He had no more than turned the corner of the porch where the scythe leaned which he had borrowed 3 months ago to cut away the weeds thru which he walked, when Supten rode up on the old stallion. He did not wonder how Sutpen had got the word. He merely took it for granted that this was what had got the other out at this hour, and he stood while Sutpen dismounted and he [handed him the reins *del.*] took the reins from the other with on his gaunt face an expression almost imbecile with a kind of weary triumph, saying, "Hit's a gal, Kernel. I be dawg if you aint as old as I am —" until Sutpen passed him without a word and entered the house.

He was standing there and heard what Sutpen said as he looked down at the pallet. Something seemed to stop him for an instant before going on. The sun was now up, the swift sun of Mississippi latitudes, and [he *del.*] it seemed to him that he stood beneath a strange sky, in a strange scene, familiar only as things are familiar in dream, like the dream of falling to one who has never climbed. 'I kaint have heard what I thot I heard,' he thot quietly. 'I know I kaint.' Yet the voice, the known voice which had spoken the words was going on, talking now to the old negress about a colt foaled that a.m. 'That's why he was up so early,' he thot. 'That was hit. Hit aint me and mine. Hit aint even hisn that got him outen bed and down hyer——'

Sutpen emerged. He descended into the weeds, moving with that heavy deliberation which would have been haste [if he *del.*] when he was young. He hardly looked at Wash stooped a little among the weeds beside the house. "Dicey will stay and tend to her. You better ——" Then he seemed to see Wash. He paused. "What?" he said.

"You said ——" To his own ears Wash's voice sounded flat, ducklike, like a deaf man's. "You said efn she was a mare, you could give her a better stall than thisn."

"Well?" Sutpen said. [Wash *del.*] His eyes widened and narrowed, almost like a man's fists flexing and shuting, as Wash, still stooping, advanced toward him — that [*illeg.*], equable, servile man whom in 20 years he had never known to make an unhidden volitional movement beyond that necessary to walk. "Stand back," Sutpen said suddenly, sharply: "don't you touch me."

"I'm going to tech you, Kernel." Wash said in that flat voice, advancing.

Sutpen did not retreat; he did not glance behind him, tho the old negress now peered around the crazy [6] door with the black gargoyle face of a worn gnome. He raised the hand which held the riding whip. "Stand back, Wash," he said. Then he struck. The old negress leaped down into the weeds with the agility of a goat, and fled. Sutpen slashed Wash again across the face, knocking him to his knees. When he rose and advanced once more, he held in his hands the scythe which he had borrowed from Sutpen 3 months ago and which Sutpen would never need again.

When he reentered the house his granddaughter stirred on the pallet and called his name fretfully. "What was that?"

"What was what, honey?" [he sa *del.*]

"That ere racket out there."

"T'warnt nothing," he said gently. He touched her forehead clumsily. "Do you want ara thing?"

"I want a sup of water," she said querulously.
"I been laying here wanting a sup of water for a long time, but don't nobody pay me no mind."

"Sho now," he said soothingly. He fetched the dipper and raised her head to drink and laid her back and watched her turn to the child with an absolutely stonelike face. But a moment later he saw that she was crying quietly. "Now, now," he said. "I wouldn't do that. Old Dicey says hit's a right fine gal." But she continued to cry quietly, almost sullenly, and he rose and stood uncomfortably above the pallet for a time, [before he moved away and drew a chair up to the window and sat down. *del.*] thinking as he had thot when his own wife lay so and then his daughter in turn: 'Women. Hit's a mystery to me. To ara man. They seem to want em and yit when they git em they cry about hit.' Then he moved away and drew a chair up to the window and sat down.

Through all that long, bright, sunny forenoon he sat there, waiting. Now and then he rose and tiptoed to the pallet. But his granddaughter slept now, her face sullen and calm, the [child *del.*] bundle which was the child in the crook of her arm. Then he returned to the chair and sat again, waiting. <*marg.* wondering why it was so long, until he remembered that it was Sunday> He was sitting there at [better than noon *del.*] <midafternoon> when they found the body, when a halfgrown white boy came around the corner of the house upon it and gave a choked cry and looked up and saw Wash sitting in the window and gave him a wild mesmerised glare before he turned and fled. [Then Wash rose again and tiptoed to the pallet and stood for a while, and returned. *del.*] <*marg.* Then he rose again and tiptoed to the pallet. "Milly," he said. "Air you hungry?" She didn't answer. Nevertheless, he built up the fire and prepared what food there was: [sowbelly, *del.*] fatback, cold corn pone; he poured water into the stale coffee pot and heated it. But she would not eat when he carried her [and he found that he too ha *del.*] so he ate quietly, alone, and left the soiled [*illeg.*] dish where it lay and returned to the chair>

Now he seemed to sense, feel, the men who would gather, with horses and dogs and the guns which they would not need. [They would be led, directed, by men *del.*]—the curious, and the vengeful: men of Sutpen's own kind, who had made the company about his table in the time when he had yet to approach nearer to the house than the scuppernong arbor—men who had also shown the lesser men like him how to fight in battle, who maybe also had signed papers from the generals saying that they were among the first of the brave; who had also galloped in the old days arrogant and proud on the fine horses on the fine plantations—symbols also of admiration and hope; instruments <too> of despair and grief.

That was who they would expect him to run from. It seemed to him that he had no more to run from [7] than he had to run to. If he ran, he would merely be fleeing one set of bragging and evil shadows for another just like them, since they were all of a kind throughout all the earth which he knew, and he was old, too old to flee far even if he were to flee. He could never escape them, no matter how much or how far he ran: a man going on 60 could not run that far. Not far enough to escape beyond the boundaries of earth where such men lived, set the order and the rule of living. He saw now for the first time, after 5 years, how it was that Yankees or any other living men had managed to whip them: the gallant, the proud, the brave; the acknowledged and chosen best among them all to carry courage and honor and pride. Maybe if he had gone to the war with them he would have discovered them [without having to see all that he had *del.*] sooner. But if he had discovered them sooner, what would he have done with his life since? how could he have borne for 5 years to remember what his life had been before?

Now it was getting toward sunset. The child had whimpered and wailed; when he [tiptoed *del.*] went to the pallet he saw that his granddaughter was feeding it, her face still bemused, sullen, inscrutable. "Air you hungry yit?" he said.

"I dont want nothing."

"You ought to eat."

She didn't answer, musing upon the child. He returned to his chair and found that the sun had set. 'Hit kaint be much longer,' he thot. He could sense them quite near now, the curious and the vengeful. He could even seem to hear what they were saying about him: *Old Wash Jones he come a tumble at last. He thot he had Sutpen but Sutpen fooled him. He thot he had Kernel where* [*Kernel* del.] *he would have to marry the gal or pay up. And Kernel refused.* "But I never expected that, Kernel!" he cried aloud, catching himself at the sound of his own voice, looking quickly to see his granddaughter looking at him.

"Kernel?" she said. "Is he ——"

Hit aint nothing," he said. "I was just thinking and talked out before I knowed hit."

She looked down again, bemused, sullen, indistinct now. "I reckon so. I reckon you'll have to talk louder than that before he'll hyer you."

"Sho now," he said. "Dont you worry now." But already thinking was going smoothly on: "You know I never. You know how I aint never expected or asked ara thing from ara living man but what I expected from you. And I never asked that. I didn't think it would need. I said, *I dont need to. What need has a fellow like Wash Jones to question or doubt that man that General Lee himself says in a handwrote ticket that he was brave?* [His kind looked on my kind as less than niggers,' he thot. 'All right. He was born to do it. Hit's times when I thot myself that maybe they was right. But hit waited for him to look Brave,' he thot. "Better if his kind and my kind too ——' He became still, motionless *del.*] Brave,' he thot. [Better if his kind and mine too had never drawn the breath of life on this earth. *del.*] 'Better if nara a one of them had ever rid back home in '65': thinking *Better if his kind and mine too had never drawn the breath of life on this earth. Better that all who remain of us be blasted from the face of earth than that another Wash Jones should see his whole life shredded from him and shrivel away like shucks thrown into the fire*

He ceased, became still, motionless. He heard the horses, suddenly and plainly; presently he saw the lantern. Yet he did not stir. He listened to the voices and the sounds of underbrush as they [*illeg.*] about the house. He watched the lantern come on until the light fell upon Sutpen's body, where the group halted, the horses tall, the men on foot shadowy—legs, horse and man, the glint and shadow of guns. A voice said, "Jones." [8]

"I'm here," he said quietly. "That you, Major?"

"Come out."

"I'm coming. I just want to see to my granddaughter."

"We'll see to her. Come out."

"Sho, Major. Just a minute."

"Show a light, then. Light your lamp."

"Sho. In just a minute." He was already moving, swift and silent. From the pallet his granddaughter spoke, fretfully;

"What is it? Why dont you light the lamp."

"Sho," he said, soothingly, quietly: ["Hit wont need no light," *del.*] He went unerringly to the crack in the chimney where he kept the butcher knife. His hand touched it; the one thing in his sloven life and house in which he took care and pride, since it was razor sharp. He approached the pallet, his granddaughter's voice.

"Light the lamp, grandpaw."

"Hit wont need no light, honey. Hit wont take but a minute," he said, kneeling, fumbling, whispering now. "Where air you?"

"Right here," she said fretfully. "What —" Then his hand touched her face. "Grandpaw!" she said. "Grand —"

"Jones!" the man outside said. "Come out of there!"

"In just a minute, Major," he said. Now he moved swiftly. He knew where in the dark the kerosene can was, just as he knew that it was full, since it was not 2 days back that he had fetched it home, [waiting for *del.*] holding it at the store until he got a ride, since the 5 gallons were heavy. It took him no time at all to empty it; besides the rather crazy house itself was like tinder: the coals on the hearth, the walls, [seemed to *del.*] exploded in a single blue glare against which the waiting men saw him in a wild instant springing toward them with the scythe in his hands before the horses reared and whirled. They checked the horses and turned them, yet still against the now glazing [hou *del.*] shack the gaunt figure ran toward them, swinging the scythe.

"Jones!"
["Wash!" the Major shouted. "Stop! Stop, or I'll shoot! "Jones! *Wash!*" Yet still, against the furious glare of the fire, the gaunt figure running toward the wild eyes of the horses and the guns *del.*]
["Shoot!" Wash shouted. "Hit's done been purified." *del.*]

"Jones!" the sheriff shouted; stop! Stop, or I'll shoot. Jones! *Jones!*" Yet still the gaunt, wild figure came on, against the furious glare of the blazing shack. With the scythe lifted it bore down upon them, upon the wild glinting eyes of the plunging horses and the last gleaming of gun barrels, without a word, without a sound. [9]

808 *Requiem for a Nun,* 1951

The history of *Requiem for a Nun* may be divided into four distinct phases: the play that Faulkner originally conceived as a vehicle for Ruth Ford, his actress friend; the novel, including the addition of the prose prologues, published by Random House in 1951; the stage adaptation that Faulkner completed shortly after the publication of the novel; and the revised play adaptation by Ruth Ford, brought to the stage in 1957 and published by Random House in 1959.

The Brodsky Collection contains 34 pages (27 leaves), plus six additional pieces of unattached cut-and-paste inserts, that Faulkner discarded as he worked on the progressive drafts of what became the play section of the novel. While the text, understandably, is not continuous in all instances, the random pages invite grouping into four clusters of identifiable segments of the action: the conclusion of Act I, Scene III; a lengthy section from the first half of Act II, Scene I; a brief passage from later in that same scene; and an extended portion of the end of Act II, Scene III. Representing advancing stages of the compositional process, the materials include original autograph manuscript, additional holograph pages that are clearly revisions of previous material, and at least two separate typescripts. Almost all of the manuscripts were further revised before publication.

Several of the holograph passages are written on sheets of letterhead stationery of *View,* a New York-based magazine of the arts edited at that time by Charles Henri Ford, the brother of Ruth Ford, for whom Faulkner created the role of Temple Drake. Miss Ford has no recollection of Faulkner's working on the play during any of his visits to her apartment, which her brother shared when he was in New York; but she surmises that Faulkner probably picked up the *View* letterheads on one of the occasions when he visited her home, perhaps in February 1950, when Faulkner's trip to New York coincided with his work on the early part of the play. This indirect link of these manuscript pages to Miss Ford might suggest on first consideration that the pages belong to the play version that Faulkner wrote after the publication of the novel. A close examination of the materials, however, reveals that many of the passages, including key interlineations, are unique to the novel. The pagination also conforms to the novel and not the post-novel play. Finally, the holograph pages exhibit characteristics (false starts, deletions, marginal insertions, rephrasings) of Faulkner's initial, free-flowing writing process rather than the revisionary process.

That these pages relate to the novel (or even the pre-novel play) and not the subsequent adaptation is further supported by the fact that these *Requiem* materials came to the Brodsky Collection from the files of Saxe Commins, Faulkner's Random House editor and literary executor, who oversaw Faulkner's work on the novel but had no involvement in the stage adaptation of the book.

Leaves 1–2, 23–24, and 26–33 display a Hammermill Bond watermark. Leaves 4–9, 11, 13–14, 16–18, 20–22, and 25 are sheets of stationery showing the *View* letterhead; these sheets bear a Plover Bond watermark. The remaining leaves carry no watermark. All of the pages, excluding the scissored fragments, measure 11 by 8½ inches.

———*Requiem for a Nun,* ribbon typescript, 1 page, numbered "1-3-28." Cf. pp. 95–97 of the Random House edition. (Leaf 1R)

(HE turns, crosses again to the door without stopping nor looking back, exits, closes the door behind him. She is not watching him either now. For a moment after the door has closed, she doesn't move. Then she makes a gesture something like Gowan's in Scene 2, except that she merely presses her palms for a moment hard against her face, her face calm, expressionless, cold, drops her hands, turns, picks up the crushed cigarette from beside the tray and puts it into the tray and takes up the tray and crosses to the fireplace, glancing down at the sleeping child as SHE passes the sofa, empties the tray into the fireplace and returns to the table and puts the tray on it and this time pauses at the sofa and stoops and tucks the blanket closer about the sleeping child and then goes on to the telephone and lifts the receiver.)

TEMPLE *(into phone)* Three two nine, please [. . . . . . *del.*].

(while she stands waiting for the answer, there is a slight movement beyond the open doors at rear, in the darkness, [the[n] Gowan, dressed except for his coat and vest and perhaps tie, comes quietly into view and stands just inside the other room at the door, *del.*] just enough silent movement to tell us that something or someone is there or has moved there. Temple is unaware of it [) *del.*]. Then:)

(Into phone)

Maggie? Temple . . . Yes, suddenly . . . Oh, I don't know; perhaps we got bored with sunshine . . . of course, I may drop in tomorrow. I wanted to leave a message for Gavin . . . I know; he just left here. Something I forgot . . . if you'll ask him to call me when he comes in . . . Yes . . . Wasn't it. Yes . . . If you will . . . Thank you.

(SHE puts the receiver down and starts to turn back into the room when the telephone rings. SHE turns back, takes up the receiver)

Hello . . . Yes. Coincidence again; I had my hand on it; I had just called Maggie . . . Oh, the filling station. I didn't think you had had time. I can be ready in fifteen minutes. Your car, or ours? . . . how much will I have to tell? *(hurriedly)* Oh, I know; you've already tole me eight or ten times. But maybe I didn't hear it right. How much will I have to tell?

(SHE listens, quiet, frozen-faced, then slowly begins to lower the receiver toward the stand: quietly, without inflection)

Oh, God. Oh, God.

———*Requiem for a Nun,* ribbon typescript, 1 page, numbered "1-3-29." Cf. p. 97 of the Random House edition. (Leaf 2R)

TEMPLE *(Cont)* (She puts the receiver down, crosses [the room *del.*] to the sofa, takes up the sleeping child, snaps off the lamp and exits, carrying the child, snaps off another light switch at the door, so that the room is lighted now only by the light which falls into it from the hall. Then the shadow inside the door and rear moves again, and Gowan enters, dressed except for his coat and vest and tie. He has obviously taken no sleeping pill. He approaches the phone and stands quietly beside it, facing the door through which Temple went out, and obviously listening. Now the hall light snaps off, and the room is in complete darkness.

GOWAN'S VOICE *(quietly)* Three two nine, please. . . . . Good evening, Aunt Maggie [? *del.*]. [How are you *del.*] Gowan. As soon as Uncle Gavin comes in, will you ask him to call me? . . . . . Yes, I'll be right here. Thank you.

(Sound of receiver being put back)

CURTAIN

———*Requiem for a Nun,* ribbon typescript, 1 page, numbered "2-1-3." Cf. pp. 114–117 of the Random House edition. (Leaf 3R)

TEMPLE [The blindfold. The firing squad. Or is metaphor wrong? Or maybe it's the joke. But don't apologize; a joke that has to be diagrammed is like trying to excuse an egg, isn't it? The only thing you can do is, bury them both, quick.

(The GOVERNOR approaches the flame to TEMPLE's cigarette. SHE leans and accepts the light, then sits back)

Thanks.

(The GOVERNOR closes the lighter, sits down in the tall chair behind the desk, still holding the lighter in his hand, his hands resting on the desk before him. STEVENS sits down in the other chair, across from TEMPLE, laying the pack of cigarettes on the desk beside him)

GOVERNOR What has Mrs. Gowan Stevens to tell me? *del.*]

TEMPLE Not Mrs. Gowan Stevens: Temple Drake. You remember Temple Drake: the all-Mississippi debutante whose finishing school was the Memphis sporting house—about eight years ago, remember? not that anyone, certainly not the sovereign state of Mississippi's first paid servant, need be reminded of that, provided they could read newspapers five years ago or were kin to someone who could read five years ago or even had a friend who could or even just hear or even just remember or just believe the worst or even just hope for it.

GOVERNOR I think I remember. What does Temple Drake have to tell me, then?

TEMPLE Everything, of course. To save our murderess. But first, how much? How much that you don't already know? It's two o'clock in the morning; you want to—maybe even need to—sleep some, even if you are our first paid servant; maybe because of that—

(SHE stops: only a second; her tone is still brittle, emotionless)

———*Requiem for a Nun,* autograph manuscript in blue ink, canceled; 1 page, numbered "1." Cf. pp. 115–117 of the Random House edition. (Leaf 16V)

GOV. What has Mrs Gowan Stevens to tell me?

T. *(to S)* Go on. Tell him.

(the Gov. looks from one to the other of them)

Aren't you my mouthpiece—isn't that what you call them? Dont lawyers always tell their patients—I mean clients— not to say anything at all, but to let the laywers do it?

GOV *(to T)* That's only until the client is on the witness stand.

T Am I on the witness stand?

G — You have come all the way here from Jefferson at [this *del.*] 2 oclock in the morning. What would you call it?

T All right. (speech p 2-1-3)

G — speech 2-1-3

T [Everything. *del.*] Apparently everything. But first, how much? Isn't that always the state's witness's first demand? how much? I mean, how much that you dont already know? It's 2 oclock in the morning; you want—maybe even need—to sleep some, even if you are our first paid servant; who knows? maybe even because of that——

———*Requiem for a Nun,* autograph manuscript fragment in blue ink, canceled; unnumbered. Cf. pp. 115–116 of the Random House edition. (Leaf 21R)

TEMPLE *(to Stevens)* Go on. Tell him.

(the Gov. looks from one to the other)

Aren't you my mouthpiece?—isn't that how you say it? Dont lawyers always tell their patients—I mean clients—not to say anything at all, let the lawyer do the talking?

GOV. *(to Temple)* That's only until the client enters the witness stand.

T So this is the witness stand.

G You have come all the way here from Jefferson at 2 oclock in the morning. What would you call it?

T All right. But not Mrs Gowan Stevens: Temple Drake. You remember Temple Drake: the all-Mississippi debutante whose finishing school was the Memphis sporting house—about 8 years ago, remember? not that anyone, certainly not the sovereign

———*Requiem for a Nun,* autograph manuscript in blue ink, canceled; 1 page, numbered "2-1-4." Cf. pp. 116–117 of the Random House edition. (Leaf 17V)

TEMPLE *(cont)* State of Mississippi's first paid servant, need be reminded of that, provided they could read newspapers 8 years ago or were kin to someone who could read 8 years ago or even had a friend who could or even just hear or even just remember or just believe the worst or even just hope for it.

GOV. I think I remember. What does Temple Drake have to tell me, then?

TEMPLE Apparently everything. <To save our patient tomorrow morning.> But first, how much? Isn't that what the state's evidence witness always [wants to know? *del.*] demands? how much? I mean, how much of it that you dont already know? So that I wont have to waste our time telling you that over. It's 2 oclock in the morning; you want to—maybe even need to—sleep some, even if you are our first paid servant: maybe even because of that—— You see? I'm already lying. What does it matter to me how much sleep the state's first paid servant loses, anymore than it matters to the first paid servant, a part of whose job is being paid to lose sleep over the Nancy Mannigoes and Temple Drakes whose troubles he is paid to bear or anyway listen to?

STEVENS. Not lying, maybe. Just stalling.

TEMPLE. Stalling, then, if you prefer that. So maybe if his Honor or his Excellency or whatever they call him, will answer this question, we can get on.

STEVENS Let the question go. Tell him, instead. [Tell him about Nancy Mannigoe.

TEMPLE. In time. Who's on the witness stand here? you or me? How can I tell him until I know how much? How much I will have to tell, say, speak out loud so that anyone with ears can hear it, what I mean about Temple Drake

GOVERNOR Hush, Gavin. *del.*]

TEMPLE *(to Stevens)* Who's on this witness stand?—you, or I?

———*Requiem for a Nun,* autograph manuscript in blue ink, 1 page, numbered "2-1-3." Cf. pp. 114–116 of the Random House edition. (Leaf 4R)

But of course, [we dont need a blindfold <here,> *del.*] the only one waiting execution is back there in Jefferson. So all we need to do here is, fire away, and hope that at least the volley rids us of the metaphor.

GOV. Metaphor?

TEMP. The blindfold. The firing squad. Or is metaphor wrong? Or maybe it's the joke. But don't apologise: a joke that has to be explained is like having to excuse an egg, isn't it? The only thing you can do is, bury them both, quick.

(the Gov. approaches the flame to Temple's cigarette. She leans and accepts the light, then sits back)

Thanks.

(the Gov. closes the lighter, sits down in the tall chair behind the desk, still holding the lighter in his hand, his hands resting on the desk before him. Stevens sits down in the other chair across from Temple, lays the pack of cigarettes on the desk beside him)

GOV. What has Mrs <Gowan> Stevens to tell me?

TEMP. Not tell you: ask you. No: that's wrong. [We *del.*] I could have asked you to revoke or commute [the sentence *del.*] or whatever you do to a sentence to hang when we—Uncle Gavin telephoned you tonight. *(to Stevens)* Go on. Tell him. Aren't you the mouthpiece?—isn't that how you say it? <*marg.* (to Gov)> Dont lawyers always tell their patients—I mean clients—never to say anything at all: to let them do all the talking?

GOV. That's only [until *del.*] <before> the client enters the witness stand.

TEMP. So this is the witness stand.

GOV. You have come all the way here from Jefferson at 2 oclock in the a.m. What would you call it?

———*Requiem for a Nun,* autograph manuscript in blue ink, 1 page, numbered "2-1-4." Cf. pp. 116–117 of the Random House edition. (Leaf 5R)

TEMPLE All right. Touche then. But not Mrs Gowan Stevens: Temple Drake. You remember Temple Drake: the all-Mississippi debutante whose finishing school was the Memphis sporting house—about 8 years ago, remember? Not that anyone, certainly not the sovereign state of Mississippi's first paid servant, need be reminded of that, provided they could read newspapers 8 years ago or were kin to someone who could [read or even just hear *del.*] read 8 years ago or even had a friend who could or even just hear or even just remember or just believe the worst or even just hope for it.

GOV. I think I remember. What has Temple Drake to tell me, then?

TEMP. That's not first. The first thing is, how much will I have to tell? I mean, how much of it that you dont already know, so that I wont be wasting all our time telling that over? It's 2 oclock in the morning; you want to—maybe even need to—sleep some, even if you are our first paid ser-[vant, a part of whose job is <being paid> to lose sleep over the Nancy Mannigos and Temple Drakes? *del.*] vant: maybe even because of that—— You see? I'm already lying. What does it matter to me how much sleep the state's first paid servant loses, anymore than it matters to the first paid servant, a part of whose job is being paid to lose sleep over the Nancy Mannigos & the Temple Drakes?

STEVENS Not lying.

TEMPLE All right. Stalling, then. So maybe if His Excellency—his honor will answer the question, we can get on.

STEVENS Why not let the question go, and just tell him?

GOV. Ask me your question. How much of what do I already know?

TEMP. *(after a moment; she doesn't answer, staring at the Gov: then)*

———*Requiem for a Nun,* autograph manuscript in blue ink, canceled; 1 page, numbered "2-1-[4 *del.*]5." Cf. pp. 117–119 of the Random House edition. (Leaf 6R)

GOVERNOR *(to Temple)* Ask me your question, then.

TEMPLE *(a moment: she doesn't answer, staring at the Governor: then)* Gavin's right. Maybe you are the one to ask the questions. Only, make it as painless as possible. Because it's going to be a little . . . painful, to put it euphoniously—at least 'euphoniously' is right, isn't it?—no matter who bragged about blindfolds.

GOVERNOR Tell me about Nancy Mannigoe. Mannigoe. How does she spell it?

TEMPLE. She doesn't. She cant. She cant read or write either. The court spelled it M-a-n-n-i-g-o-e, which may be wrong, though it wont matter after tomorrow morning—that is, unless—

[Governor *del.* Stevens *del.*] **Governor** Ah yes, Manigault, the old Charleston name.

STEVENS Further back than that. Maingault. Nancy's heritage—or anyway her name—runs Norman blood.

GOVERNOR *(to Temple)* Tell me about her.

TEMPLE You are so wise. She was a whore, a tramp. We—my husband and I—hired her to nurse our children. She murdered one of them. She is to be hung tomorrow morning. Her lawyer and I, the 2 interested parties—the lawyer who lost the case, and the mother who lost the child—have come here at 2 oclock in the morning to ask you to save her life.

GOVERNOR Why?

TEMPLE Why am I, the woman whose child she [killed *del.*] murdered, [even *del.*] asking you to save you? Because she is crazy.

STEVENS That's not the why the goveror means.

———*Requiem for a Nun,* autograph manuscript in blue ink, 1 page, numbered "2-1-6." Cf. pp. 118–120 of the Random House edition. (Leaf 7R)

TEMP. You are so wise. She was a whore—a tramp. We—my husband and I—took her out of the gutter to nurse our children. She murdered one of them. She is to be hung tomorrow morning. We—her lawyer and I—[have come here *del.*] the two interested parties—the one who lost the case, and the one who lost the child—have come to ask you to save her.

GOV. Why?

TEMP. Why am I, the woman whose child she murdered, asking you to save her? Because I have forgiven her.

STEVENS That's not the why the gov. means.

TEMP. Because she is crazy.

STEVENS That's not it either.

TEMPLE *(quickly: puffing rapidly at the cigarette)* I know it. You mean, why I—we hired a whore and dopefiend to nurse our children. *(rapidly through the puffing)* To give her another chance—a human being, even a nigger whore and dopefiend—

(she puffs rapidly, speaking now through the smoke [in *del.*] quickly, in a sort of despair)

Ah yes, not even stalling now. Why cant you [just *del.*] stop lying? You know: just stop it for a while like you can stop dancing or playing tennis for one hour or a day. You know: not to reform, quit it: just stop it for a while?

GOV *(gently)* That's right. You have come this far, this late at night. Just tell me.

TEMP. [Yes *del.*]

(she puffs rapidly at cigarette, leans and crushes it out in ashtray and sits erect again. She speaks in a hard rapid brittle emotionless voice)

———*Requiem for a Nun,* autograph manuscript in blue ink, 1 page, unnumbered. Cf. pp. 119–120 of the Random House edition. (Leaf 22R)

(she stops again, puffing rapidly at the cig)

STE. Nor that either.

TEM. *(puffing rapidly, speaking thru puffing)* Oh yes, not even stalling now. Why cant you stop lying? You know: just stop for a little while like you can stop dancing or playing tennis for an hour or a day or during a whole

Lent. You know: not reform: just quit for a while, rest up for a new tune or set or lie? All right. It was to have some one to talk to. And so now you will want to know why <I had to have> a dopefiend and a whore to talk [too *del.*] to [. *del.*]—

[**GOV** That's right. You have come this far, this late at night. Just tell me. *del.*]

[All right. That's what I had to come all the *del.*] that nobody else would do—that Temple Drake, the white woman, the all-Miss. debutante, descendant of [governors *del.*] statesmen and soldiers high in the annals of the sovereign state, could find nobody else [to talk to but *del.*] in all Miss. to [listen to her *del.*] get sympathy from but a negro dopefield whore already damned before she

———*Requiem for a Nun,* autograph manuscript in blue ink, 1 page, numbered "2-1-[5 *del.*]7." Cf. pp. 119–121 of the Random House edition. (Leaf 8R)

[**TEMPLE** *(quickly, puffing rapidly at the cigarette)* Oh, you [want to know more about [*illeg.*] why I—we know she is crazy. *del.*] want to know more about Nancy.

(puffing rapidly at the cigarette) *del.*]

[Blank space with residue of glue, indicating that a five-inch paste-on insert once occupied this position]

[back twice since. Is that what you want?

STEVENS. No. He wants what he asked you. Why? [You're not even stalling now.

TEMPLE. So I'm not even stalling now. I'm just lying. *del.*]

GOVERNOR *(quickly)* Yes. Why did you hire her to nurse your little children?

TEMPLE I tried to tell you—

GOVERNOR —A whore & dopefiend, you said yourself she was crazy. *del.*]

———*Requiem for a Nun,* autograph manuscript in blue ink, 1 page, numbered "2-1-8." Cf. pp. 121–122 of the Random House edition. (Leaf 9R)

TEMP. *(cont)* back twice since—

(she stops speaking, presses both hands to her face, then removes them)

No, no handkerchief. Lawyer Stevens and I made a dry run on handkerchiefs before we left home tonight. Where was I?

GOV. The banker.

(quotes)

'It was already 2 dollars'——

TEMP. So now I've got to tell all of it. Because that was just Nancy Mannigoe. Temple Drake was in more than just a 2 dollar Sat. night house. But then, I said touche, didn't I?

———*Requiem for a Nun,* ribbon typescript fragment with autograph addition in blue ink, numbered "2-1-[8 *del.*]9." Cf. p. 123 of the Random House edition. (Leaf 10R)

TEMPLE *(Cont'd)* couldn't he? In fact, he couldn't have been elected Governor of even Mississippi if he hadn't been able to read at least three years in advance, could he?

STEVENS Temple.

TEMP. *(to Stevens)* Why not? It's just stalling, isn't it?

———*Requiem for a Nun,* autograph manuscript in blue ink, 1 page, numbered "2-1-[9 *del.*]10." Cf. pp. 123–125 of the Random House edition. (Leaf 11R)

[**TEMP.** couldn't he? In fact, he couldn't have been elected Gov. of even Miss. if he hadn't been able to read and write at least 3 years in advance, could he?

STEV. Temple.

TEMP *(to S)* Why not? It's just stalling, isn't it?

GOV. *(to S)* Hush, Gavin. *(to T)* Coup de grace not only means mercy, but is. Deliver it. Give her the cigarette, Gavin. *del.*] So here we are, right back where we started from, and so we can start over. How much will I have to tell, [you? *del.*] say, speak out loud so that anybody with ears can hear it, about Temple Drake that I never thot [*sic*] that anything on earth, least of all the [death of my child *del.*] <murder of my child and the> execution of a nigger dopefiend whore, would ever make me tell? That I came here at 2 oclock in the a.m. to wake you up to listen to, after 8 years of being safe or at least quiet? You know: how much will I have to tell, to make it good and painful of course, but quick too, so that you can revoke or commute the sentence or whatever you do to it, and we can all go back home to sleep or at least to bed? Painful of course, but only painful enough—— I think you said 'euphoniously' was right, didn't you?

GOV. Death is plenty painful. A shameful one, even more so.—which is not too euphonious, even at best.

TEMP. Oh, death. We're not talking about death now. We're talking about Temple Drake. [All *del.*] Nancy Mannigoe <*marg.* has no shame. All she> has to do is, die. But touche for me too; haven't I come all the way here at 2 oclock in the a.m. because Nancy M. is the one who has nothing to do but die?

STEV Tell him, then.

TEMP He hasn't answered my question yet. *(to Gov)* How much will I have to tell?

———*Requiem for a Nun,* ribbon typescript fragment, unnumbered. Cf. p. 124 of the Random House edition. (Leaf 12R)

(After a moment)
There again. I'm not even [lying *del.*] stalling now: I'm faulting—what do they call it? burking. You know: here we are at the fence again; we've got to jump it this time, or crash. You know: slack the snaffle, let her mouth it a little, take

———*Requiem for a Nun,* ribbon typescrit fragment, unnumbered. Cf. p. 124 of the Random House edition. (Leaf 15R)

hold, a light hold, just enough to have something to jump against; then touch her. [So here goes. Temple Drake, the foolish virgin, that is, as far as anyone at least disproved, a virgin, but a fool certainly; seventeen and more of a fool than simply being a virgin or even being seventeen could have excused or accounted for; indeed, being capable of that height of folly which even seven or three, let alone virginity, could hardly have matched; getting off the train as soon as she could persuade someone to stop it, to make the rest of the trip in an automobile; not to get anywhere any sooner: just to ride in the automobile: and that mainly because all the other girls were either not brave enough to be that foolish or not virgin enough to—

STEVENS —or too lucky to have a boy-friend who owned or at least could borrow his mother's car. That was her husband. *del.*]

———*Requiem for a Nun,* autograph manuscript in blue ink, 1 page, numbered "2-1-11." Cf. pp. 117, 126, 127–129 of the Random House edition. (Leaf 14R)

[2-1-4
TEMPLE *(cont)*
(she stops etc.)

S Not lying, maybe. Stalling.

T All right. Stalling then, if you prefer that. So maybe if you will answer the question, we can get on. How much

T. 2-1-9 *(to S)* The Va. gentleman, etc.

GOV. I know who Temple Drake was: the young woman student at the University 8 years ago who left the school one day on a special train of students to attend a baseball game at another college, and disappeared from the train somewhere during the [trip *del.*] run, vanished, nobody knew where, until she appeared 6 weeks later as witness in a murder trial in Jefferson— *del.*]

TEMP. <Oh yes,> [—produced by the Memphis lawyer of the man that she knew had done the murder, *del.*] <*marg.* for the very good reason that she saw him do it,> so that she could swear away the life of the man who was falsely accused of it. Oh yes, that's the one. And now I've already told you something you nor nobody else but the Memphis lawyer knew, and [it's *del.*] I haven't even started. You see? I cant even bargain with you. You havent even said yes or no yet, whether you [will *del.*] <can> save her or not, whether you want to save her or not, will consider saving her or not, which, if either of us, Temple Drake or Mrs Gowan Stevens[, *del.*] either, if they had any sense, would demand first of you.

GOV. Do you want to ask that first?

TEMP. I can't. I dont dare. You might say No.

GOV. Then you wouldn't have to tell me about Temple Drake.

TEMP. I've got to do that. I've got to say it all, or I wouldn't be here. But, unless I can still believe that you might say Yes, I don't see how I can. Which is another touche for somebody. God maybe—if there is one. You see? That's what's so terrible. We dont even need him. Simple evil is [just *del.*] enough.

———*Requiem for a Nun,* autograph manuscript in blue ink, 1 page, numbered "2-1-1[0 *ov.* 1]A." Cf. pp. 126–127 of the Random House edition. (Leaf 13R)

GOV. I know who Temple Drake was: the young woman student at the University 8 years ago who left the school one morning on a special train of students to attend a baseball game at another college, and disappeared from the train somewhere during the run and vanished, nobody knew where, until she reappeared 6 weeks later as a witness in a murder trial in Jefferson [—*del.*], [where *del.*]

[TEMP. — produced by the Memphis lawyer of the man——*del.*] [it was learned that she had been abducted *del.*] produced by the lawyer of the man whom [*sic*], it was then learned, had abducted her and held her prisoner—

TEMP. —in the Memphis sporting house: dont forget that.

GOV —in order to produce her to prove his alibi in the murder—

TEMP —Produced by the lawyer of the man [she *del.*] that she knew had done the murder——

STEVENS Wait, let me [interrupt too, *del.*] have a [share *del.*] share in the interrupting too. She got off the train [at an intermediate stop *del.*] at the instigation of a young man who met the train with an automobile at an intermediate stop, the plan being to drive on [*illeg. del.*] to the ball game in the car, except that the young man was drunk at the time and got drunker during the trip, as a result of which he wrecked the car and stranded the two of them at the moonshiner's house where the murder took place and from which the [ab *del.*] [criminal *del.*] <murderer—> abductor you spoke of kidnapped her to Memphis, to hold her until he would need his alibi. Afterward he—the young man with the automobile—<her escort and protector at the moment of the abduction> married her. He is her husband now. He is my nephew. [*(to Temple)* del.] *(to Temp)* Go on.

TEMP. *(to Ste)* You too. So wise too. Why cant you believe in truth? At least, that I'm trying to tell it. At least trying now to tell it. *(to Gov)* Where was I?

GOV *(quotes)* Produced by the lawyer of the man whom [*sic*] she knew had done the murder—

———*Requiem for a Nun,* autograph manuscript in blue ink, 1 page, numbered "2-1-12." Cf. pp. 129–130 of the Random House edition. (Leaf 16R)

TEMP. *(cont)* Even after 8 years, it's still enough. It was 8 years ago that Uncle Gavin said—oh yes, he was there too: <*marg.* didn't you just hear him?> he would have told you all of this [over the *del.*] or anyway most of this over the telephone and you could be in bed asleep right this minute—said how there is a corruption even just looking at evil, even by accident, that you cant haggle, traffic with putrefaction—you cannot, you dont dare. . . .

(she stops. A moment)

GOV Take the cigarette now. *(to Stevens)* Gavin—

(Stevens moves to offer cigarette)

TEMP. No thanks. It's too late now. Because here we go. If we [dont clear it, we'll crash through. But anyway, we're going. *del.*] <cant jump the fence, we can> at least break through it—

STEVENS *(interrupts)* Which means that [at least *del.*] <anyway> one of us will get over standing up.

(as Temple reacts)

Oh yes, I'm going to ride this one too. Go ahead. Temple Drake—

TEMPLE [You're doing splendidly. Dont let me stop you. *del.*] —Temple Drake, the foolish virgin, that is, a virgin as far as anybody went on record to disprove, but a fool certainly by anybody's computation; 17 and more of a fool than simply being a virgin or even being 17 could excuse or account for; indeed, showing herself capable of a height of folly which even 7 or 3, let alone mere virginity, could scarcely

———*Requiem for a Nun,* autograph manuscript in blue ink, 1 page, numbered "2-1-13." Cf. pp. 130–133 of the Random House edition. (Leaf 17R)

TEMP. have matched——

STEV. Give the brute a chance. Try at least to ride him at the fence and not just through it.

TEMP. Oh, you mean the Va. gentleman. *(to Gov)* That's my husband. He went to the Univ. of Va., trained, Uncle G would say, at Va. not only in drinking but in gentility too——

STEV. —and ran out of both [simu *del.*] at the same time that day 8 years ago when he took you off the train and wrecked the car at the moonshiner's house.

TEMP. But [at least *del.*] he had a relapse into one of them, at least. At least, he married me as soon as he could. You dont mind my telling his excellency or his honor that, do you?

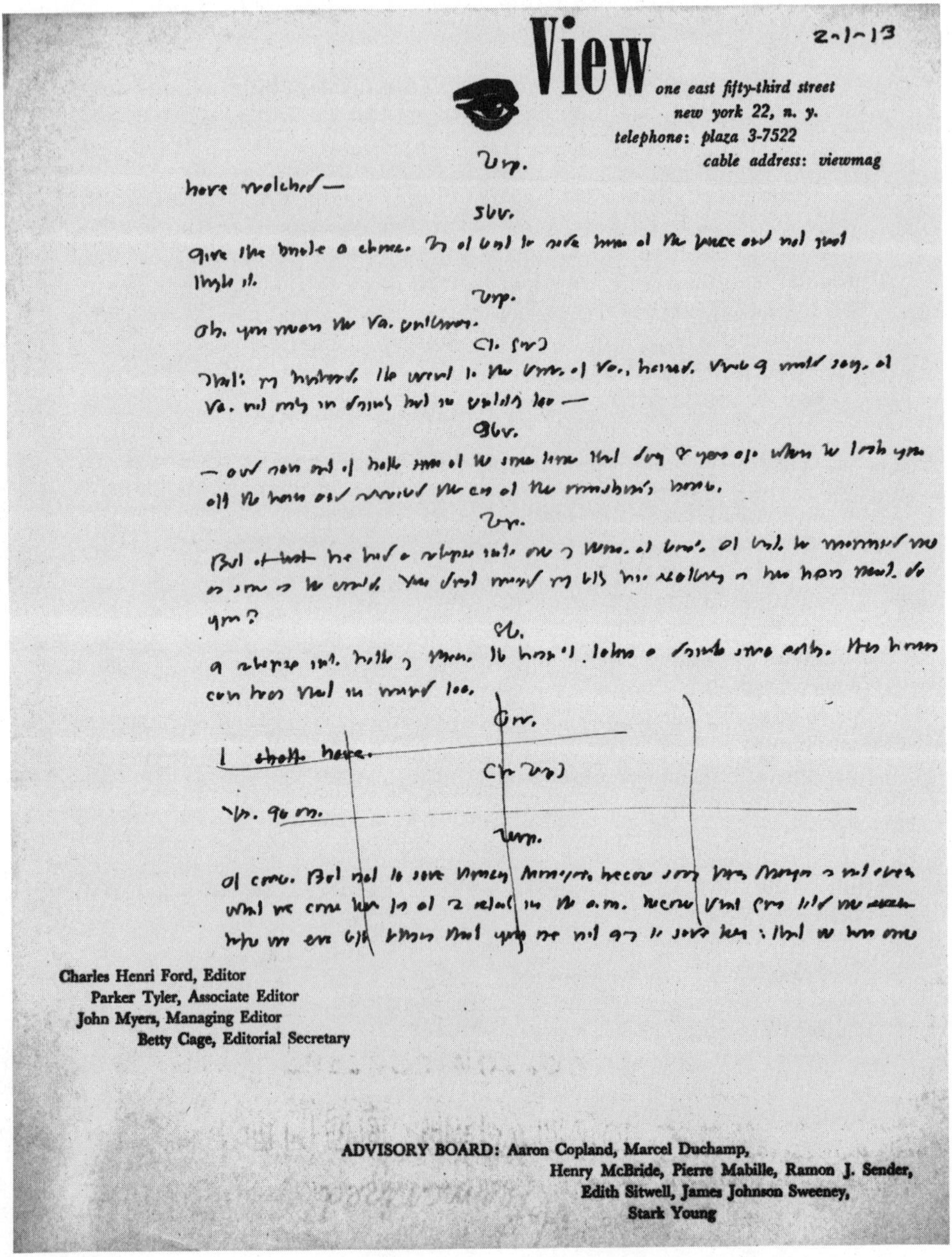

View
one east fifty-third street
new york 22, n. y.
telephone: plaza 3-7522
cable address: viewmag

Charles Henri Ford, Editor
Parker Tyler, Associate Editor
John Myers, Managing Editor
Betty Cage, Editorial Secretary

ADVISORY BOARD: Aaron Copland, Marcel Duchamp,
Henry McBride, Pierre Mabille, Ramon J. Sender,
Edith Sitwell, James Johnson Sweeney,
Stark Young

42. Manuscript page of *Requiem for a Nun,* c. 1950

STE. A relapse into both of them. He hasn't taken a drink since either. His honor can bear that in mind too.

[**GOV.** I [shall *del.*] have. *(to Temp)* Yes. Go on.

TEMP. Of course. But not to save Nancy Mannigoe, because saving Nancy Mannigoe is not even what we came here for at 2 oclock in the a.m. because Uncle Gavin told me [even *del.*] before we even left Jefferson that you are not going to save her: that we have come *del.*]

———*Requiem for a Nun,* autograph manuscript in blue ink, 1 page, numbered "2-1-14." Cf. pp. 131–133 of the Random House edition. (Leaf 18R)

[**TEMP** here and waked you up just to give Tem. Drake a good fair honest chance to suffer. You know. *del.*]

GOV I shall. I have.

(he does just enough of a pause to make them both stop and look at him)

I almost wish——

(they are both watching him)

I notice [your husband *del.*] <he> is not with you.

STE *(mildly yet quickly)* Wont there still be time for that later?

TEM. *(quickly too, [defiant* del.], *terse)* [No. Why? *del.*] Who?

GOV Your husband.

TEMP *(quick, hard)* Why?

GOV You have one here to plead for the life of [a dopefiend and *del.*] <the> murderer of your child. Your husband was its parent too.

TEMP. *(hard & harsh)* You're wrong. [Saving N M is not even what *del.*] we [came *del.*] didn't come here at 2 a m to save N M. N.M. is not even concerned in this because N M's lawyer told me before we ever left Jefferson that you were not going to save N.M.

———*Requiem for a Nun,* ribbon typescript fragment, unnumbered. Cf. p. 136 in Random House edition. (Leaf 19R)

TEMPLE Oh yes, already bad and lost before she ever started for the ball game. Because she only went to the ball game because she would have to make a train trip to get there, so that she could slip off the train the first time it stopped so she could get into the automobile to make the rest of the hundred-mile trip with a young man who could be depended on to be wrong about how much he could drink. You know: an optimist. I don't mean the young man, he was just doing the best he knew, could. He didn't want to make the trip anyway, the automobile was Temple's idea. She was the optimist, eternally hopeful; not that she had foreseen, planned ahead either; she simply had every trust and confidence in her parents' acquaintance with evil, and was simply doing the best thing she could invent or think of that she knew her father and brothers would have forbidden her to do. And they were right and so of course she was right, though still having to fight a little for her rights and destiny even then, even driving the car for a while after we began to realize that the young man had been mistaken about the drink, driving and insisting on the wrong turn which got u—them lost—

STEVENS *(To GOVERNOR)* It was my nephew who knew about the moonshiner.

———*Requiem for a Nun,* autograph manuscript in blue ink, 1 page, numbered "2-1-16." Cf. pp. 140–141 of the Random House edition. (Leaf 20R)

GOV. Dont call it a barrel. Call it a tunnel. That's a thoroughfare, because the other end is open too. Go through it. Not a seducer—

TEMP. Not even that. [It *del.*] <He> was worse than a father or an uncle. It was even worse than being [an insurance co. orphan. It *del.*] the wealthy ward of the most indulgent insurance co: carried to Memphis and shut up in that Manuel street sporting house like a 10-year-old [girl *del.*] <bride> in a [Catholic *del.*] <Spanish> convent, with the madam herself

———*Requiem for a Nun,* ribbon typescript, 1 page, numbered "2-1-[22 *del.*]27." Cf. pp. 161–163 of the Random House edition. (Leaf 24R)

STEVENS *(cont)* The letters were not first. The first thing was the gratitude, for the reason that the gratitude was a part of the past which had had to come into existence and begin to become past, in order to produce the letters—the past which she had brought with her into the edifice of marriage and respectability for the reason that she couldn't help herself, had no 'out', as she would say; not refusing—as Hemingway said—to accept it because it was too late for that now, she had already accepted it and it had left its ineradicable scar, but at least to reconcile with it by constant and unflagging rectitude, for the sake of the husband and children [who[m *del.*] <whom>, you will agree she was justified in thinking, that roof might have sheltered *del.*] whom (not herself: the husband and children, the children who were innocent, the husband who had what he probably considered his supreme sacrifice to expiate his instrumentality in the past), you will agree she might have been justified in thinking, that roof might have protected from it. Only[, *del.*]—

(the lights flicker again. This time, they do not flare up again, but steady at the slightly dimmer point, and hold there)

—she had not been in the house very long before she discovered that that roof was not going to protect anybody from anything; [that the past was *del.*] not only that the past was already in the house with her and not only was she not going to reconcile with it, but now she could not even flee from it, which up to now she had known that, if worst came to worst, she always could. Because she still had the arms and legs and the eyes, but now there was a child on the way[; now she kn *del.*] and so now she was doomed; she knew now that she was going to spend a good part of the rest of her days (nights too) being forgiven for that past, and no recourse from it now as long as she lived, or anyway until that child was born and grew up and created a past of its own from which she could not protect it;—the rest of her life [in *del.*] (and now we have even come to the husband, my nephew) in being not only constantly reminded—well, maybe not specifically reminded, but say made—kept—aware of the past so that she could be forgiven for it and so be grateful for the forgiveness, but in having to employ steadily and unflaggingly more and more of what tact she had (and the patience which she probably didn't know she had, since until now she had had no occasion to discover it) to make her gratitude (in which she probably had had as little experience as she had in patience) [meet, match, the *del.*] be acceptable to, meet, match, the high standards of, the forgiver. Do you accept that?

GOVERNOR Yes. Go on.

STEVENS But she was not afraid[, *del.*]. She had no doubts of her capacity to continue to supply whatever degrees of gratitude the increasing appetite of its addict might demand. So she carried on, coped, not only accepting, arsorbing the forgiveness and supplying the gratitude on constant demand, [and doing *del.*] but doing whatever she could to make the gratitude palatable, swallowable; still carrying on and coping even when she realised that the more gratitude she gave, the more unpalatable to the swallower it would become. Because of the child, you see. Because you never really give up hope, you

———*Requiem for a Nun,* ribbon typescript and autograph manuscript in blue ink, 1 page, numbered "2-1-[22 *del.*]27." Cf. pp. 161–163 of the Random House edition. (Leaf 23R)

[STEVENS *(cont)* heir) was not only her shackle, but her salvation too, the hand reached down from [haven too *del.*] heaven too, since the child's own innocence would save not only it, but her too; that God—if there was one—would save the child because it was innocent and defenseless

GOVERNOR I accept it. Go on. *del.*]

STEVENS *(cont)* The letters were not first. The first thing was the gratitude; and now we have even come to the husband, my nephew[; *ov.* .] and when I say 'past' I mean that part of it which her husband knows so far—which apparently was enough [for him *del.*] by his estimation. Because it was not long before she discovered, realised, that she was going to spend a good part of the rest of her days (and nights too) being forgiven for it; in being not only constantly reminded—well, maybe not specifically reminded, but say made—kept—aware of it [so that she could *del.*] <in order to be> be [*sic*] forgiven for it and so be grateful for the forgiveness, but in having to employ steadily an unflaggingly more and more of what tact she had—and the patience which she probably didnt know she had since until now she had had no occasion to need patience—to make her gratitude—in which she had probably had as little experience as with patience—[to me *del.*] acceptable to, meet with, match, the high standards of the forgiver. But she was not too concerned. [She had no doubts of her capacity to continue to supply whatever degree of gratitude the increasing appetite of its addict would demand, which she was probably willing to do *del.*] Her husband—my nephew—had made what he probably considered [his *del.*] <the> supreme sacrifice [in *del.*] to expiate his part in her past; she had no doubts of her capacity to continue to supply whatever increasing degree of gratitude the increasing appetite of its addict would demand, in return for the sacrifice which, so she believed, she had accepted for the same reason. Besides, she still had the two legs and the eyes; she could walk away, escape, from it at any time, even though her past history had shown her that she probably would not use the legs and the eyes to escape from threat and danger. Do you accept that?

GOV. All right. Go on.

STE. Then she discovered that the child [was on the way. *del.*]—the first one—was on the way. That gave her to pause. Now she could not escape. She had waited too long. For a moment she must have known even frenzy. But you never really give up hope, you know, not even after you finally realise that people can bear anything, and therefore, the whole sum of everything can, probably will, [happen to you *del.*] maybe even must, happen to you. Whereupon she saw that the child was not only her shackle, but her salvation too: the hand reaching down

———*Requiem for a Nun,* autograph manuscript in blue ink, 1 page, numbered "2-1-28." Cf. pp. 163, 162 of the Random House edition. (Leaf 25R)

STE. *(cont)* from heaven to save not only the child but her too because of, by means of, the child's innocence: that God—if there was one—would save the child because it was innocent, even though she knew better, all her observation having shown her that God either would not or could not—anyway, did not—save innocence just because it was innocent; that when he said 'Suffer little children to come unto Me', He meant exactly that: He meant suffer: that the adults, the fathers, the old in and capable of sin, must be ready and willing, nay, eager to suffer at any time, that the little children shall come unto Him unanguished, unterrified, undefiled. Do you accept that?

GOV. Go on.

STE. Then the child came, a little boy, a son, the son and heir; what had been merely a theory and a hope, was now a fact, an actuality, tender and defenseless: she saw now, when it was too late, to be [a fact *del.*] an incontrovertible fact what before had been merely an instinct: that God did not [protect and shield innocence *del.*] save innocence just because it was innocent—

[rule]

STE. Then she discovered that the child,—the first one—was on the way.

———*Requiem for a Nun,* autograph manuscript in pencil, 1 page, unnumbered. Cf. p. 202 of the Random House edition. (Leaf 7V)

GOWAN ([*rises quickly* del.] <*grimly*>) [That [*illeg.*] it. *del.*] Hiding under desks. Maybe I didn't start hiding soon enough. Maybe I should have started 8 years ago, anyway, but not just under a desk, but in a 1000 foot mine shaft, in some place like Siberia or Kamchatka—and hope that right wo—

STEVENS [Sit down *del.*] Stop it, Temple.

———*Requiem for a Nun,* ribbon typescript, canceled; 1 page, numbered "2-3-47A." Cf. pp. 202-204 of the Random House edition. (Leaf 28R)

STEVENS *(sharply: to Temple)* Stop it.

GOWAN Maybe we both didn't start hiding soon enough—about eight years ago—not in desk drawers either, but one of us in a cave in Siberia and the other in Kamchatka—and I suppose that's right, isn't it?

TEMPLE *(to Gowan)* I'm sorry. [I would have told you. *del.*] I didn't mean hiding—

GOWAN [Sure—but when? *del.*] Dont be. Just draw on your eight years' interest for that.

(quickly: to Stevens) Okay, okay, so you can tell me to shut up too.

(to Temple) I'm sorry too. I didn't mean it either. Maybe I'll need a little time myself to lose the habit of eight years of gratitude. [Well—

(to Stevens) I guess that's all, isn't it?

(he starts to come around the table)

TEMPLE *(watching him)* I would have told you.

(quickly: before he can answer)

All right, I'll say it for you: '[Sure but *del.*] Sure—but when?' *del.*] Alphonse and Gaston—only we're both trying to get through the door first. Well—

(to Stevens) I guess that's all, isn't it?

(he starts to come around the table)

TEMPLE *(watching him)* I would have told you.

GOWAN *(with a kind of gentleness)* Sure—but when?

(coming on around the desk) You see how easy it is? You could have been doing it for eight years: every time I would say 'Say thank you', all you would need would be to [say, 'For what' Okay—but when?' *del.*] answer 'Okay—but when?'

(comes around the table) I guess I'll get along and gather up Bucky.

TEMPLE Where is he?

GOWAN Where we always leave our children in clutches: with our—

STEVENS Maybe I can say Shut up this time.

GOWAN

———*Requiem for a Nun,* ribbon typescript, 1 page, numbered "2-3-48." Cf. pp. 205–207 of the Random House edition. (Leaf 29R)

TEMPLE *(cont)* or whenever it'll be when we are through with this and. . . .

(she stops: a moment: then to Stevens) You see. I started to say 'get back to chewing on the old hair shirt again'. Then I knew that was wrong, so I started to say 'On the new hair shirt'. Then I knew that that was wrong too, because it wont last that long; it will be quick, just painful, like a piece of glass or a box of carpet tacks—

GOWAN *(to Temple)* I said, stop it.

(to Stevens) Why dont you give her the cigarette now?

(Stevens [wor *del.*] takes up the pack, works the end of a cigarette out, and extends it. Gowan picks up the lighter from the desk, snaps it on as Temple takes the cigarette, turns as by reflex to the lighter, before she seems to realise that it is Gowan who has snapped it on and now holds it out. She stops, the cigarette suspended [) *ov.*:] [to no one) *del.*]

TEMPLE *(to no one)* Oh God. Again.

STEVENS Unless you mean 'Thank God'. Go on. Say it.

TEMPLE *(to Gowan)* Thanks.

(then she seems to forget the unlighted cigarette, turns to Stevens; after a moment Gowan snaps the lighter shut and puts it back on the desk)

All right. He said No. [didn't he? *del.*]

[[STEVENS *del.*] GOWAN *(before Stevens can answer)* Yes.

TEMPLE Did he say why?

[STEVENS *del.*] GOWAN He cant.

TEMPLE *(to Stevens)* The governor, with all the legal power to pardon or at least reprieve—cant?

STEVENS Yes, cant. He wasn't talking about law, any more than Nancy was, that I was, who could have plead [*sic*] insanity for her at any time and saved her life without bringing you here at two oclock in the morning—*del.*]

———*Requiem for a Nun,* ribbon typescript fragment, canceled; numbered "2-3-48" (on verso of paste-on continuation of "2-3-49A"). Cf. p. 207 of the Random House edition. (Leaf 32V)

GOWAN *(before Stevens can answer)* Yes.

TEMPLE [Did he say why? *del.*] So

GOWAN Yes. He cant.

TEMPLE Cant?

(to Stevens) The governor, with all the legal power [of *del.*] to pardon or at least reprieve, cant?

———*Requiem for a Nun,* ribbon typescript, 1 page, numbered "2-3-48A." Cf. pp. 207–209 of the Random House edition. (Leaf 30R)

[GOWAN *(before* [Temple *del.*] *Stevens can answer)* Yes.

TEMPLE *(to Gowan; this is not bitterness, but tension, trying to control hysteria actually)* So you were under the desk all the time. But all right. Did he say why?

GOWAN Yes. He cant.

TEMPLE Cant?

(to Stevens) The Governor of a state, with all the legal power to pardon or at least reprieve, cant?

GOWAN That's law. If it was just law, Uncle Gavin could have plead [*sic*] insanity for her at any time, without bringing you here at two oclock in the morning——*del.*]

TEMPLE And the other parent too; dont forget that. I dont know yet how he did it, and besides, it doesn't matter. But just dont forget it.

STEVENS <All right.> He wasn't even talking about justice. He was talking about a child, a little boy——

TEMPLE *(turning on him)* That's right. Make it good: the same little boy to hold whose normal and natural home together, the murderess, the nigger, the dopefiend-whore, didn't hesitate to cast the last gambit she knew and had: her own debased and worthless life. Oh yes, I know that answer too; that was brought out here tonight too: that a little child shall not suffer in order to come unto Me. So good can come out of evil.

STEVENS It not only can, it must.

TEMPLE So touche, then. Because what kind of natural and normal [house *del.*] home can that little boy have where his father may at any time tell him he has no father?

[**GOWAN** *(sharper)* Boots. *del.*]

STEVENS Haven't you been answering that question every day for eight years? Didn't Nancy answer it for you when she told you how you fought back, not for yourself, but for that little boy? Not to show the father that he was wrong, nor even to prove to the little boy that the father was wrong, [but to let the *del.*] but to let the little boy learn with his own eyes that nothing, not even that, which could possibly enter that house, could ever harm him?

———*Requiem for a Nun,* ribbon typescript fragment, numbered "2-3-49." Cf. pp. 209–210 of the Random House edition. (Leaf 31R)

TEMPLE But I quit. Nancy told you that too.

STEVENS She doesn't think so now. Isn't that what she's going to prove Friday morning?

TEMPLE Friday. The black day. The unlucky day. The day you never start on a journey. Except that Nancy's journey didn't begin at daylight or sunup or whenever it is polite or tactful to hang people, day after tomorrow. Her journey began that morning I got on that train at the University [——*del.*] eight years ago [—*del.*] [*(she stops, reacts)* Oh God, oh God, that was Friday too, that baseball game was on Friday too *del.*]

GOWAN [*(interrupts)* del.] That was Friday too. That baseball game was on Friday too.

TEMPLE (*wildly*) You see? Dont you see? It's nowhere near enough yet. Of course he [cant *del.*] [wouldn't save it. It's nowhere near through yet *del.*] wouldn't save her. If he did that, it would be over, Gowan could throw me out or I could throw Gowan out or the judge would throw us both out and give Bucky to an orphanage, and it would be all over. But now it can go on, tomorrow and tomorrow and tomorrow, forever and forever and forever.

———*Requiem for a Nun,* ribbon typescript (including paste-on continuation), 1 page, numbered "2-3-49A." Cf. pp. 210–211 of the Random House edition. (Leaf 32R)

(to Gowan) Tell me exactly what he said. You were here; you must have heard it. How long were you here? I mean, before we got here. [M]aybe before we even left Jefferson? No, you couldn't have been: you were still in bed asleep or at least pretending to, when I brought Bucky in and put him with you.

(whirls: to Stevens) So that was it: the . . . leaking valve, I believe you called it, at the filling station when we changed the wheel: to give him [time to pas *del.*] a chance to pass [by *del.*] us, get ahead of us——

STEVENS Maybe a little ahead of us. The Governor said what he had to say about this a week ago.

TEMPLE Yes, about the same time you sent me that telegram. What did he say?

STEVENS He said, 'Who am I, to have the brazen temerity and hardihood to set the puny appanage of my office in the balance against that simple undeviable aim? Who am I, to render null and abrogate the purchase she made with that that [*sic*] poor crazed lost and worthless life?'

TEMPLE So it was not even in hopes of saving her life, that [you br *del.*] I came here at two oclock in the morning. It wasn't even to be told that he had already decided not to save her. The reason I came here was to [tell [to a stranger something which even my husband didn't know *del.*] before a stranger something which *del.*] confess not only to my husband but in the presence of two strangers, something I had spent eight years trying to expiate so that my husband wouldn't have to know it. Dont you see that's just suffering? Not for anything: just suffering?

———*Requiem for a Nun,* ribbon typescript, 1 page, numbered "2-3-50." Cf. pp. 211–212 of the Random House edition. (Leaf 33R)

STEVENS You came here to affirm the very thing which Nancy is going to die tomorrow morning to postulate: that little children, as long as they are little children, shall be intact, unanguished, untorn, unterrified.

TEMPLE *(a moment: quietly)* All right. I've done that. Can we go home now?

STEVENS Of course. It's late.

(he starts, pauses, turns and takes up the pack of cigarettes from the desk to put it into his pocket)

GOWAN Maybe she wants one now.

(Stevens starts to offer the pack; only Gowan seems to remember that

Temple already has an unlighted cigarette still in her hand; even she looks at it stupidly for a moment as Gowan snaps on the Governor's lighter again and holds it out. Temple leans and lights the cigarette)

TEMPLE Thanks.

(But she puffs only once, forgets the cigarette again, does not even seem aware when she puts it into the tray and turns as Gowan comes around the desk, takes up her gloves and bag which she has forgotten also, and holds them out to her)

GOWAN *(roughly almost)* Here.

TEMPLE *(taking them)* Thanks.

(She begins to move toward the steps where she and Stevens entered, Stevens at her side, Gowan slightly in the rear[) *del.*]. As she reaches the first step, she stumbles slightly, like a sleep walker; nevertheless, it is not Stevens beside her but Gowan from the rear who comes in and steadies her elbow a second before, still in that dazed sleep walker fashion, she frees it and goes on, down the first step)

TEMPLE *(to no one)* To save my soul—if I have a soul. If there is a God to save it—a God who wants it——

CURTAIN

———*Requiem for a Nun,* autograph manuscript in pencil, 1 page, unnumbered. Cf. pp. 202–203 of the Random House edition. (Leaf 6V)

Stop it.

GOWAN Maybe we both didn't start hiding soon enough—about 8 years ago—not in desk drawers either, but in two mine shafts—one in Siberia and the other at the South Pole maybe.

TEMPLE All right. I didn't mean hiding. I'm sorry.

GOWAN Dont be. Just draw on your 8 years' interest for that.

(to Stevens) All right, all right; Tell me to shut up too. <*(to no one)*> In fact, this may be a good time for me to start saying sorry. <Just give me time.> 8 years of gratitude may be a habit a little hard to break.

(to Stevens again) I guess that's all, isn't it? We can go home now?

TEMPLE *(to G)* I would have told you.

G Sure—but when?

(he moves, starts to come around the desk): to no one)

You see how easy it is? You could have been doing it for eight years yourself: every time I would say 'Say thank you' you could have answered, 'Sure—but when?'

———*Requiem for a Nun,* ribbon typescript, 1 page, unnumbered. Cf. pp. 202–204 of the Random House edition. (Leaf 26R)

[**GOWAN** But do you want to? You might let me finish first.

(to Temple) I was going to say, with our kinfolks. He's at Maggie's

2 - 3 - 50

STEVENS
You came here to affirm the very thing which Nancy is going to die tomorrow morning to postulate: that little children, as long as they are little children, shall be intact, unanguished, untorn, unterrified.

TEMPLE (a moment: quietly)
All right. I've done that. Can we go home now?

STEVENS
Of course. It's late.
(he starts, pauses, turns and takes up the pack of cigarettes from the desk to put it into his pocket)

GOWAN
Maybe she wants one now.
(Stevens starts to offer the pack; only Gowan seems to remember that Temple already has an unlighted cigarette still in her hand; even she looks at it stupidly for a moment as Gowan snaps on the Governor's lighter again and holds it out. Temple leans and lights the cigarette)

TEMPLE
Thanks.
(But she puffs only once, forgets the cigarette again, does not even seem aware when she puts it into the tray and turns as Gowan comes around the desk, takes up her gloves and bag which she has forgotten also, and holds them out to her)

GOWAN (roughly almost)
Here.

TEMPLE (taking them)
Thanks.
(She begins to move toward the steps where she and Stevens entered, Stevens at her side, Gowan slightly in the rear/. As she reaches the first step, she stumbles slightly, like a sleep walker; nevertheless, it is not Stevens beside her but Gowan from the rear who comes in and steadies her elbow a second before , still in that dazed sleep walker fashion, she frees it and goes on, down the first step)

TEMPLE (to no one)
To save my soul - if I have a soul. If there is a God to save it - a God who wants it--p---

CURTAIN

43. Page of typescript of *Requiem for a Nun,* c. 1950

STEVENS We'll all go.

GOWAN *(pauses)* Okay. *(to Temple) del.*]

STEVENS *(to Temple)* Stop it.

GOWAN Maybe we both didn't start hiding soon enough—about eight years ago—not in desk drawers either, but in two [mi *del.*] abandoned mine-shafts, one in Siberia and the other at the South Pole maybe.

TEMPLE All right. I didn't mean hiding. I'm sorry.

GOWAN Dont be. Just draw on your eight years' interest for that.

(to Stevens) All right, all right; tell me to shut up too.

(to no one[) del.] *directly)* In fact, this may be the time for me to start saying sorry for the next eight-year term. Just give me a little time. Eight years of gratitude may be a habit a little hard to break. So here goes.

(to Temple) I'm sorry[. *del.*], [Boots. *del.*] Forget it.

TEMPLE I would have told you.

GOWAN [Sure—but when?

(he moves, starts to come around the table[) *del.*]: again speaking directly to no one)

You see how easy it is? You could have been doing that for eight years yourself; every time I said, 'Say sorry please', [yo *del.*] all you would have to do would be to answer: 'Sure—but when?'

(he comes round to the front of the desk)

I guess that's all, isn't it. We can go home now?

TEMPLE Wait. *del.*]

———*Requiem for a Nun,* autograph manuscript in pencil, 1 page, unnumbered. Cf. p. 203 of the Random House edition. (Leaf 5V)

GOWAN You did. Forget it.

[(to no one) *del.*]

You see how easy it is? You could have been doing that yourself for 8 years: every time I would say 'Say sorry please' all you would need would be to answer: 'I did. Forget it.'

———*Requiem for a Nun,* ribbon typescript, 1 page, unnumbered. Cf. pp. 203–205 of the Random House edition. (Leaf 27R)

GOWAN You did Forget it. You see how easy it is? You could have [done *del.*] been doing that yourself for eight years: every time I would say 'Say sorry, please' all you would need would be to answer: 'I did. Forget it.' [I guess that's all, isn't it? We can *del.*]

(To Stevens) I guess that's all, isn't it? We can go home now.

TEMPLE Wait.

(They look at one another) Where are you going?

GOWAN I said home, didn't it [*i.e.* I]? To pick up Bucky and carry him back to his own bed again.

(they look at one another) You're not even going to ask me where he is now?

(answers himself) Where we always leave our children when the clutch comes——

[GO *del.*] STEVENS *(to Gowan)* Maybe I'd better say shut up, this time.

GOWAN Let me finish first though. I was going to say, 'with [our kinfolk *del.*] our handiest kinfolks.' He's at Maggie's.

STEVENS I think we can all go now. Come on.

GOWAN Okay.

(he comes around the desk, stops again. To Temple)

[Do you want to ride back with me, or with Gavin? *del.*] Make up your mind. Do you want to ride back with me, or Gavin?

STEVENS *(to Gowan)* Go on. You can pick up Bucky.

GOWAN Right.

(he turns, starts toward the stairs Front, stops)

That's right, I'm probably still supposed to use the spy's entrance.

(he turns back, starts back toward door at rear, sees Temple's gloves and bag on the table, stops, picks them up and holds them out to her: roughly almost)

Here. This is evidence; you dont want to forget them.

(Temple takes the gloves and bag. Gowan goes on toward the door at rear)

TEMPLE *(after him)* Did you have a hat and coat?

(he doesn't answer. He goes on, exits)

Oh God. Again.

[(Stevens to *del.*]

STEVENS

———*Requiem for a Nun,* ribbon typescript, 1 page, unnumbered. Cf. pp. 206–207 of the Random House edition. (Leaf 28V)

STEVENS *(touches her arm)* Come on.

TEMPLE *(not moving yet)* Tomorrow and tomorrow and tomorrow——

STEVENS He will wreck the car again against the wrong tree, at the wrong place, and you will have to forgive him again—until he wrecks the car again at the wrong place, against the wrong tree——

TEMPLE I was driving it too. I was driving it some of the time too.

STEVENS *(gently)* Then let that comfort you.

(*takes her arms again, turns her*)

Come on. It's late.

TEMPLE *(holds back, frees her arm)* Wait. He said no.

STEVENS Yes.

TEMPLE Did he say why?

STEVENS Yes. He cant.

TEMPLE Cant? The Governor of a state, with all the legal power to pardon or at least reprieve, cant?

STEVENS That's just law. If it was only law, I could have plead [*sic*] [her *del.*] insanity for her at any time, without bringing you here [—— *del.*] at two oclock in the morning——

927 "Weekend Revisited," c. 1953, autograph manuscript in blue ink, 1 page, on 9-by-8⅞-inch fragment of yellow ruled paper, unwatermarked.

This passage of fourteen lines was discarded and not used in the published version of the story ("Mr. Acarius," *Saturday Evening Post,* October 9, 1965; 26ff.; *Uncollected Stories,* pp. 435–448). The opening quotation is taken from James Joyce's short story, "Counterparts," in *Dubliners.*

'The barometer of his emotional nature was set for a spell of riot.'

The words on the printed page were true. They had been true for weeks now and he had known it, known that truth long before he had stumbled by chance on the printed page which bore them. The trouble was, they were not true in the way, the sense, not only of what they actually said, but as the writer himself probably intended them.

It was the word itself—riot—which was wrong. It was exactly backward. Here it was used obviously in its military sense, when the thirster for glory hopes to convert to riot what had been simple retreat. And that was not what he wanted. It was exactly what he didn't want. If he had had to be a thirster for glory, if he had had no other means [than the thirster for glory's meaning of riot, *del.*] to gain the retreat he wanted, intended, than the thirster for glory's meaning of riot, he might even deny himself the retreat.

928 "Weekend Revisited," c. 1953, autograph manuscript in blue ink, 1 page, on 10-by-8-inch fragment of yellow ruled paper, unwatermarked.

This draft is an early (perhaps the first) version of the opening four paragraphs of the story. In later drafts the unnamed protagonist becomes Mr. Aquinius and eventually Mr. Acarius.

He waited until toward the end of the p.m., though he and his doctor had been classmates and still [knew th *del.*] saw each other several times a week in the homes of the same friends and in the bars and lounges and dining rooms of the same clubs, and he knew he would be sent almost directly in. Which he was, almost immediately, to stand in his good Madison Ave. suit looking down at his friend sitting behind the desk, [buried to t *del.*] still in whites and buried to the elbows in the paper end of the day's work, a reflector cocked rakishly over one ear and the other serpentined implements of his calling dangling about him.

'I want to get drunk,' he said.

'All right,' the doctor said, <not looking up,> scribbling busily at the foot of

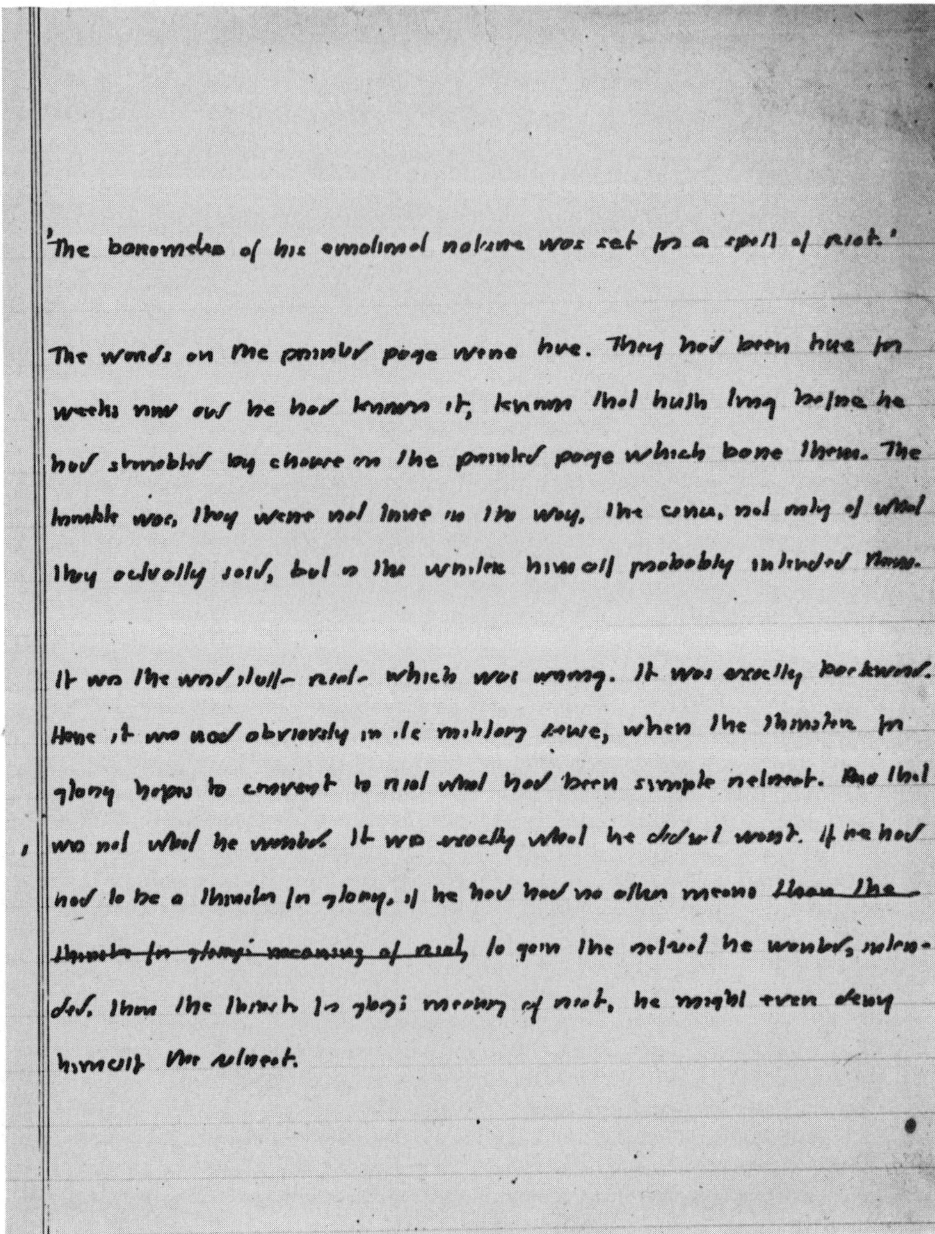

'The barometer of his emotional nature was set for a spell of riot.'

The words on the printed page were true. They had been true for weeks now and he had known it, known that truth long before he had stumbled by chance on the printed page which bore them. The trouble was, they were not true in the way, the sense, not only of what they actually said, but as the writer himself probably intended them.

It was the word itself—riot—which was wrong. It was exactly backward. Here it was used obviously in its military sense, when the thirster for glory hopes to convert to riot what had been simple retreat. And that was not what he wanted. It was exactly what he didn't want. If he had had to be a thirster for glory, if he had had no other means ~~than the thirster for glory's meaning of riot,~~ to gain the retreat he wanted, needed, than the thirster for glory's meaning of riot, he might even deny himself the retreat.

44. Manuscript page of "Weekend Revisited" ("Mr. Acarius"), c. 1953

what was probably a chart. 'Give me 10 minutes. Or why dont you go on to the club and I'll meet you there.'

But he didn't move. He said quietly: '[Look at *del.*] Ab. Look at me.'

929 "Weekend Revisited," c. 1953, ribbon typescript, canceled; 1 page, numbered "2," 11 by 8½ inches, Certificate Bond.

This draft of paragraphs 4-11 of the story has been x-ed out with a red grease pencil.

But Mr Aquinius didn't move. He said, 'Ab. Look at me' in such a tone that the doctor first paused, then started, then thrust his upper body completely away from the desk in order to stare up at Mr Aquinius standing over him.

'Say that again,' the doctor said. Mr Aquinius did so. 'I mean in English,' the doctor said.

'I [am *del.*] [was *del.*] <was> fifty years old yesterday,' Mr Aquinius said. 'I have just exactly [enough *del.*] what money I shall need to supply my wants and pleasures until the bomb falls. Except that when that happens—I mean the bomb of course—nothing will have happened to me in all my life. If there is any rubble left, it will be only the carcass of my Capehart and the frames of my Picassos, because there will never have been anything of me to have left any smudge or stain. [So far *del.*] Until now, that has contented me. Or rather, I have been willing to accept it. But not anymore. Before I have quitted this scene, vanished from the recollection of a few head waiters and the membership lists of a few clubs——'

'Along with the headwaiters and the clubs,' the doctor said. 'Predicating the bomb, [' *del.*] of course.'

'Be quiet and listen,' Mr Aquinius said. 'Before that shall have happened, I want to experience man, the human race.'

'Find yourself a mistress,' the doctor said.

'I tried that. Maybe what I want is debasement too.'

'Then in Christ's name get married,' the doctor said. 'What better way than that to run the whole gamut from [gar *del.*]

1032 *A Fable,* 1954

Printed below are 30 pages (on 17 leaves) of discarded pages reflecting various stages in the composition of *A Fable.* Included are autograph manuscript, both ribbon and carbon typescript, and typescript with holograph corrections. Several of the pages were canceled with a huge X in red grease pencil as Faulkner went on to more advanced drafts, frequently on the versos of these same leaves. While in every instance but one a corresponding passage in the novel can be identified, the published text varies considerably from these materials.

Five of the pages are carbon copies lifted from a typescript of the version of *Notes on a Horsethief* that was issued by Levee Press in 1950. Faulkner rewrote that story when he incorporated it into *A Fable.*

A number of these manuscript pages carry altered pagination, evidencing the manner in which Faulkner (often with Saxe Commins's advice and assistance) experimented with different placements for various episodes in the plot. For example, one page that belongs to the description of the military funeral of the old marshal—eventually page "650," a part of the epilogue of the novel—was formerly page "41."

Leaves 1–2, 4, 11, 15, and 17 are watermarked "Hammermill Bond"; leaves 3 and 5–6 are "Howard Bond"; leaves 12 and 16 are "Royal Writing"; leaf 13 is "Certificate Bond"; and leaf 14 is "Strathmore." Leaves 7–10 bear no watermark. All of the leaves measure 11 by 8½ inches.

Faulkner left all of these materials with Saxe Commins, at whose Princeton home Faulkner did much of his writing on *A Fable.*

———*A Fable,* ribbon typescript, canceled; 1 page, numbered "135." Not used in published version. (Leaf 15R)

which Mannock and Bishop hurled javelin-like down the air, which anterior to that, anterior to wings and engines, was the lance set home and level as sunlight and bright as lightning above the thunder of horses and, anterior to that, the flung simple javelin itself older than England, older than Europe in the long dust, the chiaroscuro, the swordy tumult of the olden race's self's long dim beginning: King David a boy, unknowing he was kingly, had one simple stone in a leather sling and it was enough: one simple single frail wing-shedding Nieuport's bullet yet his vast loomed night-fearsome Gotha crashed; King David not so young now and thought soft among the silken dulcimers, king and prince he could afford to take off his field marshal's badges and lead a squadron, not leading a squadron well so much as leading the best squadron since the squadron he led performed miracles of glorious valor simply because he led it; not always quite sahib and sometimes even less [pukka *del.*] than that pukka but so was Prince Hal, never quite as good not as he really wanted wished perhaps but as he bragged to be, and even if he never would really let you forget he had put off the rank, never did quite stop using the fact that he had left the red tabs at home, nevertheless, the best to lead; not the best pilot, never to be a real pukka bung-ho gosport pilot and maybe never really anymore a first rate one but none better to command a wing, incomparable because his luck was always in and those he led partook of it; he would survive scatheless an old man splendid in scarlet and barnacles and badges, crowned, not like matchless Joshua dead after matchless Jericho: the flight commander godlike and supreme, invincible fierce and feared even [dead, against the mere *del.*]

———*A Fable,* ribbon typescript, canceled; 1 page, numbered "136." Cf. pp. 88–89 of published version. (Leaf 1R)

dead, against the mere air-flaming memory of whose record incredible in its terror and its briefness Pfalz and Fokker, Albatros and Halberstadter and L.V.G. would flame and melt like moths, King David conferring on him dead the V.C. which David himself could [give but *del.*] bestow but not wear, could touch only in the giving of it away and kingly in the humility of that proud and humble act investing that bit of bronze no larger than the flattened bullet dangling from the blood-stained swatch which bound the wound it made, with a vaster value yet redounding [to *del.*] on both and all, conferring a fiercer immortality yet on the dead man's still lethal shade;—in Valhalla's halls perhaps there was no other uniform save the gaudy modest ribbons of the nations' exultant pride, anterior to any Whitehall, let alone any voice from it; in that anteroom no thumb-tacked board to carry the scrawled appendix-ed postings: *Transfers: As of This Date: To Royal Air Force: The Following:*. Because these were old, he hadn't realised how old out of the long long dust anterior to Europe, to all West, invincible in passive unproud abasement, enduring, until the King had written: *We Reposing Trust and Confidence in Our Trusty and Well Beloved Gerald* because that was when he learned that nothing mattered, simply nothing, nothing defeated you, simply nothing, so long as you never ceased not resisting what you had been and defending what you are.

Then tomorrow; he was just leaving the mess after dinner to go to his hut to write his mother when Bridesman entered from the office and saw him and said, 'Levine. Jobs tomorrow. Eleven oclock.'

———*A Fable,* ribbon typescript with deletions, canceled; 1 page, numbered "168." Cf. pp. 105–106 of published version. (Leaf 2R)

saw it, a two seater, he didn't know what kind because he had never seen a German two seater in the air before nor any other German for that matter and then Bridesman came vertically down in front of him and putting his nose down after Bridesman he discovered that the major had vanished and then he forgot that too, he and Bridesman going almost straight down now and the German was right under them now going west and he could see Bridesman's tracer going right into it until Bridesman pulled out and away and then his own tracer but he never could seem to get onto it before he had to pull out and away too and then the archie seemed to be waiting for him as though the hun were simply shooting it up here without caring whom it hit nor even watching to see, one seemed to burst between his upper and lower planes; he thought: *Maybe the reason I dont hear any clang is because this one is going to shoot me down before I have time* and then he found the two seater again, not the aeroplane but the white bursts and an S.E. (it would have to be the major; Bridesman couldn't possibly have got that far by now) diving toward it so that would be where it was and then Bridesman was just off his wing tip again, the two of them going full out now in the pocking cloud of black archie like two sparrows through a swirl of dead leaves. And then he saw the balloons and then he noticed or remembered or perhaps simply saw the sun.

[That was all too: the two seater in its aureole of white archie flying perfectly straight exactly between the two German balloons and the major above and behind it and he and Bridesman a mile back and still higher in their cloud of *del.*]

———*A Fable,* ribbon typescript, canceled; 1 page, numberd "31." Cf. pp. 131–132 of published version. (Leaf 3R)

against the fence beyond which the fatigue parties wrestling slowly among their interminable tinsel coils paused to look quietly and incuriously back at them and [on the catwalks *del.*] the gaudy midnight Senegalese, lounging in lethargic disdain among their machineguns above both the white people engaged in labor inside the pen and the one engaged in anguish outside it, smoked cigarettes and stroked idly the edges of bayonets with broad dark spatulae of thumbs and didn't bother to look at them at all. Nor could even the aviator stationed in the hard blue wind have said exactly where among them the facing about began as, like the blind headless earth-brute which apparently without any organ either to perceive alarm or select a course to evade it can move at instantaneous notice at instantaneous speed in either direction, the crowd began to flow back toward the city, turning and beginning to move all at one instant, inextricable and without confusion as a flock of birds all leave a tree as one bird, hurrying again, weary and indefatigable, indomitable in their capacity not alone for endurance but for frenzy as well, streaming immediately once more between two lines of troops stretching the whole distance back to the city—apparently a whole brigade of cavalry this time facing across the road a like number of infantry, without packs again but with bayonets still and grenades too now and at one point the nozzle and [loop *del.*] looped hose of a flame thrower and at the end of the lane where it emerged from the city the tank again half-seen beyond the flank

———*A Fable,* carbon typescript with autograph and typescript revisions, canceled; 1 page, numbered "21." Cf. pp. 154–155 of published version. (Leaf 4R)

so completely out of sight that when the railroad detectives reached the scene the next morning, it was as if the flood itself had washed the three of them away: a hummock, a small island in the swamp not a mile from the [<collapsed trestle> *del.*] collapsed trestle, where a work train [with a crew *del.*] and crew had arrived the next day to restore the crossing, and from which the white groom returned at dawn on the second day with a block and tackle bearing the railroad company's stencil, with which the crippled horse was suspended and immobilised; and the next time the white one was gone two days, returning on the second night with a pirogue with feed for the horse and food for themselves, and plaster of Paris and splints and canvas strips for a cradle, and the runner said, <cried:> 'Yes, but [the *del.*] money, the money for [this, *del.*] all this [? *ov.*—] [and *del.*] <T *ov.* t>he old Negro told that: the Cockney horse-groom who had never been further from London than Epsom or Doncaster, who in two years in America became a Mason[: *del.*] [<and> *del.*], a primitive Baptist[: *del.*], [and found himself to be one of the best natural players at or manipulators of dice *del.*] and in the two weeks up from Buenos Aires in the forecastle of an American freigher, [revealed *del.*]

discovered or anyway revealed himself to be one of the world's best players at or manipulators of dice: who, on that first night of his return to the scene of the wreck, had picked up the block-and-tackle simply because he happened to pass it, [because *del.*] his <true> destination [had been *del.*] <being> the <bunk> car in which the Negro work-gang slept, waking them, the white man in his clothes still heavy with mud and water, and the black ones in undershirts or dungaree pants or in nothing at all, squatting around the smoking lantern and the banknotes and the coins and the clicking and scuttering dice; and after that, the trestle repaired and the work-gang and that source of income departed, he (the white one) would go as far as New Orleans, bucking the professional games on baize-covered tables, beneath electric lights.

[Telling it, *del.*] [n *del.*] <N>ot how[: *del.*], <only> the simple chronology: the weeks and then months [until there were six of them, *del.*] while the ruined hip knitted and the

———*A Fable,* ribbon typescript with autograph and typescript revisions, 1 page, numbered [*ts* "23-A" *del.*] *ams* "227." Cf. p. 156 of published version. (Leaf 4V)

long since drawn [*the* del.] *and then forgot it the line of his rectitude to include the magnificent ruined horse and all who were willing to serve it* <*marg.* no italics>—would know how far he would sometimes go before he found another spread blanket beneath a smoked lantern or, as a last resort, the electric-lit baize table, where, although in their leathern cup the dice were as beyond impugnment as Caesar's wife, the counters—chips, money—still accrued, whether or not to the benison of his [need *del.*] gift or to the simple compulsion of his need.

Then months, not only within <daily> earshot of the trains [once more thundering across the repaired trestle but [of *del.*] of the search-parties themselves, *del.*]

———*A Fable,* ribbon typescript with revisions, canceled; 1 page, unnumbered. Cf. p. 160 of published version. (Leaf 5R)

'Good morning,' the deputy said. And (Oklahoma now[: before he warrantless now he overtook the pursuit: *del.*]<—> the little bleak stations between a cattle chute and a water tank, the men in broad dusty hats and heeled boots clustered quietly before the post-tacked placards offering a reward for a horse such as even America had never seen before[) *del.*]—when [he *del.*] warrantless now he overtook the pursuit, joining it as the private young man with money had used to attend Marlborough's wars—and indeed meeting among them who a month ago had been his companions in arms the same cold fronted unanimity [of *del.*] half of contempt and half of jealous fear which the private young men met among Marlborough's professional[s *del.*] guardsmen

———*A Fable,* ribbon typescript, canceled; 1 page, unnumbered. Cf. p. 165 of published version. (Leaf 6R)

lawyer on the telephone [*again* del.] *to* [*his client* del.] *<the exdeputy> in New Orleans who said, 'Stay there. If any other charges are brought they'll have to originate there. You must be where you can protect him.'*

'Pah,' the lawyer said. 'The one who will need protection here is the first man who lays a hand on him—granted of course anybody who ever saw him before [*ever does* del.] *sees him again to lay anything on him. He was a fool. If he had stayed here he could have had the sheriff's badge without even* [having *del.*] *running for it.'*

'Then stay for that,' the exdeputy said. 'What grounds did they free him on?'

'Grounds?' the lawyer said. 'They didn't use grounds. They just freed him.'

———*A Fable,* carbon typescript, canceled; 1 page, numbered "33." Cf. pp. 168–169 of published version. (Leaf 7R)

the coat, the worn brushed dusty broadcloth garment which—not the man, the coat, and not the whole coat but the elbow-deep suitcase-roomy tails of it—the county and state police of five contiguous commonwealths had been blockading roads and searching farm wagons and automobiles and freight trains and the Jim Crow cars of passenger ones and depot lavatories and charging in pairs and threes with shotguns and drawn pistols through the pool halls and burial association lodges and the kitchens and bedrooms of Negro tenements for sixty-five hours now trying to find: as did the town: so that before the turnkey and his shackled prize had left the jail hardly they were beginning to gather behind them a growing tail of men and youths and small boys like that of a rising kite which in the street leading to the square the turnkey could still tell himself he was leading and which crossing the square toward the courthouse he even still looked like he was, walking fast now so that no slack remained at all in the chain joining him to his captive when that failed too; he broke and even took one step actually running but no more, stopping and turning to face the pressing crowd all in one blind motion like the hopeless and furious repudiation of the boy turning once more whole stainless and absolved, to hurl his toy pistol into the very face of the charging elephants, victim no more of terror but of pride, and cried in a thin forlorn voice which itself was like the manless voice of a boy:

'Stop, men! This hyer's the Law!' who without doubt if they had run at him would have stood his ground, drawing his pistol and not even cocking it, dying without struggle beneath the trampling feet in that one last high moment of his badge and warrant (a small mild ordinary man whom you have seen walking in his ten thousands the streets of little American towns and many not so little either not just in the vast central Valley

———*A Fable,* carbon typescript, canceled; 1 page, numbered "34." Cf. 169–170 of published version. (Leaf 8R)

but on the eastern and western watersheds and the high ozonic mountain plateaus too, who had received his job and office out of that inexhaustible reservoir of nepotism from which during the hundred-odd years since the republic's founding almost that many millions of its children had received not just their daily bread but a little something over for Saturday and Christmas too since coeval with the republic it was one of the prime foundation-stones: from the current sheriff whose remote kinswoman to his unending surprise and unbelief even ten years afterward he had somehow managed to marry;— so quiet so mild and so ordinary that nobody really noticed, let alone remarked, the manner in which he accepted and affirmed the oath when he was sworn into his office; to them here was merely somebody else's nameless and unknown cousin by blood or maybe only by marriage promising to be as brave and honest and loyal as anyone could or should expect for the next four years in somebody else's job) as the male mayfly concentrates his whole one day of life into the one evening act of procreation and then relinquishes it; only they were not running at him but walking and only walking toward him because he was between them and the courthouse—and that was probably when he realized that what he preceeded was not even an idle concourse, let alone a simple predictable mob and perhaps in the same instant that he was not discovering they were there but had merely forgotten they would be, flowing into the square from all directions, out of the stores and the stairways leading to the second-storey offices of the doctors and lawyers and dentists and not converging on him because the two wings of its front were already passing him; at this rate before they ever reached the courthouse he and his captive would not even be in front of it but somewhere back in the ruck: except that a voice said, speaking to him by name in a tolerant

———*A Fable,* carbon typescript, canceled; 1 page, unnumbered. Cf. p. 172 of published version. (Leaf 9R)

so that he have something for his highwayman-opposite to rob him of and in that nightly losing earn his daily bread) while what for the moment anyway sufficed for Man poured steadily and without even temerity into the tabernacle the shrine itself of his last tribal mysteries, approaching not only without challenge but not even aware of it, not even fearless or intolerant of challenge but not even aware that they were absolutely incapable of conceiving of anyone or anything capable of the temerity to try let alone capable of the challenge because it was theirs, they had built it, conceived it and sweated it up: not out of any need or agony or long agony of invincible hope because he was not aware of any need or any long history of agony or that he participated in any long chronicle of frustrated yearning but because he wanted it, like it, could afford it or anyway was going to have it whether he could afford it or not, to be no symbol (cradle either) of any mammalian apex, harbor where the incredible cockleshell of any invincible dream made soundings from the chartless latitudes of his lost beginnings and where like that of the enduring sea the voice of any affirmation roared murmuring home about the atoll-dais (that railed arena actually remote as God from any mere heat and fury of puny battle since of man or long agony of man's invincible hope because was not aware of any need or any long history of agony or that he participated in any long chronicle of frustrated yearning but because he wanted it, like it, could afford it or anyway was going to have it whether he could afford it or not, to be no symbol (cradle either) of any mammalian apex, harbor where the incredible cockleshell of any invincible dream made soundings from the chartless latitudes of any lost beginnings and where like that of the enduring sea the voice of any affirmation roared murmuring home about the atoll-dais (that railed arena actually remote as God from any mere heat and fury of puny battle since here shrank and trembled no mere petty right but blind justice reigned ruthless and inattentive amid the [*sic*]

———*A Fable,* carbon typescript, canceled; 1 page, numbered "39." Cf. pp. 172–173 of published version. (Leaf 10R)

the deathless invincible smells of his invincible victories: his stale tobacco spit and his sweat) of his unanimity because to begin with he was not he but they and they only by election because what he was was I and in the first place he was not a mammal and as for chartless latitudes he not only knew exactly where he came from six thousand years ago but that in three score and ten or thereabouts he was going back there and as for affirmation the mark of a free man was his right to say no for no other reason except no: which answered unanimity too and the floor was his, he had built it, paid for it, who could spit on it if not he, perhaps the lawyer had even read Dickens and Hugo once long ago when he was a young man when though there had stood already these many months nevermore evictable from his vision the beckoning image of himself among the first (perhaps the first) of farmers-general in the boundless tillage of human folly it was not yet so peremptory and looked across the flimsy barrier into no brick-and-plaster-[*sic*] barn built yesterday by the grandfathers of orderly and decorous Missouri farmers but back a hundred and fifty years into a stone hall older than Orleans or Capet or Charlemagne entered without fear of challenge not because it (man) could not conceive of challenge but because it had itself liquidated challenge into that one same flood where the silks and lilies of a thousand years which were to have endured ten and the sabots until yesterday reeking only of plowed land and manure and the caps of Mediterranean fishermen and the smocks of cobblers and porters and road-stiffening with the drying crimson smears of hands clothing the ravening unfathered nakedness which rent the silks and lilies and the smeared hands and the faces too gaunt insatiable and bemazed all commingled in one furious inextricable maelstrom fierce as nightmare, red as dawn but (the lawyer) without fear then and with something now even more

———*A Fable,* carbon typescript with autograph and typescript revisions, canceled; 1 page, numbered "120-Z-19." Cf. pp. 172–173 of published version. (Leaf 11R)

[*but not even fearless of nor even intolerant of challenge, not even conscious that they were absolutely incapable of conceiving of anyone or anything capable of the temerity to challenge try, let alone capable of the challenge, ringing with measured unhurried thunder the corridor the stairs then the room itself* del.] [*(the lawyer) standing with his new prize inside the railing's flimsy sanctuary watching while at least for the moment* del.] *would suffice for man pour steadily and without* [abashment *del.*] *awe or even diffidence into the tabernacle and shrine itself of his tribal mysteries, approaching it not merely without challenge but not even fearless of or intolerant of challenge, not even aware that they were absolutely incapable of conceiving of anyone or anything capable of the temerity to try, let alone capable of the challenge, ringing with measured unhurried thunder the corridor the stairs then the room itself because it was* [*theirs, they* del.] <*his, he*> *had built it, conceived it out of the long travail of his aspirations and sweated it up out of the agony of his hope, symbol (cradle too) of his mammalian apex, harbor where the incredible cockleshell of his invincible dream made soundings made soundings* [sic] *from the chartless latitutdes of his beginnings and like that of the enduring sea the voice of his affirmation roared murmuring home about the atoll-dais of his unanimity—that railed arena actually remote as God from any heat and fury of puny battle since no mere petty right shrank and trembled here but blind justice reigned ruthless and inattentive above the deathless invincible smells of his invincible* [*agonies: his* del.]

———*A Fable,* autograph manuscript with deletions, 1 page, unnumbered. Cf. pp. 261–262 of published version. (Leaf 12)

[So they thought. But not I. I knew better then. *del.*] That was what they believed then: not that man had failed rapacity but that man had failed man, his own frail traitor flesh had let him down; the blood would still run but cooling now, into the second phase of his brief and furious span where the filling of his belly is [taller than *del.*] better than glory or a throne, on into the third and last one where anticipation of the latrine will be more moving than even the spread of a girl's hair on a pillow. That's what they thought, believed, was to be your destiny·and end. And 10 years from now they will still believe that. Because your time, your moment, will not have come yet.

———*A Fable,* ribbon typescript with autograph and typescript revisions, 1 page, numbered [*ts "70" del.*] *ams* "392." Cf. p. 262 of published version. (Leaf 13V)

new century, the new age, another age virgin and pristine and even unremembering of man's old passions and failures: the new decade of centuries since he discovered God for a second and then lost Him, postulated by a new digit in the accompting of his hope and need; more than twenty years even to the day, the moment when you will appear again without past, as though you had never been, because by that time[, during that time, *del.*] you will no longer exist for them save in mutual remembering since not only the old class but all of them who had [the unfinished *del.*] what they call the unfinished charade's original witnesses[, *del.*] will be diverged by duty and scattered by career to the ends of what Frenchmen anyway consider (no matter how [thinly spread) *del.*] thin the paté on the savage bread) the civilised earth, and you will be a lay figure not only without life but integrated as myth only in rare confederance: the property of no single one because the common property of all, possessing unity and integration only when its custodians happen to meet and match fragments—a fading tradition belonging impartially not even to Africa any more but to the Empire, so that for twenty years, miniscule and diffused, attenuate and untensile, you will lie lightly across the face of France from Mozambique to [Michelon *del.*] Miquelon and Devil's Island to the Treaty Ports like a thin barely[- *del.*] remembered odor, a fading word, a symbol, a habit, a thought, uncryptic, harmless, into which

———*A Fable,* ribbon typescript, 1 page, numbered [*ts* "71" *del.*] *ams* "393." Cf. p. 262 of published version. (Leaf 14V)

new St Cyr classes replace the successors of our old coeval one and are replaced in their turn to die (in glory when they can find it) or sell or be cashiered[: *del.*]—an effigy cut by a jigsaw for souvenirs and becoming whole only when the holders of the meaningless scraps meet over café or mess tables in Brazzaville or Saigon or Cayenne or Tananrive (yes, Paris too) and dovetail them for a moment or an hour like boys matching and [exchangi *del.*] swapping the pictures of the actresses and generals and presidents from the packets of tobacco or cigarettes.

<'>Oh yes, harmless now, unchanged in fact, not even any older; still fragile and, because of the fragility, durable; and because of both, as harmless and interdict as smallpox to its recovered own; durable, harmless, and no longer even a fool now but rapacity's own who would endure as does the idiot scion of any other great ducal [house *del.*] or royal servant of rapacity[; *del.*]—[a shadow *del.*] not even <a shadow> of a breathing man but instead a thing synthetic and contrived not by one but by three: the trinity: like that composite shadow of the [juxtaposed objects *del.*] homely domestic objects juxtaposed and reconciled by the nurse's hand between the nursery lamp and wall for the [child *del.*] drowsing child to take with it into slumber: a balloon: a duck: Punchinello: *la gloire:* slumber itself: the head of a cat[: *del.*]—a shadow, [empty now even of *del.*] <from behind which> what little it ever had for [a *del.*] substance, progenitor, has vanished now, cast backward upon that curtain, that arid gauze behind Oran, not by the sun but by that old spurned quartermaster captaincy, the refusal—or evadement—of which was what first struck them with [terror and with rage *del.*]

———*A Fable,* ribbon typescript with autograph and typescript revisions, 1 page, numbered *ams* ["72" *del.*] "394." Cf. pp. 262–263 of published version. (Leaf 15V)

terror and with rage: not so much that you had been offered it but that you had apparently evaded it—not refused it: evaded it, until after the twenty years, of the three of you—the youth, the two powerful kinsmen, and the indomitable and fading parchment—only it will be along [*sic*] longer real, and it so only because of some myopic civilian clerk in the Quai d'Orsay who cannot close a record and balance a sheet and turn a page[: *del.*]—not refused: [escaped; the oldest of comedies: the youth *del.*] escaped, the shopworn and now harmless [parchment *del.*] [vellum with its fading dangling seals and ribbons *del.*] vellum vainly dangling its fading seals and ribbons along the perimeter of your life in the oldest of comedies: [the youth *del.*] <the youth> fleeing, the forsaken aging [yet indomitable betrothed pursuing, *del.*] <yet indomitable betrothed pursuing,> abject, constant, undismayable, [undeflectable, terrifying not *del.*] <undeflectable, terrifying not> in threat but in fidelity, [and they who feared you once *del.*] until they who feared you once [have now watched you pass *del.*] will have watched you pass out of enmity to amazement, to contempt, to unreality, and at last out of your race and kind too into the dusty-room of literature.

'But not I,' he said, looming, visible only as a gaunt gigantic shape, sick, furious tender and composed, murmuring: 'I know. I knew that first moment eleven years ago when I looked and saw you standing there in that gate, even if I shant be there to see it—my last medical survey, you know: that marvelous and amazing thing, a human life, spanned and then [out-spanned *del.*]—what is the Boer word? Out-spanned

———*A Fable,* ribbon typescript with autograph and typescript revisions, 1 page, numbered [*ts* "73" *del.*] *ams* "395." Cf. p. 263 of published version. (Leaf 1V)

—out-spanned by one dry and sterile printed page of doctors' jargon. They are wrong of course, I mean in the Quai d'Orsay. They didn't want to post me here at all, since doing so in their opinion would simply double the year's labor of whatever clerk[; *del.*]<—>who knows?<—>perhaps that same one still trying to charge off somewhere [your captain's commission. *del.*] <that aging captaincy.> But I shall save him this, anyway; one printed dossier-page might well contain my life, but it will have to be longer than the distance from Paris here. Because you may need me, I was about to say again but it will not be again because this was no need but a simple substitution <for> which <not I was needed but only> the immutable phenomenon of military seniority, [would have supplied *del.*] and the need which I will fill will be from the [seniority *del.*] inviolable seniority of hope [for man's condition *del.*] in the condition of man.—That's right,' he said, though the other had made no sound: 'laugh, at that dream, that vain hope too. Because you will not need me; remember, you dont even need to tell me for me to know where you are going: east, into the east, where the warning to and the hope for man's condition has always risen in the shape [and with the voice *del.*] of man; I was about to say "to find whom or what you will need to be your instrument" but I refrained in time. So you dont need to laugh at that, since I know better too: who go into the east only to return from it in the shape of the <living> hope [*insert.* .] [of man's condition *del.*] [man. *del.*] Though you may laugh now because I thought for a moment that you might go to Paris first. Then you can stop[, *del.*] <*insert.* .> <B *ov.* b>ecause I know better now. [The east, the morning[; *del.*], even the pagan dead li *del.*] [morning, which even the pagan *del.*]

———*A Fable,* ribbon typescript with autograph deletions, 1 page, numbered "428-A." Cf. pp. 282–283 of published version. (Leaf 7V)

['Yes sir,' the aide said.

['Not since *del.*] 'That was all evacuated in '14 sir.'

'Then she and her husband dont know [what *del.*] whether they have a farm or not,' the old general said.

'No sir,' the aide said. 'As of Monday morning St Meregould was somewhere between the lines.'

'Ah,' the old general said. Then he said again: 'Yes?' *del.*]

'Was, sir,' the aide said. (We need research here. The aide names a village which by 1919 will be on the railway branch running from Verdun to the main line between Chalons and Vitry-le-Francois or Bar-le-Duc, which the party bringing out the body of the Unknown Soldier will pass) 'That country was all evacuated in '14. On Monday morning (the village) was (behind or under) the enemy's front line.'

'Then she and her husband dont know whether they have a farm or not,' the old general said.

'No sir,' the aide said.

'Ah,' the old general said. Then he said[, *del.*] again: 'Yes?'

———*A Fable,* ribbon typescript with autograph deletions, 1 page, numbered [*ts* "116" *del.*] *ams* "441." Cf. pp. 290–291, 300–301 of published version. (Leaf 2V)

[ered while her closed hand fumbled at mine and she tried to speak, the hand still gripping, holding on to it even after I had given my word, my promise, my oath——'

The hand, the closed one, flicked, jerked, so fast that the eye almost failed to register, the object seeming to gleam once in the air before it even appeared, already tumbling across the vacant top of the desk until it sprang open as though of its own accord and came to rest—a small locket of chased worn gold, opening like a hunting-case watch upon the twin medallions, miniatures, painted on ivory. 'Not for you: for him *del.*],' she said. 'So you actually had a mother. You really did. When I first looked inside it that night, I thought the second face was your wife or sweetheart or mistress, and I hated you. But I know better now and I apologise for imputing to your character a capacity so weak as to have earned the human warmth of hatred. And so I did wait too late to produce it, after all. No. That's wrong too. Any moment would have been too late; any moment I might have selected to use it as a weapon the pistol would have misfired, the knife-blade shattered at the stroke. But at least it's not too late for him to receive it. At least you can tell me that. Come. Say it: 'At least it's not too late for him.'

'It's not too late,' the old general said.

'So he must die.' They looked at one another. 'Your own son.'

'Then will he not merely inherit from

———*A Fable,* ribbon typescript with autograph deletions, 1 page, numbered *ams* "441." Cf. pp. 290–292, 300 of published version. (Leaf 8V)

[while her [hand *del.*] closed hand fumbled at mine and she *del.*] [keep *del.*] [hide into what privacy we could that outraged betrayed abandoned and forsaken nakedness while her closed hand fumbled at mine and she tried to speak, the hand still gripping, holding on to it even after I had given my word, my promise, my oath——' *del.*]

The hand, the closed one, flicked, jerked, so fast that the eye almost failed to register, the object seeming to gleam once in the air before it even appeared, already tumbling across the vacant top of the desk until it sprang open as though of its own accord and came to rest—a small locket of chased worn gold, opening like a hunting-case watch upon twin medallions, miniatures, painted on ivory. ['No,' she said quickly. 'Dont touch it yet; it was not for you: for him. *del.*] ['Dont touch it yet,' she said. 'It wasn't for you, but for him. No, that's wrong too: it was for this. I must have known then, even at only nine, that I would have to bring it to you some day, just as I must have known even then how vain the bringing it to you would be *del.*] ['No,' she said, 'Dont touch it yet; it wasn't for you, it was for him. No, that's wrong too; it was already for you, for this, that day thirty [years ago *del.*] five years ago; I must have known then even at only nine that someday I would bring it to you, just as I must have known even then how vain the bringing it to you would be. A doom, a fate; in order to [bring *del.*] discharge the need to bring that locket to you, I must bring within your orbit the very object which would constitute the need *del.*]

———*A Fable,* ribbon typescript with autograph revisions, 1 page, numbered "441-B." Cf. pp. 291–292 of published version. (Leaf 9V)

beyond the range of threat or annoyance, would instead accomplish the exact opposite—and this by becoming—or what remained after our passage to Beirut—a dowry.).

'Because we could have stayed there, in our mountains, our country, among people who knew us and whom we knew. We could have stayed there at the inn, in the village where we were because people are really kind, they really are capable of pity and compassion for the helpless and weak because it is pity and compassion and the helpless and weak are helpless and weak and people though of course you cannot, dare not believe that: who can, dare believe only that people are to be bought and led and used for a purpose and then thrown away. We did stay there for almost ten years. We worked of course, at the inn—the kitchen, with the milk cows: in [the village too *del.*]—for—the village too; already Marya had a way with unmartial creatures such as cows and geese which were content to be simply cows and geese and not lions or stags. But then so would we have worked at home: which was where they for all their kindness, perhaps because of the kindness, tried to persuade us to return. But not I, not me: mine was the curse; I wearing that secret [locket *del.*] <token> now, not to remember and cherish, no tender memento of plighted devotion and faith but lying against my secret flesh beneath by dress like a brand, a fever, a goad driving me (and him too since I was his mother now) on westward where she herself was facing when she drew her last breath, on to wherever it was that I must go dragging them both behind me (oh yes, a mother already at nine and ten and eleven and on to nineteen in Beirut when I found

———*A Fable,* ribbon typescript with autograph revisions, 1 page, numbered "441-C." Cf. pp. 292–293 of published version. (Leaf 10V)

them a father too, not only to an infant brother but an idiot sister two years my senior)—to wherever and whatever that spot would be where the brand, the fever could be extinguished and assuaged—France: a word, a name <a designation> significant yet unfoundationed like the ones for grace or [purity *del.*] Tuesday or quarantine, bizarre and infrequent not just to us but to the dour and ignorant people among whom, orphaned and homeless, we had found haven until soon we were known to the whole village, that whole other valley from our own native one on which we had all three turned our backs, with interest and curiosity but with a little of pride too as the the [*sic*] three little Franchini: the three who were going to—on their way—dedicated for—France as others might be to some distant and irrevocable condition or state like a nunnery or [hypnosis *del.*]: <the top of Mount Everest:> not to heaven; everyone believes he will be on his way there just as soon as he has time to set seriously about it: but rather some more peculiar and individual and esoteric place to which no one really wants to go save in idle theory yet which reflects a certain communal glory on all who witnessed the departure or its preparations.

'Yes, I. To bring you [the locket *del.*] <the token>, I must bring the reason for it too; to need to bring you [the locket *del.*] <the token>, I must bring with me into your orbit the very object [which *del.*] [whose need only this locket could serve. No, worse: *del.*] which would constitute that need. No, worse: by bringing into your orbit the object whose need only this [locket *del.*] <token> could serve, I myself [would *del.*] created the need which [only *del.*]the [locket *del.*] <token>, the last cast I would have, would be incapable of discharging. Bringing them both of

———*A Fable,* ribbon typescript with autograph revisions, 1 page, numbered "441-K." Cf. p. 297 of published version. (Leaf 11V)

['Yes, he was free of you now. That is, you were free of him since he would be the one who had better fear. Because if any minuscule of threat to you remained in his capacity he [c *del.*]<w>ould [cure *del.*] <rid> himself of it now by the oldest and most immemorial of methods: a wife: responsibility: so many physical responsibilities to discharge that he would have no time over to dream of his moral rights capacity, he would rid himself of it now by the oldest and [most *del.*] surest [way *del.*] method of all: responsibility. *del.*]

'Yes, [I thought *del.*] he was free of you at last, or so I thought. Or you were free of him that is, since he was the one [of the two of you *del.*] who had better be afraid. [Because *del.*] <I *ov.* i>f any minuscule of [threat to you *del.*] <danger still> remained [still *del.*] in him [yet *del.*], <to you,> he [would cure *del.*] himself [of *del.*] <would eradicate> that [now *del.*] by the [oldest and *del.*] surest method of all: <marriage:> by [acquiring to *del.*] <burdening> himself so much [physical *del.*] <physical> responsibility [that he would have no time over to *del.*] [<to> *del.*] [to keep him physically busy *del.*] that he would have no time over to dream of his moral [rights *del.*] rights: a grown man now and a French citizen, he could, would take to himself a wife—a family, children: that strongest and most indissoluble bond of all to anneal [him to *del.*] <him> harmless forevermore to his present and commit him irrevocably to his future and cauterise him inevictably from the griefs and anguishes (of which he had none in the sense I meant because he still had never heard of you) of his past. But I was wrong as always in regard to you, wrong steadily and constantly and forever in all my ideas relating to what I thought you thought or felt or feared from him; this time most wrong of all since apparently [to your fear equipping with *del.*]

———*A Fable,* ribbon typescript with autograph interlineation, 1 page, unnumbered. Cf. p. 298 of published version. (Leaf 5V)

ts [ing twice the [conditions *del.*] <candidates> we proposed and in such way that we could never tell if it was the candidate or the condition he said no to. And so perhaps it was both of them: your son indeed who had inherited both from you: the repudiation of the second and the choicy choosing of the first: who had been created not in marriage and then in passion but lacking the one so that the second had to be enough because it was all, and he in his turn felt, desired, believed that he deserved, no less to match his own inheritance with.

'And wrong here too, even in this: as if he were your son indeed although as far as I knew then he didn't even know that you existed: who demanded not even revenge but vengeance: declining refusing the two brides we picked [for *del.*] as not just solvent but virtuous too and still in that way I spoke of which was still not so much refusal of the candidate as negation of the state, so that we only thought it was not just now: not for always; that he still wanted merely a little more of that young man's tieless and bachelor freedom which he had regained but yesterday when he doffed the uniform *del.*]

ams< [['But he refused them. *del.*] Or was it even worse than that to you: your own son truly, demanding not even revenge on you but vengeance:

~~Yes, he was free of you now. That is, you were free of him since he would be the one who had better fear. Because if any minuscule of threat to you remained in~~ his ~~capacity he could cure~~ [would rid] ~~himself of it now by the oldest and most immemorial of methods: a wife: responsibility: so many physical responsibilities to discharge that he would have no time over to dream of his moral rights capacity, he would rid himself of it now by the oldest and surest way method of all: responsibility.~~

'Yes, ~~I thought~~ he was free of you at last, or so I thought. Or you were free of him that is, since he was the one of ~~...~~ who had better be afraid. ~~Because~~ If any minuscule of ~~threat to you~~ [danger] remained ~~...~~ [still] in him ~~yet~~ [to you], he ~~would cure~~ [would eradicate] himself ~~of~~ that ~~now~~ by the ~~oldest and~~ surest method of all: [marriage:] by ~~acquiring to~~ [burdening] himself so much ~~physical~~ [physical] responsibility ~~that he would have no time over to~~ [to] ~~to keep him physically busy~~ that he would have no time over to dream of his moral ~~rights~~ rights: a grown man now and a French citizen, he could, would take to himself a wife---a family, children: that strongest and most indissoluble bond of all to anneal ~~him to~~ [him] harmless forevermore to his present and commit him irrevocably to his future and cauterise him inevictably from the griefs and anguishes (of which he had none in the sense I meant because he still had never heard of you) of his past. But I was wrong as always in regard to you, wrong steadily and constantly and forever in all my ideas relating to what I thought you thought or felt or feared from him; this time most wrong of all since apparently ~~to your fear equipping with~~

441-K.

45. Manuscript page of *A Fable*, c. 1952

refusing the two we had picked who were not only solvent but virtuous. In this one here who had not even sold the one for the other but in traficking [*sic*] one had trafficked them both away? I didn't know. We didn't know; only that he had refused, declined, and still in that way I told you of [so that we *del.*] less of refusal than negation: so that we merely thought he was not ready yet, still wanting a little more of that young man's bachelor and tieless freedom which he had only regained [yesterday *del.*]—regained? found—yesterday when he doffed the uniform. So we could wait too *del.*] [*blank space*] make room for your victories. So he had lost his home. We all had of course but he was the primary one because he had been the reason for the home—when suddenly I—we, Marya and I—believed that we saw that [clearly too *del.*] [too. You had not dispossessed him of his home; you certainly had not instigated the invasion which drove us—him—out of it, but already all France, all helpless, embattled Europe (ah yes, Germany the enemy too: you have proved even to them now to respect you anyway) was full of your name, your face—it's [*sic*]—our—freedom's saviour: so who to say if you had *del.*] too. Not that you had dispossessed him of his home; you certainly had not instigated the invasion which drove him—us—out of it.>

———*A Fable,* ribbon typescript with autograph and typescript revisions, 1 page, unnumbered. Cf. pp. 298–299 of published version. (Leaf 6V)

negation, as though your own son truly, demanding not even revenge but vengeance. But we—I—didn't know that yet: he just refused, declined and so we only thought that marriage for him was not just now, not for always; that he still wanted merely a little more of [a *del.*] <the> young man's tieless and bachelor freedom which he had only found again yesterday when he doffed that uniform. So we could wait too, and we did, and more time passed but we still thought there was enough of it since marriage lasts long enough to have plenty of room for time behind it. Then [suddenly *del.*]—suddenly: with no warning to us who knew only bread[, not politics and glory *del.*] and work: not politics and glory—it was 1914 and whether there had been time [or *del.*] enough or [he had *del.*] not and he had been right to wait or not didn't matter. Because he didn't wait now either, not even for his class to be recalled but gone that first week still stinking of the mothballs. But even then he was no quicker, faster than we were; you know where the farm is—was (still is because it will have to be there in order to be the basis of what you will grant me or us or him) so I dont need to tell you where, nor how we left it either since a part of your trade is [getting *del.*] coping with the confused and anguished civilian homeless in order to have room for your victories

———*A Fable,* ribbon typescript with autograph and typescript revisions, 1 page, numbered [*ts* "52-A" *del.*] *ams* "512." Cf. p. 343 of published version. (Leaf 3V)

'Now turn and look at it,' the old general said. But he already had, was—down the declivity's black pitch to where the city lay trembling and myriad with lights in a bowl of night, thicker and denser than the stars in its concentration of anguish and unrepose as though all of darkness and terror had poured down in one wash, one wave to lie palpitant and unassuageable in the *Place de Ville*. 'Look at it, listen to it, remember it: a moment: then close the window on it. Disregard that anguish. You caused them [to suffer it but *del.*] <to fear and suffer but> tomorrow you will have discharged them of [it *del.*] <both> and they will only [need to *del.*] hate you: once for [having caused them the anguish, *del.*] <the rage they owe you for giving them the terror,> once for the gratitude they will owe you for [having relieved them of it, *del.*] <taking it away,> and once [because you will be *del.*] <for the fact that you are> beyond range of [both. *del.*] <either.> So close the window on that and be yourself discharged[, *del.*]. Now look beyond it. The earth, all half of earth as far as horizon demi-circles. It's dark of course but only dark from here; its darkness is only that anonymity

———*A Fable,* autograph manuscript with revisions, 1 page, unnumbered. Cf. p. 426 of published version. (Leaf 16)

saying in her bright serene and carrying voice: 'Sister! Here is the young Englishman come for the medal. There are 2 of them, coming up the lane.'

'A friend with him?' the [other woman *del.*] sister said.

'Not a friend,' [the *del.*] Marya said. 'This one is looking for a tree.'

'A tree? the sister said.

'Yes,' [the *del.*] Marya said. 'See him?

———*A Fable,* ribbon typescript with autograph and typescript revisions, canceled; 1 page, numbered "38." Cf. pp. 431–433 of published version. (Leaf 17R)

three of them[, *del.*] <now,> three bits <instead of two> of graved and symbolic bronze dangling from the three candy-striped ribbons, bright as carnivals and gaudy as sunsets, on the breast of the filthy dinner jacket as, [bra *del.*] facing them he braced the two crutches into his armpits and with the hand he still had, removed the ruined homburg in a gesture sweeping and invulnerable and clapped it back on at its raked angle and turned, the single leg once more strong and steady and tireless between the tireless rhythmic swing and recover of the crutches, [tireless and persevering *del.*] back down the lane toward where he had appeared in it, [tireless *del.*] <unwearyable> and persevering, the infinitestimal progress out of all proportion to the [tireless *del.*] fury of [the m *del.*] its motion, getting smaller and small [*sic*] with distance until he appeared <as though> fixed <against a panorama> in furious progressless unrest, not lonely: just solitary, invincibly single. Then he was gone.

'Yes,' Marya said. 'He can move fast enough. He will be there in plenty of time.'

† † †

It was a gray day though not a gray year[, *del.*]. In fact, time had not been gray since that day six years ago when the dead hero whom the quiet hatless crowds which lined both sides of the Champs Elysee and the dignitaries composing the cortege had come to honor, had driven adumbration from the face of Western Europe and indeed the western world. Only the day itself was gray, as though in dirge [for him to whom it owed *del.*]

———*A Fable,* ribbon typescript with autograph and typescript revisions, canceled; 1 page, numbered [*ts* "41" *del.*] *ams* "650." Cf. pp. 434–435 in published version. (Leaf 17V)

[Though they were not first because first behind the caisson *del.*] [and enduring arch crowned it, as though into immolation or suttee *del.*]

tatives of the republics, the uncovered crowd itself flowing in behind the last of them—up the avenue toward where the vast and triumphal and enduring arch crowned [its *del.*] <the> crest, as though into immolation or suttee.

It lifted toward the gray sky, invincible and impervious, to endure forever not because it was stone but as though because of its absolute and invincible rightness and symmetry, crowning the city; on the marble floor exactly beneath [the *del.*] its arched and soaring center burned the small perpetual flame above the forever nameless sleep of the unknown [soldier *del.*] fetched down five years ago from Verdun, the crowd flowing steadily and quietly to enclose it and the empty space facing it as the cortege halted and only the caisson came on until it too faced the arch and the flame, and stopped, the cortege shifting in hushed protocol into its place too, [and *del.*] becoming still too so that there was only silence and the gray day and that minute's thud of the distant gun.

Then a man stepped forward, in full dress and medalled too: the first man in France: poet, philosopher, statesman, orator, to stand for a moment bareheaded facing the caisson while the distant gun thudded another minute into eternity. Then the man spoke.

'Marshal,' he said[. *del.*] and waited for the day to grieve and another thud from the distant gun. Then louder this time, urgent; not peremptory: a cry: 'Marshall!' And still no answer: only the dirge of day, the dirge of France, the dirge of Europe and from beyond the seas too where [he had *del.*] he beneath the draped flag on the caisson had led men to

1171 "By the People," 1955, carbon typescript with autograph revisions, 26 pages, 11 by 8½ inches, unwatermarked. Signed in typescript on page 1: "William Faulkner / % Harold Ober, / New York."

In this copy of the story that was subsequently published in the October 1955 issue of *Mademoiselle,* Faulkner has altered by hand the name of the central character from "Yarbry" to "Snopes." Two pages of the typescript, 5 and 5-A, represent an advanced stage of composition (apparently a rewrite of the previous page 5) and thus carry the name "Snopes" instead of "Yarbry."

Faulkner reworked this material extensively when he incorporated it into *The Mansion* (pp. 294–321) in 1959. The original magazine version was reprinted in *Prize Stories 1957: The O. Henry Awards* and *40 Best Stories from Mademoiselle 1935–1960,* but it is curiously omitted from *Uncollected Stories of William Faulkner.*

BY THE PEOPLE

In the old days Ratliff's vehicle had been a Model T Ford two-seater, called a roadster then, with the tin turtleback removed and in its place a gable-roofed [box *del.*] wooden box like a biggish dog-kennel though painted to resemble a human house of two storeys, with two tiers of painted windows on each side, in each of which a painted housewife simpered across a painted sewing machine, the box itself containing the actual machine for which Ratliff was agent salesman and upkeeper. It could be seen enveloped in its own dust (our County was not paved then) not only on the highways but the remotest back roads too, or parked beside the mailbox before the remotest back-country dog-trot cabins, Ratliff (he was a slender man, not overly tall, who [had *del.*] despite his sun-burned face and neck and hands and wrists, had a workless, almost a white collar look to him, yet he could remove the machine and carry it to whatever spot the prospective client wished and then carry it back and lift [it *del.*] and insert it into its kennel single-handed) sitting in one of the circle of chairs in the shady yard, affable, bland, courteous, neatly shaved in his tieless faded perfectly clean blue shirt, while the ladies, come from both directions up at [*i.e.* and] down the road on the signal of his dust-cloud, tried the machine in turn.

Or (the dusty Model T) among the tethered wagons and saddle horses in front of country stores, Ratliff now [squatting among the whittling group along the gallery, among *del.*] one of the squatting whittling group along the gallery, among men now because he was a universal: among men a man, among ladies a gentleman; sitting among the guffaws now because there was that about him too: still affable, still bland, but discoursive now, with a humor which was not sardonic so much as tolerant, and an aptness which quite often was not just wit but wisdom too. Or in town, in Jefferson itself, the still dusty [1] Model T drawn up at the curb behind a Buick or Reo or Maxwell or (there was one in Jefferson even then) Packard, Ratliff in the parlor now among the antimacassars and bell-domed wax flowers and synthetic seashells while the doctor's or [L *del.*]<1>awyer's or merchant's or banker's wife tried the machine; or later, after supper, among the lawyers and merchants and bankers, not to mention the drummers, emissaries from the metropolitan outland itself, gathered in the chairs along the banquette of the hotel, affable (Ratliff), bland, courteous still, not exactly discoursive now but simply bearing his part in the conversation since he was indeed a universal: his diction still rather that of Varner's store in Franchman's Bend than Jefferson, the vehicle of his wit still that of his tieless state, but the wit itself and the wisdom which it did not always conceal was that of any man who had watched human folly yet still remained capable of believing in human aspiration.

Though that was in the old days, because our country was electrified now and what sewing machines ladies used now ran from wall-plugs or light-sockets—what machines they still used [now *del.*] because now they did not need to make their own and their children's and husband's [clothes *del.*] garments, buying them instead from the mail order; the R.F.D. carrier was now by proxy tailor and sempstress to rural America; time had passed, time and alteration and change: the Model T was now a vehicle of that popular make known to Ratliff (and all the rest of Mississippi which wore a necktie only on Sunday) as a Shivvy, with starter and electric lights and quickly demountable wheels—a pickup truck now because the miniature house was now twice as big and only from the upstairs windows did the painted woman simper across a sewing machine because in the lower ones, the parlor ones, what she faced was a painted organ, the house containing now not only the old sewing machine (out of loyalty perhaps or perhaps as a memento of the old time) but the organ too, its (their) new kennel so contrived that the roof folded back to one side and one wall to the other, [2] metamorphosing into a padded seat and a neat ladder leading to the ground, so that (to have removed the organ from the truck and then replace it singlehanded would have been more than our County would expect even Ratliff to be capable of) the prospect or client need only pick up her skirts and mount the ladder and sit on the padded seat to try the organ—a compact smallish one, pumped with foot pedals, 'parlor-size', the company which made it called it, adding 'suitable also for small or rural churches', manufactured by the Remish Musical Company of South Bend, Indiana, to whom Ratliff, as though forewarned of the day when electricity and the mail order business would strike the foundations of his old vocation from beneath his feet, had applied for the agency and to or for whom he had been so faithful or at least so industrious or anyway so beguiling that five years later half our County was dotted with them, whose owners boasted to each other not of owning organs but owning Remishes, making of the manufacturer's name a common noun and then, ten years later, an upper-case [one *del.*] designation: a small collection of houses near a small store a few miles from Frenchman's Bend designating itself suddenly a town and naming itself Remish; nor was that all: now, twenty years later, boy children from that section were bearing into puberty and even manhood Remish as their christian names.

And in Jefferson too, as time <passed—> —the progress which mechanised the country, and the war which drained the young people into aircraft and tank factories and army camps and Pacific [I *del.*]<i>slands, no more to return to the farms even with mufti buttonholes for the ruptured ducks, leaving the old people free enough and lonely enough to move in to Jefferson among the electric stoves and dishwashers, the Remishes dispossessed now by radio and television cabinets; oh yes, that was Ratliff too, he was agent for radio and TV now, whom time had once more devocationed or at least to the extent of altering his tools. Because that was all that alteration did: Ratliff himself unchanged by time or progress [3] or metamorphosis or anything else that morning when Uncle Gavin, apparently having found him or trapped or treed or bayed him somewhere on the Square, brought him (Uncle Gavin never invited or led anyone into the office: he brought them there as you put a cow or a horse into a stall) upstairs into the office. Not Ratliff: he was not changed at all, looking no different from what he had that day twenty and more years ago when I, about eight then, had first seen him—the same tanned out-of-doors face, bland, affable, courteous, incorrigibly bachelor, with his neatly-shaved face and neck and the neat tieless faded blue shirt which might have been the same one he had worn then, Uncle Gavin entering first and Ratliff not following so much as drawn along in the vacuum of Uncle Gavin's [passage *del.*] wake. And Uncle Gavin too, who was more than just a member of the same race and county and political party as Ratliff but rather as if he, Uncle Gavin, were the obverse of the very same die which had stamped Ratliff—the M.A., Harvard and Ph.D., Heidelberg (incorrigibly bachelor too and even still although when I came home in '43 on my last home leave for the Pacific, I found a new aunt), who by avocation was County Attorney of Yoknapatawpha County but whose true dedicated vocation was meddling in other peoples' business—not to discover the truth nor even the facts, because he said himself that he was not interested in either, nor do I think it was for the justice he occasionally found there and which he professed to be his aim; it was just to know *why* they did what they did or had done, and this not for the chance to moralise to me about it nor even to prove anything to himself, but just to know, from pure curiosity—coming into the room and swinging a chair out for Ratliff in passing on behind the desk, where he sat down and said,

'All right. Just what happened out there at that picnic that day?'

I knew what he was talking about. Who, that is, since he had been talking about little else all [summer *del.*] <spring> since this was election [4] year: the Honorable Clarence Eggleston Snopes, Member of the Mississippi Legislature—'Senator' Snopes to the people who for twenty-five years had been electing him steadily and unflaggingly to public office, first from a single Beat of our County, then from the County itself, and now (compounded by their spiritual or at least[, *del.*] political kin in the rest of the counties comprising our Congressional District) to the House of Representatives in Washington as soon as he notified them that that was what he wanted them to do. And why not Senator, since he had as much right to the implication of Statesman now as he would when, having found his way around Congress, he would notify them to elect him to the Senate itself—until last week, at the annual Varner's Mill picnic where by tradition our candidates always opened their campaigns, Snopes not only failed to appear on the speakers' platform, he disappeared from the scene itself even before dinner was served; and the next day word spread over the County that he had not only withdrawn from the race for Congress, he was even withdrawing from public life altogether when his present term in the State legislature was up.

He was a cadet (one of them) and, [since his advent into the *del.*] moving now in the metropolitan aura of [Jackson itself, *del.*] the State Capitol itself, almost a deified figurehead of a vast sprawling clan of a family or even tribe in the densely-populated southeastern part of the County, distantly kin by marriage to Uncle Billy Varner himself who was patriarch and undisputed chief of that whole section (the Snopeses had by now spread and overlapped into Jefferson, where one of them was president of the Merchants' and Farmers' Bank and was himself a local power[. But that was in Jefferson *del.*] in Jefferson. But that was Jefferson, and Uncle Billy Varner was absolute and supreme, emperor king arbiter and despot of every one who still lived or claimed to live in the [Frenchman's Bend section of Beat Four.), who (Snopes) as a young man had been leader of a roistering gang of cousins and toadies which fought and drank and beat Negroes and terrified young girls until (the story ran) Uncle Billy became irritated or exasperated enough to order the local J.P. to appoint Snopes his constable—whereupon [he *del.*] his, Snopeses [*sic*], whole life, existence, destiny, fate, found itself *del.*] [5] Frenchman's Bend section of Beat Four.), who—Snopes—as a young man had been leader of a roistering gang of cousins and toadies who fought and drank and beat Negroes and terrified young girls until (the story ran) Uncle Billy became irritated or exasperated enough to order the local J.P. to appoint Snopes his constable—whereupon his, Snopeses, whole life, existence, destiny, fate, found itself, became one and intact as the rocket finds itself and becomes one with its destiny at the first nudge, touch, taste of empyrean. [5-A]

Though that—metaphor, symbol, analogy, whatever it is—wasn't quite right. Because his career didn't go quite that fast, not at first anyway. At first it was almost like he was just looking around, discovering at first merely where he was, then in a kind of slow incredulous amazement at the vista opening before him; just amazed at first, before the exultation and the triumph began, at that limitless and incredible prospect. Because at first be even behaved himself. At first people thought that, having been as bad as he was with nothing to back him but the numerical unanimity of his old lawless pack, with the whole challengeless majesty of organised law to support him, he would be outrageous. But he wasn't. Instead, he became the defender of the civic mores and the public peace. Of course, the first few Negroes who ran afoul of his new official capacity suffered for it. But there was something impersonal even about this. Before his elevation he and his gang had beaten up Negroes as a matter of principle: not as individual Negroes nor even, Uncle Gavin said, as representatives of a race alien because it was black and hence enemy *per se,* but (Uncle Gavin said that [Yarbry *del.*] <Snopes> and his gang did not know this because they dared not know it, they could not have borne to know it) for fear of it, not because its representatives were black but because as a race it threatened their white economy of material waste by threatening it with obsolescence by their—the black man's—capacity which the white man had taught them: of being able to do more with less—less of tools, less of luxury, less of waste. But not now. Not [any more *del.*] anymore now. Now when he manhandled a Negro with the blackjack he carried or the butt of the pistol which he now officially wore, it was with a kind of detachment, as though he were using not the Negro's black skin nor even his human flesh but simply his present condition as a [flou *del.*] temporary flouter of the law, to reaffirm to himself ([Yarbry *del.*]) <Snopes> again just how far his official power extended and just how strong [he *del.*] it was.

Because they were not always Negroes. In fact, [6] one of the first victims of his new condition was the lieutenant who had been his second-in-command in the old gang; if anything, he was even more ruthless and savage in this instance because the man had obviously tried to take advantage of their old relationship; it was as though he, [Yarbry *del.*] <Snopes> had invested a kind of incorruptibility and integrity into his natural and normal instinct for [outrage and *del.*] violence and [anguish *del.*] physical anguish. So he had changed. And, Uncle Gavin said, since before his elevation into grace everybody had believed him incapable of it, now that he had changed the same ones believed at once that the new condition was for perpetuity, for the rest of his life. They still believed this even though they knew (it was no rumor: [Yarbry *del.*] <Snopes> himself bragged of it) that he had joined the Ku Klux Klan when it appeared in our County (it never got very far and didn't last very long; it was believed that it would not have lasted even that long except for him), taken in because they needed him or could use him or, as Uncle Gavin said, probably because there was no way to have kept him out since it was his dish as he was its—just one more integer, muscle-man, what in a few years people would begin to mean by 'goon', until Uncle Billy Varner's irritation or exasperation or choler made him constable, so that within a year the further rumor, whisper was that he was now an office[r] in the Klavern or whatever they called it, and in two years was himself the Dragon or Kleagle or whatever that was: who having been appointed by his grandmother's distant cousin-by-marriage to be custodian of the public peace, had now decreed himself arbiter of its individual morality too.

Which was probably when he saw for the first time clearly the long mounting corridor of his destiny, the broadening field for his capacity and how to use his natural talents: not to beat, [ma *del.*] hammer men into submission but to use them; not to expend them like ammunition nor fatten and consume them like hogs, but to use them like mules and oxen, with one eye constant [7] for tomorrow and next year; using not just their competence to vote but their capacity for passion and greed and alarm, as if he had been at the business of politics all his life instead of just a few years as a rural constable. And doing it by simple instinct, without preceptor or example, because Huey Long had not risen far enough yet into the national cognizance to be more than just a portent, a warning.

So when he announced for the State legislature, the County knew that he would need no other platform for election than that tenuous connection with

Uncle Billy Varner; in fact, the County decided [that his *del.*] immediately that his candidacy was not even his own doing but Uncle Billy's, whose irritation had now reached the point where the irritant must be removed completely from his sight. But they were wrong. He had a platform—which was the moment when some of us, a few of us, discovered that we had better fear him, tremble and beware. His platform was his own, it was one which only his amoral temerity would have dared because it left him apostate to his own constituency, so that his election was due only partly to Uncle Billy's influence, since the slim deciding margin of his vote came from people not only beyond the range of Uncle Billy's [power *del.*] autocracy, but from people who under any other conditions would have voted for almost any other [candidate first *del.*] member of the human race first: he came out publicly against the Ku Klux Klan[s *del.*]. He had been its Kleagle, Dragon, whatever the title was, right up to the day he announced his candidacy—or so the County thought. But now he was its mortal enemy, stumping the County apparently not to win an office but to destroy a dragon, winning his race by a scant margin of votes coming mostly from Jefferson itself—school-teachers, young professional people, women—the literate and liberal innocents who believed that decency and right and personal liberty would prevail simply because they were decent and right, who until now had had no political unanimity and had not even bothered always to vote until at last the thing they hated produced for them what [they *del.*] [8] in their innocence they believed to be a champion. So he went to Jackson not as a winning candidate for a county office but as dedicated champion of a cause, walking into the legislative halls in an aura half the White Knight's purity and half the shocked consternation of his own kind from whom he had apparently wrenched himself violently free. Because he did indeed destroy the Ku Klux Klan in our County; as one veteran ranking klansman said[. *del.*], 'Durn it, if we cant beat a handful of school-teachers and editors and sunday school superintendents, how in hell can we hope to [fight *del.*] beat a whole race of niggers and catholics and jews?'

He was swept through the portals of destiny and opportunity on the momentum of a delusion, a delusion which lasted through his first term or two while he remained quiet, simply watching and listening[, to learn parliamentary procedure *del.*]—to learn parliamentary proceedure the County thought, not discovering until later than what he was teaching himself was how to recognise chances, opportunities when they appeared—and which continued even after he began to talk, himself still the White Knight who had destroyed bigotry and intolerance in Yoknapatawpha County in the eyes of the impractical liberals who had elected him, long after [the *del.*] our County and the Stae too realised that he was preaching the same hatred of Negroes and Catholic and Jews which had been the tenets of that organization which he had destroyed in order to get where he now was; when the Silver Shirts were organised, he was one of the first in Mississippi to join it—not, our County now knew, having begun at last to get a kind of horrified inkling of what he portended or anyway aimed at, because of the principles which the Silver Shirts professed, but simply because he apparently considered it more durable than the old Klan which he had wrecked. That was it: to join things, anything, any organization to which enough people belonged, which he might compel or control or coerce through the emotions such as salvation or patriotism or simply political gravy; he had been a member of the [9] Baptist Church in Frenchman's Bend; he was now affiliated in Jackson, where, we heard, he now taught a Sunday school class; in Yoknapatawpha County we heard, with a shock of a kind of hysterical and terrified laughter, that he was contemplating resigning his seat in the Legislature to do a hitch in the army or navy and so be eligible for the American Legion.

Shock, because we realised now, not just how ruthless and limitless his ambition was, but that it had always been so; horror to only a few of us besides the original handful who had given him his majority. Because the mass of the country voters (yes, a lot in the town too) were now his frantic followers and disciples, ready to elect him to any office he wanted, right up to that ultimate one which (we now believed) was his goal: Governor of the State. That was what we all thought he wanted now. Huey Long now dominated the horizon of every Southern politician's ambition and aspiration. It seemed only natural that ours should pattern on him, so that even when [Yarbry *del.*] <Snopes> took as his own Long's Soak-the-rich battlecry, we still believed his sights were set no higher than the Governor's mansion. Because although at this time Mississippi had no particular rich to soak—no industries, no oil or gas—the idea of taking from the rich that which they deserved no more than he did, being no more intelligent or industrious but merely luckier, struck straight to the voting competence of every share-cropper and tenant-farmer not only in Yoknapatawpha County but in all Mississippi too; [Yarbry *del.*] <Snopes> could have been elected Governor of Mississippi on the simple platform of soaking the rich in Louisiana or Alabama, or for that matter in Maine or Oregon either.

So our shock at the rumor that he had contemplated for a moment taking over the Mississippi command of the American Legion was nothing to that one when we learned three years ago that the most powerful political faction in the State, the faction which was sure to bring in its man [10] as Governor, had offered to run Yarbry <Snopes> for lieutenant governor, and he had refused. He gave no reason though after his refusal he needed to give none because now all of us knew what his aim, his ambition, was and had been all the time: Washington, Congress; horror to only a few of us, a handful, because it was triumph and exultation to these who had already ridden his coat-tails up from the (comparatively) minor hog-trough at Jackson and who now would ride them up to that vast and limitless one in Washington itself. And to that few, that handful, there was more than just shock and horror: there was dread and fear too of the demagogue, the opportunist who had used and then discarded the Ku Klux Klan when it no longer served him, and the Baptist Church as long as he thought, believed it would or could or might serve him, who had used W.P.A. and N.R.A. and A.A.A. and C.C.C. and all the other agencies established in the dream or hope that the people should not suffer, or at least all suffer alike, in a time of economc crisis and fear, either for them or against them as the political breeze indicated since he turned against the very party which fathered them as soon as he decided he could better himself by defalcation, ringing the halls which had once echoed the voices of true statesmen and humanitarians with his own voice full of racial and religious and economic intolerance (once the strongest plank in his platform was soaking the rich; now the loudest one was the menace of organised labor), not from conviction but simply for the votes which would serve his will for aggrandisement and power, with nothing now to stand between him and Washington itself but the political [descendan *del.*] heirs of the handful of innocents who had taken him at face value twenty years ago when they believed he had destroyed the Klan in our County because it was evil and must not endure.

'Who wont be enough now, anymore than they were before,' Uncle Gavin said. 'Because he will only fool them again.'

'Then let's all of us jump in and stop him,' I said. 'You're County Attorney; you carry weight. You, and the others like you, [11] of your age—'

'No,' Uncle Gavin said. 'It's too late for us. We cant now. It was the ones of my age and generation who carried on the good work of getting things into the shape they're in now; maybe we are afraid to stick our necks out again. Or if not afraid, at least ashamed. No: not afraid: we are just too old. Call it we are just tired, don't have the confidence, dont believe in ourselves.'

'You can still believe in evil though.'

'Just to know it exists, to hate it, is not enough. You['ve *del.*]—somebody—has got to do something about it. But it wont be us; call it exhaustion, to save our faces. So it will have to be you and your generation. And you probably cant either. All you can probably do is, fail standing up.'

'Meaning the ones like me that dont have enough sense to know there are things you cant do?'

'If you like it that way,' Uncle Gavin said. 'All I know is, it wont be us.'

And some of us seemed to believe he was right. I mean, at least to the extent of believing that none of his age and generation were going to do anything to stop [Yarbry *del.*] <Snopes> from going to Congress, and so some of my age and generation would have to. Because one of the first to announce for office at all, announced against [Yarbry *del.*] <Snopes>—a man from one of the eastern countries in our district who was not even much older than me: only a little braver. He announced for Congress even before [Yarbry *del.*] <Snopes> did. But then [Yarbry *del.*] <Snopes> always did that: waited until the other candidate or candidates had announced, and he had taught us to know why now: that by doing that, waiting to be the last, he did not even [have] to invent a platform because by that time his opponents had supplied him with one. As this one did in his turn, [Yarbry *del.*] <Snopes> using him in his turn, using his valor as an instrument to defeat him with. [12]

His name was Devries. In 1941 he was a second lieutenant in the National Guard infantry; in 1948 when he got back home he was a major with enough ribbons to make a four-in-hand tie which he had acquired while commanding Negro troops, having been posted to Negro troops by some brass-hatted theorist in Personnel probably, under the premise that, being a Southerner, Devries would 'understand' Negroes; and (Devries) commanded them well for that reason: that, being a Southerner, he knew that no white man understood Negroes so long as the white man compelled the Negro to be first a Negro and only then a man, since this, the impenetrability, was the Negro's only defence for survival. Then in 1951 he went to Korea, once more to command troops containing Negroes, and came out this time a full colonel, with next to the last ribbon and a [work *del.*] mechanical leg and now on his way to Washington to get the last ribbon, the top one, the tale about that being how he finished his tour and was already posted stateside when the general pinned the next to the last medal on him, but instead he dropped the medal into his [dufflebag *del.*] foot-locker and put back on the battle fatigues and worried them until they let him go back up once more and one night he turned the rest of the regiment over to the exec. and with a Negro sergeant <and a runner> crawled out to where [th *del.*] what remained of the other battalion had been trapped by a barrage [in *del.*] and was under attack in a ravine, and sent them back with the runner and he and the sergeant held off one attack single-handed until the men were clear, then he, Devries, was carrying the sergeant back when he was hit too and this time a hulking giant of an Arkansas cottonfield hand crawled out and picked them both up and brought them in and when he came out of the other with his remaining leg he worried enough people enough until they sent for the field hand and he had the nurse dig the medal out of the foot-locker and said to the field hand: 'raise me up, you big bastard' and the Negro did so and Devries pinned the medal on him. [13]

That was who was going to run against [Yarbry *del.*] <Snopes> for Congress, and now it was us, the ones of my age and time, who felt the exultation, who had been soldiers too in that decade between 1942 and 1952, as well as the ones who had soldiers in 1917 and [–18 *del.*] '18 and found out that the earth extended a little further than the Yoknapatawpha Counties; Devries would have us, the weight of the veterans' organizations the possibility of which [Yarbry *del.*] <Snopes> himself had toyed with for a moment years ago and then dismissed as not worth the effort; and not only us but the uncoordinated political innocents who had nothing but the belief that demagoguery and intolerance and bigotry and opportunism must not endure, whom [Yarbry *del.*] <Snopes> had betrayed twenty years ago; triumph and exultation too until Uncle Gavin said: 'No. You're wrong. You cant beat him—it. You think you are merely faced with a situation. You are not. You are preparing to beat your brains out against one of the foundation stones of our national character itself: the premise that politics and political office are not the method by which we can govern ourselves in peace and security and support our place in the family of nations with dignity and honor, but instead are our national refuge for our incompetents who have failed at everything else to make a living for themselves and their families. The surest way to be elected to office in America is to have seven or eight children and to have lost your [leg *del.*] arm or leg in a sawmill accident, both of which—the reckless optimism which begot seven or eight children with nothing to support them by but a sawmill, and the incredible ineptitude which put an arm or a leg in range of a moving saw—should have damned you. No, you cant beat him, not him, not the Honorable [Homer X Yarbry *del.*] <Clarence Eggleston Snopes>. He will be elected to Congress for the simple reason that if he fails there is nothing else he can do, and Uncle Billy Varner and the rest of his vast interlocking kin have no intention whatever of [suppo *del.*] boarding and feeding him for the rest of his life. You will see.' [14]

So again it looked like Uncle Gavin was right. [Yarbry *del.*] <Snopes> still had not announced his candidacy. We knew why; we simply could not for-guess how he intended to use Devries' past for his, [Yarbry's *del.*] <Snopeses [*sic*]>, platform. We were not long in doubt; also, we realised how much he actually was to be feared; I mean in his capacity to manipulate men. Because this time he did not even leap forth and declare himself a champion. This time he forced, compelled, the ones whose champion he was going to offer himself to be, to come and beg him to be the champion—and more: not just to be the knight but actually to name and establish the cause. Though we still didn't know just how he did it: only that suddenly the whole Country knew that he was <not only> not going to run for Congress, he was going to retire from public life altogether, we, the ones of us who hoped that this was so, feeling the same shock of incredulous astonishment as did those who feared it was. So it was not just those who had followed him like sheep to the polls for twenty-[years *del.*] five years who hung on each word with which he explained his stand—words tinged even with a kind of mild surprise that explanations should be needed:

'Why, I'm an old man now (he was just past fifty) and it's time I stepped aside. Especially since you got a brave young man like this—this Captain Devries—'

'Colonel Devries,' they told him.

'Excuse me: Colonel Devries.—to represent you, to carry on the work which I have tried to do for the betterment of our folks and county—'

'You mean, you endorse him? you will support him?'

'Of course,' [Yarbry *del.*] <Snopes> said. 'Us old fellers have done the best we could for you. But now maybe what we need in Congress is young men. Of course General Devries—' [15]

'Colonel Devries,' they told him.

'Colonel Devries.—is a little younger maybe than I would have chose myself. But time will cure that. Of course he's got some ideas that I will never agree with [than *del.*] and that lots of other old fogies like me in Mississippi and the South will never agree with either. But maybe we are all too old now, out of date, and the things that we believed in and stood up and suffered for if necessary, aint true anymore and his new ideas are the right ones for [Mississ *del.*] Yoknapatawpha County and Mississippi and the South——'

'What ideas?' they asked. And that was it. He told them, and that was all: this man, Colonel Devries (nor any more inadvertent mistakes about his rank) who had become so attached to Negroes by commanding them in war that he had volunteered twice to return to battle in order to consort with them, who had risked his life to save one and then had his life saved in turn by another—a brave man (had not his government and country recorded and affirmed that by the medals it gave him, including that highest one in its power?) and an honorable one (that medal meant that too; did not its very name include the word 'Honor'?) what course would—could—dared he take, once he was a member of that Congress already passing laws to break down forever the normal and natural (natural? God Himself had ordained and decreed them) barriers between the white man and the black one——That was all; as Uncle Gavin said, he was already elected, the County and the District would not even need [the money *del.*] to spend the money to have the ballots cast and counted; that Medal of Honor which Congress had awarded him for risking death to defend the principles on which it was founded and by which it existed, had destroyed forever his chance to serve in the Congress which awarded the medal.

'You see?' Uncle Gavin said. 'What did I tell you?'

'But there must be something we can do—something somebody can do.' [16]

'Then do it,' Uncle Gavin said.

'Tell us how,' I said. 'You say if the old only could and the young only knew. Tell us. We'll do it.'

['Will you believe me if I tell you *del.*]

'If I tell you, will you believe me?'

'Yes,' I said. 'Tell us.'

'Join him. One of the first—no: the first, the absolute primary one—tenet and rule of politics is, If you cant beat 'em, join 'em.'

'*Join* him?' I said. 'Join *him?*'

'All right,' Uncle Gavin said. 'Then stay out of range of him and hope for a madman like Long's.'

'Meaning that no sane man, no man driven merely by principles of decency and dignity and right, can stop him?'

'Then you tell me,' Uncle Gavin said. That would be all; [Yarbry *del.*] <Snopes> wouldn't even need to make a campaign, a race; only to get up on the platform at Varner's Mill picnic and remind folks to be sure his name was spelled right on the ballots; Devries could have quit now, and there were some who thought he should have. Except that how could he, with that medal—all five or six of them—for guts and valor in the trunk in the attic or wherever he kept them. He even came to Jefferson, into [Yarbry's *del.*] <Snopeses [*sic*]> own bailiwick and made his [speech as if nothing had happened although we knew that he knew as well as we that Yarbry had beat him with that first speech which, a eulogy of his courage, had doomed him forever not just to the sixth congressional district of Mississippi but to all Mississippi and the whole South too as a lover of Negroes and hence subversive to our whole way of life. *del.*] [17] speech as if nothing had happened although we who came to hear him (the ex-soldiers, the liberals, the innocents, the women) knew that he knew that [Yarbry *del.*] <Snopes> had beat him with that first speech which, a eulogy of his courage, had doomed him forever not just in [the *del.*] one Congressional District of Mississippi but in all Mississippi and the whole South too, as a lover of Negroes and hence subversive to our [whole *del.*] <entire> way of life.

It was even sad: the man who had already been beat in advance by the very medal which would never let him quit and withdraw from the race. Then it was past sadness and had become pain to us who had to watch him. Because even those of us who never had had and, praise God, never would have a mechanical leg knew what it must have been—not in the back seat of a car around the Square or along the streets or even the highways themselves, letting the constituency, the votes walk out to the car to shake his hand as had become [Yarbry's *del.*] <Snopes's> [habit *del.*] custom as the long monotony of his success incremented, but walking, swinging that dead mechanical excrescence or bracing it to stand for an hour on a platform to [speak *del.*] speak, rationalising for an office which he already knew he had lost while still trying to keep all rumor of the chafed and outraged stump out of the face which ratiocinated, until at last we who would still vote for him dreaded having to see him and still keep all rumor of that stump out of our faces too, beginning to wish that the whole thing was over, wondering how we ourselves might [*illeg. del.*] end it in simple mercy, advance the election date and get it over so he could go home and throw the leg away, burn, destroy it, and be just peacefully maimed. Then the day approached for Uncle Billy Varner's picnic at his sawmill on the river, the day on which by tradition every candidate in our district announced himself, and we caught at that straw: that once [Yarbry *del.*] <Snopes> had declared himself, Devries might feel that he could withdraw his name and still save his face.

Except that he didn't have to. After the dinner was eaten and the speakers had gathered on the platform, [Yarbry *del.*] <Snopes> was not even [18] among them; shortly afterward the rumor spread that he had even left the grounds; the next day [th *del.*] word spread over the whole County that he had not only withdrawn from the race, he had announced his retirement from all public life; and now, a week later, until Gavin finally managed to run down or tree or bay Ratliff somewhere on the Square, and brought (not led: brought) him into the office and said, 'All right. Now just exactly what happened out there that day?'

'Out where what day, Lawyer?' Ratliff said.

'You know what I mean. At Uncle Billy's picnic last week when [old Yarbry *del.*] <Clarence Snopes> withdrew from the race for Congress.'

'Oh, that,' Ratliff said. 'Why, that was what you might call a kind of a hand of God, holp a little of course by them twin boys of Colonel Devrieses [*sic*] sister.'

'Colonel Devries' nephews?' Uncle Gavin said. 'He brought his whole family all the way over here from Minton County, to hear him announce for a race everybody knew he had already lost?'

'Why, now, that was kind of curious, come to think of it,' Ratliff said. 'Yes sir, it must have been that hand of God, because Colonel Devries sholy couldn't have knowed about that thicket, especially as he likely never seen Varner's Mill before in his life, could he?'

'Varner's Mill,' Uncle Gavin said. 'Thicket. Twin boys. Stop it now. Just tell me.'

'It was a dog thicket,' Ratliff said. 'I was about to say that of course you know what a dog thicket is, except that on second thought I reckon you dont because I never heard of one neither until I seen this one—a clump of gum and hickory and ash and pinoak switches on the bank jest above the mill-pond[, which *del.*] <so it will be> is convenient for the customers or members[, *del.*] like having a reservoy of fountain pen ink right next to the writing room—'

'Wait,' Uncle Gavin said. 'You said dog thicket.' [19]

'That's what I'm trying to tell you,' Ratliff said. 'A dog way-station. Kind of a dog postoffice, you might say. Ever dog in Beat Four uses it at least once a day, and ever dog in the Congressional District, let alone Yoknapatawpha County, has stopped there at least once in his life to leave his visiting card. You know: two dogs comes trotting up and takes a snuff and Number One says, "I be dawg if here aint that old bob-tail blue tick from up on Tallahatchie. What you reckon he's doing way down here?" "No it aint," Number Two says, "This here is that ere fyce that Eck Grier swapped Bookright for that half a day's work shingling the church that time, dont you remember?" and Number One says, "No, that fyce come after. This here is that old Tallahatchie blue tick." You know: that sort of thing.'

'All right,' Uncle Gavin said. 'That sort of thing. I understand. Go on.'

'That's all,' Ratliff said. 'That picnic and ever vote in twenty mile that owned a span of mules or a pickup or had a neighbor or a cousin that owned one, milling around the grove while Senator [Yarbry *del.*] <Snopes> circulated amongst them getting out the ballot until time would come to stand up on the platform in that ere pigeon-tailed coat and tell the folks where to put the X-mark, until some underhanded son-of-a-gun (I wont say scoundrel because it must a been Colonel Devries his-self since never nobody else knowed who them twin boys was, let alone what they was doing that fur from [home *del.*] Minton County—leastways not them foreign twin boys and that ere local dog thicket in the same breath) suggested to them boys what might happen say if someboby about that size would shoo the dogs away from that thicket long enough to cut off a handful of them switches down close to the ground and kind of walk up behind Senator [Yarbry *del.*] <Snopes> where he was busy getting out the votes, and draw them damp switches light and easy across the back of his britches-legs; light and easy, because apparently he [20] never even noticed the first eight or ten dogs atall until he felt his britches getting wet and broke for the nighest car, with them augmenting dogs strung out behind him like the knots in a kite-tail until he got the door slammed and the glass rolled up, them dogs still circling around the car like the spotted horses and swan-boats on a flying jenny, except that they was travelling on jest three legs, being already [cocked and *del.*] loaded and cocked and aimed you might say, until they finally found the owner of the car and got the key and druv Senator [Yarbry *del.*] <Snopes> home, finally outdistancing the last dog in about two miles, and stopped in the yard where they was safe at last since evidently the [Yarbry *del.*] <Snopes> dogs had went to the picnic too, while somebody went in the house and fetched out a pair of dry britches for Senator [Yarbry *del.*] <Snopes> to change into in the car. But even [the *del.*] <with> fresh dry britches he never went back to the picnic; likely he figgered that even then it would be too much risk and strain. And I reckon he was right; it would be kind of a strain, trying to keep your mind on withdrawing from a political race and all the time having to keep at least one eye over your shoulder for dogs.'

'So that was why he withdrew,' Uncle Gavin said.

'I reckon he figgered that to convince folks how they ought to vote him to Congrss and all the time standing on one foot trying to kick dogs away from the other leg, was a little too much to expect of even Mississippi voters,' Ratliff said.

'But why withdraw?' Uncle Gavin said. 'Nobody knew about it. Come to think of it, there were folks right there at the picnic that didn't know what had happened.' Then he stopped. He looked at Ratliff. He said: 'Or at least. . . .'

'That's right,' Ratliff said, 'Or at least. That was the trade.'[21]

'Trade?' Uncle Gavin said.

'It was likely that same low-minded scoundrel again,' Ratliff said. 'Anyway, somebody made a trade that if Senator [Yarbry *del.*] <Snopes> would withdraw from that race for Congress, the folks that had seen them dogs would forget it, and the ones that hadn't seen wouldn't never need to know atall.'

'But he could have beat that,' Uncle Gavin said. 'Talked himself out of that too—the man who used the Ku Klux Klan while he needed it and then betrayed it when they would help him too, who used and betrayed and made capital of everything else he ever touched, to be stopped or even checked at the height of his career just by a few dogs——'

'Oh, [Yarbry,' Ratliff said. *del.*] Senator [Yarbry *del.*] <Snopes>,' Ratliff said. 'I thought we was talking about Uncle Billy Varner.'

'Uncle Billy Varner?' Uncle Gavin said.

'That's right,' Ratliff said. 'It was Uncle Billy his-self that that low-minded rascal must a went to. Leastways, Uncle Billy his-self sent word back that same afternoon that Senator [Yarbry *del.*] <Snopes> had withdrawed; he never seem to notified Senator [Yarbry *del.*] <Snopes> atall. Oh yes,[' he said quickly,' *del.*] they told Uncle Billy the same thing you jest said: how it wouldn't hurt him; they even used your exact words about them dogs, only a little stronger. But Uncle Billy said No, that Senator [Yarbry *del.*] <Snopes> wasn't going to run for nothing in Beat Four.

'"But he aint running in jest Beat Four," they said. "He aint even running in jest Yoknapatawpha County now. He's running in a whole one-eighth of the State of Mississippi," and Uncle Billy said,

'"Durn the whole [ten *del.*] <hundred> eighths of Mississippi and Yoknapatawpha County too. I aint going to have Beat Four and Frenchman's Bend represented nowhere by nobody that ere a dog that passes cant tell from a fencepost."'

Now Uncle Gavin was looking at Ratliff. He had been [22] looking at Ratliff for some time. 'So he not only knew the twin nephews and the dog thicket, he knew Uncle Billy Varner too.'

Though apparently Ratliff hadn't noticed it yet. 'That's right,' he said.

'So it worked,' Uncle Gavin said.

'That's right,' Ratliff said. 'Something had to be done, so whos——' Then he stopped. He sat perfectly still while he and Uncle Gavin looked at each other.

'You started to say We,' Uncle Gavin said. 'Then you tried to change it to He. What you meant was I.' They looked at one another. 'Who told those boys about the dog thicket, V.K.?'

'Why Colone Devries, I reckon,' Ratliff said. 'He was a soldier in the War and Korea both; likely it wasn't nothing for him to think up a little political strategy.'

'Colonel Devries coped with snipers and night patrols and camouflaged attacks,' Uncle Gavin said. 'Not with demagogues.' They looked at one another. 'All right,' Uncle Gavin said. 'You started to say?'

'He used what he had, where he was,' Ratliff said.

'That's not enough,' Uncle Gavin said. They looked at one another. 'Sometimes,' Uncle Gavin said.

'Sometimes,' Ratliff said. Then he said, 'Well—' He rose, lean and easy, perfectly courteous, perfectly inscrutable; now he was looking at me. 'You mind that ere big oat field in the bend below Uncle Billy's pasture, Major? It stayed full of geese all last winter. Why dont you come out and shoot some of them when the season opens?'

'I'd like to,' I said. Then he turned to the door [23] and put his hand on the knob, only he stopped again and turned until he and Uncle Gavin were once more looking at each other. Then Uncle Gavin said, not loud:

'O Cincinnatus.'

'Good day, Lawyer,' Ratliff said.

'Good day,' Uncle Gavin said. Then Ratliff was gone, and now I looked at Uncle Gavin until presently he drew a sheet of paper to him and began to write busily on it, not fast: just busily while I watched him; I didn't speak very loud either:

'"So it will have to be you, the young ones,"' I said. '"Because it wont be us——"'

'Good day, Charles,' Uncle Gavin said, still writing.

'"—we are too old, too tired, dont believe in ourselves—"'

'Damn it,' Uncle Gavin said, 'I said Good day.'

So I got up too then, but I still didn't go. Then I gave him back something else he had said to me once: 'The United States, America—the greatest country in the world, if we can just keep on affording it. Only let "afford it" read "depend on God." Because He saved us this time, using Ratliff of course.

Only next time Ratliff may be off selling somebody a radio or an organ or a sewing machine, and God wont be able to put His Hand on him quick enough. So what we need is, to trust in God without depending on Him. We need to fix things so He can depend on us. Then He wont need to waste Himself having to be everywhere at once.' Then Uncle Gavin looked up at me—the face I had known and loved as long as I could remember. Oh yes, I loved and respected Father too, but Father just talked to me while Uncle Gavin listened to me, intent and quiet no matter how foolish what I was saying began to sound even to me, listening until I had finished, then saying: 'Well, I cant say yet whether it's reasonable [24] or not. But I know a good way to find out. Let's try it.' Not 'you try it' but 'let's us try it'.

'Yes,' he said. 'So do I.'

'Then good day,' I said.

'Good day,' Uncle Gavin said. [25]

1177 *Big Woods,* 1955, autograph manuscript in blue ink, 1 page, 13⅜ by 8 inches, Royal Writing yellow ruled paper. Cf. p. 104 of published version.

That was when he really knew that he was lost. First he had to find a place of secrecy when the sickness came. It was deep in the swamp, where he could leave no trail. At first his arm swelled so rapidly that the mud cracked off as fast as he plastered it on. But by the next night the swelling had stopped and even the sickness had begun to pass. And [that was *del.*] the arm began to smell. At first he thought of running again (he could have run again now) but that would never have [*illeg.*] the odor

IV

Non-Fiction

UPON RECEIVING the Nobel Prize for Literature on December 10, 1950, Faulkner became a world figure. From that time until his death in July 1962, he traveled the world as a cultural emissary and a recipient of literary accolades bestowed upon him by various countries. At home he engaged in public debate, most explicitly and persistently over the crucial issue of civil rights. Although he continued to produce fiction, he increasingly turned his energies to other forms of writing, notably the public address and the non-fiction essay.

Of the fourteen major speeches Faulkner composed beginning with the Nobel Prize Acceptance Address, all but one—the acceptance of the Silver Medal of the Athens Academy—are represented in the Brodsky Collection either in autograph manuscript, typescript, or mimeograph form. The texts of five of these are not sufficiently different from printed versions to merit republication, but the other eight, printed below, represent in-progress drafts, with revisions, or variant texts considerably different from those previously published. Of extraordinary significance in this regard is the Andrés Bello Award speech, which, until quite recently, was known to exist only in the Spanish text which Faulkner delivered in Caracas, Venezuela, in April 1961.

During this same period Faulkner also wrote at least eighteen essays that vary from personal impressions and a foreword to a collection of his fiction to semi-autobiographical pieces and polemics against the evils of racial inequality. Published here for the first time are variant texts (or portions thereof) of eight of these essays. Three other essay manuscripts in the Collection ("A Letter to the Leaders in the Negro Race" ["If I Were a Negro"], the review of Hemingway's *The Old Man and the Sea,* and the clarifying statement on *A Fable*) are identical or very similar to the published versions and thus have been omitted.

The Faulkner that emerges from a number of these non-fiction statements is a man of distinctive conviction and courage. Often as controversial as they are illuminating, in relation both to the mind of Faulkner and to the time in which he lived, these speeches and essays express an urgent concern and compassion toward man, the individual, whose very uniqueness and freedom are constantly being threatened by forces of oppression and mediocrity.

▶ Address to the Graduating Class, University High School, May 28, 1951, ribbon typescript with autograph revisions in blue ink, 3 pages, 11 by 8½ inches, Nekoosa Bond.

This typescript, the one which Faulkner read at the commencement exercises, then handed over to Phil Mullen, editor of the *Oxford Eagle,* appeared in the May 31, 1951 edition of that weekly newspaper. Mullen retained the typescript until 1982. See Louis Daniel Brodsky, "On the Road to the Mullen Holdings: A Faulkner Collector's Odyssey," in *New Directions in Faulkner Studies: Faulkner and Yoknapatawpha, 1983,* ed. Doreen Fowler and Ann J. Abadie (Jackson: University Press of Mississippi, 1984), 254–269.

Years ago, before any of you were born, a wise Frenchman said, 'If youth knew; if age could.' We all know what he meant: that when you are young, you have the power to do anything, but you dont know what to do. Then, when you have got old and experience and observation have taught you [what to do, *del.*] <answers,> you are tired, frightened; you dont care, you want to be left alone as long as you yourself are safe; you no longer have the capacity or the will to grieve over any wrongs but your own.

So you young men and women in this room tonight, and in [a *del.*] thousands of other rooms like this one about the earth today, have the power to change the world, rid it forever of war and injustice and suffering, provided you know how, know what to do. And so, according to the old Frenchman, since you cant know what to do because you are young, then anyone standing here with a head full of white hair, should be able to tell you.

But maybe this one is not as old and white as his white hairs pretend or claim. Because he cant give you a glib answer or pattern either. But he can[n *del.*] tell you this, because he believes this. What threatens us today is fear. Not the atom bomb, nor even fear of [the atom bomb *del.*] it, because if the bomb fell on Oxford tonight, all it could do would be to kill us, which is nothing, since in doing that, it will have robbed itself of its only power over us: which is fear of it, the being afraid of it. Our danger is not that. Our danger is the forces in the world today which are trying to use man's fear to rob him of his individuality, his soul, trying to reduce him to an unthinking mass by fear and bribery—giving him free food which he has not earned, easy [1] and valueless money which he has not worked for;—the [tyrants *del.*] economies or ideologies or political [parties, *del.*] <systems,> communist or socialist or democratic, whatever they wish to call themselves, the tyrants and the politicians, American or European or Asiatic, whatever they call themselves, who would reduce man to one obedient mass for their own aggrandisement and power, or because they themselves are baffled and afraid, afraid of, or incapable of, believing in man's capacity for courage <and endurance> and [honor and compassion *del.*] and sacrifice.

That is what we must resist, if we are to change the world [and save man. *del.*] <for man's peace and security.> It is not [the mass *del.*] men in the mass who can and will save Man. It is Man himself, created in the image of God so that he shall have the power and the will to choose right from wrong and so be able to save himself because he is [worthy *del.*] <worth> saving;—Man, the individual, men and women, who will refuse always to be tricked or frightened or bribed into surrendering, not just the right but the duty too, to choose between justice and injustice, courage and cowardice, sacrifice and greed, pity and self;—who will believe always not only in the right of man to be free of injustice and rapacity and deception, but the duty and responsibility of man to see that justice and truth and pity and compassion are done.

So, never be afraid. Never be afraid to raise your voice for honesty and truth and compassion, against injustice and lying and greed. If you, not just you in this room tonight, but in all the thousands of other rooms like this one about the world [2] today and tomorrow and next week, will do this, not as a class or classes, but as individuals, men and women, you will change the earth. In one generation all the Napoleons and Hitlers and [Alexand *del.*] Caesars and Mussolinis and Stalins and all the other tyrants who want power and aggrandisement, [or *del.*] <and> the simple politicians and time-servers who themselves are merely baffled or ignorant or afraid, who have used, or are using, or [will *del.*] hope to use, man's fear and greed for man's enslavement, will have vanished from the face of it.

834 Speech of Acceptance upon receiving the Legion of Honor, October 26, 1951, autograph manuscript (in French) in pencil, 1 page, 8¼ by 7⅜ inches, yellow ruled note paper, unwatermarked.

Whether this copy, which Faulkner gave to his editor, is the actual copy of the speech Faulkner delivered in New Orleans at the induction ceremony or a recopy made two weeks later is unknown. At the top of the sheet appears this penciled inscription: "For Saxe Commins / William Faulkner / 12 Nov 1951 / New York, N.Y." A facsimile of this document appears in *Princeton University Library Chronicle* (Spring 1957), and a transcription of the text, with slight alterations in spelling, punctuation, and paragraph indentation, was published in *Essays, Speeches & Public Letters.*

Un artiste doit recevoir avec humilite ce dignite conferré a lui par cette payes la quelle a ete toujours la mere universelle des artists.

Un Americain doit cherir avec la tendresse toujours chacque souvenir de cette pays le quelle a ete toujours la soeur d'Amerique.

Un homme libre doit g<u>arder avec l'esperence et l'orgeuil aussi l'accolade de cette pays la quelle etait la mere de la liberte de l'homme et de l'espirit humaine

1032 ["Commencement Address Given by William Faulkner at Pine Manor Junior College, Wellesley, Massachusetts, June 8, 1953"], ribbon typescript deleted with red grease pencil, 1 page, 11 by 8½ inches, Certificate Bond.

This four-line false start of the Pine Manor Commencement Address appears at the top of page "[70 *del.*] 392" of the manuscript of *A Fable*. See page 173.

What's wrong with this world is, it's not finished yet. It is not finished in the sense that it is not completed yet. It is not completed to that point where man can put his final signature

▶ "COMMENCEMENT ADDRESS DELIVERED BY WILLIAM FAULKNER AT PINE MANOR JUNIOR COLLEGE, WELLESLEY, MASSACHUSETTS JUNE 8, 1953," second issue, mimeographed typescript, 10 pages.

This issue of Faulkner's Pine Manor speech was apparently copied from the first printing (mimeographed typescript, 11 pages) distributed at commencement time by the Pine Manor Alumni Office, and rereleased by Random House c. mid-June 1953 for publicity and press syndication purposes. However, in this second printing (presumably in all copies) four passages have been deleted in pencil by Random House secretary, Jean Ennis, doubtless at the request of Faulkner, who was already revising the speech for *Atlantic Monthly,* which would publish it under the title "Faith or Fear" in its August 1953 issue. Thus, containing less text than the first issue, while as yet not incorporating the further stylistic changes made for the *Atlantic* text, this second issue represents an intermediary stage in the publication history of this document.

COMMENCEMENT ADDRESS DELIVERED BY WILLIAM FAULKNER
AT PINE MANOR JUNIOR COLLEGE, WELLESLEY,
MASSACHUSETTS
JUNE 8, 1953

What's wrong with this world is, it's not finished yet. [I don't mean in the atom-hydrogen bomb sense. *del.*] I mean it is not completed to that point where man can put his final signature to the job and say, "It is finished. We made it, and it works."

Because only man can complete it. Not God, but man. It is not only man's high destiny, but proof of his immortality too, that his is the choice between ending the world, effacing it from the long annal of time and space, and completing it. This is not only his right, but his privilege too. It rises phoenix-like from its own ashes with each generation, until it is our turn now in our flash and flick of time and space which we call today, in this and in all the quadrangular stations in time and space today and yesterday and tomorrow, where a handful of aged people like me, who should know but no longer can, are facing young people like you who can do, if they only knew where and how, to perform this purpose, accept this privilege, bear this right.

In the beginning, God created the earth. He created it completely furnished for man. Then he created man completely equipped to cope with the earth, by means of free will and the capacity for decision and the ability to learn by making mistakes and learning from them because he had a memory with which to remember and so learn from his errors, and so in time make his [1] own peaceful destiny of the earth. Then God stopped. It was not an experiment. God didn't merely believe in man, He knew man. He knew that man was competent for a soul because he was capable of saving that soul. He knew that man was capable of saving not only his soul but himself too. That man was capable of starting from scratch and coping with the earth and with himself both; capable of teaching himself to be civilized, to live with his fellow man in amity, without anguish to himself or causing anguish and grief to his fellows, and of appreciating the value of security and peace and freedom, since our dreams at night, the very slow evolution of our bodies themselves, remind us constantly of the time when we did not have them. He did not mean freedom from fear, because man does not have the right to be free of fear. We are not so weak and timorous as to need to be free of fear; we need only use our capacity to not be afraid of it and so relegate fear to its proper perspective. He meant security and peace in which to not be afraid, freedom in which to decree and then establish security and peace. And He demanded of man only that we work to deserve and gain these things—liberty, freedom of the body and spirit both, security for the weak and helpless and peace and freedom for all—because these were the most valuable things He could set within our capacity and reach.

[But almost at once we began to show that we were not going to do this. That apparently we really preferred to achieve our destiny in the litter of our own baseness. That we really liked belligerence and savagery and injustice, and would continue so right into our final twilight where the last whelming wave of oblivion would still leave in sight a few snatching hands, not [2] struggling with, fighting against their doom but still grasping and snatching at one last crumb of lust or greed long after the body itself, already finished and lifeless, could any longer even respond to it. *del.*]

During all this, the angels (with one exception; God had probably trouble with this one before) merely looked on and watched—the serene and blameless seraphim, that white and shining congeries who, with the exception of that one whose arrogance and pride God had already had to curb, were content merely to bask for eternity in the reflected glory of the miracle of man, content merely to watch, uninvolved and not even caring, while man ran his worthless and unregretted course toward and at last into that twilight where he would be no more. Because they were white, immaculate, negative, without past, without thought or grief or regrets or hopes, except that one—the splendid dark incorrigible one, who possessed the arrogance and pride to demand with, and the temerity to object with, and the ambition to substitute with—not only to decline to accept a condition just because it was a fact, but to want to substitute another condition in its place.

But this one's opinion of man was even worse than that of the negative and shining ones. This one not only believed that man was incapable of anything but baseness, this one believed that baseness had been inculcated in man to be used for base personal aggrandisement by them of a higher and more ruthless baseness. So God used this too. He did not merely cast this one out of heaven, to plunge for eternity through endless space with one last fading shriek, as He could have done. Instead, [3] He did more. [The ambitious and arrogant one wanted to be god and king; very well, let him. So God created a kingdom for him, a kingdom which would set off and frame his dark splendor like a black jewel in a casket of living crimson. Because God knew that, Alexander-like, that ambition would not remain there where it was already god and king of all in its view, and that sooner or later it would have to invade the earth, trying to find what Alexander in his turn would cry for. *del.*]

So God even used the ambition. He already presaw the long roster of the ambition's ruthless avatars—Genghis and Caesar and William and Hitler and Barca and Stalin and Bonaparte and Hughey Long. Then He did more. He not only used the ambition and the ruthless[ness] and the arrogance to show man what to revolt against, He used the temerity to revolt and the will to change what one does not like too. Because He presaw the long roster of the other avatars of that rebellious and uncompromising pride also, the long roster of names longer and more enduring than those of the tyrants and oppressors. They are the long annal of the man [*sic*] and women who have anguished over man's condition and who have held up to us not only the mirror of our follies and greeds and lusts and fears, but have reminded us constantly of the tremendous shape of our godhead too—the godhead and immortality which we cannot repudiate even if we dared, since not we can rid ourselves of it but only it can rid itself of us—the philosophers and artists, the articulate and grieving who have reminded us always of our capacity for honor and courage and compassion and pity and sacrifice. [4]

But they can only remind us that we are capable of revolt and change. They do not need, we do not need anyone to tell us what we must revolt against and efface from the earth if we are to live in peace and security on it, because we already know that. They can only remind us that man can revolt and change by telling, showing, reminding us how he has revolted and changed and, in the end, must. And, in that sense, they can even show us how to do it. But they can only show us how, not lead us, since to be led, we must surrender our free will and our capacity and right to make decisions out of our own personal soul. If we are to be led into peace and security by some individual gauleiter or gang of them, like a drove of sheep through a gate in a fence, it will not only be merely from one enclosure to another, through merely another fence with another closable gate in it, all history has shown us that it will be the gauleiter's enclosure and fence and his hand which closes and locks the gate, and *that* kind of peace and security will be exactly the sort of peace and security which a flock of sheep deserve.

So He used that split part of the dark proud one's character to remind us of our heritage of free will and decision; He used the poets and philosophers to remind us, out of our own recorded anguish, of our capacity for courage and endurance. But it is we ourselves who must employ them. This time it is you, here, in this room and in all the others like it about the world at this time and occasion in your lives. It is us, we, not as groups or classes but as individuals, simple men and women individually free and capable of freedom and decision, to decide, affirm simply [5] and firmly and forever never to be led like sheep into peace and security, but ourselves, us, simple men and women simply and mutually confederated for a time, a purpose, an end, for the simple reason that reason and heart have both shown us that we want the same thing and must have it and intend to have it [. *ov.* :] [to cast down that fence and gate and all the other fences and gates until no barrier to freedom and liberty and security remains save that single one which stipulates that freedom and liberty stop exactly at the point where the next individual freedom and liberty begins. *del.*]

To do it ourselves, as individuals, not because we have to merely in order to survive, but because we wish to, will to out of our heritage of free will and decision, the possession of which has given us the right to say how we shall live, and the long proof of our recorded immortality to remind us that we have the courage to elect that right and that course.

The answer is very simple. I don't mean easy, but simple. It is so simple in fact that one's first reaction is something like this: "Aw, shucks, if that's all it takes, what you will get for it can't be very valuable, very enduring." There is an anecdote about Tolstoy, I think it was, who said in the middle of a discussion on this subject: "All right, I'll start being good tomorrow—if you will too." Which was wit, and had, as wit often does, truth in it—a profound truth in fact to all of them who are incapable of belief in man. But not to them who can and do believe in man. To them, it is only wit, the despairing repudiation of man by a man exhausted into despair by his own [6] anguish over man's condition. They are the ones who can say, not *The answer is simple, but how difficult,* but instead rather *The answer is not easy, but very simple.* We do not need, the end does not even require, that we dedicate ourselves from this moment on to be Joans of Arc with trumpets and banners and battle-dust toward an end which we will not even see since it will merely be a setting for the monument of our martyrdom. It can be done within, concommitant with, the normal life which everyone wants and everyone should have. In fact, that normal life which everyone wants and deserves and can have—provided of course we work for it, are willing to make a reasonable amount of sacrifice commensurate with how much it is worth and how much we want and deserve it—can be dedicated to this end and be much more efficacious than all the loud voices and the cries and the banners and trumpets and dust.

Because it begins at home. We all know what 'home' means. Home is not necessarily a place fixed in geography. It can be moved, provided the old proven values which made it home and lacking which it cannot be home, are taken along too. It does not necessarily mean or demand physical ease, least of all, never in fact, physical security and ease in the terms of governmental benevolence. But it does mean security for the spirit, for love and fidelity to have peace and security in which to love and be faithful, for the devotion and sacrifice to have something worthy of the devotion and the sacrifice. Home means not just today, but tomorrow and tomorrow, and then again tomorrow and tomorrow. It means someone to offer the love and fidelity [7] and respect to that are worthy of it, someone to be compatible with, whose dreams and hopes are your dreams and hopes, who wants and will work and sacrifice also that the thing which the two of you have together shall last forever; someone whom you not only love but like too, which is more, since it must outlast what when we are young we mean by love because without the liking and the respect, the love itself will not last.

Home is not merely four walls—a house, a yard on a particular street, with a number on the gate. It can be a rented room or an apartment—any four walls which house a marriage or a career or both marriage and career at once. But it must be all the rooms or apartments; all the houses on that street and all the streets in that association of streets until they become a whole, in [*i.e.* an] integer, of people who have the same aspirations and hopes and problems and duties. Perhaps that collection, association, integer, is set in the little spot of geography which produced us in the image of, to be the inheritors of, their problems and dreams. But this is not necessary either; it can be anywhere, so long as we accept it as home; we can even move it, providing and demanding only that we are willing to accept the new problems and duties and aspirations with which we have replaced the old ones which we left behind us, will accept the hopes and aspirations of the people already there, who had established that place as an integer worthy of being served, and are willing to accept our hopes and aspirations in return for their duties and problems. Because the duties and problems were already ours: we merely changed their designations; [8] we cannot shed obligations by moving, because if it is home we want, we do not want to escape them. They are in fact still the same ones, performed and solved for the same reason and result: the same peace and security in which love and devotion can be love and devotion without fear of violence and outrage and change.

If we accept this to mean 'home,' we do not need to look further than home to find where to start to work, to begin to change, to begin to rid ourselves of the fears and pressures which are making simple existence more and more uncertain and without dignity or peace or security, and which, to those who are incapable of believing in man, will in the end rid man of his problems by ridding him of himself. Let us do what is within our power. It will not be easy, of course: just simple. Let us think first of, work first toward, saving the integer, association, collection which we call home. In fact, we must break ourselves of thinking in the terms foisted on us by the split-offs of that old dark spirit's ambition and ruthlessness: the empty clanging terms of 'nation' and 'fatherland' or 'race' or 'color' or 'creed.' We need look no further than. home; we need only work for what we want and deserve here. Home—the house or even the rented room so long as it includes all the houses and rented rooms in which hope and aspire the same hopes and aspirations—the street, then all the streets where dwell that voluntary association of people, simple men and women mutually confederated by identical hopes and aspirations and problems and duties and needs, to that point where they can say, "These simple things—security and freedom and peace—are not [9] only possible, not only can and must be, but they shall be." Home: not where *I* live or *it* lives, but where *we* live: a thousand then tens of thousands of little integers scattered and fixed firmer and more impregnable and more solid than rocks or citadels about the earth, so that the ruthless and ambitious split-offs of the ancient dark spirit shall look at the one and say, "There is nothing for us here," then look further, at the rest of them fixed and founded like fortresses about the whole inhabited earth, and say, "There is nothing for us any more anywhere. Man—simple unfrightened invincible men and women—has beaten us." Then man can put that final signature to his job and say, "We finished it, and it works." [10]

943 Pine Manor Commencement Address, mid-June, 1953, ribbon typescript with holograph revisions in blue-black ink, 2 pages, 11 by 8½ inches, Certificate Bond and Strathmore respectively, numbered "1" and "2."

This copy, which comprises virtually the first four paragraphs of Faulkner's address, reflects the revisions Faulkner made in preparing the speech for publication in the August 1953 issue of *Atlantic.* These two pages are quite possibly the first two pages of the copy from which Faulkner read at the commencement exercises. In the transcription below the asterisks indicate typescript revisions presumably made during the original stage of composition, as opposed to the autograph changes that Faulkner made when revising the speech for the *Atlantic.*

What's wrong with this world is, it's not finished yet. [I dont mean in the atom-hydrogen bomb sense. I mean *del.*] [I *ov.* i]t is not completed to that point where man can put his final signature to the job and say, 'It is finished. We made it, and it works.'

Because only man can complete it. Not God, but man. It is [not only *del.*] man's high destiny, [but *del.*] <and> proof of his immortality too, that his is the choice between ending the world, effacing it from the long annal of time and space, and completing it. This is not only his right, but his privilege too. [It rises phoenix-like from its own ashes [in *del.*] <with> each generation *del.*] <Like the phoenix, it rises from the ashes of its own failure with each generation,> until it is <y>our turn now in <y>our flash and flick of time and space which we call today, in this and in all the [quadrangular *del.*] stations in time and space today and yesterday and tomorrow, where a handful of aged people like me, who should know but no longer can, are facing young people like you who can do, if they only knew where and how, to perform this [purpose *del.*] <duty>, accept this privilege, bear this right.

In the beginning, God created the earth. He created it completely furnished for man. Then He created man completely equipped to cope with the earth, by means of free will and the capacity for decision and the ability to learn by making mistakes [because *del.*]* and learning from them because he had a memory with which to remember and so learn from his errors, and so in time make his own peaceful destiny on the earth. [Then God stopped. *del.*] It was not an experiment. God didn't merely believe in man, He knew man. He knew that man was competent for a soul because he was capable of saving that soul[. *del.*] <and, with it, himself.> [He knew that man was capable of saving not [1] only his soul but himself too. That *del.*] <He knew that> man was capable of starting from scratch and coping with the earth and with himself both; capable of teaching himself to be civilised, to live with his fellow man in amity, without anguish to himself or causing anguish and grief to [his fellows, *del.*] <others,> and of appreciating the value [of] security and peace and freedom, since [his *del.*] <our>* dreams at night, the very slow evolution of [his body itself, *del.*] <our bodies themselves,>* remind[ed *del.*]* [him *del.*] <us>* constantly of the time when [he *del.*] <we>* did not have them. He did not mean freedom from fear, because man does not have the right to be free of fear. We are not so weak and timorous as to need to be free of fear; we need only use our capacity to not be afraid of it and so relegate fear to its proper perspective. He meant security and peace in which to not be afraid, freedom in which to decree and then establish security and peace. And He demanded of man only that we work to deserve and gain these things—liberty, freedom of the body and spirit both, security for the weak and helpless and peace [and freedom *del.*] for all—because these [things *del.*]* were the most valuable things He could set within our capacity and reach.

[But almost at once we began to show that we were not going to do this. That apparently we really preferred to achieve our destiny in the litter of our own baseness. That we really liked belligerence and savagery and injustice, and would continue so right into our final twilight where the last whelming wave of oblivion would still leave in sight a few snatching hands, not struggling with, fighting against their doom but still *del.*] [2]

1002 "Foreword" to *The Faulkner Reader,* November 1953, ribbon typescript with autograph revisions in black ink, 5 pages, 11 by 8½ inches, Hammermill Bond (1, 1-A) and unwatermarked (2–4).

This typescript exhibits Faulkner's final set of revisions on this essay. Pages 1 and 1-A (in elite type) apparently represent an expanded version of a previous page 1 and are combined in this copy with pages 2–4 (pica type) of the earlier version.

My grandfather had a moderate though reasonably diffuse and catholic library; I realise now that I got most of my early education in it. It was a little limited in its fiction content, since his taste was for simple straight-forward romantic excitement like Scott or Dumas. But there was a heterogeneous scattering of other volumes, chosen apparently at random and by my grandmother, since the fly-leaves bore her name and the dates in the 1880's and -'90's of that time when even in a town as big as Memphis, Tennessee, ladies stopped in their carriages in the street in front of the stores and shops and clerks and even proprietors came out to receive their commands—that time when women did most of the book-buying and the reading too, naming their children Byron and Clarissa and St Elmo and Lothair after the romantic [heroes and her *del.*] and tragic heroes and heroines and the even more romantic [writers *del.*] creators of them.

He knew that
~~only his soul but himself too. That~~ man was capable of starting
from scratch and coping with the earth and with himself both;
capable of teaching himself to be civilised, to live with his
fellow man in amity, without anguish to himself or causing an-
others,
guish and grief to ~~his fellows~~, and of appreciating the value
our
security and peace and freedom, since ~~his~~ dreams at night, the
our bodies themselves, us
very slow evolution of ~~his body itself~~, remind ~~him~~ constantly
we
of the time when ~~he~~ did not have them. He did not mean freedom
from fear, because man does not have the right to be free of
fear. We are not so weak and timorous as to need to be free of
fear; we need only use our capacity to not be afraid of it and
so relegate fear to its proper perspective. He meant security
and peace in which to not be afraid, freedom in which to decree
and then establish security and peace. And He demanded of man
only that we work to deserve and gain these things---liberty,
freedom of the body and spirit both, security for the weak and
helpless and peace ~~and freedom~~ for all---because these ~~things~~
were the most valuable things He could set within our capacity
and reach.

~~But almost at once we began to show that we were not going to do this. That apparently we really preferred to achieve our destiny in the litter of our own baseness. That we really liked belligerence and savagery and injustice, and would continue so right into our final twilight where the last whelming wave of oblivion would still leave in sight a few snatching hands, not struggling with, fighting against their doom but still~~

2.

46. Canceled page of the Pine Manor commencement speech, 1953

One of these books was by a Pole. I dont even remember the spelling of his name, but I think it was Sienkiewicez—a story of the time of King John Sobeiski, when the Poles, almost single-handed, kept the Turks from over-running central Europe. This one, like all books of that period, at least the ones my grandfather owned [all his *del.*] <had a> preface[s *del.*], <a> foreword[s *del.*]. I never read <any> of them; I was too eager to get on to what the people themselves were doing and anguishing and triumphing over. But I did read the foreword in this one, the first one I ever took time to read; I dont know why now. It went something like this:

This book was written at the expense of considerable effort, to uplift men's hearts [. *del.*] [1] and I thought: *What a nice thing to have thought to say.* But no more than that. I didn't even think, *Maybe some day I will write a book too and what a shame I didn't think of that first so I could put it on the front page of mine.* Because I hadn't thought of writing books then. The future didn't extend that far. This was [1-A] 1915 and -16, I had seen an aeroplane and my mind was filled with names: Ball, and Immelman and Boelcke, and Guynemer and Bishop, and I was waiting, biding, until I would be old enough or free enough or anyway could get to France and become glorious and beribboned too.

Then that had passed[, *del.*]. [I *ov.* i]t was 1923 and I wrote a book and discovered that my doom, fate, was to keep on writing books: not for any exterior or ulterior purpose: just writing the books for the sake of writing the books; obviously, since the publisher considered them worth the financial risk of being printed, someone would read them. But that was unimportant too as measured against the need to get them written, though naturally one hope[d *ov.* s] that who read them would find them true and honest and even perhaps moving. Because one was too busy writing the books <during the time> while the demon which drove him still considered him worthy of, deserving of, the anguish of being driven, while the blood and glands and flesh still remained strong and potent, the heart and the [comprehension *del.*] <imagination> still remained undulled to follies and lusts and heroisms of men and women; still writing the books because they had to be written after the blood and glands began to slow and cool a little and the heart began to tell him, *You dont know the answer either and you will never find it,* but still writing the books because the demon was still kind: only a little more severe and unpitying: until suddenly one day he saw that that [old half-forgotten Pole *del.*] [2] old half-forgotten Pole had had the answer all the time.

To uplift man's heart; the same for all of us: for the ones who are trying to be artists, the ones who are trying to write simple entertainment, the ones who write to shock, and the ones who are simply escaping themselves and their own private anguishes.

Some of us dont know that this is what we are writing [of *del.*] for. Some of us will know it and deny it, lest we be accused and self-[condemned *del.*] convicted and -condemned of sentimentality, which people nowadays for some reason are ashamed to be tainted with; some of us seem to have curious ideas of just where the heart is located, confusing it with other and baser glands and organs and activities. But we all write for this one purpose.

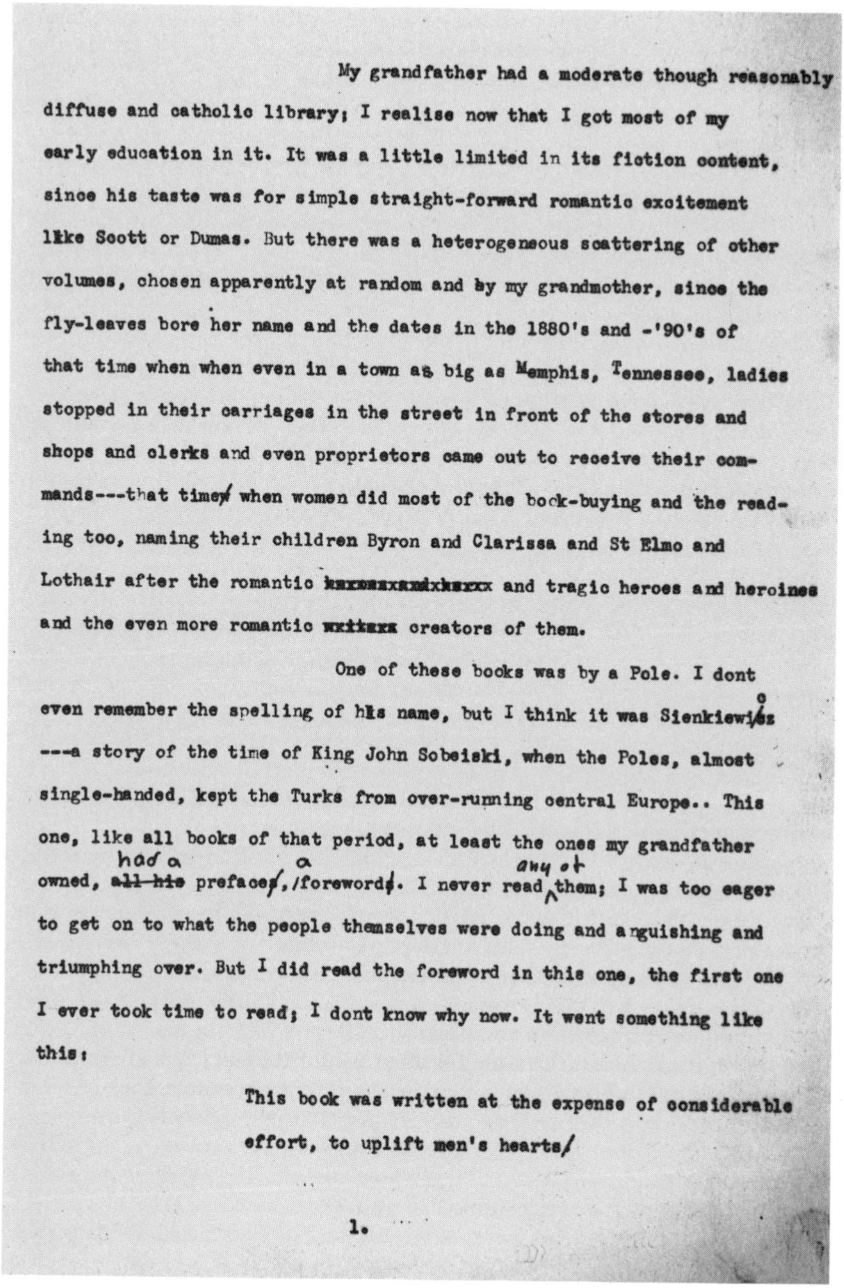

My grandfather had a moderate though reasonably diffuse and catholic library; I realise now that I got most of my early education in it. It was a little limited in its fiction content, since his taste was for simple straight-forward romantic excitement like Scott or Dumas. But there was a heterogeneous scattering of other volumes, chosen apparently at random and by my grandmother, since the fly-leaves bore her name and the dates in the 1880's and -'90's of that time when when even in a town as big as Memphis, Tennessee, ladies stopped in their carriages in the street in front of the stores and shops and clerks and even proprietors came out to receive their commands---that time when women did most of the book-buying and the reading too, naming their children Byron and Clarissa and St Elmo and Lothair after the romantic ~~xxxxxxxxxxxxx~~ and tragic heroes and heroines and the even more romantic ~~xxxxxx~~ creators of them.

One of these books was by a Pole. I dont even remember the spelling of his name, but I think it was Sienkiewicz---a story of the time of King John Sobeiski, when the Poles, almost single-handed, kept the Turks from over-running central Europe.. This one, like all books of that period, at least the ones my grandfather owned, ~~all his~~ had a preface, a foreword. I never read any of them; I was too eager to get on to what the people themselves were doing and anguishing and triumphing over. But I did read the foreword in this one, the first one I ever took time to read; I dont know why now. It went something like this:

This book was written at the expense of considerable effort, to uplift men's hearts/

1.

47. Typescript of opening of "Foreword" to *The Faulkner Reader*, 1953

This does not mean that we are trying to change man, improve him, though this is the hope—maybe even the intention—of some of us. On the contrary, in its last analysis, this hope and desire to uplift man's heart is completely selfish, completely personal. He would lift up man's heart for his own benefit because in that way he can say No to death. He is saying No to death for himself by means of the hearts which he has [uplifted *del.*] hoped to uplift, or even by means [to *del.*] of the mere base glands which he has disturbed to that extent where they can say No to death on their own account by knowing, realising, having been told and believing it: *At least we are not vegetables[;* the *del.*] [3] *because the hearts and glands capable of partaking in this excitement are not those of vegetables, and will, must, endure.*

So he who, from the isolation of cold impersonal print, can engender this excitement, himself partakes of the immortality which he has engendered. Some day he will be no more, which will not matter then, because isolated and itself invulnerable in the cold print remains that [which *del.*] capable of engendering still the old deathless excitement in hearts and glands whose owners and custodians are generations from even the air he breathed and anguished in; if it was capable once, he knows that it will be capable and potent still long after there remains of him only a dead and fading name. [4]

996 "Mississippi," 1954, autograph manuscript in blue ink, 1 page, unnumbered, on torn fragment 10 by 8½ inches, unwatermarked.

This manuscript, the text of which corresponds to paragraphs 9–13 of the published essay, appears to be an early version, quite possibly the first, of this section of the work that appeared in the April 1954 issue of *Holiday.* The bottom left and the bottom right portions of the leaf have been torn away.

So that this happened: not much money in Mississippi then (1901 & 2 & 3 & 4) so that Santa Claus was only at Xmas time, not like now, and for the rest of the year children played with what they could make or find or contrive, the indomitable old women still holding together a few of the old house slaves, women too who, like the white ones, declined, refused, to give up the old ways, the child himself remembering one, <Caroline> free these many years but who had declined to leave, to him at that time older than God himself, who called his grandfather 'colonel' but still called the child's father and brother and sister by their christian names: [Caroline *del.*]: a matriarch with a score of descendants (and probably that many more whom she had outlived), one of them a boy too, whether her grandson or great grandson even she did not remember, born in the same week with the child and both bearing the same [name *del.*] (the white boy's grandfather's) name, suckled at the same black breast and sleeping and eating together and playing together the game which was the most important thing the boy knew since at that time, at 4 & 5 & 6, his [life was *del.*] world was a female world and he had heard nothing else since he could remember: playing over again in miniature the war, the old irremediable and inescapable and escapeless battles: Corinth and Vicksburg and Brice's Crossroads, which was not too far from where the boy (both of

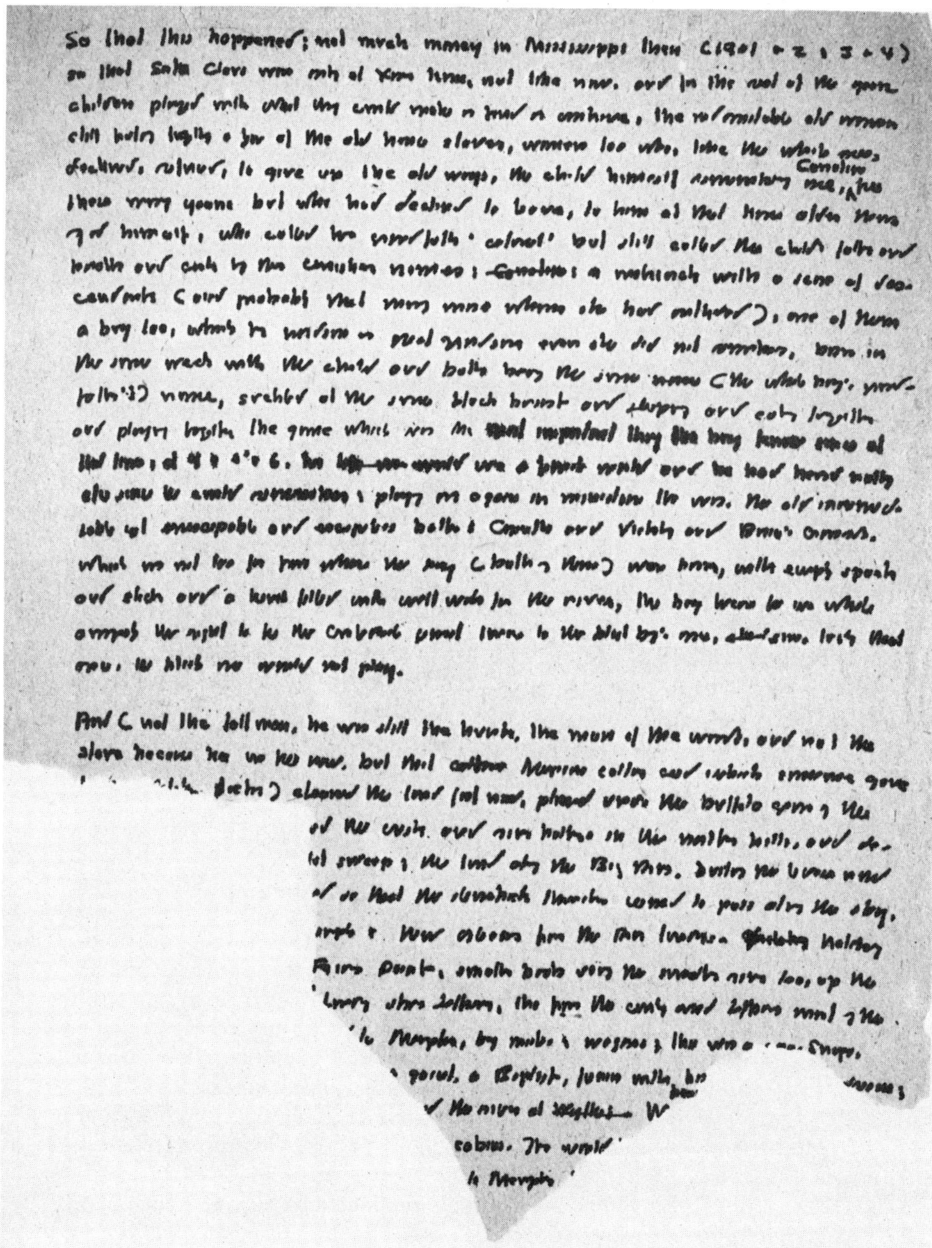

48. Page of early draft of "Mississippi," 1954

them) was born, with empty spools and sticks and a trench filled with well water for the river, the boy because he was white arrogating the right to be the Confederate general twice to the black boy's once, [lack *del.*] since, lacking that once, the black one would not play.

And (not the tall man, he was still the hunter, the man of the woods, and not the slave because he was free now, but that [cotton *del.*] Mexican cotton seed which someone gave to the Natchez doctor) cleared the land fast now, plowed under the buffalo grass of the [ ]ed the creek and river bottoms in the northern hills, and de-[ ]al sweep of the land along the Big River, building the levees and [ ]ed so that the steamboats themselves seemed to pass along the sky. [ ]mphis & New Orleans from the river towns—[Vicksburg *del.*] Natchez [ ] Friars Point, smaller boats along the smaller rivers too, up the [ ] Landing above Jefferson, tho from the county and Jefferson most of the [ ] to Memphis, by mules & wagons; there was a pre-Snopes, [ ] a giant, a Baptist, furious with his [ ] dream; [ ]ed the river at [Wylie's—*del.*] W <han> [ ] cabins. The world [ ] to Memphis [ ]

997 "Mississippi," 1954, ribbon typescript, canceled; one page, numbered "2," 11 by 8½ inches, Certificate Bond.

This draft, which has been x-ed out with a red grease pencil, is a slightly different version of paragraphs 3b–5 of the published essay. The verso of the leaf carries a canceled typescript draft of page "2" of "Weekend Revisited" (see page 165).

hind the presidents' desks of banks and on the controlling boards of wholesale grocery corporations and deaconries of Baptist churches, buying up the decayed Georgian houses and chopping them into apartments[; *del.*]<, and on their death-beds decreed annexes and baptismal fonts to the churches as mementos to themselves [out *del.*] or perhaps out of simple terror;> they hunted too, in the camps too where the De Spains and Compsons and McCaslins and Ewells were masters in their hierarchial [*sic*] turn, shooting the does not only when the law but the master too said not do it, not even because the meat was needed, leaving the meat itself to be eaten by scavengers in the woods, shooting it simply because it was big and moving and alien, of an older time than the little grubby stores and the accumulating money; the boy a man now and in his hierarchial turn master of a camp, coping, having to cope [wit *del.*] not with the diminishing wilderness where there was less and less game, but with the Snopeses who were destroying [t *ov.* w]hat little [was left of it. *del.*] which did remain.

These elected the Bilboes and voted indefatigably for the Vardamans, naming their sons after both; their origin was in bitter hatred and fear [of the Negroes on li *del.*] and economic rivalry of the Negroes of little farms no larger than and adjacent to their own, because the Negro, remembering when he had not been free and therefore capable of valuing freedom and of fighting to retain it, could do more with less: raise more cotton with less money to spend and food to eat and fewer or inferior tools to work with: until he, the Snopes, could escape from the land, into the little grubby side-street stores where he could live not beside Negroe[s *del.*] but on [them *del.*] <him> by marking up on the inferior meat or meal or beans the price which [some of the customers *del.*] <he, the Negro,> could not even [read *del.*] always read.

1107 "A Guest's Impression of New England," 1954, autograph manuscript in blue ink, 1 page, 11 by 8½ inches, Hammermill Bond.

This draft represents a false start consisting of the first paragraph and the opening of the second sentence of the second paragraph of the three-page ribbon typescript transcribed below. This false start appears on the verso of page 3 of the typescript.

A GUEST'S IMPRESSION OF NEW ENGLAND

[What impressed me, a Southerner, most about New England, are the people. *del.*] It is not of the country, but of the people—men and women themselves so individual that they take it for granted that all other men and women are individuals too and treat them as such:—that capacity to let all other people [completely and absolutely *del.*] alone with complete and absolute dignity and courtesy

One matchless New England

1107 "A Guest's Impression of New England," 1954, ribbon typescript with autograph corrections in red grease pencil, black pencil, and blue-black ink, 3 pages, 11 by 8½ inches, Hammermill Bond.

Resulting from impressions Faulkner gleaned from his visit with Malcolm and Muriel Cowley in their Sherman, Connecticut, home in October 1948, this essay appeared, in considerably altered form, in *New England Journeys Number 2: Ford Times Special Edition, 1954.*

A GUEST'S IMPRESSION OF NEW ENGLAND

It is not the country, but the people who impressed this one—men and women themselves so individual, who hold individual integration and privacy as high and dear as liberty and freedom, that they take it for granted that all other men and women are individuals too and treat them as such, doing this simply by letting them alone with complete and absolute dignity and courtesy.

[One matchless New England Indian summer afternoon Malcolm Cowley *del.*]

This is what I mean. One matchless New England Indian summer afternoon Malcolm Cowley and I were driving through back roads in western Connecticut and Massachusetts. We got lost. We were in what a Mississippian would call mountains but which New Englanders call hills; the road was not getting worse yet: just hillier and lonelier and apparently going nowhere save upward, toward a range of hills. At last, just as we were about to turn back, we found a house, a mailbox, two men, farmers or in the costumes of farmers—sheep-lined coats and caps with ear-flaps tied over the crowns—standing beside it[. *del.*] and watching us quietly and with perfect courtesy as we drove up and stopped.

'Good afternoon,' Cowley said.

'Good afternoon,' one of the men said.

'Does this road cross the mountain?' Cowley said.

'Yes,' the man said, still with that perfect courtesy.

'Thank you,' Cowley said and drove on, the two men still watching us quietly—for perhaps fifty yards, when Cowley braked suddenly and said, 'Wait,' and backed the car down to the mailbox again [1] where the two men still watched us. 'Can 1 get over it in this car?' Cowley said.

'No," the same man said. 'I don't think you can.' So we turned around and went back the way we came.

That's what I mean. In the West, the farmer would have farmed only as a hobby[; *del.*], his true <vocation> being a used car dealer; he would have tried to sell us <for three prices> a used car which he assured us would get over that mountain[; *del.*], [indeed, *del.*] the only car <in fact> west of the Rocky Mountains which would [have done *del.*] <do> it[, *del.*]; in the Central States and the East we would have been given directions <to circumvent it> based on lightning-struck trees and houses a quarter-mile from the road with a lightning-rod on the north-east chimney and creeks where if you looked carefully you could see remains of a bridge which vanished forty years ago, which only Gabriel could have followed; in my own South the [Mississippian would have said *del.*] two Mississippians would have adopted us before Cowley could have put the car in motion again, saying (one of them; the other would already be trying to get into the car): 'Why sure, it wont be no trouble at all; Jim here will go with you and I'll telephone across the mountain to my nephew to meet you with his jeep when you get stuck; it'll pull you right on through and he'll even have a mechanic waiting to put on a new crank case for you.'

But not the New Englander, who respects your right to privacy and free will by telling, giving you only and exactly what you asked for, and no more. If you want to try to take your car across that road, that's your business and not his to ask you why. If you want to wreck it and spend the night [walk *del.*] on foot to the nearest lighted window or disturbed watch-dog, that's your business too since it's your car and your legs; if you had not wanted to do that, you would have asked him that too. Because he is free, private, not made so by the [2] [poor soil *del.*] by the hard and rock-bound land—the poor soil and the hard long winters—on which his lot was cast, but having elected <deliberately> of his own volition that stern and rock-bound land because he knew he was tough enough to cope with it, having been bred by all his tradition which sent him from Europe in order to be free, [that *del.*] to believe that there was no valid reason why life should be soft and amenable, that to be individual, and private was the thing, and that the man who could not cope with any environment had better not clutter the earth anyway; to stand out against that environment which had done its worst and failed, leaving him not only tougher and superior to it but its master. He leaves it occasionally of course, but he takes it with him too; you will find him in the middlewest, you will find him in sun glasses and [with *del.*] <straw sandals and> his shirt-tail [on the *del.*] outside [of *del.*] his pants in Los Angeles. But open the aloha [shirt *del.*] <bed jacket> and scratch him a little and you find the thin soil and the rocks and the snow and the man who had not at all been driven from his birthplace because it had beaten him at last, but <who> had quitted it because he himself was the victor and the sport was gone with his slowing blood, and now [he wanted only a hobby for his old age. *del.*] he [was *del.*] is simply using Southern California—that [lan *del.*] never never land of mystics and fire-worshippers and raw-vegetable addicts <—> as a hobby for his old age. [n.n.]

1101 "Sepulchure South: in/by Gaslight," 1954, ribbon typescript and autograph manuscript in blue ink, 6 pages, 11 by 8½ inches, Hammermill Bond (pp. 1–4) and unwatermarked (pp. 5–6).

This manuscript is an early draft of the semi-autobiographical essay that was inspired by a Walker Evans photograph and was first published in the December 1954 issue of *Harper's Bazaar.* Pages 1–3 and the first seven lines of page 4 (the first six paragraphs of the essay) are in typescript; the remainder of page 4 and pages 5–6 are in holograph.

SEPULCHURE SOUTH: IN/BY GASLIGHT

When Grandfather died, Father['s fi *del.*] [probably *del.*] spoke what was his first reaction because what he said was involuntary because if he had had time to think first, he would not have said it: 'Damn it, now we'll lose Liddy.'

Liddy was the cook. She was one of the best we had ever had and she had been with us ever since Grandmother died seven years ago and the cook before her had left, and now with another death in the family, she would move too, regretfully because she liked us too, but that was the way Negroes did: left after a death in the family, as though obeying not a superstition but a rite: the rite of [being free, the rig *del.*] <their> freedom: not freedom from having to work, that would not occur to anybody for several years yet, not until W.P.A., but the freedom to move from one job to another, taking a death in the family as the moment, instigation to move since only death was important enough to exercise a right as important as freedom.

But she would not go yet; hers and Arthur's (her husband's) departure would be done with a dignity commensurate with the dignity of Grandfather's age and position in our family and our town and the commensurate dignity of his sepulchure. Not to mention the fact that Arthur himself was now serving his apogee as a member of our family, as if he had served us for the seven years while waiting for this moment, this hour, this day: sitting (not standing: sitting) now, freshly shaved and with his hair trimmed this morning, in a clean white shirt and necktie of Father's and wearing his coat, in a chair in the back room of the jewelry store while Mr Wedlow the jeweler inscribed on the sheet

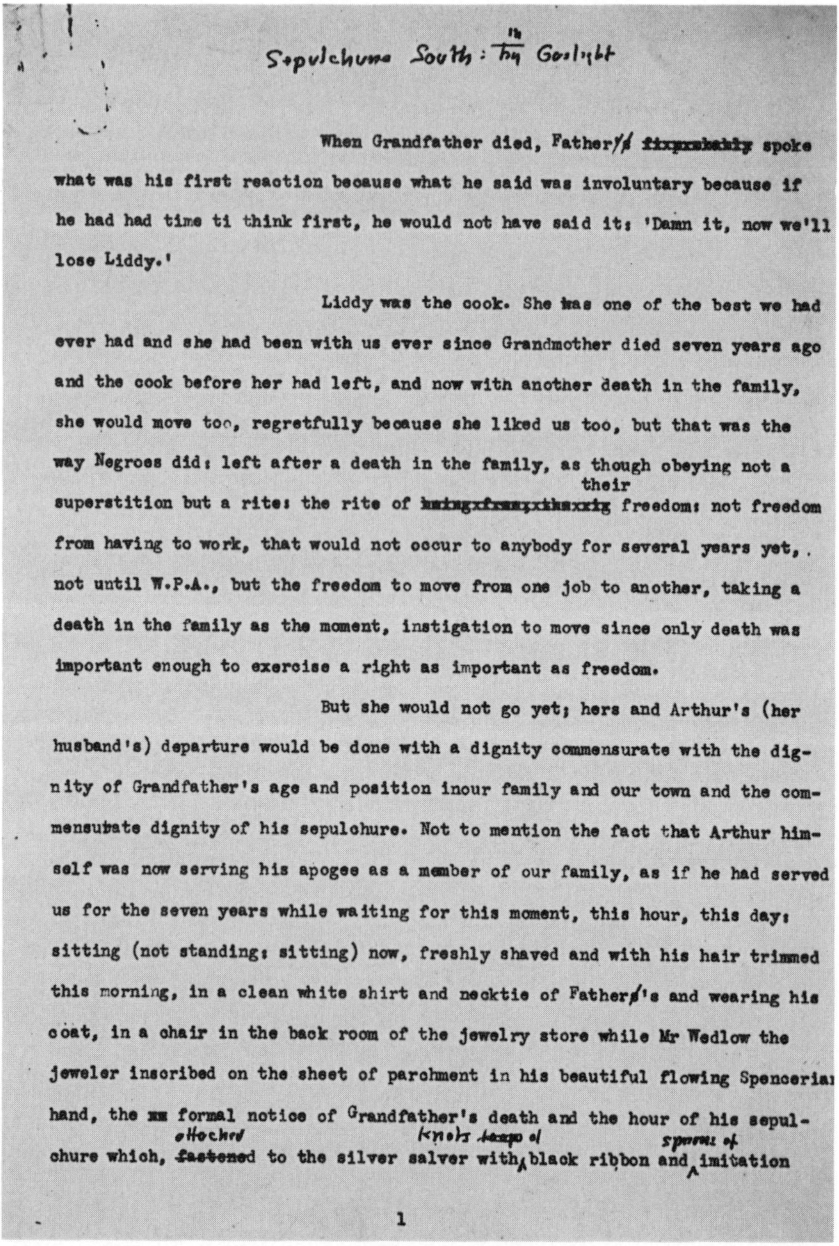

Sepulchure South: in Gaslight

When Grandfather died, Father ~~fixpxxbably~~ spoke what was his first reaction because what he said was involuntary because if he had had time ti think first, he would not have said it: 'Damn it, now we'll lose Liddy.'

Liddy was the cook. She was one of the best we had ever had and she had been with us ever since Grandmother died seven years ago and the cook before her had left, and now with another death in the family, she would move too, regretfully because she liked us too, but that was the way Negroes did: left after a death in the family, as though obeying not a superstition but a rite: the rite of ~~beingxfreexxthexxig~~ their freedom: not freedom from having to work, that would not occur to anybody for several years yet, not until W.P.A., but the freedom to move from one job to another, taking a death in the family as the moment, instigation to move since only death was important enough to exercise a right as important as freedom.

But she would not go yet; hers and Arthur's (her husband's) departure would be done with a dignity commensurate with the dignity of Grandfather's age and position inour family and our town and the commensurate dignity of his sepulchure. Not to mention the fact that Arthur himself was now serving his apogee as a member of our family, as if he had served us for the seven years while waiting for this moment, this hour, this day: sitting (not standing: sitting) now, freshly shaved and with his hair trimmed this morning, in a clean white shirt and necktie of Father's and wearing his coat, in a chair in the back room of the jewelry store while Mr Wedlow the jeweler inscribed on the sheet of parchment in his beautiful flowing Spencerian hand, the formal notice of Grandfather's death and the hour of his sepulchure which, ~~fastened~~ attached to the silver salver with knots of black ribbon and sprays of imitation

1

49. Title page of typescript of "Sepulchure South," 1954

of parchment in his beautiful flowing Spencerian hand, the [no *del.*] formal notice of Grandfather's death and the hour of his sepulchure which, [fastened *del.*] <attached> to the silver salver with <[loops *del.*] knots of> black ribbon and <sprays of> imitation [1] immortelles, Arthur would bear from door to door (not back or kitchen doors now but front doors) through our town, to ring the [front door *del.*] bell and then pass the salver in to who answered it (not a servant this time but a member of the family, since the town [knew by now th *del.*] <by this hour> needed no notification that Grandfather was dead and this was not a notice but a ritual, a rite), Arthur himself dominating that moment, [no *del.*] for this moment, during this entire morning not a servant of ours nor even an envoy from us but rather a messenger from Death itself, saying to our town: 'Pause, mortal; remember Me.'

Then Arthur would be busy for the rest of the day too, now in the coachman's coat and beaver hat which he had inherited from the husband of Liddy's pre[de *del.*]cessor who had inherited it in his turn from the husband of Liddy's precessor's precessor, meeting with the surrey the trains on which our kin <and connections> would [arrive *del.*] begin to arrive. And now the town could begin the brief ritual [calls of con *del.*] formal calls, almost wordless and that in [whisp *del.*] murmurs, whispers, because the ritual said that Mother must bear this first shock of bereavement in privacy and Father must support her, so the next of kin must receive the callers—Mother's sister and her husband from Memphis, and Aunt Alice who was Father's brother Charles's wife. And all this time the neighbor ladies would be coming to the kitchen door (not the front door: the back ones) followed by their cooks or yard boys carrying the dishes and trays of food they had prepared, for our influx of kin to eat, and for the midnight supper for the men, Father's [and Grand *del.*] friends, who would sit up all night with the body when it came back from the undertaker's.

And all tomorrow too, while the wreaths and flowers arrived, and now those who wanted to could go into the parlor and look at Grandfather framed in white satin in his gray uniform with the three gold stars on the collar [and *del.*]<, freshly shaven and with> just the barest touch of rouge on his cheeks. And tomorrow too, until after we had had our dinner, when Liddy said to us, 'Now you [2] chillen go on down to the pasture and play until I calls you.' But not to me, I was not only the oldest but a boy, [I *del.*] the third generation of oldest son from Grandfather's father; when Father's turn came it would be my turn to say before I would have time to think: [' *del.*] Damn it, now we'll lose Liddy or Julia or Florence or whatever her name would be. I must be there too, in my Sunday suit, with a band of crape on my arm, all of us except Mother and Father [in the back room which Grandfather called his office—Mother's sister and [her husband *del.*] <Uncle Fred> and Father's brother Charley and [his wife *del.*] <Aunt Alice> and [his brother *del.*] <Uncle> Rodney[, the *del.*] who had no wife—the dashing bachelor who wore silk shirts and used scented lotion *del.*] in the back room which Grandfather called his office, to which the whiskey decanter had been moved from the diningroom sideboard in deference to the funeral—Mother's sister and <her husband>

Uncle Fred and Father's brother Charley and <his wife> Aunt Alice and Uncle Rodney who had no wife—the dashing bachelor who wore silk shirts and used scented lotion, who had been Grandmother's favorite and that of a lot of other women too—the travelling salesman for the Saint Louis wholesale house who brought into our town on his [visits *del.*] brief visits a breath, an odor, a glare almost of the metropolitan outland which was not for us: the teeming cities of hotel bellhops and girl-shows and oyster-bars, my first recollection of whom was standing at the sideboard with the whiskey decanter in his hand and who had it in his hand now, only Aunt Alice's hand was on it too and we could all hear her furious whisper: 'You cannot, you shall not let them smell you like this!' and Uncle Rodney:

'All right, all right. Get me a handful of cloves from the kitchen.' So that too, the odor of cloves inextricable from that of whiskey and shaving lotion, was a part of Grandfather's passing [from *del.*] for the last time from the house too, while the ladies entered the parlor, the men stopping outside on the lawn, decorous and quiet, still wearing their hats until the music started, when they would remove them and stand again, their [3] heads bared and bowed a little in the bright early afternoon sunshine. Then Mother was in the hall, in black and heavily veiled, and Father in black, and now we crossed into the dining room where chairs had been arranged for us, the folding doors open into the parlor where the minister and the ladies waited before the coffin, we, the family of the funeral but not in it, as though Grandfather in his casket now had to be two: one for his blood descendants and one for those who were merely his friends and fellow townsmen.

Then that song, that hymn that meant nothing to me now: no lugubrious dirge to death, no reminder that Grandfather was gone and I would never see him again, because never again could it match what it had once meant to me: terror: not of death but of the un-dead; I was just 4 then; Maggie, next to me, could barely walk, the 2 of us in a throng of older children [running *del.*] half concealed in the shrubbery in the corner of the yard, I at least didn't know why, until it passed—the first I had ever watched—the black plumed hearse, the black closed hacks and carriages, at the slow and [portentous *del.*] significant pace thru the [town *del.*] street which was suddenly deserted so that I thot [*i.e.* thought] that the entire town too would be.

'What?' I said. 'A deader? What's a deader?' and they told me. I had seen dead things before—birds, toads, beatles: I had [*illeg.*] seen Sarah or her husband beat into bloody shapeless strings the snakes which I know now were harmless. But that that, that ignominy, should happen to people too, God himself would not permit. So they could not be dead, it must be something like sleep, more profound of course but no more permanent: a trick played on people by the same inimical forces and powers for evil that made Sarah and Joe have to beat the snakes or drown the [beatles, *del.*] kittens—tricked into that helpless coma until the earth was packed over them and they could never escape again, to strain and thrash and cry in agony in the dark. So that that p.m. I had a fit of something very like hysterics, clinging to Sarah's legs and panting 'I wont die! I wont! I wont!'

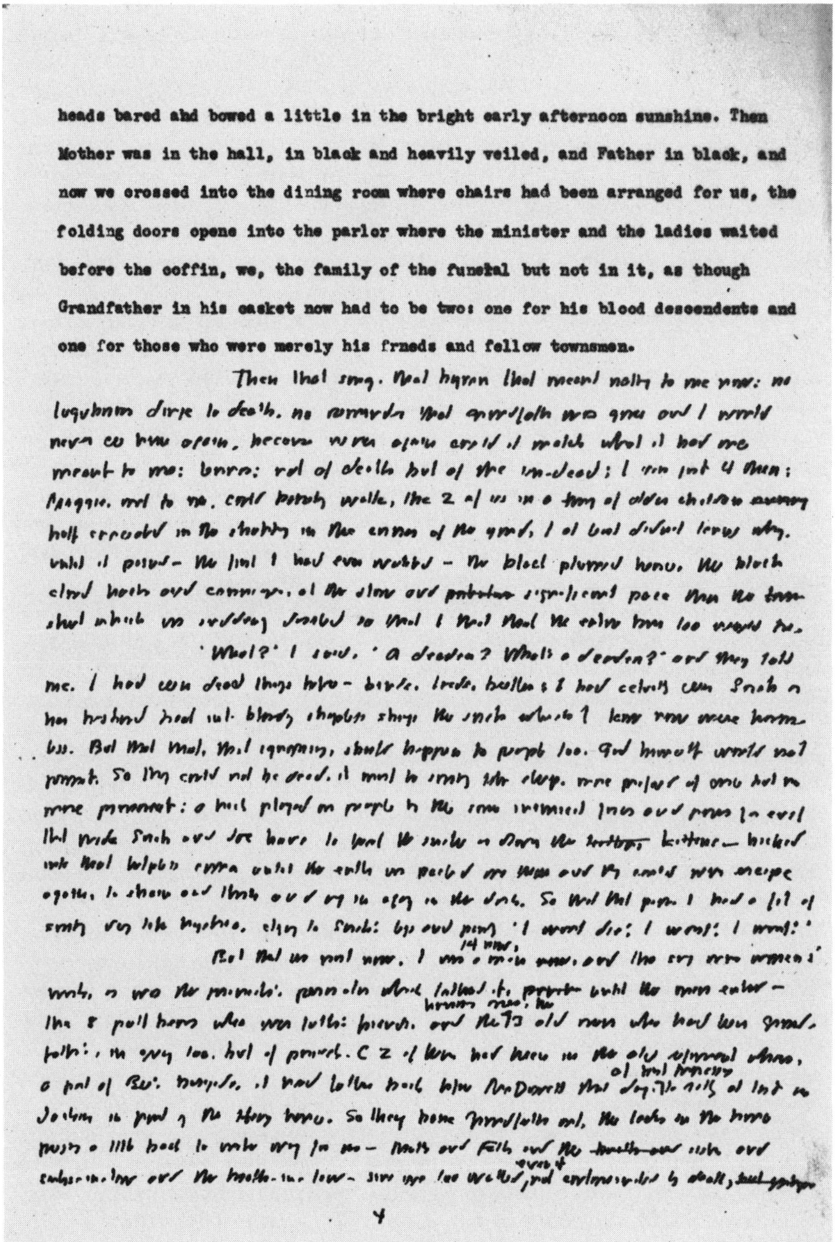

heads bared and bowed a little in the bright early afternoon sunshine. Then Mother was in the hall, in black and heavily veiled, and Father in black, and now we crossed into the dining room where chairs had been arranged for us, the folding doors opene into the parlor where the minister and the ladies waited before the coffin, we, the family of the funeral but not in it, as though Grandfather in his casket now had to be two: one for his blood descendents and one for those who were merely his frneds and fellow townsmen.

4

50. Page 4 of "Sepulchure South," 1954

But that was past now. I was <14 now,> a man [now *del.*], and the song was womens' [*sic*] work, as was the minister's peroration which followed it, [prior *del.*] until the men entered—the 8 pall bearers who were father's friends, and the <honorary ones, the> 3 old men who had been Grandfather's, in grey too, but of privates, (2 of them had been in the old regiment when, a part of Bee's brigade, it had fallen back before McDowell that day, <at first Manassas> to rally at last on Jackson in front of the Henry house. So they bore Grandfather out, the ladies in the house pressing a little back to make way for us—Mother and Father and the [brother and *del.*] sister and sisters-in-law and the brother-in-law—since we too walked, <even if> not contaminated by death, [but perhaps *del.*] [4] <*marg.* at least> within [the *del.*] <its> contamination, the men in the sunny yard not looking at the passing casket either, bareheaded, their heads bowed a little: from the street there came one muffled half-hollow sound as the bearers, amateurs at this too, got the casket into the hearse and then—the bearers—moving sharply, briskly, already dis-associating themselves <the moment> from the funeral, around the corner where the vehicle waited to carry them <but by back streets> to the cemetery in advance, to be waiting there when our slow processional arrived, [but by the back streets *del.*] so that any southern stranger in our town, seeing that black vehicle full of black clad sober faced freshly shaved men going at [a *del.*] that rapid trot up a back street, would know what it signified.

Yes, processional: the hearse, then our carriage with Mother and Father and me, then the brothers and sisters and then the cousins in 1 & 2 & 3 degrees, diminishing in distance from the hearse as their connection with Grandfather diminished, up the deserted street, across the Square empty as Sunday so that my heart swelled with snobbery and pride to think that Grandfather had been this important in the town, then along the deserted street which led to the cemetery, in [every *del.*] almost every yard of which the children stood along the fence, watching the hearse pass with that same [pleasurable *del.*] terror and excitement which I remembered, remembering [how *del.*] the terror and regret with which I had once wished we lived on Cemetery street too so that I could watch them all pass by.

And now we could already see them, gigantic and white, taller on their marble pedestals than the rose-and-honeysuckle-choked fence, looming over the very trees themselves, the magnolias and cedars and elms, gazing forever eastward with their empty marble eyes—not symbols: not angels of mercy [or *del.*] <and> winged seraphim lambs and shepherds, but the <effigies of the> actual people as they had been in life, in marble now, durable, heroic in size, towering above their dust in the [tradi *del.*] uncompromising tradition of our [harsh uncompromising *del.*] <*marg.* [grim *del.*] <strong> uncompromising [cold *del.*] <grimly> ebullient> Baptist and Methodist protestantism, carved in Italian marble in Italy by expensive Italian craftsmen and shipped the long costly way back to our South in our grim unreconstructable tradition which extended from the banker and [the *del.*] cotton planter down to the tenant farmer <*marg.* who didn't even own the mule he plowed nor the tools he worked with,> which decreed that, no matter how spartan the life, in death the significance of crass money was abolished: that Grandmother might have split stovewood up to the day of her death, yet she must enter the earth in mahogany, with silver handles—a ceremony not at all to death nor even to represent the deed at the moment of her death, but to decorum: the victim of accident or even murder represented not as in the instant of his passing but at the peak of his sublimation, as tho in death at last he denied forever the passions and mistakes of human affairs

Grandmother too; the hearse stopped now beside the raw yawn of the waiting pit and the bearers and the 3 old men in grey, with the dangling meaningless bronze medals which didn't signify valor because all the men on both sides in that war had to be valorous and were, but reunions, now carrying shotguns, appeared and bore the casket to the grave, Grandmother too in her bustle and puffed sleeves and the face which we remembered save for the empty eyes, musing at nothing while the [minister finished *del.*] casket sank and the minister finished and the first clod shuddered with that profound quiet half-hollow sound on the varnished wood and the 3 old men fired their ragged volley and raised their ragged and quavering yell. [5]

Grandmother too. I could remember that day 6 years ago, the family gathered, Father and Mother and Maggie and I in the surrey because Grandfather rode his horse, the cemetery, our lot, and Grandmother's effigy dazzling and pristine out of its packing case, [standing on *del.*] tall on the pedestal above the grave, [for us to *del.*] the undertaker with his hat off and the negro workmen who had set it up, withdrawn a little, for us, the family, to look at it and say it was well. And in other years Grandfather too <*marg.* after the long tedious carving in Italy and the long Atlantic ship> on his pedestal <at last> beside her, not as the soldier <which he was and> which I had wanted him to be but—in the old tradition of apotheosis' [sublimation *del.*] <apogee>—<the lawyer, parliamentarian;> the orator which he was not, in a frock coat, [bareheaded *del.*] the bare head thrown back, the large carven tome in one carven hand and the other extended in the immemorial gesture of declamation, and this time father and mother and [Maggie *del.*] I to come for that formal inspection to say that it was well.

And 3 or 4 times a year I would come back alone, I would not know exactly why after that to look at them, not just Grandfather and Grandmother but all of them, [looming over *del.*] looming among the lush green of summer or the royal splendor of fall or the rain and snow and barren branches of winter, until spring bloomed again, serene, motionless, [gazing at *del.*] and [*illeg. del.*] remote, gazing at nothing, not like sentinels, not defending the living from the dead by keeping the dead beneath their ton measured weight, but rather as tho [protecting the d *del.*] shielding the [helpless *del.*] <now harmless> and [harmless dust *del.*] <defenseless dust> from the anguish and grief and inhumanity of [hum *del.*] mankind [n.n.]

1121 Acceptance Address, National Book Award, January 25, 1955, carbon typescript, 3 pages, 11 by 8½ inches, unwatermarked.

This draft of Faulkner's address was typed by Harold Ober's office and was among the Faulkner files that Saxe Commins kept in his Princeton, New Jersey, home. Like the two-page, mimeographed press release issued concurrently with the delivery of the speech, this copy contains two revisions and two major insertions in Commins's hand, including the addition of a three-line conclusion. Whether these changes reflect Faulkner's wishes is debatable. Certainly, their existence establishes two different texts. The *New York Times Book Review* of February 6, 1955, and *Essays, Speeches & Public Letters* both print the Commins-emended version.

By artist I mean of course everyone who has tried to create something which was not here before him, with no other tools and material than the uncommerciable ones of the human spirit; who has tried to carve, no matter how crudely, on the wall of that final oblivion, <beyond which he will have to pass,> in the tongue of the human spirit, 'Kilroy was here.'

That is primarily, and I think in its essence, all that we ever really tried to do. And I believe we will all agree that we failed. That what we made never quite matched and never will match the shape, the dream of perfection which we inherited and which drove us and will continue to drive us, even after each failure, until anguish frees us and the hand falls still at last.

Maybe it's just as well that we are doomed to fail, since, as long as we do fail and the hand continues to hold blood, we will try again; where, if we ever did attain the dream, match the shape, scale that ultimate peak of perfection, nothing would remain but to jump off the other side of it into suicide. Which would not only deprive us of our American right to existence, not only inalienable but harmless[, *del.*] too [*insert.* ,] since by our standards, in our culture, the pursuit of art is a peaceful hobby like breeding Dalmatians, it would leave refuse in the form of, at best indigence and at worst downright crime resulting from unexhausted energy, to be scavenged and removed and disposed of. While this way, constantly and steadily occupied by, obsessed with, immersed in trying to do the impossible, faced always with the failure which we decline to recognize and [1] accept, we stay out of trouble, keep out of the way of the practical and busy people who carry the burden of America.

So all are happy—the giants of industry and commerce, the manipulators for profit or power of the mass emotions called government, who carry the tremendous load of geopolitical solvency, the two of which conjoined are America; and the harmless breeders of the spotted dogs (unharmed too, protected, immune in the inalienable right to exhibit our dogs to one another for acclaim, and even to the public too; defended in our right to collect from them at the rate of five or ten dollars for the special signed editions, and even [in the *del.*] <at the rate of> thousands to special fanciers named Picasso or Matisse).

Then something like this happens—like this, here, this afternoon; not just once and not even just once a year. Then that anguished breeder discovers that not only his fellow breeders, who must support their mutual vocation in a sort of mutual desperate defensive confederation, but other people, people whom he had considered outsiders, also hold that what he is doing is valid. And not only scattered individuals who hold his doings valid, but enough of them to confederate in their turn, for no mutual benefit of profit or defense but simply because they also believe it is not only valid but important that man should write on that wall 'Man was here also A.D. 1953 or '54 or '55', and so go on record like this this afternoon.

To tell not the individual artist but the world, the time itself, that what he did is valid. That even failure is worth while and admirable, provided only that the failure is splendid [2] enough, the dream splendid enough, unattainable enough yet forever valuable enough, since it was of perfection.

So when this happens to him (or to one of his fellows; it doesn't matter which one, since all share the validation of the mutual devotion) the thought occurs that perhaps one of the things wrong with our country is success. That there is too much success in it. Success is too easy. In our country a young man can gain it with no more than a little industry. He can gain it so quickly and easily that he has not had time to learn the humility to handle it with, or even to discover, realise, that he will need humility.

<*added:* Perhaps what we need is a dedicated handful of pioneer-martyrs who, between success and humility, are capable of choosing the second one.>

1156 "Freedom: American Style," 1955, ribbon typescript with autograph revisions in black ink and red grease pencil, 11 pages, 11 by 8½ inches, unwatermarked (pages 1, 5, 6-A, 7–10) and Hammermill Bond (pages 2–4, 6). Signed in typescript in upper left corner of page 1: "William Faulkner / % Harold Ober, / New York, N.Y."

This manuscript appears to be an intermediate version of the essay published in the July 1955 *Harper's* as "On Privacy: The American Dream: What Happened to It." This copy is considerably shorter than the magazine text, but included are five pages of material (6-A, 7–10) not contained in the early draft that Malcolm Cowley printed in *The Faulkner-Cowley File,* pp. 132–137.

FREEDOM: AMERICAN STYLE

About ten years ago [Malcolm Cowley, a good *del.*] <a New York literary critic and essayist, a good> friend of long standing, notified me that Life Magazine had offerred him a good price to write a piece about me—not about my works, but about me as a private citizen, an individual. I said No, and explained why: my belief that only a writer's works were in the public domain, the writer himself having put them there by submitting them for publication and accepting money for them, and therefore he not only would but must accept whatever the public wished to think or say or do about them from praise to burning. But that, until the writer committed a crime or ran for public office, his private life was his own and not only had he the right to defend his privacy but the public had the duty to do so, since one man's liberty must stop at exactly the point where the next one's begins; and that I believed that anyone of taste and responsibility would agree with me.

But [Cowley *del.*] <he> said No. He said: 'You are wrong. If I do the piece, I will do it with taste and responsibility. But if you refuse me, sooner or later someone will do it who will not bother about taste or responsibility either, who will care nothing about you or your status as a writer, an artist, but only as a commodity: merchandise: to be sold, to increase circulation, to make a little money.'

[He was right. Two years ago I learned ([as I recall, *del.*] <indirectly,> by chance[, *del.*]: [accident: *del.*] no direct notice <[or even *del.*]> <let alone request> either formal or in- *del.*] [1]

'Nonsense,' I said. 'Until I commit a crime or announce for office, they cant invade my privacy if I [said *del.*] <say> No.'

'They not only can,' he said, 'but [as soon as your coattails are worth the ride, they will. Just wait and see. *del.*] <once your European reputation gets back here and makes your coat-tails worth riding, they will. Wait and see.'

Well, I did. Two years ago I learned by mere chance, during a conversation with an editor in the house which publishes my books, that the same magazine had already set [of *del.*] on foot the same project which I had declined; I dont know whether the publishers were formally notified or if they just heard [about *del.*] about it by chance too, as I did. I said No again, recapitulating the same reasons which I still believed were not even arguable by anyone possessing the power of the public press since the qualities of taste and responsibility would have to be inherent in that power. The editor interrupted.

'I agree with you,' he said. 'Besides, you dont need to give reasons. The simple fact that you dont want it done is enough. Shall I do it for you?' So he did, or tried it, because my critic-friend was still right. Then I said,

'Try them again. Say "I ask you: please dont."' Then I submitted the same [I ask you: *del.*] *I ask you: please dont,* the answer implying this time, as I recall: 'I've got to. If [I refuse, they will fire me.' So after that, the only defense left me was to refuse to co-operate, have anything to do with the project, though even I realised by this time that that would do no good since at this point nothing I could do in life or death either would stop them. *del.*] [2] I refuse, they will fire me.' Which must be correct, since I got the same answer from the representative of another magazine on the same subject. So after that[— *del.*]<,> if the writer, a member of the craft, was victim too of that facet of freedom, American style—that one calling itself Freedom of the Press—[that *del.*]<which> I was victim of, the only defense left me was to refuse to co-operate, have anything to do with the project. Though even I realised by this time that that would do no good since at this point nothing I could do in life or death either would stop them.

And this time even I was right. Perhaps they—the writer and his employer—did not believe it; perhaps it is impossible for any American publisher or journalist to believe that any American (possibly anyone anywhere) <*trans.* actually does not want his name and picture in the paper> <*trans.* except when he is hiding from the police>. Or perhaps they wanted me out of it since I would only have been in the way, insisting still on responsibility regarding the material even though I had already lost the battle [for good taste regarding *del.*] <regarding the bad taste of> the invasion. (I did not read the articles; my information about them is hearsay, from my mother's shocked outrage and by telephone, telegraph and the [U.S. mail *del.*] <Federal post> from every male alcoholic in the United States; this day a year and they will all have phoned or wired or written, to move in and live with me: the unregenerate to help me drink, <it,> the reformed to save me from it.).

[So the writer came (was sent; for his sake I [3] still prefer to believe that, victim too, he had no choice *del.*]

So the writer with his party—group—crew (I dont know how many; I never saw them) came (was sent; for his sake I still prefer to believe that, victim too, he had no choice either but to come and get his material where and how he could—one of the party told my mother or permitted her to assume an outright lie to persuade her to be photographed—for the reason that he durst not return empty-handed) and departed and published his articles. Which is not the point. The point is not even that the writer is not to be blamed for what he turned up with since empty-handed he would have been fired from the job which must be valuable to him even if it does seem [4] to have deprived him of the right to choose between good and bad taste. It is not even that his employer is not to blame since to hold his (the employer's) precarious own in his precarious and towering craft like an inverted pyramid balanced on its apex, which, like the man on the tightrope, depends for balance, [and *del.*] continuation, life itself not on the compounding of mass but of speed, and which in collapsing will destroy him too, he (the employer), unless his is a really terrifying integrity, must serve the time also.

The point is—the terrifying (not shocking; we should not be shocked by it since we permitted its birth and watched it grow and condoned and validated it and even in individual cases use it at need) thing is—that it could have happened at all, was possible to have happened at all, its victim, even when accidentally warned in advance, completely helpless to prevent it; nor, even after the fact, without recourse since, unlike obscenity and degeneracy, we have no laws against bad taste because unlike degeneracy and obscenity we have not yet discovered how to sell bad taste and know that that's what we are selling; and even if there were laws the publisher could charge the judgment and court costs off income as operating loss, and the subsequent profit from increased sales to capital investment. That in American today any organization or group, simply by functioning under a phrase like Freedom of the Press or National Security or Anti-Subversion, can postulate for itself complete immunity to violate the privacy of any individual himself not a member of some federation populous enough or rich enough to frighten them off. Not artists of course; being [5] individuals, not even two of them could federate, let alone enough; besides which, artists dont count in America, there is no place for them, they have no more business in American life than [the employers of the Mr Coughlans have *del.*] <the employers *del.*> <Life Magazine [writers *del.*] has> in Faulkner's [life *del.*]. But the two other human occupations which require privacy to endure, live, and which are valuable to

I refuse, they will fire me.' Which must be correct, since I got the same answer from the representative of another magazine on the same subject. So after that, if the writer, a member of the craft, was victim too of that facet of freedom, American style---that one calling itself Freedom of the Press ---~~that~~ which I was victim of, the only defense left me was to refuse to co-operate, have anything to do with the project. Though even I realised by this time that that would do no good since at this point nothing I could do in life or death either would stop them.

And this time even I was right. Perhaps they---the writer and his employer---did not believe it; perhaps it is impossible for any American publisher or journalist to believe that any American (possibly anyone anywhere), actually does not want his name and picture in the paper except when he is hiding from the police. Or perhaps they wanted me out of it since I would only have been in the way, insisting still on responsibility regarding the material even though I had already lost the battle ~~for good taste regarding~~ regarding the bad taste of the invasion. (I did not read the articles; my information about them is hearsay, from my mother's shocked outrage and by telephone, telegraph and the Federal post from every male alcoholic in the United States; this day a year and they will all have phoned or wired or written, to move in and live with me: the unregenerate to help me drink it, the reformed to save me from it.).

[redacted]

3.

51. Page of typescript of "Freedom: American Style," 1955

American life: science and humanity: the scientists and the humanitarians—the pioneers in the science of endurance and mechanical craftsmanship and self-discipline and skill like Colonel Lindbergh compelled at last to repudiate it by the harassment of that nation which abrogated to itself the glory of his renown yet could neither protect his children nor shield his grief; the pioneers in the simple science of saving the nation like Doctor Oppenheimer, harassed and impugned by that same nation until all privacy was stripped from him and there remained only the qualities of individualism whose possession we boast since they alone differ us from animals—gratitude for kindness, [loyalty and *del.*] fidelity to friendship, chivalry toward women and the capacity to love—before which even his federated officially vetted harassers were impotent, turning away themselves (one hopes) in shame: as if the whole business had had nothing whatever to do with loyalty or disloyalty but was simply to batter and strip him completely naked of the privacy lacking which he could never have become the individual capable of saving a nation at that moment when apparently nobody else was, and so reduce him at last to one more identityless integer in that identityless anonymous unprivacied mass which seems to be our goal. [6]

And even that is only the point[, because the sickness itself goes much further back *del.*] for departure, because the sickness itself goes much further back. It goes back to that moment in our history when we decided that the old simple [6-A] moral verities over which taste and responsibility were the arbiters and the controls, were obsolete and to be discarded. It goes back to that moment when we repudiated the meaning which our fathers had stipulated for the words 'liberty' and 'freedom' on and by and to which they founded us as a nation and dedicated us as a people, keeping only the mouthsounds of them. It goes back to the moment when we substituted license in the place of liberty—license for any action which kept within the proscription of laws promulgated by confederations of the practitioners of the license and the harvesters of the material benefits; back to that moment when [we *del.*] in place of freedom we substituted immunity for any action to any recourse, provided merely that the act is performed beneath the aegis of the empty mouthsound of freedom.

At which instant truth vanished too. We didn't abolish truth; even we could not do that. It simply quit us, turned its back on us, not in scorn nor even contempt nor even (let us hope) despair. It just simply quit us, to return when whatever it will be—suffering, national disaster, maybe even (if nothing else will serve) military defeat—will have taught us to prize truth, to regain it (oh yes, we are brave and tough too; we just intend to put off having to be as long as possible) and hold it again on its own terms of taste and responsibility;—that long clean clear simple undeviable unchallengeable straight and shining line, on one side of which black is black [7] and on the other white is white, has now become an angle, a point of view having nothing to do with truth nor even with fact, but depending solely on where you are standing when you look at it. Or rather—better—where you can contrive to have him standing whom you are trying to fool or obfuscate when he looks at it.

Across the board: truth and freedom and liberty: the American sky which was once the sky of freedom, the American air which was once the living breath of liberty, now become one vast pressure to abolish them both by destroying man's individuality as a man by (in turn) destroying the last vestige of privacy without which man cannot be an individual. Our very architecture itself has warned us. Time was when you could see neither from outside in nor from inside out through the walls of our houses. Time is when you can see from inside out though still not from outside in through the walls. Time will be when you can do both, then privacy will indeed be gone; he who is individual enough to want it even to change his shirt or visit the bathroom in will be cursed by one universal American voice as subversive to the American way of life and the American flag.

If (by that time) walls themselves, opaque or not, can still stand before that furious blast, that force, that power rearing like a thunder-clap into the American zenith, multiple-faced yet mutually conjunctived, bellowing the words and phrases which we have long since emasculated of any significance or meaning other than as tools, implements for the further harassment of the private individual human spirit, by their [8] furious and immunised high priests: 'Security'. ['Subversion'. *del.*] 'Anti-[communism' *del.*] <Subversion'>. 'Christianity'. 'Prosperity'. 'The American Way'. 'The Flag'.

With odds at balance (plus a little fast footwork now and then of course) one individual can defend himself from another individual's liberty. But when powerful federations and organizations and amalgamations like publishing corporations and religious sects and political parties and legislative committees can absolve themselves of all restrictions of moral responsibility by means of such catch-phrases as 'Freedom' and 'Salvation' and 'Security' and 'Democracy', beneath which fearsome aegis the individual salaried practitioners are themselves in their turn absolved of all individual responsibility, then let us beware. Then [peopl *del.*] even people like Doctor Oppenheimer and Colonel Lindbergh and me ([Mr. Coughlan *del.*] <the Life Magazine writer> too if he [really *del.*] <actually> was compelled to choose between good taste and starvation) will have to confederate in our turn to preserve that privacy in which alone the artist and scientist and humanitarian can function. Or (to repeat) not the artist; America has never yet found any place for him who deals only in things of the human spirit except to use his notoriety to advertise cigarettes or fountain pens or automobiles or resort hotels or (if he can compromise enough to meet the standards) in radio or cinema where he can produce enough income tax to be worth attention. But the scientist and the humanitarian: the humanitarian in science and the scientist in the humanity of man, who might [9] [yet save that civilization the professionals [in *del.*] <at> which—the publishers who batten on man's lusts and follies[, by pandering to them *del.*], the politicians who [trade on *del.*] <traffic in> his stupidities and the churchmen who trade on his fears and superstitions—seem to be proving that they cant. *del.*] yet save that civilization the professionals at which—the publishers who batten on man's lust[s *del.*] and foll[ies *del.*]<y>, the politicians who traffic in his stupidity and greed and the churchmen who trade on his fear[s *del.*] and superstition[s *del.*]—seem to be proving that they cant.

1157 "Freedom: American Style," ribbon typescript, 1 page, numbered "5," 11 by 8½ inches, Hammermill Bond. Cf. pp. 67–68 of version reprinted in *Essays, Speeches & Public Letters.*

This and the following ten entries are from a 14-page draft of this essay which represents an advancement over the previous 10-page draft. Both it and this draft are intermediary stages in the evolution of this work.

have to be inherent in that power for it to be valid and allowed to endure. The editor interrupted.

'I agree with you,' he said. 'Besides, you dont need to give reasons. The simple fact that you dont want it done is enough. Shall I attend to it for you?' So he did, or tried it. Because my critic friend was still right. Then I said,

'Try them again. Say "I ask you: please dont." ' Then I submitted the same *I ask you: please dont* to the writer who was to do the piece. I dont know whether he was a staff writer designated to the job, or whether he volunteered for it or perhaps himself sold his employers on the idea. Though the first is obviously correct since my recollection is that his answer implied 'I've got to. If I refuse, they will fire me.' Which—the implication of the blackmail at least—must be correct, since I got the same answer from a staff-member of another magazine on the same subject. So after that, if the writer, a member of the craft he served, was victim too of that facet of feedom, American style—that one calling itself Freedom of the Press—which I was victim of, the only defense left me was to refuse to co-operate, to have anything to do with the project. Though by this time even I realised that that would [do no goo *del.*] not save me, since at this point nothing I could do in life or death either would stop them.

And this time even I was right. [Perhaps *del.*] It is possible of course that they—the writer and his employer—did not believe me, could not believe me, perhaps dared not believe me; impossible for any American, let alone publisher or

———"Freedom: American Style," carbon typescript, canceled; 1 leaf, verso, unnumbered, 11 by 8½ inches, Eagle-A Trojan Onion Skin. False start for page "6" of 14-page version (see following item). Recto contains duplicate carbon copy of page "6" of 14-page version.

journalist ones, to believe that anyone not hiding from the police could actually not want <*insert.* ,> [his name and picture in any printed organ no matter how modest and circumscribed its circulation *del.*] as a gift free-for-nothing, his name and picture in any printed organ, no matter how modest and circumscribed in [circulation, [<*insert.* . *del.*>] let alone an organ of this scope and size *del.*] circulation. And even one hiding from the police to have protested and tried to deny an organ of this scope and size, since its free publicity would have converted into enough dollars and cents to attract <even> the most conversant [of mouthpieces *del.*] with the angles [needful to free him *del.*] of lawyers

———"Freedom: American Style," ribbon typescript, 1 page, numbered "6," 11 by 8½ inches, Hammermill Bond. Cf. p. 68 of version reprinted in *ESPL.*

journalist ones, to believe that anyone not hiding from the police could actually not want, as a free-gift-for-nothing, his name and photograph in any printed organ, no matter how modest and circumscribed in circulation. And even one hiding from the police to have protested and tried to deny that free gift from an organ of this scope and size, since mere association with that publicity would have tempted the most conversant with angles of lawyers to defend and free him. Though I dont think that the matter ever actually reached this point. I think that two of the three of us—the publisher and the writer—knew from the first, whether I did or not, that the three of us, publisher, writer, and their victim (my startled then shocked then outraged mother too in time presently) were all victims as one, the same one victim trinity and tripartite, faced not with an idea, a principle, a choice between good taste and bad taste or responsibility or lack of it, but by a fact, a condition of American life before which we were all three helpless, beneath which we were all three doomed.

Anyway the writer with his party—crew, force, whatever they were (I dont know how many; I never saw them) came (was sent; for his sake I still prefer to believe that, victim too, he had no choice either but to come and get his material where and how he could—one of the group told my mother or permitted her to assume an outright lie to persuade her to be interviewed and photographed—for the reason that he durst not return empty-handed) and departed and published his article in the magazine and later as a book. But that is not the point.

———"Freedom: American Style," carbon typescript, canceled; 1 leaf, verso, unnumbered, 11 by 8½ inches, Eagle-A Trojan Onion Skin. False start for page "7" of 14-page version (see following item.) Recto contains duplicate carbon copy of page "7" of 14-page version.

The point is not even that the writer is not to be blamed for what he turned up with since, empty-handed, he would have been fired from the job which he durst not jeopardise even though it does deprive him of the right to choose between good and bad taste. It is not even that his employer is not to blame since, to hold his (the employer's) precarious own in his precarious and towering craft like an inverted pyramid balanced on its apex which, like the man on the tightrope, must depend for continuation, life, existence itself, on the compounding not of mass but of speed and which in collapsing will destroy him too, he (the employer), unless his is a really terrifying in[tegrity and a completely reckless repudiation of self-interest, must serve the time also. *del.*] <tegrity and an utter> contempt for self-preservation, must serve the time also.

It is not even important whether his facts and information were correct or not because the important thing is not what he printed but that he—they—printed, published it [over the subject's protest. *del.*] at all over the subject's protest. The terrifying (not shocking; we should not be shocked by it since we permitted its birth and watched it grow and condoned and validated it and even in individual cases use it for our own private ends at need) thing is, that it could have been done at all under those conditions; was possible for it to have happened at all with its subject or victim, even though accidentally warned in advance, completely helpless to prevent it

———"Freedom: American Style," ribbon typescript, 1 page, numbered "7," 11 by 8½ inches, Hammermill Bond. Cf. p. 69 of version reprinted in *ESPL*.

The point is not even that the writer is not to be blamed for what he turned up with, since, empty-handed, he would have been fired from the job which he durst not jeopardise even if it does deprive him of the right to choose between good and bad taste. It is not even that his employer is not to blame since, to hold his (the employer's) precarious own in his precarious and towering craft like an inverted pyramid balanced on its apex which, like the man on the tightrope, must depend for continuation, life, existence itself, on the compounding not of mass but of speed and which in collapsing will destroy him too, he (the employer), unless his is a really terrifying integrity or an utter contempt for self-preservation, must serve the time also.

Because the important thing is not what he said but that he said it. Or not that he said it or even wrote it but that he—they—printed, published it or any word of it at all over the subject's protest. The terrifying (not shocking; we cannot be shocked by it since we permitted its birth and watched it grow and condoned and validated it and even in individual cases use it for our own private ends at need) thing is, that it could have happened at all under those conditions; that it was possible for it to have happened at all with its subject or victim, even though accidentally warned in advance, completely helpless to prevent it. And that, even after the thing is done, its victim to have no recourse whatever since, unlike obscenity and sacrilege, we have no laws against bad taste, perhaps because in a democracy the majority of [people *del.*]

———"Freedom: American Style," carbon typescript, canceled; 1 leaf, verso, unnumbered, 11 by 8½ inches, Eagle-A Trojan Onion Skin. False start for page "8" of 14-page version (see following item). Recto contains duplicate carbon copy of page "8" of 14-page version.

the people who make the laws do not recognise bad taste when they see it, or perhaps because in our democracy bad taste has been converted into a marketable and therefore a taxable and [a lobbyable commodity *del.*] therefore a lobbyable commodity by the merchandising federations which at the same time create the market and the product to [glut it *del.*] serve it. And even if there were grounds for recourse, the publisher could probably charge judgment and costs off income to operating loss, and the subsequent increased sales to capital investment.

The point is that in America today any organization or group, simply by functioning under a phrase like Freedom of the Press or National Security or League Against Subversion, can postulate to itself complete immunity to violate the privacy of any individual who is not himself a member of some federation numerous enough or rich enough to frighten them off.

———"Freedom: American Style," ribbon typescript, 1 page, numbered "8," 11 by 8½ inches, Hammermill Bond. Cf. pp. 69–70 of version reprinted in *ESPL*.

the people who make the laws do not recognise bad taste when they see it, or perhaps because in our democracy bad taste has been converted into a marketable and therefore taxable and therefore lobbyable commodity by the merchandising federations which at the same simultaneous time create the market (not appetite, it did not need creation: only pandering to) and the product to serve it. And even if there were grounds for recourse, the publisher could probably charge judgment and costs [to *del.*] off income to operating loss, and the subsequent circulation gain to capital investment.

The point is that in America today any organization or group, simply by functioning under a phrase like Freedom of the Press or National Security or League Against Subversion, can postulate to itself complete immunity to violate the privacy of any individual who is not himself a member of some federation numerous enough or rich enough to frighten them off. Not writers, artists, of course; being individuals, not even two artists could ever confederate, let alone enough artists. Besides which, artists dont count in America. There is no place for them; they have no more place in American life than the employers of the weekly pictorial magazine staff writers have in Faulkner's life. But there are the other two human occupations which require, demand privacy in order to endure, live, which are valuable to American life. These are science and humanity, the scientists and the humanitarians: the pioneers in the science of endurance and mechanical craftsmanship and self-discipline and skill like Colonel Lindbergh who was compelled

———"Freedom: American Style," ribbon typescript, 1 page, numbered "9," 11 by 8½ inches, Hammermill Bond. Cf. pp. 70–71 of version reprinted in *ESPL*.

at last to repudiate it by the harassment of that nation which abrogated to itself the glory of his renown, yet could neither protect his children nor shield his grief; the pioneers in the simple science of saving the nation like Doctor Oppenheimer who was harassed and impugned by that same nation until all privacy was stripped from him and there remained only the qualities of individualism whose possession we boast since they alone differ us from animals—gratitude for kindness, fidelity to friendship, chivalry toward women and the capacity to love—before which even his federated officially vetted harassers were impotent, turning away themselves (one hopes) in shame. It was as if the whole business had [been *del.*] had nothing [to do *del.*] whatever to do with loyalty or disloyalty or security or insecurity, but was simply to batter and strip him completely naked of the privacy lacking which he could never have become the individual capable of serving a nation at that moment when apparently nobody else was, and so reduce him at last to one more identityless integer in that identityless anonymous unprivacied mass which seems to be our goal.

And even that is only a point of departure. Because the sickness itself goes much further back. It goes back to that moment in our history when we decided that the old simple moral verities over which taste and responsibility were the arbiters and controls, were obsolete and to be discarded. It goes back to that moment when we repudiated the meaning which our fathers had stipulated for the words 'liberty' and

———"Freedom: American Style," ribbon typescript, 1 page, numbered "12," 11 by 8½ inches, Hammermill Bond. Cf. pp. 73–74 of version reprinted in *ESPL.*

the further harassment of the private individual human spirit, by their furious and immunised high priests: 'Security'. 'Subversion'. 'Anti-Communism'. 'Christianity'. 'Prosperity'. 'The American Way'. 'The [American *del.*] Flag'.

With odds at balance (plus a little fast footwork now and then of course) one individual can defend himself from another individual's liberty. But when powerful federations and organizations and amalgamations like publishing corporations and religious sects and political parties and legislative committees can absolve themselves of all restrictions of moral responsibility by means of such catch-phrases as 'Freedom' and 'Salvation' and 'Security' and 'Democracy', beneath which fearsome absolution the individual salaried practitioners are themselves absolved of all individual responsibility and restraint, then let us beware. Then even people like Doctor Oppenheimer and Colonel Lindbergh and me (the weekly magazine staff writer too if he really was compelled to choose between good taste and starvation) will have to confederate in our turn to preserve that privacy in which alone the artist and scientist and humanitarian can function. [Or to preserve life itself, breathing; not just artists and scientists and humanitarians but the parents by law or biology of doctors of osteopathy. I am thinking of course of the Cleveland doctor convicted recently of the brutal slaying of his wife; three of whose parents, his wife's father and his own father and mother, with one exception did not even outlive [the trial *del.*] that trial which *del.*]

———"Freedom: American Style," carbon typescript, canceled; 1 leaf, verso, numbered "14," 11 by 8½ inches, Eagle-A Trojan Onion

Skin. False start for page "14" of 14-page version (see following item). Recto contains duplicate carbon copy of page "14" of 14-page version.

Press which [we are taught to accept *del.*] <[s *del.*]trained us to accept it> as that paladin through whose dedication truth shall prevail and justice and pity be done, belong to that the criminal's very progenitors be obliterated from the earth? And if he was innocent as he said he was, what crime did that champion of the weak and the oppressed himself participate in?

Or (to repeat) not the artist. America has never yet found any place for him who deals only in things of the human spirit except to use his notoriety to sell soap or cigarettes or fountain pens or to advertise automobiles and resort hotels, or (if he can contort fast enough to meet the standards) in radio or moving pictures where he can produce enough income tax to be worth attention. But the scientist and the humanitarian, yes: the humanitarian in science and the scientist in the humanity of man, who might yet save that civilization which the professionals at saving it—the publishers who batten on man's lust and folly, the politicians who traffic in his stupidity and greed, and the churchmen who trade on his fear and superstition—seem to be proving that they cant.

That was the American Dream. What happened to it? Where did we lose it? When shall we find it again?

———"Freedom: American Style," carbon typescript, recto of previous item, numbered "14," 11 by 8½ inches, Eagle-A Trojan Onion Skin. Duplicate of page "14" of 14-page version. Cf. pp. 74–75 of version reprinted in *ESPL*.

Press which has trained us to accept it as that dedicated paladin through whose [incorruptible integrity *del.*] <inflexible rectitude> truth shall prevail and justice and [pity *del.*] <mercy> be done, belong to that the criminal's very progenitors be [obliterated *del.*] <eliminated> from the earth in expiation of his crime? And if he was innocent as he said he was, what crime did that champion of the weak and the oppressed [himself *del.*] <itself> participate in?

Or (to repeat) not the artist. America has never yet found any place for him who deals only in things of the human spirit except to use his notoriety to sell soap or cigarettes or fountain pens or to advertise automobiles and resort hotels, or (if he can contort fast enough to meet the standards) in radio or moving pictures where he can produce enough income tax to be worth attention. But the scientist and the humanitarian, yes: the humanitarian in science and the scientist in the humanity of man, who might yet save the civilization which the professionals at saving it—the publishers who batten on man's lust and folly, the politicians who traffic in his stupidity and greed, and the churchmen who trade on his fear and superstition—seem to be proving that they cant.

That was the American Dream. What happened to it? Where did we lose it? When shall we find it again?

1157 "Freedom: American Style," ribbon typescript, 1 page, unnumbered, 11 by 8½ inches, Hammermill Bond. Cf. pp. 68–69 of version reprinted in *ESPL*.

This sheet appears to be a working draft from a more advanced stage of the 14-page version cited in the previous eleven entries.

ious own in the craft which can compel even him, head and chief of one of its components, to serve the mores of the hour in order to survive among his rival integers.

It's not what the writer said, but that he said. Or rather, that he—they—published [in a recogni *del.*] it, in a recognised organ which, to be and remain recognised, functioned on the assumption of certain inflexible standards, not only over the subject's protests but with complete immunity to them; an immunity not merely assumed to itself by the organ but an immunity already granted in advance by the public to which it sold its wares for a profit. The terrifying (not shocking; we cannot be shocked by it since we permitted its birth and watched it grow and condoned and validated it and even use it [for our own pri *del.*] individually for our own private ends at need) thing

1193 "American Segregation and the World Crisis," December 1, 1955, ribbon typescript, 1 page, 11 by 8½ inches, unwatermarked.

This three-paragraph typescript represents an addition to the address Faulkner had made to the Southern Historical Association on November 10, 1955, in Memphis, Tennessee. Unsolicited, this manuscript was typed by Faulkner at Rowan Oak in the presence of James W. Silver, the coordinator of the Memphis meeting, who had come to seek Faulkner's permission to include Faulkner's address in a pamphlet entitled *Three Views of the Segregation Decisions*. At the bottom of the page Silver has recorded in red pencil the following notation: "Statement typed by / William Faulkner / 12/1/55."

The question is no longer of white against black. It is no longer whether or not white blood shall remain pure, it is whether or not white people shall remain free.

We accept insult and contumely and the risk of violence because we will not sit quietly by and see our native land, the South, not just Mississippi but all the South, wreck and ruin itself twice in less than a hundred years, over the Negro question.

We speak now against the day when our Southern people who will resist to the last these inevitable changes in social relations, will, when they have been forced to accept what they at one time might have accepted with dignity and goodwill, will say, 'Why didn't someone tell us [about *del.*] this [in time *del.*] before? Tell us this in time?'

1237 "On Fear: The South in Labor: Mississippi," 1956, carbon typescript with revisions, 17 pages, 11 by 8½ inches; Eagle-A Trojan Onion Skin (pp. 1–5, 14–15), Esleeck Clearcopy Onion Skin (pp. 6, 8), and unwatermarked (pp. 7, 9–13, 16–17). Signed in typescript on page 1: "William Faulkner / % Harold Ober, / New York."

This typescript represents an intermediate version of the essay that appeared, with further revisions, in the June 1956 issue of *Harper's Magazine.* Faulkner intended the piece as a part of a projected series entitled "The American Dream: What Happened to It."

The versos of pages 9 and 12 of this typescript contain canceled typescript fragments of the same essay (see pages 248–249). On the versos of pages 8, 14, and 15 are canceled typescript drafts of letters Faulkner wrote, respectively, to the Editor of the Memphis *Commercial Appeal* and W. C. Neill (see Volume II of *Faulkner: A Comprehensive Guide to the Brodsky Collection,* pp. 188, 190). The ideas, and some of the phrasing, of these letters were incorporated into the "On Fear" essay.

ON FEAR

[DEEP *del.*] <*marg.* THE> SOUTH IN LABOR: MISSISSIPPI

(The American Dream: What Happened To It?)

Immediately after the Supreme Court decision abolishing segregation in schools, the talk began in Mississippi of ways and means to increase taxes to raise the standard of the Negro schools to match the white ones. I wrote the following letter to the open forum page of our most widely-read Memphis paper:

'We Mississippians already know that our present schools are not good enough. Our young men and women themselves prove that to us every year by the fact that, when the best of them want the best of education which they are entitled to and competent for, not only in the humanities but in the professions and crafts—law and medicine and engineering—too, they must go out of the state to get it. And quite often, too often, they dont come back.

'So our present schools are not even good enough for white people: our present State reservoir of education is not of high enough quality to assuage the thirst of even our white young men and women. In which case, how can it possibly assuage the thirst and need of the Negro, who obviously is thirstier, needs it worse, else the Federal Government would not have had to pass a law compelling Mississippi (among others of course) to make the best of our education available to him. [1]

'That is, our present schools are not even good enough for white people. So what do we do? make them good enough, improve them to the best possible? No. We beat the bushes, rake and scrape to raise additional taxes to establish another system at best only equal to that one which is already not good enough, which therefore wont be good enough for Negroes either: we will have two identical systems neither of which are good enough for anybody.'

A few days after my letter was printed in the paper, I received by post the carbon copy of a letter addressed to the same forum page of the Memphis paper. It reads as follows: 'When Weeping Willie Faulkner splashes his tears about the inadequacy of Mississippi schools. . . . we question his gumption in these respects' etc. From there it went on to cite certain facts of which all Southerners are justly proud: that the seed-stock of education in our land was preserved through the evil times following the Civil War when our land was a defeated and occupied country, by dedicated teachers who got little in return for their dedication. Then, after a brief sneer at the quality of my writing and the profit motive which was the obvious reason why I was a writer, he closed by saying: 'I suggest that Weeping Willie dry his tears and work up a little thirst for knowledge about the basic economy of his state.'

Later, after this letter was printed in the Memphis paper in its turn, I received from the writer of it a letter addressed to him by a correspondent in another small Miss-[2]ississippi town, consisting in general of a sneer at the Nobel Prize which was awarded me, and commending the Weeping Willie writer for his promptness in taking to task anyone traitorous enough to hold education more important than the color of the educatee's skin. Attached to it was the Weeping Willie writer's reply. It said in effect: 'In my opinion Faulkner is the most capable commentator on Southern facts of life to date . . . If we could insult him into acquiring an insight into the basic economy of our region, he could (sic) do us a hell of a lot of good in our fight against integration.'

My answer was that I didn't believe that insult is a very sound method of teaching anybody anything, of persuading anyone to think or act as the insulter believes [he *del.*] they should. I repeated that what we needed in Mississippi was the best possible schools, to make the best possible use of the men and women we produced, regardless of what color they were. And even if we could not have a school system which would do that, at least let us have one which would make no distinction among pupils except that of simple ability, since our principal and perhaps desperate need in America today was that all Americans at least should be on the side of America; that if all Americans were on the same side, we would not need to fear that other nations and ideologies would doubt us when we talked of human freedom.

But this is beside the point. The point is, what is behind this. The tragedy is not the impasse, but what is behind the impasse—the impasse of the two apparently irreconciliable facts which we are faced with in the South: the one be-[3]ing the decree of our national government that there be absolute equality in education among all citizens, the other being the white people in the South who say that white and Negro pupils shall never sit in the same classroom. [Because these two facts must be reconciled *del.*] Only apparently irreconciliable, because they must be reconciled since the only alternative to change is death. In fact, there are people in the South, Southerners born, who not only believe they can be reconciled but who love our land—not love white people specifically nor love Negroes specifically, but our land, our country: our climate and geography, the qualities in our people, white and Negro too, for honesty and fairness, the splendors in our traditions, the glories in our past—enough to try to reconcile them, even at the cost of displeasing both sides: the contempt of the Northern radicals who believe we dont do enough, the contumely and threats of our own Southern reactionaries who are convinced that anything we do is already too much.

The tragedy is, the reason behind the fact, the fear behind the fact that some of the white people in the South—people who otherwise are rational, cultured, gentle, generous and kindly—will—must—fight against every inch which the Negro gains in social betterment: the fear behind the desperation which could drive rational and successful men (my correspondent, the Weeping Willie one, is a banker, perhaps president of a—perhaps the—bank in another small Mississippi town like my own) to grasp at such straws for weapons as contumely and threat and insult to change the views or anyway the voice which dares to suggest that betterment of the Negro's condition [4] does not necessarily presage the doom of the white race.[in the *del.*] Nor is the tragedy the fear so much as the tawdry quality of the fear—fear not of the Negro as an individual Negro nor even as a race, but as an economic class or stratum or factor, since what the Negro threatens is not the <Southern> white man's social system but the <Southern> white man's economic system—that economic system which the white man knows and dares not admit to himself is established on an obsolescence—the artificial inequality of man—and so is itself already obsolete and hence doomed. He knows that only three hundred years ago the Negro's naked grandfather was eating rotten elephant or hippo meat in an African rain-forest, yet in only three hundred years the Negro produced Dr Ralph Bunche and George Washington Carver and Booker T. Washington. The white man knows that only ninety years ago not one percent. of the Negro race could own a deed to land, let alone read that deed; yet in only ninety years, although his only contact with a county courthouse is the window through which he pays the taxes for which he has no representation, he can own his land and farm it with inferior stock and worn-out [ge *del.*] tools and gear—equipment which any white man would starve with—and raise children and feed and clothe them and send them to what schools are available and even now and then send them North where they can have equal scholastic opportunity, and end his life holding his head up because he owes no man, with even enough over to pay for his coffin and funeral. That's what the white man in the South is afraid of: that the Negro, who has done so much with no chance, might do so much more with an equal one that he might take the white man's economy away from him, the Negro now the banker or the merchant [5] or the planter and the white man the share-cropper or the tenant. That's why the Negro can gain our country's highest decoration for valor beyond all call of duty for saving or defending or preserving white lives on foreign battle-fields yet the Southern white man dares not let that Negro's children learn their abc's in the same classroom with the children of the white lives he saved or defended.

* * * *

Now the Supreme Court has defined exactly what it meant by what it said: that by 'equality' it meant, simply, equality, without qualifying or conditional adjectives: not 'separate but equal' nor 'equally separate', but simply, equal:

and now the Mississippi voices are talking of something which does not even eixst anymore.

In the first half of the nineteenth century, before slavery was abolished by law in the United States, Thomas Jefferson and Abraham Lincoln both held that the Negro was not yet competent for equality.

That was more than ninety years ago now, and nobody can say whether their opinions would be different now or not.

But assume that they would not have changed their belief, and that that opinion is right. Assume that the Negro is still not competent for equality, which is something which neither he nor the white man knows until we try it. [6]

But we do know that, with the support of the Federal Government, the Negro is going to gain the right to try and see if he is fit or not for equality. And if the Southern white man cannot trust him with something as mild as equality, what is the Southern white man going to do when he has power—the power of his own fifteen millions of unanimity back[ed] by the Federal Government which has compelled his right to test his capacity from those who are on record through white organizations for that sole purpose, that they will go to any length short of violence to stop him, when the only check on that power will be that Federal Government which is already the Negro's ally?

In 1849, Senator John C. Calhoun made his address in favor of secession if the Wilmot Proviso was ever adopted. On Oct. 12th of that year, Senator Jefferson Davis wrote a public letter to the South, saying: 'The generation which avoids its responsibility on this subject sows the wind and leaves the whirlwind as a harvest to its children. Let us get together and build manufacturies, enter upon industrial pursuits, and prepare for our own self-sustenance.'

At that time the Constitution guarantee the Negro as property along with all other property, and Senator Calhoun and Senator Davis had the then undisputed validity of States' Rights to back their position. Now the Constitution guarantees the Negro equal right to equality, and the states' rights which the Mississippi voices are talking about do not exist anymore. We—Mississippi—sold our states' rights back to the Federal Government when we accepted the first cotton [7] price-support subsidy twenty years ago. Our economy is not agricultural any longer. Our economy is the Federal Government. We no longer farm in Mississippi cotton-fields. We farm now in Washington corridors and Congessional committee-rooms.

We—the South—didn't heed Senator Davis's words then. But we had better do it now. If we are to watch our native land wracked and ruined twice in less than a hundred years over the Negro question, let us be sure this time that we know where we are going afterward.

* * * *

There are many voices in Mississippi. There is that of one of our United States senators, who, although [what he advocates does not quite match the oath he took when he entered into his high office several years ago, at least has made no attempt to hide his iden *del.*] he is not speaking for the United States Senate and what he advocates does not quite match the oath he took when he entered into his high office several years ago, at least has made no attempt to hide his identity and his condition. And there is the voice of one of our circuit judges, who, although he is not now speaking from the Bench and what he advocates also stands a little awry to his oath that before the law all men are equal and the weak shall be succored and defended, makes no attempt either to conceal his identity and condition. And there are the voices of the ordinary citizens who, although they do not claim to speak specifically for the white Citizens' [8] Councils and the NAACP, do not try to hide their sentiments and their convictions; not to mention those of the schoolmen—teachers and professors and pupils—though, since most Mississippi schools are State-owned or -supported, they dont always dare to sign their names to the open letters.

There are all the voices in fact, except one. That one voice which should silence them all, being the superior of all since it is the living articulation of the glory and the sovereignty of God and the hope and aspiration of man. The Church, which is the strongest unified force in our Southern life since all Southerners are not white and are not democrats, but all Southerners are religious and all religions serve [one *del.*] <the same> single God. Where is that voice now, the only reference to which I have seen was in an open forum letter to our Memphis paper which said that to his (the writer's) knowledge, none of the people who begged leave to doubt that one segment of the human race was forever doomed to be inferior to all the other segments just because the Old Testament five thousand years [ago] said it was, were communicants of any church.

Where is that voice now, which should have propounded perhaps two but certainly one of these still-unanswered questions?

1. The Constitution of the U.S. says: Before the law, there shall be no artifical inequality—race creed or money—among citizens of the United States.
2. Morality says: Do unto others as you would have others do unto you.
3. Christianity says: I am the only distinction among men since whosoever believeth in Me, shall never die. [9]

Where is this voice now, in our time of trouble and indecision? Is it trying by its silence to tell us that it has no validity and wants [no *del.*] <none> outside the sanctuary behind its symbolical spire?

* * * *

When I first learned about the Till affair I said, thought—knowing my country and its people—: *They did not intend to kill him: only to whip and perhaps frighten him. Instead of cringing, he talked back to them and so in that sense participated as an agent in his own destruction.* According to the recent piece in LOOK magazine, that assumption was right, assuming [that *del.*] the circumstances as stated in the LOOK piece to be fairly correct, since a magazine would think pretty hard before deliberately leaving itself actionable for a specific accusation of homicide.

If these were the circumstances, this is what ineradicably remains: two adults, armed, in the dark, kidnap a fourteen-year-old boy and take him away to frighten him. Instead of which, the fourteen-year-old boy not only refuses to be frightened, but, unarmed, alone, in the dark, so frightens the two armed adults that they must destroy him.

What are we Mississippians afraid of? Why do we have so low an opinion of ourselves that we are afraid of people who by all our standards are our inferiors?—economically: i.e., they have so much less than we have that they must work for us not on their terms but on ours; educationally: i.e., their [10] schools are so much worse than ours that the Federal Government has to threaten to intervene to give them equal conditions; politically: i.e., they have no recourse in law for protection from nor restitution for injustice and violence.

Why do we have so low an opinion of our blood and traditions as to fear that, as soon as the Negro enters our house by the front door, he will propose marriage to our daughter and she will immediately accept him?

Our ancestors were not afraid like this—our grandfathers who fought at First and Second Manassas and Sharpsburg and Shiloh and Franklin and Chickamauga and Chancellorsville and the Wilderness; let alone those who survived that and had the additional and even greater courage and endurance to resist and survive Reconstruction, and so preserved to us something of our present heritage. Why are we, descendants of that blood and inheritors of that courage, afraid? What are we afraid of? What has happened to us in only a hundred years?

* * * *

For the sake of argument, let us agree that all white Southerners (all white Americans maybe) curse the day when the first Briton or Yankee sailed the first shipload of manacled Negroes across the Middle Passage and auctioned them into American slavery. Because that doesn't matter now. To live anywhere in the world today and be against equality because of race or color, is like living in Alaska and being against snow. [11] We have already got snow. And as with the Alaskan, merely to live in armistice with it is not enough. Like the Alaskan, we had better use it.

Suddenly about five years ago and with no warning to myself, I adopted the habit of travel. Since then I have seen (a little of some, a little more of others) the Pacific islands, Asia, the Middle East, [Europe *del.*] <North Africa> and Europe. The countries I saw were not communist of course, but they were more: they were not even communist-inclined, where it seemed to me they should have been. And I wondered why. Then suddenly I said to myself with a kind of amazement: It's because of America. These people still believe in the American dream: they do not know yet that something [has *del.*] happened to it. They believe in us and are willing to trust and follow us not because of our material power: Russia has that: but because of the idea of individual human freedom and liberty and equality on which our nation was founded, which our founding fathers postulated the word 'America' to mean.

And, five years later, the countries which are still free of communism are still free simply because of that: that belief in individual liberty and equality and freedom which is the one idea powerful enough to stalemate the idea of communism. And we can thank our gods for that since we have no other weapon to fight communism with; in diplomacy we are children to communist diplomats, and in production we will always lag since under monolithic government all production can go to the aggrandisement of the State. But then, we dont need anything [12] more since that simple belief of man that he can be free is the strongest force on earth and all we need to do is use it.

Because it makes a glib and simple picture, we like to think of the world situation today as a precarious and explosive balance of two irreconcilable ideologies confronting each other: which precarious balance, once it totters, will drag the whole universe into the abyss along with it. That's not so. Only one of the opposed forces is an ideology. The other one is that simple fact of Man: that simple belief of individual man that he can and should and will be free. And if we who are still free want to continue so, all of us who are still free had better confederate and confederate fast with all others who still have a choice to be free—confederate not as black people nor white people nor blue or pink or green people, but as people who still are free, with all other people who are still free; confederate together and stick together too, if we want a world or even a part of a world in which individual man can be free, to continue to endure.

And we had better take in with us as many as we can get of the nonwhite peoples of the earth who are not completely free yet but who want and intend to be, before that other force which is opposed to individual freedom, befools and gets them. Time was when the nonwhite man was content to—anyway, did—accept his instinct for freedom as an unrealisable dream. But not anymore: the white man himself taught him different with that phase of his—the white man's—own culture which took the form of colonial expansion and exploitation based and morally condoned on the premise of inequality not because of individual incompe-[13]tence but of mass race or color. As a result of which, in only ten years we have watched the nonwhite peoples expel, by bloody violence when necessary, the white man from all the portions of the Middle East and Asia which he once dominated, into which vacuum has already begun to move that other and inimical power which people who believe in freedom are at war with—that power which says to the nonwhite man: 'We dont offer you freedom because there is no such thing as freedom; your white overlords whom you have just thrown out have already proved that to you. But we offer you equality, at least equality in slavedom; if you are to be slaves, at least you can be slaves to your own color and race and religon.'

We, the western white man who does believe that there exists an individual freedom above and beyond this mere equality of slavedom, must teach the nonwhite peoples this while there is yet a little time left. We, America, who are the strongest national force opposing communism and monolithicism, must teach all other peoples, white and nonwhite, slave or (for a little while yet) still free. We, America, have the best opportunity to do this because we can [do it here, *del.*] begin here, at home: we will not need to send costly freedom task-forces into alien and inimical nonwhite places already convinced that there is no such thing as freedom and liberty and equality <and peace> for nonwhite people too, or we would practise it at home. Because our nonwhite minority is already on our side; we dont need to sell the Negro on America and freedom because he is already sold; even when ignorant from inferior or no education, even despite the record of his history of inequality, he still believes in our concepts of [14] freedom and democracy.

That is what America has done for them in only three hundred years. Not done *to* them: done *for* them because to our shame we have made little effort so far to teach them to be Americans, let alone to use their capacities and capabilities to make us a stronger and more unified America;—the people who only three hundred years ago [were eating carrion in African jungles *del.*] lived beside one of the largest bodies of inland water on earth and never thought of sail, who yearly had to move by whole villages and tribes from famine and pestilence and enemies without once thinking of wheel, yet in three hundred years have become skilled artisans and craftsmen capable of holding their own in a culture of technocracy; the people who only three hundred years ago were eating the carrion in the tropical jungles yet in only three hundred years have produced the Phi Beta Kappas and the Doctor Bunches and the Carvers and the Booker Washingtons and the poets and musicians; who have yet to produce a Fuchs or Rosenberg or Gold or Burgess or [Meredith *del.*] McLean or Hiss, and where for every Robeson or Richard Wright there are a thousand white ones.

The Bunches and Washingtons and Carvers and the musicians and the poets who were not just good men and women but good teachers too, teaching him—the Negro—[what *del.*] by precept and example what a lot of our white people have not learned yet: that to gain equality, one must deserve it, and to deserve equality, one must understand what it is: that there is no such thing as equality *per se,* but only equality *to*: equal right and oppor-[15]tunity to make the best one can of one's life within one's capacity and capability, without fear of injustice or oppression or violence. If we had given him this equality ninety or fifty or even ten years ago, there would have been no Supreme Court ruling about segregation in 1954.

But we didn't. [It is our southern white *del.*] We dared not: it is our southern white man's shame that in our present economy the Negro must not have economic equality; our double shame that we fear that giving him more social equality will jeopardise his present economic status; our triple shame that even then, to justify our stand, we must becloud the issue with the bugaboo of miscegenation; what a commentary that the one remaining place on earth where the white man can flee and have his uncorrupted blood protected and defended by law, is in Africa—Africa: the source and origin of the threat whose present presence in America will have driven the white man to flee it.

Soon now all of us—not just Southerners nor even just Americans, but all people who are still free and want to remain so—are going to have to make a choice, lest the next (and last) confrontation we face will be, not communists against anti-communists, but simply the remaining handful of white people against the massed myriads of all the people on earth who are not white. We will have to choose not between color nor race nor religion nor between East and West either, but simply between being slaves and being free. And we will have to choose completely and for good; the time is already [16] past now when we can choose a little of each, a little of both[, *del.*]. We can choose a state of slavedom, and if we are powerful enough to be among the top two or three or ten, we can have a certain amount of license—until someone more powerful rises and has us machine-gunned against a cellar wall. But we cannot choose freedom established on a hierarchy of degrees of freedom, on a caste system of equality like military rank. We must be free not because we claim freedom, but because we practise it; our freedom must be buttressed by an homogeny equally and unchallengeably free, no matter what color they are, so that all the other inimical forces everywhere—systems political or religious or racial or national—will not just respect us because we practise freedom, they will fear us because we do.

———"On Fear: The South in Labor: Mississippi," 1956, carbon typescript, canceled; 1 page, unnumbered, 11 by 8½ inches, unwatermarked. On verso of page 9 of a complete typescript of this same essay (see page 244).

We have already got that snow. And the time is near when just to live in amity with that snow may not be enough, when we will [have to use *del.*] <even need> that snow if we wish to survive.

Of the countries outside the northern half of the western hemisphere [which only *del.*] <, the only ones which more than> the most arrant optimism could say definitely will not be communist in ten years, are the [other *del.*] <rest of the> aryan members of the British Commonwealth. And if the other nations of the earth which are still free, do not remain free, then England will no longer endure

———"On Fear: The South in Labor: Mississippi," 1956, carbon typescript, canceled; 1 page, unnumbered, 11 by 8½ inches, unwatermarked. On verso of page 12 of a complete typescript of this same essay (see page 245).

We have already got [the *del.*] snow. And as with the Alaskan, merely to live in amity, armistice, with it is not enough. Like the Alaskan, we had better use it.

Of the countries outside the northern half of the western hemisphere which are still more or less free of communism, the only ones which any save the most arrant optimist could say definitely will not be communist in ten years, are the English-speaking ones. And if the other nations of the earth which are still free, do not remain free, then [Eng *del.*] England will no longer endure as a free [nation *del.*] people. And if all the rest of the world becomes communist, it will be the end of America too as we know it: we will be strangled by simple economic blockade since there will be no one anywhere anymore to sell our products to.

And the only reason

1347 Address upon presentation of the Gold Medal for Fiction to John Dos Passos, May 22, 1957, carbon typescript with autograph corrections in black ink, 1 page, 11 by 8½ inches, unwatermarked "copy" paper.

This typescript reflects Faulkner's concern with distilling and refining the brief conclusion of his speech to purge it of residual stiltedness. Ironically, when his turn came after excessive delay, his patience betraying him, Faulkner resorted to delivering only a part of the last of three paragraphs celebrating the achievement of Dos Passos.

The artist, the writer, must never have any doubts about where he intends to go; the aim, the dream, must be that high to be worth that destination and the anguish of the effort to reach it. But he must have humility regarding his competence to get there, about his methods, his craft and his craftsmanship in it.

So the fact that the artist has no more actual place in the American culture of today than he has in the American economy of today, no place at all in the warp and woof, the thews and sinews, the mosaic of the American dream as it exists today, is perhaps a good thing for him since it teaches him humility in advance, gets him into the habit of humility well ahead whether he would or no; in which case, none of us has been better trained in humility than this man whom the Academy is honoring today. Which proves also that that man, that artist, who can accept the humility, will, must, in time, sooner or later, work through the humility and the oblivion into that moment when he and the value of his life's work will be recognised and honored at least by his fellow craftsmen, as John Dos Passos[' life *del.*] and <his> life's work [is *del.*] are at this moment.

[And mine is the honor to *del.*] [partake of his *del.*] <It is my honor to> < share* in his>, [in *del.*] <by> having been chosen [[by *del.*] <of> our fellow craftsmen *del.*] to hand this medal to him. No man [has *del.*] deserve[d *del.*]<s> it more, and few have waited longer for it.

*When Saxe Commins retyped this corrected copy of Faulkner's speech, he interpreted as a long dash what appears to be a mark instructing the printer to close up text, thus making the copy read "to ________ share" and producing an unintelligible syntax. This confusing form is perpetuated in *Essays, Speeches & Public Letters.* Our reading of the passage is consistent with that printed in *Proceedings of the American Academy of Arts and Letters and the National Institute of Arts and Letters* (1958).

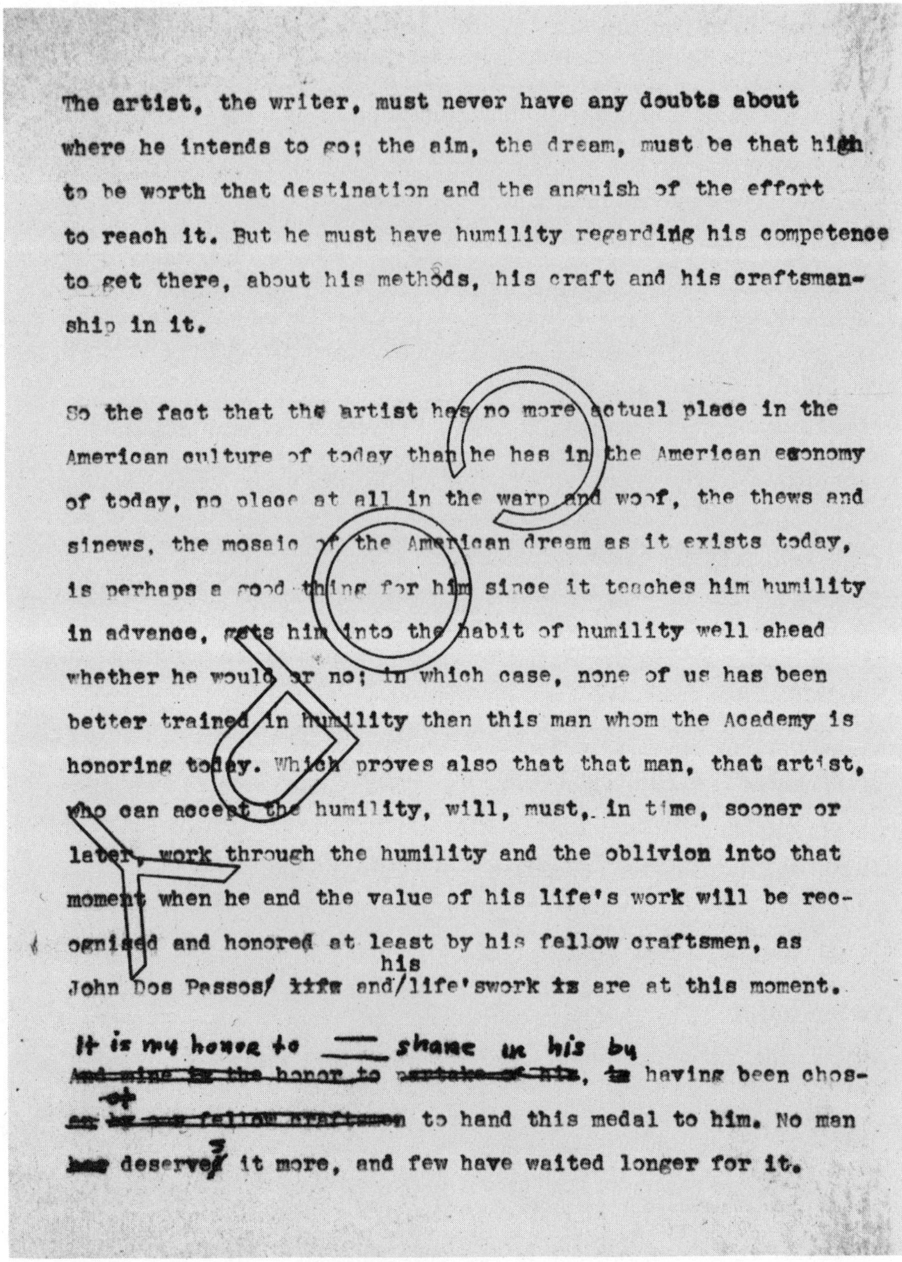

The artist, the writer, must never have any doubts about where he intends to go; the aim, the dream, must be that high to be worth that destination and the anguish of the effort to reach it. But he must have humility regarding his competence to get there, about his methods, his craft and his craftsmanship in it.

So the fact that the artist has no more actual place in the American culture of today than he has in the American economy of today, no place at all in the warp and woof, the thews and sinews, the mosaic of the American dream as it exists today, is perhaps a good thing for him since it teaches him humility in advance, gets him into the habit of humility well ahead whether he would or no; in which case, none of us has been better trained in humility than this man whom the Academy is honoring today. Which proves also that that man, that artist, who can accept the humility, will, must, in time, sooner or later, work through the humility and the oblivion into that moment when he and the value of his life's work will be recognized and honored at least by his fellow craftsmen, as his John Dos Passos' ~~life~~ and/life'swork ~~is~~ are at this moment.

It is my honor to ___ share in his by
~~And mine is the honor to partake of his~~, ~~is~~ having been chos-
~~en~~ of ~~by his fellow craftsmen~~ to hand this medal to him. No man ~~has~~ deserves it more, and few have waited longer for it.

52. Faulkner's presentation of Gold Medal of Fiction to John Dos Passos, 1957

► Acceptance Speech, Andrés Bello Award, April 6, 1961, autograph manuscript in pencil, 1 page, 10½ by 8 inches, watermarked with United States Information Service American eagle and shield.

This manuscript is the original draft of the speech Faulkner wrote in English and delivered in Spanish (from a copy translated by Hugh Jencks, Faulkner's interpreter) at the Ministry of Education in Caracas, Venezuela. The manuscript was discovered among the papers formerly in the possession of William and Victoria Franklin Fielden, Faulkner's son-in-law and stepdaughter, his hosts on the visit Faulkner made to Venezuela under the auspices of the Department of State. The text is written on the verso of a letter to Faulkner from Cecil L. Sanford, Cultural Attache, American Embassy, Caracas, dated April 4, 1961. For a more detailed discussion of this speech see Louis Daniel Brodsky, "The 1961 Andrés Bello Award: William Faulkner's Original Acceptance Speech," *Studies in Bibliography,* 39 (1986), 277–281, in which article the speech had its first publication in English.

The artist, whether he would have chosen so or not, finds that he has [become *del.*] <been> dedicated to a single course and one from which he will never escape. This is, he tries, with every means in his possession, his imagination, experience and observation, to put into some more durable form than his own fragile and ephemeral life—in paint or music or marble or the covers of a book—that which he has learned in his brief spell of breathing—the passion and hope, the beauty and horror and humor[—*ov.,*] of frail and fragile and indomitable man struggling and suffering and triumphing [in the human cond *del.*] amid the conflicts of his own heart, in the human condition. He is not to solve this dilemma nor does he even hope to survive it save in the shape and significance, the memories, of the marble and paint and music and ordered words which [to *del.*] someday he must leave behind him.

This of course is his immortality, perhaps the only one. Perhaps the very drive which has compelled him to that dedication was simply the desire to leave [written *del.*] inscribed beside that final door into oblivion through which he first must pass, the words 'Kilroy was here.'

So, as I stand here today, I have already tasted that immortality. That I, a country-bred [w *del.*] alien [from thousands of miles away *del.*] who followed that dedication thousands of miles away, to seek and try to capture and imitate for a moment in a handful of printed pages, the truth of man's hope in the human dilemma, have received here in Venezuela the official accolade which [*sic*] says in effect [Yes. What you *del.*] found and tried to imitate, was truth. [*transferred by guideline to end of passage*] Your [search *del.*] <dedication> was not spent in vain. What you sought and [found . . . truth. *brought down by guideline*]

► Impressions of Danzas Venezuela, c. April 7, 1961, autograph manuscript in blue ink, 1 page, 11 by 8½ inches, Keith Onionskin.

Faulkner's original draft of impressions of a performance of indigenous music and dance at the Teatro Municipal, Caracas, Venezuela, on the evening

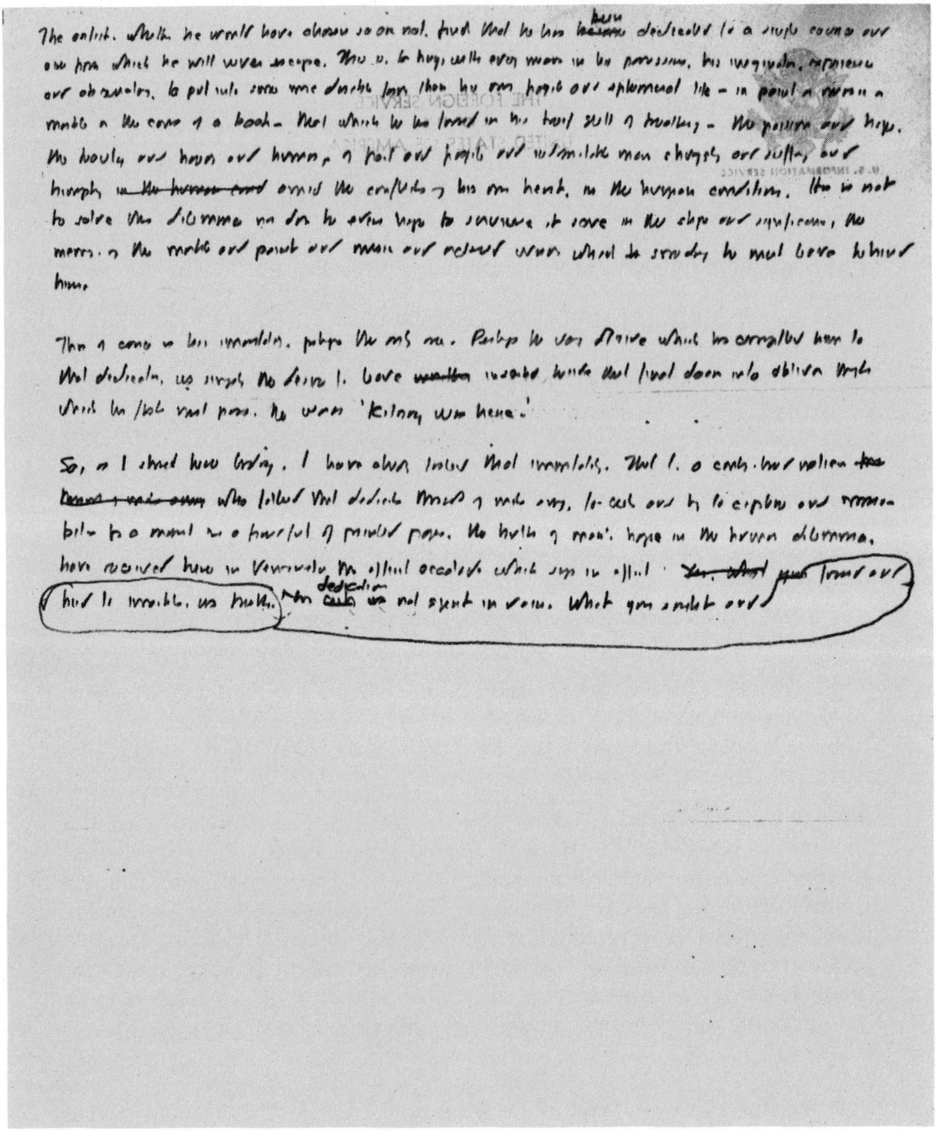

53. Faulkner's Andrés Bello Award acceptance speech, 1961

of April 6, 1961. See Louis Daniel Brodsky, "William Faulkner's 'Danzas Venezuela': The Original Manuscript," *Studies in Bibliography,* 40 (1987), 226–229.

I saw the spirit & history of Venezuela caught and held for a moment [in bri *del.*] with skill and grace, in bright and happy motion [*transferred by guideline to follow* to see the *at end of the next paragraph*]

Of course I was aware of the honor which was offered me, but ever since I reached Venezuela I had been offered [honors *del.*] the warmest of sympathy and honors, and so I was not surprised by it this time. What I experienced was more than the honor. It was this opportunity to see the [I saw . . . motion *brought down by guideline*]

This done with grace and skill by the young men and women who gave the impression that they did it for love of it, for their pride in the spirit and history of their country which they showed to the foreigner who will take home with him that remembrance, [never to forget the gesture *del.*] and with fuller knowledge of Venezuela which he had already come to admire, never to forget the gesture nor the inspiration of it, or the young men and women [who performed it *del.*] [in *del.*] <from> the [words *del.*] <poetry> of Andres Blanco [& senora Oss *del.*] which senora Ossona portrayed so wonderfully, nor senora Ramon y Rivera who directed it and the young men & women who performed it. I thank them all.

Anyone who had received as many honors as myself since reaching Venezuela, might have supposed that there was no new honor he could be worthy of. He would have been wrong. In this performance of Danzas Venezuela I saw not merely another warm and generous honor, <gesture from one American country to a visitor from another one,> I saw the spirit and history of Venezuela caught and held [for a moment *del.*] in a bright and [happy *del.*] warm moment of grace and skill and happiness, by young men and women who gave one the impression that they were doing it out of love for what they were doing, to show to this stranger, this foreigner, so that he could carry back home with him the [remembrance of *del.*] fuller poetic knowledge of a country which he had already come to admire [and respect *del.*], never to forget the gesture nor the inspiration of it from the poetry of Andres Blanco and the other Venezuelan poets whose [names *del.*] perhaps had no names, which senora Ossona translated [so wonderfully into *del.*] <into spectacular and significant> motion, nor senora Ramon y Rivera who directed it and the young men and women who performed it. He thanks them all. He will not forget [it nor them. *del.*] the experience nor those who made it possible.

► Acceptance Address, Gold Medal for Fiction, May 24, 1962, carbon typescript, 1 page, 11 by 8½ inches, Eaton's Corrasable Bond.

This typescript of Faulkner's speech to members of the American Academy of Arts and Letters and the National Institute of Arts and Letters was given by Faulkner to Joseph Blotner in gratitude for Blotner's assistance in composing

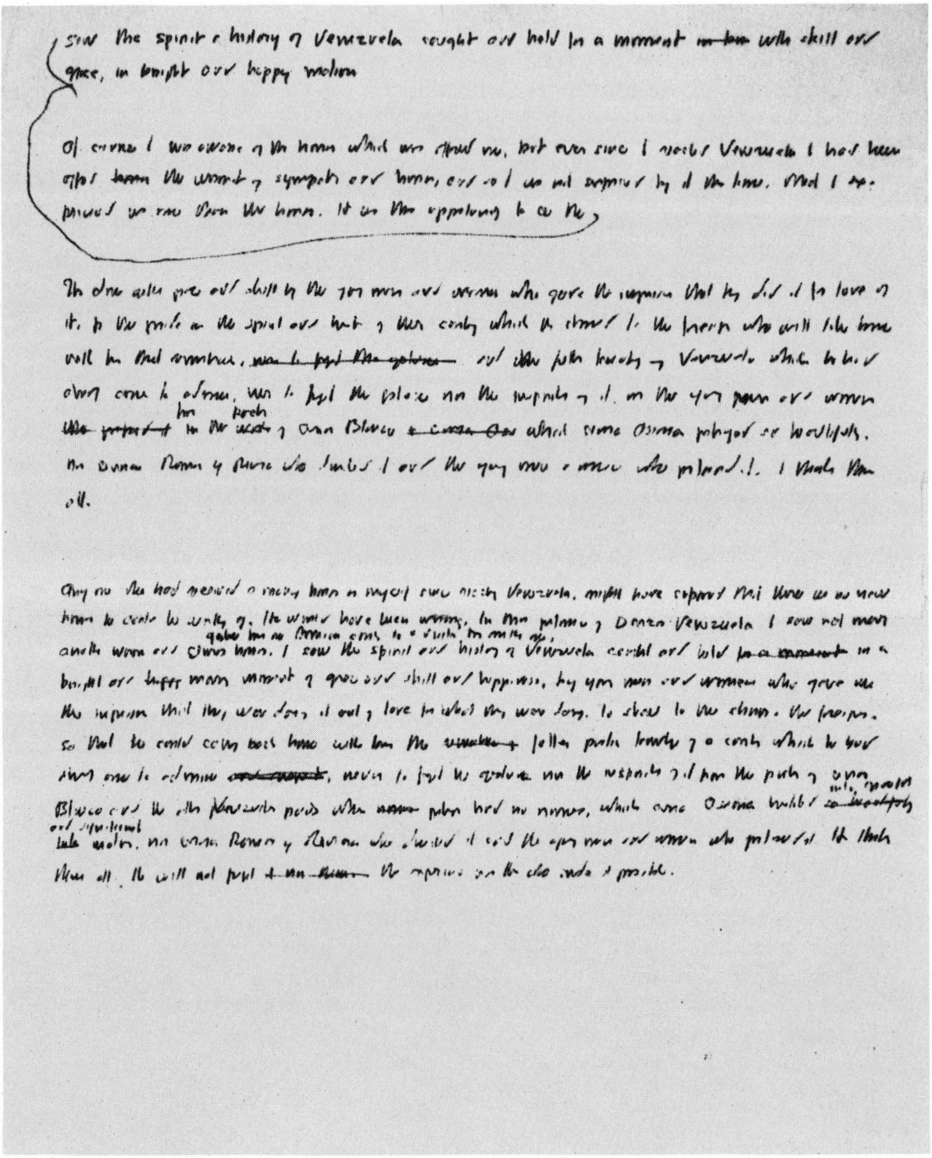

54. Faulkner's impressions of Danzas Venezuela, 1961

the speech. This copy is identical to the ribbon copy which Faulkner read and deposited with the Academy-Institute. For a detailed treatment of the composition of this speech, see Louis Daniel Brodsky, "Ghostwriting the Ghostwriter: William Faulkner's 1962 Gold Medal Speech," *Studies in Bibliography,* 41 (1988), 315–321.

This award has, to me, a double value. It is not only a comforting recognition of some considerable years of reasonably hard and arduous, anyway consistently dedicated, work. It also recognises and affirms, and so preserves, a quantity in our American legend and dream well worth preserving.

I mean a quantity in our past: that past which was a happier time in the sense that we were innocent of many of the strains and anguishes and fears which these atomic days have compelled on us. This award evokes the faded airs and dimming rotogravures which record that vanished splendor still inherent in the names of Saint Louis and Leipzig, [so that *del.*] the quantity which they celebrated and signified [is *del.*] recorded still today in the labels of wine bottles and ointment jars.

I think that those gold medals, royal and unique [among the *del.*] above the myriad spawn of their progeny which were the shining ribbons fluttering and flashing among the booths and stall of forgotten county fairs in recognition and accolade of a piece of tatting or an apple pie, did much more than record a victory. They affirmed the premise that there are no degrees of best; that one man's best is the equal of any other best, no matter how asunder in time [and *del.*] <or> space [and *del.*] <or> comparison, and should be honored as such.

We should keep that quantity, more than ever now, when roads [are *del.*] <get> shorter and easier between aim and [goal *del.*] <gain> and goals become less demanding and more easily attained, and there is less and less [room *del.*] <space> between elbows and more and more pressure on the individual to relinquish into one faceless serration like a mouthful of teeth, simply in order to [breathe. *del.*] find room to breathe. We should remember those times when the idea of an individuality of excellence compounded of resourcefulness and independence and uniqueness not only deserved a blue ribbon but got one. Let the past abolish the past when—and if—it can substitute something better; not us to abolish the past simply because it was.

V
Plays

Only slightly less prominent than his interest in drawing and poetry was Faulkner's early involvement with drama. The 1920–1921 *Ole Miss* lists Faulkner as "property man" for the Marionettes, the campus dramatic club organized by Ben Wasson, Lucy Somerville, and others; and for each of the next three years, as the successive yearbooks show, Faulkner was included among the organization's "honorary members." Actually, Faulkner's contributions to the Marionettes were far more extensive than the yearbook phrases suggest. In late 1920 he wrote a one-act play, appropriately entitled *Marionettes,* hand-lettering and -illustrating six copies as gifts for particular friends. Shortly thereafter, in January 1921, he assisted Lucy Somerville in directing a production of Norman Lee Swartout's popular farce, *The Arrival of Kitty,* for performance in Oxford's Lyric Theatre. In addition to his various activities with the Marionettes, Faulkner wrote dramatic criticism for the campus newspaper, *The Mississippian.* The January 13, 1922 issue carried Faulkner's review of Edna St. Vincent Millay's experimental play, *Aria da Capo;* and the February 3, 1922 number printed his extended treatment of Eugene O'Neill and American drama. During this period, as Joseph Blotner has documented, Faulkner read many plays (he especially admired George Bernard Shaw's *Candida*), discussed them with his friends, and on at least one occasion boasted that he "could write a play like *Hamlet.*" He never followed up on this contention, abandoning drama for poetry and fiction, but Shakespearean parallels figure strongly in such novels as *The Sound and the Fury* and *Light in August.* Moreover, in Hollywood, first in the 1930s and again in the '40s and '50s, Faulkner applied and extended his earlier experience with the technical and structural requirements of the play format. Eventually his interest in dramatic form culminated in the publication of the hybrid play-novel, *Requiem for a Nun* (1951), and his subsequent attempts to adapt that work to the stage. Faulkner also had limited experience with a newly-emerging form, the teleplay, collaborating on the script of his own story, "The Brooch," for presentation on the *Lux Video Theatre* in April 1953.

▶ "Requiem" (play), 1951

Even as *Requiem for a Nun* was in galley form, Faulkner and Ruth Ford were already making plans for a stage adaptation of the novel. In early July 1951, still more than two months before the publication of the novel, Faulkner spent two weeks in New York writing synopses of the acts, conferring with Ford and and Lemuel Ayers, the prospective producer, and beginning work on the script. Faulkner completed his adaptation in October and November in Cambridge, Massachusetts, working there with Albert Marre, Ford's choice as director of the play. Plans called for the play to open in January 1952, but failure to secure the necessary financing led to one postponement after another. When hopes for a Paris production collapsed in April, Faulkner withdrew from the project, leaving Ford to make whatever arrangements she could. Her persistence eventually paid off, though not until November 1957 (following Albert Camus' French adaptation in 1956), when the play ran for a month in London. In January 1959 Ford finally succeeded in bringing the play to Broadway, but it was closed after only forty-three performances. By the time of the London and New York productions, however, Faulkner's script had undergone many changes at the hand of Ford, with more than half of Faulkner's lines being replaced (usually with passages from Faulkner's novel) or rearranged. The Random House edition of the play version (1959) accurately though unobtrusively calls attention to these revisions by identifying the work as "A play from the novel of William Faulkner adapted to the stage by Ruth Ford." Until now Faulkner's own adaptation of his novel has remained unpublished.

The copy of Faulkner's play in the Brodsky Collection is a mimeographed typescript, 85 pages, bound in printed blue wrappers with brass clasps. The title page shows " *'REQUIEM'* / by William Faulkner" and, in the lower right corner, "Lemuel Ayers / 200 West 57th Street / New York City."

REQUIEM

The action of the play takes place in the present time in the City of Jefferson, Yoknapatawpha County, Mississippi—before and after the trial of one, Nancy Mannigoe, for murder.

ACT ONE

Scene 1

10 A.M. November 13th. Interior the Judge's Chambers, opening off the courtroom, Jefferson, Yoknapatawpha County, Mississippi. A door rear center; Tubs and a Deputy Sheriff stand beside the door which Tubs is holding slightly open while they listen to what is going on in the courtroom. They are both country types between 40 and 50. They are carelessly dressed in unpressed clothes. The Deputy wears a pistol strapped to his waist under his coat. The tail of his coat is hiked carelessly up over the handle of the pistol. He wears a Sheriff's badge on the front of his coat which we can't see now because their backs are to the audience.

JUDGE *(offstage)* Read the indictment.

CLERK'S VOICE *(offstage)* That you, Nancy Mannigoe, did on the ninth day of September wilfully and with malice aforethought kill and murder the infant child of Mr. and Mrs. Gowan Stevens in the town of Jefferson and the County of Yoknapatawpha. . .

JUDGE'S VOICE *(offstage)* How do you plead, Mr. Stevens, guilty or not guilty?

NANCY'S VOICE *(offstage)* Guilty, Lord.

A second of aghast silence, then an uproar of many voices begins. The sound of the judge's gavel stops it.

CLERK'S VOICE *(offstage)* Order! Order! Order in the courtroom.

The uproar continues.

JUDGE'S VOICE *(offstage)* Clear the room, clear the courtroom.

The uproar ceases.

JUDGE'S VOICE *(offstage)* The court will recess for thirty minutes. Mr. Stevens, come with me. Sheriff, bring the prisoner.

The Deputy closes the door quickly.

TUBS What is it? What happened?

DEPUTY The darn nigger said she was guilty.

TUBS Well, she is, ain't she?

DEPUTY Sure. But you can't plead guilty to an indictment for murder. When the Judge asks you, are you guilty or ain't you guilty, you're supposed to say not guilty. That's the rule.

TUBS What's going to happen now?

DEPUTY Plenty. Judge Dukinfield is the maddest man in Mississippi. At this rate, this trial can last for a month.

TUBS A month! That'll be a darn shame.

DEPUTY Sure. For you and Judge Dukinfield. You all get paid by the month. I just get paid by the day as long as the jury's settin'. I wouldn't mind if it took them clean till Christmas to hang her.

TUBS I hadn't thought of that.

Tubs and the Deputy spring back from the door in alarm and just in time, as the door is flung violently open and the Judge enters, followed by the prisoner who is Nancy Mannigoe and Mr. Gavin Stevens.

The Judge is a man of about 60. He wears a neat though sober clothing. He has a pair of glasses on a black ribbon or cord which are always falling off his nose.

Nancy is a Negress in the thirties, though she could be any age between 20 and 40. Her face shows that she has lived pretty hard. It is calm, impenetrable, almost bemused. During this scene she acts as though she had no interest in what was going on; unless someone is addressing her directly, she looks off as though she were looking out the window or staring at some empty corner of the room itself. It is almost as though she were alone in the room. She is—or has been until recently—a domestic servant, nurse to two white children, the second of whom, an infant, she smothered in its cradle, for which act she is now on trial for her life. But she has probably done many things else—chopped cotton, cooked for working gangs—any sort of manual labor within her capabilities, or rather, limitations in time and availability, since her principal reputation in the little Mississippi town where she was born is that of a tramp—a drunkard, a casual prostitute, being beaten by some man or cutting or being cut by his wife or his other sweetheart. She has probably been married, at least once.

Stevens is about 50. He looks more like a poet than a lawyer and actually is: a bachelor, descendant of one of the pioneer Yoknapatawpha County families, Harvard and Heidelberg educated, and returned to his native soil to be a sort of bucolic Cincinnatus, champion not so much of truth as of justice, or of justice as he sees it, constantly involving himself, often for no pay, in affairs of equity and passion and even crime too among his people, white and Negro both, sometimes directly contrary to his office of County Attorney which he has held for years, as is the present business.

The Judge crosses angrily towards his desk.

DEPUTY Excuse me, Judge. Ain't this a little irregular?

JUDGE Very. That's what I'm going to do now: make it regular. We will excuse you and Mr. Tubs, too. I will not abscond with your prisoner.

Tubs and the Deputy exit and shut the door.

JUDGE *(sitting down)* Now, Mr. Stevens, what's going on here?

STEVENS I'm sorry, Judge. *(to Nancy)* Nancy, don't you remember what I told you? When they ask you "Guilty or Not Guilty?" you're supposed to say "Not Guilty."

JUDGE So you wait until now to rehearse and instruct your client.

NANCY If I'm the one that done it, how can I say "Not Guilty"?

JUDGE Stop it! Stop it! Have you no control at all over your client? If I thought for one minute that you had put this woman up to this . . .

STEVENS Maybe justice did it.

JUDGE Justice? To me?

STEVENS To whom else would I say justice if not to you?

JUDGE Let me tell you something, Mr. Stevens. You, as County Attorney of this county, have no business in my court to begin with. And if that were not enough, here you are, a white man, defending the Negro who murdered your own niece's child. You are already guilty of contempt of court by permitting that disgraceful scene. And now you are threatening me with the word justice. Just what is going on here anyway—or do you know?

STEVENS Maybe I don't know. But I believe there is somebody out there in that room who does.

JUDGE A witness? Then he should be put on the stand in an orthorox manner.

STEVENS It's not he—it's she.

JUDGE She?

STEVENS It's my niece—the mother of this child. Don't you remember who Mrs. Gowan Stevens was? She was Temple Drake. Now do you remember? About eight years ago, the young woman, the student at the university, who vanished from that baseball excursion train, and reappeared six weeks later in that courtroom right out there as a witness in a murder trial.

JUDGE Yes—I remember.

STEVENS —Who hired as a nurse for her children this woman who—*(to Nancy)* I'm sorry, Nancy, but this is true. *(continues to the Judge)*—who was notorious in this town as a tramp, a drunkard, who had a police record for brawling and fighting, for leading an irregular life. Yet for six years she made a good and faithful servant, then suddenly after six years, for no reason that the Sheriff or any of his investigators have ever discovered, she murdered the six-months old baby. Why?

JUDGE Isn't that obvious? She was crazy.

NANCY I ain't crazy. I'm just guilty.

STEVENS Even if she is crazy, why did she wait six years? Something happened that night that none of us have been able to learn yet.

JUDGE Just what do you want? What are you trying to do?

STEVENS I told you—ask my niece to come in here.

JUDGE There's nobody in the courtroom now. I ordered it cleared.

STEVENS If she is still there, will you accept that as an indication that maybe I'm right?

JUDGE *(after a moment)* All right. See if she's there.

Stevens goes to the door, opens it enough to speak through it.

STEVENS Mr. Tubs, if my niece is still here, will you ask her to come in?

TUBS Sure, she's right here.

JUDGE You can thank your stars that this is off the record. If this town ever learns that you are trying to drag this murdered baby's mother into this thing—

STEVENS I hate this more than you do, you're just a white man—I'm her uncle.

Temple and Gowan enter.

Temple is in the middle twenties. She is smartly dressed. She is in mourning but she is not making a parade of it. She is on her guard like a poker player, but her main audience is the Judge. To him she is acting the part of a bereaved mother who has got to go through the necessary unpleasantness of the consequence of the bereavement.

Gowan is three or four years older. He is almost a type; there were many of him in America, the South, between the two great wars: only children of financially secure parents living in city apartment hotels, alumni of the best colleges, South or East, where they belonged to the right clubs; married now and raising families yet still alumni of their schools, performing acceptably jobs they themselves did not ask for, usually concerned with money; cotton futures, or stocks, or bonds. But this face is a little different, a little more than that. Something has happened to it—tragedy—something, against which it had had no warning, and to cope with which (as it discovered) no equipment, which it has accepted and is trying, really and sincerely and selflessly (perhaps for the first time in its life) to do its best with according to its code.

Judge gets up.

JUDGE Won't you sit down, Mrs. Stevens? Bring her a chair.

TEMPLE Thank you.

JUDGE Your uncle seems to think you know something about this tragic affair that hasn't come out yet. He suggests that we discuss it.

TEMPLE Of course. Anything. If Uncle Gavin would just give me some idea what it is.

GOWAN Discuss what? What *is* there to discuss?

TEMPLE Hush, Gowan. Let Uncle Gavin tell us.

GOWAN He's dragged you in here—he'd better make it good. But first get that woman out of here.

JUDGE Of course. *(to Stevens)* Will you call Mr. Tubs?

TEMPLE Not on my account.

JUDGE You don't want her out of the room?

TEMPLE If anything Uncle Gavin wants to ask me would be unpleasant for Nancy, by all means send her out, but don't do it on our account. My husband and I don't want revenge. We're past that now.

JUDGE Well, Mr. Stevens?

STEVENS Let her stay.

GOWAN Wait.

Steps quickly to door, jerks it open. The Deputy is kneeling down with his eye on the keyhole. A second, then the Deputy breaks and runs.

JUDGE Sheriff, arrest that man!

Gowan closes the door.

GOWAN Okay. Now what is this? What's going on here?

STEVENS I want to know three things: Why did you hire this sort of woman to nurse your children in the first place? Why did she make a good servant for six years? Then what happened that night after six years that caused her to murder your baby?

TEMPLE I can't answer the second or third question. I think I see now why Uncle Gavin sent for me. Because maybe I can answer the first one.

Though if Temple Drake's past is to be put in evidence for Nancy, isn't this a queer time and place for it? *(to Judge)* My father is a judge too. That's where I got my knowledge of court procedure. Maybe you have even heard of him, Judge Drake. I imagine that all judges know one another just like all doctors do, don't they?

JUDGE Of course. Everybody knows Judge Drake, Mrs. Stevens. Your Uncle says that this is not evidence in the proper meaning of the term.

TEMPLE I see. It's just a confession then.

JUDGE Your Uncle will have to answer that. I seem to be the one who knows the least about this of all of us.

TEMPLE Don't look so down-hearted, Uncle Gavin. How do you say it? I throw myself on the mercy of the court, *(to Stevens)* and answer the first question, which is the one that I can answer and hope that Uncle Gavin can find in it whatever he needs to answer the other two. So to do that, I'll have to go back to Temple Drake, whom I had believed, hoped for eight years was dead. But apparently I was wrong. It's going to be a little difficult. You know: you can begin a story by saying "One summer when I was spending a few weeks in a Gulfport or Cape Cod hotel" and go on from there; it's all fixed and established and understood, and all you have to do is just tell the rest of it. But you can't go on from there when you begin the story by saying "One spring when I happened to be spending six weeks in a Memphis whorehouse," can you—that is, if you happen to be Mrs. socialite Gowan Stevens. Because that startles people; they don't even listen to the rest of it for saying "What? Where?"

GOWAN Come on. Let's get out of here.

TEMPLE Stop it, Gowan. Haven't we all agreed that Temple Drake's unfortunate misadventure is no secret? That's agreed, isn't it? Temple Drake, the all-Mississippi debutante whose finishing school was the Memphis sporting-house. You remember: about eight years ago. Not that anyone need be reminded of that, provided they could read newspapers eight years ago or even were kin to somebody who could read eight years ago or even were a kin to somebody who could read or even just hear or even just remember or just believe the worst or even just hope for it.

JUDGE *(to Stevens)* Do we have to have this?

TEMPLE Yes, because this is the answer to the first question. I was seventeen years old. I was on my way to a baseball game. I should have stayed on the train. I didn't. I was a foolish kid. I went to a moonshiner's house in time to see a murder committed. The murderer kidnapped me and carried me to Memphis and locked me up in a room on the top floor of a house. The house was a brothel but I was seventeen years old then and a fool, didn't even know it. The murderer sent me back down here to this very courtroom and I committed what I know now was perjury, under oath on the witness stand because I was frightened. Because he told me that if I didn't swear to the lie, he would tell where I spent those six weeks. I was just seventeen then, and I didn't know that people were really kind and good and forgiving. But I have learned better since and when I came back here and was married and safe my husband told me of a Negro woman lying in the gutter—you remember, Uncle Gavin, what was his name?—the cashier in the bank, the pillar of the church or anyway in the name of his childless wife; and this Monday morning and still drunk, Nancy comes up while he is unlocking the front door of the bank and fifty people standing at his back to get in, and Nancy comes into the crowd and right up to him, and says, "Where's my two dollars, white man?" and he turned and struck her, knocked her across the pavement and into the gutter and then ran after her, stomping and kicking at her face or anyway her voice which was still saying "Where's my two dollars, white man?" until the crowd caught and held him still kicking at the face lying in the gutter, spitting blood and teeth and still saying, "It was two dollars more than two weeks ago and you done been back twice since." And I thought that there, but for the grace of God who had given me a white skin instead of a black one, was Temple Drake. So when my son was born and I needed a nurse for him I sent for Nancy for—not absolution; I didn't want to absolve Temple Drake; it was for—what is the word I want?

JUDGE Expiation?

TEMPLE No. Expiation is not it either. People had excused me after I with a white skin had told a lie which freed a wanton murderer, of a poor ignorant harmless country-man. I thought that the least I could do was to hold out my hand to someone whose only crime was that her skin was black.

JUDGE And this was your recompense for it—the murder of your child.

TEMPLE Not recompense. Maybe expiation is the right word after all. I was a fool, a. . . . coward. I was just lucky. Because people were . . . good . . . kind. You don't just deserve that. You should have to earn it. I failed to. I failed in . . . what do you call it? Integrity. Maybe you not only mustn't fail in integrity: you don't dare.

JUDGE Do you mean that you would do this all over again?

TEMPLE How can I answer that? I was the child's mother. How can you even ask it of me?

JUDGE That's true. I am ashamed of myself to have asked it. I apologize. But even that will be easier to answer to the people of this county, than for your uncle to justify what he has attempted to do here this morning. *(to Stevens)* Well? That only answers your first question, which is exactly what your niece told you to begin with.

STEVENS *(to Nancy)* Nancy, tell the judge what really happened there that night.

JUDGE Stop. I'll put an end to this, even if you won't. You dragged your niece in here and forced her to undergo this. Now are you going to impugn her veracity?

STEVENS Tell him, Nancy.

TEMPLE Yes, Nancy, tell him.

STEVENS Tell him, Nancy, this is your last chance.

NANCY About midnight it began to rain—

TEMPLE Is that all you want with us, Judge? We can go now?

JUDGE Yes.

Temple and Gowan exit.

JUDGE Will you now instruct your client to plead properly to this charge?

NANCY Guilty, Lord.

JUDGE *(bangs his fist on the table like a gavel)* I warn you for the last time. If you cannot control your client, then you had better go back to your County Attorney's office and stick to your trespass and right-of-way and sewage disposal squabbles, and I will appoint counsel for her who can control her.

NANCY Mr. Stevens, what did I do that was wrong?

STEVENS You said "Guilty." You can't say that.

NANCY What will the Judge say if I says "Not Guilty"?

STEVENS He'll say to take you back to the jail and hang you by the neck until you're dead. And may God have mercy on your soul. Is that what you want, Nancy?

NANCY Yes, Lord.

CURTAIN

ACT ONE

Scene 2

Gowan Stevens' living room. 6:00 P.M. November 13th.

Living-room, a center table with a lamp, chairs, a sofa left rear, floor-lamp, wall-bracket lamps, a door left enters from the hall, double doors rear stand open on a dining room, a fireplace right with gas logs. The atmosphere of the room is smart, modern, up-to-date, yet the room itself has the air of another time—the high ceiling, the cornices, some of the furniture; it has the air of being in an old house, an ante-bellum house descended at last to a spinster survivor who has modernized it (vide the gas fire and the two overstuffed chairs) into apartments rented to young couples or families who can afford to pay that much rent in order to live on the right street among other young couples who belong to the right church and the country club.

Sound of feet, then the lights come on as if someone about to enter had pressed a wall switch, then the door left opens and Temple enters, followed by Gowan and Gavin. Temple's air is brittle and tense, yet controlled. Her face shows nothing as she crosses to the center table and stops. Gowan and Stevens wear their overcoats, carrying their hats. Stevens stops just inside the room. Gowan drops his hat onto the sofa in passing and goes on to where Temple stands at the table, stripping off one of her gloves.

TEMPLE *(takes cigarette from box on the table; mimics the prisoner; her voice, harsh, reveals for the first time repressed, controlled, hysteria)* Yes, God. Guilty, God. Thank you, God. If that's your attitude, toward being hung, what else can you expect from a judge and jury except to accommodate you?

GOWAN Stop it, Boots. Hush now. Soon as I light the fire, I'll buy a drink. *(to Stevens)* Or maybe Gavin will do the fire while I do the butler.

TEMPLE *(takes up lighter)* I'll do the fire. You get the drinks. Then Uncle Gavin won't have to stay. Then he can get on home, where they are probably already waiting for him.

She crosses to the hearth and kneels and turns the gas valve, the lighter ready in her other hand.

GOWAN *(anxiously)* Now, Boots.

TEMPLE *(snaps lighter, holds flame to the jet)* Will you for God's sake please get me a drink?

GOWAN Sure, honey. *(he turns; to Stevens)* Drop your coat anywhere.

He exits into the dining-room. Stevens does not move, watching Temple as the log takes fire.

TEMPLE *(still kneeling, her back to Stevens)* If you're coming to stay, why don't you sit down? Or vice versa. Backward. Only, it's the first one that's backward; if you're not sitting down, why don't you go? Let me be bereaved and vindicated, but at least let me do it in privacy, since God knows if any one of the excretions should take place in privacy, triumph should be the one—

Stevens watches her. Then he crosses to her, taking the handkerchief from his breast pocket, stops behind her and extends the handkerchief down where she can see it. She looks at it, then up at him. Her face is quite calm.

TEMPLE What's that for?

STEVENS It's all right. It's dry too. *(still extending the handkerchief)* For tomorrow, then.

TEMPLE *(rises quickly)* Oh, for cinders. On the train. We're going by air; hadn't Gowan told you? We leave from the Memphis airport at midnight; we're driving up after supper. Then California tomorrow morning; maybe we'll even go on to Hawaii in the spring. No; wrong season: Canada, maybe. Lake Louise in May and June—

STEVENS Where will you go then?

TEMPLE What?

STEVENS When Judge Dukinfield asks her that question next time, she will say not guilty. Sometime next spring, while you are in Hawaii or at Lake Louise, the sheriff of Yoknapatawpha County will hang her in the Jefferson jail. Where will you go then?

TEMPLE Nonsense. They won't hang her. They can't. She's crazy. That's obvious.

STEVENS I can't prove insanity yet.

TEMPLE Meaning without my help. You tried that this morning and apparently failed. Yet here you are again. All right. What do you want?

STEVENS To talk to you.

TEMPLE Gowan will be back in a moment, then you can get it off your chest. But you'll have to talk fast; we've got to pack and then drive up to the Memphis airport—

STEVENS Not to Gowan; to you.

They watch one another. Temple is now weary, alert, watchful.

TEMPLE Then it'll have to be fast indeed, to happen inside the emptying of one ice tray.

STEVENS Then send him away. Or I'll come back later.

TEMPLE Is this a threat, or a bluff?

STEVENS It's neither.

TEMPLE So it must be a bluff. I'll call it.

They both hear the sound from beyond the dining-room doors which indicates that Gowan is approaching. Temple lowers her voice again, rapidly.

TEMPLE Put it this way then. I don't know what you want, because I don't care. Because whatever it is, you won't get it from me. *(the sound is near now—footsteps, clink of glass)* Now Gowan'll offer you a drink, and then he'll ask you what you want here too. Maybe you will tell him—

Gowan enters with the tray containing water, ice, three glasses. The bottle of whiskey is in his side overcoat pocket. He sets the tray on the table.

GOWAN Tell me what? *(sets tray on the table)* That's right; three. I'm going to have one myself, for a change. After six years. *(he mixes three highballs)* Not one drop in six years. So I can't think of a better time to start than now. A stirrup cup, you know; California, here I come.

He offers the tray to Temple, who takes a glass. Then he offers the tray to Stevens.

STEVENS You have another reason too, if you need it.

GOWAN *(as Stevens takes a glass)* Yeah? *(then he understands the significance. He is sarcastic now)* You mean the arraignment. Thanks for reminding me—us. We're so unaccustomed to having our children murdered that we might have forgotten about it except for you. *(he sets the tray back on the table and takes up the third glass. To Stevens)* Drink up. Is it too weak? Here—

Gowan sets his glass back on the table, rapidly takes up the bottle and approaches it to Stevens' glass.

STEVENS *(quickly refusing)* No thanks. It's all right.

GOWAN *(sets the bottle back on the tray, but does not take up his own drink, as though he were not aware himself that he had not done so. Temple has not touched hers* *either)* Now this time maybe Defense Attorney Stevens will tell us what he wants out of my wife?

TEMPLE To say goodbye.

GOWAN Then say it. One more for the road, and where's your hat, huh?

He takes the tumbler from Stevens and turns back to the table.

TEMPLE *(sets her untasted glass back on the tray)* And put ice in it this time, and maybe even a little water. But first, take Uncle Gavin's coat. Maybe that's what has tied his tongue.

GOWAN *(takes bottle from his pocket and makes a highball for Stevens in the tumbler)* That won't be necessary. If he can raise his arm in a courtroom to defend that client, he can certainly bend the elbow of it in nothing but a wool sleeve to take a drink with the bereaved parents. And while we're on the subject, you drink up too. I thought you couldn't even wait to get home for one.

TEMPLE I don't want it—I want some milk.

GOWAN *(with simulated hopeless bafflement of female vagaries; his whole attitude in this scene is a show, to cover his unease, worry, grief, etc., he knows there is something behind this murder which has not come out yet, too)* You would. *(to Stevens)* You see, you can't beat them? You can't even keep up. *(to Temple)* Don't say hot, too.

TEMPLE Please.

GOWAN *(starts out)* Okay.

STEVENS What about yourself? Your drink.

GOWAN *(going)* I drink by the calendar, not the clock. It's a little too early for me yet. Don't let Uncle Gavin get away until I get back. Lock the door, if you have to. Or maybe just telephone that nigger freedom agent. What's his name?

He exits. They don't move until the slap of the pantry door sounds.

TEMPLE *(rapid and hard)* How much do you know? Don't lie to me—don't you see there's no time.

STEVENS No time for what? Before your plane leaves tonight? She has a little time yet—four months until March—the 13th of March.

TEMPLE You know what I mean. What did your client tell you? Since this morning? It can't be much or—

She stops herself; she has gone too far and now realizes it.

STEVENS Or? *(she doesn't answer)* You can't stop there; you see yourself it's too late now. That I've got to finish for you; "It can't be much, or not merely her lawyer with a question, but a policeman with a summons or a warrant, would have followed me home."

TEMPLE *(impatiently)* All right, all right; don't you realize that even heating a glass of milk won't take forever? What did she tell you? Don't say nothing, now; don't tell me to my face that it was me that spilled it.

STEVENS She has told me nothing.

TEMPLE Swear. *(quickly)* Oh, God. I talk about no time, and it's me playing button button. She's told you nothing yet.

STEVENS Yes.

TEMPLE All right. Now, don't you see it's you who've given yourself away? She's never going to tell you anything.

STEVENS And you too. So there is something she could tell about that night.

TEMPLE Except that she's not going to.

STEVENS Suppose she does.

TEMPLE No. And you know that yourself. That's why you're here. I've learned something myself, recently; that not all human beings, but only some of them, stink. Sometimes, not even a dopefiend nigger whore hired up out of the gutter. She will tell you nothing, nor will I. So take your drink for the road, Uncle Gavin. Where's your hat?

STEVENS Not even when in about two or three weeks Judge Dukinfield says to her, to be taken back to the Yoknapatawpha jail and on the something something of something be there hanged by the neck until you are dead, and may God have mercy on your soul?

They stare at each other.

TEMPLE They won't do that. They can't. She's crazy.

STEVENS Nobody capable of the physical act of murder is so crazy they don't have what they call reasons.

TEMPLE All right. But it won't happen. It can't. There is some price for your sins that you don't have to pay. They—it—are not usurers.

STEVENS It? God?

TEMPLE If there was God, He would have saved my baby. Didn't He say Himself—or so it was reported—"Suffer little children to. . ."

Her voice dies away. Stevens watches her.

STEVENS He said, "Suffer."

TEMPLE There is some price you don't have to pay. I have lost a child—my baby. That's enough.

STEVENS Enough to pay for the fact that the man who is now your husband got drunk and deserted you in the hands of a criminal who kept you prisoner in a Memphis brothel—

TEMPLE Leave Gowan out of it.

STEVENS He got drunk and deserted you in a situation where you could be kidnapped. And the murder of your little baby is enough to pay for that.

TEMPLE *(defiant)* Yes.

STEVENS So whatever it was that happened that night, did come out of that Memphis experience.

TEMPLE A lie. No, that doesn't matter either; whether I call it a lie or not, or whether you believe it or not. Because it won't happen.

STEVENS But suppose it does. The moment when it will be too late, when Judge Dukinfield will say, "Hanged by the neck till you are dead, and may God have mercy on your soul"?

TEMPLE No!

STEVENS But suppose it does.

They stare at each other.

TEMPLE Still no.

STEVENS You mean, even then you won't tell what happened that night?

TEMPLE Not even then. And let God—if there is one—have mercy on my soul, too—if I have one. Which He could do very simply by saving Nancy—or, for that matter, just by saving my baby that night, He could have saved all of us. So you see, it was not only not a threat, it didn't even hold together as a bluff. So I'm even going to give you a second chance to try it on Gowan—*(they both hear Gowan approaching)* So at least there's no doubt about my own stinking, is there?

GOWAN *(enters, carrying the hot milk, a salt shaker and a napkin, and comes to the table)* What are you talking about now?

TEMPLE Nothing. I was telling Uncle Gavin that he had something of Virginia or some sort of gentleman in him too that he must have inherited from you through your grandfather, and that I'm going up to give Bucky his bath and supper. *(she touches the glass for heat, then takes it up to Gowan)* Thank you, dear.

GOWAN Right, dear. *(to Stevens)* You see? Not just a napkin; the right napkin. That's how I'm trained. *(he stops suddenly, noticing Temple, who has done nothing apparently; just standing there holding the milk. But he seems to know what is going on; to her)* What's this for?

TEMPLE I don't know. *(he moves; they kiss, not long but not a peck either; definitely a kiss between a man and a woman. Then, carrying the milk Temple crosses toward the hall door. To Stevens)* Goodbye then until next June. Bucky will send you and Maggie a postcard. *(she goes on to the door, pauses and looks back at Stevens)* I may even be wrong about Temple Drake's odor too; if you should happen to hear something you haven't heard yet and it's true, I may even ratify it. Maybe you can even believe that—if you can believe you are going to hear anything that you haven't heard yet.

STEVENS Do you?

TEMPLE *(after a moment)* Not from me, Uncle Gavin. If someone wants to go to heaven, who am I to stop them? Good night. Goodbye.

She exits, closes the door. Stevens, very grave, turns back and sets his highball down on the tray.

GOWAN Drink up. After all, I've got to eat supper and do some packing too. How about it?

STEVENS About what? The packing, or the drink? What about you? I thought you were going to have one.

GOWAN Oh, sure. Sure. *(takes up the small filled glass)* Maybe you had better go on and leave us to our revenge.

STEVENS I wish it could comfort you.

GOWAN I wish to God it could. I wish to God that what I wanted was only revenge. An eye for an eye—were ever words emptier? Only, you have lost the eye to know it.

STEVENS Yet she still has to die.

GOWAN Why not? Even if she would be any loss—a nigger whore, a drunkard, a dope fiend—

STEVENS —a vagabond, a tramp, hopeless until one day Mr. and Mrs. Gowan Stevens out of simple pity and humanity picked her up out of the gutter to give her one more chance—*(Gowan stands motionless, his hand tightening slowly about the glass. Stevens watches him. . .)* And then in return for it—

GOWAN Look, Uncle Gavin. Why don't you go for God's sake home? Or to hell, or anywhere out of here?

STEVENS I am, in a minute. Is that why you think—why you would still say she has to die?

GOWAN I don't. I had nothing to do with it. I wasn't even the plaintiff. I didn't even instigate—that's the word, isn't it?—the suit. My only connection with it was, I happened by chance to be the father of the child she—Who in hell ever called that a drink?

He dashes the whiskey, glass and all, into the ice bowl, quickly catches up one of the empty tumblers in one hand and, at the same time, tilts the whiskey bottle over it, pouring. At first he makes no sound, but at once it is obvious that he is laughing; laughter which begins normally enough, but he still pours whiskey into the glass, which in a moment now will overflow, except that Stevens reaches his hand and grasps the bottle and stops it.

STEVENS Stop it, now. Here.

He takes the bottle from Gowan, sets it down, takes the tumbler and tilts part of its contents in the other empty one, leaving at least a reasonable, a believable, drink, and hands it to Gowan. Gowan takes it, stopping the crazy laughter, gets hold of himself again.

GOWAN *(holding the glass untasted)* Six years. Six years on the wagon—and this is what I got for it. You see? Six years without the drink, and so I got whatever it was I was buying by not drinking, and now I've got whatever it was I was paying for and it's paid for and so I can drink again. And now I don't want the drink. You see? Like whatever it was I was buying I not only didn't want, but what I was paying for it wasn't worth anything, wasn't even any loss. So I have a laugh coming. Because I got a bargain even in what I didn't want. I got a cut rate. I had two children. I had to pay only one of them to find out it wasn't really costing me anything—Half price; a child, and a dopefiend nigger whore on a public gallows. That's all I had to pay for immunity.

STEVENS There's no such thing.

GOWAN From the past. From my folly. My drunkenness. My cowardice, if you like.

STEVENS There's no such thing as past either.

GOWAN That is a laugh, that one. Only, not so loud, huh?—disturb Miss Drake—Miss Temple Drake.—Sure, cowardice. Only, for euphony, call it simple overtraining. You know? Gowan Stevens, trained at Virginia to drink like a gentleman, gets drunk as ten gentlemen, takes a country college girl, a maiden; who knows? maybe even a virgin, cross country by car to another country college ball game, gets drunker than twenty gentlemen, gets lost, gets still drunker than forty gentlemen, wrecks the car, pass eighty gentlemen now, passes completely out while the maiden, the virgin is being kidnapped into a Memphis whorehouse—*(he mumbles an indistinguishable word)*

STEVENS What?

GOWAN Sure; cowardice. Call it cowardice; what's a little euphony between old married people?

STEVENS Not the marrying hereafterward, at least. What—

GOWAN Sure. Marrying her was purest Old Virginia. That was indeed the hundred and sixty gentlemen.

STEVENS The intent was, by any other standards too. The prisoner in the whorehouse; I didn't quite hear—

GOWAN *(quickly; reaching for it)* Where's your glass? Dump that slop—here—

STEVENS *(holds glass)* This will do. What was that you said before about held prisoner in the whorehouse?

GOWAN *(harshly)* That's all. You heard it.

STEVENS You said "and loved it." *(they stare at each other)* Is that what you can never forgive her for? Not for having been the instrument creating that moment in your life which you can never recall nor forget nor explain nor condone nor even stop thinking about, but because she herself didn't even suffer, but on the contrary, even liked it—that month or whatever it was like the episode in the movie of the white girl held prisoner in the cave by the Bedouin prince?—That you had to lose not only your bachelor freedom, but your man's self-respect in the chastity of his wife and your child too, to pay for something your wife hadn't even lost, didn't even regret, didn't even miss? Is that why this poor lost doomed crazy Negro woman must die?

GOWAN Go on. Get out of here.

STEVENS In a minute. Or else you'll have to blow your own brains out; stop having to remember, stop having to be forever unable to forget; nothing; to plunge into nothing and sink and drown forever and forever, never again to have to remember, never again to wake in the night writhing and sweating because you cannot, can never not, stop remembering? What else happened during that month, that time while that madman held her prisoner there in the Memphis whorehouse, that nobody but you and she knew about, maybe not even know about?

Still staring at Stevens, slowly and deliberately Gowan sets the glass of whiskey back on the tray and takes up the bottle and swings it bottom up back over his head. The stopper is out and at once the whiskey begins to pour out of it, down his arm and sleeve and onto the floor. He does not seem to be aware of it even. His voice is tense, barely articulate.

GOWAN So help me, Christ. . . . So help me, Christ.

A moment, then Stevens moves, without haste, taking his coat as he passes the sofa, and goes on to the door and exits. Gowan stands a moment longer with the poised bottle, now empty. Then he draws a long shuddering breath, seems to rouse, wake, sets the empty bottle back on the tray, notices his untasted whiskey glass, takes it up, a moment; then turns and throws the glass crashing into the fireplace, against the burning gas logs, and stands, his back to the audience, and draws another long shuddering breath and then draws both hands hard down on his face. Then turns, looking at his wet sleeve, takes out his handkerchief and dabs at his sleeve as he comes back to the table, puts the handkerchief back in his pocket and takes the folded napkin from the small tray beside the saltcellar and wipes his sleeve with it, sees he is doing no good, tosses the crumpled napkin back onto the whiskey tray; and now, outwardly quite calm again, as though nothing had happened, he gathers the glasses back onto the tray, puts the small tray and the napkins onto it too and takes up the tray and walks quietly toward the dining-room door as the lights begin to go down.

CURTAIN

ACT TWO

Scene 1

Temple's upstairs sitting room. 10 P.M. March 11th.

The nursery opens directly off this room. The hall door opens. Temple enters, followed by Stevens. She now wears a long housecoat; her hair is tied back with a ribbon as though prepared for bed. This time Stevens carries the topcoat and the hat too; his suit is different. Apparenly she has already warned Stevens to be quiet; his air anyway shows it. She enters, stops, lets him pass her.

TEMPLE Close the nursery door, please.

Stevens crosses to the nursery door and looks inside.

STEVENS You're letting Bucky sleep in the room his sister was murdered in. So this is a plant.

TEMPLE Why not? Don't the philosophers and other gynecologists tell me that women will strike back with any weapon, even their children?

STEVENS Does that include the sleeping pill you gave Gowan? I suppose you really did give him one, didn't you?

TEMPLE If I didn't, I have certainly wasted a good lie—at a time when I'm probably going to need the best lies of which Temple Drake is capable.

STEVENS You came all the way back from California, almost without notice. You have given your husband a sleeping pill to keep him out of the way—

TEMPLE If I would stop struggling how much time we could save. I came all the way back from California but I still can't seem to quit. Do you believe in coincidence?

STEVENS I can. Yes.

TEMPLE *(at table, takes up a folded yellow telegraph form, opens it, reads:)* "Dated Jefferson, March sixth. 'You have a week yet until the thirteenth. But where will you go then?' signed Gavin." *(she folds the paper back into its old creases, folds it still again. Stevens watches her)* Do you remember last winter—last winter? Oh God, last year, last aeon, last world, when I still believed that, no matter what you had done, there was still some last price, last drop of blood, that wouldn't be demanded of you—when you said, "After they hang her, where will you go then?"

STEVENS I remember.

TEMPLE It was the day before yesterday—God, not even seventy-two hours yet—in the afternoon, Bucky and I were on the beach. I was reading and he was—oh, talking, babbling—you know: "Is California far from Jefferson, Mamma?" and I say "Yes darling"—you know: still reading or trying to, and he says, "Will we stay here until after they hang Nancy, Mamma?" and it's already too late then, I should have seen it coming, but it's too late now; I say, "Yes, darling," and then he drops it right in my lap, right out of the mouths of—how is it?—babes and sucklings: "Where will we go then, Mamma?" So we came back to the hotel and I got plane reservations for the next day and here we are and I got Gowan—I hope—safely in bed with a barbital, and telephoned you. Well?

STEVENS What?

TEMPLE Let's for God's sake stop. She hasn't told you anything yet? Swear it. *(quickly)* Oh God, why won't I stop? Why should we waste time lying to each other, when the time for lying hasn't even started yet? So let's start. I mean formally.

STEVENS Formally?

TEMPLE By the rules. You're just the lawyer. Don't we have to have a—what do you call it? Notary public? *(Stevens stares at her. Temple, impatient at his stupidity)* For the deposition or whatever you call it. Have I had to come all the way back here from California to teach the prisoner's own lawyer how to suck his eggs? It doesn't matter what she told you or didn't tell you, what I know about that night or what you think I know. Because we won't even need it. All we need is the affidavit. That she is crazy. Has been for years.

STEVENS I thought of that too. But I couldn't do it without you. If this is what you wanted, you should have done it three months ago. It's too late now. The trial is over. She has been convicted and sentenced. In the eyes of the law, she is already dead. In the eyes of the law, Nancy Mannigoe doesn't even exist.

TEMPLE Yes?

STEVENS We haven't got one.

TEMPLE Yes? That's right. Try to listen. Really try. I am the affidavit. I wasn't here then. But now I am. What else did I come all the way back from California for? When I was . . . . . safe, free. Maybe you need a drink to clear your head—

STEVENS No. I'm dizzy enough with just perjury and contempt of court.

TEMPLE What perjury?

STEVENS After my client is not only convicted but sentenced to death too, I turn up with the victim's mother, offering evidence to set the whole trial aside—

TEMPLE Tell them I forgot this part of it. Or tell them I changed my mind. Tell them the district attorney bribed me to keep my mouth shut—

STEVENS *(peremptory, commanding)* Temple.

TEMPLE Or better still; won't it be obvious? A mother whose child was murdered in its crib, wanting vengeance, capable of suppressing any fact to get vengeance, even when she has the vengeance, realizing she can't go through with it, can't sacrifice a human life, even a nigger whore's?

STEVENS Stop it, Temple. *(she stops)* We produce—turn up with—a sworn statement that this murderess was crazy when she committed the crime.

TEMPLE You were listening, weren't you?

STEVENS Based on what? *(she stares at him)* On what proof? What are we going to affirm now, that for some reason, any reason, we—you—didn't see fit to bring up until after she was—

TEMPLE How do I know? You're the lawyer. What do you want—need—in it? Don't you have samples in your law books to tell you that you can copy and have me swear to? Good ones. Certain ones, such a good one that nobody, not even an untrained lawyer, can blunder on a hole in? *(he stares at her. She stares back)* What do you want, then? What more do you want?

STEVENS The truth. What happened here that night. If that means Temple Drake, then I want Temple Drake.

TEMPLE No! Mrs. Gowan Stevens maybe. But not Temple Drake.

STEVENS Yes. Temple Drake. The truth.

TEMPLE Truth? We're trying to save a condemned murderess, whose lawyer has already admitted that he has failed. What has truth got to do with it? *(quickly) We? We're* trying? I. I'm trying. I, the mother of the baby she murdered. Not you, the lawyer, but I, Mrs. Gowan Stevens, the mother. Can't you get it through your head that I will do anything, *anything?*

STEVENS Except one. *(they watch each other)* Which is all, everything. We're not concerned with death. That's nothing. Any handful of petty facts and sworn documents can cope with that. That's finished now; we can even forget it. What we are trying to deal with now is injustice, falsehood. Only truth can cope with that. Or love.

TEMPLE Love. Oh God. Love.

STEVENS Call it pity, then. Or call it simply the desire for the right to sleep at night.

TEMPLE You prate of sleep, to me, who learned six years ago how not even to realize anymore that I didn't mind not sleeping at night?

STEVENS Yet you came back, after—as you put it—you were safe, free.

TEMPLE Will you, for Christ's sake stop? *(they watch each other)* All right. What do you want? What in God's name do you want?

STEVENS I told you. What happened that night. The truth.

TEMPLE And I told you that what you keep harping on as truth, has nothing to do with this. When you go before the. . . . what do you call this next collection [of] trained lawyers? the Supreme Court, isn't it? . . . what you will need will be fact, papers, sworn documents, that no other trained lawyer can punch holes in.

STEVENS We're not going to the Supreme Court. That's all finished. If that would have done, you would not have needed to come back. We're going to the Governor.

TEMPLE The Governor?

STEVENS Yes, the last. Perhaps he won't save her either. He probably won't.

TEMPLE Then why ask him? Why?

STEVENS I've told you. Truth.

TEMPLE *(in quiet amazement)* For no more than that. For no better reason than that. Just to get it told, breathed aloud, into words, sound. Just to be heard by, told to, someone, anyone, any stranger none of whose business it is, can possibly be, simply because he is capable of hearing, comprehending it. The Governor. We don't even need papers. I just talk, tell what I have believed for eight years I would never tell anyone. I go to him, a stranger, and tell him. . . . .

STEVENS Yes. What really happened here that night.

TEMPLE Why blink your own rhetoric? Why don't you go on and tell me it's for the good of my soul—if I have one?

STEVENS I did. I said, "so you can sleep at night."

TEMPLE And I told you I forgot six years ago even what it was to miss the sleep. *(turns her head and looks toward the nursery door)* So it was a plant, after all. I just didn't seem to realize who it was planted for. *(a moment)* So I threw my remaining child at you. And so you threw it back.

STEVENS But without waking him.

TEMPLE Aha. Got you, lawyer. What would be better for his peace and sleep than to hang his sister's murderer?

STEVENS No matter now, by what means, what lie?

TEMPLE Nor even whose lie.

STEVENS Yet you came back.

TEMPLE Mrs. Gowan Stevens did.

STEVENS Temple Drake did. Mrs. Gowan Stevens is not even fighting in this class. This is Temple Drake's.

TEMPLE Temple Drake is dead.

STEVENS The past is never dead. It's not even past.

TEMPLE All right. How much will I have to tell?

STEVENS Everything.

TEMPLE By which logic, this Temple Drake we are so concerned about, isn't even *is* yet. How much has she told you about that night?

STEVENS Nothing.

TEMPLE Swear.

STEVENS Would you believe me?

TEMPLE No. But swear anyway.

STEVENS I swear.

TEMPLE All right. How much do you *think* you know?

STEVENS There was a man there.

TEMPLE *(quickly)* Gowan.

STEVENS Let's agree that this is for your life too. So nobody but a fool would expect you to fight by Queensberry rules. But only a fool would believe you foolish enough to mistake a straw for a cudgel. Gowan wasn't there then. He and Bucky had already left four hours ago for New Orleans—*(they watch each other)* It wasn't your fault; you just had to use tools—implements—that failed you. It was Gowan himself who gave you away—something he said to me without knowing he was doing it, which showed who planned that trip, to get not only Gowan, but Bucky too out of this house. I'm surprised that you didn't send Nancy away too—*(he stops, obviously reacts to something he sees in Temple's face)* Why, you did. You did try, and she refused. Yes. There was a man here that night.

TEMPLE Prove it.

STEVENS I can't. Don't I keep on saying that Nancy has refused to tell me anything about that night?

TEMPLE Then listen to me. Listen carefully, because I don't intend to say this again. Temple Drake is dead. Temple Drake will have been dead six years longer than Nancy Mannigoe will ever be. If there is anything—anything at all—that Mrs. Gowan Stevens can sign or swear to or lie to, to save Nancy Mannigoe, we will do it. But if all Nancy Mannigoe has left to save her, is Temple Drake, then God help Nancy Mannigoe. Now get out of here. And close the front door when you go out. It's getting cold.

Stevens exits. Temple stands watching the door. When Stevens is gone, Gowan appears quietly in the dining room door, in his shirtsleeves, tieless, his collar open. He watches Temple as she stands a moment longer. Then she makes a gesture something like Gowan's in scene [2], except that she merely presses her hands hard against her cheeks, stands a moment, then drops her hands and crosses purposefully to the telephone, Gowan still watching her, and lifts the receiver.

TEMPLE *(into the phone)* Three-two-nine, please. *(she does not see Gowan yet. He approaches her, carrying something in his closed hand. He is right behind her when the phone answers)* Hello. Maggie? This is Temple. When Uncle Gavin—

Gowan reaches roughly past her, grasps her hand holding the receiver and claps the receiver back on the stand, cutting off the connection; at the same time he flips the capsule from his other hand onto the table.

GOWAN There's your pill too. Why don't you even tell me about the man that Gavin says was here that night? Come on. You won't even have to think hard. Just tell me he was an uncle of Buck's that you just forgot to tell me about.

TEMPLE Would you believe me if I said there wasn't one?

GOWAN Sure I would. Anything you say. I always have. That's what has sunk us. I even believed right up until tonight that it was me that planned that fishing trip. Everybody but me knew better, even the neighbors knew better, but that was all right, nobody needed to be fooled but me and I was already on my back when I came in. Thanks though. But I can still see, even if I don't know until six years afterward what I was looking at. But try the truth maybe; there surely must be something you can tell me that I won't believe. Maybe Gavin was right and his business wasn't with my wife, but with Temple Drake. Maybe it was Bucky's papa, huh, just dropped in on the way through town—

TEMPLE Gowan. *(he stops talking, looking at her)* Why can't you just hush? *(indicates the sleeping child)*

GOWAN Don't worry, you were the one who seems to worry about waking him. I'm not going to make that much noise. I'm not going to hit you. I never hit a woman in my life, not even a whore, not even a Memphis whore, an ex-Memphis whore—Jesus, what do you know, they say there are two women every man is entitled to hit once: his wife, and his whore. And just look at me: I can hit both of mine at one time, with one swing, one lick—

TEMPLE Try to stop. Try to.

GOWAN Okay. Maybe if you had a drink, I would stop. Do you want a drink?

TEMPLE I don't want one.

GOWAN Come on. I'll fix you one.

TEMPLE I don't want one.

GOWAN *(produces pack of cigarettes from his trousers pocket and offers one)* Then have a cigarette, then. For Christ's sake, do something. Don't just stand there. *(Temple takes the cigarette. He produces a lighter from the same pocket and snaps it on)* Here. *(she accepts the light. He puts the lighter back into his pocket, drops the pack of cigarettes onto the table)* Okay, I've stopped. Now we can start even. If we just could, of course. But with all these big-wheel international truths knocking around here tonight, it's no wonder you and I can't get together on a little petty fact like how a man's wife just treating herself to a little extra-curricular poontang should cause the murder of their child—

TEMPLE That's right. Go ahead. Then maybe we can stop.

GOWAN Because you really do believe it, don't you? That there really is some price, some point where you can stop paying, some last nickel you've got in the world that they won't ask of you, that you won't have to pay for just one mistake—mistake—mistake? Jesus, let's laugh. Come on, laugh. Don't just stand there—

TEMPLE *(sharply)* Gowan! Stop it! You've got to stop.

GOWAN That's right. Slap me, try that. Hit me. Then maybe I will hit you back and then you can start forgiving me for a change. You know, for the whole thing; getting drunk that day eight years ago, not because I wanted to get drunk, but because I was afraid, afraid that I, the big wheel, Joe College himself, president of his frat at Charlottesville, who could even call the madams of New York City cathouses by their first names, couldn't handle a seventeen-year-old Mississippi country girl who had never been away from home until she entered the freshman class at the State University—had to get drunk to have enough courage to persuade you to slip out of that damned baseball excursion train.

TEMPLE Did you twist my arm?

GOWAN What?

TEMPLE Not persuade. Suggest.

GOWAN Will you shut up? Will you?

TEMPLE I was driving the car some of the time too.

GOWAN Reckon I was too drunk even for me.

TEMPLE I could have got out and walked. I could have slipped out of that house that night, and hid in the woods. Except that I didn't.

GOWAN You couldn't.

TEMPLE I didn't.

GOWAN *(almost beside himself)* Try to shut up—try hard! I could hit you, remember. Okay?

TEMPLE Yes.

GOWAN Yes, got you into a spot where Dick Tracy himself would have envied me the chance to defend your honor. But not me. I have to get drunk a third time, so I won't even have to watch him kidnap you, let alone try to stop him.

TEMPLE You couldn't have. He had a pistol.

GOWAN *(with seething restraint)* Didn't you hear me? I said okay. Okay?

TEMPLE Yes.

GOWAN Then say it.

TEMPLE Okay.

GOWAN Won't you leave me anything? Do you want to take everything I've got? Let me have a good whine while I'm at it. Tell me what you probably think I've been telling myself all these six years: how, if it hadn't been for you, I might have married a good girl—a decent girl that never heard of hot pants until her husband taught her—*(he stops, drags his hands down his face again as in the scene with Gavin)* God, we must have loved each other once. We must have. Can't you remember?

TEMPLE Yes.

GOWAN Yes what?

TEMPLE Loved one another once. We must have.

GOWAN Can't you remember! Can't you? *(she doesn't answer)* Come here.

TEMPLE *(she doesn't move)* Take the capsule and go to bed.

GOWAN We're both going. We won't want the capsule either. Come here.

TEMPLE *(not moving)* No.

GOWAN All right. If you want it this way, you can have it. You're not going to use that telephone. There was a man here that night—

TEMPLE No.

GOWAN *(pays no attention)*—since Uncle Gavin knows it, I suppose everybody else in Jefferson does too—except me of course. Though I still don't see how that brought about the murder of a six-months-old baby. Maybe Nancy caught you laying him, and killed Dee Dee in spite or excitement or something. Or maybe the excitement wasn't Nancy's; that in your hurry you forgot to move Dee Dee out of the bed, and in the general thrashing around—You see? You see what I am capable of? I don't even have to half try . . .

TEMPLE No.

GOWAN No what? Go on. Say it. There was no man there. *(Temple says nothing)* Go on. Can't you say it? *(Temple says nothing)* All right then. At least you didn't tell Gavin what happened here that night. So I don't want to know what happened. And so nobody else shall. Not ever. You're not going to call Uncle Gavin and agree to go tell the Governor or anybody else anything. You said it yourself, and you'll never speak a truer word: if all Nancy Mannigoe's got to save her is Temple Drake, then God help Nancy Mannigoe. Okay?

TEMPLE No.

GOWAN Oh yes. You see, I'm even giving you one more chance. If there is any reason for grief and suffering, it's so that you will learn at least not to make the same mistake again, and to have consideration—whether you ever understand them or not—for the mistakes that other people make, and to believe that they are going to try not to make the same ones anymore too. But I still believe that there is some drop of blood you won't have to pay for what you did and can't recall. So you are not going to touch that telephone. Because if you do, I'm gone. *(quickly)* Wait. You could have quit at any time these six years. You still can. But if you pick up that telephone and call Uncle Gavin, it will be too late. It will be me that's gone. Okay? *(she doesn't answer)* Say yes, Temple.

TEMPLE I can't.

GOWAN Say yes, Temple. We loved each other once. Didn't we?

TEMPLE We must have.

GOWAN Then say it. You said it once.

TEMPLE We loved each other once.

GOWAN Then prove it. If she must die, let her. If something happened here that night that would save her and she won't tell it, then who are you—

TEMPLE I can't.

GOWAN Temple—*(they watch one another a moment. Then Temple turns toward the telephone. Gowan moves faster, reaches it first, and puts his hand on the receiver)* Remember.

TEMPLE Please move your hand, Gowan. (*they watch one another. Then he* *removes his hand. Temple takes the receiver; into the phone)* Three-two-nine, please. . . .

CURTAIN

ACT TWO

Scene 2

Office of the Governor of the state. 2:00 A.M. March 12th.

It is the office of the Governor of the Commonwealth, late at night, about 2 A.M.—a clock on the wall says two minutes past two; a massive flat-topped desk bare except for an ashtray and a telephone, behind it a high-backed heavy chair like a throne; on the wall behind and above the chair, is the emblem, official badge, of the State, sovereignty (a mythical one, since this is rather the State of which Yoknapatawpha County is a unit), an eagle, the blind scales of justice, a device in Latin perhaps, against a flag. There are two other chairs in front of the desk, turned slightly to face each other, the length of the desk between them. In the rear wall is a small private door, closed.

The Governor stands in front of the high chair, between it and the desk, beneath the emblem on the wall. He is symbolic too: no known person, neither old nor young; he might be someone's idea not of God but of Gabriel, perhaps, the Gabriel not before the Crucifixion but after it. He has obviously just been routed out of bed or at least out of his study or dressing-room; he wears a dressing gown, though there is a collar and tie beneath it, and his hair is neatly combed.

Temple and Stevens have just entered. Temple wears the same fur coat, hat, bag, gloves, etc. Stevens is dressed the same, is carrying his hat. They are moving toward the two chairs at either end of the desk.

STEVENS Good morning, Henry. Here we are.
GOVERNOR Yes. Sit down. *(as Temple sits down)* Does Mrs. Stevens smoke?
STEVENS Yes. Thank you.

He takes a pack of cigarettes from his topcoat pocket, as though he had come prepared for the need, emergency. He works one of them free and extends the pack to Temple. The Governor puts one hand into his dressing-gown pocket and withdraws it, holding something in his closed fist.

TEMPLE *(takes the cigarette)* What, no blindfold? *(the Governor extends his hand across the desk. It contains a lighter. Temple puts the cigarette into her mouth. The Governor snaps on the lighter)* But of course, the only one waiting execution is back there in Jefferson. So all we need to do here is, fire away, and hope that at least the volley rids us of the metaphor.

GOVERNOR Metaphor?

TEMPLE The blindfold. The firing squad. Or is metaphor wrong? Or maybe it's the joke. But don't apologize: a joke that has to be diagrammed is like having to excuse an egg, isn't it? The only thing you can do is, bury them both, quick. *(the Governor approaches the flame to Temple's cigarette. She leans and accepts the light, then sits back)* Thanks.

The Governor closes the lighter, sits down in the tall chair behind the desk, still holding the lighter in his hand, his hands resting on the desk before him. Stevens sits down in the other chair facing Temple at the other end of the desk, and lays the pack of cigarettes on the desk beside him.

GOVERNOR What has Mrs. Gowan Stevens to tell me?

TEMPLE Not Mrs. Gowan Stevens: Temple Drake.

GOVERNOR What has Temple Drake to tell me then?

TEMPLE Not tell you, ask you. You can see what an amateur I am at this. I mean, begging for a life. I didn't even . . . dicker: that's the word, isn't it? . . . with you first. You haven't said yet whether you'll save her or not—which, if either of us, Temple Drake or Mrs. Gowan Stevens either, had any sense, would have been the first thing we would demand of you.

GOVERNOR How can I answer you until you tell me what you want to ask.

TEMPLE The life of Nancy Mannigoe. Didn't Uncle Gavin tell you that too?

GOVERNOR Mannigoe? How does she spell it?

TEMPLE She doesn't. She can't. She can't read or write either. You are to hang her under Mannigoe. Which may be wrong too, though after tomorrow morning it won't matter.

GOVERNOR Oh yes, Manigault. The old Charleston name.

STEVENS Older than that. Maingault. Nancy's heritage—or anyway her patronym—runs Norman blood.

TEMPLE That's right. We—her lawyer and I—have come to ask you to save her.

GOVERNOR Yes. Why?

TEMPLE Why am I, the mother of the child she murdered, asking you to save her? Because I have forgiven her. *(they watch her, saying nothing)* Because she is crazy. *(they watch her, waiting)* All right. What you mean is, not why I am asking you to save her, but why I—we hired a whore and a tramp and a dope fiend to nurse our children. To give her another chance—a human being too, even a dope fiend nigger whore—

STEVENS *(rises and reaches for his hat)* Good night, Henry. Sorry we bothered you.

TEMPLE Stop it. *(Stevens pauses)* Sit down. Don't you see that this can go on all night?

STEVENS And all tomorrow. And then tomorrow. And then it will be the thirteenth of March.

TEMPLE You've said that twice since six this afternoon. Can't you at least be original?

STEVENS Have you got time before the thirteenth of March for originality?

TEMPLE Oh God, oh God, sit down. *(Stevens doesn't move yet)* What do you want? My promise? Oath?

STEVENS Not to me.

TEMPLE Oh yes, to myself. All right. But at least you can give me one. Don't threaten me with the hat again. *(Stevens sits down again)* It wasn't Mrs. Gowan Stevens that hired Nancy. It was Temple Drake. Not the socialite Gowan Stevenses hiring a dope fiend to nurse their children, but Temple Drake hiring a two-dollar whore to have somebody to talk to because a two-dollar whore was the only animal in Jefferson that spoke the same language. So we've got to the trade, the deal. What am I going to get for this?—How much will I have to tell about Temple Drake just to save Nancy Mannigoe? I mean, will telling everything about Temple Drake save Nancy Mannigoe?

GOVERNOR Do you want to ask that first?

TEMPLE I don't know. Do I? You might say No. Then I wouldn't have to tell any of it. Could get up now and go back to Jefferson. *(to Stevens)* Hand me that hat, Gavin. Maybe it's my time to try it on for size. . . . *(neither of them moves)* All right. Because it won't take long now because it will only take one word to save Nancy Mannigoe, which you can say at any time—for all I know, you may have already said it when Uncle Gavin talked to you on the phone tonight—maybe you did; did you? or is it against the rules to answer that yet too?—so that all we had to come here and wake you up at two o'clock in the morning was just to give Temple Drake a good fair honest chance to writhe. You know: anguish: just anguish for the sake of anguish, like that Russian or somebody who wrote a book about suffering; not suffering about or for anything, just suffering, like somebody unconscious not really breathing for anything but just breathing. Or maybe that's wrong too and nobody really cares, suffers, anymore about suffering than they do about truth or justice or Temple Drake's writhing and squirming or Nancy Mannigoe's worthless nigger life—

GOVERNOR Give her a cigarette, Gavin.

TEMPLE No thanks. Because we're too near the end now. *(to Stevens)* You could almost go on down and start the engine and have it warming up while I finish. *(to Governor)* Because all you have to do now is just be still and listen. Or not even listen if you don't want to, but just be still, just wait. Then we can all go to bed and turn off the light, and then night: dark; sleep even maybe, when with the same arm you turn off the light and pull the covers up with, you can put away forever Temple Drake and whatever it is you have done about her, and Nancy Mannigoe and whatever it is you have done about her—if you're going to do anything, if it even matters whether you will do anything or not, and none of it will have to bother any of us anymore. I think I will have the cigarette after all, please. *(cigarette business)* So now we have come to the letters. . . . the blackmail. The blackmail was because I wrote the letters. And I wrote the letters because I fell in love.

GOVERNOR Oh yes, with the man that kidnapped you.

TEMPLE No, no, you underestimate Temple Drake. This was still another one.

STEVENS Not another one. There was only one. The thing who kidnapped her wasn't even a man. I investigated him myself. His name was Vitelli. They called him Popeye. He wasn't a seducer, he was just a murderer. He didn't want a girl . . . .he couldn't have used one. He needed a witness for his alibi.

TEMPLE A little black thing like a cockroach who shut me up in the Manuel Street cathouse like a ten-year-old bride in a Spanish convent, with the Madam herself more eagle-eyed than any mamma, and the Negro maid to guard the door while Madam was away, gone wherever the madams of cathouses go on their afternoons: to pay police fines or protection or to the bank to put the money in or maybe just visiting, which would not be so bad because the maid would unlock the door and come in and we would . . . . *(her voice fades; for an instant she sits in a sort of motionless and quiet despair, then speaks again)* Oh yes, that was why, someone to talk to: even at just seventeen, an amateur, the only one she could find who could speak her language was still a Negro maid in the industry of whoring. *(again rapid and glib and calm)* A prisoner, but guilded, because he really did, he wanted her to be happy—

STEVENS Contented.

TEMPLE Happy.

STEVENS Contented.

TEMPLE *(to Governor)* Your honor, for God's sake—

STEVENS He was going to need her someday, maybe soon. It might be quick and it could be bad. *(to Temple)* Just say all right, and go on.

TEMPLE I will, if you'll just for God's sake—Where was I? Oh yes.—with every wish granted before expressed even: perfume by the quart, a fur coat, with nowhere to wear it since he wouldn't let her out, and in May too, too warm to wear a fur coat even if he had let her out—and a nasty mind would have said he waited until May to buy the fur coat, but they would have been wrong; nothing was too good for her really—snazzy underwear, negligees, too many of them and the wrong shade, just as the perfume was wrong too, doing all the shopping, choosing, selecting himself, but at least the perfume was in quarts; at least his taste was based on the bid end of an underworld big shot's wallet. Because he really did, he really did want me to be . . . . happy— *(she stops speaking, suddenly and sharply, almost as though in terror: a gasp, almost)*

STEVENS Go on. Say it. All right.

TEMPLE *(rapid and glib again; she is getting ready to evade or perhaps downright lie; Stevens and the Governor both know it, though the Governor knows that he won't detect the lie himself, and that their only hope is, that Stevens may)* Because I still had the two arms and legs and eyes; I could have climbed down the rain spout at any time, the only difference being that I didn't. I would never leave the room except late at night, when he would come in a closed car the size of an undertaker's wagon, and he and the chauffeur on the front seat, and me and the madam in the back, rushing at forty and fifty and sixty miles an hour up and down the back alleys of the red light district. Which—the back alleys—was all I ever saw of them too. I was not even permitted to meet or visit with or even see the other girls in my own house, not even to sit with them after work and listen to the shop talk while they counted their chips or blisters or whatever they would do sitting on one another's beds in the elected dormitory . . . . *(she pauses, hesitates, falters)* room. You know: like the dormitory, sorority house at school: the same smell: of women, young women all busy thinking constantly not about men but man: not any more seriously: just a little stronger, a little calmer, less excited, accustomed, un-amazed,—sitting on the temporarily idle beds discussing the exigencies—that's purely the right one, isn't it?—of their trade. But not Temple: shut up in that room twenty-four hours a day, with nothing to do but hold fashion shows in the fur coat and the flash pants with nothing to look at them but a dingy two-foot mirror and a hired nigger maid; hanging bone-dry and safe in the middle of sin and pleasure like being suspended twenty fathoms down in an ocean diving bell. *(she begins to speak, staccato and rapid)* So I met a man, and I wrote him some letters, and eight years later the letters turned up again since they were the sort of letters that would still be worth turning up eight years afterward, whereupon my foolish though moral nigger maid—

STEVENS Temple . . . .

Temple stops rigid, then continues suddenly to speak.

TEMPLE *(to Stevens)* Come on. Let's get out of here. *(to Governor)* Don't you see I can't? that I've got to have something left? I wrote the letters; I said so. And now I *am* going to trade.

STEVENS No. You can't dodge this. This is why your little child had to die. I'm only helping you carry your twig—stick—post—whatever you call your symbolical wood, up whatever you call your symbolical hill. Besides, it's only a hill: not a precipice. *(to Governor)* She fell in love. Her husband knows none of this from here on. There is no reason why he ever should, since this is still off the record.

GOVERNOR I see. Go on.

STEVENS The man was known as Arkansas Red—He was simply an employee of Vitelli's—the Houseman, bouncer, at the night club on the edge of the town which Vitelli owned and which was his Memphis headquarters. He—Red—died shortly afterward in the alley behind Temple's—house, of a bullet from Vitelli's pistol. He—Vitelli—would bring Red there himself.

GOVERNOR What? Would *bring* him there?

STEVENS Yes. Vitelli. What a name for him. A hybrid, impotent. He was hanged the next year, to be sure. But even that was wrong; his very effacement debasing, flouting, even what dignity man has been able to lend to necessary human abolishment. He should have been crushed somehow under a vast and mindless boot, like a spider. He didn't sell her: you violate and outrage his very memory with that crass and material impugnment. He was a purist, an amateur always: he did not even murder for base profit. It was not even for simple lust. He was a gourmet, a sybarite, centuries perhaps hemispheres before his time; in spirit and glands he was of that age of princely despots to whom the ability even to read was vulgar and plebeian and reclining on silk amid silken airs and scents, had eunuch slaves for that office, commanding death to the slave at the end of each reading, each evening, that none else alive, even a eunuch slave, shall have shared in, partaken of, remembered, the poem's evocation.

GOVERNOR Wait. You said this Vitelli would bring the young man each time. Are you trying to tell me that Vitelli would remain in the room with them each . . .

STEVENS I thought that's what we were both telling you. Yes. Oh, yes, he would bring Red there, and remain to watch, and she fell in love with Red, since what else did she have left, what simple else simply to cover the nakedness with. That was why he brought him. You can see now what I meant by connoisseur and gourmet.

GOVERNOR And what you meant by spider and cockroach too. But he, Vitelli, is dead.

STEVENS Oh, yes, he's dead; we haven't come here for vengeance.—So she wrote the letters . . . .

TEMPLE Yes. The letters. They were good letters. I mean, you would have wondered how an amateur just seventeen and not even through freshman in college, could have learned the . . . . right words. But then I was a fast learner; even just one lesson would have been enough, let alone three or four or a dozen or two or three dozen. So I wrote them, I don't know how many, enough, more than enough because just any one of them would have been enough, writing one each time . . . . afterward, after they—he left, and sometimes two or three when it would be two or three days between, when he—they wouldn't—you know something to do, be doing, filling the time, better than the fashion parades in front of a two-foot glass with nobody to be disturbed even by the—pants, or even no pants—

GOVERNOR *(to Stevens)* He's dead too—this Vitelli.

STEVENS Oh, yes, he's dead too; they both are. We haven't come here for vengeance either.

GOVERNOR *(to Temple)* Go on.

TEMPLE So I wrote some letters and the man I wrote them to dies and so I had to reform and so I married another man, and bore two children and hired another reformed whore to help me nurse them, except that both of us found out that I hadn't reformed, and so the other reformed whore had to murder one of my children to save me this time. And so it wasn't even Nancy who murdered my baby. It was me. So now all we have to do is go back to Jefferson and turn her out and lock me up in the cell. *(to Stevens)* Come on. I won't stop you this time.

STEVENS No. You've still got to tell him why.

TEMPLE Oh yes, I know; just suffering. Not for anything; just suffering. Like taking the calomel and the ipecac.

GOVERNOR *(to Stevens)* Hush, Gavin. *(to Temple)* Go on. You wrote the letters to the young man, and the young man died—

TEMPLE Oh yes, died, shot from a car while he was slipping up the alley behind the house, to climb up the same drain pipe I could have climbed down at any time and got away, to see me—the one time, the first time, the only time when we thought we had dodged him, fooled him, could be alone together, just the two of us, after all the . . . . If love can be—ever—

GOVERNOR *(gently)* Yes. Tell me.

TEMPLE And thank you for calling it love too. If love can be, mean anything, except the newness, the learning, the peace, the privacy; no shame; not even conscious that you are naked because you are just using the nakedness because that's a part of it, like the hands; then he was dead, killed, shot down right in the middle of it thinking about me, when in just one more minute he would have been in the room with me, when all of him except his body was already in the room with me and the door locked at last just for the two of us alone. Is that it? Is that what you want?

GOVERNOR Yes. Go on.

TEMPLE That's all. He dies. And then it was all right. You know people are lucky, they are wonderful. At first you think you can bear only so much. Then you find out that you can bear anything, you really can, and then it won't even matter because suddenly it will be as though it never happened. Somebody—Hemingway, wasn't it?—wrote a book about how it never actually happened to a girl—woman, if she just refused to accept it, no matter who remembered, bragged. Besides, both of the ones who could remember, were dead. So it was all right. Then Gowan came to Paris—my father had taken me to Europe—and we were married, at the Embassy, with a reception afterward at the Crillon and if that couldn't fumigate an American female past, what this side of heaven could? Not to mention a new automobile and a honeymoon in a rented hideaway built for his European mistress by a Mohammedan prince at Cap Ferrat. Only, I was wrong.

STEVENS *(to Temple)* Wait. *(to Governor)* Henry, will you have them send Gowan in.

GOVERNOR *(into intercom)* Albert, ask Mr. Stevens to come in.

TEMPLE Oh God!

STEVENS The governor is just saving Nancy. I'm on Nancy's side. I'm trying to save all of you.

The door opens. Gowan enters.

GOVERNOR *(into intercom)* Thank you, Albert. You can go on to bed now. *(to Gowan)* Sit down.

GOWAN No thanks. I won't stay that long. *(to Stevens)* O.K. You sent for me. What do you want?

STEVENS I want you to hear this too.

GOWAN By force, eh?

STEVENS If you want to put it that way.

GOWAN You and who else? He's just sent his gorilla to bed.

STEVENS Then leave if you want to. Go on.

GOWAN It's too late now. If you had just let me alone I would be up in Jefferson in bed. But not now. *(to Temple)* O.K. Go on. But remember I warned you.

STEVENS We'll remember. Now be quiet and listen. Only you were both wrong because you thought that marriage would be enough. Not the Embassy and the Crillon and Cap Ferrat, but just the marriage: to kneel down together—the two of you, and say "We have sinned, forgive us." And maybe there would be love this time—the peace, the quiet, the no-shame that you had missed that other time—love, and more than love too: not depending on just love to hold two people together, make them better than either one would have been alone, but tragedy, suffering, having suffered and caused grief; having something to live with even when, because, you knew both of you could never forget it. And something even stronger than that, stronger than tragedy, to hold two people together: forgiveness. Except that that seemed to be wrong too. So that you thought that maybe it wasn't the forgiveness that was wrong but the gratitude; and maybe the only thing worse than having to give gratitude constantly all the time, was having to accept it. Which was exactly backward. What was wrong was—

TEMPLE Your honor—

GOVERNOR Hush, Gavin. Let her.

STEVENS I can do it better. Remember I have lived in Jefferson for the last six years too, I was watching this too. *(to Governor)* What was wrong wasn't Temple's past. It wasn't even her husband's conscience. It was his vanity: the Virginia-trained aristocrat caught with his gentility around his knees like the guest in the trick Hollywood bathroom. So the forgiving wasn't enough for him. Because after about a year, his restiveness under the onus of accepting the gratitude for the forgiving began to take the form of doubting the paternity of their first child. It had happened once that she had admitted. How many times might it have happened that she had not told him about?

GOWAN What the hell are you trying to do? Make out that I was the real murderer?

TEMPLE Your Honor, can't you for God's sake—

GOVERNOR Both of you hush. Let her tell it.

TEMPLE Which is what I'm trying to do, if they'll just for God's sake let me. Where were we? Oh yes, we're in Jefferson now, back home. You know: face it: the disgrace: the shame of having spent a six-weeks' holiday in a whorehouse, even though you had managed to convince everybody that it was just an innocent lark, all except one that is, because at first all you had was just a husband, except that was not enough for you, not when your name was or anyway had been Temple Drake; you and your husband presenting a common front to stink because at that time, for a little while anyway, you really did think that Temple Drake was dead, like that gir—woman in that book who said that it had not happened to you if you just refused to accept it; but not enough for Temple Drake, not enough for her: using her children as an excuse to hire out of the gutter itself an ex-dopefiend nigger whore in order to have somebody to talk to for the simple reason that an ex-dopefiend nigger whore was the only animal in Jefferson, Mississippi, that spoke Temple Drake's language.

JUDGE Yes. The letters, the blackmail.

TEMPLE Not yet. Our dear uncle advocate Stevens insists that you've got to know the why of Nancy Mannigoe. Here it is. A confidante, someone, anyone, to talk to, tell it to. You know: the long afternoons, with the last electric button pressed on the last cooking or washing or sweeping gadget and the baby safely asleep for a while, and the two ex-sisters in sin swapping trade or anyway avocational secrets over Coca-Colas in the quiet kitchen. You know: somebody to talk to, as we all seem to need, want, have to have: not to converse, communicate with nor even agree with, but just to keep quiet and listen. Which is all that people really want, really need; in order to keep on behaving themselves, keep out of one another's hair; maybe if the world was just populated with a kind of creature half of which were not deaf but just dumb, couldn't do anything but listen without being able to escape or talk back, there wouldn't even be any war. Which was what Temple Drake had and so you would have thought that would have been enough and that now even Temple Drake might have been expected to behave. Only it wasn't. Because Hemingway was right: all you've got to do is, refuse to accept it. Only, you've got to . . . . refuse . . . .

STEVENS Now the letters. The man.

TEMPLE Only you've got to refuse. But I didn't. I did worse than that. I did more.

GOWAN Well, well, so I am going to hear something good after all.

STEVENS You're right. You are. You're going to hear about a man. The one she wrote the letters to, this is his younger brother. You probably see it now, don't you? Even the first one stuck out like a sore thumb.

GOVERNOR The first what?

GOWAN Were there so many that even Uncle Stevens can't keep them straight?

STEVENS The one she wrote the letters to. Red. Don't you know anything at all about women? I never saw Red, nor the brother either. But all three of them, the brothers and her husband, that means you, probably all look enough alike—or anyway act enough alike, maybe by simply making enough impossible unfulfillable demands on her or being drawn by her enough to accept, risk, almost incredible conditions—to be at least first cousins. Where have you been all your life?

GOVERNOR All right, all right. Tell me.

STEVENS He turned up with the letters—the old too-private letters she had written to his brother eight years ago and had forgotten about, or anyway had assumed for eight years—six anyway, during which she had come to believe that God, if He was anything at all, was at least a gentleman, above mere horse-play—that they no longer existed. At first of course, all he wanted, planned on, intended, was money—to sell the letters back to whoever wrote them and collect the dough and beat it, get the hell out. But I don't know. You have got to remember that in his veins ran the same blood which had not only instigated, motivated, a handful of scrawled paper which even eight years later the writer would pay any price rather than have her husband read them. Bringing back to her without warning, no time for preparation, not just the old letters but the old time too, not just the old love but perhaps the one love since it had been too brief for satiety, too violent in its widowing even to have formed a protecting scab. But more than that, he was a man—by that six years of comparison—a man, a man, so single, so hard and ruthless, so impeccable in amorality, as to have a kind of integrity, purity, who would not only never need nor intend to forgive anyone anything, he would never even realize that anyone expected him to forgive anyone anything; who wouldn't even bother to forgive her if it ever dawned on him that he had the opportunity, but instead would simply black her eyes and knock a few teeth out and fling her into the gutter: so that she could rest secure forever in the knowledge that, until she found herself with a black eye and or spitting teeth in the gutter, he would never even know he had anything to forgive her for. Not to mention Nancy: the long afternoons, two and three and four and five and then six years of them, the two of them in the quiet kitchen with the last button pressed and the child and then the two children asleep in its or their cribs or playing in its or their playpens in the yard, and suddenly Nancy says, "Since he can't be happy unless he's telling himself that his own children ain't his, make him sure enough happy. Fix him up with one that he can't have no doubt about whether it's his or not—"

TEMPLE Make him stop, God!

GOWAN Sure, make him stop. Make them all stop if you can. *(to Temple)* You've got one more chance. You can stop now. Don't tell it. Don't tell anymore.

STEVENS Tell him, Temple.

The lights begin to go down. The stage is in complete darkness.

ACT TWO

Scene 3

Interior, Temple's private sitting or dressing room. 9:30 P.M. September 13th *ante.*

The closet door stands open. Garments are scattered over the floor about it, indicating that the closet has been searched, not hurriedly so much as savagely and ruthlessly and thoroughly. A desk against the rear wall is open and shows traces of the same savage and ruthless search. A table, center, bears Temple's hat, gloves and bag, also a bag such as is associated with infants; two bags, obviously Temple's, are packed and closed and sit on the floor beside the table. The whole room indicates Temple's imminent departure, and that something has been vainly yet savagely and completely, perhaps even frantically, searched for.

When the lights go up, Pete is standing in the open closet door, holding a final garment, a negligee, in his hands. He is about 25. He does not look like a criminal. That is, he is not a standardized recognizable criminal or gangster type, quite. He looks almost like the general conception of a college man, or a successful young automobile or appliance salesman. His clothes are ordinary, neither flashy nor sharp, simply what everybody wears. But there is a definite "untamed" air to him. He is handsome, attractive to women, not at all unpredictable because you—or they—know exactly what he will do, you just hope he won't do it this time. He has a hard, ruthless quality, not immoral but unmoral.

He wears a lightweight summer suit, his hat is shoved onto the back of his head so that, engaged as he is at present, he looks exactly like a youthful city detective in a tough moving picture. He is searching the flimsy negligee, quickly and, without gentleness, drops it and turns, finds his feet entangled in the other garments on the floor and, without pausing, kicks himself free and crosses to the desk and stands looking down at the litter on it which he has already searched thoroughly and savagely once, with a sort of bleak and contemptuous disgust.

Temple enters, left. She wears a dark suit for traveling beneath a lightweight open coat, is hatless, carries the fur coat which we have seen, and a child's robe or blanket over the same arm, and a filled milk bottle in the other hand. She pauses long enough to glance at the littered room. Then she comes on in and approaches the table. Pete turns his head; except for that, he doesn't move.

PETE Well?

TEMPLE No. The people where she lives say they haven't seen her since she left to come to work this morning.

PETE I could have told you that. *(he glances at his wrist watch)* We've still got time. Where does she live?

TEMPLE *(at the table)* And then what? Hold a lighted cigarette against the sole of her foot?

PETE It's fifty dollars, even if you are accustomed yourself to thinking in hundreds. Besides the jewelry. What do you suggest then? Call the cops?

TEMPLE No. You won't have to run. I'm giving you an out.

PETE An out?

TEMPLE No dough, no snatch. Isn't that how you would say it?

PETE Maybe I don't get you.

TEMPLE You can quit now. Clear out. Leave. Get out from under. Save yourself. Then all you'll have to do is, wait till my husband gets back, and start over.

PETE Maybe I still don't get you.

TEMPLE You've still got the letters, haven't you?

PETE Oh, the letters. *(he reaches inside his coat, takes out the packet of letters and tosses it onto the table)* There you are.

TEMPLE I told you two days ago I didn't want them.

PETE Sure. That was two days ago.

They watch each other a moment. Then Temple dumps the fur coat and robe from her arm, onto the table, sets the bottle carefully on the table, takes up the packet of letters and extends her other hand to Pete.

TEMPLE Give me your lighter.

Pete produces the lighter from his pocket and hands it to her. That is, he extends it, not moving otherwise, so that she has to take a step or two toward him to reach and take it. Then she turns and crosses to the hearth, snaps the lighter on. It misses fire two or three times, then lights. Pete has not moved, watching her. She stands motionless a moment, the packet of letters in one hand, the burning lighter in the other. Then she turns her head and looks back at him. For another moment they watch each other.

PETE Go ahead. Burn them. The other time I gave them to you, you turned them down so you could always change your mind and back out. Burn them. *(they watch each other for another moment. Then she turns her head and stands now, her face averted, the lighter still burning. Pete watches her for another moment)* Then put that junk down and come here.

She snaps out the lighter, turns, crosses to the table, putting the packet of letters and the lighter on the table as she passes it, and goes on to where Pete has not moved. At this moment, Nancy appears in the door, left. Neither of them sees her. Pete puts his arms around Temple.

PETE I offered you an out too. *(he draws her closer)* Baby.

TEMPLE Don't call me that.

PETE *(tightens his arms, caressing and savage too)* Red did. I'm as good a man as he was. Ain't I?

They kiss. Nancy moves quietly through the door and stops just inside the room, watching them. She now wears the standardized department-store maid-servant's uniform, but without cap and apron, beneath a lightweight open topcoat; on her head is a battered almost shapeless felt hat which must have once belonged to a man. Pete breaks the kiss.

PETE Come on. Let's get out of here. I've even got moral or something. I don't even want to put my hands on you in this house—

He sees Nancy across Temple's shoulder, and reacts. Temple reacts to him, turns quickly and sees Nancy too. Nancy comes on into the room.

TEMPLE *(to Nancy)* What are you doing here?

NANCY I brought my foot. So he can hold that cigarette against it.

TEMPLE So you're not just a thief: you're a spy too.

PETE Maybe she's not a thief either. Maybe she brought it back. *(they watch Nancy, who doesn't answer)* Or maybe she didn't. Maybe we had better use that cigarette. *(to Nancy)* How about it? Is that what you came back for, sure enough?

TEMPLE *(to Pete)* Hush. Take the bags and go to the car.

PETE *(meaningly)* I'll wait for you. There may be a little something I can do here, after all.

TEMPLE Go on, I tell you! Let's for God's sake get away from here. Go on!

Pete watches Nancy for a moment longer, who stands facing them but not looking at anything, motionless, almost bemused, her face sad, brooding and inscrutable. Then Pete turns, goes to the table, picks up the lighter, seems about to pass on, then pauses again and takes up the packet of letters, pauses again, then drops the letters back on the table.

PETE Maybe you better not forget these, huh?
TEMPLE Go on!

He takes up the two packed bags and crosses to the French window, passing Nancy, who is still looking at nothing and no one.

PETE *(to Nancy)* Not that I wouldn't like to, you know. For less than fifty bucks even. For old lang syne. *(he transfers the bags to one hand, opens the French window, starts to exit, pauses and looks back at Temple)* I'll be listening, in case you change your mind about the cigarette.

He exits, draws the door to after himself. Just before it closes, Nancy speaks.

NANCY Wait.

Pete stops, begins to open the door again.

TEMPLE *(quickly: to Pete)* Go on! Go on! For God's sake go on!

Pete exits, shuts the door after himself. Nancy and Temple face each other.

NANCY Maybe I was wrong to think that just hiding that money and diamonds was going to stop you. Maybe I ought to have given it to him yesterday as soon as I found where you had hid it. Then wouldn't nobody between here and Chicago or Texas seen anything of him but his dust.

TEMPLE So you did steal it. And you saw what good that did, didn't you?

NANCY If you can call it stealing, then so can I. Because wasn't but part of it yours to begin with. Just the diamonds was yours. Not to mention that money is almost two thousand dollars, that you told me was just two hundred and that you told him was even less than that, just fifty. No wonder he wasn't worried—about just fifty dollars. He knows that all he's got to do is, just wait and keep his hand on you and maybe just mash hard enough with it, and you'll get another passel of money and diamonds too out of your husband or your pa.

Temple steps quickly forward and slaps Nancy across the face. Nancy steps back. As she does so, the packet of money and the jewel box fall to the floor from inside her topcoat. Temple stops, looking down at the money and jewels. Nancy recovers.

NANCY Maybe if I was to take it out to where he's waiting in that car right now, and say, here, man, take your money—

TEMPLE Try it. Pick it up and take it out to him, and see. If you'll wait until I finish packing, you can even carry the bag.

NANCY I know. It ain't even the letters any more. Maybe it never was. It was already there in whoever could write the kind of letters that even eight years afterward could still make grief and ruin. The letters never did matter. You could have got them back at any time; he even tried to give them to you twice—

TEMPLE How much spying have you been doing?

NANCY All of it.—You wouldn't even needed money and diamonds to get them back. A woman don't need it. All she needs is womanishness to get anything she wants from men. You could have done that right here in the house, without even tricking your husband into going off fishing.

TEMPLE A perfect example of whore morality. But then, if I can say whore, so can you, can't you? Maybe the difference is, I decline to be one in my husband's house.

NANCY I ain't talking about your husband. I ain't even talking about you. I'm talking about two little children.

TEMPLE So am I. Why else do you think I sent Bunny on to his grandmother, except to get him out of a house where the man he has been taught to call his father, may at any moment decide to tell him he has none? As clever a spy as you must surely have heard my husband—

NANCY *(interrupts)* I've heard him. And I heard you too. You fought back—that time. Not for yourself, but for that little child. But now you have quit.

TEMPLE Quit?

NANCY Yes. You gave up. You gave up the child too. Willing to risk never seeing him again maybe. *(Temple doesn't answer)* Now answer me this one. Who are you going to leave the other one with?

TEMPLE Leave her with? A six-months-old baby?

NANCY That's right. Of course you can't leave her. Not with nobody. You can't no more leave a six-months-old baby with nobody while you run away from your husband with another man, than you can take a six-months-old baby with you on that trip. That's what I'm talking about. So maybe you'll just leave it in there in that cradle; it'll cry for a while, but it's too little to cry very loud and so maybe won't nobody hear it and come meddling, especially with the house shut up and locked until Mr. Gowan gets back next week, and probably by that time it will have hushed—

TEMPLE Are you really trying to make me hit you again?

NANCY Or maybe taking her with you will be just as easy, at least until the first time you write Mr. Gowan or your pa for money and they don't send it as quick as your new man thinks they ought to, and he throws you and the baby both out. Then you can just drop it into a garbage can and no more trouble to you or anybody, because then you will be rid of both of them— *(Temple makes a convulsive movement, then catches herself)* Hit me. Light you a cigarette too. I told you and him both I brought my foot. Here it is. *(she raises her foot slightly)* I've tried everything else; I reckon I can try that too.

TEMPLE *(repressed, furious)* Hush. I tell you for the last time. Hush.

NANCY I've hushed. *(she doesn't move. She is not looking at Temple. There is a slight change in her voice or manner, though we only realize later that she is not addressing Temple)* I've tried. I've tried everything I know. You can see that.

TEMPLE Which nobody will dispute. You threatened me with my children, and even with my husband. You even stole my elopement money. Oh yes, nobody will dispute that you tried. Though at least you brought the money back. Pick it up.

NANCY You said you don't need it.

TEMPLE I don't. Pick it up.

NANCY No more do I need it.

TEMPLE Pick it up, anyway. You can keep your next week's pay out of it when you give it back to Mr. Gowan.

Nancy stoops and gathers up the money, and gathers the jewelry back into its box, and puts them on the table.

TEMPLE *(quieter)* Nancy. *(Nancy looks at her)* I'm sorry. Why do you force me to this—hitting and screaming at you, when you have always been so good to my children and me—my husband too—all of us—trying to hold us together in a household, a family, that anybody should have known all the time couldn't possibly hold together? Even in decency, let alone happiness?

NANCY I reckon I'm ignorant. I don't know that yet. Besides, I ain't talking about any household or happiness neither—

TEMPLE *(with sharp command)* Nancy!

NANCY —I'm talking about two little children—

TEMPLE I said, hush.

NANCY I can't hush. I'm going to ask you one more time. Are you going to do it?

TEMPLE Yes!

NANCY Maybe I am ignorant. You got to say it out in words yourself, so I can hear them. Say, I'm going to do it.

TEMPLE You heard me. I'm going to do it.

NANCY Money or no money

TEMPLE Money or no money.

NANCY Children or no children. *(Temple doesn't answer)* To leave one with a man that's willing to believe the child ain't got no father, willing to take the other one to a man that don't even want no children—*(they stare at one another)* If you can do it, you can say it.

TEMPLE Yes! Children or no children! Now get out of here. Take your part of that money, and get out. Here—

Temple goes quickly to the table, removes two or three bills from the mass of banknotes, and hands them to Nancy, who takes them. Temple takes up the rest of the money, takes up her bag from the table and opens it. Nancy crosses quietly toward the nursery, picking up the milk bottle from the table as she passes, and goes on. With the open bag in one hand and the money in the other, Temple notices Nancy's movements.

TEMPLE What are you dong?

NANCY *(still moving)* This bottle has got cold. I'm going to warm it in the bathroom.

Then Nancy stops and looks back at Temple, with something so strange in her look that Temple, about to resume putting the money into the bag, pauses too, watching Nancy. When Nancy speaks, it is like the former speech: we don't realize until afterward what it signifies.

NANCY I tried everything I knowed. You can see that.
TEMPLE *(peremptory, commanding)* Nancy.
NANCY *(quietly, turning on)* I've hushed.

She exits through the door into the nursery. Temple finishes putting the money into the bag, and closes it and puts it back on the table. Then she turns to the baby's bag. She tidies it, checks rapidly over its contents, takes up the jewel box and stows it in the bag and closes the bag. All this takes about two minutes; she has just closed the bag when Nancy emerges quietly from the nursery, without the milk bottle, and crosses, pausing at the table only long enough to put back on it the money Temple gave her, then starts on toward the opposite door through which she first entered the room.

TEMPLE Now what? *(Nancy goes on toward the other door. Temple watches her)* Nancy. *(Nancy pauses, still not looking back)* Don't think too hard of me. *(Nancy waits, immobile, looking at nothing. When Temple doesn't continue, she moves again toward the door)* If I—it ever comes up, I'll tell everybody you did your best. You tried. But you were right. It wasn't even the letters. It was me. *(Nancy moves on)* Goodbye, Nancy. *(Nancy reaches the door)* You've got your key. I'll leave your money here on the table. You can get it *(Nancy exits)* Nancy!

There is no answer. Temple looks for a moment longer at the empty door, moves, takes up the money Nancy left, glances about, crosses to the littered desk and takes up a paperweight and returns to the table and puts the money beneath the weight; now moving rapidly and with determination, she takes up the blanket from the table and crosses to the nursery door and exits through it. An instant, then Nancy appears quietly in the opposite door and stands in it. Another second, perhaps two, then Temple screams. The lights flare sharply up, then begin to dim, fading swiftly back toward complete darkness. Just before it does so, Temple reenters from the nursery. She is now frantic. She stops, sees Nancy; the two of them stand so, staring at one another, Temple clutching both hands to her head. She screams again, the stage fading into complete darkness over the scream.

The stage is in complete darkness.

ACT THREE

Scene 1

Same as Act Two, Scene 2. Governor's office. 3:09 A.M. March 12th.

The scene is directly after the flashback.

TEMPLE And that's all. The police came, and the murderess, still sitting in the chair beside the door saying, "Yes, Lord, I done it," and the same thing in the jail and in the courthouse too: Uncle Gavin had rehearsed her telling her that when they ask you to answer to a murder charge all you can say is "Not guilty," because if you don't, they can't even have a trial. They would have to rush out into the street and find another murderer before they could take the next official step. Except that she didn't say it. She said, "Guilty, Lord," throwing back 2000 years of corpus juris and rules of evidence and all the rest of it like when you reach out your hand and turn over a chip and expose an antbed. Then the jury said "Guilty" and the judge said "Hang" and then she moved the chip again; the judge said, "And may God have mercy on your soul" and Nancy answered: "Yes, Lord." And that is all this time. And so now you can tell us. It won't be difficult. Just one word—

GOWAN *(springs to his feet, the chair crashing over backward; to Temple)* Bitch. *(to no one directly)* So this is what I get for—

STEVENS *(sharply)* For what? For not taking a drink in eight years? Pick up the chair.

GOWAN *(to Stevens)* Pick it up yourself, if you want it up. Or let him— *(meaning the Governor)* do it. *(to the Governor)* Don't worry. If I start breaking things, you can always ring for your nigger.

GOVERNOR *(sharply peremptory)* Stevens.

GOWAN *(to the Governor)* I apologize. You know how it is. After six years, you can get used to your wife having been a whore—that is, in this golden age of morality and enlightenment, at least you'd better get used to it. But even after six years, you still don't have to like it. *(to Temple)* And you too. Try to forget it too. *(looks at Stevens)* Anybody else? We have only a limited supply, and naturally our old customers come first.

TEMPLE *(to Gowan)* I would have told you.

GOWAN You did. I said forget it, didn't I? You see how easy it is? You could have been doing that yourself for six years now; every time I would say "Say sorry, please" all you would need would be to answer, "I did. Forget it." *(to Stevens)* I guess that's all, isn't it? We can say good night to his lordship and go home now. *(he turns, starts to come around the desk)*

GOVERNOR Pick up the chair.

GOWAN *(pauses, then does a burlesque "take")* Oh I see. His lordship's a politician. He doesn't believe in anything unless he can pick it up and count it.

He stoops and sets the chair back up, starts around the desk again.

TEMPLE Wait. *(Gowan comes on around the desk, stops again, looks at Temple)* Where are you going?

GOWAN I said home, didn't I? To pick up your other child and carry him back to his own bed again. *(they look at one another)* What? You're not even going to ask me where he is now, what I even did with him when this flight out of Egypt started? *(answers himself before she can speak)* Where do we always leave our children when the clutch—

STEVENS *(to Gowan)* Maybe I'll say shut up, this time.

GOWAN *(to Stevens)* Except let me finish first. *(to Temple)* I was going to say, "with our handiest kinfolks." I carried him to Maggie's. *(to Stevens)* I suppose we can go home now, can't we? There can't be any more, can there? Don't tell me that in just twenty-five years, let alone in that six weeks, she could have produced two pasts for me to have to listen to.

STEVENS *(to Gowan)* You can.

TEMPLE *(to Gowan)* Wait. *(to the Governor)* You can get rid of us all now. Just one word, and then we can all go home and go to bed and turn off the light. And then, night, dark; sleep even maybe, because with the same arm you turn off the light and pull the covers up, you can put away forever Temple Drake and whatever it was you did about her, and Nancy Mannigoe and whatever it was you did about her, if it really matters whether you do anything or not, and none of it will ever have to bother us anymore. Just one word will do it. Are you going to save her?

GOVERNOR No.

TEMPLE Will you tell me why?

GOVERNOR Yes. I can't.

TEMPLE The Governor, with all the legal power to pardon or at least reprieve—can't?

GOVERNOR Yes—can't. We're not talking about law now, any more than the murderess herself was, than her lawyer was, who could have pleaded insanity for her at any time and so saved her life without bringing her victim's mother here at two o'clock in the morning to plead for her. We're not even talking about justice. We're talking about a child, a little boy—the same little boy, to hold whose natural and normal home together, the murderess didn't hesitate to cast the last gambit she knew and possessed—her own debased and worthless breathing—

TEMPLE So now you're telling me that good can come from evil.

GOVERNOR More than that. It not only can, it must. Now you answer my question. Didn't she? *(Temple doesn't answer)* Now you will say, what kind of home can that little boy have where his father may at any time tell him he has none? I don't need to answer that, because you have been answering it yourself, not just six years ago but every day since. Didn't. . .the—

STEVENS Nancy.

GOVERNOR Nancy—answer it for you when she told you how you had fought back, not for yourself, but for that little boy? Not to show the father that he was wrong, not even to prove to the little boy that the father was wrong, but to let the little boy learn with his own eyes that nothing, nothing, not even that, which could ever possibly enter that house, could ever harm him?

TEMPLE But I quit. Nancy told you that too.

GOVERNOR And answered it too. Or will, tomorrow morning. *(to Stevens)* That's the day, isn't it? Friday?

STEVENS Yes.

TEMPLE Friday. The black day. The day you never start on a journey. Except that Nancy's trip didn't start at daylight or sunup or whenever it's polite and tactful to hang people, day after tomorrow. Her journey started that morning eight years ago when I got on that special train at the University—

GOWAN That was Friday.

TEMPLE What?

GOWAN That baseball game was on Friday.

TEMPLE Oh God. Oh God. *(wildly)* You see? Don't you see? *(to Stevens)* You said how there is a corruption even in just looking at evil, even by accident; that you can't haggle, traffic, with putrefaction—you can't, you don't dare? You were only partly right. *(quickly)* No: not even that much; that's nowhere near enough; it's not that you must never even look on evil and corruption; sometimes you can't help it, you are not always warned in time. It's not even that you must resist it always. Because you've got to start much sooner than that. You've got to be already prepared to resist it, say No to it, long before you see it; you must have already said No to it long before you know what it is. Of course he won't save her. If he did that, it would be over— *(while she is speaking, Stevens turns to the desk, takes up his hat and is about to turn away when he sees the pack of cigarettes, pauses and takes it up and puts it in his coat pocket, then turns to Temple and touches her arm. Temple ignores him)*—then Gowan wouldn't have to wait to throw me out tonight because the judge would throw us both out tomorrow and give Bucky to an orphanage, and it would be all over and we could even go to sleep. But not now. I've got to stay awake forever now.

STEVENS Temple.

TEMPLE *(to Stevens: still watching the Governor)* No. Not yet. *(to the Governor)* Say it again; I seem to have to have everything said twice tonight before I seem to believe it. You won't save her.

GOVERNOR Who am I, to have the brazen temerity and hardihood to set the puny appanage of my office in the balance against that simple undeviable aim? Who am I, to render null and abrogate the purchase she made with that poor crazed lost and worthless life?

TEMPLE So it was not in hope of saving her life that I had to come here at two o'clock in the morning. It wasn't even to be told that you had already decided not to save her. It wasn't even to trick me into a confession that would supply my husband with court evidence because all the court evidence he will need is the letters, if anybody knew where they were, which doesn't matter either because all he has to do is just quit, walk out—

GOWAN And now is a good time to do it—*(he starts to move toward the stairs by which Temple and Stevens entered)*

GOVERNOR Yes. The letters. You don't have any idea where they are?

TEMPLE You asked that before. What does it matter? *(continuing the other thought)* It was just to confess, not even to my husband but to two strangers, something I had spent six years trying to pay for so that nobody would have to know about it. Don't you see? That's just suffering? Not for anything: just suffering?

GOWAN *(he has paused for an instant)* Unless the guy decides to sell them to me direct this time. Which he may not do, since I won't swap him a lay for them. *(he goes on around the desk, now heading toward the door at rear where he entered)*

STEVENS I have them.

TEMPLE What? *(Gowan stops)*

STEVENS *(to Temple)* Don't you remember? Nancy was in the room that night when you came back? The letters were on the table. She took them and gave them to me.

Gowan begins to laugh, harsh and bitter, mirthless. He goes on again toward the rear door.

GOWAN Not even a lay.

STEVENS Where are you going?

GOWAN *(walking)* To get drunk—unless I have forgotten how in eight years. Or have you a suggestion?

STEVENS What about Bucky?

GOWAN So what about him? He's at your house—or your sister's. Isn't that safe? They don't murder babies there too, do they?

STEVENS You're not going to pick him up and bring him back home?

GOWAN How can I, if I'm drunk? If I'm that drunk, I may not get back to Jefferson myself. *(he exits)*

STEVENS *(to Temple)* So you're spared that, anyway. Tomorrow and tomorrow and tomorrow, until he wrecks the car again against the wrong tree in the wrong place and forgives you for it and accepts the gratitude for the next six years until he wrecks the car again in the wrong place, against the wrong tree.

TEMPLE I was driving too. I was driving some of the time too.

STEVENS *(softly insistent)* But you are spared that now.

TEMPLE Oh yes. I'm spared that now. *(Stevens picks up the handkerchief and extends it)* Thank you. *(she sees him toss it back to the Governor instead of keeping it, and realizes whose it is)* Oh. Well, thank him too—His Honor or His Excellency—and now maybe we can all go home.

GOVERNOR Yes. Try to sleep—

TEMPLE *(briskly now, turns and takes up her gloves and bag, turning)* Oh yes, I know that one too; to be bright and fresh in the morning to take the official blackball to the jail. In Jefferson everything going to the graveyard passes the jail or going anywhere else for that matter, passing right in front of the barred windows of the bull-pen where the Negro prisoners—the crapshooters and the whiskey peddlers and vagrants and the murderers and murderesses too can look out and enjoy it, enjoy the funerals too. So whenever you pass the jail, you can see them—no, not then, you don't see them at all, you just see the hands holding to the bars in the windows, not napping nor fidgeting not even gripping the bars like white hands would be, but just lying there among the spaces, not just at rest, because they are more than that. They are even restful, already shaped to the handles of the plows and axes and hoes, and the mops and brooms, and the rockers of white babies' cradles, until even the steel bars fit them without trouble or anguish. So what you see are just the hands not even the eyes, just the hands lying there among the bars and looking out, the hands that can see the shape of the plow or hoe before daylight comes; and even in the dark, without even having to turn on the light, can find the child, the baby—not her child but yours, the white one—and then find the trouble and the discomfort to—the hunger, the wet didy, the unfastened safety pin—and see how to cure it—You see, if I could just cry. At least I should have won that privilege. Only I didn't. Because it's just suffering. *(she goes on toward the stairs by which she and Stevens entered)* Coming, Gavin? Tell his lordship good-night. I've got to put Bucky back in his own bed.

STEVENS *(moves too)* Yes. Good night, Henry.

GOVERNOR Good night.

Stevens follows Temple, who has now reached the top of the stairs. She seems to falter, stumble slightly. Stevens moves faster, to take her arm, but she has already recovered herself, beginning to descend, walking a little blindly, like a sleepwalker.

TEMPLE To save my soul—if I have a soul—if there is a God to save it—a God who wants it—

CURTAIN

ACT THREE

Scene 2

Interior, the Jail. 10:30 A.M. March 12th.

The common room, or "bull-pen." It is on the second floor. A heavy barred door at left is the entrance to it, to the entire cell-block, which—the cells—are indicated by a row of steel doors, each with its own individual small barred window, lining the right wall. A narrow passage at the far end of the right wall leads to more cells. A single big heavily barred window in the rear wall looks down into the street. It is mid-morning of a sunny day.

The door, left, opens with a heavy clashing of the steel, and swings back and outward.

Mr. Tubs enters.

MR. TUBS Come in, come in.

Temple and Stevens enter. Temple has changed her dress, but wears the fur coat and the same hat, gloves and bag. Stevens is dressed exactly as he was in Act Two. Mr. Tubs speaks to Temple as she passes him.

MR. TUBS You're late, this morning. I been watching Lawyer here standing out there on the corner for fifteen minutes, waiting for you. But then, getting home last night from that long California trip, is a excuse for oversleeping. I reckon Gowan's still at it, huh?

TEMPLE No. He's still out of town for a few days.

MR. TUBS Why I heard you all three come in on Number Six yesterday evening—

STEVENS *(interrupts)* He had to leave again last night. If you'll bring Nancy out, we won't keep you.

MR. TUBS Sure, sure. *(he draws the door in and locks it, already talking again, turns, still talking, pauses again)* Well— *(to Stevens)* Singing school will be over after tonight, huh? *(to Temple)* You don't know about this, you ain't up with what's—*(he stops himself quickly, he is about to commit what he would call a very bad impoliteness, what in the tenets of his class and kind would be the most grave of gaucherie and bad taste; referring directly to a recent bereavement in the presence of the bereaved, particularly one of this nature, even though by this time tomorrow the State itself will have made restitution with the perpetrator's life. He tries to rectify it)* Not that I wouldn't too, if I'd a been the ma of the very—*(stopping himself again, this is getting worse than ever; now he not only is looking at Stevens, but actually addressing him)* Every Sunday night, and every night since last Sunday except last night—come to think of it, Lawyer, where was you last night? We missed you—Lawyer here and Na—the prisoner have been singing hymns in her cell. The first time, he just stood out there on the sidewalk while she stood in that window yonder. Which was all right, not doing no harm, just singing church hymns. Because all of us home folks here in Jefferson and Yoknapatawpha County both know Lawyer Stevens, even if some of us might have thought he got a little out of line— *(again it is getting out of hand; he realizes it, but there is nothing he can do now; he is like someone walking a foot-log; all he can do is move as fast as he dares until he can reach solid ground or at least pass another log to leap to)* defending a nigger murderer, let alone when it was his own niece was mur— *(and reaches another log and leaps to it without stopping: at least one running at right angles for a little distance into simple generality)*—maybe suppose some stranger say, some durn Yankee tourist, happened to be passing through in a car, when we get enough durn criticism from Yankees like it is—besides, a white man standing out there in the cold, while a durned nigger murderer is up here all warm and comfortable; so it happened that me and Mrs. Tubs hadn't went to prayer meeting that night, so we invited him to come in; and to tell the truth, we come to enjoy it too. Because as soon as they found out there wasn't going to be no objection to it, the other nigger prisoners (I got five more right now, but I taken them out back and locked them up in the coal house so you could have some privacy) joined in too, and by the second or third Sunday night, folks was stopping along the street to listen to them instead of going to regular church. Of course, the other niggers would just be in and out over Saturday and Sunday night for fighting or gambling or vagrance or drunk, so just about the time they would begin to get in tune, the whole choir would be a complete turnover. In fact, I had a idea at one time to have the Marshal comb the nigger dives and joints not for drunks and gamblers, but basses and baritones. *(he starts to laugh, guffaws once, then catches himself; he looks at Temple* *with something almost gentle, almost articulate, in his face, taking (as though) by the horns, facing frankly and openly the dilemma of his own inescapable vice)* Excuse me, Mrs. Stevens. I talk too much. All I want to say is, this whole county, not a man or woman, wife or mother either in the whole state of Mississippi, that don't—don't feel— *(stopping again, looking at Temple)* There I am, still at it, still talking too much. Wouldn't you like for Mrs. Tubs to bring you up a cup of coffee or maybe a Coca-Cola? She's usually got a bottle or two of sody pop in the icebox.

TEMPLE No, thank you, Mr. Tubs. If we could just see Nancy—

MR. TUBS *(turning)* Sure, sure.

He crosses toward the rear, right, toward a passage. Temple watches him until he disappears into the passage. Then she looks at Stevens.

TEMPLE So you don't know where he is, either.

STEVENS He's not drunk.

TEMPLE So what? I'm already spared, you know. . . So you haven't been able to give him the letters yet.

STEVENS How could I, if I don't know where he is either?

TEMPLE Don't worry though. You won't have to; he won't need them. Didn't we already agree that I am already spared?

STEVENS That's correct.

She turns again and looks toward the passage where the jail disappeared; she seems to be listening.

TEMPLE The blindfold again. Out of a Coca-Cola bottle this time, or a cup of county-owned coffee. People. They're really innately, inherently gentle and compassionate and kind. That's what wrings, wrenches. . .something. Your entrails maybe. The member of the mob who holds up the whole business for seconds or even minutes while he dislodges a family of bugs or lizards from the log he is about to put on the fire—You see the trouble is you can't quit. Do you remember that other one? A man this time—it happened right here in this room—don't you remember? The Negro sawmill hand—his wife had just died—they had been married only two weeks and he buried her and so at first he tried just walking the country roads at night to get tired enough to sleep, only that failed, and then he tried getting drunk so he could sleep, and that failed, and then he tried fighting, and then he cut a white man's throat with a razor in a dice game and so at last he could sleep for a little while. Which was where the sheriff found him. Asleep on the wooden floor of the house he had rented for his wife—his bride,—his marriage, his life, his old age. Only that waked him up, and so in the jail that afternoon, all of a sudden it took the jailor and a deputy and five other Negro prisoners just to throw him down and hold him while they locked the chains on him—lying there on the floor with more than a half dozen men panting to hold him down, and what do you think he said? "Look like I just can't quit thinking. Look like I just can't quit."

There is the clash and the clang of another steel door beyond the passage.

She stops as Nancy emerges from the passage, followed by Mr. Tubs, who passes Nancy and comes on, still carrying the keys like a lantern.

TUBS Okay, Lawyer. How much time you want? Thirty minutes? A hour?

STEVENS Ten minutes should be enough.

TUBS *(moving on toward the exit left)* Okay. *(to Temple)* You sure you don't want that coffee or Coca-Cola? I could bring you up a rocking chair—

TEMPLE Thank you just the same, Mr. Tubs.

TUBS Okay. *(at the exit door, unlocking it)* Ten minutes then.

He opens the door, exits, clashes the door to behind him, locks it; his footsteps die away. Nancy has stopped where the Jailor passed her, about six feet beyond Temple and Stevens. Her face is calm, unchanged. She is dressed exactly as before; she even wears the hat. She is looking at Stevens, though Temple does not realize it yet.

TEMPLE Nancy—

Almost at the same moment, Nancy herself speaks, to Stevens, so that it takes Temple a fraction of a second to catch on to what they are talking about.

NANCY *(to Stevens)* Did you give them to him?

When Stevens answers, Temple is still that fraction of a second late, turning to him.

STEVENS Yes. This morning. Just as you told me to.

Again Temple is that fraction late, trying to catch up.

NANCY Then I reckon they're burned up by now.

STEVENS Yes.

TEMPLE *(wildly)* The letters? *(to Stevens)* You have already given them to him? *(wildly)* You lied to me. *(she begins to laugh, wildly and hysterically, striving for control)* Don't you see? It's all a waste? You lied to me when you didn't have to, you gave him the letters when he didn't even need them—it's all a waste, of lying and letters to—and even all this too: just a waste?

STEVENS *(sharply)* Temple.

NANCY He ain't read them. He burned them.

TEMPLE Gowan? Burned them?

NANCY Maybe there was a heap of things he wasn't raised not to do, but reading other folks's letters ain't one of them, least of his wife's, from another man. He burned them up.

TEMPLE Oh God, you're lying. You're going to die tomorrow morning, yet you're lying too. Besides, haven't we just agreed that he doesn't even need the letters?

STEVENS Hush. Listen.

NANCY *(in the same flat, level voice)* He can't quit now. If he had read them, maybe he could. But he burned them up, quick, so he wouldn't even have to not read them anymore. Any quitting now, you'll have to do it.

TEMPLE I won't believe you. I won't. You're lying. You made it up. Because I'm spared, I'm free. Just tomorrow and tomorrow, with nothing in them? Don't you see, I don't dare believe anything else? I don't dare risk it?

STEVENS Temple.

TEMPLE *(catches herself; with an effort)* Yes. All right. *(to Nancy)* I came back—

NANCY From California, they tell me. I used to think maybe I would get there too, some day. But I waited too late to get around to it.

TEMPLE So did I. Too late and too long. Too late when I went to California, and too late when I came back. That's it: too late and too long, not only for you, but for me too; already too late when both of us should have got around to running, like from death itself, from the very air anybody breathed named Drake or Mannigoe.

NANCY Only, we didn't. And you come back, yesterday evening. I heard that too. And I know where you were last night, you and him both. *(indicating Stevens)* You went to see the Mayor.

TEMPLE Oh, God, the Mayor. No: the Governor, the Big Man himself, in Jackson. Of course; you knew that as soon as you realized that Mr. Gavin wouldn't be here last night to help you sing, didn't you? In fact, the only thing you can't know about it is what the Governor told us. You can't know that yet, no matter how clairvoyant you are, because we—the Governor and Mr. Gavin and I—were not even talking about you; the reason I—we had to go and see him was not to beg or plead or bind or loose, but because it would be my right, my duty, my privilege—Don't look at me, Nancy.

NANCY I'm not looking at you. Besides, it's all right. I know what the Governor told you. Maybe I could have told you last night what he would say, and saved you the trip. Maybe I ought to have—sent you the word as soon as I heard you were back home, and knowed what you and him—*(again she indicates Stevens with that barely discernible movement of her head, her hands still folded across her middle as though she still wore the absent apron)*—both would probably be up to. Only, I didn't. But it's all right—

TEMPLE Why didn't you? Yes, look at me. This is worse, but the other is terrible.

NANCY What?

TEMPLE Why didn't you send me the word?

NANCY Because that would have been hoping: the hardest thing of all to break, get rid of, let go of, the last thing of all poor sinning man will turn aloose. Maybe it's because that's all he's got. Leastways, he holds onto it, hangs onto it. Even with salvation laying right in his hand, and all he's got to do is, choose between it; even with salvation already in his hand and all he needs is just to shut his fingers, old sin is still too strong for him, and sometimes before he even knows it, he has throws salvation away just grabbing back at hoping. But it's all right—

STEVENS You mean, when you have salvation, you don't have hope?

NANCY You don't even need it. All you need, all you have to do, is just believe. So maybe—

STEVENS Believe what?

NANCY Just believe. —So maybe it's just as well that all I did last night, was just to guess where you all went. But I know now, and I know what the Big Man told you. And it's all right. I finished all that a long time back, that same day in the judge's court. No: before that even: in the nursery that night, before I even lifted my hand—

TEMPLE *(convulsively)* Hush. Hush.

NANCY All right. I've hushed. Because it's all right. I can get low for Jesus too. I can get low for Him too.

TEMPLE Hush! Hush! At least, don't blaspheme. But who am I to challenge the language you talk about Him in.

NANCY What's wrong with what I said? Jesus is a man too. He's got to be. Menfolks listens to somebody because of what he says. Women don't. They don't care what he said. They listens because of what he is.

TEMPLE Then let Him talk to me. I can get low for Him too, if that's all He wants, demands, asks. I'll do anything He wants if He'll just tell me what to do. No: how to do it. I know what to do, what I must do, what I've got to do. But how? You couldn't even be any worse off. And this time tomorrow, you won't be anything at all. But not me. Because there's tomorrow, and tomorrow. All you've got to do is, just to die. But let Him tell me what to do. No: that's wrong; I know what to do, what I'm going to do; I found that out that same night in the nursery too. But let Him tell me how. How? Tomorrow, and tomorrow, and still tomorrow. How?

NANCY Trust in Him.

TEMPLE Trust in Him. Look what He has already done to me. Which is all right; maybe I deserved it; at least I'm not the one to criticize or dictate to Him. But look what He did to you. Yet you can still say that. Why? Why? Is it because there isn't anything else?

NANCY I don't know. But you got to trust Him. Maybe that's your pay for the suffering.

STEVENS Whose suffering, and whose pay? Just each one's for his own?

NANCY Everybody's. All suffering. All poor sinning man's.

STEVENS The salvation of the world is in man's suffering. Is that it?

NANCY Yes sir.

STEVENS How?

NANCY I don't know. Maybe when folks are suffering, they will be too busy to get into devilment, won't have time to worry and meddle one another.

TEMPLE But why must it be suffering? He's omnipotent, or so they tell us. Why couldn't He have invented something else? Or, if it's got to be suffering, why can't it be just your own? Why can't you buy back your own sins with your own agony? Why did you and my little baby both have to suffer just because I decided to go to a baseball game years ago? Do you have to suffer everybody else's anguish just to believe in God? What kind of God is it that has to blackmail His customers with the whole world's grief and ruin?

NANCY He don't want you to suffer. He don't like suffering neither. But

He can't help Himself. He's like a man that's got too many mules. All of a sudden one morning, he looks around and sees more mules than he can count at one time even, let alone find work for, and all he knows is that they are his, because at least don't nobody else want to claim them, and that the pasture fence was still holding them last night where they can't harm themselves nor nobody else the least possible. And that when Monday morning comes, he can walk in there and hem some of them up and even catch them if he's careful about not never turning his back on the ones he ain't hemmed up. And that, once the gear is on them, they will do his work and do it good, only he's still got to be careful about getting too close to them, or forgetting that another one of them is behind him, even when he is feeding them. Even when it's Saturday noon again, and he is turning them back into the pasture, where even a mule can know it's got until Monday morning anyway to run free in mule sin and mule pleasure.

STEVENS You have got to sin, too?

NANCY You ain't *got* to. You can't help it. And He knows that. But you can suffer. And He knows that too. He don't tell you not to sin, He just asks you not to. And He don't tell you to suffer. But He gives you the chance. He gives you the best He can think of, that you are capable of doing. And He will save you.

STEVENS You too? A murderess? In heaven? *(Nancy doesn't answer nor stir)* A heaven where that little child will remember nothing of your hands but gentleness because now this earth will have been nothing but a dream that didn't matter? Is that it?

TEMPLE Is there a heaven, Nancy?

NANCY I don't know. I believes.

TEMPLE Believe what?

NANCY I don't know. But I believes.

They all pause at the sound of feet approaching beyond the exit door; all are looking at the door as the key clashes again in the lock and the door swings out and Mr. Tubs enters, drawing the door to behind him.

MR. TUBS *(locking the door)* Ten minutes, Lawyer. You named it, you know: not me.

STEVENS I'll come back later.

MR. TUBS *(turns and crosses toward them)* Provided you don't put it off too late. What I mean, if you wait until tonight to come back, you might have some company; and if you put it off until tomorrow, you won't have no client. *(to Nancy)* I found that preacher you want. He'll be here about sundown, he said. He sounds like he might even be another good baritone. And you can't have too many, especially as after tonight you won't need none, huh? No hard feelings, Nancy. You committed as horrible a crime as this county ever seen, but you're fixing to pay the law for it, and if the child's own mother—*(he falters, almost pauses, catches himself and continues briskly, moving again)* There, talking too much again. Come on, if Lawyer's through with you. You can start taking your time at daylight tomorrow morning, because you might have a long hard trip.

He passes her and goes briskly on toward the alcove at rear. Nancy turns to follow.

TEMPLE *(quickly)* Nancy. *(Nancy doesn't pause. Temple continues, rapidly)* What about me? Even if there is one and somebody waiting in it to forgive me, there's still tomorrow and tomorrow. And suppose tomorrow and tomorrow, and then nobody there, nobody waiting to forgive me—

NANCY *(moving on after the Jailor)* Believe.

TEMPLE Believe what, Nancy? Tell me.

NANCY Believe.

She exits into the alcove behind the Jailor. The steel door offstage clangs, the key clashes. Then the Jailor reappears, approaches, and crosses toward the exit. He unlocks the door and opens it out again, pauses.

JAILOR Yes, sir. A long hard way. If I was ever fool enough to commit a killing that would get my neck into a noose, the last thing I would want to see would be a preacher. I'd a heap rather believe there wasn't nothing after death than to risk the station where I was probably going to get off.

He waits, holding the door, looking back at them. Temple stands motionless until Stevens touches her arm slightly. Then she moves, stumbles slightly and infinitesimally, so infinitesimally and so quickly recovered that the Jailor has barely time to react to it, though he does so: with quick concern, with that quality about him almost gentle, almost articulate, turning from the door, even leaving it open as he starts quickly toward her.

JAILOR Here; you set down on the bench; I'll get you a glass of water. *(to Stevens)* Durn it, Lawyer, why did you have to bring her—

TEMPLE *(recovered)* I'm all right.

JAILOR You sure?

TEMPLE Yes, sure.

JAILOR Okay. I sure don't blame you, though. Durned if I see how even a murdering nigger can stand this smell.

He goes on to the door and exits, invisible now, though still waiting for them to follow, so he can lock it.

TEMPLE *(begins to move toward the door)* Anyone to save it. Anyone who wants it. If there is none, I'm sunk. We all are. Doomed. Damned. Finished.

STEVENS *(begins to follow)* Of course we are. Hasn't He been telling us that for going on two thousand years?

JAILOR'S VOICE *(offstage, suddenly, surprised)* Why, howdy, Gowan. Thought you was out of town. Here's your wife, just coming out now.

GOWAN'S VOICE *(offstage)* Did you? *(raises it, calls)* Temple.

Temple stops dead, motionless; Stevens stops too. He cannot see her face.

STEVENS *(taking the handkerchief from his breast pocket)* Not just the first one, but the last one. *(he extends the handkerchief)* Tomorrow and tomorrow, until he wrecks the car again against the wrong tree, in the wrong place—

TEMPLE *(glances down and sees the proffered handkerchief)* No thanks. *(she raises her head, moves again toward the door and into it. Her voice is calm)* Yes, Gowan. Coming.

She exits. Stevens follows. The door swings in and clashes and clangs as the Jailor locks it; the sound of their footsteps dies away beyond it.

CURTAIN

841 "Innocent's Return," c. 1951, 10 pages plus two title pages and a cast of characters page, 11 by 8½ inches, in black clasped folder with paste-on label stating "INNOCENT'S RETURN / by / William Faulkner / and / Joan Williams / HAROLD OBER ASSOCIATES / 40 East 49th Street / New York." Second title page notes: "Alternate title: ALL CLEAR."

This curious piece, a one-act comedy that may have been intended for television adaptation, dates from the period when Faulkner was serving as a literary mentor for Joan Williams, an aspiring young writer. Interestingly, Williams has indicated that she had nothing at all to do with the composition of the script and, in fact, never saw the work. Apparently Faulkner credited Williams with joint authorship as a means of securing a publication credit for his young friend and protégé.

INNOCENT'S RETURN

Cast

HENRY MORGAN About 45–50, member of a prosperous publishing house or firm, dominated by his forceful wife, is contented in his marriage, has probably never dreamed of such as this happening to him.

PRISCILLA Henry's wife, about 40, youngish club-woman type, childless, still handsome.

JACKIE GORDAN (Her stage name) A successful nightclub singer, making good money, good looking in a hard metropolitan way, about 25.

TONY MINETTI Jackie's husband and agent, big, handsome, in Madison Avenue clothes.

DOORMAN In the apartment house where the Morgans and the Minettis live. Resembles a big prize fighter.

TAXI DRIVER

WAITER CAPTAIN

FLORIST'S BOY

Interior corridor of apartment house of prosperous class. A practice air raid is going on, the sirens have just started, are now going full blast. A door on one side of the corridor opens hurriedly. Out of it comes Henry Morgan, a big bath towel clutched about him, his bathrobe thrown hurriedly over his shoulders. As he starts to run down the corridor, the opposite door opens, he glances into it, stops, exclaims.

HENRY Holy cow! Here!

He snatches the bathrobe from his shoulders, tosses it through the open door, and hurries on down the corridor as Jackie emerges from the opposite room, putting Henry's bathrobe on, but not before we realize that under it she wears only panties and bra, which she covers hurriedly and hastens after Henry, toward the elevator, into which other guests are hurrying, the elevator man yelling.

ELEVATOR MAN Everybody out! Hurry!

Henry and Jackie enter the elevator, the doors close.

Interior foyer of the apartment house. Much excitement. Guests hurry across the foyer beneath sign and arrow bearing words: SHELTER. The sirens are still going, wardens' and police whistles sound from outside. The front door opens, the doorman and the taxi driver enter, hurrying between them Priscilla, the doorman carries her weekend bag.

DOORMAN Gee, Mrs. Morgan, you come all the way back from Connecticut to get into this.

PRISCILLA Yes. Thank heaven, I didn't bring Mother back with me.

Tony enters behind them. As they cross the foyer, the elevator doors open, the passengers come out, among them are Henry in the bath towel, and Jackie now wearing Henry's bathrobe, with a big monogram on the pocket. At once the two couples recognize each other, stop dead still, staring. Priscilla registers Henry's bathrobe on Jackie. Henry realizes his situation.

HENRY Holy cow!

PRISCILLA The minute I turn my back.

HENRY I can explain.

DOORMAN Get on folks! Get on!

He starts to shove them toward the shelter. Tony flings him off, staring grimly at Jackie.

TONY Again.

DOORMAN *(still shoving them)* Get on! Get on!

Jackie gives Tony a defiant look, turns suddenly to Henry, kisses him quickly on the nose.

JACKIE Thank you for the bathrobe.

DOORMAN Get on! Get on!

All exit toward the shelter. The sirens are still going.

The foyer, fifteen minutes later. The ALL CLEAR has just sounded, the guests emerge from the shelter and exit from the foyer until only the two couples and the doorman remain. Priscilla, coldly and grimly angry, goes to her bag and picks it up. Henry follows.

HENRY I can explain, if you will just listen a minute.

PRISCILLA Write me a letter. I'm going back to Mother's. I might even read it.

HENRY All right then, if that's the way you want it.

PRISCILLA *(going toward the door)* Only I suggest that you get your bathrobe back first.

HENRY Sure, I'll even put in the letter how I did it.

PRISCILLA If you could see yourself now, you wouldn't wait long enough to write a letter.

Henry stares at her as she exits. Then he starts toward the elevator.

TONY *(advances grimly toward Jackie)* You come on.

Henry stops, watching, as Tony grasps Jackie roughly by the wrist and starts to drag her toward the elevator.

JACKIE *(resisting, struggling)* If you spank me again——

TONY *(dragging her on)* What for? *(indicates Henry contemptuously)* For *that?*

HENRY *(starts forward)* Look here, Mr. Minetti——

TONY *(dragging Jackie into elevator: contemptuously to Henry)* Write me a letter too. *(to the elevator man)* Twelfth floor. And don't mind the lights.

Henry wakes from his trance, starts toward the elevator. The doorman steps in front of him.

HENRY *(to doorman, tries to pass him)* Get out of the way, Mike.

DOORMAN *(soothingly)* Now, Mr. Morgan. You know you can't interfere between a man and his wife. *(the elevator doors close)* If you want to sympathize with her, why not wait until tonight and go down to that sink where she works.

Interior Henry's apartment, night. Henry is dressing in black tie, is examining in the mirror the fit of his coat, swells his chest, etc. The door bell rings.

HENRY Come in.

A florist's delivery boy enters, bearing a bunch of roses and a small carton. Henry takes the carton, opens the carton, takes out a carnation and puts it in his buttonhole.

HENRY You look like a man of the world. What's your opinion of a pretty young woman who would wear a strange man's bathrobe in public?

BOY Gee, that sounds serious, don't it?

HENRY I rather think so myself. In that case, what would you do about it?

BOY Well, gee, if I was the guy, I'd sure try to find out if it was serious or not.

HENRY I rather think so myself.

He gives the boy a dollar tip. The boy exits.

Interior. Small, intimate, and expensive nightclub. Jackie is at the microphone beside the piano, finishing a number. In the background the headwaiter waits, carrying the bunch of roses which the florist's boy delivered to Henry. When Jackie's number is over, applause comes, she bows, the waiter comes in and hands her the roses.

WAITER There at table number three. He's already ordered champagne.

JACKIE *(looks out, recognizes Henry off[stage], reacts)* Oh yes, I know him. It's Mr. Morgan, my neighbor. *(quickly, as an idea strikes her)* Where's Tony?

WAITER Right here at his table. You want him?

JACKIE *(glances toward Tony's table)* No no. I just thought maybe he hadn't waited for me tonight. Bring Mr. Morgan up here.

WAITER Right.

He exits. Henry enters.

JACKIE Good evening, Mr. Morgan. I never did thank you for saving my modesty this afternoon.

HENRY Not quite. That one on the nose was just an installment—I hope. Or am I wrong?

JACKIE And for the beautiful roses too.

HENRY You could thank me for that by drinking a bottle of champagne with me. It's waiting at my table now.

JACKIE *(with false hesitation, leading him on)* I really shouldn't drink where my public can see me.

HENRY Then where can we go that's private? Your dressing room, maybe?

JACKIE Champagne? In my dressing room? Do we know one another that well?

HENRY We knew one another well enough for you to wear my bathrobe this afternoon, didn't we? *(they look at each other a moment. Then Henry turns triumphantly)* Waiter! Take my champagne to Miss Gordan's dressing room, will you?

Jackie has taken out her compact, opens the mirror, looks into it.

INSERT: The compact mirror, Tony's face reflected in it as Jackie makes sure again that he is missing none of this.

Jackie and Henry exit.

Interior. Jackie's dressing room, a negligee over the back of a chair. The waiter is about to open the champagne. Henry waves him off, opens the bottle himself, and starts to fill a glass.

JACKIE While you're doing that——

She takes up the negligee and goes toward screen. Henry watches her, turning his head. The pouring champagne begins to miss the glass, Henry recovers hurriedly, fills the glass. Jackie emerges from behind the screen, making up her face. Henry reacts: he had expected her to have on the negligee.

HENRY I thought maybe you were getting into something more comfortable.

JACKIE What's more comforting than champagne?

HENRY Besides, the evening's young yet, isn't it?——

Rapid footsteps sound from the corridor, approaching the door. Jackie reacts.

JACKIE It's Tony!

HENRY Who?

JACKIE My husband.

Henry leaps to the door, tries to hold it as Tony pushes at it, struggles valiantly as Tony pushes the door in about a foot, then shoves the door violently open, flinging Henry back into the wall. Tony enters angrily, paying no attention to Henry, approaches Jackie.

TONY *(to Jackie)* Not that one. Not that shrimp again.

JACKIE You were just sulking. Did you expect me to sit around all evening, holding your chin up off the floor?

TONY Maybe you call this sulking.

He grasps her by the wrist, whirls the chair around, sits down, and jerks Jackie face-down across his lap.

JACKIE *(struggling)* Don't you dare!

TONY *(gives her the first spank)* What are you going to do about it?

Jackie screams. Henry leaps forward, grasps Tony's raised hand.

HENRY Don't touch her!

TONY *(his hand raised to spank)* For crying out loud.

Jackie looks up to see what's going on. Tony gives Henry a backhanded blow across the face, knocks him aside, spanks Jackie again. Again Henry leaps in, tries to pull Jackie off Tony's lap. Henry's nose is bleeding.

JACKIE *(to Henry)* Will you beat it? Don't you know anything about privacy?

TONY Yeah, get out. Beat it.

He spanks Jackie again. Henry falls slowly back, watching them.

HENRY *(murmurs)* Privacy.

He finds his nose bleeding, takes out handkerchief as he exits.

TONY *(still spanking Jackie: with each blow)* Didn't I warn you this afternoon? Huh? Huh?

Interior. Henry's apartment, CLOSE on door as it opens and Henry enters slowly, dejected, holding the handkerchief to his nose. Without looking into the room yet, he removes the handkerchief, glances at it, returns it tenderly to his nose, comes on into the room, closes the door, and for the first time, looks up. He stops and reacts.

WIDER ANGLE—Room. Priscilla sits in her usual easy chair at one end of the table, knitting. On the other end of the table the evening paper and Henry's pipe lie. In front of the other easy chair are his slippers.

PRISCILLA *(not even looking up)* Of course you forgot to telephone them to start my yogurt again tomorrow morning.

HENRY No, dear. I mean, yes, dear.

He crosses to the telephone and takes it up. A moment:

HENRY *(into phone)* Get me the dairy, please.

END

VI
Biographical Documents

In hindsight, one can justifiably claim that Faulkner's greatest literary achievements had been accomplished by the end of the 1930s. The decade of the forties, on the other hand, was for Faulkner of an altogether different tenor. As a result of the failure of his novels and stories to earn him a sustained livelihood, Faulkner spent almost half of the 1940s working as a scenarist at Warner Bros. in Burbank, California. The two payroll notices reproduced in this section mark the beginning and the end of a very dispiriting, unproductive (from a literary standpoint) stint in Hollywood. Two other items—the report card he signed for his daughter Jill and the set of instructions for curing pork he typed out for his son-in-law—suggest the more tranquil, domestic side of life which characterized the second half of the forties for Faulkner.

By the end of 1950 both Hollywood and Rowan Oak, marked as they were by a degree of privacy, no matter how antithetical their geographies and life styles, were already being irreversibly displaced. A Random House publicity circular from 1951, Phil Stone's copy of the Ford Foundation *Omnibus* script, and the records of the People-To-People committee that Faulkner co-chaired for President Eisenhower document just three of a multiplicity of distractions and responsibilities that Faulkner assumed in attempting to fulfill the role of an international Man of Letters.

Although he continued to write fiction, as two ancillary items relating to his 1954 novel, *A Fable,* suggest, his most energetic efforts during these years took the form of polemical essays, letters to editors, public speeches, and interviews. This extra-literary aspect of this stage of Faulkner's career is represented by the "Beer Broadside," Faulkner's contribution to the debate over the question of the legalization of the sale of beer in Oxford. This period is also marked by Faulkner's involvement with Joan Williams, a young writer who became first Faulkner's protégé and then his mistress. Reproduced below are two story fragments that Faulkner typed out for Joan as examples of the narrative process.

The reservation card from the Algonquin Hotel in New York City, bearing five Faulkner signatures and documenting periodic stays between November 1958 and May 1962, only hints at the peripatetic nature of Faulkner's activities during the last decade of his life. At the other extreme is the "First Experimental Balch Hangar-Flying Squadron" citation, conceived and executed in collaboration with Joseph Blotner and Frederick Gwynn, Faulkner's two closest friends during his 1956–1958 tenure as writer-in-residence at the University of Virginia. This mock-serious document symbolizes Faulkner's lifelong penchant for male camaraderie which had begun in the 1910s and '20s with Phil Stone, flourished during the '30s and '40s with various hunting and drinking cronies, but by the last years of his life had greatly diminished.

▶ Warner Bros. "Employee's Starting Record" for William Faulkner, July 27, 1942, 1 page, 3¾ by 5¹⁵⁄₁₆ inches.

This document records Faulkner's starting date with the studio as July 27, 1942, and lists his salary as $300 (per week). During his first assignment at Warner Bros., which lasted until late November 1942, Faulkner concentrated all his energies on writing a screenplay entitled *The De Gaulle Story* for producer Robert Buckner. For a history of this project, and the texts of the successive scripts, see Volume III of *Faulkner: A Comprehensive Guide to the Brodsky Collection.*

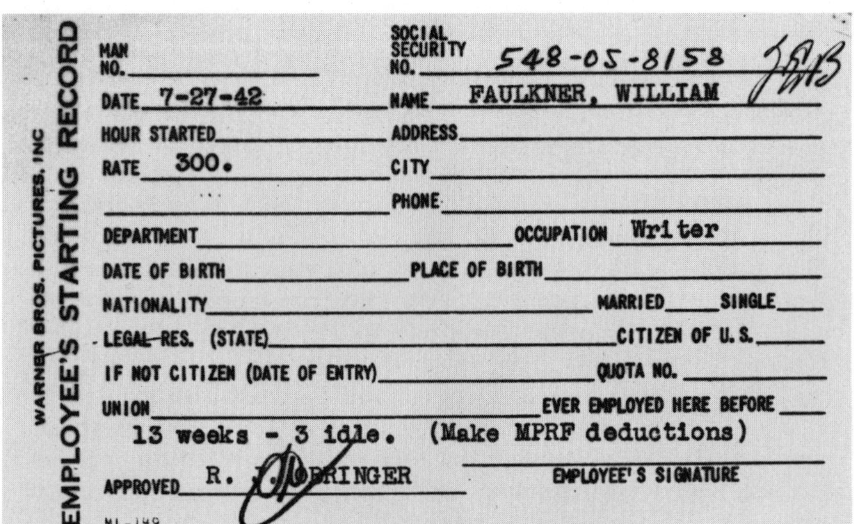

WARNER BROS. PICTURES, INC
EMPLOYEE'S STARTING RECORD

MAN NO. ____ SOCIAL SECURITY NO. 548-05-8158 JB
DATE 7-27-42 NAME FAULKNER, WILLIAM
HOUR STARTED ____ ADDRESS ____
RATE 300. CITY ____
PHONE ____
DEPARTMENT ____ OCCUPATION Writer
DATE OF BIRTH ____ PLACE OF BIRTH ____
NATIONALITY ____ MARRIED ____ SINGLE ____
LEGAL RES. (STATE) ____ CITIZEN OF U.S. ____
IF NOT CITIZEN (DATE OF ENTRY) ____ QUOTA NO. ____
UNION ____ EVER EMPLOYED HERE BEFORE ____
13 weeks - 3 idle. (Make MPRF deductions)
APPROVED R. J. OBRINGER ____ EMPLOYEE'S SIGNATURE
ML-149

55. Faulkner's Warner Bros. Starting Record, 1942

▶ "Report on visit to Consolidated Aircraft Factory re 'Liberator.' Nov. 14, 1942." Ribbon typescript, 1 page, 11 by 8½ inches, Sebo yellow copy paper; with typed signature in upper left corner: "William Faulkner." Accompanied by "LIBERATOR / Notes," ribbon typescript, 2 pages, 11 by 8½ inches, Sebo yellow copy paper.

These joint documents derive from Faulkner's November 13, 1942 visit to an aircraft factory in San Diego and record his background research for a proposed movie script to be titled *Liberator Story* or *The Life and Death of a Bomber.* Although Faulkner wrote a story outline for Warner Bros. in January 1943, it was never developed into a screenplay. Faulkner's outline was first published in *Country Lawyer and Other Stories for the Screen,* ed. Louis Daniel Brodsky and Robert W. Hamblin (Jackson: University Press of Mississippi, 1987), pp. 61–81.

REPORT ON VISIT TO CONSOLIDATED AIRCRAFT FACTORY RE "LIBERATOR." NOV. 14, 1942.

Arrived San Diego Friday afternoon, 13th, with Mr. Berry, of Location Dept.

Received permission to enter plant 10:00 A.M., Saturday. Consolidated Publicity Department sent a car for Berry and myself. We were received very courteously by Mr. Collier, were furnished a conscientious guide, all personal contacts with publicity department very pleasant. Berry and I were conducted through factory, trip took from 10:00 A.M.–2:00 P.M., with one hour out for lunch as factory guests.

My impression is that we were given a more or less standardized tour. Mr. Collier referred to it as a 'General Knudsen Quickie.' Except for more detail, being permitted to pause and look longer and to ask any questions about what I was looking at that occurred to me, I saw not much more than was shown in the picture, 'Wings for the Eagle.' There were certain secret processes, etc. which I did not expect to be shown. Mr. Collier mentioned that I had not been shown certain things. I was permitted, courteously and without challenge, to examine as long as I liked any phase of the work which I was shown. Notes on what I saw and on the points I was given information about are attached herewith.

My impression, from private assumption and from comments volunteered by Mr. Collier, is that Consolidated intends to go as far toward getting a picture of publicity value to Consolidated, as Lockheed did for 'Wings for the Eagle,' and for the same reason. Whether they will go further than Lockheed did, I do not know. I was given permission to return.

I had no chance to talk to people: workers, foremen, etc. I would like to do this. They were busy at the time, and I had the impression that I was being, not hurried through, but conducted through and then out. I was not refused permission to talk to anyone. I imagine I will be allowed to.

As the attached notes show, I was given a comprehensive view of the general birth and construction of an aeroplane.

I asked permission to enter and examine a finished aeroplane. This was refused at the time by the guide, pending ratification from some other authority. It was indicated that I would be given this permission later, not definitely permitted, but the guide said he thought it could be done.

Returned to Los Angeles 11:30 P.M. Saturday.

LIBERATOR

Notes

Sources. Blue prints, drafting department.
  Requisitions, card system: order, requisition, manufacture, inspections, additional work, to stock room.
Nose. Tip to instrument panel. Bombardier's office.
  Bomb releases, bombsight base, guns and mounts, bomb selector switches and panel, nose wheel.
Wing. Center section between two outboard engines, from instrument panel to rear end of bomb-bay.
  Fuselage. Flight and engine instruments, flight controls, navigator's office, bomb-bay, bomb-sight case, navigator's hatch, gun-blisters and mounts, inner wiring and control cables.
  Wing. Engine mounts, under-carriage gear, flaps.
  Wing-tips. Ailerons.
Tail. From bomb-bay to end. Tail gunner's turret, elevators and rudder, tail skid gun blisters.
Assembly Wing. Controls and wiring installed, superchargers, gear, guns, engines.
  Nose. Bombardier's instruments, wiring, guns.
  Tail. Guns, wiring, cables, tail wheel.
Swing Shift.
Women. Do all types of work, drop hammer, spot welding, painting and doping, sewing linen. Man & wife not permitted to work at same job. (Department?)
  Nursery problem.
  Will they want to quit after war?
  Medical care, examinations for applicants.
  General air of plant: seems efficient but free and easy, people seem con-

tented. Perhaps with the wages and free from draft they should be.
Plant protection. From air and ground.
Eating on lot.
Would like to talk with some of workers, foremen, etc.
Noticed first general air of calmness, confidence. People all seemed happy, perhaps proud of the ships they are making. Busy but not frenzied. Set up seems simplified, not complex, to a layman like myself. Quite clean and pleasant working conditions and surroundings. People do not seem to be in one another's way, work busily yet quietly, not necessary to shout orders, etc., all seem to know what to do.

Spot welding. Why of it.
Armor plate.
Engines and mounts.
Testing personnel.
Private ferrying organization.
Army and Navy: Catalinas and Coronados. Navy plant. Older, veterans, quieter, as if they had been at job long enough for novelty to be gone, but pride remains.
Indoor testing of hulls.

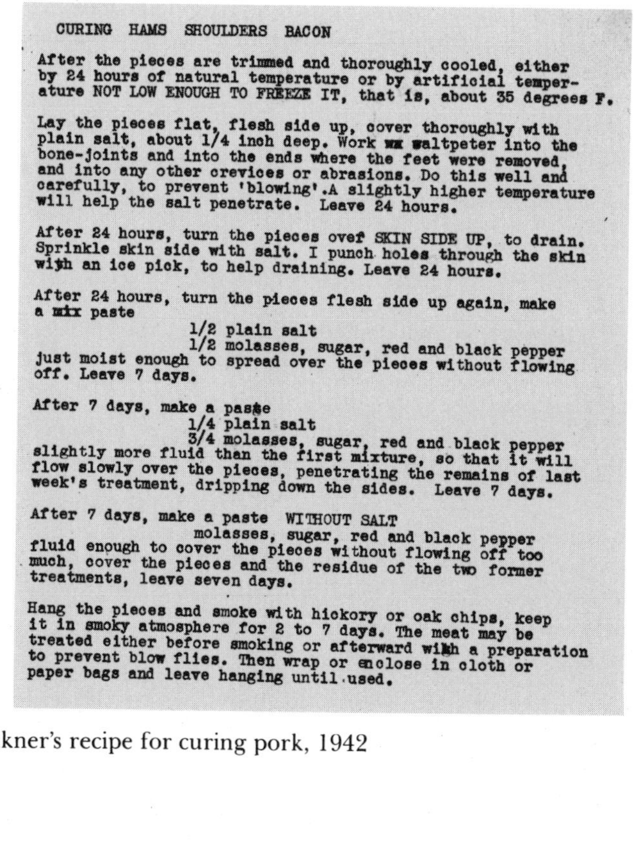

CURING HAMS SHOULDERS BACON

After the pieces are trimmed and thoroughly cooled, either by 24 hours of natural temperature or by artificial temperature NOT LOW ENOUGH TO FREEZE IT, that is, about 35 degrees F.

Lay the pieces flat, flesh side up, cover thoroughly with plain salt, about 1/4 inch deep. Work ~~xx~~ saltpeter into the bone-joints and into the ends where the feet were removed, and into any other crevices or abrasions. Do this well and carefully, to prevent 'blowing'. A slightly higher temperature will help the salt penetrate. Leave 24 hours.

After 24 hours, turn the pieces over SKIN SIDE UP, to drain. Sprinkle skin side with salt. I punch holes through the skin with an ice pick, to help draining. Leave 24 hours.

After 24 hours, turn the pieces flesh side up again, make a ~~mix~~ paste
1/2 plain salt
1/2 molasses, sugar, red and black pepper
just moist enough to spread over the pieces without flowing off. Leave 7 days.

After 7 days, make a paste
1/4 plain salt
3/4 molasses, sugar, red and black pepper
slightly more fluid than the first mixture, so that it will flow slowly over the pieces, penetrating the remains of last week's treatment, dripping down the sides. Leave 7 days.

After 7 days, make a paste WITHOUT SALT
molasses, sugar, red and black pepper
fluid enough to cover the pieces without flowing off too much, cover the pieces and the residue of the two former treatments, leave seven days.

Hang the pieces and smoke with hickory or oak chips, keep it in smoky atmosphere for 2 to 7 days. The meat may be treated either before smoking or afterward with a preparation to prevent blow flies. Then wrap or enclose in cloth or paper bags and leave hanging until used.

56. Faulkner's recipe for curing pork, 1942

▶ "CURING HAMS SHOULDERS BACON," c. December 1942, ribbon typescript, 1 page, 11 by 8½ inches, Highway Bond.

At the request of his son-in-law, William Fielden, who, with his wife Victoria, was then living at Rowan Oak, Faulkner typed out these instructions outlining his own personal recipe for curing pork. Butchering and curing were standard practices by which Faulkner provided meat for his family during the 1930s and '40s. For a detailed discussion of this item, see Louis Daniel Brodsky, "'Pappy' Faulkner's Recipe for Curing Pork," *Faulkner Journal,* II (Fall 1986), 73–74.

CURING HAMS SHOULDERS BACON

After the pieces are trimmed and thoroughly cooled, either by 24 hours of natural temperature or by artificial temperature NOT LOW ENOUGH TO FREEZE IT, that is, about 35 degrees F.

Lay the pieces flat, flesh side up, cover thoroughly with plain salt, about ¼ inch deep. Work saltpeter into the bone-joints and into the ends where the feet were removed, and into any other crevices or abrasions. Do this well and carefully, to prevent 'blowing'. A slightly higher temperature will help the salt penetrate. Leave 24 hours.

After 24 hours, turn the pieces over SKIN SIDE UP, to drain. Sprinkle skin side with salt. I punch holes through the skin with an ice pick, to help draining. Leave 24 hours.

After 24 hours, turn the pieces flesh side up again, make a [mix *del.*] paste
½ plain salt
½ molasses, sugar, red and black pepper just moist enough to spread over the pieces without flowing off. Leave 7 days.

After 7 days, make a paste
¼ plain salt
¾ molasses, sugar, red and black pepper slightly more fluid than the first mixture, so that it will flow slowly over the pieces, penetrating the remains of last week's treatment, dripping down the sides. Leave 7 days.

After 7 days, make a paste WITHOUT SALT
molasses, sugar, red and black pepper fluid enough to cover the pieces without flowing off too much, cover the pieces and the residue of the two former treatments, leave seven days.

Hang the pieces and smoke with hickory or oak chips, keep it in smoky atmosphere for 2 to 7 days. The meat may be treated either before smoking or afterward with a preparation to prevent blow flies. Then wrap or enclose in cloth or paper bags and leave hanging until used.

▶ Warner Bros. "Off Payroll Notice" for William Faulkner, September 19, 1945, 1 page, 3¾ by 5⅝ inches.

Coming in the wake of Faulkner's growing frustration at Warner Bros., climaxed by his failure to produce an acceptable screenplay of *Stallion Road*, this document records the studio's response to Faulkner's quitting his job and returning to Oxford. To avoid a legal confrontation over the terms of Faulkner's contract, which technically did not expire until July 27, 1949, the studio placed Faulkner on a six-months' suspension of duties.

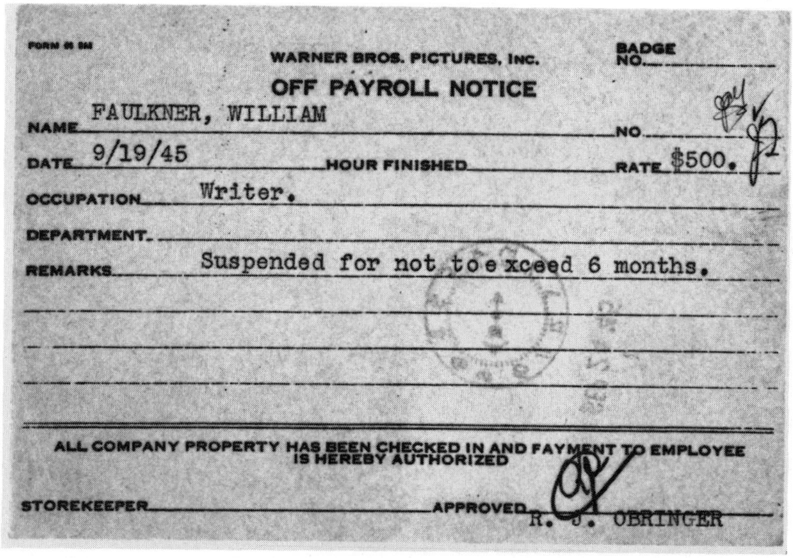
FORM 88 5M
WARNER BROS. PICTURES, INC.
OFF PAYROLL NOTICE
BADGE NO.
NAME FAULKNER, WILLIAM NO.
DATE 9/19/45 HOUR FINISHED RATE $500.
OCCUPATION Writer.
DEPARTMENT
REMARKS Suspended for not to exceed 6 months.
ALL COMPANY PROPERTY HAS BEEN CHECKED IN AND PAYMENT TO EMPLOYEE IS HEREBY AUTHORIZED
STOREKEEPER APPROVED R. J. OBRINGER

57. Faulkner's Warner Bros. Off Payroll Notice, 1945

▶ "Pupil's Report Card" for Jill Faulkner, 1945–1946, 4 pages (1 folded leaf).

On this Class 7A report card for Faulkner's daughter, issued by University High School, Mississippi, Faulkner's signature appears in the slots allocated for the third, fourth, and fifth terms under the section designated "Signature of Parent or Guardian." These periods relate roughly to the December–June time frame when Faulkner, having abrogated his Warner Bros. contract by leaving Burbank without permission in mid-September 1945, was back home in Oxford.

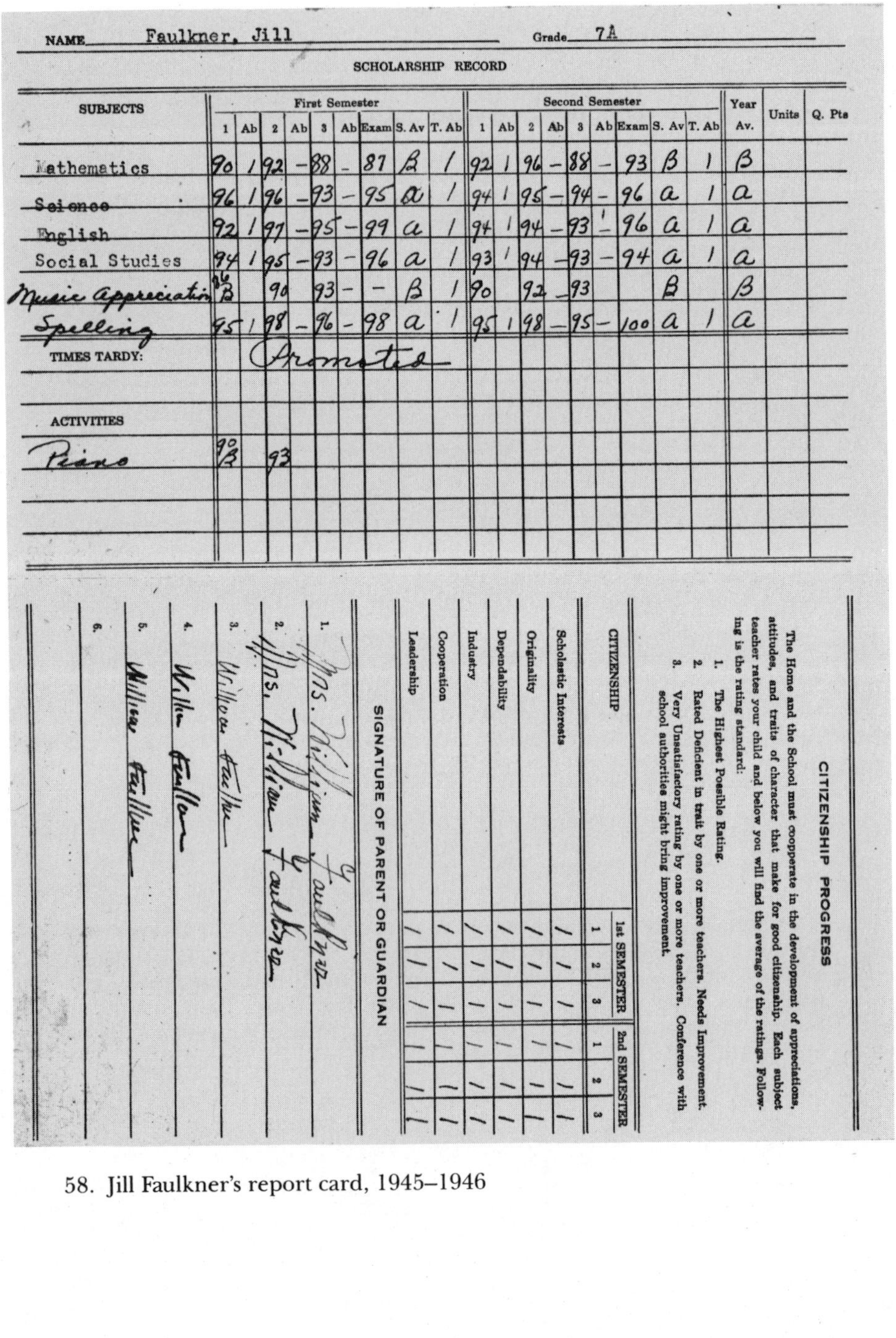

NAME Faulkner, Jill Grade 7A

SCHOLARSHIP RECORD

SUBJECTS	First Semester 1	Ab	2	Ab	3	Ab	Exam	S. Av	T. Ab	Second Semester 1	Ab	2	Ab	3	Ab	Exam	S. Av	T. Ab	Year Av.	Units	Q. Pts
Mathematics	90	1	92	–	88	–	87	B	1	92	1	96	–	88	–	93	B	1	B		
~~Science~~	96	1	96	–	93	–	95	a	1	94	1	95	–	94	–	96	a	1	a		
English	92	1	97	–	95	–	99	a	1	94	1	94	–	93	1 –	96	a	1	a		
Social Studies	94	1	95	–	93	–	96	a	1	93	1	94	–	93	–	94	a	1	a		
Music appreciation	86 B		90		93	–	–	B	1	90		92	–	93			B		B		
Spelling	95	1	98	–	96	–	98	a	1	95	1	98	–	95	–	100	a	1	a		
TIMES TARDY:	Promoted																				
ACTIVITIES																					
Piano	90 B		93																		

CITIZENSHIP PROGRESS

The Home and the School must cooperate in the development of appreciations, attitudes, and traits of character that make for good citizenship. Each subject teacher rates your child and below you will find the average of the ratings. Following is the rating standard:

1. The Highest Possible Rating.
2. Rated Deficient in trait by one or more teachers. Needs Improvement.
3. Very Unsatisfactory rating by one or more teachers. Conference with school authorities might bring improvement.

CITIZENSHIP	1st SEMESTER 1	2	3	2nd SEMESTER 1	2	3
Scholastic Interests	1	1	1	1	1	1
Originality	1	1	1	1	1	1
Dependability	1	1	1	1	1	1
Industry	1	1	1	1	1	1
Cooperation	1	1	1	1	1	1
Leadership	1	1	1	1	1	1

SIGNATURE OF PARENT OR GUARDIAN

1. Mrs. William Faulkner
2. Mrs. William Faulkner
3. William Faulkner
4. William Faulkner
5. William Faulkner
6.

58. Jill Faulkner's report card, 1945–1946

▶ "To the Voters of Oxford," c. late August or early September 1950, printed notice, 1 page,

This copy of a circular prepared by three Protestant ministers in Oxford originally belonged to Faulkner, who subsequently gave it to James W. Silver. The verso contains a number of penciled notations on particular Bible verses and hymns (presumably notes someone recorded during a sermon)—a fact which suggests that copies of this broadside were passed out in some of the Oxford churches. Faulkner's "Beer Broadside" was written as a rejoinder to, and copied the format of, this document.

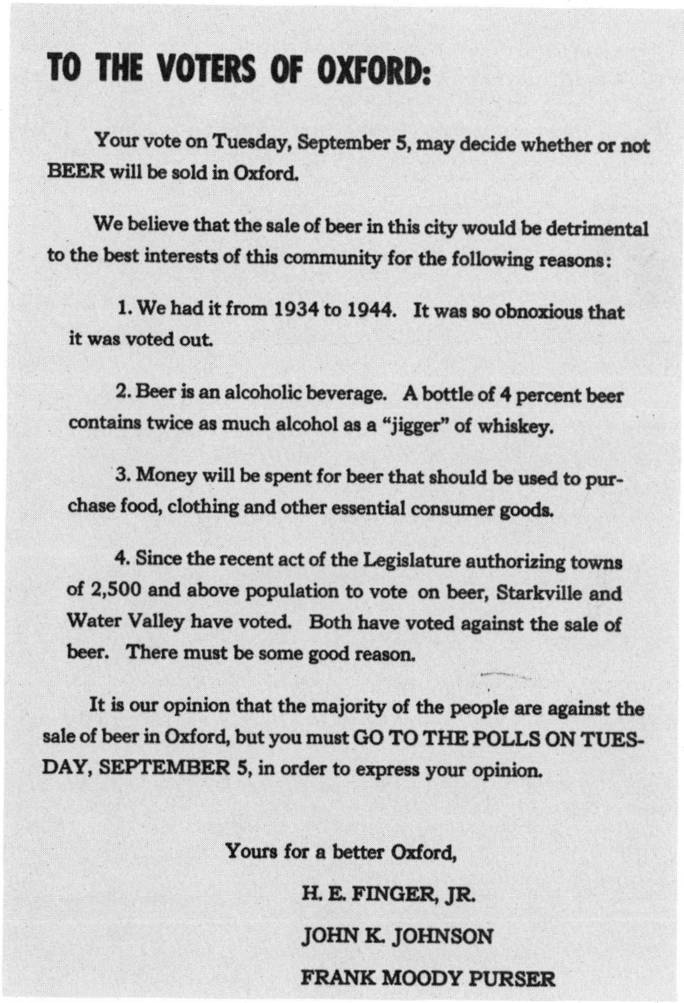

TO THE VOTERS OF OXFORD:

Your vote on Tuesday, September 5, may decide whether or not BEER will be sold in Oxford.

We believe that the sale of beer in this city would be detrimental to the best interests of this community for the following reasons:

1. We had it from 1934 to 1944. It was so obnoxious that it was voted out.

2. Beer is an alcoholic beverage. A bottle of 4 percent beer contains twice as much alcohol as a "jigger" of whiskey.

3. Money will be spent for beer that should be used to purchase food, clothing and other essential consumer goods.

4. Since the recent act of the Legislature authorizing towns of 2,500 and above population to vote on beer, Starkville and Water Valley have voted. Both have voted against the sale of beer. There must be some good reason.

It is our opinion that the majority of the people are against the sale of beer in Oxford, but you must GO TO THE POLLS ON TUESDAY, SEPTEMBER 5, in order to express your opinion.

Yours for a better Oxford,

H. E. FINGER, JR.

JOHN K. JOHNSON

FRANK MOODY PURSER

59. Ministers' anti-beer broadside, 1950

725 "To the Voters of Oxford," c. late August or early September 1950, printed notice, 1 page, 11 by 8½ inches, Nekoosa Bond.

Faulkner's "Beer Broadside," while supporting the legalized sale of beer in "dry" Oxford, Mississippi, was also a satiric barb directed at three Protestant ministers who, in Faulkner's view, had interposed clerical views in a matter of civil politics. This lampoon, printed at Faulkner's expense in the Oxford *Eagle* shop and handed out by Faulkner and members of his family, had for its prototype a broadside quite similar in format that the Reverends Finger, Johnson, and Purser had distributed through their respective congregations.

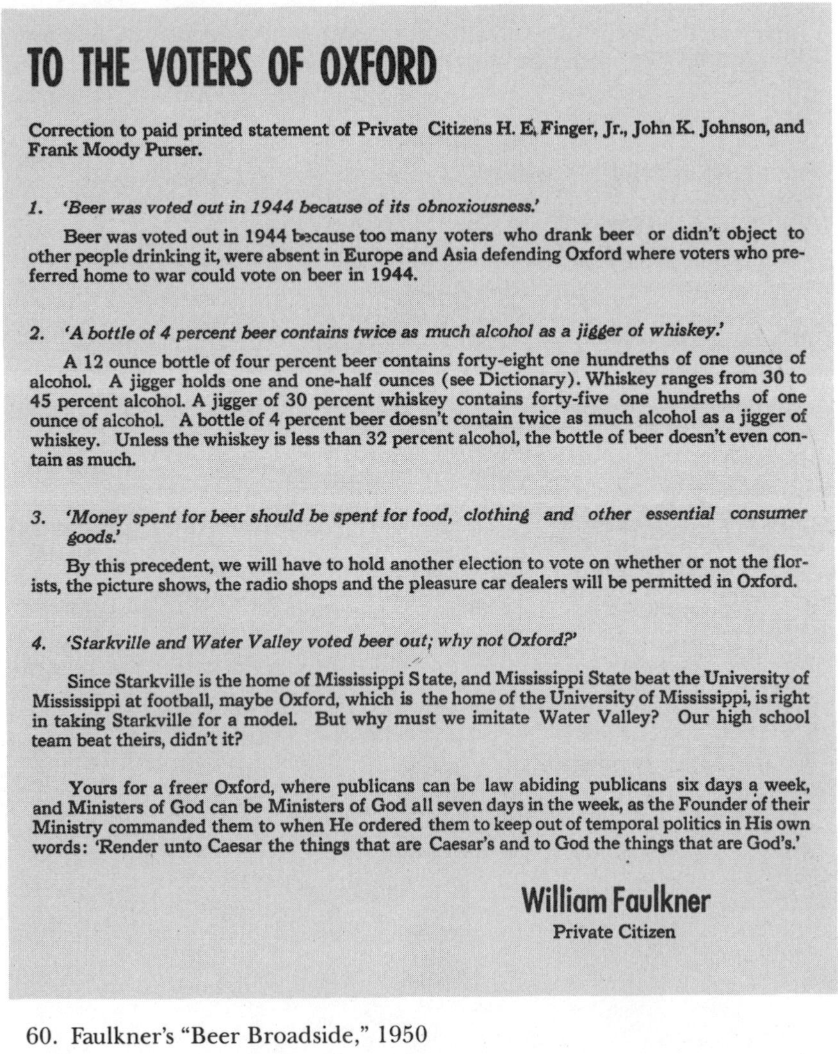

TO THE VOTERS OF OXFORD

Correction to paid printed statement of Private Citizens H. E. Finger, Jr., John K. Johnson, and Frank Moody Purser.

1. *'Beer was voted out in 1944 because of its obnoxiousness.'*

Beer was voted out in 1944 because too many voters who drank beer or didn't object to other people drinking it, were absent in Europe and Asia defending Oxford where voters who preferred home to war could vote on beer in 1944.

2. *'A bottle of 4 percent beer contains twice as much alcohol as a jigger of whiskey.'*

A 12 ounce bottle of four percent beer contains forty-eight one hundreths of one ounce of alcohol. A jigger holds one and one-half ounces (see Dictionary). Whiskey ranges from 30 to 45 percent alcohol. A jigger of 30 percent whiskey contains forty-five one hundreths of one ounce of alcohol. A bottle of 4 percent beer doesn't contain twice as much alcohol as a jigger of whiskey. Unless the whiskey is less than 32 percent alcohol, the bottle of beer doesn't even contain as much.

3. *'Money spent for beer should be spent for food, clothing and other essential consumer goods.'*

By this precedent, we will have to hold another election to vote on whether or not the florists, the picture shows, the radio shops and the pleasure car dealers will be permitted in Oxford.

4. *'Starkville and Water Valley voted beer out; why not Oxford?'*

Since Starkville is the home of Mississippi State, and Mississippi State beat the University of Mississippi at football, maybe Oxford, which is the home of the University of Mississippi, is right in taking Starkville for a model. But why must we imitate Water Valley? Our high school team beat theirs, didn't it?

Yours for a freer Oxford, where publicans can be law abiding publicans six days a week, and Ministers of God can be Ministers of God all seven days in the week, as the Founder of their Ministry commanded them to when He ordered them to keep out of temporal politics in His own words: 'Render unto Caesar the things that are Caesar's and to God the things that are God's.'

William Faulkner
Private Citizen

60. Faulkner's "Beer Broadside," 1950

792 "WILLIAM FAULKNER," c. April 1951, mimeographed typescript, 6 pages, 11 by 8½ inches.

Presenting a detailed account of Faulkner's life as well as his literary achievements, this announcement was distributed by the Publicity Department of Random House to newspapers and book stores as part of the advance promotion of *Requiem for a Nun* (published September 27, 1951). Interestingly, the essay contains numerous factual errors, including the apocryphal stories about Faulkner's heroic actions as a flyer in World War I. This publicity notice was likely drafted by Saxe Commins, Faulkner's editor, who retained this copy in his Princeton, New Jersey, home files.

WILLIAM FAULKNER

Winner in 1950 of: The Nobel Prize for Literature
The National Book Award for Fiction
The William Dean Howells Medal for Fiction
of the American Academy of Arts and Letters.

WILLIAM FAULKNER was born in New Albany, Mississippi, on September 25, 1897, the eldest of four sons born to Murry Charles and Maud Butler Faulkner. (One of his brothers, John, also became a novelist.) He was named after his great-grandfather, Colonel William Falkner (as the family name is variously spelled), who fought in the Civil War, built railroads, and wrote a popular novel, THE WHITE ROSE OF MEMPHIS. Early in Faulkner's childhood, the family moved to Oxford, Mississippi, where his father owned a livery stable and served as business manager of the University of Mississippi.

Faulkner's schooling was intermittent after the fifth grade and he left high school, without graduating, to work in his grandfather's bank. He entered the University of Mississippi as a special student at sixteen. He was a "slave" of Swinburne at the time. "Whatever it was in Swinburne," he said later, "it completely satisfied me and filled my inner life." Two years later, at the start of World War I, he dropped out of school to join the Canadian Air Corps and was transferred to Oxford, England, where he was in training as a noncommissioned officer for more than a year. He spent his spare time taking courses at Oxford and reading in the University Library. It was there that he started to read and study the Elizabethan poets, whom he still likes for their "beautiful awareness, power, and masculinity." He became a lieutenant in the British Royal Air Force, was sent to France as an observer, crashed twice and was injured once. He remained abroad until after the Armistice. Upon his return to Oxford, he enrolled, officially, at the University of Mississippi but withdrew after a year or so without taking a degree.

It was in the summer of 1920 that Stark Young, a Mississippi novelist, advised him to go to New York. There he persuaded Miss Elizabeth Prall, then head of the Book Department at Lord & Taylor's, to give him a job as clerk. After a few miserable months, Faulkner returned to Mississippi. He worked briefly at odd jobs—roof painting, carpentry, and paper hanging. He became postmaster of the University in 1922 but was dismissed two years later for reading while on duty. During this period he enriched his mind, he says, largely by "undirected and uncorrelated reading." Poetry was his chief interest; and among his favorite poets were Shakespeare, Spenser, the Elizabethans, Shelley, Keats and Housman.

With the money he had saved while working as postmaster, Faulkner went to New Orleans. There he visited Miss Prall, who had recently married Sherwood Anderson and had settled in New Orleans. He and Anderson became friends, and for a time he shared the Anderson apartment in the Vieux Carré. It was at the suggestion of Anderson that Faulkner attempted his first novel. The book was completed in six weeks and Anderson agreed to show the manuscript to his publishers on the condition that he wouldn't have to read it first. He kept his word and the novel, SOLDIER'S [*sic*] PAY, the story of a disfigured flier's return after World War I, eventually was published in 1926 by Liveright. His next book, MOSQUITOES, a satire on New Orleans Bohemians, was published in 1927.

In 1929, Mr. Faulkner was married to Mrs. Estelle Oldham Franklin, a widow with two children. That same year his third novel, SARTORIS, was published. This was the first of a series of interconnected novels (by 1950 numbering twelve) and short stories dealing with the life, people and history of the fictional Mississippi county of Yoknapatawpha and its chief town of Jefferson—a locale that bore a close physical resemblance to the town of Oxford in Lafayette County. THE SOUND AND THE FURY, written before SARTORIS but published late in 1929, was the first of Faulkner's books to win widespread critical acclaim. It also had Jefferson, the fictional counterpart of Oxford, for its locale. These four novels involved two changes of publishers.

Unable to earn a living by writing, Faulkner took a job as night superintendent of a power plant. There, writing on an upturned wheelbarrow in the small hours of the morning, he revised THE SOUND AND THE FURY, and at the same time deliberately set about writing a pure horror story, aimed at the collection of royalties, which he called SANCTUARY. After the establishment of his reputation by THE SOUND AND THE FURY and AS I LAY DYING, he rewrote SANCTUARY also, so that now it is a part of the Jefferson cycle. Published in 1931, SANCTUARY marked the turning point in Faulkner's career: it won him a large popular following and financial security. The year 1931 also saw the publication of his first collection of short stories, THESE THIRTEEN. His next book, LIGHT IN AUGUST, was published in 1932. That same year Faulkner went to Hollywood, for the first time, to adapt one of his stories for the film, TODAY WE LIVE (1933); on later visits, he helped write the screenplay of THE ROAD TO GLORY (1936) and made the adaptation for SLAVE SHIP (1937), TO HAVE AND HAVE NOT (1944), and THE BIG SLEEP (1946). His second book of poems, A GREEN BOUGH, came out in 1933. THE MARBLE FAUN, his first book of poems, had been published in 1924 with money supplied by a friend. It aroused so little interest that most of the hundred copies were sold to a bookstore at ten cents each. DOCTOR MARTINO AND OTHER STORIES, published in 1934, was followed in 1935 by PYLON, a novel about barnstorming aviators. He returned to the Yoknapatawpha cycle with ABSALOM, ABSALOM! (1936), THE UNVANQUISHED (1938) and THE WILD PALMS (1939). THE HAMLET was published in 1940 and was followed by GO DOWN, MOSES in 1942. INTRUDER IN THE DUST, published in 1948, was later made into an immensely successful motion picture of the same title. KNIGHT'S GAMBIT (1949), a collection of his detective stories, was followed in 1950 by his COLLECTED STORIES.

During the past decade, critics have been hailing this 53-year-old Mississippian as "a genius whose works promise an enduring life . . . our greatest living writer . . . our only genius." His work has been compared to that of Henry James, Franz Kafka and Feodor Dostoevski. Among professional writers the name of Faulkner is as venerated as it is in college English seminars. Above all, he is a superlative storyteller, as Richard Rovere points out in his fine introduction to the Modern Library's edition of LIGHT IN AUGUST: "No other American writer can match him in the old art of catching the ear of the passerby." The last word, and the best, comes from Eudora Welty: "His stories seem to race with time, race with the world . . . The reason Faulkner's unwieldy-looking sentences can race is of course their high organization. And Faulkner is highly organized and his evocation does seem to come out of the place where music comes. Don't let his turbulence ever blind us, his structure is there—daring structure. Faulkner deals with such aspects of the human being as dignity and corruptibility and ridicule and defeat and endurance—especially endurance."

On November 10, 1950, the awarding of the 1949 *Nobel Prize for Literature* to Faulkner was announced. The award cited "his powerful and artistically independent contribution to the new American novel." In his acceptance speech in Stockholm on December 10, 1950, Faulkner said the tragedy today is "a general and universal fear" with "only the question: When will I be blown up?" As a result, young writers have "forgotten the problems of the human heart in conflict with itself, which alone can make good writing because only that is worth writing about." "I believe that man will not merely endure, he will prevail," Mr. Faulkner added. "He is immortal . . . because he has a spirit capable of compassion and sacrifice and endurance." This was the fourth time that an American had received the Nobel Prize for Literature.

On March 6, 1951, Faulkner was awarded the 1950 *National Book Award Gold Medal for Fiction* for COLLECTED STORIES OF WILLIAM FAULKNER, which Random House published on August 21, 1950. This fiction award is one of three annual prizes sponsored by The American Book Publishers Council, Inc., The American Booksellers Association, Inc., and The Book Manufacturers Institute, Inc. to honor "the most distinguished books of 1950." The other two awards are for Non-fiction and Poetry. In 1950 Faulkner also received the Howells Medal of the American Academy of Arts and Letters, of which he is a member. Other organizations to which he belongs are the National Institute of Arts and Letters and Sigma Alpha Epsilon. He won the first prize in the O. Henry Memorial Short Story Award contests of 1939 and 1949.

William Faulkner is short in stature and slight of build. His eyes are black and his hair is gray. Although reportedly shy and taciturn with strangers, the Southern novelist is said to become animated in the company of friends, revealing a ready wit and a talent for inventing "outlandish" tales. His Oxford home is a century-old plantation house and he also owns a thirty-five-acre farm in the hills. Flying used to be a favorite pastime, but he now finds relaxation chiefly in hunting and fishing. The mornings he reserves for work, writing with a pen in minute script the first drafts of his manuscripts on the right-hand side of legal-sized sheets of paper, using the left-hand side for revisions. After typing a copy for his publisher, Random House, he puts the original in a safety-deposit vault. He does not read reviews of his books and avoids literary circles. "I am not a literary man," he told one interviewer, "I am a farmer who just likes to tell stories."

Random House has announced for Fall, 1951 publication a new novel, REQUIEM FOR A NUN. It will be the first novel Faulkner has published since 1948. In April, 1951, Random House will also reissue in the Modern Library ABSALOM, ABSALOM!, which many critics consider Faulkner's finest novel. The Modern Library edition will have an introduction by Harvey Breit.

PUBLICITY DEPARTMENT
RANDOM HOUSE, INC.
457 Madison Avenue
New York 22, N.Y.

▶ "TUESDAY," c. 1952, autograph manuscript in pencil and red grease pencil, 1 page, 11 by 8½ inches, Hammermill Bond.

This manuscript presents an early, abbreviated draft of the Tuesday portion of the plot outline for *A Fable* that Faulkner printed on the wall of his office at Rowan Oak. This outline appears on the verso of Faulkner's penciled map of the Brown's Hotel section of London (see page 22).

▶ Story fragments, c. 1952, ribbon typescript with revisions, 1 leaf (recto and verso), 11 by 8½ inches, Eaton's Berkshire.

These two brief passages, typed by Faulkner, describe a famous, middle-aged writer who has fallen in love with a 22-year-old woman. As early as September 1950 Faulkner suggested to Joan Williams that she write such a story, and he likely intended these passages as lessons in narrative for his young protégé. A revised version of the second of these passages (on verso of leaf) appears in Williams' novel, *The Wintering* (pp. 119–120), the central character of which, Jeffrey Almoner, is partly based on Faulkner.

The writer had received all awards there were, a fact he gave little thought to being still too busy being an artist. But now thinking of himself as this person, he could not help but smile at the incident of himself having lied to drive forty miles on a hot morning to meet a bus bringing a twenty-two year

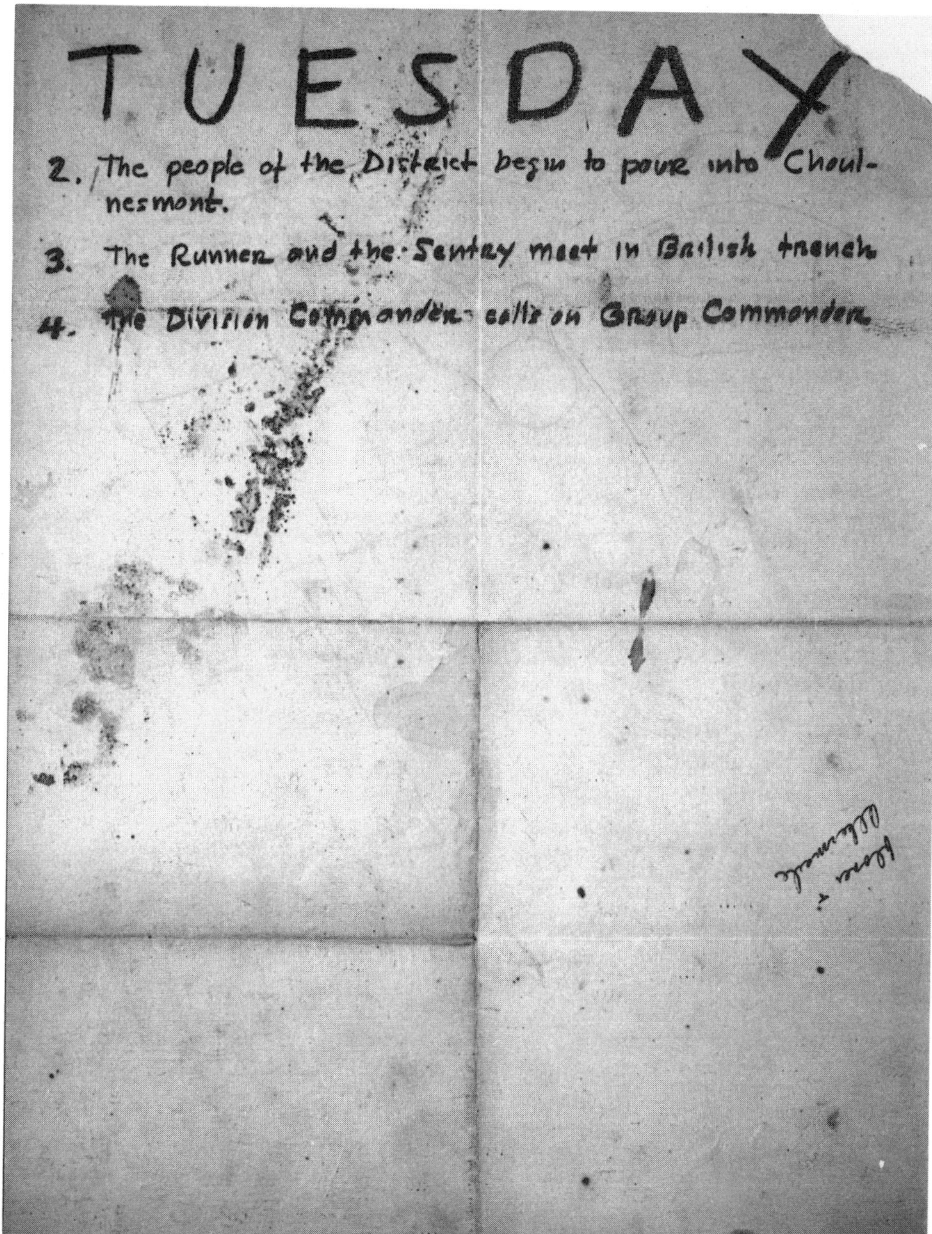
TUESDAY

2. The people of the District begin to pour into Choul-
nesmont.

3. The Runner and the Sentry meet in British trench

4. The Division Commander calls on Group Commander.

61. Faulkner's draft of "Tuesday" outline *(A Fable),* c. 1952

old girl forty miles to meet him secretly too. [Perhaps it was not even so much the incident he smiled at, he told himself <admitted> *del.*] <[Or, *del.*] Perhaps, he admitted, [perhaps *del.*] it was [only *del.*] not even so much the incident as it was> his own satisfaction at finding himself a white-haired bloke and still capable not only of love, but of a fool-young fearfulness at the thought that his love might not keep a rendezvous.

Or perhaps it was just the happiness who brought to a white-haired bloke to find he was still capable not only of love, but of a fool

* * *

'She picked out a bad hour for the subway.'

'She didn't take the subway. I put her in a cab.' Then suddenly, before he even knew he was going to say it: 'Bob, she is a modest and [gentle and *del.*] tender and charming young woman. Not many can wear that, but she can.[' *del.*] Sometimes it frightens me to think that one as old and battered as I am should have the responsibility [for *del.*] of that tenderness and the [luck *del.*] incredible luck of the responsibility.'

'You are lucky,' the other said, turning quickly toward him. 'But dont be afraid. Just deserve it. She is more than that. She's a good girl. Oh, I dont mean in the conventional morality sense. I mean, she's honest and honorable and gentle, and I believe she is capable of generosity and [fi *del.*] affection and fidelity. When you first introduced us, I knew she was pretty. But I was looking at her tonight and suddenly I knew she was beautiful.'

[']Yes, I discovered that myself one night three years ago in an elevator. But let's dont talk about it. All I have to do is just think of her name, and it breaks my heart.'

[']It should break your heart. But let's <*insert.* dont>

[All right. We wont *del.*] talk about it. Let's have a drink.'

896 "BILL FAULKNER AND THE NOBEL PRIZE," c. October 1952, carbon typescript, 10 pages, 11 by 8½ inches.

This shooting script, written in part by Phil "Moon" Mullen, editor of the *Oxford Eagle,* was used in filming the television documentary produced by the Ford Foundation and aired on CBS's *Omnibus* in December 1952. This copy belonged to Phil Stone and shows in his hand penciled revisions of three speeches by Faulkner and one by Stone.

BILL FAULKNER AND THE NOBEL PRIZE

FADE IN 1. Filling the screen, the works of William Faulkner, and translations, on bookshelves.	MUSIC:	Atmospheric, moody, Southern in theme. . . . fades to background. . . .

2. DISSOLVE behind this a medium shot of William Faulkner in work clothes working on his plantation.

FAULKNER'S VOICE: . . . until after the honeysuckle got all mixed up in it the whole thing came to symbolize night and unrest. I seemed to be lying neither asleep nor awake looking down a long corridor of grey halflight where all stable things had become shadowy paradoxical all I had done shadows. . . .

The image of Faulkner dissolves out, leaving only the books.

MUSIC: up. . . .

3. Oxford, Mississippi. Court House Square on a Saturday afternoon. Trucks and cars on the street and alterations in process on the courthouse saying progress and vitality. Citizens, students, country people, negroes, in groups or moving about, unhurried, in languid harmony with the timeless.

MUSIC: segue to march by High School band in the distance. . . .

coming closer. . . .

4. The High School band marching down the street, playing, the cute drum-majorettes prancing.

5. A group of country people on the sidewalk, watching. A man reading a newspaper, the *Oxford Eagle.*

6. Masthead of the *Oxford Eagle.*

MUSIC: fades out.

7. DISSOLVE TO interior of *Eagle* office. A close shot of Moon Mullen rattling the typewriter at top speed. He doesn't speak but his voice is heard.

SOUND: fast smooth typing.

MOON'S VOICE: If you look at a town simply as arithmetic, four thousand people isn't many—

8. The street again. A truck shot from a car, fairly close on the people watching the parade.

MUSIC: band music up as background. . . .

	MOON: —four thousand, living here all the time—
9. Facade of the mellow old administration building of the University.	—not counting the students at the University.
10. DISSOLVE TO a glimpse of the sleek modern interior of the new University Library.	
11. Back to a close shot of Moon Mullen typing.	But all the lives in even a small town is too many to set down in a novel. So a writer—
12. A sequence of close up of faces full of character DISSOLVED one upon the other.	—overlays one life with another, till they become a meaning—
13. The University Monument to the Civil War dead, Union and Confederate.	—many meanings. **ALASTAIR COOKE'S VOICE:** [*blank*]
(Inscription on stone)?	
14. Close shot of Mr. Ike Roberts sitting in his "office" on the sidewalk outside the Colonial Hotel.	**MOON'S VOICE:** As a writer chooses a few of the few to give a timeless life to—
15. The shelf of William Faulkner's works.	—so does history, choosing a few of the few, for what they have done and meant.
16. Moon Mullen typing.	Here, in Oxford, Lafayette County, Mississippi—
17. Faulkner's plantation. A long shot with negroes picking cotton. Camera PANS to a medium long shot. A tractor pulling a trailer stops. Faulkner gets out, unhitches the trailer.	we have a citizen who refers to himself as a farmer. A farmer who also writes.
18. Long shot of William Faulkner's home.	His family is old South, and he's never been gone from Lafayette County for long. Yoknapatawpha County he calls it in his books.
19. Outside a shed on the plantation. A medium shot. Faulkner pauses in his farm chores as some neighbors with a child and some dogs come up. Bill lights his pipe and they	His friends are the friends of his boyhood, and what he writes about he has always known. **ALASTAIR COOKE'S VOICE:** On No-

sit down for a friendly relaxed talk. The child likes him. He scratches a dog's back with his toe as he smokes and listens to the good talk.

vember tenth, nineteen hundred and fifty, it was announced from Stockholm that the Nobel Prize for literature had been awarded to William Faulkner.

20. The *Oxford Eagle* office. Moon Mullen is still typing. The phone rings. He answers it. As he listens, his face shows amazement, delighted amazement. He hangs up. Excited. Grabs pencil, paper, box camera, film, and rushes out.

21. DISSOLVE TO driveway in front of William Faulkner's house. Moon drives up, hops out. Loading his camera, he hurries toward the door. Hears someone out back and goes around the house.

22. A truck in the back yard. A negro heaves some farm gear onto the truck and climbs in with it.

23. In the driver's seat of the truck, Faulkner lights his pipe and is about to drive away when he hears Moon calling. Looks back.

SYNC

MOON: Hey Bill!

24. Moon hurries toward the truck.

MOON: Y'all have won the Nobel Prize!

25. Faulkner in the truck.

FAULKNER: So they tell me, Moon.

26. As the truck starts to move on, Moon calls.

MOON: When can I take your picture for the paper?

Faulkner waves and the truck drives away over the bumpy driveway.

Moon is disappointed.

27. DISSOLVE TO footage and sound track of the conferring of the Nobel Prize in Stockholm to William Faulkner of Oxford, Mississippi.

28. DISSOLVE TO footage and sound track of a passage of Faulkner's acceptance speech.

29. DISSOLVE TO footage and music sound track of Faulkner's informal visit with the King of Sweden and his family.

30. DISSOLVE TO a showcase in the Mary Buie Museum in Oxford, a case displaying the decorated parchment of the Nobel Award, and the medal.

MUSIC: From the sound track of the Swedish film. . . .

31. A medium shot in the Museum. Moon Mullen is happily taking a picture of the proud display in the case.

MUSIC: segue to street noises in Oxford.

32. Street in Oxford. Walking along through the crowd, back in his old clothes, Faulkner nods to an acquaintance, pauses to shake hands with a farmer. Ad Lib comment about crops. Calls to a passing woman (Phil Stone's secretary) who pauses.

Faulkner says so long to the farmer and crosses the street.

SYNC

FARMER & FAULKNER: Ad Lib.

FAULKNER: Morning, Miss Ann. Is Phil Stone in his office?

MISS ANN: Yes he is, Mr. Faulkner.

33. Exterior of Phil Stone's law office. Faulkner walks up the path and goes inside.

34. Interior of office. Stone glances up from his desk, smiles warmly as Faulkner comes in, shakes hands, and sits down, relaxed.

SYNC

STONE: Well Bill, you made it. I'm mighty proud.

FAULKNER: [You share in *del.*] <We made> it, Phil.

STONE: How was Sweden?

FAULKNER: Fine.

35. A closer shot. Stone picks up a typed page.

STONE: Moon wanted me to write something about you for the paper.

36. A close shot of Phil Stone holding the typed page.

STONE: I told about our families being friends for generations—and how we became friends in the twenties with our heads full of Keats and Shelley, and the Imagist poets. How I had confidence way back that you were a fine writer—in spite of the rejection slips. How you stoked the furnace at the University, and painted the roof of the Law building. About your trip to Europe to try to get recognition like Frost and Eliot and Pound did. And the way Sherwood Anderson bullied Horace Liveright into publishing *Soldiers' Pay.*

37. A close shot of Faulkner listening as Stone continues.

I told how discouraged we both were when nobody much read it. And how Mack Reed tried to sell copies in his drug store, and the next half dozen fine books nobody much read then either, until *Sanctuary.* With only your mother, and me, and Mack Reed believing in you.

38. A close shot of Stone as he hands the page out to Faulkner. Then he watches as Faulkner reads.

Here, you read it, far as I've gone.

39. A medium close shot including Stone and Faulkner. Faulkner finishes reading and hands the page back to Stone. Faulkner rises.

FAULKNER: [Thank you, Phil, for all those years. And for this. *del.*] <So you're the one I have to thank for having to wear a necktie now.>

STONE: [Maybe I should add *del.*] Mr. Ike Roberts to <*insert.* o> [those who *del.*] <he> believed in you. [Ike always did, Bill. *del.*]

FAULKNER: As a hunter, [I'm proud to say. *del.*] <Mr Ike is too busy to read books.>

40. A full shot of the office. Faulkner goes out. Stone glances over his manuscript. His secretary comes in for dictation. She sits and transcribes as Stone paces the floor and dictates.

STONE: Perhaps I shouldn't say this: this I am about to say. Very likely Bill had rather I shouldn't have said what I have already said and I wouldn't have if Moon Mullen hadn't talked me into it. But Bill and I are getting to be old men now and perhaps someone who knows should say it, someone who knows that he is even greater as a man than he is as a writer. A lot of us talk about decency, about honor, about loyalty, about gratitude. Bill doesn't talk about these things; he lives them. Other people may persecute you and revile you but this would only bring Bill quickly to your side if you are his friend.

41. DISSOLVE TO Ike Roberts' office outside the Colonial Hotel. Faulkner sits beside the gentle old man.

IKE: Mack Reed was asking if you come back yet. Where you been?

FAULKNER: Sweden.

IKE: You got some kind of prize I hear. That's good. (Pause) Long time to deer season. Month or two anyway.

FAULKNER: We'll get us a big one this year, you watch.

IKE: Maybe so, Bill. (Pause) You go say hello to Mack Reed, and come on back here to my office. I'll tell you a new yarn. About *four* bear this time. Ed Hewlett told it to me.

Faulkner rises, an affectionate hand on old Ike's arm. Walks away.

Ike gestures for someone down the street.

42. A PAN shot as Moon Mullen walks up and sits down beside Ike, pencil ready. Moon writes as Ike speaks.

MOON: Okay, Mr. Ike, go on.

IKE: Bill Faulkner is a full hand at anything he does. The rule is, that the hunter stays on the stand from sun-up until he hears the three long blows on the horn from the man who is following the dogs. Bill will stay on the stand until after sundown, if he doesn't hear the horn, and someone will have to go by and get him. He'll pick up the smutty end of a log as quick as anyone when the fire needs attention.

43. DISSOLVE TO exterior of Gathright-Reed Drug Store as Faulkner goes inside.

44. Interior drug store. Faulkner comes in, waits while Mack Reed finishes with a customer.

45. A medium close shot. Mack Reed sees Faulkner. They shake hands warmly.

REED: Bill, glad to see you back. Through your great honor Oxford and Lafayette County is honored. I'm glad you don't want to live anywhere else.

FAULKNER: I'm glad I don't, too, Mack. Have you still got any of those books you tried to sell?

REED: No sir. I finally sold them all. Took me eleven years, even offering a discount. Now I hear collectors are paying big prices for them.

FAULKNER: It's funny how things have happened.

REED: It's wonderful how things have come out. Wonderful, and just, Bill.

46. Street. Moon Mullen comes along looking about for Faulkner. He speaks to a High School girl.

MOON: Nancy Lee, have y'all seen Mr. Faulkner?

NANCY LEE: Huh-uh, Mistah Moon, not fo' days.

MOON: Have you heard he was aiming to talk to the High School at his daughter's graduation?

NANCY LEE: Uh-huh, sho nuff, Jill tol' me he was.

Moon hurries on.

47. DISSOLVE TO a close shot of William Faulkner behind a lectern, speaking.

FAULKNER: —What threatens us today is fear. Not the atom bomb, or even fear of it. Our danger is not that. Our danger is the forces in the world today which are trying to use man's fear to rob him of his individuality, his soul, trying to reduce him to an unthinking mass by fear and bribery—giving him free food which he has not earned, easy and valueless money which he has not worked for;—the economies or ideologies or political systems—whatever they call themselves—who would reduce man to one obedient mass for their own aggrandisement and power, or because they themselves are baffled and afraid, afraid of or incapable of, believing in man's capacity for courage and endurance and sacrifice.

48. A medium close shot of High School girls in cap and gown in the audience, listening.

49. A medium close shot of High School boys in cap and gown, listening.

It is not men in the mass who can and will save Man. It is Man himself, created in the image of God so that he shall have the will to choose right from wrong—Man, the individual, men and women—

50. Soda fountain. Boys and girls sipping their sodas, thoughtful. The voice continues, perhaps in their memories, perhaps over a radio, it is not explained.

—who will refuse always to be tricked or frightened or bribed into surrendering.

So never be afraid.

51. Mrs. Maud Faulkner, William's mother, sitting on her porch, listening, smiling.

Never be afraid to raise your voice for honesty and truth and compassion, against injustice and lying and greed. If you will do this, not as a class or classes, but as individuals, men and women, you will change the earth. All the tyrants, and the merely baffled or ignorant or afraid, using man's fear and greed for man's enslavement, will have vanished from the face of it.

52. DISSOLVE TO Faulkner's plantation. A long shot. Faulkner and the negroes spreading lime.

MUSIC: to finish. . . .

53. A medium shot. Faulkner working beside one of the old negroes—perhaps Fathers.

FATHERS: Mistah Bill, you mean folks way off read them home-written books y'all write? An' give you rewards? My my. You don' take care you up an' be famous some day 'fore you know it.

54. A long slow DISSOLVE TO Faulkner's library. Shelves of his works and their translations filling the screen.

ALASTAIR COOKE'S VOICE: William Faulkner, of Oxford, Lafayette County, Mississippi—a farmer who looks deep into the heart of life and writes what he sees there—beauty, evanescent and intense, violence and tragedy, innocence, and hope—and fatality.

55. A long slow DISSOLVE TO a close shot of William Faulkner, pausing in his farm labor.

56. A close up as he looks out and away.

FADE OUT

THE END

1033 "Acknowledgment" section of *A Fable,* 1954, ribbon typescript with autograph corrections in blue ink, 1 page, 11 by 8½ inches, Nekoosa.

It appears that Saxe Commins typed this draft of the "Acknowledgment" to be included in the setting copy (page VI) of *A Fable,* made a few emendations of his own, and then gave the copy to Faulkner, who made more extensive revisions. In the transcription that follows, Faulkner's alterations are denoted by asterisks.

<*marg.* To*> William Bacher and Henry Hathaway of Beverly Hills, California, <who*> had the basic idea from which [this book *del.*] <[this book came *del.*]> <*marg. A Fable*> grew into its present form, [and it was in *del.**] <to*> James Street['s *del.*] <, in whose*> [book *del.*] <volume>, *Look Away,* [that *del.**] I read the story of the hanged man and the bird, [which I have used. To these three gentlemen I wish to make grateful acknowledgment. *del.**] <*added:* and to Hodding Carter and Ben Wasson of the Levee Press, who published in a limited edition the original version of the stolen racehorse,*> <*added:* I wish to make grateful acknowledgment.>

[W.F. *del.**]

▶ "WHITE HOUSE CONFERENCE on A Program for People-to-People Partnership," June 1956, mimeographed typescript, 1 page, 11 by 8½ inches.

This announcement may have been enclosed with the June 1956 letter from President Dwight D. Eisenhower enlisting Faulkner's support of the People-To-People Program. The conference was held on September 11-13, 1956, and Faulkner served as chairman of the writers' group in attendance.

WHITE HOUSE CONFERENCE
ON
A PROGRAM FOR PEOPLE-TO-PEOPLE PARTNERSHIP

The purpose of the Conference is to enlist your help in an important task. That task is to encourage American citizens to develop their contacts with the peoples of other lands as a means of promoting understanding, peace and progress.

Friendship between peoples is built on understanding, and understanding is nurtured by exchange of information and ideas and by neighborly association.

For such association Americans are by nature well fitted. On their own initiative, they have forged ahead in business and industry, in science, and in the arts.

The international political situation presents a new challenge to Americans as individuals. Through his own efforts and through group action, every American can do much to win the friendship of other peoples and in so doing strengthen the cause of freedom and world peace.

Said President Eisenhower: ". . .if our American ideology is eventually to win out in the great struggle being waged between the two opposing ways of life, it must have the active support of thousands of independent private groups and institutions and millions of individual Americans acting through person-to-person communication in foreign lands."

Many institutions and groups are already doing extensive work of this nature, but a tremendous potential exists for further activity. What is now envisaged is, first, an effort to increase the national consciousness of these vast possibilities and, then, to achieve a growing volume of friendly contact and communication—and understanding—between Americans and other peoples throughout the world.

1265 Transcribed remarks of the Writers' Committee of the People-To-People Program, November 29, 1956, carbon typescript, 26 pages, 11 by 8½ inches.

In June 1956 Faulkner was invited by President Dwight D. Eisenhower to serve as chairman of the Writers' Committee of the People-To-People Program. The purpose of the writers' group was to make recommendations concerning ways that American ideas and values might be communicated to people in other nations. Faulkner enlisted literary critic Harvey Breit as co-chairman, and the committee met at Breit's home in New York City on November 29, 1956. Among the writers attending the meeting were Saul Bellow, Donald Hall, Edna Ferber, Robert Hillyer, Elmer Rice, John Steinbeck, and William Carlos Williams. The discussion was recorded (in a truncated style that is frequently difficult to comprehend) by Jean Ennis, a Random House secretary.

GENERAL DISCUSSION

FAULKNER: The gentlemen from Washington have been assigned to us not to lead us or suggest, but to answer any questions we want to ask. There are some things about this business that we are all agreed on, and one is that most committees, maybe all, are the last despair and cry of impotence. I can't say we will pass a revolution . . . Another thing is that artists, writers, painters, and musicians have spent all, we have spent all our lives already doing this very job which President Eisenhower discovered last year is a critical necessity. So there is not much more we can do. . . . Harvey Breit and our beautiful slave girl, Jean Ennis, and I have gone over the correspondence, and we have tried to pick up something we can more or less agree on and discuss. If we can devote the first half-hour to basic issues, then we can listen to any suggestions. We should have a moderator. (Breit chosen).

BREIT: The thing that Mr. Faulkner has asked us to discuss is the idea not so much of exporting as of importing, just what we can do and propose to the President. Floor is open to talk of that kind.

CHUTE: Important writers, or any kind of people?

HALL: A random selection of people?

FAULKNER: It seems to me if we just import other writers, we are talking to people already on our side. All the writers have the same idea of freedom and liberty. We must get the people who are our enemies, to approach them instead of sending them the propaganda we have . . . Just sending doesn't work, just brings up a fiasco. Let's bring our enemies here to see this country as it is, instead of a false picture. Let them see what it is here that makes us write.

———:* Isn't there always the danger of people seeing what they want to see? In World War I, our veterans all came back with a little of the color of France, but they also came back talking about those horrible "frogs."

FAULKNER: Yes, that's true, but I think it should be considered that they were in France in an unusual situation, which was war. Let's bring them here, give them jobs, let their children see what children do here.

———: How would it be possible to bring about?

*Blank spaces throughout text indicate unidentified speakers.

FAULKNER: Let the government use the money that it puts up for the propaganda.

———: Do we know whether they will be willing to do it?

FAULKNER: No, we can only suggest this is what we think.

———: What about observers from Russia who were brought over to watch our elections. Did anything come about? They found it very interesting.

FERBER: They said, "The police kept us from doing it the way we wanted to. There they were."

RICE: Admirable objective. How and why is it the function of writers to get into it? We must have little to do with position we are in.

STEINBECK: What about Hungarians who appealed to writers?

———: Churches, trade unions in better position to organize any importation.

———: Needham can tell you more about that. We are only one committee. There are committees representing all American pursuits. We are just writers. Aim is the same, to give our enemies a picture of this country which will cure them of being enemies, and the propaganda won't do it, doesn't do it.

———: How bring over families who don't know any English? Children will not be able to read comic books, etc.

FAULKNER: Can pick up pretty fast. Labor should take care of the language problem, with head of family who has job in labor. May take an interpreter. Won't be any more difficult than sending our American propaganda abroad into foreign languages.

———: I worked with Radio Free Europe and agencies. Main trouble is semantics. Lost signals. Make a definite study of making contact.

FAULKNER: Let them come here and learn it. First thing we should abolish all American passports and make them stop talking. . . .

———: What about American representation abroad?

FAULKNER: I don't think it does much good. In many cases, it probably doesn't do any harm. More important to let enemy come here and see.

———: Official representation?

FAULKNER: If Mathes and Needham will excuse me, they are under the shadow of people in Congress who got elected because they could build the most roads or something. They can put pressure on people like them. Our State Department is not free.

———: Change in laws. People admitted now are people so insensitive . . . or with no political history.

FAULKNER: Do away with McCarran Act and passports. We should bring in people who are Communists, as well.

———: That would mean a revision of McCarran Act.

———: Recruitment not only from Communist but partially Communist population. This is possible, but only with revision of Act.

BREIT: Idea here is not to even try what is realistic. We arrive at what we think should be done and screen . . . and committee can bat that up to President, that this is what we honestly think.

———: Suggest revision of immigration laws.

FAULKNER: We can suggest anything.

———: President suggested that 4 years ago.

———: Are people supposed to come for visit or stay?

FAULKNER: Stay and bring whole family for time of one year. Then he has chance to buy icebox and automobile. He makes payments when he goes. If and when he comes back, he can finish paying out value of new car, etc.

———: Opposition? (from his government when he goes back)

FAULKNER: No, he must go back so new ones may come over. Hope he will see enough to stay here.

———: Wouldn't any family under these conditions be subject to a particular kind of pressure, interviews from newspapers, etc., which would make it completely unfeasible?

FAULKNER: After the first year he wouldn't be news anymore.

———. I don't think that would be so bad. In college, constant . . . exchange students. Imagine something like that. Never much publicity about that. Would this be anymore special than exchange of students? It would stop being news immediately.

FAULKNER: Agreed, just so they came here and saw this country as it is, not as we would like them to think. For some reason, it continues in spite of all its faults and stupidities. Let them see the faults and stupidities too.

———: Isn't that job taken care of by certain agencies?

FAULKNER: No, they just seem to be exchanging scholars and students. They are on our side already. We want to bring our enemies.

CHUTE: Is it correct to say that scholars and students are on our side?

FAULKNER: Yes, I doubt if anyone listens much to scholars. Better that they did.

HALL: More might be accomplished by bringing half as many people for 2 years, because of language barrier.

FAULKNER: Maybe for 5 years.

———: Would have to have permission from their own government of some sort. Does this imply some sort of liasion with governments over there, or would these people be already on their way out? Would they have to [be] rescued or appropriation with governments over there?

FAULKNER: Governments over there probably wouldn't cooperate. Think of fiasco that came from Voice of America which told people in other countries that they could be free, that this country would help people. Never did. But if Voice of America could tell these people to come to this country anyway you can . . . you will have a house, a job.

———: Where will they go after this? If we say for a year or two, if we limit them and ask them . . .

FAULKNER: Only reason is to make room for another family. If we can do this, OK.

———: Point is we don't want them to stay. If they stay, they're not doing much good.

FERBER: Then they would go back and tell their friends how dandy it is here and how bad it is at home. They would get their heads chopped off.

FAULKNER: Would get them chopped off anyway. If enough of them went back every year and said . . . Exchange student has to use a certain amount of discretion when he goes back. The people would come under the same conditions as exchange students.

———: Would it be right to invite sons and daughters of the most influential people, say children of Nehru, Kruschev, who would really not get their heads chopped off so easily, and they would come back with reports. Question is whom we get here are people who will really be heard and be given some recognition for what they have really witnessed here.

FAULKNER: Yes, of course people like Nehru doesn't have to come to this country to know what it is. His own job at home is to consolidate his own power. He must use man. He knows just now what he would see here. He is bound to be that intelligent. Just like the average informed American has a good idea what goes on in Russia.

BELLOW: May we ask the gentlemen from the State Department whether any such program has been proposed?

FAULKNER: Yes, what about it?

GOVT.: There are in existence a large number of exchange programs, not only the official ones but unofficial ones. A great many people are constantly coming to this country, scholars, etc. But quite a few businesses bring people to this country for experience of one kind or another, and foundations. Some have been very much interested in supporting leadership of all kinds and make it possible for them to come to this country. All this in a way amounts to not more than a drop in the bucket to what could be done. I've never heard a proposal like Mr. Faulkner's. A great many people are thinking in terms of how to step up movements of people from abroad to this country, hoping that when they get here they will have meaningful experiences. One thing that troubles me a little is what this does in terms of individuals. I know in India the young Indian comes to this country and it takes him quite a long time to get adjusted, stays awhile and must get readjusted. Our culture is so different from that of others. It means two major periods of adjustment in a young person's life. Don't want to be negative. They certainly raise enormous number of questions.

RICE: When I was in China, met people who had been in America. In the main they fell into two categories. So completely Westernized they were aliens when they came back. Regarded by fellow Chinese as aliens. Other group reacted so violently against West that they were more so than Nationalists, who had never been abroad. Most fell into one or more of these categories. What effect on the people who came over there? Students, technicians.

BREIT: When I was away study being made by Indian Government about the reaction of Indians who had been in America for a period of time. They were troubled that a great many of the Indians who came here want back. They had been sent out of small villages to school here. They came back and were disappointing to the village in many instances because of that long period of adjustment they had to make and couldn't make. It is a human problem, but that man (going back to West) has to solve that. We can't solve all the problems.

If our end is to show people what America is, then what his problem is when he goes back, I think, he has to take problems back to him.

RICE: We cannot treat them as guinea pigs.

BREIT: I think these men are mature.

———: What of Russian farmers who were over here?

———: Little bits of maladjustment can be very good for people. I wouldn't be sorry about upsetting things. It is a wonderful idea of bringing our enemies here. It can only be done with some kind of appropriation with governments over there. People who generally part of regime . . . they will not get invitation. . . . Just leave the country without considering what will happen to them. You don't know America; come over and look at it—see them, talk to them. You can't measure the effect of that kind of experience immediately, but it can be quite tremendous.

———: Anyone who comes out of satellite countries with a visa, his government will make sure he is not to be twisted. I think there is the story of all immigrants. They come over for a year and hate this country, stay 1½ years and go back, lusting to go home. Then can't stand it. Has nothing to do with politics, but people hate it the first year.

———: If the government is interested in this program, a rather careful selection of the people who come over here will be made. They have to be fairly tough, able to make a readjustment.

COMMINS: How determine that?

———: Yes, but it seems anyone who knows people might be able to judge in that respect, in individual terms you could. He would be penalized if he were of a certain character when he got back. He would be in a very bad way. That is one of the dangers. I think we are being inhuman in that sense. That we have to know, not in matters of status or class, but the character of the individuals we're inviting.

———: Up to the recent events in Eastern Europe, there was a trend of letting people out from those countries. I'd rather . . . a great many people came out of these countries and it was a great experience for them to be in the West for the first time. Not officials, some actors, some writers, who came out and until this thing happened in Poland and Hungary, there was a whole trend in letting people out. They were not penalized. It may happen again. Don't know when and how, but that was the whole trend until August of this year. I have 3 friends who could not leave the country since 1945. They went to Paris, not officials, not Communists, just Hungarians, let them out for 2 or 3 weeks and they went back, and they loved every minute of it, in Paris, and allowed to speak about it. May change again.

BELLOW: Very well to bring them out . . . assuming they don't know what the situation is in Hungary and Poland, and they don't know what it is in U.S. is wrong. They must know comparative situations at home and in the West. What would be achieved really by this?

FAULKNER: This—knowing and experiencing are two different things. You think you know what life is like in a country but you have to go there to know what it is really like.

———: Instruct them in differences. If you think you are going to show them in larger sense . . .

FAULKNER: Not to show—let them find out. Only one of the 100 will find it. You can't teach people anything, all you can do is show them. Propaganda pictures of America that we bombard them with. They aren't sold. They don't know the true story. Let them come out here and find out what it is.

———: It is kind of significant that the Russians sent ballet companies to China years and years ago. It apparently did have quite an effect on the Chinese thinking about Russia. Something they understood and felt some response to.

———: Will such a family be housed and supported and kept at whatever level we think is proper on a monetary level?

FAULKNER: No, he would be given a job by labor commensurate with his ability, and his family would have to live on that and spend rest on credit, just like the American families. All government does is bring them here.

———: Never found a lack of interest in this country nor a dislike except on a political plane where governmental functions involved. Farming people have nothing but the greatest interest and friendship. Interest is there. On political level, different matter.

BREIT: Because of Hungary thing it has just the other day (newspapers have not carried it particularly) that a big old company called Pan-Texas made an offer to the international rescue agency that it would take care of 1,000 Hungarians. Would give jobs, house them, take untrained workers and train them and at same time support them. Through what happened in Hungary, it is possible that we as writers committee made this suggestion . . . some door has been opened. Perhaps plants throughout country would give them jobs. By a mechanism by which this plan could be put into practice. Not just for refugees.

———: Would they take Communists?

BREIT: Great virtue if it can be done. It may loosen up a lot of things.

FAULKNER: It would take some pressure on labor. Labor likes what it has got. They don't want any part of this. Meany got up in Washington and said he wasn't going to let us boys have anything to do with this. Have not talked to Reuther.

GOVT.: Background. Why and how Eisenhower brought this whole thing up.

FAULKNER: Not necessary. Writers have been doing this all their lives. They struck on this. He simply expressed a need which we all recognize.

WILLIAMS: But wouldn't it be well to hear this gentleman, who has something to say? I'd like to hear him very much.

GOVT.: On behalf of those of us who labor in Washington, Eisenhower found out that the information arm of the U.S. had not been what it ought to have been. The main reason for that was Congress not appropriating enough money for last 10 years. He saw the money that the other side was spending, Russia for example. He went to Congress and asked for more money. Answer was no. How can we solve problem about information of U.S. all over the world? The only way he thought was to go to the people here. People-to-

People program. Exchange of persons. It's a vast and complex mechanism which has been operating some time now, but we need more of it. That is why this suggestion you make might be very appropriate, at this time. But there are obstacles to be overcome. Main one is the high-level policy on exchanges between East and West. It is an easy matter to exchange a person from Italy and Arkansas, but not so easy to exchange one from New York and Poland because of the policies. Your friend, Mr. Meany, and his whole movement are very influential as you said on Congress to let us not have any kind of this exchange as yet. Eisenhower hopes that all through U.S. with all kinds of media on a private non-governmental operation, the information program of the country could, in effect, be expanded. Don't know if this helps.

FAULKNER: Certainly all agree with that.

———: One thing occurred to me that does this apply to people who are in Russia alone, but applies to Eastern people who may be invited as well and people in Europe that may be affected by Russian propaganda?

GOVT.: Yes, it does apply world-wide.

———: Would Eisenhower with that point of view . . . if writers threw away their strongest weapon, which remains export.

———: Satellite countries ask for books. I sent some twice to Moscow but they never got there.

BREIT: Go on to some of the other things we are all thinking about as writers. More specialized thing that we could possibly do. Maybe that would take in the export of certain things and come back to first question.

No American writer is going to change his way of writing to please his own country, but every American feels thinking in America could be heard all over, and impression could be favorable. What we most want to see is cheapest and widest distribution . . . Russia would be place to have cheap distribution. Cost of things is so important there.

During war, Army printed great number of pocketbooks. Very popular with Army, also with Allies. Still in existence. Very cheap edition. They don't want only the good things, anything about the country—how it lives, what they eat, how they pay for things. Could we declare state of emergency, say this is war, get publishers to cooperate? Book committee as such, what could publishers do?

———: What else is being done by government to distribute books?

GOVT.: Private book campaigns. There are a number of programs overseas which are by no means extensive enough. The government is instrumental in clearing copyrights to permit cheap editions overseas, we help foreign publishers get use of large editions of foreign books, help with translations. Certainly they should be reviewed. There is an advisory committee on information which has a very large sub-committee made up of leading publishers who periodically review all efforts overseas leading to greater distribution of American books. But a great deal is already being done; more could be done.

NEW SPEAKER: On two occasions, students crossed from East Germany and asked for books. One guaranteed at least 500 readers for every American book I could send. Sent Bantam books. Deposited in West Germany and students came over for Communist rallies and took them back. Distribution they can get is fantastic. Small and concealable (pocketbooks). This is an enormous turn-over at a very small cost. Has nothing to do with governments at all. Had to do with private people. At a certain address in West Germany books were picked up and taken over by students to Eastern side.

RICE: Have been very much impressed by what U.S. Information Service is doing abroad under difficult conditions. Was in Belgrade, people were most alive and alert. Doing everything possible to get information about America. Had excellent small library at U.S. Information Service and hundreds of people coming in to take out books. Same at University of Belgrade. Had library there that was as good as average public library in small town in America.

———: Did you hear anything of distribution of these books?

RICE: Some English, some American. Had excellent representation of world literature with emphasis on contemporary as well as classic. They're crying for books, eager for information about America. U.S. Information Service had about $8.00 a year to spend, so they'd buy 4 books. With a very very small amount of money, the output of those books could be enormously increased, and it is amazing the effect of these books. People you talk to are really informed about it. They read everything. That could be stepped up enormously. A group of writers could and should do this. Books were worn out with use.

WILLIAMS: Government spending a certain amount of money for translation and distribution of chief books. No censorship . . .

CHUTE: . . . Small traveling book fair. Reasonable attendance.

COMMINS: Russians have done a very big job in that direction.

RICE: A great many American writers are well known in Russia. Don't know much of distribution into foreign countries. Runs into millions. Government pouring millions into it and our government is pouring pennies.

STEINBECK: U.S. has guaranteed certain foreign publishers against loss. In practically no case has there been any loss.

———: Could you ask Mr. Klopfer to report on the last meeting of the Books Committee?

KLOPFER: I will give a short and negative report. Meeting where we were . . . informed by George Brett, Chairman, that we were a group who had been asked to serve. We started throwing this thing around exactly as you are at this meeting. George said first thing and 7 other big industrialists decided when they had a meeting of a sub-committee was that if Mr. Eisenhower were serious about this thing, the first thing that should be done was to form a non-profit corporation so that we could operate and not talk in a void. Brett, Charlie Wilson of GE, and a few very famous names put this up to the President. What's happened, I don't know.

———: Jim Donovan . . . his office undertook to set up, and handle all the legality connected with setting it up. Understand his work is through now and they're planning to incorporate, in New York papers are being checked. Should come into being before too long.

KLOPFER: These gentlemen felt there should be an organization through which we could implement whatever suggestions would be approved by the President and State Department.

———: Could non-profit organization have same use as common carriers?

KLOPFER: Yes, they were after a $2 million first to show government was serious too. Not just going through motions. As meeting is concerned, we started off our function for books, etc. How to get more books into more countries and reviewed what has been done by government and agencies, but it is a drop in the bucket. No matter what we do it will be. There is an insatiable demand for books. George Brett came up with suggestion of possibility of raiding American homes to get books. That seems to me . . . you know what comes out of attics.

KLOPFER: We left our meeting rather indecisive as to whether organization . . . whether it would function, how to get more books. By that time we quit. It was a very indecisive thing. Small group has since doubled. Dovetails right into what you fellows are talking about.

KLOPFER: Yes, important thing. Don't think with all fairness to State Department . . . Other agencies they're . . . trying to get books, model library, model bookshop on periphery. But not doing anything in comparison to what Russia is doing. Spending on literature millions. Translating into Chinese, Afghanistan, any language, where they can distribute. 150,000 copies of Kruschev's latest propaganda line. Like any written word, are gobbling it up.

———: Look at impact of tour such as Porgy and Bess on foreign countries. On Paris and on London. We must give this attention as one of most potent weapons in world.

RICE: Best good-will was tour of Porgy & Bess, sensational. Everyone who saw it was overwhelmed. Gave them a new slant on America. Government wouldn't do one thing about that.

BREIT: Russia passed for them to come over there.

RICE: U.S. Government wouldn't even sanction the thing. Diary of Anne Frank in translation, was a European thing. Native thinking carried people away. Eyes lighted up when they talk about it. But government won't do these things. Also they censor books that go abroad from U.S. Information Service. Government ought to ask people who believe in freedom, they ought to learn the principles of freedom themselves. Maybe we should spend some with propaganda in Washington.

———: The government is at the mercy of any congressman who gets up on the floor and wants to make a denunciation.

RICE: A little imagination in Washington would go a long way.

———: Why not a series of City Center productions sent abroad?

RICE: Impact of Boston Symphony.

———: Italians eager to get American books.

———: They believe what they read, impact of printed works.

———: Paperbacks to be bought in quantity and sold at cost?

COMMINS: Is being done. Not doing it in sufficient volume.

Whole thing comes down to subsidy.

If we did as the Russians did, we would be spending many, many times what we are now, but can we do that and still remain the kind of government we are?

PROPOSALS

PROPOSAL I (Faulkner) — *A larger, better distribution of books, plays, movies, etc., all the arts.*

PROPOSAL II — (a) *Suggest revision of McCarran Act.* (Faulkner)
(b) *Free Ezra Pound.* (Williams)

PROPOSAL III (West) — *All the passports and red tape be abolished, and we take as many Hungarian refugees as we can by airlift to this country right away.*

PROPOSAL IV (Hall) — *Try to bring unfriendly people over for a duration of time, having them live a normal life. People from England, France, Italy—people from everywhere with unfriendly atmosphere.*

DISCUSSION OF PROPOSALS

(Verbatim from notes)

BREIT: On basis of discussion we had and talk, I won't even try to say what we emphasized, what seemed to be met with most approval. I think that maybe somebody here could say 1 or 2 or 3 proposals we could all agree on. A minimum set of proposals that we would draw up and not necessarily send on to Washington, but send out to each other for all of us to consider and see which of us will sign what part of the proposals. I would like to hear proposals now.

FAULKNER: PROPOSAL I — *A larger, better distribution of books, plays, movies, etc., all the arts.*
These already are in the process of being distributed now, but to do it . . .

BREIT: I'd like to add along with sending out plays, you send out some of our good writers who have never had a popular audience—a play by Bill Williams or a play by Herman Wilson, and that could hit certain audiences too, I think.

———: It should be borne in mind that some things would be very effective abroad which have limited audience in this country.

———: In some cases, it has been quite striking.

COMMINS: It seems the problem is not of selection but one of universal distribution. Central problems are volume and distribution. Once we get machinery and money . . . We should be assured temporary money will be forthcoming. Once that is done, volume of work, existing work which portrays America in all its aspects . . . and then the means of distribution.

———: If books are available, I am sure they can be distributed through peoples of the countries.

BREIT: Through American Book Shop, you get 100 paperbacks for (sum) CARE has been taking care of that. All you writers are in those books, a Steinbeck, Faulkner. I called and asked how many distributed—a pathetic number.

———: There you come into competition with local European publishers.

———: Let's talk about distribution behind Iron Curtain.

———: What about trying to distribute through French, Italian publishers as the distributing agents? There they would get a cut, particularly paperbacks.

BREIT: Could be intensified. Paperbacks have wide distribution abroad through regular book channels, through arrangement with local distributors.

———: Also propose withdrawal of McCarran Act . . .

STEINBECK: Since the whole person-to-person thing is illegal under the law as it stands today, not a thing can be done. Exchange of people is completely infeasible now, as the law stands.

COMMINS: That should not prevent us from proposing it. It should be suggested.

FAULKNER: PROPOSAL II — *Suggest revision of McCarran Act.*
Free Ezra Pound. (Williams)

———: Not quite as hopeless person-to-person as Steinbeck says. It doesn't have to start on a mass basis. Some propaganda is more effective if it is selective rather than a mass thing. We can't prevent the Russians on that basis. . . . to at least start a person-to-person thing, at least with certain key persons over there. I think the advantage this committee may have is it has all the prestige of people like Faulkner and Steinbeck, others. People who would be much more trusted than people in government. Therefore, if program like this was started in name of this committee, in spite of McCarran Act, in spite of their own acts; to start some kind of exchange of persons on that level. A carefully selected people who ought to know what America is like and who could be much more effective than just a family of a farmer. I think if you ask some scientists, intellectuals to stay for a year, they may come. Doesn't have to be mass movement—just come and look and then go back. May be more effective than asking a lot of people who couldn't come or who couldn't leave. Wouldn't know what to do with them. If the idea is to impress our enemies, as Mr. Faulkner has called them . . . People over there who are interested in America, whatever their politics may be. I think it is perfectly possible to start something on that basis.

STEINBECK: Case of Aaronberg. He knew better, but he misreported for the sake of his position in the Soviet Union.

COMMINS: Men who came over here to observe elections said tendency in America for widespread distribution of stocks makes people slave tremendously.

———: But Aaronberg, we don't know what he was thinking.

STEINBECK: He showed me some French painting which he had to conceal.

———: If you could reach some of those people.

INGE: Don't think we should overlook plastic arts because American painters are causing more excitement there than any other country, like Pollock.

FAULKNER: Communication already in process.

HALL: Is importing enemies an original idea?

STEINBECK: There are two kinds of enemies: people who are enemies because they are a part of the government, and people who are exposed to certain situation. They're not strong in any direction, except they want to live. Are not active enemies.

WILLIAMS: You lose track of what Trabori's just said . . . reveals process. In export, or books by import, chosen men who would be good reporters for us. Selected . . .

TRABORI: Not only authors, but people who could be artists . . .

BREIT: Using the word "enemy" in its two definitions. If we said that, taking Bill's original proposal, could take in families, selected people Trabori is talking about—painters, writers, the Aaronberg thing is a good example. A lot of borderline writers in Far East. Flirt with America. Talk as if they knew it but don't know it at all. Scholars and students exchange all the time, but not writers.

FAULKNER: Who we ought to convince are the writers.

PROPOSAL III (A. West) — *That all the passports and red tape be abolished, and we take as many Hungarian refugees as we can by airlift to this country right away.*

CHUTE: Other side of the question . . . more American writers willing to go abroad, answer questions, and be listened to. For instance, Karl Shapiro. They're more interested in him than anyone else because he is a poet; they valued him. The next conference in Japan is first Far Eastern conference that will be held by different nations represented. Only really strong organization operates in East . . . Japan is watching very carefully to see what American writers turn up. If past is representative, will be a very small number; and yet, they judge very strongly about what happens at a place like that.

BREIT: When I left India, at parties given by two groups, I was told: "We have met your businessmen too often. Send us your writers." Mr. Faulkner doesn't even know that I saw a book which he hasn't seen called *Faulkner at Tesaco* [*sic*].

———: That had nothing to do with stopping the Japanese with wanting us to move our troops from Japan.

FAULKNER: This happened in Japan. The first great Japanese port . . . The second big Japanese port was Communistic. Tried to convert me to Communism. The mass of people insist that the troops move. This story . . . happened to publicity officer. He had a Japanese gardener who came every day to work on his bicycle. He had a knife, with handle parallel to the blade, which he used for tearing up the brush. Clem ordered a Sears & Roebuck power saw. Showed him how to work it, and went into the house. When he came back, the gardener had disappeared. He had gone home to pick up his own saw. That is who we must cooperate with. Not just those who can read books.

STEINBECK: I once thought best propaganda would be a Montgomery-Wards catalog. You can describe America to another country by a Sears & Roebuck catalog. How we live and how we pay for it.

BREIT: Would they be able to compare?

STEINBECK: Convert it to their money.

CHUTE: Russia has not asked to join the Pen Club. We have members from the satellite countries.

FAULKNER: Give them the taste of what America is like, say by giving comic books to the children. They wouldn't need much translation. You can't do it with old people. It is the children you have to cooperate with. I'm inclined to think that after you're so many years old you can't change anyway.

HALL: PROPOSAL IV — *Try to bring unfriendly people over for a duration of time, having them live a normal life. People from England, France, Italy—people from everywhere with unfriendly atmosphere.*

STEINBECK: To convert some people who don't approve of us.

HALL: For some time it's already been in force, bringing opinion-makers for 3 months. We can have them for a year or two or more. Let's not exclude anybody.

STEINBECK: To have any effect, it should be on an age level. Nobody over 30 should be even considered because after that they are so set.

FAULKNER: Should have a family. What we want to corrupt is the family.

———: Young, unfriendly people.

It was decided to:

(1) Type and mimeograph everything said at this meeting.

(2) Form committee of 2 or 3 to write up the proposals as intelligently and lucidly as possible.

Chosen: W. Faulkner, J. Steinbeck, D. Hall.

(3) To send drafted proposals and report of meeting to everyone on the list, not just those who attended.

► Summary report of the Writers' Committee of the People-To-People Program, December 1956, mimeographed typescript, 2 pages, 11 by 8½ inches.

This report, distilled from the discussion and correspondence of the Writers' Committee chaired by Faulkner, was issued in early January 1957 over the typed signatures of William Faulkner, John Steinbeck, and Donald Hall.

A representative group of American writers led by William Faulkner, after free and open discussion, have come to the following conclusions:

We in America tend to overestimate our enemies. For example, we have believed that the Soviet state has been able to condition their people so that they are impervious to the outside world. In recent months this has been proved completely untrue in Hungary and Poland. The human animal is not conditionable to the extent that we've been led to believe. Therefore, we are convinced that free and honest communication will not fall on deaf ears.

Our failure to qualify in the cold war is the result of our failure to communicate. The first step of a dictator is to cut off communication of ideas, of people, of arts, to close borders and to stop the interchange of messages. This being so, it is to our advantage to enter into communication upon any or all levels: person-to-person, the written and spoken word, by example, and the arts which communicate without words.

The people of the world have been trained to detect means of propaganda. The only antidote to propaganda is simple honesty and the widest dissemination of truth, undirected and uncensored—especially uncensored. When communication becomes propaganda, it ceases to communicate.

In order to achieve better communication, these things should be done:

I. To reduce visa requirements to a minimum and abrogate red tape for the Hungarian people and any other people who may or will suffer the same crisis.

II. To try to bring people from all over the world who do not agree with us to this country for a duration of at least two years to live a normal American life, to see and experience what we have here that makes us like it. This will necessarily require a revision of the McCarran Act.

III. To disseminate books, plays, and moving pictures through our Government, at least to match what the Russians are doing.

These are the basic three points we feel are necessary in order for us to engage in the world-wide struggle for democracy against totalitarianism. There are other steps to be taken.

For example, we should free Ezra Pound. While the Chairman of this Committee, appointed by the President, was awarded a prize for literature by the Swedish Government and was given a decoration by the French Government, the American Government locks up one of its best poets.

To accomplish these proposals will require a liberalization of passport regulations for people coming and going and adequate government subsidy.

William Faulkner
John Steinbeck
Donald Hall

► "First Experimental Balch Hangar-Flying Squadron," April 1, 1958, document in calligraphic script, with hand-drawn, water-colored illustration, 1 page, 12 by 9 inches.

This mock-serious citation records the actions and qualifications of the three participants of a self-proclaimed drinking club Faulkner and two English professors, Joseph Blotner and Frederick Gwynn, established during Faulkner's 1956–1958 tenure as Writer-in-Residence at the University of Virginia. All three men collaborated in composing the fanciful copy; Faulkner's contributions consisted of the insignia that carried the logo "Ad Astra Per Jack Daniels" (a parody of the RAF motto, "Ad Astra Per Ardua"); the use of stars to assign rank; and the signature in sophomoric script, "E. V. Trueblood," a pseudonym Faulkner had previously employed in his short story, "Afternoon of a Cow." Four copies of this citation were rendered by a local artist (the extra copy was for Floyd Stovall, chairman of the English Department), and each was ceremoniously signed by "Trueblood" before the conferring of the awards.

► Faulkner's Hotel Algonquin registration folio, signed by Faulkner in blue ink, November 30, 1958–May 25, 1962, 1 leaf, recto and verso.

On stays at this New York hotel, Faulkner was accorded all VIP amenities, including fruit in his room and the courtesy of merely having to sign his folio in lieu of filling out a lengthy registration form. The last of the five entries on the verso of this card corresponds with Faulkner's May 24–25, 1962 trip from Charlottesville to accept the Gold Medal for Fiction from the American Academy of Arts and Letters and the National Academy of Arts and Letters.

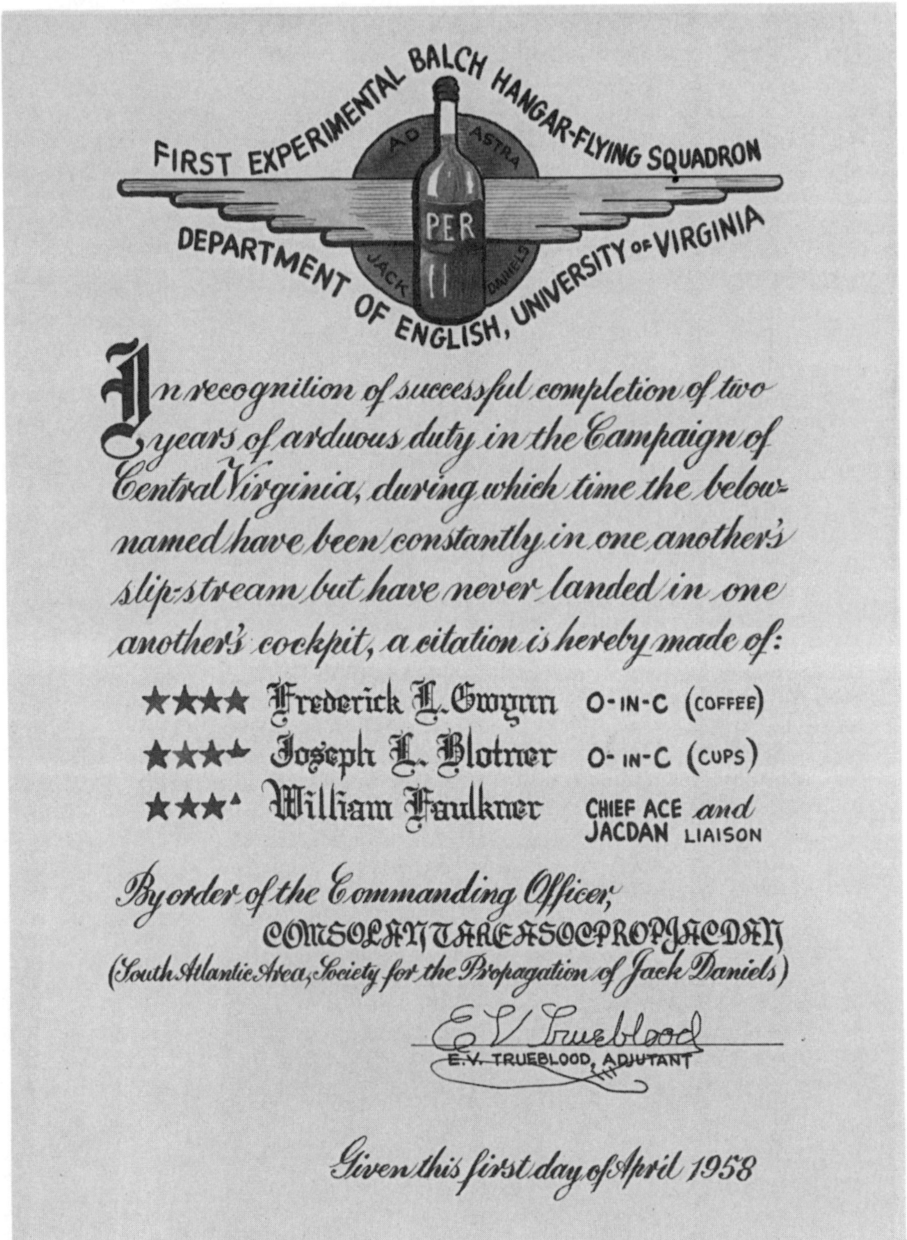

FIRST EXPERIMENTAL BALCH HANGAR-FLYING SQUADRON
AD ASTRA PER JACK DANIELS
DEPARTMENT OF ENGLISH, UNIVERSITY OF VIRGINIA

In recognition of successful completion of two years of arduous duty in the Campaign of Central Virginia, during which time the below-named have been constantly in one another's slip-stream but have never landed in one another's cockpit, a citation is hereby made of:

★★★★ Frederick L. Gwynn O-IN-C (COFFEE)
★★★★ Joseph L. Blotner O-IN-C (CUPS)
★★★★ William Faulkner CHIEF ACE *and* JACDAN LIAISON

By order of the Commanding Officer,
COMSOLANTAREASOCPROPJACDAN
(South Atlantic Area, Society for the Propagation of Jack Daniels)

E. V. Trueblood
E.V. TRUEBLOOD, ADJUTANT

Given this first day of April 1958

62. "First Experimental Balch Hangar-Flying Squadron" citation, 1958

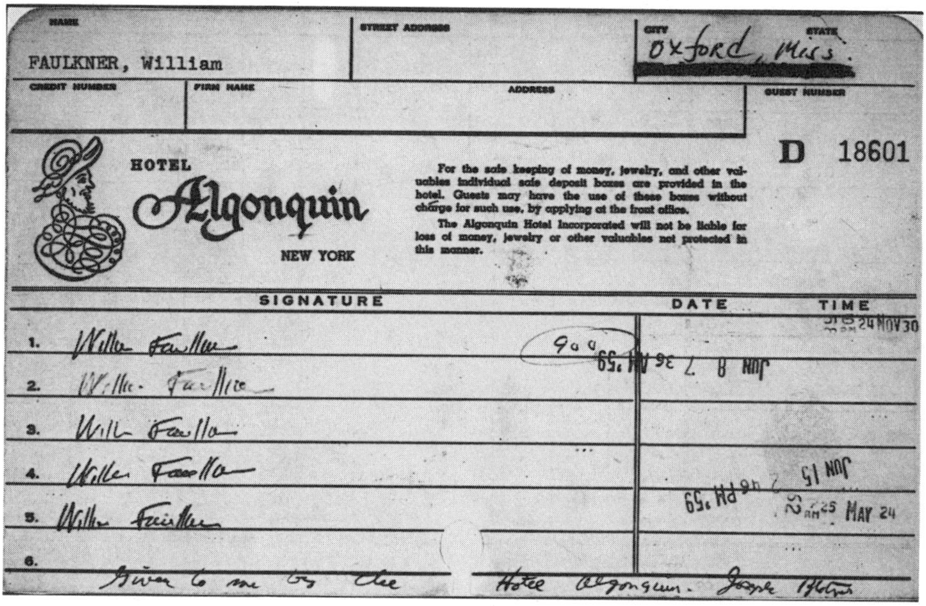

NAME: FAULKNER, William | STREET ADDRESS | CITY: Oxford, Miss. | STATE

[redacted]

CREDIT NUMBER | FIRM NAME | ADDRESS | GUEST NUMBER

D 18601

HOTEL Algonquin NEW YORK

For the safe keeping of money, jewelry, and other valuables individual safe deposit boxes are provided in the hotel. Guests may have the use of these boxes without charge for such use, by applying at the front office.

The Algonquin Hotel Incorporated will not be liable for loss of money, jewelry or other valuables not protected in this manner.

	SIGNATURE	DATE	TIME
1.	William Faulkner	900	24 NOV 30
2.	William Faulkner	JUN 8 7 36 AM '59	
3.	William Faulkner		
4.	William Faulkner	JUN 15 2 46 PM '59	
5.	William Faulkner		25 AM MAY 24
6.			

Given to me by the Hotel Algonquin. Joseph Blotner

63. Recto of Faulkner's Hotel Algonquin registration folio

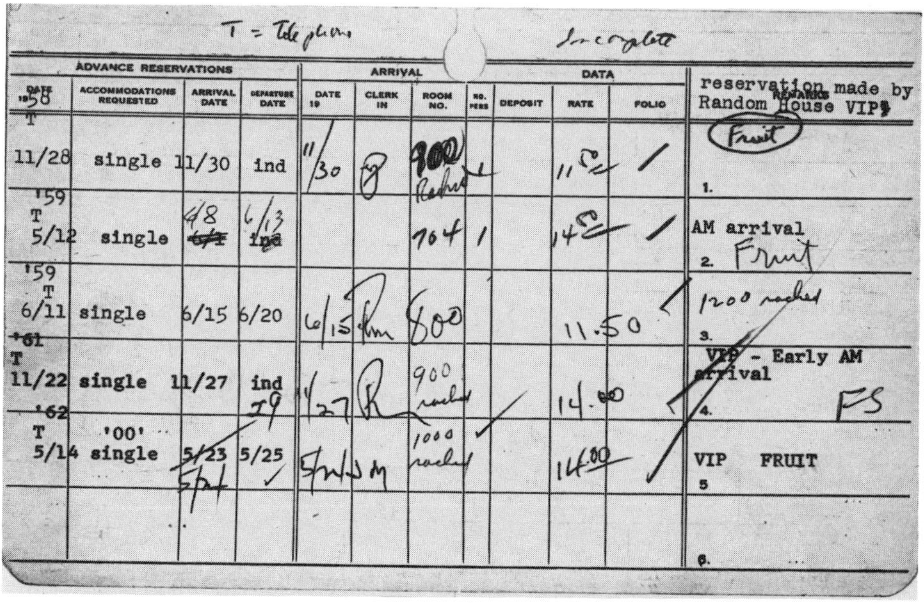

T = Telephone

Incomplete

ADVANCE RESERVATIONS: DATE 19	ACCOMMODATIONS REQUESTED	ARRIVAL DATE	DEPARTURE DATE	ARRIVAL: DATE 19	CLERK IN	ROOM NO.	NO. PERS	DATA: DEPOSIT	RATE	FOLIO	REMARKS
'58 T 11/28	single	11/30	ind	11/30	[illegible]	900 Radio	1		11.50	/	reservation made by Random House VIP Fruit 1.
'59 T 5/12	single	6/8 ~~6/1~~	6/13 ~~ind~~			704	1		14.00	/	AM arrival 2. Fruit
'59 T 6/11	single	6/15	6/20	6/15	[illegible]	800			11.50	✓	1200 reached 3.
'61 T 11/22	single	11/27	ind 19	11/27	R	900 reached			14.00		VIP - Early AM arrival 4. FS
'62 T 5/14	'00' single	~~5/23~~ 5/24	5/25 ✓	5/24	JM	1000 reached			14.00	/	VIP FRUIT 5
											6.

64. Verso of Faulkner's Hotel Algonquin registration folio

VII
Last Wills and Testaments

In the course of his lifetime Faulkner executed six different Last Wills and Testaments. The first, now in the possession of Jill Faulkner Summers, was drawn up in 1924. Others followed in 1934, 1940, 1951, 1954, and 1960. All of the wills except the last were prepared by Phil Stone, the Oxford lawyer who was Faulkner's close personal friend and early mentor. The final will, prepared by a Charlottesville, Virginia, law firm, was probated at the Oxford courthouse following Faulkner's death in 1962. The Brodsky Collection contains the middle four wills, each of which is reproduced below.

The provisions of these successive wills reveal Faulkner as a man with a strong sense of responsibility and loyalty toward family, friends, and employees. While the principal beneficiaries are Faulkner's wife Estelle and daughter Jill, there are also provisions, in some cases quite generous, for his mother Maud; for his stepchildren, Victoria and Malcolm Franklin; for his brothers Murry and John; for his niece Dean, the daughter of the brother who was killed in a plane crash in 1935; and for his nephews James (Jimmy) and Murry (Chooky).

These documents provide particularly strong evidence of the close friendship that existed between Faulkner and Stone throughout their lives. During the period of Jill's minority Stone, along with Faulkner's brother Murray, was named to serve as an executor of Faulkner's estate and as a testamentary guardian of Jill until her twenty-first birthday. In addition, Faulkner arranged for Stone to receive a manuscript of one of Faulkner's novels and for a personal loan to Stone to be canceled.

Faulkner also made provisions for a number of the black employees who assisted him with the operation of Greenfield Farm. Principal among these was Ned Barnett, the aged retainer who had served four generations of the Faulkner family and whose character and behavior supplied details for Faulkner's portrayals of Simon Strother in *Sartoris,* Lucas Beauchamp in *Intruder in the Dust,* and Ned McCaslin in *The Reivers.* Other blacks mentioned in one or more of Faulkner's wills are Payne Wilson and Lawrence, Alvis, and Charlie McJunkin.

If the earliest wills express in unambiguous, colloquial language Faulkner's simple wishes to assign his meager assets and as yet relatively undiscovered literary legacies, the formulaic, all-inclusively qualified, impersonal will drafted in 1960 by highly specialized corporate lawyers also expressed Faulkner's requirements: to guard the Faulkner Foundation against the liability of estate and inheritance taxes. Taken in their totality, the six wills parallel and mirror Faulkner's evolution from a poor, small-town, aspiring writer to the world-renowned artist whose works had finally brought the financial rewards and security for which he had unremittingly worked and hoped. In this regard, these documents showcase a unique, if partial, history of the man and the artist, his life and literary career.

363 Last Will and Testament of William Faulkner, dated "June __, 1934," unsigned carbon typescript, 3 pages, 14 by 8½ inches, Myriad Chemco.

I, William Faulkner, being the same person as William Falkner, a resident of Oxford, Lafayette County, Mississippi, being over the age of twenty-one years and of sound and disposing mind, do hereby make this my Last Will and Testament, hereby revoking all other wills by me previously made.

I

I hereby will and bequeath all of my property of every kind whatsoever, with the exceptions hereinafter set out, to my wife, Mrs. Estelle Faulkner, for use during her natural life or until remarried. At her death I will and devise all of said property to my daughter, Jill Faulkner. My wife, Estelle Faulkner, is only to have the use of said property and the income thereof, the principal of same to be held intact for my daughter, Jill Faulkner.

II

I hereby will and bequeath to my mother, Mrs. Maude [*sic*] Falkner, all revenue of any sort whatever from my novel *Soldiers' Pay* and the novel *Sanctuary*. This bequest also includes the sale of my manuscript from either of said novels and includes all revenue of any sort from said novels.

III

I will and devise my present home to my wife, Estelle Faulkner, for her life or until remarriage and, at her death, or remarriage, to my daughter, Jill Faulkner. During the life of my wife or until her remarriage she and all her children are to have said property as a home. This last provision also includes her two children, Victoria Franklin and Malcolm Franklin.

IV

I hereby appoint my brother, M.C. Falkner, and my friend, Phil Stone, as Testamentary Guardians of my daughter, Jill Faulkner, and they are to supervise and handle, under the instructions of the Chancery Court of Lafayette County, Mississippi, all the property of my daughter, Jill Faulkner, until she becomes twenty-one years of age. This also includes certain Life Insurance which I have and the proceeds of which are payable at my death directly to my said daughter, Jill Faulkner.

V

I hereby constitute and appoint as Executors of this said Will and Testament my brother, M.C. Falkner, and my friend, Phil Stone.

VI

The said Executors and Testamentary Guardians are to have full power to sell or incumber any of my property or to reinvest the proceeds of same, and of any property that shall go to my said daughter, Jill Faulkner, subject to the approval of the Chancery Court of Lafayette County, Mississippi.

The said Executors and Testamentary Guardians are to have full power, with the approval of the Chancery Court of Lafayette County, Mississippi, to sell any part of the capital of my estate and use same for the benefit of my said wife, Estelle Faulkner, if in the judgment of either of my Executors the same should become necessary, but this shall be done only upon the order of the Court.

VII

This Will has been this day executed by me in duplicate, and the duplicate original thereof has been this day turned over by me to my said friend Phil Stone for safekeeping, both this Will and the duplicate thereof being originals.

Witness my signature at Oxford, Mississippi, this June __, 1934.

/t/ William Faulkner

/t/ Mary A. Stone, Witness

/t/ R. L. Holley, Witness

/t/ R. L. Sullivan, Witness

We, Mary A. Stone, R.L. Holley, and R.L. Sullivan, subscribing witnesses to the above Last Will of William Faulkner, do hereby certify that said Testator signed and declared the same to be his Last Will and Testament in our presence and that we each signed the same as subscribing witnesses thereto at the request of said Testator, in his presence and in the presence of each other.

We further certify that at the time of the execution of said Last Will and Testament the said William Faulkner was over the age of twenty-one years and of sound and disposing mind.

Witness our signatures this June __, 1934.

/t/ Mary A. Stone

/t/ R. L. Holley

/t/ R. L. Sullivan

499 Last Will and Testament of William Faulkner, dated March 27, 1940, signed carbon typescript, 6 pages, 14 by 8½ inches, Valid Onion Skin. Signed and dated on each page in brown ink: "William Faulkner / 3/27/40."

I, William Faulkner, being the same person as William Falkner, a resident of Oxford, Lafayette County, Mississippi, being over the age of twenty-one years and of sound and disposing mind, do hereby make this my Last Will and Testament, hereby revoking all other Wills by me previously made.

Item 1

I hereby will and bequeath all of my property of every kind whatsoever, with the exceptions hereinafter set out, to my wife, Mrs. Estelle Faulkner, for use during her natural life or until remarried. At her death or remarriage, I will and devise all of said property to my daughter, Jill Faulkner. My wife, Estelle Faulkner, is only to have the use of said property and the income thereof, the principal of same to be held intact for my daughter, Jill Faulkner.

Item 2

I will and devise my present home to my wife, Estelle Faulkner, for her life or until remarriage and, at her death or remarriage, to my daughter, Jill Faulkner. During the life of my wife or until her remarriage she and all of her children are to have said property as a home. This last provision also includes her two children, Victoria Franklin Selby and Malcolm Franklin.

Item 3

I hereby appoint my brother, M. C. Falkner, and my friend, Phil Stone, as Testamentary Guardians of my daughter, Jill Faulkner, and they are to supervise and handle, under the instructions of the Chancery Court of Lafayette County, Mississippi, all the property of my daughter, Jill Faulkner, until she becomes twenty-one years of age. This also includes certain Life Insurance which I have and the proceeds of which are payable at my death directly to my said daughter, Jill Faulkner.

Item 4

I hereby constitute and appoint as Executors of this said Will and Testament my brother, M. C. Falkner, and my friend, Phil Stone.

Item 5

The said Executors and Testamentary Guardians are to have full power to sell or incumber any of my property or to re-invest the proceeds of same, and of any property that shall go to my said daughter, Jill Faulkner, subject to the approval of the Chancery Court of Lafayette County, Mississippi.

The said Executors and Testamentary Guardians are to have full power, with the approval of the Chancery Court of Lafayette County, Mississippi, to sell any part of the capital of my estate and use same for the benefit of my said wife, Estelle Faulkner, if in the judgment of either of my Executors the same should become necessary, but this shall be done only upon the order of the Court.

Item 6

I have with the Penn Mutual Life Insurance Company a policy in the face value of Ten Thousand ($10,000.00) Dollars, one-half of which is payable to my daughter, Jill Faulkner, and the other one-half of which I am having made payable to my mother, Mrs. Maude Falkner, if she survives me, otherwise payable to my Executors. In the event my said mother should fail to survive me, then the above named Phil Stone and M. C. Falkner, as my Executors and Trustees, are further empowered to use the said one-half proceeds of said insurance policy in need, according to the judgment of these Trustees, who are hereby given full power without restrictions, save their own judgment, to further the education and other needs of my niece, Dean Falkner, if her revenue from other sources be not sufficient for such purposes.

Item 7

Except as set out in Item 6 above, all property left by this Will to my mother, Mrs. Maude Falkner, shall at her death go back into my estate to be handled by my Executors and Testamentary Guardians as set out herein. The same shall be true as to all property herein devised to my mother, Mrs. Maude Falkner, in the event that she should die before my death. However, if my mother, Mrs. Maude Falkner, should outlive me, she is to have full and free use during her lifetime of the property herein devised to her without any restriction whatever.

Item 8

My mother, Mrs. Maude Falkner, is to have one-half of all revenue derived in any manner from my published books or sales of my manuscripts until her death if she outlives me. If she outlives me, upon her death this half shall go to my niece, Dean Falkner, and shall be handled as hereinabove set out in Item 6.

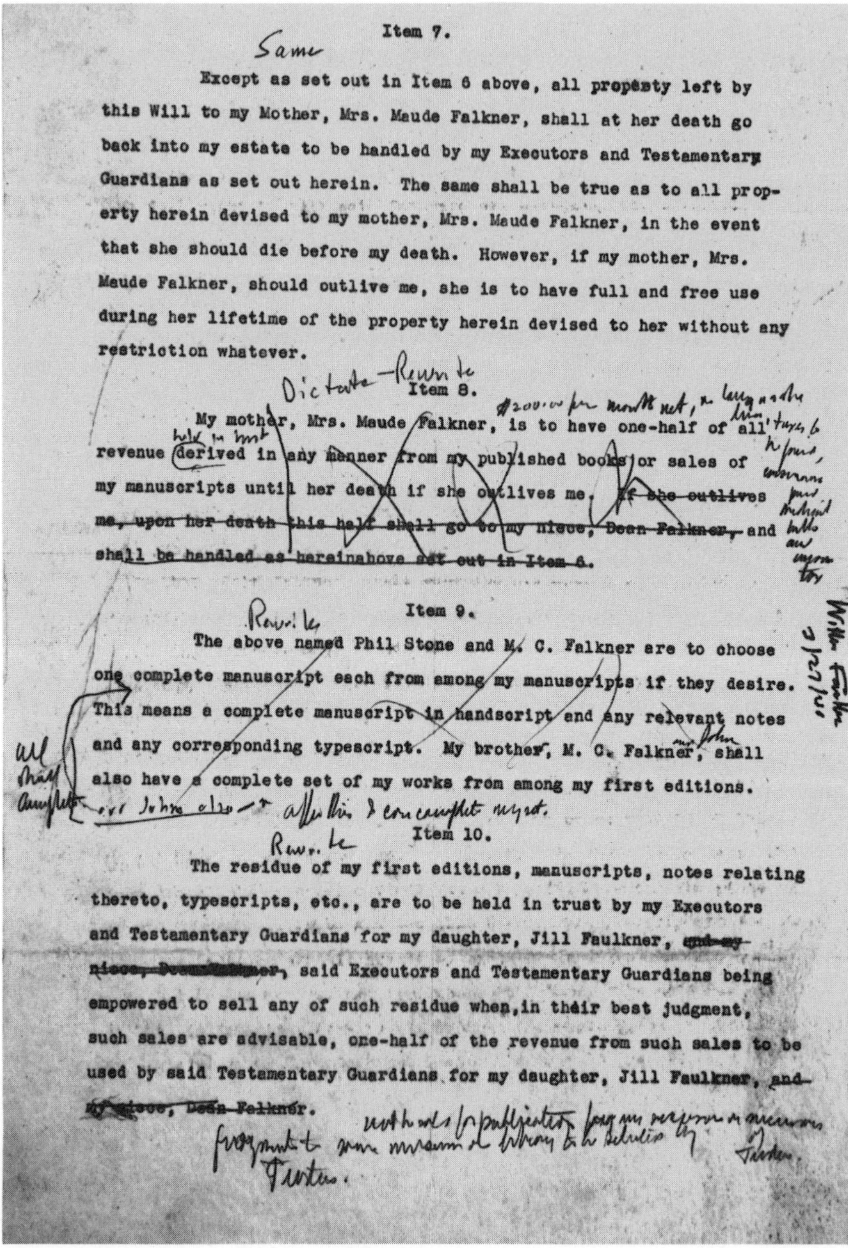

Item 7.

Same

Except as set out in Item 6 above, all propesty left by this Will to my Mother, Mrs. Maude Falkner, shall at her death go back into my estate to be handled by my Executors and Testamentary Guardians as set out herein. The same shall be true as to all property herein devised to my mother, Mrs. Maude Falkner, in the event that she should die before my death. However, if my mother, Mrs. Maude Falkner, should outlive me, she is to have full and free use during her lifetime of the property herein devised to her without any restriction whatever.

Dictate—Rewrite

Item 8.

My mother, Mrs. Maude Falkner, is to have one-half of all revenue derived in any manner from my published books or sales of my manuscripts until her death if she outlives me. ~~If she outlives me, upon her death this half shall go to my niece, Dean Falkner,~~ and shall ~~be handled as hereinabove set out in Item 6.~~

Item 9.

Rewrite

The above named Phil Stone and M. C. Falkner are to choose one complete manuscript each from among my manuscripts if they desire. This means a complete manuscript in handscript and any relevant notes and any corresponding typescript. My brother, M. C. Falkner, shall also have a complete set of my works from among my first editions.

Item 10.

Rewrite

The residue of my first editions, manuscripts, notes relating thereto, typescripts, etc., are to be held in trust by my Executors and Testamentary Guardians for my daughter, Jill Faulkner, ~~and my niece, Dean Falkner,~~ said Executors and Testamentary Guardians being empowered to sell any of such residue when, in their best judgment, such sales are advisable, one-half of the revenue from such sales to be used by said Testamentary Guardians for my daughter, Jill Faulkner, ~~and my niece, Dean Falkner~~.

65. Page of Faulkner's 1940 Last Will and Testament, with revisions entered by Phil Stone in 1951

Item 9

The above named Phil Stone and M. C. Falkner are to choose one complete manuscript each from among my manuscripts if they desire. This means a complete manuscript in handscript and any relevant notes and any corresponding typescript. My brother, M. C. Falkner, shall also have a complete set of my works from among my first editions.

Item 10

The residue of my first editions, manuscripts, notes relating thereto, typescripts, etc., are to be held in trust by my Executors and Testamentary Guardians for my daughter, Jill Faulkner, and my niece, Dean Falkner, said Executors and Testamentary Guardians being empowered to sell any of such residue when, in their best judgment, such sales are advisable, one-half of the revenue from such sales to be used by said Testamentary Guardians for my daughter, Jill Faulkner, and my niece, Dean Falkner.

Item 11

My brother, John Falkner, and his descendants are to have the use of the farm northeast of Oxford which I now own, rent free, and use of all equipment and livestock on it necessary for working said farm, free of charge. However, my Executors and Testamentary Guardians shall have full right to sell said farm and all equipment and livestock at any time they consider in their judgment such sale to be necessary for the well-being of my other legatees. My brother, John Falkner, is to have the first option to purchase all of said property at a purchase price to be fixed as near as possible in accordance with what my brother, John Falkner, can pay. This option is to expire when my Executors and Testamentary Guardians think it advisable to sell said property or, in any event, it shall expire when my daughter, Jill Faulkner, becomes of legal age. If said property, or any part thereof, has not been sold when my daughter, Jill Faulkner, becomes of legal age, then all of said property shall go to my daughter, Jill Falkner. In the event my brother, John Falkner, shall exercise his option to purchase said property, he shall be credited on such purchase price with the value of all improvements made by him and all taxes paid by him from the time of my death until the exercise by him of such option, but if he does not exercise such option, he shall not recover for any such improvements made or taxes paid. The above devise is made with the understanding that Ned Barnett, colored, if he outlives me, is to have the house he now lives in, rent free, as long as he remains on this farm. If at my death the title to said farm is clear in my name, the said Barnett is to receive clear title to said house and the piece of ground on which it rests and the line between his property and the other property is to be established by my Executors and Testamentary Guardians and is not to infringe upon other buildings. The said Ned Barnett is also to have rent free to cultivate a five-acre piece of ground to be selected by my Executors and Testamentary Guardians and is to have such until his death, at which time all of said property will revert to my estate. My Executors and Testamentary Guardians are also to see that the said Barnett is to have use of such livestock and tools as are on said farm and necessary to cultivate the land left to him. At the death of the said Ned Barnett, my Executors are to use whatever funds necessary from my estate to send his body where he wishes and to give him a decent funeral and burial. The amount to be spent therefor is to be determined solely by my said Executors. If the said Ned Barnett should leave said farm and my family, then my said Executors are to pay him from my estate Five ($5.00) Dollars per month until his death.

Item 12

My brother, M. C. Falkner, is to have my silver cigarette case.

Item 13

My daughter, Jill Faulkner, is to have my Zeiss binoculars, Lica camera, No. 12 Browning shot gun, .270 Winchester rifle, .30 Winchester carbine, .25–20 Savage rifle, .22 Savage rifle with telescope sights, and .22 Colt pistol. My wife's son, Malcolm Franklin, and my brother John's sons, James and Murray, are to have proper use of any of these items, and my daughter, Jill Faulkner, shall have the right to dispose of these items by gift before she becomes of age when in the judgment of my Executors she has sufficient discretion to make such gifts.

Item 14

In case of any disagreement as to procedure and policy between my two Executors, either of them shall have the right to apply to the Chancery Court of Lafayette County, Mississippi, for direction on all matters, and the order of said Court thereon shall be binding on both my Executors.

Item 15

This Will has been this day executed by me in duplicate, and the duplicate original thereof has been this day turned over by me to my said friend, Phil Stone, for safekeeping, both this Will and the duplicate thereof being originals.

Witness my signature at Oxford, Mississippi, this March 27, 1940.

/s/ William Faulkner
/t/ William Faulkner

Witnesses:

/s/ B. W. Jones
/s/ Estelle K. Patton

We, B. W. Jones and Estelle K. Patton, subscribing witnesses to the above Last Will and Testament of William Faulkner, do hereby certify that said Testator signed and declared the same to be his Last Will and Testament in our presence and that we each signed the same as subscribing witnesses thereto at the request of said Testator, in his presence and in the presence of each other. We further certify that at the time of the

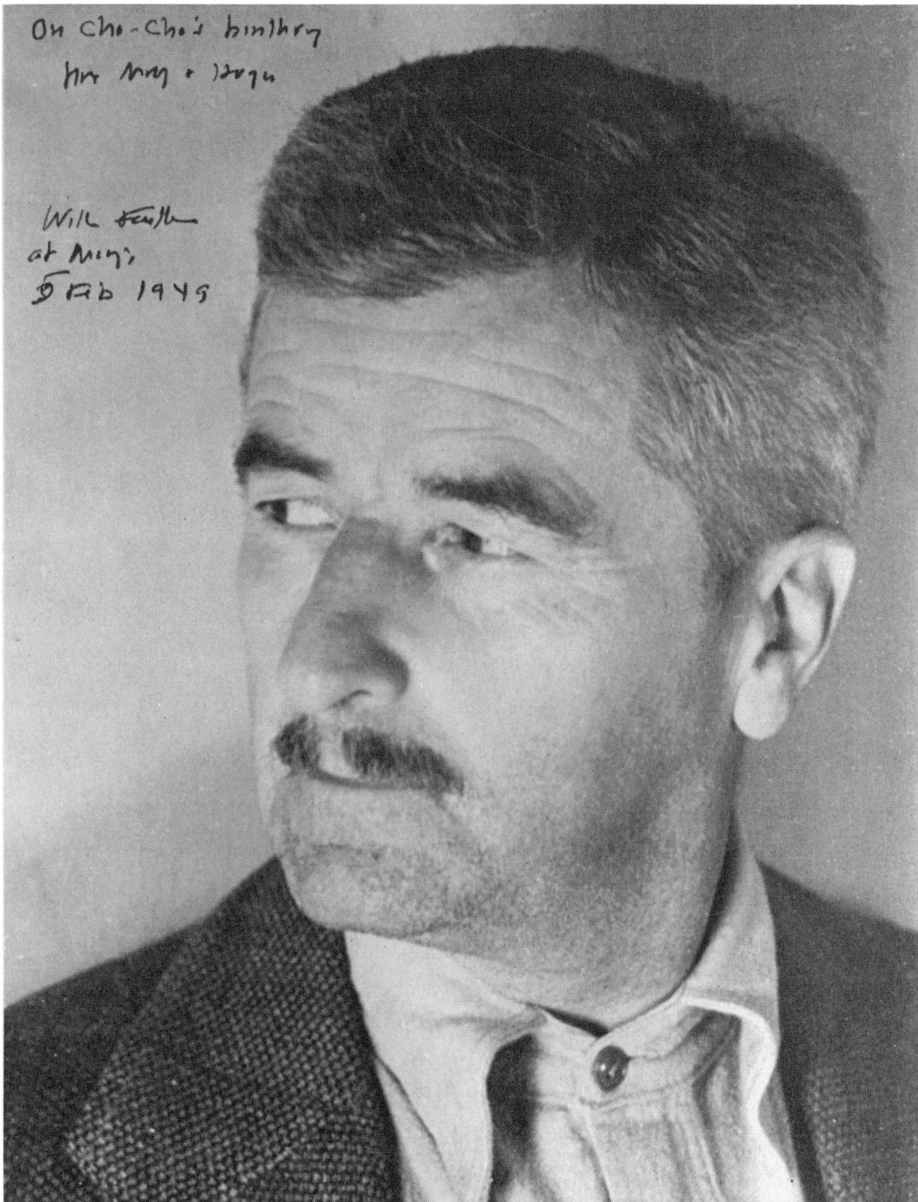

66. Faulkner, 1949

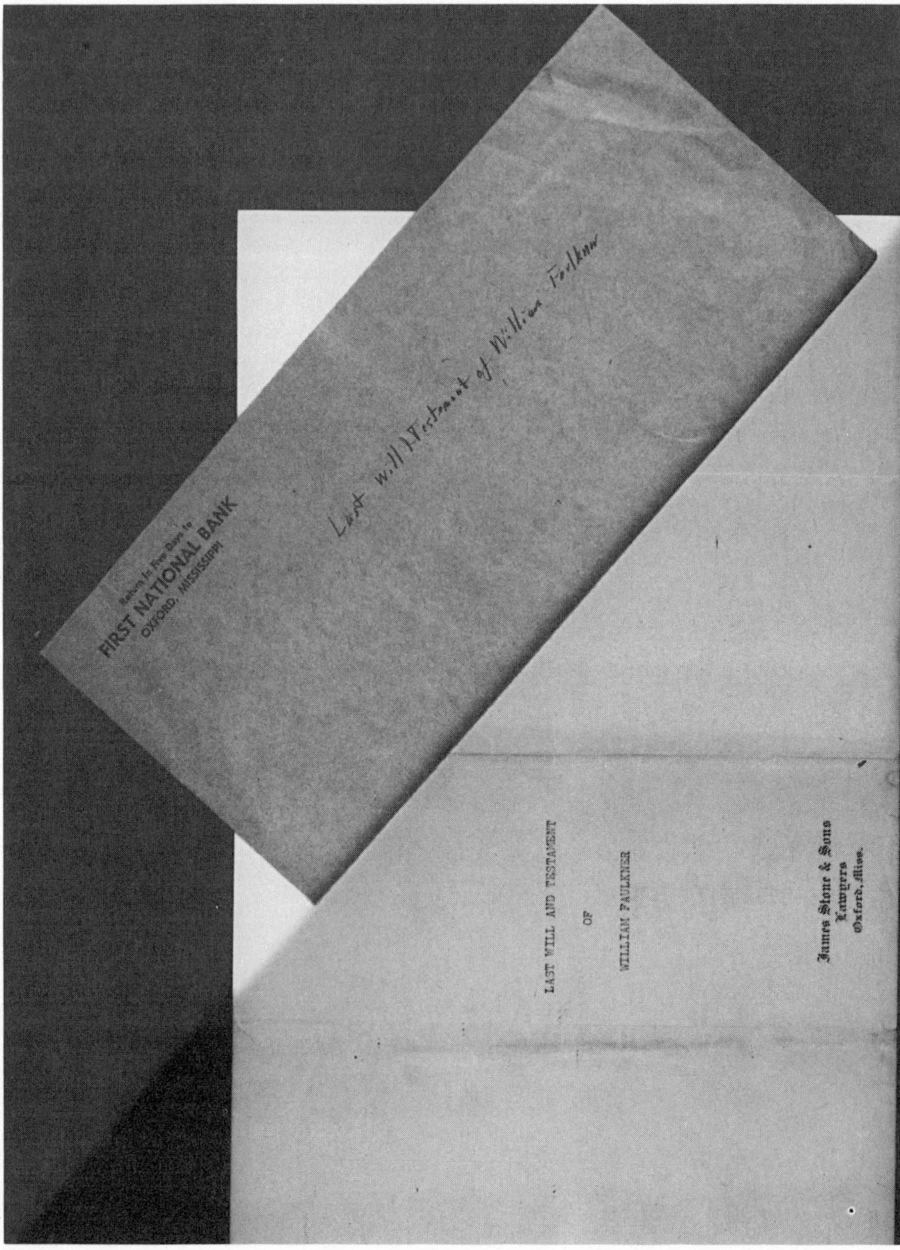

67. Envelope and title page for Faulkner's 1951 Last Will and Testament

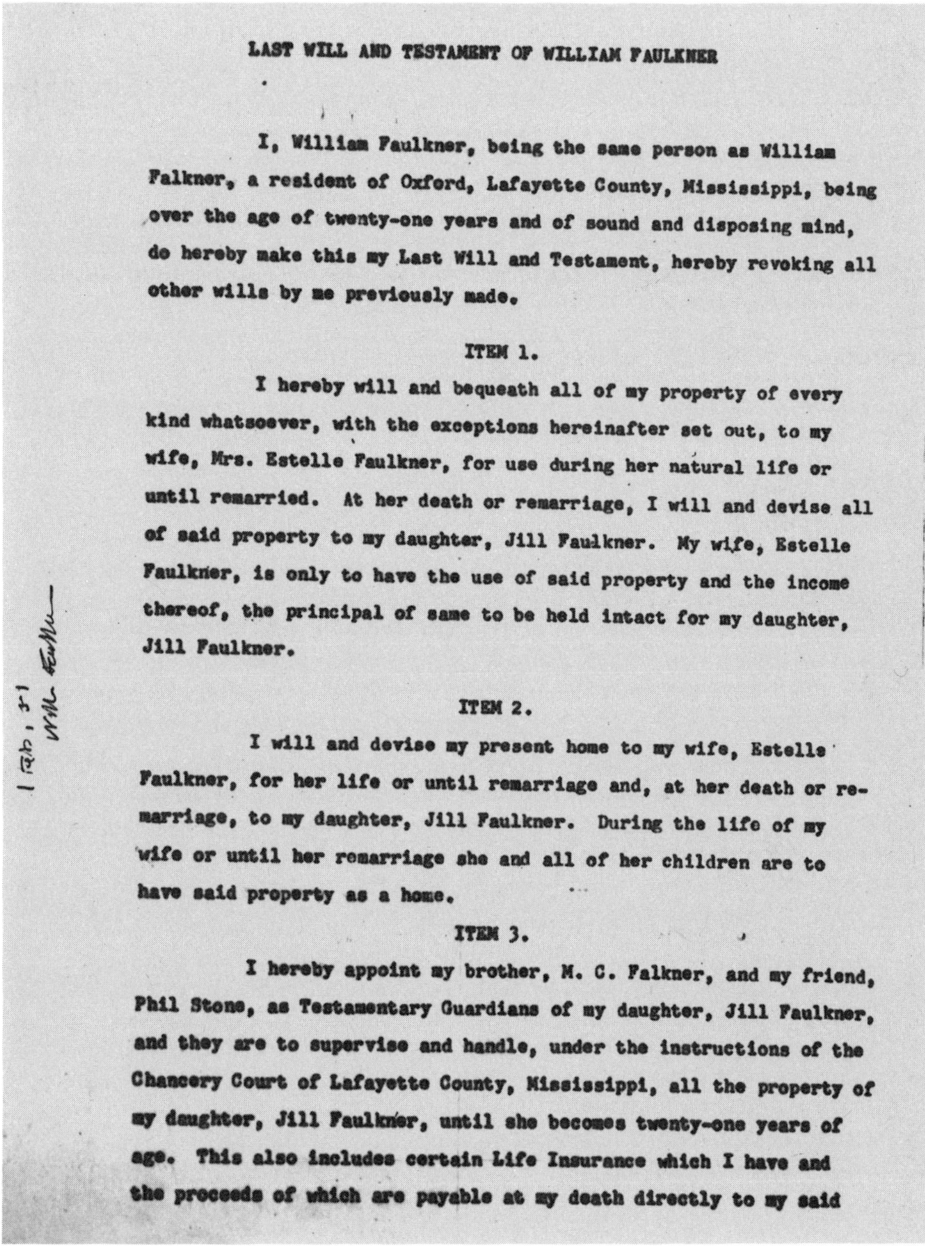

LAST WILL AND TESTAMENT OF WILLIAM FAULKNER

I, William Faulkner, being the same person as William Falkner, a resident of Oxford, Lafayette County, Mississippi, being over the age of twenty-one years and of sound and disposing mind, do hereby make this my Last Will and Testament, hereby revoking all other wills by me previously made.

ITEM 1.

I hereby will and bequeath all of my property of every kind whatsoever, with the exceptions hereinafter set out, to my wife, Mrs. Estelle Faulkner, for use during her natural life or until remarried. At her death or remarriage, I will and devise all of said property to my daughter, Jill Faulkner. My wife, Estelle Faulkner, is only to have the use of said property and the income thereof, the principal of same to be held intact for my daughter, Jill Faulkner.

ITEM 2.

I will and devise my present home to my wife, Estelle Faulkner, for her life or until remarriage and, at her death or remarriage, to my daughter, Jill Faulkner. During the life of my wife or until her remarriage she and all of her children are to have said property as a home.

ITEM 3.

I hereby appoint my brother, M. C. Falkner, and my friend, Phil Stone, as Testamentary Guardians of my daughter, Jill Faulkner, and they are to supervise and handle, under the instructions of the Chancery Court of Lafayette County, Mississippi, all the property of my daughter, Jill Faulkner, until she becomes twenty-one years of age. This also includes certain Life Insurance which I have and the proceeds of which are payable at my death directly to my said

68. Page 1 of Faulkner's 1951 Last Will and Testament

execution of said Last Will and Testament, the said William Faulkner was over the age of twenty-one years and of sound and disposing mind.

Witness out signatures this March 27th , 1940.

/s/ B. W. Jones
/s/ Estelle K. Patton

766 Last Will and Testament of William Faulkner, dated February 1, 1951, signed ribbon typescript, 7 pages, 14 by 8½ inches, unwatermarked. Each page signed in blue ink: "1 Feb. 1951 / William Faulkner." All pages except the first and sixth include interlineal autograph revisions entered before signing.

I, William Faulkner, being the same person as William Falkner, a resident of Oxford, Lafayette County, Mississippi, being over the age of twenty-one years and of sound and disposing mind, do hereby make this my Last Will and Testament, hereby revoking all other wills by me previously made.

Item 1

I hereby will and bequeath all of my property of every kind whatsoever, with the exceptions hereinafter set out, to my wife, Mrs. Estelle Faulkner, for use during her natural life or until remarried. At her death or remarriage, I will and devise all of said property to my daughter, Jill Faulkner. My wife, Estelle Faulkner, is only to have the use of said property and the income thereof, the principal of same to be held intact for my daughter, Jill Faulkner.

Item 2

I will and devise my present home to my wife, Estelle Faulkner, for her life or until remarriage and, at her death or remarriage, to my daughter, Jill Faulkner. During the life of my wife or until her remarriage she and all of her children are to have said property as a home.

Item 3

I hereby appoint my brother, M. C. Falkner, and my friend, Phil Stone, as Testamentary Guardians of my daughter, Jill Faulkner, and they are to supervise and handle, under the instructions of the Chancery Court of Lafayette County, Mississippi, all the property of my daughter, Jill Faulkner, until she becomes twenty-one years of age. This also includes certain Life Insurance which I have and the proceeds of which are payable at my death directly to my said daughter, Jill Faulkner.

Item 4

I hereby constitute and appoint as Executors of this said Will and Testament my brother, M. C. Falkner, and my friend, Phil Stone.

Item 5

The said Executors and Testamentary Guardians are to have full power to sell or incumber any of my property or to reinvest the proceeds of same, and of any property that shall go to my said daughter, Jill Faulkner, subject to the approval of the Chancery Court of Lafayette County, Mississippi.

The said Executors and Testamentary Guardians are to have full power, with the approval of the Chancery Court of Lafayette County, Mississippi, to sell any part of the capital of my estate and use same for the benefit of my said wife, Estelle Faulkner, if in the judgment of either of my Executors the same should become necessary, but this shall be done only upon the order of the Court.

Item 6

I have with the Penn Mutual Life Insurance Company a policy in the face value of Ten Thousand ($10,000.00) Dollars, one-half of which is payable to my daughter, Jill Faulkner, and the other one-half of which I am having made payable to my mother, Mrs. Maude Falkner, if she survives me, otherwise payable to my Executors. In the event my mother should fail to survive me, the above-named Executors and Trustees are further empowered to use the one-half of the above insurance made payable to my mother, [or so much thereof as they may deem necessary, *del.*] for the education of my niece, Dean Falkner Meadow. [If my mother is not living at the time of my death the above-named Executors and Trustees shall turn said fund above set aside for Dean Falkner Meadow, or such part thereof as may remain unspent, over to my daughter, Jill Faulkner, upon the said Jill Faulkner becoming of legal age. In the event any part of said fund shall be so turned over to my said daughter, it is my wish that my said daughter should use said fund, or such part as she may deem advisable, for the education of my said niece. The said Jill Faulkner shall then handle said fund without making any bond and without making any accounting to any Court or to anyone. Neither the above-named Executors and Trustees, nor the said Jill Faulkner, is required to spend any part of said fund for the education of my said niece if said Executors and Trustees (or the said Jill Faulkner, if any part of said fund has been turned over to her) shall determine that the revenues of said niece received from other sources are sufficient for such purpose, and said Executors and Trustees (or the said Jill Faulkner, if said fund has been turned over to her) shall be the sole judges (or judge) of the necessity of such expenditure. Any part of such fund as may not have been expended for the education of my said niece shall go to my daughter, Jill Faulkner. *del.*] <*marg.* If my mother does not survive me, her half of said insurance policy shall be applied by the Trustees herein to further or complete the education of my niece Dean Falkner Meadow. If this fund is not available to the amount of $5,000.00 for the purpose of educating my said niece, my Executors shall add to it from my estate sufficient money to amount to $5,000.00. Any of this sum as may be left over from this amount after completion or stoppage of her education shall be turned over to her in cash when she reaches twenty-five years of age.>

Item 7

Except as set out in Item 6 above, all property left by this Will to my mother, Mrs. Maude Falkner, shall at her death go back into my estate to be handled by my Executors and Testamentary Guardians as set out herein. The same shall be true as to all property herein devised to my mother, Mrs. Maude Falkner, in the event that she should die before my death. However, if my mother, Mrs. Maude Falkner, should outlive me, she is to have full and free use during her lifetime of the property herein devised to her without any restriction whatever.

Item 8

My Executors and Trustees are to pay to my mother, if she survives me, the sum of Two Hundred Dollars ($200.00) per month as long as she shall live. They shall also pay all taxes, insurance, and utility bills upon the homestead of my mother and all income taxes on the above monthly payments. These amounts are to be paid out of any part of the income or corpus of my estate and are to take precedence over any legacy or bequest herein made. <This item shall not apply until the insurance left her by item 6 has been exhausted.>

Item 9

The above-named Phil Stone and M. C. Falkner and my brother, J. W. T. Falkner III, shall each choose one complete manuscript from my manuscripts if they desire. This means a complete manuscript in handscript and any relevant notes and typescript pertaining to such manuscript as may be chosen. Also the above-named M. C. Falkner and J. W. T. Falkner III shall each have from my first editions such volumes as shall give each of them a complete set of my works. After they have made their choice the said Phil Stone shall have from my first editions remaining such volumes as may be necessary to give him a complete set of my works.

Item 10

The residue of my first editions, manuscripts, notes relating thereof, typescripts, etc., are to be held in trust by my Executors and Testamentary Guardians for my daughter, Jill Faulkner, said Executors and Testamentary Guardians being empowered to sell any of such residue when, in their best judgment, such sales are advisable, the revenue from such sales to be used by said Testamentary Guardians for my daughter, Jill Faulkner. In case both of said Testamentary Guardians should die and a successor to them should be appointed by a Court, such successor or successors shall not have the power to sell or publish any part of the above-mentioned material, but such material as may remain unsold shall be turned over to some museum or library, or museums or libraries, as may be selected by the Court.

Item 11

My nephews, J. M. Falkner and M. C. Falkner II, are to have the use of the farm northeast of Oxford which I now own, rent free, and the use of all equipment and livestock on it necessary for working said farm, free of all charge <for five years from my death>. They are to have the first option to purchase all of said property within five (5) years from the date of my death at a price to be fixed by my Executors as near as possible in accordance with what my said nephews are able to pay. This option is subject to the provision hereinafter set out. In the event my said nephews shall exercise this option to buy this property, they shall be credited on such purchase price with the value of all improvements made by them and all taxes paid by them from the time of my death, but if they do not exercise such option within the time set out then they shall not recover for any such improvements made or taxes paid. This option is subject to the full rights of my Executors and Testamentary Guardians to sell said farm and all equipment and livestock at any time they consider, in their judgment, such sales be necessary for the well-being of my wife, my daughter, or my mother. This option is also subject to the right of Payne Wilson to use the land he is now using on said farm at a yearly rental of Fifty and No/100 Dollars ($50.00), and the said Payne Wilson shall not be dispossessed from said property now being used by him as long as he pays said rent promptly each year. This option is also subject to the right of Lawrence Arenza McJunkin to remain upon said property as long as he chooses and without rent and, in the event my said nephews shall exercise their option to buy said property, it is my wish that they will continue to employ the said McJunkin as I now do.

Item 12

My brother, M. C. Falkner, is to have my silver cigarette case.

Item 13

My daughter, Jill Faulkner, is to have my Zeiss binoculars, Leica camera, No. 12 Browning shotgun, .30 Springfield rifle, .30 Winchester carbine, .25-20 Savage rifle, .22 Winchester rifle with telescope sights, and .22 Colt pistol. My wife's son, Malcolm Franklin, and my two nephews, J. M. Falkner and M. C. Falkner II, are each to have one firearm to be selected by my daughter, Jill Faulkner.

Item 14

I hereby bequeath to my Godson, Philip Stone, my Bulova watch.

Item 15

If my friend, Phil Stone, shall, at the time of my death, owe me any amount, including any note payable to my mother, Mrs. M. C. Falkner, said indebtedness shall be canceled. However, if the said Phil Stone shall insist on paying such indebtedness, if any exists at the time of my death (and he probably will), he is to pay the same either to my mother, my daughter, or to the Trust Fund hereinafter mentioned, or to pay any part thereof, in such proportions as he may see fit to any or all of the parties above-mentioned and to said Trust Fund.

Item 16

There is hereto attached an original copy of a trust instrument, the original of which will be found in my safety deposit box in the First National Bank of

Oxford, Mississippi, and said instrument controls a fund for the purpose therein set forth and it is hereby made controlling over any and every part of this Will.

Item 17

In case of any disagreement as to procedure and policy between my two Executors, either of them shall have the right to apply to the Chancery Court of Lafayette County, Mississippi, for direction on all matters and the order of said Court thereon shall be binding on both my Executors.

Item 18

This Will has been this day executed by me in duplicate, and the duplicate original thereof has been this day turned over by me to my said friend, Phil Stone, for safekeeping, both this Will and the duplicate thereof being originals.

<All interlineations and changes were made before signing.>

Witness my signature at Oxford, Mississippi, this February 1st, 1951.

/s/ William Faulkner
/t/ William Faulkner

WITNESSES:

/s/ Loutie Lyles
/s/ Lillie Sue King

We, Loutie Lyles and Lillie Sue King, subscribing witnesses to the above Last Will and Testament of William Faulkner, do hereby certify that said Testator signed and declared the same to be his Last Will and Testament in our presence and that we each signed the same as subscribing witnesses thereto at the request of said Testator, in his presence and in the presence of each other. We further certify that at the time of the execution of said Last Will and Testament, the said William Faulkner was over the age of twenty-one years and of sound and disposing mind.

Witness our signatures this February [*blank*], 1951.

/s/ Loutie Lyles
/s/ Lillie Sue King

766 Codicil to Last Will and Testament of William Faulkner, dated February 1, 1951, signed carbon typescript, 3 pages, 14 by 8½ inches, unwatermarked.

STATE OF MISSISSIPPI
COUNTY OF LAFAYETTE

I, William Falkner of Oxford, Mississippi, do hereby declare that I have placed on deposit to the credit of a checking account in the First National Bank of Oxford, Mississippi, styled "William Falkner, Prize Account," in the sum of Twenty-five Thousand ($25,000.00) dollars, and it is my intention and desire to create a trust of the amount of the credit balance of the funds of said account at the time of my death in accordance with the terms and conditions hereinafter stated;

I hereby create and declare a trust of the amount of the credit balance of the above-stated account in said bank at the time of my death vesting fiduciary title thereto in the following trustees, viz.: my brother M. C. (Jack) Falkner, my cousin J. W. T. (John Junior) Falkner IV, and my friend Mack Ried [*sic*] of Oxford, Mississippi, for the purpose of retaining and investing the amount of said balance of said account at the time of my death for the benefit of the trust estate as hereinafter set forth.

In case the annual income of the estate of my daughter Jill Falkner shall at any time produce less that Six Thousand ($6,000.00) [dollars] per annum revenue for my said daughter, then and in that case upon presentation of proof of said fact satisfactory to a majority of the trustees above named, then and in that case the trustees shall pay over to and for the benefit of my said daughter Jill Falkner a sum sufficient to increase her income for the specific year that such fact exist and such proof is presented to increase the annual income of my said daughter for said year to the sum of Six Thousand ($6,000.00) dollars. Said disbursement to supplement such annual income for my daughter shall first be paid from the accumulated revenue from the estate in the hands of the trustees at said time, then and in that case there be no accumulated revenue from the estate in the hands of the trustees at that time, then and in that case the trustees shall withdraw from the corpus of the trust estate thereby reducing the principal thereof accordingly, a sum sufficient to supplement the income of my said daughter for the current year as aforesaid.

The trustees above named shall use and disburse all revenue of the said trust estate for charitable purposes in Lafayette County, Mississippi, it being the intention of this trust declaration to create a "Falkner Memorial," for disbursement of only the revenue of said trust estate after my death for charitable purposes.

To accomplish the purposes of the creation of this trust the said trustees are authorized to invest funds of the corpus of the estate and any accumulated revenue in such investments as may be determined in the discretion of said trustees and to disburse the revenue for charitable purposes in the discretion of said trustees.

In all decisions affecting the control, use, investment and disbursement of trust funds a majority vote of said trustees shall control; however, it is my belief and earnest hope that all matters coming before the trustees affecting the trust estate may be decided by a unanimous agreement of said trustees.

This declaration of trust is made a part of my Last Will and Testament of date the __1__ day of __February__, 1951, a copy of which is attached to said Will, made a part thereof as fully as if written at length therein, and marked as exhibit (A) thereto, and referred to in paragraph __16__ set forth in said Will.

The original of this trust and a copy of my Last Will above mentioned is placed and is to be retained in my safety lock box at the First National Bank, and after my death said papers shall be retained by the trustees in a safety lock box that may be selected by said trustees.

The corpus and all accumulated revenue of the trust estate while not invested shall be deposited by the trustees, when title is vested in the said trustees, in a bank selected by the trustees and preferably the First National Bank of Oxford, Mississippi, to the credit of an account styled as above stated, and withdrawals therefrom shall be made by checks on said account signed by a majority of said trustees.

The trustees appointed herein shall have the right of naming successors in the following manner: the three trustees shall each make appointments by naming a successor designated by each trustee to succeed himself in case of death upon the condition and under the requirement that when a succeeding trustee shall take office as such after the death of the trustee whom he is to succeed, my daughter Jill shall automatically thereupon become a trustee of the trust estate, thus increasing the total trustees to four. This policy of selection of succeeding trustees shall be followed in the future thereafter; my daughter Jill Falkner shall continue to serve as a trustee during her natural life.

I, William Falkner, of Lafayette County, Mississippi, being over the age of twenty-one years, of sound and disposing mind and memory, do hereby make, publish, and declare this instrument of three typewritten pages to be, and hereafter become a part and parcel of my Last Will above mentioned as fully as if written at length therein.

Witness my signature at Oxford, Mississippi, this 1 day of February , 1951.

/s/ William Faulkner

Witnesses

/s/ Loutie Lyles
/s/ Lillie Sue King
/s/ Phil Stone

925 Codicil to Last Will and Testament of William Faulkner, dated January 23, 1953, unsigned carbon typescript, 2 pages, 14 by 8½ inches, Eagle-A Trojan Onion Skin.

CODICIL

I, William Faulkner, being over the age of twenty-one years and of sound and disposing mind, hereby execute and declare this Codicil to my Last Will and Testament dated February 1, 1951, revoking said Last Will and Testament to the following extent and to that extent only:

I hereby nominate and appoint Saxe Commins of New York, New York, my literary executor, and he is to have full and complete authority over the control of my book royalties, manuscript reprints, and all things concerning the republishing of any of my work and the sale or loan of any of my manuscripts. He is to have no authority over the management of the rest of my estate.

Items 4, 5, 9, and 10 of my Last Will and Testament of February 1, 1951, are hereby revoked to that extent and to that extent only, except that the gifts made in Item No. 9 of said Will to Phil Stone, M. C. Falkner, and J. W. T. Falkner III, are to remain as given in said Will.

Witness my signature this January 26, 1953.

____

/t/ William Faulkner

We, ____________ and ____________, hereby certify that the above named William Faulkner executed and declared said Codicil to be his Codicil in our presence, and that we signed our names as subscribing witnesses thereto at the request of the Testator in his presence and in the presence of each other.

We also certify that at the time of the execution of said Codicil, the said William Faulkner was over the age of twenty-one years and was of sound and disposing mind.

Witness our signatures at Oxford, Mississippi, this January 26, 1953.

____

Witness

____

Witness

1072 Last Will and Testament of William Faulkner, dated "August __, 1954," unsigned carbon typescript, 6 pages, 14 by 8½ inches, Eagle-A Trojan Onion Skin.

I, William Faulkner, being the same person as William Falkner, a resident of Oxford, Lafayette County, Mississippi, being over the age of twenty-one years and of sound and disposing mind, do hereby make this my Last Will and Testament, hereby revoking all other Wills and Codicils by me previously made.

Item 1

I hereby will and bequeath all of my property of every kind whatsoever, with the exceptions hereinafter set out, to my wife, Mrs. Estelle Faulkner, for use during her natural life or until remarried. At her death or remarriage, I will and devise all of said property to my daughter, Jill Faulkner. My wife, Estelle Faulkner, is only to have the use of said property and the income thereof, the principal of same to be held intact for my daughter, Jill Faulkner.

Item 2

I hereby bequeath to my daughter, Jill Faulkner, all other property, any Life Insurance which I have and the proceeds of which are payable at my death directly to my said daughter, Jill Faulkner.

Item 3

I hereby appoint my daughter, Jill Faulkner, as Executrix of this Last Will and Testament, and she is to serve without making any bond and without making accounting to any court or to any person.

Item 4

I hereby give to my said Executrix the power and authority to sell any part of the capital of my estate and to use same for the benefit of my said wife, Estelle Faulkner, if, in the judgment of my said Executrix, it should be necessary to do so, and such judgment of my Executrix shall not be questioned by any person or any court.

Item 5

I devise and bequeath Five Thousand Dollars ($5,000.00) to further or complete the education of my niece, Dean Falkner Meadow. My Executrix is hereby empowered to furnish from any part of my estate sufficient funds to bring the total amount payable to my niece, Dean Falkner Meadow, to Five Thousand Dollars ($5,000.00). Any part of such sum of Five Thousand Dollars ($5,000.00) as may be left over after the completion or stoppage of the education of said Dean Falkner Meadow shall be turned over to her in cash when she reaches twenty-five years of age.

Item 6

If my Executrix should find the burden of my estate too onerous, she is hereby authorized and empowered to select some person, persons, bank, or corporation to administer my estate and to vest such person, persons, bank, or corporation with all power granted under this will to my Executrix.

Item 7

My Executrix is to pay to my mother, if she survives me, the sum of Two Hundred Dollars ($200.00) per month as long as my said mother shall live. My Executrix shall also pay all taxes, insurance, and utility bills upon the homestead of my mother and all income taxes on the above-mentioned monthly payments to my said mother. These amounts are to be paid out of any part of the income or corpus of my estate and are to take precedence over any legacy or bequest herein made. All sums accrued to my said mother from this bequest shall, on her death, revert to my estate.

Item 8

I hereby nominate and appoint Saxe Commins, of New York, New York, my Literary Executor, and he is to have full and complete authority over the control of my book royalties, manuscript reprints, and all things concerning the republishing of any of my work and the sale or loan of any of my manuscripts except as hereinafter set out in this paragraph. He is to have no authority over the management of the rest of my estate. Phil Stone and M. C.

Falkner and my brother, J. W. T. Falkner III, shall each choose one complete manuscript from my manuscripts if they so desire. This means a complete manuscript in handscript and any relevant notes and typescript pertaining to such manuscript as may be chosen. Also, the above-named M. C. Falkner and J. W. T. Falkner III shall each have from my first editions such volumes as shall give each of them a complete set of my works. After they have made their choice the said Phil Stone shall have from my first editions remaining such volumes as may be necessary to give him a complete set of my works.

Item 9

The residue of my first editions, manuscripts, notes relating thereto, typescripts, etc., are to be the property of my daughter, Jill Faulkner, and she shall have the right to sell any of such residue without any supervision from any court or any person.

Item 10

My nephews, J. M. Falkner and M. C. Falkner II, are to have the first option to purchase all of said property, the farm and gear and livestock, within one (1) year from the date of my death at a price to be fixed by my Executrix as near as possible in accordance with what my said nephews are able to pay. This option is subject to the provision hereinafter set out. In the event my said nephews shall exercise this option to buy this property, they shall be credited on such purchase price with the value of all improvements made by them and all taxes paid by them from the time of my death, but if they do not exercise such option within the time set out then they shall not recover for any such improvements made or taxes paid. This option is subject to the right of my Executrix to sell said farm and all equipment and livestock at any time that she may see fit. But this option is subject also to the right of Payne Wilson to use the land he is now using on said farm at a yearly rental of Fifty Dollars ($50.00), and the said Payne Wilson should not be dispossessed from said property now being used by him as long as he pays said rent promptly each year, either during the life of this option or as long as the title to said property shall remain in my daughter, Jill Faulkner. Even if said Payne Wilson fails to pay the rent, he shall not be dispossessed of the house in which he is living, but shall live in said house rent free; but my daughter, Jill Faulkner, may rent said land formerly used for farming by Payne Wilson if, in her opinion, this is practical or necessary. The above provisions of this paragraph are also subject to the right of Lawrence Arenza McJunkin to remain upon said property as long as he chooses, subject to the present arrangement with Charlie McJunkin as manager, so long as my daughter, Jill Faulkner, shall keep said farm property, provided that said Lawrence Arenza McJunkin, Alvis McJunkin, and Charlie McJunkin meet any other competitive offer for profitable rent of said farm.

Item 11

My brother, M. C. Falkner, is to have my silver cigarette case.

Item 12

My daughter, Jill Faulkner, is to have my Zeiss binoculars, Leica camera, No. 12 Browning shotgun, .30 Springfield rifle, .30 Winchester carbine, .25-20 Savage rifle, .22 Winchester rifle with telescope sights, and .22 Colt pistol. My wife's son, Malcolm Franklin, and my two nephews, J. M. Falkner and M. C. Falkner II, are each to have one firearm to be selected by them.

Item 13

I hereby bequeath to my Godson, Philip Stone, my Bulova watch.

Item 14

If my friend, Phil Stone, shall, at the time of my death, owe me any amount, including any note payable to my mother, Mrs. M. C. Falkner, said indebtedness shall be canceled. However, if the said Phil Stone shall insist on paying such indebtedness, if any exists at the time of my death (and he probably will), he is to pay the same either to my mother, my daughter, or to the Trust Fund hereinafter mentioned, or to pay any part thereof, in such proportions as he may see fit, to any or all the parties above-mentioned and to said Trust Fund.

Item 15

There is hereto attached an original copy of a trust instrument, the original of which will be found in my safety deposit box in the First National Bank of Oxford, Mississippi, and said instrument controls a fund for the purpose therein set forth and it is hereby made controlling over any and every part of this Will.

Item 16

This Will has been this day executed by me in duplicate, and the duplicate original thereof has been this day turned over by me to my said friend, Phil Stone, for safekeeping, both this Will and the duplicate thereof being originals.

Witness my signature at Oxford, Mississippi, this August ____, 1954.

____

/t/ William Faulkner

WITNESSES:

____

____

We, ____________ and ____________, subscribing witnesses to the above Last Will and Testament of William Faulkner, do hereby certify that said Testator signed and declared the same to be his Last Will and Testament in our presence and that we each signed the same as subscribing witnesses thereto at the request of said Testator, in his presence and in the presence of each other. We further certify that at the time of the execution of said Last

Will and Testament, the said William Faulkner was over the age of twenty-one years and of sound and disposing mind.

Witness our signatures this August ____, 1954.

____

____

1417 Codicil to Last Will and Testament of William Faulkner, dated October 10, 1958, signed carbon typescript, 3 pages, 14 by 8½ inches, Manifold Nekoosa.

CODICIL

I, William Faulkner, being over the age of twenty-one years and of sound and disposing mind, and a resident of Oxford, Lafayette County, Mississippi, do hereby make and declare this Codicil to my Last Will and Testament.

Pursuant to an Agreement, dated April 1, 1957, between me and Twentieth Century-Fox Film Corporation, a Delaware corporation, I have heretofore granted to said Twentieth Century-Fox Film Corporation the worldwide motion picture and related rights in and to the novel entitled *The Hamlet,* written by me.

A portion of said novel was published as a short story under the title "Spotted Horses" in the June, 1931 issue of *Scribner's Magazine* and was registered for copyright in the name of Charles Scribner's Sons on May 19, 1931, under Entry No. B:114704 in the Office of the United States Register of Copyrights, Washington, D. C.

A portion of said novel was published as a short story under the title "The Hound" in the August, 1931 issue of *Harper's Magazine* and was registered for copyright in the name of Harper and Bros. on July 18, 1931, under Entry No. B:121709 in the Office of the United States Register of Copyrights, Washington, D. C.

A portion of said novel was published as a short story under the title "Lizards in Jamshyd's Courtyard" in the February 27, 1932 issue of *The Saturday Evening Post* and was registered for copyright in the name of the Curtis Publishing Company on February 23, 1932, under Entry No. B:145466 in the Office of the United States Register of Copyrights, Washington, D. C.

A portion of said novel was published as a short story under the title "Fool About a Horse" in the August, 1936 issue of *Scribner's Magazine* and was registered for copyright in the name of Charles Scribner's Sons on July 24, 1936, under Entry No. B:307463 in the Office of the United States Register of Copyrights, Washington, D. C.

Said novel was published in book form under the title *The Hamlet* by Random House and was registered for copyright in the name of Random

House, Inc., on April 11, 1940, under Entry No. A:138683 in the Office of the United States Register of Copyrights, Washington, D. C.

All of the aforementioned copyrights have heretofore been assigned to me.

If, under the Copyright Act of the United States or any other applicable law, there shall at any time or from time to time accrue in favor of my executor the right to renew or extend any United States or any other copyright in said novel *The Hamlet,* or in any portions thereof, published under the respective titles and separately copyrighted as hereinabove specified, then, in consideration of the execution by said Twentieth Century-Fox Film Corporation of the aforesaid Agreement, dated April 1, 1957, I direct my executor to renew or extend each such copyright within the period required by law, and promptly after each such renewal or extension, and, without cost or expense to said Twentieth Century-Fox Film Corporation, I direct my executor to assign to said Twentieth Century-Fox Film Corporation for such renewed or extended term all of the rights in said novel (or in any such portion thereof) covered by the aforesaid Agreement, dated April 1, 1957.

This Codicil has this day been executed in duplicate, each of which is an original.

Witness my signature at Oxford, Mississippi, this [March ___ *del.*] <October 10>, 1958.

/s/ William Faulkner
/t/ William Faulkner

We, T. H. Freeland II and Mrs. Elaine F. Hoffman have this day signed our names as subscribing witnesses to the foregoing Codicil, as subscribing witnesses thereto, at the request of the said Testator, in his presence, and in the presence of each other. Said Testator declared in our presence that he had executed this Codicil and at the time of the execution of said Codicil said Testator was over the age of twenty-one years and of sound and disposing mind.

This [March ___ *del.*]< October 10>, 1958.

/s/ T. H. Freeland II
Witness

/s/ Elaine F. Hoffman
Witness

INDEX

Absalom, Absalom!, 91, 327, 328
"After Fifty Years," 46, 54–55
"After the Concert," 26, 60
"Afternoon of a Cow," 355
American Academy of Arts and Letters, 253
"American Segregation and the World Crisis," 239
Anderson, Sherwood, 326, 335
Andrés Bello Award Acceptance Speech, 201, 251
Anthology of Magazine Verse for 1925, 43
Anthology of Poems from the Seventeen Previously Published Braithwaite Anthologies, 43
Anthology of the Younger Poets, An, 76
"Apres-Midi d'un Faune, L'," 26, 34–35, 43, 52–53
Aria da Capo, 257
Arrival of Kitty, The, 257
As I Lay Dying, 326
"As when from dark the vernal equinox," 26, 89
"Aubade," 27
Ayers, Lemuel, 258

Bacher, William, 339
Baird, Helen, 26
"Ballade des Femmes Perdues, Une," 43, 53–54
"'Bama poems," 26–34
Barnett, Ned, 359, 365–66
"Beer Broadside," 315, 323–24
Bellow, Saul, 341, 344, 345
Big Sleep, The, 326
Big Woods, 91, 199
"Bill Faulkner and the Nobel Prize," 330–39
"Black bird swung in the white rose tree, The," 27, 30–32
Blotner, Joseph, 23, 24, 253, 316, 355
Borsten, Orin, 19
Breit, Harvey, 328, 341–42, 344–47, 349–53
Brodsky, Louis Daniel, 34, 35, 39, 74, 75, 92, 115, 202, 251, 253, 255, 317, 320
"Brooch, The," 257
Brown, Calvin, 92
Brown, Mrs. Calvin, 92
Buckner, Robert, 316
"By the People," 91, 183–99

Camus, Albert, 258
Canadian Royal Air Force, 3, 16, 35, 325
Candida, 257
Carter, Hodding, 339
Cartoons, 3, 4–14
"Cathay," 43, 50
Cézanne, Paul, 3
Collected Stories of William Faulkner, 327
Collins, Carvel, 57
Commins, Saxe, 21, 22, 26, 91, 138, 166, 203, 226, 249, 325, 339, 345, 348–52, 376, 378
Cooke, Alistair, 332, 339
"Counterparts," 163
Country Lawyer and Other Stories for the Screen, 317
Cowley, Malcolm, 217–18, 227–28
Cowley, Muriel, 217
"Curing Hams Shoulders Bacon," 320

"Dancer, The," 26, 59, 60
Daniel, Robert W., 72
Danzas Venezuela, 251, 253
De Gaulle Story, The, 316
"Dead Dancer, A," 26, 35, 39–42, 46, 56–57
"December: To Elise," 76, 84
Doctor Martino and Other Stories, 327
Dos Passos, John, 249
Dostoevski, Feodor, 327
Double Dealer, 43
Dubliners, 163

Eisenhower, Pres. Dwight D., 315, 340
"Elder Watson in Heaven," 74–75
Eliot, T. S., 335
Elmer, 3
Ennis, Jean, 204, 341
"Eunice," 27, 32–34
Evans, Walker, 219

Fable, A, 22, 91, 165–83, 201, 315, 328, 339
"Faith or Fear," 204
Falkner, Dean, 359, 363, 365, 371, 378
Falkner, J. M., 359, 366, 372, 373, 379, 380
Falkner, J. W. T., III, 325, 359, 365, 372, 377, 379
Falkner, J. W. T., IV, 375
Falkner, M. C., 359, 361, 362, 363, 365,

366, 370, 372, 373, 375, 377, 378–79
Falkner, M. C., II, 359, 366, 372, 373, 379, 380
Falkner, Maud, 3, 16, 25, 35, 325, 338, 359, 360, 363, 371, 372, 373, 378, 380
Falkner, Murry C., 325
Falkner, W. C., 325
Faulkner, Estelle, 19, 26, 58, 326, 359–63, 370–71, 377–78
Faulkner Foundation, 360
Faulkner, Jill, 315, 321, 359, 360–63, 365–66, 370–73, 375–80
Faulkner, Jimmy, *see* Falkner, J. M.
Faulkner, John, *see* Faulkner, J. W. T., III
Faulkner Reader, The, 210
Faulkner, William, —biographical documents, 315–57; —career, 3–4, 25–26, 91–92, 201, 257, 315–16, 359–60; —cartoons and drawings, 3–23; —fiction, 91–199; —last wills and testaments, 359–82; —non-fiction, 201–55; —plays, 257–314; —poetry, 25–89; *see also* titles of individual works
Ferber, Edna, 341–43
Fielden, Victoria Franklin, 251, 320, 359, 360, 362
Fielden, William, 251, 320
Finger, H. E., Jr., 323–24
"First Experimental Balch Hangar-Flying Squadron," 316, 357
"Fool About a Horse," 381
Ford, Charles Henri, 138
Ford, Ruth, 92, 137, 138, 257–58
"Foreword" to *The Faulkner Reader,* 210, 212–14
Franklin, Malcolm, 19, 359, 360, 362, 366, 373, 380
Franklin, Victoria, *see* Fielden, Victoria Franklin
"Freedom: American Style," 227–39
Freeland, T. H., II, 382
Frost, Robert, 335

"Gallows, The," 76, 80, 82
Go Down, Moses, 327
Gold Medal for Fiction Acceptance Address, 253, 255, 355
Gold Medal for Fiction Presentation Address, 249
Green Bough, A, 26, 43, 59, 76, 84, 326
"Green grow the rushes O," 27, 30
Greenfield Farm, 359, 365, 372–73, 379
"Guest's Impression of New England, A," 217–19
Gwynn, Frederick, 23, 316, 355

Hall, Donald, 341, 343, 352–55
Hamblin, Robert W., 34, 317
Hamlet, 257
Hamlet, The, 25, 327, 381–82
Hathaway, Henry, 339
"He furrows the brown earth, doubly sweet," 76, 78–79
Held, John, Jr., 3
Helen: A Courtship, 4, 26, 76, 84
Hemingway, Ernest, 201
Hewlett, Ed, 336
Hillyer, Robert, 341
Hoffman, Elaine F., 382
Holley, R. L., 361–62
"Hound, The," 381
Housman, A. E., 27, 326
Hurst, G. G., 6, 9, 12
"Hymn," 27

"I give the world to love you," 27, 29
"If I Were a Negro," 201
"Indian Summer," 76, 77–78
"Innocent's Return," 309–14
Intruder in the Dust, 327, 359

James, Henry, 327
Jencks, Hugh, 251
Johnson, John K., 323–24
Jones, B. W., 366, 370
Jones, Mrs. Homer K., 75
Joyce, James, 163

Kafka, Franz, 327
Keats, John, 326, 334
King, Lillie Sue, 374, 376
Klopfer, Donald, 348–49
Knight's Gambit, 327

Last Wills and Testaments, 359–82
"Leaving Her," 26, 84–85, 89
Legion of Honor Acceptance Speech, 203
"Letter to the Leaders in the Negro Race, A," 201
"Liberator Story," 317
"Life and Death of a Bomber, The," 317, 318–19
Light in August, 257, 326
"Lilacs, The," 16, 26, 35–39, 43, 46–50
Lilacs, The, 4, 18, 25, 43–57
Lincoln, Abraham, 14
Liveright, Horace, 335
"Lizards in Jamshyd's Courtyard," 381
"Love Song of J. Alfred Prufrock, The," 70
Lyles, Loutie, 374, 376

McJunkin, Alvis, 359, 379
McJunkin, Charlie, 359, 379
McJunkin, Lawrence, 359, 373, 379
McLean, Alabama ("'Bama"), 26
Mansion, The, 25, 184
Marble Faun, The, 4, 25, 26, 57, 58–59, 326–27
"March," 76, 84
Marionettes, 257
Marionettes, The 43, 257
Marre, Albert, 258
Massey, Linton R., 76
Mayday, 4
Millay, Edna St. Vincent, 257
"Mississippi," 214–17
"Mississippi Hills: My Epitaph," 76, 80
Mississippi Poems, 26, 75–84
Mississippi Verse, 76
Mississippian, The, 43, 46, 257
"Moon of death, moon of bright despair," 76, 77
Mosquitoes, 326
Mullen, Phil, 202, 330, 331–33, 335–38
"My Epitaph," 76

National Book Award Acceptance Speech, 225–27
National Institute of Arts and Letters, 253
Neill, W. C., 240
Nobel Prize Acceptance Speech, 201
Notes on a Horsethief, 165
"November 11th," 76, 82

"O Atthis," 43, 51–52
Ober, Harold, 184, 226, 227, 240, 309
"Ode to the Louver," 89
Old Man and the Sea, The, 201
"Old Man Says:, An," 27, 32
Oldham, Mrs. Lemuel, 27
Ole Miss, 3–4, 13, 43, 257
Omnibus, 315, 330
"On Fear: The South in Labor: Mississippi," 239–49
"On Privacy: The American Dream: What Happened to It," 227
O'Neill, Eugene, 257
Orpheus, and Other Poems, 58
"Out of Nazareth," 3

Pan, 4
"Pastoral," 27
Patton, Estelle K., 366, 370
People-To-People program, 315, 340–54, 357
"Pierrot, Sitting Beside the Body of Colombine, Suddenly Sees Himself in a Mirror," 72–74
Pine Manor Commencement Address, 203–10
"Poet Goes Blind, The," 76, 79–80
Portable Faulkner, The, 4, 18
Pound, Ezra, 335, 355
Prall, Elizabeth, 325–26
"Pregnacy," 75, 76, 82
"Preludes," 70
Purser, Frank Moody, 323–24
Pylon, 327

Ramey, Myrtle, 4, 15, 26, 75, 76
Reed, Mack, 335–37, 375
Reivers, The, 359
"Requiem," 257–309
Requiem for a Nun (novel), 91, 137–63, 257, 325, 328
Requiem for a Nun (play), 137–38, 257–309
Rice, Elmer, 341–42, 344–45, 348–49
Road to Glory, The, 326
Roberts, Ike, 332, 335–36
Rovere, Richard, 327
Royal Air Force, 23

Salmagundi, 43
Sanctuary, 326, 360
Sanford, Cecil L., 251
"Sapphics," 46, 55–56
Sartoris, 326, 359
Sensibar, Judith L., 58
"Sepulchure South," 219–25
Shakespeare, William, 236
"Shall I recall this tree, when I am old," 76, 77
Shapiro, Karl, 352
Shaw, George Bernard, 257
Shelley, Percy Bysshe, 326, 334
Silver, James W., 91, 239, 321
Silver Medal of the Athens Academy, 201
Soldiers' Pay, 76, 326, 360
Somerville, Lucy, 257
Sound and the Fury, The, 257, 326
Southern Historical Association, 239
Spenser, Edmund, 326
"Spotted Horses," 381
Spratling, William, 3
Stallion Road, 320
Steinbeck, John, 341–42, 348, 351–55
Stone, Emily, 57
Stone fragments, 57–72
Stone, Mary A., 361–62
Stone, Phil, 4, 18, 25, 26, 43, 46, 57–58, 75–76, 89, 91, 315, 316, 330, 334–36,

359, 361–63, 365, 370, 372–73, 376–80
Stone, Philip, 91, 92, 373, 380
Stovall, Floyd, 355
Street, James, 339
Sullivan, R. L., 361–62
Summers, Jill Faulkner, *see* Faulkner, Jill
"Sun lay long upon the hills, The," 27–28
Swartout, Norman Lee, 257
Swinburne, Algernon, 27, 325
"Symphony, A," 26, 63

These Thirteen, 326
This Earth, 76
Three Views of the Segregation Decisions, 239
"To a Co-ed," 43, 51
To Have and Have Not, 326
"To the Voters of Oxford" (Faulkner's), 323–24
"To the Voters of Oxford" (ministers'), 323–24
Today We Live, 326
Town, The, 25
"Turn again, Dick Whittington," 27, 28–29
Twentieth Century-Fox Film Corporation, 381–82

University High Commencement Address, 202–03
Unvanquished, The, 327

View, 138
Vision in Spring, 26, 58, 59, 60, 63

Warner Bros. Pictures, 315, 317, 321
"Wash," 91, 114–37
Wasson, Ben, 15, 257, 339
Wasson, Ben F., Sr., 72
Wasson, Mrs. Ben F., Sr., 72, 74
"Weekend Revisited," 91, 163–65
Welty, Eudora, 327
"When evening shadows grew around," 27, 29
"When I rose up with morning," 27, 28
"When I was young and proud and gay," 27, 29–30
White Rose of Memphis, The, 325
"Wild Geese," 76, 78
Wild Palms, The, 327
Wilde, Meta Carpenter, 19
William Faulkner: Early Prose and Poetry, 43, 46
Williams, Joan, 21, 309, 315, 328
Williams, William Carlos, 341, 346, 348, 350, 352
Wilson, Herman, 350
Wilson, Payne, 359, 373, 379
Wilson, Robert A., 85
Wings for the Eagle, 317
Wintering, The, 328
Wishing-Tree, The, 4, 91, 92–114
Wright, Ella, 14

Young, Stark, 325